By Richard M. Watt

THE KINGS DEPART
DARE CALL IT TREASON

The Kings Depart

THE TRAGEDY OF GERMANY:
VERSAILLES AND
THE GERMAN REVOLUTION

by
RICHARD M. WATT

A CLARION BOOK

PUBLISHED BY SIMON AND SCHUSTER

A Clarion Book
Published by Simon and Schuster
Rockefeller Center, 630 Fifth Avenue
New York, New York 10020

Copyright © 1968 by Richard M. Watt
First paperback printing, 1970
SBN 671-20534-X

Library of Congress Catalog Card Number: 68-22973
Manufactured in the United States of America

Contents

The Kings Depart

PART 1

Yet when we achieved and the new world dawned,
the old men came out again and took our victory
to remake in the likeness of the former world
they knew . . .

—T. E. LAWRENCE

Chapter One

Stand Not upon the Order
of Your Going

Bʏ Sunday, June 29, 1919, most of the principal figures of the peace conference had left Paris. The three men who almost had it in their power to remake the modern world had gathered together for the last time. They would not meet again.

On the afternoon before, they had signed the treaty of peace with Germany in the Hall of Mirrors at Versailles. As with almost everything else at this six-months-long conference, even the ending had been somehow unsatisfactory. The only thing to be said in favor of the ceremony was that it was mercifully brief—less than an hour from the moment when old Georges Clemenceau stood up to announce, *"La séance est ouverte,"* until the last name had been scrawled on the vellum pages of the signature copy of the treaty of peace. The Allied signatories had sat at tables arranged in a horseshoe shape in the middle of the long, narrow room; the rest of the room had been packed with nearly a thousand members of the press and other invited spectators. There had been trouble with the crowd: they could not see the treaty being signed, nor could they hear the proceedings, and the solemnity of the occasion had been marred throughout by unseemly cries of "Down in front!" from the far ends of the room. This, together with the noise of cameras, the shuffling of feet and the whispering of innumerable private conversations, created a background noise which sounded to one observer "like water running into a tin bath."[1]

Finally everyone had signed; that is, everyone except the Chinese, who, it was well known, had been exploited shamefully in the Shantung compromise and who therefore had refused to put their names to the treaty. The two German delegates had been brought in for the signing and then escorted out, by way of side doors, while the others remained seated—an effect which had miscarried. Most of the delegates now felt that the Germans had been gratuitously insulted by the French. The selection of the Hall of Mirrors for the occasion, the same room in which Wilhelm I had been crowned German emperor in 1871, had been a calculated indignity. The final humiliation of being shunted in and out of the hall without ceremony or *politesse* of any kind had brought the Germans the unexpected sympathy of the spectators. A United States plenipotentiary, Colonel Edward House, observed that it was "not unlike what was done in olden times when the conqueror dragged the conquered at his chariot wheels."[2]

Finally, at three-fifty, Clemenceau rose to his feet and announced in a voice made inaudible by the general din, "*La séance est levée.*" Then from the Paris forts and the hills around Versailles a racket of artillery salutes began, and in the parks the fountains were suddenly switched on. When Lloyd George, Clemenceau and Woodrow Wilson appeared on the terrace to watch the fountains, they were nearly bowled over by a vast swarm of sightseers who swept through the cordons of police and troops. Only with great difficulty were they rescued from the crowd and returned to the palace.

The next day Paris seemed suddenly deserted. There were still separate peace treaties to be concluded with Austria, Hungary, Bulgaria and Turkey, but this was a task which could safely be left to subordinates. The major outlines of the "new" Europe had already been established in the Treaty of Versailles. The lesser treaties had only to conform with what had already been decided. Lloyd George left for London, where, in the evening, he was accorded the unusual honor of being met at Victoria Station by the King and the Prince of Wales. Woodrow Wilson had left Paris the night before, aboard the private train of Raymond Poincaré, the President of the French Republic—a man Wilson hated. The American party was bound for Brest, where the liner *George Washington* waited with an escort of a battleship and four destroyers to convey the President back to the United States. Woodrow Wilson's departure from Paris had been very different from the scene of delirious enthusiasm which had marked his arrival. By contrast, a French general noted, the small crowd of onlookers at the railway station "was very reserved, almost cold. There were a few cries of 'Vive Wilson!,' but they were very scattered."[3]

Upon most of those who had been delegates to the Paris Peace Conference there now suddenly descended a mood of gloom and despair. "How splendid it would have been had we blazed a better trail," Colonel House wrote in his diary.[4] "What a wretched mess it is," General Tasker Bliss wrote his wife.[5] The young British diplomat Harold Nicolson noted the words "To bed, sick of life" in his daily journal.[6]

The three principal figures at the conference were not immune from these doubts. Georges Clemenceau was under attack from the powerful forces of the French right, who accused him of having been outwitted by the wily "Anglo-Saxons." He would not long withstand the combined attacks of the Army and the political forces led by President Poincaré.

Lloyd George, in a compartment of a private train racing across closed signal blocks between Paris and Boulogne, knew that he was heading into a storm of criticism for his failure to obtain the huge reparations payments from the Germans which he had promised the British public in the election campaigns of the previous December. Nor did it appear that the cherished British dream of bringing the Kaiser to trial in London and hanging him there would come to pass. But Lloyd George had deeper concerns. He had come to fear that the treaty was too harsh and unworkable, that perhaps it condemned Europe to another gigantic war. "We do not quite appreciate the importance and magnitude of the events in which we have been taking part," he confessed to a friend.[7] And earlier he had told Sir William Wiseman that the treaty was "all a great pity. We shall have to do the same thing all over again in twenty-five years at three times the cost."[8]

For Woodrow Wilson there must surely have been an especially agonizing form of apprehension. He had first come to Paris with keen anticipation, for the Paris Peace Conference represented the opportunity he had always dreamed of—to completely remake the world according to the liberal and democratic concepts to which he had dedicated his life. But he had found the task so vast, so overlaid with conflicting claims and interests, so tinctured with hatreds and fears and greeds, that he was forced to settle for a patchwork compromise which satisfied no one. Hopefully, his League of Nations, which had been established as an integral part of the treaty of peace, would eventually resolve some of the more onerous provisions—but this was only a hope. Wilson had arrived in Paris as indisputably the most powerful man in the world; six months later he was retiring with his power nearly destroyed—together with his health, hopes and prestige. Wilson could not even count upon his nation's accepting what he had agreed to at Paris. The Senate's Foreign Relations Committee was in the hands of political enemies whom he had mortally offended and who would do anything to prevent ratification of a Wilsonian treaty. So now Woodrow Wilson stood looking out an open train window and told his wife, "Well, it is finished, and, as no one is satisfied, it makes me hope we have made a just peace; but it is all in the lap of the gods."[9]

In December of 1918, when they had first met in Paris, it had seemed that the task of making peace would be easy. The Allies* had extracted "armistices" from their enemies which were, in effect, surrenders. Every one of the enemy monarchs had fallen before the power of the democracies, and their places had been taken by new regimes eager to proclaim a government acceptable to the victors. East of Paris were a thousand miles of hunger and chaos, over which it seemed that the Allies—the sole possessors of navies, food, weapons and disciplined armies (totaling more than twelve million men)—must surely have absolute control.

It seemed inconceivable that any man, any party, any nation could dispute the dictates of the three principal victors. And yet the peace treaty had not turned out in the way that any of the principals had wanted. The dreams of a world of happy peoples, each assembled into an entity of its own nationality and living in its own historical geographic location, were now seen to have been imbecilic wishes which could not and would not come true.

The cause of the failure of the Treaty of Versailles to create a permanent peace has been variously assessed. Generally speaking, the British place the blame on France, whose designs for the emasculation of Germany triggered off such resentment in Germany that World War II became almost inevitable. Americans tend to hold both Clemenceau and Lloyd George responsible as the cynical

---

* Throughout the period during which the United States was a combatant in World War I, as well as during the subsequent peace negotiations, the United States's policy was to insist that it was not one of the "Allies"—among whom various secret treaties had been concluded to which the United States was opposed. Accordingly, the cumbersome phrase "Allied and Associated Powers" was created to describe the United States and its co-belligerents. For the purposes of simplicity, this book will use the term "Allies" to describe the entire collection of victorious nations.

and corrupt Europeans who frustrated the altruistic proposals of the United States. The French, on the other hand, blame the "Anglo-Saxons" for hoodwinking Clemenceau into a treaty which failed to insure France's security against a resurgent Germany and thus made possible the awful revenge of a humiliated people. But the single name most inextricably bound up with the Treaty of Versailles, and consequently with its failure, is that of Thomas Woodrow Wilson.

When he first appeared in Paris for the peace conference, Woodrow Wilson (he had dropped the "Thomas" as a youth) was sixty-one years old. His appearance favored him; slender, of medium height, with a lean, ascetic face, a stern jaw and carefully combed gray hair, he looked almost like a noble caricature of what he was, the scholarly son of a stern Scotch-Irish Presbyterian minister.

Wilson had been born in Virginia in 1856 and had grown up in the South during and after the Civil War. His enthusiasms had always been bookish and theoretical. As the son of an austere Presbyterian divine, he had not been particularly popular with other boys; he could not throw a ball properly; as a young man he had been subject to repeated breakdowns of health during periods of stress. In 1875 he entered Princeton University, where he majored in political science. Then, in order, he attended the University of Virginia Law School, failed as an attorney in Atlanta, returned to scholastic life at Johns Hopkins, taught history at Bryn Mawr and at Wesleyan, and erupted into national notice as a phenomenally influential young professor of jurisprudence and political economy at Princeton. Suddenly Wilson had found himself; his subsequent academic career was nothing less than spectacular.

His success was certainly no accident. Wilson had spent years practicing and polishing his oratorical style. His lecture preparation far exceeded that which was common for university teachers of his time. His enthusiasm for politics and political history was contagious, and his views were argued with exceptional lucidity. It was not unusual for his students to burst into applause at the conclusion of one of his lectures. Although Wilson was regarded as one of the toughest and most demanding professors at Princeton, his courses were jammed with students. Year after year he was named the most popular teacher at Princeton, and his reputation grew until promising students entered the university simply in order to study under him. He was in demand to speak to alumni groups all over the nation, and the combination of his oratory and his vision of "Princeton in the Nation's Service" was so spectacular that a Wilsonian speech generally attracted widespread notice in the press. He was at various times offered the presidency of six different universities. To keep him at Princeton, a group of alumni volunteered privately to supplement his annual salary, which was already higher than that of any other member of the faculty. In short, Wilson became a national figure in the field of political science. It is probable that no American university professor before or since has ever been as well known as Woodrow Wilson.

In 1902, at the age of forty-six, Wilson was named president of Princeton University. At the time of his appointment, the university had noticeably slipped from the position of academic eminence it had once held. The Princeton student was generally regarded as a careless fellow, well-dressed and well-mannered but more interested in his club than in his scholarship. Classes were casually attended, and most of the faculty contented themselves with delivering the identical series of lectures year after year. The university had come to be noted as a rich man's school to which admission was easy, where the academic pace was slow and where nothing was allowed to interfere with the demands of social · activity. Wilson himself called it "an intellectual country club."[10]

Woodrow Wilson cut through this like a cold wind. He demanded academic excellence and he got it. The class admitted in 1902 lost a quarter of its members in a year. Wilson insisted that the faculty improve their courses, and he hired fifty young "preceptors" to give personal tutorial attention to the undergraduates. He reformed the Princeton curriculum completely and attracted outstanding men to the faculty. He proposed a costly and controversial system of residence quadrangles which he claimed would "remedy the great evil"[11] caused by the Princeton club system. To support his various projects he demanded money in sums which his board of trustees had never before dreamed. And as the result of Wilson's determination, Princeton abruptly became more famous than it had ever been—and with it its president.

All this was not done without exacting a price from Wilson himself. He worked endless hours. For years he did not even have a secretary (the university could not afford one), and he composed the bulk of his letters and speeches in his own shorthand and transcribed them himself on his own typewriter. Under this work load his health broke down repeatedly. In May of 1906 he awoke one morning to find that he had temporarily lost the sight of his left eye. Two specialists advised him that he had arteriosclerosis and must retire immediately. But Wilson shrugged off their advice and continued as before. He traveled all over the country, not only speaking of his work at Princeton but, in the broader sense, likening his struggles for the "democratization" of Princeton to the need for a similar effort in national politics. "In planning for Princeton . . . we are planning for the country." To the distress of many Princeton alumni, he attacked the forces of "special privilege" who had "obtained control of our commerce and our industries."[12] As an expert in government history and law, Wilson claimed that the American political system had fallen into the hands of party bosses, monopolists and the moneyed forces of special interest. His political speeches, so superbly prepared and delivered, made the president of Princeton a famous American orator—particularly because he had the ability to make the solution to complex problems so simple. "Democracy," was the Wilson message: Let there be democracy and more democracy, reform Princeton, the nation and ultimately the world, simply by letting the voice of the people be heard. His critics claimed that Wilson oversimplified and that in practice the solutions were much more complex. But he painted a captivating vision. Persons who heard him went away spellbound. He began to receive letters from listeners who said that they had never heard the problems of American society explained so clearly and with such sincerity. He received invitations to speak at the rate of three a day. Obscure people (and some not so obscure) began to plead that he consider running for public office. In February, 1906, Colonel George Harvey, an influential Democrat and the publisher of *Harper's Weekly*, introduced Wilson at a New York dinner with the words, "It is with a sense almost of rapture that I contemplate even the remotest possibility of casting a ballot for the president of Princeton University to become President of the United States."[13]

But, under the scrutiny of eminence, Woodrow Wilson's personality was now seen to have certain serious defects. Some thought that his sudden rise to prominence had given him delusions of grandeur; more probably, it simply aggravated his latent tendency toward authoritarianism. An idealist, Wilson conceived of himself as being perpetually on the side of the angels, struggling in a lonely battle against the forces of cynical compromise, special interest and sheer stupidity. An avowed democrat ("the only cure for the ills of democracy is more democracy"), he saw nothing contradictory in his personally dictatorial tendencies. (To a trustee of Princeton who mentioned the board's difficulty in agreeing upon the site for a new building he said, "Thompson, as long as I am president of Princeton, I propose to dictate the architectural policy of the university.")[14]

But perhaps the most complex characteristic of this brilliant man was his need for personal friendships. All his life he craved the love and devotion of a few (and only a few) close friends. But there were complications to this need. To be a friend of Wilson one had to go to him and actually declare, "I like you," or, better, "I am your friend and I will follow you."[15] Even the statement of this messianic credo did not insure the apostle's continued reception at the side of the master. Some quirk of Wilson's character demanded the complete and unswerving agreement of his friends on any matter which he felt to be important. He possessed an immense capacity for suspicion, and, like many men who pride themselves on their frankness, he could not bear frankness on the part of others. He could not conceive of any point of view opposed to his; should a friend disagree with him, Wilson instantly concluded that the man was now a mortal enemy. For many years his dearest friend was Professor John Grier Hibben. They were inseparable. Almost every day Wilson and the Hibbens took tea together. But at the height of the residence-quadrangle controversy Hibben felt compelled by conscience to vote against Wilson proposals. That evening when the Hibbens appeared at Wilson's residence the president of Princeton shut the door upon them, and shortly afterward he ceased even to speak to Hibben. His attitude toward compromise and equivocation was equally difficult. He abhorred both—but only in others. His own compromises were readily defensible (indeed, they were not recognized as such), but similar actions by other men were pitilessly castigated as moral weakness of the highest order.

These personal defects, which ultimately grew to serious proportions, would have crippled the career of a less well-educated or cultivated man. But such was Wilson's effectiveness as the articulate spokesman of progressivism and the foe of monopoly and special privilege that his objectionable personal characteristics were successfully masked to the majority of Americans.

Wilson left Princeton in 1910 at the request of the board of trustees. He had been one of the most successful presidents the university ever had, and his speeches throughout the nation had brought Princeton renown, but the price of this had been a series of increasingly violent disputes with the trustees, the alumni and the faculty. The culmination was a year-long struggle over the allocation of funds for the construction of a postgraduate school.

When Wilson was elected president of Princeton his only serious rival for the post had been Andrew West, a professor of classics. Like Wilson, West was popular with the alumni and was regarded as a scholar of great distinction. Wilson apparently felt sympathetic toward West's disappointment and encouraged him to remain at Princeton. West agreed, with the understanding that he would be given the title of dean and the responsibility for the development and construction of a graduate school, which had long been an interest of his. Although West was offered the presidency of the Massachusetts Institute of Technology in 1906, he remained at Princeton at Wilson's urging to work on the graduate-school program. Wilson even contributed an enthusiastic preface to a graduate-school brochure which West wrote to stimulate the project.

As time went on, it became apparent to West that if his graduate school was ever going to be built he would have to raise much of the money himself, since Wilson's own projects consumed practically all of the university's funds. The gradually independent attitude which West adopted was extremely distasteful to Wilson, who was also critical of what he regarded as the rather lavish plans which West had for the graduate-school buildings. In addition, Wilson did not care for the site which West had in mind—an area adjoining the Princeton golf course, a mile from the center of the university campus. Wilson let it be known that he would oppose the construction of a graduate school if it were located on that site.

The conflict came to a head in 1909, when Dean West obtained from an old pupil, William C. Proctor of Cincinnati, the offer of $500,000 toward the construction of the graduate school—provided it was built on the golf-course site. This enraged Wilson, who chose to regard it as a personal attack. Despite the fact that the sum offered was, for the time, an enormous one, he demanded that the Princeton trustees refuse the money on threat of his resignation. The trustees very reluctantly agreed, but the whole matter soon became known to the Princeton alumni, who could not understand the dispute and could not comprehend how Wilson could refuse this generous gift on what seemed to them to be a minor matter of personal preference. Wilson defended himself before the alumni in a series of addresses which became increasingly intemperate and ill-advised. He accused the forces of wealth of attempting to control

the educational process and described the Proctor gift as an attempt
"to take the guidance of the University out of my hands entirely."[16]
It quickly became evident to most alumni that Wilson's objections
were based on a personal hatred of Dean West. The alumni and the
trustees became deeply divided on the issue. As opposition hardened, so did Wilson's own position.

In May, 1910, at the height of the controversy, Wilson received a
telegram from Dean West informing him that a Princeton alumnus,
Isaac C. Wyman, had died and bequeathed to Princeton the sum of
two million dollars to be spent for the construction of a graduate
school. Dean West himself was named one of the trustees of the
estate. At this, Proctor renewed his offer. It was obvious that the
graduate school would be built on the golf-course site. The Princeton trustees informed Wilson that they would not refuse this immense bequest, and in October, 1910, his resignation was requested.
Professor John Grier Hibben was appointed his successor; Wilson
refused to attend his former friend's inauguration.

To his good fortune, Woodrow Wilson now had other opportunities. His relationship with Colonel George Harvey had deepened,
and Harvey encouraged Wilson to make himself available as the
Democratic nominee for the governorship of New Jersey.

He had long wanted to put his theories of government to actual
test in the political world. As a Southerner, brought up in the Reconstruction years, Wilson was a staunch Democrat. In New Jersey
the Democratic Party was split into two factions—the unsavory
"organization" group, dominated by the city political bosses, and,
contending against it, a weak liberal, or reform, wing. The machine
politicians were by far the stronger faction, and Wilson, strangely,
saw nothing inconsistent with his progressive principles in running
as their candidate for the 1910 New Jersey gubernatorial nomination. Nor, once he had secured the nomination through them, did he
see anything equivocal in repudiating the machine leaders and all
they stood for—even though he had previously given a solemn
pledge of loyalty to "Boss" Smith of Jersey City. He promised that,
if elected, he would surely never consider "fighting and breaking
down the existing Democratic organization and replacing it with
one of [his] own."[17]

Wilson's repudiation of the bosses secured him the delighted support of the liberal wing of the Democratic Party; with it, victory in
the election became certain. Even the sullen machine politicians

could do nothing but support him, for Wilson was, after all, their own nominee. (He was later to describe them in enduring terms as "warts on the body politic.") Only occasionally could the machine counterattack. At a Democratic Party dinner "Boss" Jim Nugent jumped to his feet to propose a toast: "Gentlemen, I give you the Governor of New Jersey . . . " All rose. ". . . a liar and an ingrate!"[18]

Despite the tactics which Wilson used to obtain his election, there was no denying his success as governor of New Jersey. In a few months he drafted, got passed and signed a torrent of liberal legislation—a direct-primaries law, an employers'-liability act, a public-utilities-commission act and a series of antitrust laws known as "the Seven Sisters." He was becoming a truly famous political figure; against the opposition of the bosses and the trusts he had succeeded in fulfilling the image which was developing around him as "the defender of the helpless, the simple, the innocent, against the economic and social mighty of this world."[19] And in 1911 Governor Wilson received an invitation to meet in New York City with Edward Mandell House of Texas.

In the crevices of American political life there is often found a peculiar species, a type of shrewd and knowledgeable man who wants nothing out of life but the opportunity to guide and influence a great man toward the pinnacle of political power. Edward House was one of this strange breed. At the time he first met Wilson, House was fifty-three years old, two years younger than the New Jersey Governor. In appearance he was an almost ludicrous antithesis of what a Texan should look like—short, bald and with a face whose most noticeable characteristics were a receding chin and cheekbones so pronounced that they gave his face a Mongolian cast. In manner too House was distinctly un-Texan—mysterious, silent, almost humble.

Born the son of a wealthy Galveston planter and trader, House had in his youth become fascinated with history and politics, and, as the heir to a modest fortune, he had the leisure to follow his enthusiasms. By his early thirties he had begun masterminding the careers and campaigns of a succession of Texas politicians. Carefully avoiding any notoriety whatsoever, this quiet little man served as the sub-rosa campaign manager for four successive Texas governors. It was one of these who awarded him the honorary rank of "colonel" on the gubernatorial staff, a title which House detested but which he could not shake off.

By 1911 House was a power within the Democratic Party, and state-house politics had begun to bore him. He had become an acknowledged master in the art of making Texas governors, even against what seemed like hopeless odds. He had solved, to his own satisfaction, the riddle of practical politics, which he described as "largely a matter of organization. You've got to have a good, clean feller to put before the voters. After that it's organization."[20] He had continued to practice his fetish of anonymity; in his most recent campaign House had elected a governor without ever having his own name mentioned in a Texas newspaper. But he was now spending more time away from Austin. He had become increasingly concerned with the faults of the American political system as he saw them: he believed that certain business interests, notably the railroads, were not being effectively checked in their monopoly abuses. Gradually House began to explore the possibilities of steering the destinies of some Democratic candidate toward the ultimate prize, the Presidency. Woodrow Wilson, by 1911, was seriously spoken of as a possible Democratic Presidential nominee for the 1912 campaign. Although House had never met Wilson, he liked what he had heard of him. Thus, when Woodrow Wilson and Edward House finally met in New York City on November 24, 1911, their lives were ready to complement each other like pieces of a jigsaw puzzle. The Governor had ambitions, and he was currently in need of a devoted adherent. He was soon to thrust aside George Harvey, the man who had introduced Wilson to politics, had guided his early career and now had for months run the phrase "Woodrow Wilson for President" over the *Harper's* banner.

The first meeting between House and Wilson was followed by a series of dinners and luncheons. To their mutual delight and astonishment, the two men found that they agreed on virtually every conceivable subject. House had assiduously, absorbed everything which anyone could tell him about Wilson and had been prepared to find him a difficult and egotistic man. But this feature of Wilson's character was little in evidence. Wilson remarked, "My dear fellow, we have known each other all our lives."[21] For House the meeting with Wilson was a call to greatness. "Never before," he exulted to his brother-in-law, "have I found both the man and the opportunity!"[22]

In November of 1912 Woodrow Wilson was elected to the Presidency. It was not, to be sure, an overwhelming electoral triumph.

Great good fortune attended his campaign. Although Colonel House had done his best, the Democratic Party convention went through no fewer than forty-five ballots before it finally nominated Wilson, and even then the Democratic nomination did not appear to be much of a prize. The nation was predominantly Republican; only one Democratic President had been elected since the Civil War. But, providentially for Woodrow Wilson, the Republicans fell out among themselves. Theodore Roosevelt announced himself as the "Bull Moose" candidate and split the Republican ticket. The vote for Woodrow Wilson was a plurality, not a majority, and he carried only fourteen states, all in the South; nonetheless, he was elected, and he brought in with him a Democratic Congress.

Wilson's first years in office were devoted to the passage of a good deal of what was then considered to be mildly radical legislation—a tariff-reduction act, a sweeping currency-reform law and the Clayton Anti-Trust Act. This legislation did nothing to enhance his popularity in the Eastern manufacturing cities, but it won Wilson considerable support in the Midwest and in the rural areas. The common people had caught the Wilson message—the vision of a bright and free world which could be created simply by throwing off the old shackles. His speeches, always superbly written and delivered, invariably reflected a lofty moral tone which countless Americans found irresistible. Congress was less impressed. Many of its members, even a number of leading Democrats, complained that Wilson did not talk to them—he lectured from on high. His speeches had, in truth, taken on an increasingly pastoral ring. In his inaugural address he summoned the crowd closer to the rostrum with the words "Let the people come forward."[23] Himself a nonsmoker and nondrinker, he irritated certain Congressmen when, upon visiting the White House, they were never offered the customary cigar or drink. It became well known that the President did not receive advice gladly, particularly when his mind was already made up. And it was observed that there were very few men of first caliber among Wilson's Cabinet officers and closest associates. It seemed that he could not shake off the role of professor, in which his was always the superior intellect.

Wilson's only intimate associate continued to be Edward House. The little Colonel had been offered practically any Cabinet seat he wanted, but had shrewdly declined. House felt sure that his influence with the President would not survive in an official relationship. On the plea that his health could not stand the humid Washington climate, he lived in New York—an arrangement which kept him out of the way of day-to-day governmental controversy. Nonetheless, he devoted himself almost exclusively to the service of the President. Letters and telephone calls were exchanged almost daily. House knew exactly how to deal with Wilson and took great care never to argue with him, never to appear to be giving advice, and never to try to change his mind. He once advised a young friend, "The President gets easily annoyed and allows policy to be swayed by annoyance. . . . Never begin by arguing. Discover a common hate, exploit it, get the President warmed up and then start in on your business."[24] He also knew Wilson's craving for intimate friendship, and his notes to the President (always beginning "Dear Governor") generally ended with the word "Affectionately" or "Devotedly." His tenderness was amply repaid. Wilson publicly stated, "Mr. House is my second personality. He is my independent self. His thoughts and mine are one."[25]

In August of 1914, when World War I began, there was no question but that the United States would remain neutral. No one was more determined on this course than Woodrow Wilson. The thought of leading his nation into a European war (or any war, for that matter) was utterly abhorrent to him. Wilson was even reluctant to make the United States militarily prepared for war, on the grounds that the very act of preparation might itself bring America into the conflict. He dispatched House on unofficial missions to Europe to see whether there might not be some way in which the President of the United States might mediate an end to the war. The American people approved his position and reelected Wilson in 1916 on the campaign slogan "He kept us out of war."

Nonetheless, it became increasingly obvious that the United States could not remain neutral indefinitely. American vessels were being sunk by German submarines, and a Presidential statement that there was "such a thing as being too proud to fight" was widely attacked as being sheer cowardice. In April of 1917 Wilson came to the agonizing conclusion that he must ask Congress for a declaration of war. But he would not lead the nation into war without a noble purpose. In his message to Congress he stated that the United States wanted "no conquest, no dominion . . . no indemnities." She sought only to make the world safe for democracy against the evil forces of German autocracy and not, he made clear, against the German people. When the war was over, there would be a new age for mankind. The forces of evil would be overthrown, and nations, bound by covenants of peace and friendship, would never war again.

As the President returned to the White House, weeping women knelt and prayed at his passage. He had rallied America and world to a vast moral crusade—and he was their undisputed leader.

Wilson had not met the other leaders of the major nations ranged against Germany. He quickly determined that the interests of the United States would best be served if he maintained his freedom of action. Contact with the Allied leaders could be left to House; Wilson would adopt an attitude of personal reserve toward them. It was not difficult. The heads of government of the major Allies were not men to whom Woodrow Wilson would normally have been attracted, and he viewed their policies with distinct suspicion.

One of these men was a short, robustly handsome Welshman with a theatrical flowing mane of white hair—David Lloyd George, Prime Minister of Great Britain and, at fifty-six, the youngest of the major Allied plenipotentiaries who were to sign the Treaty of Versailles. Lloyd George was an unusual man in many respects, not the least of which was that he had risen from near-poverty to the summit of British political power in an age when British politics were still dominated by the sons of wealth and privilege. He had grown up in the Welsh village of Llanystumdwy, raised by his widowed mother and an uncle who was the local shoemaker. At sixteen Lloyd George had become an articled clerk to a lawyer. He had been lucky to pass the week-long preliminary examinations. They had required a proficiency in French, and there was not a single person in his village who had ever heard so much as a word of French. The boy and his uncle had bought a secondhand grammar and dictionary and taught themselves the language.

By the time he was twenty-one, Lloyd George had passed the solicitor's qualifying examinations and begun to practice on his own. Politically he was a Liberal, a natural thing for a poor youth in Wales, where only the Anglicized gentry were Tory. But despite the secret sympathy of his peers, being a Liberal in Llanystumdwy was not easy. It was, Lloyd George claimed, "the blackest Tory parish in the land."[26] Any cottager who acknowledged himself to be a Liberal could count on instantly receiving a notice of dismissal from his landlord. "They were turned out by the score on the roadside because they had dared to vote according to their consciences. . . . It is my first memory of politics."[27]

In 1890 Lloyd George, then twenty-seven, ran for Parliament. He had developed a flaming oratorical style which electrified the voters. He could be vicious. Typical was his attack on the Tories as "the whole kennelry of gorged Aristocracy and of their fawning minions."[28] By a margin of eighteen votes he beat the local squire and became a member of Parliament.

Within a few years after taking his seat in the House of Commons, Lloyd George had become the leader of the pivotal Welsh bloc of the Liberal Party in the house. By 1906 he had become a Cabinet member, as chancellor of the exchequer in the Liberal government of Sir Henry Campbell-Bannerman. In this capacity he formulated a revolutionary national budget, named the "People's Budget," which called for increased taxes on land and property to support a program of social reform. Coupled with this budget (furiously attacked by the Tories as a socialist assault on property) was Lloyd George's National Insurance scheme to compensate workers for wages lost due to sickness and, in some cases, due to unemployment. These measures were subject to the most violent attacks and, it is commonly agreed, were carried through only by the Chancellor of the Exchequer's determination and ability.

When war came in 1914, Lloyd George successfully steered the British financial system through the first days of the struggle, devised the taxation and borrowing schemes to finance the war, and formulated the first war budget. Then came mid-1915 and a series of British battlefield frustrations in France, coupled with an agonizing shortage of munitions, especially artillery shells. A coalition government was formed and Lloyd George given the newly created Cabinet post of minister of munitions. He took over a ministry consisting of a table, a chair and two stenographers. (When Colonel House, visiting Great Britain, arrived to meet Lloyd George, the two men had a friendly argument about which one would sit on the chair and which on the table.) Within a few months his energy and determination had created a staff of twenty-five thousand persons, filling a hundred London hotels and clubs and directing every facet of British military production. He negotiated agreements with the trade unions to permit the use of unorganized labor in the factories, and he dragooned hordes of women into industry to enlarge the munitions-making labor force. He brought into his ministry a huge corps of the leading British businessmen, put them in charge of various subdivisions of the manufacturing effort and demanded only one thing of them: results. Energy, man hours and money were all of no consequence—"What you spare in money you spend in blood," he told Parliament.[29]

Still, at the end of 1916 the Allied war effort had yet to show any worthwhile results. Lloyd George was appalled by the awful slaughter of the Somme and had become convinced that the British failures were caused by the lack of determined direction from the top. In his view the Prime Minister, Asquith, was too prone to follow unquestioningly the advice of his generals, whom Lloyd George considered—not altogether without reason—a mediocre and hidebound lot. In December, 1916, Asquith was maneuvered out of power, and David Lloyd George kissed hands with King George V and received the seals of office as His Majesty's first minister. The generals hated him, the King disliked and distrusted him, the Conservatives tolerated him only reluctantly, and the Liberals supported him with faint heart, but the shock of his personality was instantly felt at all levels. He appointed a War Cabinet consisting of only five persons, including himself. These men met every day, sometimes twice a day. The function of this small group was to serve as the central direction for the entire British war effort—including the military. The official Cabinet, with its cumbersome membership of twenty-two separate ministers, was relegated to the task of executing the decisions of the War Cabinet.

The War Cabinet, apart from its generally acknowledged success, was the perfect ground for the type of leadership at which Lloyd George excelled. He always preferred to do business in person and with small groups. He had a weakness for the snap decision which might have been fatal in another man. His memory was phenomenal, and he had an unusual ability to hold in his mind and interrelate a host of facts. He could quickly become expert on almost any subject. His memoranda were undistinguished, but as a personal negotiator he was without peer. No one could make his way more cannily through the maze of conflicting interests with which he dealt—labor, industry, public opinion and the military men who hated him. A member of his Cabinet marveled at his ability to frame "with telepathic instinct the argument or appeal best suited to the vanity, weakness or self-interest of his immediate auditor."[30] No man could be more charming than Lloyd George, when he chose, and no man could manipulate people better. Moreover, his confidence in himself, his determination to drive through his plans, his perception and his common sense were all of the first rank. There were other virtues in Lloyd George's character. Not the least of them, as Winston Churchill pointed out, was "his complete freedom at the height of his power, responsibility and good fortune from anything in the nature of pomposity or superior airs. He was always natural and simple. He was always exactly the same to those who knew him well: ready to argue any point, to listen to disagreeable facts even when controversially presented. One could say anything to him on the terms that he could say anything back."[31]

David Lloyd George suffered, however, from one glaring defect. He was a very difficult man to trust. There was a curious air about him as if he had no principles, only temporary opinions. In his dealings with other men he betrayed a perpetual fondness for the oblique or circuitous approach. He gave the impression that he acted not from conviction, but from expediency. His greatest relaxation, one from which he derived genuine pleasure, was gathering for an evening with a group of Welsh preachers and singing Welsh hymns. At the same time, in his relationships with women he was practically a satyr, and more than once he was cited as a corespondent in a divorce case. Behind his back he was sometimes called "the Goat."

Lloyd George was, however, no hypocrite. He was frank to admit that nothing he had ever seen in life had led him to put much faith in idealism or the brotherhood of man. He was acutely aware of the fact that he was the first British prime minister who had not been born in the favored classes. He was not bitter about this, merely realistic. He had made his way to the top through ability, an incredible capacity for work, and his own cleverness. "No one," he said, "ever called down to me, 'Come up here, there is a place for you beside me.' "[32]

In all of this, Lloyd George was a product of his nation's political outlook. The British expected little more than the most ordinary virtues in their politicians. To them a Woodrow Wilson with his sententious progressivism would have been more than faintly ridiculous. And, this being the case in England, how much more it was in France, where the premier of the time was the aged Georges Clemenceau.

The "Tiger" was now a stubby, grizzled man of seventy-six. A medical doctor by education, a republican by conviction, a misanthrope by nature, this old man had had one ruling passion in his life: his Germanophobia. As long ago as 1871 he had helped to prepare the defenses of Paris against the surrounding Germans during the Franco-Prussian War. Then, in the years following, he had been the major extragovernmental figure in the turgid politics of the Third Republic. More than any other man he had been responsible for the overthrow of ministry after ministry, until ultimately there was no more hated man in French political life. This bothered Clemenceau not at all. When the Tiger had been premier, he had not hesitated to resort to every device of reaction—police spies, manufactured dossiers, and a Parliament controlled by its members' fears of what the old man knew about them. Clemenceau's recall to the premiership had been unthinkable until the fall of 1917, when an exhausted France had nearly collapsed in the aftermath of a military mutiny and revelations of civil treason Then, every other card having been played, the hated Clemenceau was asked to form a ministry. Everything about him was open to question—everything except his patriotism and his ruthless determination. In a few weeks he had silenced the pacifists, crushed the influence of the left wing and assumed near-dictatorial direction of the French war effort.

These, then, were the men whom Wilson was to face. They were men whose hides were thick and tough. Their careers had been marked by near-ruinous scandals, neither forgiven nor forgotten. Clemenceau had never been able satisfactorily to explain his involvement in the Panama scandals of 1893, just as there was still a cloud over Lloyd George for his imprudent connection with the English Marconi Company profiteering of 1912.

Compared to the backgrounds of these men, Woodrow Wilson's career had been almost simple, the controversies he had known minor. Where he had walked, the waters had opened before him. And the greatest of his successes was his effectiveness as a wartime leader. Perhaps he had failed to keep America out of war, but none could fault his Administration's management of the United States's war effort. Wilson husbanded his own energies and was careful to avoid doing too much himself. His appointments to key economic positions were unanimously acclaimed: Bernard Baruch managing the economy as head of the War Industries Board; William Gibbs McAdoo running the railroads, in addition to his duties at the Treasury; Charles Schwab a director of ship construction . . .

The role of Colonel House remained fundamentally the same as before, except that his contacts with the Allied leaders overseas grew even closer. Every day House's New York apartment was

jammed with visitors who recognized the pivotal influence which he
had upon the President. The British Foreign Office had even sent a
sort of "ambassador" to Colonel House. He was young Sir William
Wiseman (who doubled as British intelligence chief in the United
States) and he occupied the apartment directly over House's on
East Fifty-third Street. On the desk in House's study sat a telephone
with direct connection to the White House and the State Department. This last was probably redundant. For all practical purposes,
Wilson and House *were* the State Department. The President had
little respect for Robert Lansing, whom he had selected to replace
William Jennings Bryan as secretary of state. Lansing was a lawyer,
and the President did not like lawyers. Wilson had appointed him,
as he said, "to put diplomatic notes in proper form."[33]

Wilson reserved to himself a position as moral leader of the
common peoples of the world. In chiseled prose of dignity and force
he reiterated the position in which America found itself—a mighty
nation, hating war, totally uncontaminated with the responsibility
for its outbreak, which had been thrust into the fight because of the
bestial atrocities of the enemy. His words were not directed merely
at the people of the United States. Wilson had made another outstanding appointment, by naming George Creel director of the
Committee on Public Information. Creel was a dynamic publicist,
whose most spectacular feat was the worldwide distribution of more
than sixty million books, pamphlets, placards and leaflets, translated
into dozens of languages, featuring the uncomplicated speeches and
writings of the President of the United States. Wilson's name
quickly became identified throughout the world with freedom and
with an unselfish concern for small nations and dispossessed nationalities. To be sure, the other Allies had attempted to cast themselves
as liberators of mankind, but their attempts had been far less
successful—particularly after November, 1917, when the Bolshevik
revolution took place in Russia. In a devastating propaganda move,
Leon Trotsky threw open the secret archives of the old imperial
government and published in the pages of *Izvestia* the secret
treaties and agreements which France, Great Britain, Italy and
czarist Russia had concluded among themselves for dividing the
possessions of the Central Powers after the war. There for all the
world to read was the Treaty of London, which gave Italy huge
pieces of the Austro-Hungarian Empire; the Franco-Russian agreement for mutual support in determining Germany's postwar frontiers; the agreement to give the Japanese most of Germany's posses-

sions in the Pacific; and a web of understandings which cut apart the Ottoman Empire.

The secret treaties were the inevitable result of three years of frightful warfare, in which the Allies had come within a hair's-breadth of losing the war. They had felt compelled to make any concession so long as it procured another ally. Nevertheless, such agreements were difficult to explain. For years the peoples of the European nations had suspected that their interests were being bargained away in secret negotiations over which they had no control and of which they had no knowledge; now the Bolsheviks had shown that the suspicions were true.

Partly to counteract these revelations and partly to state the aims of the United States, Woodrow Wilson appeared before a joint session of Congress on January 8, 1918. In a low, quiet voice the President introduced his statement, "What we demand in this war . . . is nothing peculiar to ourselves. It is that the world be made fit and safe to live in. . . . All the peoples of the world are in effect partners in this interest."[34] Then he proceeded to enunciate "Fourteen Points" for which the United States was fighting. They were direct and simple: a demand that future world agreements be "open covenants of peace, openly arrived at"; an insistence upon "absolute freedom of the seas"; a demand for the restoration of Alsace-Lorraine to France; a promise of the creation of "an independent Polish State"; and, as the fourteenth point, the formation of "a general association of nations."

The Fourteen Points were sped abroad by the activity of Creel's Committee on Public Information. Almost everywhere they were hailed with vast enthusiasm, for they were superb propaganda. Their brevity allowed them to be reprinted on placard-size posters. Their simplicity made it easy to translate them into foreign languages. Their freedom from self-interest made them morally unassailable. They were spread throughout the Allied nations and the neutral countries and, by balloon, airplane, and leaflet shells, introduced into the enemy countries. It soon became apparent that the Fourteen Points were almost as impressive to foes as to friends. Who could argue against the principles of justice or against "an impartial adjustment of colonial claims"?

However, the contrast between the Fourteen Points and the war aims announced by the European Allies was startling. When Clemenceau had been asked for the war aims of his government, he replied simply, "I make war." The statement had an heroic ring to it, but left much to be desired as an objective for which more than a million Frenchmen had already died. The British had, of necessity, been circumspect in the announcement of their detailed war aims. They could not very well commit themselves to the self-determination of peoples; the rebellious Irish would quickly seize upon this, and, besides, certain of the secret treaties obviously violated the principles of self-determination. Nor did it suit Great Britain's interests to promise freedom of the seas or to make definite commitments regarding colonies.

The Fourteen Points, on the other hand, seemed to be detailed and specific. They held the promise of redressing every grievance and settling every wrong. With them, Woodrow Wilson suddenly snatched the moral initiative from the European Allies. However much this might gall the French and the British, they were now overshadowed by this slender scholar from the New World who had, in Lloyd George's bitter words, been "loitering in the way"[35] for three years while the British and the French had fought the war.

There were certain ambiguities in the Fourteen Points which went largely unobserved at the time. Several of the Points were mutually contradictory. For example, the one relating to Poland called for the new nation to be "inhabited by indisputably Polish populations, which should be assured a free and secure access to the sea." It was little noted that this access to the sea had to be made across territory which was indisputably populated by Germans. Point eight called for the invaded portions of France to be "restored." Presumably this restoration would be done, or paid for, by the Germans, but what about "restorations" to the other Allied nations which had damages to submit? Did Wilson mean that these claims would not be allowed, or were they to be allowed on the same basis as any which might be negotiated for France?

The enthusiastic reception accorded the Fourteen Points encouraged Wilson to amplify, interpret and add to them in subsequent addresses. In two such speeches he enunciated what became known as the Four Principles and the Five Particulars; of these the one that was to be the most famous was the principle that peoples should be free to form their own nations on the basis of "self-determination." To the enemy nations, particularly the Austro-Hungarian Empire, this was an ominous warning. "Self-determination" implied the freeing of the Czechs, the Slovaks, the Hungarians and the Croats, among many others. Wilson's statements, combined with weariness of a war which these peoples had never wanted, began to dissolve the last ties which bound the component parts of the Empire to the Hapsburg throne.

On the morning of October 7, 1918, the Swiss minister to the United States appeared at the Department of State in Washington bearing a message from the German government addressed personally to Wilson. It was brief. Germany requested an immediate armistice and asked the President of the United States "to take steps for the restoration of peace, to notify all belligerents of this request, and to invite them to delegate plenipotentiaries for the purpose of taking up negotiations. The German Government accepts, as the basis for its negotiations, the program laid down by the President of the United States . . ."[36]

It was the culmination of the war. All along the western front the German armies were in retreat, nearly shattered by Foch's concentric attack. Bulgaria had deserted Germany and asked for armistice terms. Austria-Hungary was in its death throes. But the message was not a straightforward appeal for terms of surrender. The note had been drafted at the request of the German Army's Supreme Command, which had desperately demanded a temporary armistice as a "breathing space" during which it was hoped Germany might negotiate a favorable peace; failing this, she would resume the war. Wilson clearly saw the trap and was now faced with a decision: either he could refer the German note to the Allies for joint action or he could answer it himself. It is doubtful that he agonized much over this decision. Despite House's urging to reply only, "The President will at once confer with the Allies,"[37] Wilson decided to handle the negotiations without consulting the French or the British. He would not forgo his special position as spokesman for the peoples of the world and hand over the negotiations to the "old diplomacy."

The subsequent exchange of notes between the United States and Germany continued until October 23, by which time Wilson had, in a series of letters written over the signature of Secretary of State Lansing, secured every conceivable advantage to the Allies. It was not that he wrote the actual terms of the armistice itself; this was to be left in the hands of the Allied Supreme War Council in Paris. What he did was refuse to relay the German request for an armistice to the other Allies until such time as he was convinced that the German government was sincere in its appeal for peace. And even when he was convinced, Wilson told Germany that negotiation would be impossible if the Allies had to "deal with the military masters and monarchial autocrats of Germany."[38] The implications of this demand were not lost upon the enemy. General Erich Ludendorff was dismissed from office, and eventually the German Emperor himself was forced to flee into exile. Wilson secured the Germans' agreement to evacuate France and Belgium immediately upon the conclusion of an armistice, and he made it clear to them that any armistice would be tantamount to surrender, since the Allies would demand such military concessions as "to make a renewal of hostilities on the part of Germany impossible."[39] Only then did the American President agree to grant the Germans the Fourteen Points as a basis for peace and to send their request for an armistice to the Allied War Council in Paris.

In the meantime, the United States's allies had been given only the barest notice of Wilson's negotiations with the common enemy. Their pride had been hurt and their apprehension was acute. Technically, nothing which Wilson might say could commit them, but they had come to learn the power of a Wilsonian announcement. None of the Allied prime ministers had met Wilson, and they were terrified that the crafty Germans would trap this ingenuous and egotistic Presbyterian moralist (for that was how they then viewed him) into some agreement which would force them to an awkward renunciation. If Wilson would not consult with them, then they must consult with Wilson, however humiliating it might be. On October 9 the first ministers of Great Britain, France and Italy appealed by telegram to Wilson for "an American representative possessing the full confidence of the United States Government" to be sent to Paris so as to keep the Allies "accurately and fully informed of the point of view of the United States Government."[40]

By October 17, 1918, Colonel House had sailed for France, armed with a private code to which only he and Wilson had the key, together with a virtual power of attorney from the President as a "special representative" of the United States in such conferences "in which it may be serviceable for him to represent me."[41] The Allies had been counting on his appointment to this mission. Lloyd George and Clemenceau had met House before and they liked this quiet, confidential little man from Texas. They respected him as a negotiator who managed to give at least the impression that he knew and sympathized with their problems and fears, and that he was willing to go at least halfway to meet them.

House arrived in Paris on October 26 and, setting up headquarters in a house on the Rue de l'Université close to both the Foreign Ministry and the Ministry of War, plunged immediately into a round of informal morning meetings with Clemenceau, Lloyd George and Sonnino of Italy. The decisions made at these morning meetings were rubber-stamped by the larger and more formal sessions of the Allied War Council, which met in the afternoons around a huge table in the Trianon Palace at Versailles.

On October 23 Wilson had sent the Allies a formal memorandum referring to them his exchange of notes with the Germans and asking them to advise him whether they were willing to grant an armistice along the lines of the notes, so that he might relay their decision to Germany. Up to this point the European Allies had no legitimate cause for complaint over Wilson's handling of the situation. He had obtained every possible concession; even Clemenceau was moved to comment that Wilson's final reply to the Germans was "an excellent document."[42] But this did not mean the Allies were willing to make peace on his terms. It had not eluded such experienced politician-lawyers that if they agreed to give an armistice along the lines of the Wilson notes to Germany, they would in effect be making a contract to conclude a peace treaty on the basis of Wilson's Fourteen Points. House was under no illusion that this would be palatable to the Allies. It was the moment for the supreme test of his negotiating skill.

On the afternoon of October 29 all niceties were swept aside as Clemenceau turned to Lloyd George in the strained intimacy of an office in the French Foreign Ministry and questioned, "Have you ever been asked whether you accept the Fourteen Points? I have never been asked."

"I have not been asked, either," replied Lloyd George. Then, turning to Colonel House, he asked if it was House's understanding that the Allies would be committed to the Fourteen Points if they gave an armistice.

"That is my view," replied House calmly.

"Then," said Clemenceau, feigning a deprecating ignorance of the exact nature of the Wilsonian pronouncement, "I want to hear the Fourteen Points."[43]

For this moment House had prepared himself well. In particular, he was aware of the ambiguities of many of the Fourteen Points and knew that this imprecision would allow the Points to be evaded in the future on the grounds that they were misunderstood. He had

therefore instructed two young Americans in his mission* to draw
up a detailed "commentary" on the various points. This interpretation was now produced, and House read it aloud, taking each of the
Fourteen Points in turn. Lloyd George himself, his face a wry study,
repeated aloud several of the more distasteful provisions—particularly point two, a call for freedom of the seas in peace and war,
which would make a blockade by the Royal Navy illegal in any
future war. "It is impossible for me to conclude an armistice if I
must accept this clause," he said.[44] The other Allies, Clemenceau
and Sonnino, also spoke out against being bound in their peacemaking by Wilson's pronouncements. Many of the Fourteen Points
had interpretations which they did not entirely welcome. The
French, for example, had no intention of abandoning what Wilson
castigated as the "old diplomacy," with its secret understandings
and interlocking alliances. If it had not been for these, France
would have been alone and friendless in 1914. The French found it
unthinkable that they should abandon these diplomatic guarantees
at the behest of the President of the United States. "I cannot
agree," Clemenceau protested, "never to make a private or secret
diplomatic agreement of any kind."[45] And there were a multitude of
other objections, especially to the provision that there be "no punitive damages" imposed on the vanquished—for British and French
public opinion had already been conditioned to anticipate huge
reparations payments.

To each objection Colonel House had a quiet, carefully considered reply. His voice remained low and confident, his expression
was tranquil, his tone courteous, unimpassioned and sympathetic,
but he would not budge from his position. The Allies must accept
each and all of the Fourteen Points; on this he was absolutely
determined. Finally the conference wore itself down into desultory
wrangling. It was apparent that the Allies would not accept House's
demands. Then into the quiet of the waning afternoon House threw
the first of two trumps, beginning with a little speech—only a few
words, but still unusual in length for this customarily silent Texan.
Since the Allies would not agree to the Fourteen Points, perhaps the
United States "would have to take up direct negotiations with
Germany."[46]

But this would mean, the horror-struck Allied leaders said, a
separate peace between the United States and the Central Powers.

---

* Walter Lippmann of U. S. Army Military Intelligence and Frank Cobb, an editor
of the New York *World*.

"It might," House replied.[47] With this, the conference came to a complete deadlock. It was suggested that it be adjourned for the day while all the parties reconsidered their positions.

The following morning, October 30, House met privately with Lloyd George and Clemenceau at the latter's office in the Ministry of War on the Rue St.-Dominique. It transpired that each of the Europeans was preparing a lengthy draft of reservations, stipulations and amendments to the Fourteen Points. This was in no way acceptable to House. The Allies could not rewrite the Wilsonian principles. He would not permit them to emasculate the United States's program, and he now played his second trump. If the Allies would not agree to accept the Fourteen Points, Wilson would simply have to advise the world of the Allied reservations.

This was a bombshell. Lloyd George and Clemenceau could not possibly allow themselves to be put into the position of refusing a victorious armistice and compelling their nations to continue a now pointless war—especially when their reasons for doing so would be interpreted by world opinion as a cynical rejection of such exalted principles as freedom of the seas and the abolition of secret diplomacy. The adroit little Colonel had placed them in a position from which there was no escape. These knowledgeable politicians sensed the special role which Wilson had come to assume as the spokesman for the common people of the world against the "old diplomacy," against power politics, against entrenched privilege.

Sullenly the Allies surrendered. They forwarded to Washington a memorandum in which their capitulation was almost complete. The Allies declared "their willingness to make peace with the Government of Germany on the terms of peace laid down in the President's address to Congress of January, 1918, and the principles of settlement enunciated in his subsequent addresses." House allowed them only two reservations—one to the effect that "freedom of the seas" was "open to various interpretations, some of which they could not accept," the other that the Germans should understand that compensation would "be made by Germany for all damage done to the civilian population of the Allies."[48] The Italians had protested this. They wanted to take exception to Wilson's ninth point, which stipulated that Italy's frontiers should be drawn along "already recognizable lines of nationality." The secret Treaty of London concluded between Britain and Italy and endorsed by France had promised Italy a slice of the Dalmatian coastline, which was not Italian by any test. But the British and the French brushed the

Italian protests aside. They were already having enough trouble with Wilson; now was not the time to bring up the secret treaties.

The Allies' note of acceptance was forwarded to Wilson on November 5. He immediately advised the Germans of their decision. By November 8 the German delegation had appeared in the famous railway carriage in the Forest of Compiègne, where they were given the Allied terms of armistice. On November 11 the armistice took effect; the Germans were compelled to evacuate France, to retire behind the Rhine and to surrender the bulk of their aircraft, artillery and machine guns and the most modern elements of their fleet.

Let us now pause to examine the role of President Wilson in all these events, and the astounding success of his policies. Here was a man who in the space of only eight years had come from a New Jersey college campus to world power. When he had entered the White House he had been advised by a famous specialist that his arteriosclerosis would not permit him to survive a single term. Now he had been President for six years, and his personal physician claimed that his health had never been better. For three years he had kept the world's greatest industrial nation out of a global war into which every other major power had been drawn. When America had finally joined the Allies, the war was so advanced that, despite every effort to rush its manpower into battle, the United States had suffered casualties only slightly larger than those of Bulgaria. Despite this, the President of the United States was now the world's most revered statesman, he had becomes the spokesman for the Allied nations while simultaneously preserving his own complete freedom of action, and when Germany ultimately sued for an armistice it was to Wilson that she appealed. Moreover, the President had conducted the negotiations with such skill that Germany agreed to an armistice which deprived her of virtually every means of defense and which was, in effect, a surrender. He had played his hand so adroitly that the leaders of the European Allies, for all their cunning, craft and experience, had been forced to concede that Wilson was more powerful in their own nations than they were themselves.

Even the most knowledgeable of experts were astounded at the United States's diplomatic victory. "Frankly," Walter Lippmann wrote to Colonel House, "I did not believe it was humanly feasible, under conditions as they seemed to be in Europe, to win so glorious a victory. This is a climax of a course that has been as wise as it was brilliant, and as shrewd as it was prophetic."[49] But now, at the absolute zenith of his achievement, Woodrow Wilson fell into a series of errors in judgment which would prove disastrous. Prior to the last months of 1918 he had been successful in everything. From this point on he would be successful in almost nothing.

One of Wilson's great political feats during his six years in office had been his bringing a Democratic majority into Congress and keeping it there. In the autumn of 1918 Congressional elections were at hand. Because the war had not yet ended and because Wilson had long before announced that politics was "adjourned" for the duration of the war, it was anticipated that campaigning would be suitably restrained, with a minimum of attacks on the record of the Administration. It was generally assumed that Democratic majorities would be returned to Congress, but on October 25 Wilson himself threw a rock into this placid political pool. He issued an appeal to all Americans in the form of an open letter, pleading for the reelection of a Democratic majority and castigating the Republican Congressional opposition for having been "anti-Administration" and having "sought to take the choice of policy and the conduct of the war out of my hands."[50]

This attack was gratuitous, unnecessary and grossly unfair. Countless Republican politicians and industrialists had loyally served in the wartime government on a completely bipartisan basis. They had faithfully observed the President's injunction against political acrimony. Now they were being suddenly treated as outsiders—indeed, virtually as traitors. They rose in wrath against this treatment, and the elections were bitter and furiously fought.

The Republican Party leadership was delighted with this turn of events. They had begun to fear that they had deferred too much to Woodrow Wilson. In his increasing power and prestige they saw a threat to their future—the possibility that Wilson would be elected for a third term in 1920. They fell to with a will.

On November 5 the nation went to the polls and elected to the Senate of the United States twenty-five Republicans and fifteen Democrats. When the new Senate met, there would be forty-eight Republicans, forty-seven Democrats and one Progressive. It was a thin Republican margin, but it was enough. For the new chairman of the crucial Committee on Foreign Relations would be Wilson's bitter enemy, Senator Henry Cabot Lodge of Massachusetts.

Chapter Two

A Prophet Is Not

The armistice had come with unexpected abruptness. Churchill's warning in 1917 that "peace may yet steal in upon us like a thief in the night" had not proved wholly incorrect. The fighting was done, and there now arose an instant clamor for a peace treaty—a treaty to get the boys home, a treaty to restore ruined France and Belgium, a treaty to punish the defeated and reward the victors, a treaty to reorder the world and make another war impossible.

Looking back from an age when peace treaties have been concluded five years or longer after the termination of war, the haste with which the peace conference to end World War I was called seems incredible. Even before the site of the conference was selected (at first Wilson was anxious to hold it in Switzerland, but he was persuaded by the French to accept Paris), before an agenda and rules of procedure had been adopted, before it had been decided whether the peace treaty was to be drawn up as a "preliminary" or a permanent treaty, every nation was speedily completing its own preparations for peacemaking.

The reason for this haste lay not only in the fact that every nation was anxious to demobilize. Each of the principal victorious powers also felt itself to be thoroughly prepared for peacemaking. The great powers had been conducting their own extensive studies, for periods of a year or more, to determine what sort of peace should be made and how it should be drafted. The British, the French and the Italians had large committees at work studying every aspect of peace. In the United States, as early as September, 1917, Wilson had appointed a group separate from the State Department to prepare for the conference. At first the committee consisted of only a few men (Walter Lippmann was its secretary) working from rooms in the main building of the New York Public Library. But within a few months "the Inquiry," as the group came to be known, had expanded to include a horde of hastily mobilized university professors specializing in every facet of history, ethnography, economics and diplomatic affairs. Operating under the supervision of Colonel House's brother-in-law, Sidney Mezes, and conducted in the greatest secrecy, the Inquiry swiftly outgrew its library offices and moved uptown into the American Geographical Society building on West 156th Street.

The Inquiry had seemed a splendid idea. Its task was to research every possible question or problem which could arise at the peace conference and to develop historical studies, position papers and recommendations for the guidance of the American negotiators. Special attention was to be paid to tracing the ethnic lines of division which (it was supposed) separated one European nationality from another. But it soon transpired that there were very few American academes who possessed any great knowledge of these subjects. A certain amount of "making do" had to be done. For example, nobody could find an expert on Finland and the Baltic lands, so a young instructor in American history, Samuel Eliot Morison, was given the job despite the fact that he could neither speak nor read any of the languages. There had been organizational troubles, too. Sidney Mezes proved to be hopeless as an administrator; his qualifications for the job would seem to have been questionable, since Mezes' field of study had been the philosophy of religion, which he had taught at the University of Texas. At one point it seemed as if the whole project might collapse over the personality of Walter Lippmann, who had managed to offend most of the Inquiry scholars.* The secrecy in which the Inquiry was supposed to work was quickly lost, with the result that the State Department (which had anticipated that *it* was going to work up

---

* One of the most distinguished of the Inquiry's members, David Hunter Miller, complained that "he never knew of anyone who worked with Lippmann who did not hate him." Colonel House seemed sympathetic but privately explained to an Inquiry member that the Administration "had to co-operate with the extreme liberals of the country and that he could think of none who had so much influence and at the same time was so easy to get along with as Lippmann." House added, "Don't you think that he is the least vocal of that crowd?"[1]

the background papers for the peace conference) learned of the project. In the following months the jealous State Department attempted to infiltrate the Inquiry, and the scholars devoted considerable effort to keeping the State men out.

Ultimately a considerable amount of worthwhile work did get done. Mezes was pushed aside; Lippmann resigned. The papers and studies were eventually completed, although it was found that drawing any clear-cut ethnographic or demographic line through Europe was a horrifyingly difficult task. Perhaps the most notable success was in the field of cartography: more than three thousand maps were collected or specially drawn. Another triumph was the reference library which the Inquiry assembled. Every major university library was ransacked and an excellent reference system established. Everything was perfectly indexed and catalogued.

By the end of the war, it seemed that the United States delegation should be able to answer any possible problem or question. There seemed no point in waiting further. Only a few days after the armistice, Woodrow Wilson announced that the peace conference would begin shortly and that he himself would attend.

Wilson's decision to attend the Paris Peace Conference cannot be dissociated from the conference's ultimate failure; it was the first and most crucial of the mistakes that doomed the treaty. Wilson had won a staggering victory in compelling the Allies to accept the Fourteen Points as the basis of a peace treaty. His victory had been so overwhelming that he could not possibly expect to gain more; indeed, he could only lose. Any observer of the process of diplomatic negotiation knows that it is only another term for bargaining. Moreover, it is bargaining conducted among gentlemen, and this in itself presents a problem. However tough-minded they may be, there is an inevitable tendency among the well-bred to avoid offense, to seek the happy phrase, to leave unsaid the abrasive truth which should really be spoken. Moreover, when face to face with his peers for prolonged periods, even the most powerful man feels compelled to make at least some concessions. It is embarrassing (and certainly ungentlemanly) to take constantly and never to give. Only a dictator is immune to the afflictions of gentility and is thus able to become overwhelmingly successful in personal negotiation.

All of this Woodrow Wilson either did not know or ignored. Both Secretary of State Lansing and Colonel House had urged him not to attend the conference, or at least not to take personal part in the discussions. Had Wilson followed this advice he would surely have retained a tremendous advantage. As the elected head of the strongest nation in the world, the creditor of every ally, the political master of the land which was feeding the world, the man who had dictated the basis of the peace, he could remain high above the sordid disputes which would inevitably take place in Paris. Uncompromised, unapproachable, unassailable and unhurried, he could have issued instructions from Washington to his representatives in Paris, who would then have no further discretion. The American negotiators would be free from the agonizing doubt of those who know (and of whom it is known) that they have the authority to make great compromises. They would have blunt, categoric instructions in which they could take refuge against any appeal or blandishment. Meanwhile, Wilsonian statements, couched in his superb prose, polished and repolished, would resound from Washington, where the President could also keep a watchful eye on the Senate.

Instead, Wilson flatly declined the counsel of his subordinates. Ever suspicious, he chose to view the advice against his going to Paris as being largely inspired by the Europeans who feared him or by those Americans who coveted the glory of leading the United States delegation in Paris. He would not cheat the world of his mission—to bring laws unto mankind. Anyway, it was easier for him to go than to stay ("Half my time and more is occupied in decoding dispatches"[2]—dispatches which House sent to him in their private code). Thus, amid the misgivings of such men as Lansing ("I am convinced that he is making one of the greatest mistakes of his career"[3]) and the fears of House ("Instead of becoming the great arbiter of human freedom, he becomes merely a negotiator dealing with other negotiators"[4]), Woodrow Wilson set sail for France. With him he bore, in supreme self-confidence, his messianic ideal. Ahead of him lay Paris, toward which, observed Winston Churchill, "the American peace argosy wended on across the waters bearing a man who had not only to encounter the moral obliquity of Europe but to produce world salvation in a form acceptable to (domestic) political enemies whom he had newly and deeply offended. Upon him centered the hopes of the world . . . and behind him, the sullen veto of the Senate."[5]

The President and his party sailed from Hoboken on Wednesday morning, December 4, 1918, aboard a captured German liner re-named the *George Washington*. Escorted by the battleship *Pennsylvania* and four destroyers, the vessel took the southern route across the Atlantic. It was, on the whole, a most pleasant journey. The ship was comfortable and big—a necessary feature in view of the fact that on board were many of the members of the Inquiry, a vast collection of the Inquiry's documents, its huge reference library, various foreign ambassadors to the United States and their wives, and, of course, the commissioners of the American delegation.

The composition of this latter group must be accounted as another great Wilsonian mistake. It had been agreed among the major powers that each should be entitled to five "commissioners." Wilson had named himself as one of the American five. The others were the ubiquitous House, already in Paris; Secretary of State Lansing, whose position had practically evolved to that of a nonentity; General Tasker Bliss, already in Paris as the United States member of the Supreme War Council; and Henry White, an elderly career diplomat. All these men were competent, respected and informed. But none was a member of the Senate, and only White was a Republican—and he had not been active in party affairs for at least a decade.

Wilson was not unaware of the potential consequences of his selection of commissioners. He surely knew the enmity which Senator Lodge bore toward him. Less than a year before, Wilson had canceled his attendance at a Washington church celebration when he learned that Lodge was to speak there. He was aware that there was rising within the Senate and the Republican Party a bloc determined to defeat any treaty which Wilson might bring home. Lodge's friend and Wilson's enemy, Theodore Roosevelt, had only just issued the ominous statement, "Our Allies and our enemies and Mr. Wilson himself should all understand that Mr. Wilson has no authority to speak for the American people at this time. His leadership has just been repudiated by them."[6] But Woodrow Wilson was not a man to be impressed by such a statement. He hated Lodge, he hated Roosevelt, and he hated the Republican Party. He could easily have disarmed the opposition by the simple inclusion of one or two prominent Republicans among his commissioners. Thomas W. Gregory, Wilson's Attorney General, had given the President a list of several Republicans, including former Secretary of State Elihu Root and former President William Howard Taft. Gregory noted that the choice of any of them would "absolutely insure the approval of the Senate" to whatever treaty the President brought back. "These men," he wrote, "agree in sum with your policies, they would be of valuable assistance and would not obstruct."[7] Nevertheless, Wilson refused to appoint these men (with whom he had no personal differences) to the commission; he would have it his own way, would brook no objections and would suffer no counsel from those who did not acknowledge themselves to be his willing subordinates.

It was this last which constituted the principal chink in Wilson's armor. He did not really understand men. He was a scholar, a theoretician, a writer; in no sense was he an effective negotiator on a personal basis. For all his experience as a debater, he lacked the sensitivity necessary to deal with other men *as equals* and, on this level, to persuade, conciliate or flatter them into agreement. Since the time of his appointment as president of Princeton, Wilson had rarely had the experience of dealing with men on a plane of power equivalent to his own; he had always demanded to be the master, and he had forgotten (if indeed, he had ever known) the art of tactful imposition of his will upon an equal. Moreover, in recent years he had been so successful in his written statements that he had become unaccustomed to dealing on a face-to-face basis without a prepared statement or speech.

Bearing this load of concealed weakness, the *George Washington* proceeded across the Atlantic. It was in the course of this passage that a disturbing question first became evident to the delegation's membership. Although there was a wealth of information available to them, there was apparently no, clear-cut American program for the peace conference. Commissioners Lansing and White confessed that they "knew of no plan or schedule of procedure,"[8] and none of the American delegates knew precisely who was in charge of what. The suspicion began to grow that the President regarded peacemaking as his personal crusade, to which his subordinates would be admitted only for the purpose of providing information.

Only once was there anything approaching a general conference among the delegates. On December 10, as the *George Washington* and its escort steamed past the Azores, a brash young member of the delegation's staff, William C. Bullitt, went up to the President and told him that the delegation did not seem to have any clear idea of the President's program. Wilson, surprisingly, took this statement in good part and immediately summoned a number of staff members into the sitting room of his cabin, where he sketched out his ideas in a manner which impressed most of his listeners as being disturbingly "vague" and "impromptu."[9] He opened with the observation that the United States delegation must be prepared to find that they would be "the only disinterested people" at the peace conference. The foreign delegates, Wilson advised, did not represent their own people. He went on to outline his position on the League of Nations, which he obviously conceived to be the most important of the individual items to be placed before the peace conference. The United States must be prepared to fight for a new order in the world "agreeably, if we can, disagreeably if necessary." The Presidential conclusion was an exhortation for his subordinates to give him "a guaranteed position." "Tell me what's right," he said, "and I'll fight for it."[10]

Woodrow Wilson's arrival in Paris on the morning of December 14 was, and probably still remains, the greatest triumphal progress which a human being has ever made. The *George Washington* steamed into Brest the day before and the Presidential party was drawn to Paris aboard the private train of the President of the French Republic. There, at the Porte Dauphine Station, Wilson was met by Poincaré, Clemenceau and other military and diplomatic figures. Together with Poincaré, he took his place in an open carriage closely escorted by the Garde Républicaine and drove forth to a parade on the Bois de Boulogne, then down the Champs Élysées into the Place de la Concorde. The crowds were so vast that they were frightening; they were so dense that in places they pushed the files of troops lining the route out into the street, and it was only with difficulty that the Presidential carriage could be forced through. For the first time since 1871 the huge chains beneath the Arc de Triomphe were taken down, and Wilson, truly the conquering hero, was driven through. Placards hailing *"Wilson le juste"* were posted everywhere. Weeping, shouting and crying "Veelson!," millions of Parisians fought for a better view of this savior from the New World. It was a scene of mass delirium. Herbert Hoover, a man not given to overstatements, observed:

> *To them no such man of moral and political power and no such an evangel of peace had appeared since Christ preached the Sermon on the Mount. Everywhere men believed that a new era had come to all mankind . . . Woodrow Wilson had reached the zenith of intellectual and spiritual leadership of the whole world, never hitherto known in history.*[11]

In haste and with a certain amount of inevitable confusion, the American delegates moved into their quarters. The President and

Mrs. Wilson occupied a sumptuous residence, the palace of Prince Murat. Colonel House and the other commissioners were given apartments and offices in the Hotel Crillon. The Army Signal Corps at once installed a private telephone line connecting House with the President. Additional office space was provided by turning over a building across the square, 4 Place de la Concorde, to the American delegation. Most of the clerical assistance was provided by Army enlisted men or Navy yeomen. A British diplomatic visitor commented, "The whole place is like a battleship and smells odd."[12]

There now began a period of confused waiting which proved as trying as it was unnecessary. Incredibly, there had been almost no preliminary discussions among the Allies about the procedures for the peace conference. There had been one pre-conference meeting, held in London on December 2–3, but House had been ill and unable to attend it. No American delegate had been sent in his place. Thus when Wilson arrived in Paris on December 14 he seems to have been operating under the impression that the conference would convene within a few days. This was clearly impossible. The British were having an election. The votes would not be counted until December 28, and, much to Wilson's annoyance, Lloyd George refused to come to Paris until then. The French had not even appointed their commissioners to the peace conference. All this left Wilson in the distinctly embarrassing position of a guest of honor who has arrived an hour too early for a party. No one knew quite what to do with him, and so a series of state receptions, visitations and tours to England and Italy were hastily arranged. These were successful in the sense that Wilson received the same measure of public adulation which had been accorded him on his entry into Paris. But they were unsuccessful in several other respects. Wilson, during his Italian trip, conceived the impression that Orlando and Sonnino, the Premier and the Foreign Minister of Italy, were preventing him from speaking to large audiences of Romans. He was sure that they feared his power to sway the Italian people, and this infuriated him. On his state visit to Britain, it was Wilson's turn to be offensive. Before two successive state receptions, surrounded by "Field Marshals and Generals . . ., Admirals . . ., Ambassadors of every land, . . . all arrayed in resplendant uniforms of every cut and color,"[13] Wilson made a speech which Lloyd George described as being characterized only by "perfect enunciation, measured emphasis, and cold tones"; there was "no glow of friendship" in it, and when he sat down "there was a perceptible chill of disappointment."[14] Despite a tactful suggestion from Lloyd George, Wilson refused to make even a passing reference to Britain's wartime sufferings and accomplishments. This refusal seemed to the British an unwarranted insult, and it marred the intended effect of the President's subsequent speeches in England.

But if Wilson could find little constructive to do during these winter weeks, it must not be supposed that Lloyd George and Clemenceau were idle. For one thing, they had now met Wilson for the first time and were much relieved by what they saw. Ominous tales of the American's powers had filtered across the seas. He had been depicted as an awesome personality, a sort of philosopher king, but these Europeans had not found him especially impressive. He did not frighten them. Both Clemenceau and Lloyd George made it a matter of pressing business to find out as much as they could about Wilson's personality, his habits of mind and his objectives at Paris. Lloyd George called in all the British diplomats who knew Wilson and questioned them closely as to the President's personality. It was rumored that the British were carefully studying an extensive analysis of the Wilsonian character which had been secretly prepared by a Republican lawyer in the United States.

Wilson had also been subject to the most careful observation by the Europeans during his first meetings with them. Even the irascible Clemenceau made the greatest effort to steer clear of any subject which could possibly be controversial. Wilson was allowed to do most of the talking, and it was instantly noted that he "opened at once with the question of the League of Nations and had given the impression that that was the only thing he cared about."[15]

But, in addition to observing Wilson, the Europeans had been busy doing the one thing which Wilson had not done—insuring themselves of mastery within their own political houses. Only three days after the armistice, Lloyd George had announced a general election for December 14. There followed four weeks of furious campaigning. The British electorate was maddened with thoughts of vengeance against the Hun, and there was no real way in which a politician could avoid committing himself on this issue. There was an overwhelming demand that Germany be made to pay the entire cost of the war ("We will get out of her all you can squeeze out of a lemon and a bit more . . . squeeze her until you can hear the pips squeak")[16] and that the Kaiser be brought to London to be tried and hanged. Lloyd George himself could not get away with only a vague promise to "make Britain a fit country for heroes to live in." To his discredit, he led his nation to believe that at the peace conference his government would "demand the whole cost of the war," adding, *sotto voce* as it were, "up to the limit of [Germany's] capacity."[17] The election, which came to be known as the "Khaki Election" because of the large number of servicemen who won seats in the House of Commons, presented David Lloyd George a victory of overwhelming proportions. When the votes were counted on December 28 it was found that almost every one of his candidates had won. His supporters now held 526 out of 707 seats in the House. Winston Churchill, himself reelected, was awestruck at the scope of the Lloyd George victory. "Nearly every candidate who had obtained his [Lloyd George's] benediction was returned; nearly every one who did not seek or receive it was rejected [and] barely ninety of his Liberal or Labor opponents found seats in the House of Commons."[18]

The next day, December 29, it was Clemenceau's turn to secure his political footing. He appeared before the French Chamber of Deputies to explain what would be his policies at the peace conference. He observed that there was abroad in the world a movement to renounce the "old diplomacy" and to substitute for it a world organization of some kind. Instead of the old power balances and instead of treaties of alliance there was proposed a sort of supranational organization which was to prevent future war. Be that as it might, he, Clemenceau, had no intention of casting aside those diplomatic devices that had served France so well in the past. As for Wilson's cherished League of Nations: "America is distant," he noted. "It has taken her a long time to get here."[19] He would welcome the League, but only as a "supplementary guarantee."[20] The Tiger ended his speech with an offhand slash at Wilson, whom he described as a man of *"noble candeur,"* a phrase which can best be translated as something approaching simple-mindedness. This statement drew shouts of "Shame!" from the Socialist deputies, and the words were altered to read *"noble grandeur"* in the official minutes.[21] Nevertheless, Clemenceau got what he wanted from the deputies—a vote of four to one backing his policy.

The significance of it all did not elude House, who wrote in his diary that this "was about as bad an augury for the success of progressive principles at the Peace Conference as we could have," and that "the situation strategically could not be worse."[22]

* * *

However profitable these December and January weeks had been for Lloyd George and Clemenceau, the peace conference had not started, nor had much been done by way of preparing for it. There was not even a joint committee at work drafting an agenda. Indeed, there had been only one attempt to get a plan of procedure accepted—this by the French, who, as the host nation, considered it a point of honor to be the first to propose an agenda for the conference. As early as December 2 they had submitted to Wilson in Washington a fairly detailed plan now known by the name of the French ambassador who presented it, Jusserand. The Jusserand Plan, a straightforward document which paid only the barest lip service to the enlightened principles of the Fourteen Points, called for a preliminary treaty of peace to be drafted by the United States, Great Britain, France and Italy without consultation with any of the smaller nations. After all matters of consequence had been decided, the Germans, together with the lesser Allied powers, would be summoned to a formal congress to approve what had already been decided. As a cynical afterthought, the Jusserand proposal acknowledged that the congress "could place itself, as has sometimes been done in the past, under the invocation of some of the great principles leading to justice, morals and liberty."[23]

This plan was totally unacceptable to Wilson. It was the "old diplomacy" incarnate and, moreover, was almost insulting to him personally. He would not even dignify the tactless document with his refusal. The French, of course, put this down to "that repugnance of the Anglo-Saxons to the systematized constructions of the Latin mind."[24]

One aspect of the Jusserand Plan, however, was subscribed to by all of the Allies: there was to be no "conference" in the traditional sense of victors negotiating a peace settlement with vanquished. For this decision, they owed much to their research into historical precedents. The last comprehensive European peace settlement on a scale approaching the present deliberations had been the Congress of Vienna in 1815. Into that assembly, it was recalled, defeated France had managed to introduce her Foreign Minister, Talleyrand, who had quickly broken the victors' unity and obtained sweeping concessions for France. The parallel between the Congress of Vienna and the Paris Peace Conference was obvious. It was unanimously agreed that there could be no question of inviting Germany to the peace conference until a complete treaty had been drawn up. Until the treaty was finished the Germans must be held at arm's length; they would get no nearer than Spa, in Belgium, where the Allied Armistice Commission was in continuous session.

By mid-January of 1919 most of the national delegations had arrived in Paris, and the peace conference was ready to convene. The conference was beginning, as a British observer noted, like "a riot in a parrot house."[25] There was too much of everything: too many problems, too many nations attending (thirty-two separate delegations—twenty-seven nations plus five British dominions), too many people (the official *Composition et fonctionnement* contained more than a thousand names, and these were only the upper-echelon officials) and too much research. They had not been able to agree upon an agenda, but this had not prevented each nation's study groups from laboring at their own individual peace objectives. Swollen corps of experts in diplomatic history, geography and ethnography had analyzed every conceivable aspect of the peace to come. The results of their researches filled endless volumes and countless filing cabinets. The experts and specialists overflowed every hotel in Paris. The British had taken over the Astoria and the Majestic, had turned out the French staffs and replaced them with British servants from scullery boy to maître d'hôtel, and a team of Scotland Yard detectives. The profusion of experts, staff reports and studies was so vast, so stupefying, that no one man could possibly read or comprehend it all. It was apparent that the principal delegates would either drown in research or simply ignore it.

Because the victors held it in their power to remake the world, to draw new borders, to create new states, a horde of claimants, suitors and special pleaders had descended upon Paris. They represented the "new" nations, such as Poland and Czechoslovakia, which had already created themselves from the wreckage of defeated states. But these were not all. Paris was jammed with representatives of would-be nations—Balts, Ukrainians, Sinn Feiners, Hindus, Koreans, Arabs, Aaland Islanders, Armenians, Kurds and countless others. Ceaselessly they importuned the major powers, reminding them of past services or acquainting them with ancient national existences the legitimacy of which was, in many cases, exceedingly suspect. As iron filings are drawn to a magnet, these nationality groups were drawn to Woodrow Wilson. He was, after all, the spokesman for "self-determination," and his daily appointment calendar was crowded with an endless stream of interviews with determined nationalities.

A method of procedure obviously had to be decided upon. The pressures of public opinion and the magnitude of the events had already begun to exert an unsettling effect upon the minds of the principals. What had seemed so simple in the confines of their respective Cabinet rooms was already becoming somewhat less certain. Nor, within the American delegation, was the situation helped by the methods of Woodrow Wilson. The various United States commissioners were rarely called together for strategy conferences. Only Colonel House, who had the direct telephone line from his suite at the Crillon to Wilson's office at the Murat Palace, was regularly informed of the President's private conversations with Clemenceau and other foreign statesmen. From time to time Wilson arrived unannounced at the Crillon, where, ignoring the offices of Secretary of State Lansing on the first floor, he would take the elevator directly to House's quarters on the third floor. "No plan of work has been prepared," complained Lansing in his diary. "He [Wilson] has not even given us a list of subjects to be considered. . . . We putter around in an aimless sort of way and get nowhere."[26]

On Sunday, January 12, the four principal powers—Great Britain, France, Italy and the United States—at last convened a meeting of an already existing organization, the Supreme War Council. Each of the powers was represented by two persons, the head of the delegation and his foreign minister. The four powers agreed to add Japan to their group, and thus it became known, from the number of its members, as the Council of Ten. They agreed also on the establishment of a general secretariat for the peace conference under the supervision of a Frenchman, M. Paul Dutasta. After sketching out a few rules of procedure, they decided that the first "plenary" (full) session of the peace conference would be held the following Saturday, and they then adjourned.

On January 18 the peace conference began, in a hall at the French Foreign Ministry on the Quai d'Orsay. Known as the Clock Salon (there was a small clock mounted in the ornamented mantelpiece), but renamed the Salon of Peace for the occasion, the huge room was furnished with a large horseshoe table, at which the delegates were seated. Behind them were separate tables for the secretariats of the individual nations.

The session was almost totally ceremonial. Poincaré, as the host, opened the meeting. He spoke for half an hour, discussing in turn and at length the courageous and humanitarian qualities of each of the victorious nations. From this he graduated to a predictable and pitiless condemnation of the Germanic spirit of conquest; then, his tone softening, he paid homage to the United States and "the lofty moral and political truths of which President Wilson has nobly made himself the interpreter." He did not overlook the question of reparations to France, advising the delegates that the French would "seek nothing but justice"—which he defined as "restitution and reparation for the peoples and individuals who have been despoiled or maltreated."[27]

The next to speak was Woodrow Wilson, formally attired for the occasion—striped trousers, high collar, cravat with pink pin—who nominated Georges Clemenceau as president of the peace conference. The nomination was seconded in turn by Lloyd George and Baron Sonnino of Italy.

When it was the Tiger's turn to speak, the old man rose stiffly to his feet and, after a few obligatory words of thanks, suggested to the delegates the careful study of the matter of reparations. "The greater the bloody catastrophe which devastated and ruined one of the richest regions of France, the more ample and splendid should be the reparation," Clemenceau emphasized. From this he turned to a rapid survey of matters of procedure, requested that nations wishing to offer observations on any topic submit memoranda to the general secretariat, and announced that the proposed League of Nations would be the principal subject for discussion at the next meeting of the conference in plenary session. Then, in rapid-fire tempo, without pause, he asked, "No one has anything further to say? The sitting is closed."[28]

At first all went smoothly; there was little to go wrong. The various features of the treaty being obviously too complex and too detailed to permit their discussion in plenary session, a number of committees were formed to investigate such matters as control of ports, waterways and railways, international labor legislation, territorial questions, financial questions, economics, reparations, and responsibility for war. The last-named, headed by U. S. Secretary of State Lansing, had the mission of rendering a judgment against Germany so as to justify the punishment which was to be inflicted on her.

Over all these committees, which proliferated endlessly, the five principal Allies kept close control. Either they occupied every committee seat or they retained the chairmanship and a majority. The smaller nations deeply resented this, pointing out that they were left no effective voice in the treaty. Moreover, the meetings of these committees were held in strict secrecy, which hardly agreed with the first of Wilson's Points: "open covenants, openly arrived at." There was, of course, an obvious reason why the committees could not meet in public sessions: a certain amount of negotiation and compromise had to take place; if exposed to general observation, this might look suspiciously like lack of principle. And if the minutes of the committee meetings were made public the members would be forced to speak for the record; the result would be an endless series of speeches delivered for home consumption. So a reinterpretation of Wilson's first point was announced. The smaller nations were advised that "open covenants, openly arrived at" actually meant that after the committees of the Council of Ten had worked out the details the drafts would be brought before a plenary session of the conference, at which time there would be an opportunity for general discussion.

Clemenceau made the best justification for the domination of the committees by the great powers. He did not deny that the Council of Ten was making the major decisions. He merely pointed out that on the day the war came to a close the principal Allies had twelve million soldiers fighting on the field of battle. "*C'est un titre*," he declared.[29] It was generally agreed that it was indeed a title, and Clemenceau let it be known that the major powers were unwilling to discuss the matter further.

In this manner the Paris Peace Conference began its work. Every day the hordes of experts and official delegates convened in their separate committees. From the embassies, legations, hotels and pensions the technical experts journeyed across the dismally wet streets of winter Paris to the embassies, offices or legations at which their committees met. There they gathered in conference, each nation armed with its own set of statistics, its own maps, its own point of view. Where should the Upper Silesian borders of the newly established Polish nation lie? What section of Schleswig-Holstein should be considered Danish and where should the new German boundary be drawn? What should be the position of the International Labor Organization regarding child labor in Oriental nations?

The luncheon adjournments were merely continuations of the

committee meetings, each side sounding out the other on the fine technical points which were the core of their concern. A young British nationalities expert noted in his diary: "Lunch with the American Delegation. . . . I gather the following. (1) Albania. Not so pro-Albanian as I expected . . . (2) Greece. Cession of Doiran and Ghevgueli. Some idea of giving Kavalla to the Bulgars. They threw a fly over us about Cyprus [which the British were demanding for themselves as an eastern-Mediterranean base]. The fish does not rise."[30]

The Council of Ten met daily, sometimes twice a day, in a council room at the French Foreign Ministry on the Quai d'Orsay. The room was paneled in oak, with carved insets, principally cupids in flight. In one wall were two windows which looked out onto a lawn alternately soggy with rain and covered lightly with snow; two of the other walls were covered with tapestries. The dominant feature of the fourth wall was a simple marble fireplace. Set out a little from the fireplace was a Louis XV table behind which Clemenceau sat, his back to the fire. The other principal members of the Council sat in a semicircle of chairs curving from the Tiger's left and right. At the open end of this rough horseshoe was a cluster of chairs for whomever the Council was interviewing that day. Immediately behind Clemenceau sat Paul Mantoux, the official interpreter, and behind the other members sat the aides or experts whom they had brought with them—although, for security reasons, everyone was encouraged to bring as few subordinates as possible. The room was almost invariably hot and stuffy. Logs were always burning in the fireplace, and about thirty persons were usually present at any session, a number which was somewhat too large for the room.

Language did not prove to be a major problem. There were two "official" tongues, French and English. Two members of the Council of Ten in addition to the British and the Americans spoke English fluently. Clemenceau, who had once lived in the United States and had even taught school in Stamford, Connecticut, spoke perfect grammatical and idiomatic English, although with a strong French accent. Sonnino, the Italian Foreign Minister, whose mother was a Scot, spoke such perfect English that he could easily have passed for an Oxonian. Only the two Japanese did not seem able to participate in the discussions. Perhaps they understood what was transpiring well enough, but they were not sufficiently fluent in French or English to engage in the exchanges. The Council could not understand them, and once when a Japanese began to speak Clemenceau embarrassed everyone by turning to an assistant and demanding in a loud, irritated whisper, "What is the little fellow saying?"[31]

In the anteroom outside the double soundproof doors of the conference room another score or so of persons waited. Aside from the attending functionaries, there were various secretaries, assistants and experts. These last, usually bearing with them maps and reports, had been summoned by their masters to provide information on whatever specialized subject might be under discussion that day.

All in all, the Council of Ten did not provide an atmosphere in which things could be swiftly accomplished. The stuffiness of the room, the endless parade of nationalities demanding to be heard, and the large number of people present all prevented the speedy dispatch of business.

Georges Clemenceau, paunchy and sleepy-eyed, slouched his old body in his chair. Had it not been for his age, the Tiger's attire would have seemed ridiculous or eccentric. His clothes were rumpled and unpressed. To hide a skin infection he wore gray gloves which he never took off. He generally wore a black skullcap. Much of the time he seemed to be drowsing, and when he was not he was blunt and rude, never attempting to spare the feelings of his subordinates, who were obviously terrified of him.

Unlike the other principal Allied figures, Clemenceau seemed at first to show no interest in details. He left them to his underlings. Clemenceau spoke seldom, conserving his energy for the battles he knew would come. France had only two principal objectives at the Paris Peace Conference. One was to obtain security against another German invasion, which Clemenceau and practically every other Frenchmen believed was sure to come in another generation. The other was to wring from the enemy the largest possible reparations payments, an objective which would compensate France for her wartime damages while simultaneously draining the German economy of its capacity to reinvade France. Beyond these two objectives, Clemenceau cared for very little. The idealistic policies of Woodrow Wilson were his most serious obstacle. Lloyd George found it almost ludicrous the way Clemenceau observed Wilson— "like an old watchdog keeping an eye on a strange and unwelcome dog who has visited the farmyard and of whose intentions he is more than doubtful."[32]

Lloyd George himself presented a far different picture. Bright and alert, well-groomed and smiling, the Welshman generally radiated geniality. If he was not particularly well informed about details, he made up for this by his glib and articulate manner. It was difficult to believe that Lloyd George was personally very well prepared for the discussion of any particular matter. He displayed his usual penchant for the impulsive and the erratic, and he did not work very hard. This, however, was more than compensated for by his superb personal staff. Waiting in the anteroom was his private secretary, Philip Kerr, a charming, persuasive gentleman with a memory that bordered on total recall. From time to time the Prime Minister would summon Kerr inside, where he could always be depended upon to provide whatever facts were necessary to help Lloyd George through a sticky argument. The secretary to the entire British delegation was an officer of the Royal Marines, Sir Maurice Hankey, a man who must surely have been one of the most efficient secretarial administrators of all time. Every day Hankey's staff (which included such persons as A. J. Sylvester, who had won awards as the fastest shorthand writer and typist in Europe) put together a digest of the Council of Ten's activities as well as a summary of the daily reports of the senior British delegate to every committee and commission. By evening this digest was in print and in the hands of every British diplomat.

Lloyd George had not been welcomed into Paris with anything like the public adulation which had distinguished the arrival of Wilson. By comparison he had slipped in almost unnoticed and, in the words of Churchill, "somewhat dishevelled by the vulgarities and blatancies of the recent General Election. Pinned to his coattails were the posters 'Hang the Kaiser,' 'Search Their Pockets,' 'Make Them Pay,' and this sensibly detracted from the dignity of his entrance upon the scene."[33]

But hanging the Kaiser and squeezing the German lemon were both short-term political goals. Britain's position at Paris was most unusual in that two of her paramount objectives, the neutralization of the German High Seas Fleet and the elimination of German colonial competition, were already accomplished. The German fleet was interned at Scapa Flow, and the German colonies were all occupied by the Allies, mostly by various British dominion forces. What remained as goals for British diplomacy were largely debts of honor to her dominions and to certain of the Allies.

The dominions, having once been colonies themselves, now wanted colonies of their own. New Zealand had captured German

Samoa and wanted to keep it. Australia had seized New Guinea and
refused to give it up. South Africa had occupied German Southwest
Africa and had no intention of abandoning it. Great Britain found it
impossible not to support these claims. The faithful dominions had
sprung instantly to arms to defend the mother country at the
outbreak of the war, and they had contributed blood and money in
unstinting amounts. New Zealand, for example, had mobilized and
sent overseas almost ten per cent of her population; surely the
British government could not deny this little land the possession of
Samoa. The same was true of other dominions. These were obligations which the mother country must honor, even though they
would conflict with Wilson's fifth point.

Great Britain also had her secret-treaty debts to other nations,
most notably Japan and Italy. If any future treaty with Great
Britain was to mean anything, these secret treaties must be honored—even though this might not agree with the first and ninth of
Wilson's Fourteen Points. Finally, it was the traditional policy of
His Majesty's Government, and the first objective of British diplomacy, to secure a European peace of as durable a character as
possible.

These were the manifold aims of British policy at Paris, all
pursued by a consummate negotiator. Lloyd George's mind was
marvelously adaptable and his point of view ever flexible in small
things. In moments of contention he was always ready with a happy
phrase, a disarming smile, or an alternative proposal which would
permit his antagonist to save face. From the ranks of his delegation's
experts Lloyd George could produce a draft resolution for consideration by the Council at a moment's notice. He seemed to know
what Wilson or Clemenceau or Orlando of Italy or the Japanese
were going to say before they said it, and he had a shrewd reply
framed before they had half finished what they were saying.

Among Lloyd George's other remarkable attributes was his mercurial Welsh theatricality. With him on stage, no one knew what
might happen. When the future of the captured German colonies
was under discussion he suddenly brought into the conference room
the prime ministers of all the British dominions to state their case to
the astonished Council. When the partition of the Ottoman Empire
was being considered, the startled plenipotentiaries found themselves confronted by a group of swarthy Arabs dressed in an exotic
combination of desert headdress and British Army uniform, and

accompanied by the famous Lawrence of Arabia. No one could match Lloyd George in producing a startling dramatic effect.

The technique of the President of the United States, perched on his chair at the other side of the room, was very different. His scholarly features were impressive even to Lloyd George and Clemenceau. So was his alert attention to every detail of the proceedings and his ability to take pen in hand and, on the spot, draft a swift, coherent, sensible resolution for adoption by the Council. But they noted that Wilson did not do this often. He seemed to agonize over decisions and appeared too prone to urge that difficult question be given back to the committees for restudy or that the members of the Council "sleep on it" before coming to a conclusion.

Wilson had, moreover, given the Europeans the vastly irritating impression that he regarded himself "as a missionary whose function it was to rescue the poor Europeans from their age-long worship of false and fiery gods," as Lloyd George noted. "He was apt to address us in that vein, beginning with a few simple and homely truths about right being more important than might, and justice being more eternal than truth."[34] Lloyd George and Clemenceau found this only barely tolerable, as they did the President's tendency to open his remarks with the words "Friends—for we are all friends here . . ."[35]

This was not the end of the difficulties under which the President labored. One observer claimed that Wilson's mind moved a fraction more slowly than did the others'. His ideas were thought out in principle, but he had few detailed proposals, and there was a vast gulf between his extemporaneous remarks and his brilliant prepared speeches. To the observant Lloyd George, Wilson seemed "an interesting but not a difficult character study."[36] One thing about the President did puzzle Lloyd George—the President's immense capacity for hatred. The British Prime Minister claimed to have been the one who advised Wilson, in early January, of the death of Theodore Roosevelt and to have expressed the condolences of the British nation. Lloyd George knew that Roosevelt had been closely allied with Senator Henry Cabot Lodge in enmity to Wilson, but even under the circumstances he had not been prepared for "the outburst of acrid detestation which flowed from Wilson's lips."[37]

Doubtless Wilson would have made a more dynamic impression upon the other members of the Council of Ten if only he had possessed the assured backing of the United States Senate. To success-

ful politicians there is no more abject spectacle than another politician whose base of power is insecure or whose leadership has been
repudiated. The Europeans, who had once been terrified of Wilson's
influence over their own constituents, now found it difficult to
endure what Clemenceau called "*sermonettes*"[38] from this man who
might, for all they knew, be powerless to obtain the agreement of
the Senate to what he had demanded in Paris. Nor was this feeling
confined to the Council of Ten. It extended to the subordinate
committees, where Harold Nicolson, a young British diplomat,
noted that "the ghastly suspicion that the American people would
not honor the signature of their delegates was never mentioned
between us; it became the ghost at all our feasts."[39]

But if his labors in the Council of Ten lacked the authority
expected of the scholar President, there was certainly no question
about the hours which Wilson devoted to his work. He was working
incredibly hard, as much as eighteen hours a day—an ominous
matter for a man whose personal physician insisted that he was not
really capable of more than eight hours' work each day.[40] He was
delegating too little and withholding too many decisions for himself,
and the United States commission was suffering the inevitable
consequences. One of the American commissioners, General Tasker
Bliss, wrote in his diary: "There seems to be no executive head, no
minute of our meetings kept (or at least I have not been able to
obtain copies of them), and no instructions to anyone in writing of
the decisions and instructions of the Commission."[41] Unlike the
British, the American secretarial staff was notably weak in executive
skills. The President had left his principal administrative aide,
Joseph Tumulty, in Washington, and now he had no one of real
executive caliber to assist him. Much of the time he was even bereft
of the counsel of Colonel House; the Texan, whose health was never
very good, was intermittently ill with gallstone attacks. Yet Wilson
still refused to delegate anything of consequence to Robert Lansing.
As a matter of protocol the Secretary of State had been appointed
the other American member of the Council of Ten, but Wilson
would give him almost nothing to do. Lonely, ignored and embittered, Lansing occupied himself during Council meetings by
sketching remarkably good caricatures of the other delegates.

Slowly at first, and now more rapidly, too much work and care
were piling up on Wilson's shoulders: the endless streams of foreigners, obscure or prominent, deserving or charlatan, who must see
the President and would see no one else; the secret wartime treaties

among the European nations which would violate the Fourteen
Points and were already creating problems of the most serious sort;
the French newspapers of the right and center which were beginning a series of attacks on the thin-skinned President, obviously
inspired by the Clemenceau government ("American Mysticism,"
they sneered, "Idealism of Wilson: Realism of Clemenceau"[42]); and
the constant warnings from the Senate Republican leadership that
any treaty which Woodrow Wilson brought back to them might be
vetoed—especially if it contained a provision for the League of
Nations.

The creation of an association of the nations of the world was, as
everyone knew, the summit of Woodrow Wilson's ambition. Wilson's formal studies of history and government vastly exceeded
those of Lloyd George or Clemenceau, and his scholarship had
convinced him that the only salvation for the world would be a
community of nations. The League of Nations, as he conceived it,
would be an organization before which nations would bring their
complaints and grievances against others. It would inquire into the
rights and wrongs of each case and then render a peaceful judgment. Under the supervision of the League the major rivers of
Europe would float the unhampered commerce of every nation,
large or small, child labor would be restricted, secret treaties abolished, and the traffic in arms and ammunition controlled. The
League was to be Wilson's personal creation, and outsiders tam-
pered with it at their risk. When Lansing mentioned to him in early
January that he had assigned several experts to the preparation of a
draft constitution for the League of Nations, Wilson turned on him
and demanded, "Who authorized them to do this? I don't want
lawyers drafting this treaty."[43]

The idea of a league of nations was not, of course, strictly
Wilson's. Before the war a host of committees and associations had
existed to promote a system of world alliance. A torrent of plans,
drafts and preliminary League of Nations constitutions had been
drawn up. The French had a draft plan, the British had two plans
(one by General Smuts, the other by Lord Robert Cecil), and the
United States had a draft which had been prepared by House and
revised three times by Wilson. All of them had certain similarities.
They called for the compulsory arbitration of disputes, for a guarantee of territorial inviolability and for common action against trans-
gressor nations.

It was inevitable that the Europeans would view the idea of a league of nations in a somewhat different light than did Wilson. It was hard for them to believe that a world association could be formed which would be truly effective in preventing future wars. There were exceptions, of course; among the British, Smuts and Cecil were enthusiastic. But there is little evidence that the League held any particular attraction for Lloyd George. In fact, to him Wilson's enthusiasm seemed almost ludicrous. With relish Lloyd George describes a meeting of the Council of Ten during which Wilson explained to those present, including the notorious atheist Clemenceau, that the League of Nations would succeed in creating a brotherhood of man where Christianity had failed. "Why," Wilson asked them, "has Jesus Christ so far not succeeded in inducing the world to follow His teachings in these matters? It is because He taught the ideal without devising any practical means of attaining it. That is why I am proposing a practical scheme to carry out His aims." Clemenceau, says Lloyd George, "slowly opened his dark eyes to their widest dimension and swept them around the Assembly to see how the Christians gathered around the table enjoyed this exposure of the futility of their Master."[44]

Lloyd George's lack of enthusiasm for the League did not stem merely from irritation with Wilson. To the British the creation of such a league raised many problems, not the least of which were those revolving around the captured German colonies. It had been generally agreed that the colonies would be taken away from Germany, but to whom were they to be given? Several of the League of Nations' draft constitutions proposed that the German colonies be administered by the League itself—which put the British in a very difficult position, since their own dominions also claimed those colonies.

Nor was that all. The secret treaties which Britain had signed during the war had promised her allies certain other German colonies; the Japanese, for example, were to get all the former enemy islands north of the equator, together with the old German concessions in China. Now these secret obligations had to be honored, and it was difficult to reconcile them with the altruistic ideals of the League of Nations. Doubtless, Lloyd George would have preferred to conclude the treaty with Germany first and then, after the German colonies had been parceled out, to convene another conference to set up the League. But to Wilson, unencumbered with either colonial obligations or secret treaties, these British problems could be dismissed as an attempt at "mere distribution of spoils."[45]

For France the question of the League of Nations was even more complex. Clemenceau could hardly afford to regard it with indifference, since the League was in some respects a potential threat to France's safety. The Tiger was quick to point out that in years past there had been many utopian schemes to outlaw war and compel arbitration of international differences, and that none of these schemes had exerted the slightest deterrent upon the Germans in August of 1914. Clemenceau had no faith that a future league of nations would be more effective. Indeed, its very existence might lull the world into a sense of false security and prevent the negotiation of a new web of international military alliances similar to the Triple Entente which had saved France in 1914. Clemenceau was interested in the proposed League of Nations only on two conditions: that there would be an international armed force (from which Germany would obviously be excluded) to carry out the League's orders, and that this armed force would be supervised by an international general staff (on which French officers would obviously predominate)—in short, that the League would be simply a continuance of the victors' wartime alliance against Germany. Only if these conditions were fulfilled—and Clemenceau suspected that Wilson could never agree to them—would the League be of value to France. With Lloyd George, Clemenceau would have preferred first to settle the German treaty and then, at some later date, to discuss the possibility of a world organization. But, like the other Allies, France was committed to the League. It had been one of the damnable Fourteen Points, and its creation could not be delayed or avoided.

As for the Italians and the Japanese, their attitude toward the League can best be described as one of cautious reserve. If the greater powers wanted the League of Nations, then so be it. Written in the secret treaties were substantial territorial promises to Japan and Italy. They would be well content with these. As for the League of Nations, perhaps it would turn out to be a good thing. In any event, it would not do to displease Woodrow Wilson by betraying a lack of interest in it.

Thus, with the exception of the United States, the attitudes of the assembled diplomats ranged from mild enthusiasm through casual interest to mild disfavor. But all reservations had to be carefully concealed; world public opinion was in favor of the League, and though Wilson's prestige in Paris had definitely waned, no one knew for sure how it stood among the peoples of the world. They could not risk refusing him the League.

The attitude of each of the Allies toward the League was either known or suspected by Wilson. He was convinced that unless he got a League of Nations constitution written into the peace treaty with Germany there would never be a League. Backed by world opinion, Wilson had demanded the agreement of the other Allies to a treaty of peace that would contain a "Covenant" for a League of Nations. This Covenant would consist of the League's constitution and the agreement of the victor nations to join it. Many of the provisions of the peace with Germany would be administered by the League. The League and the peace treaty would be so intermeshed that they could never be split apart. This, at any rate, was the prophet's plan.

The beginning of the work of the peace conference on the League began at the second plenary session on January 25. Wilson rose and offered a resolution which proposed that a League of Nations be formed which would "be created as an integral part of the general treaty of peace." He further proposed that the conference appoint a special commission "to work out the details of the constitution and functions of the League."[46] In due course Wilson's resolution was seconded and adopted and the members of the commission were announced. The chairman of the commission was Woodrow Wilson. The other American member was Colonel House.

The commission held its first meeting on the afternoon of February 23, in House's suite at the Hotel Crillon. A green baize cloth had been spread over a large circular table in the dining room, and around this the commission members gathered and began their labors. For this opening conference Wilson and House had made painstaking preparations. They had carefully considered which among the other major powers was closest to their own thinking about the League and had decided upon the British. Accordingly, David Hunter Miller, an American expert, had been dispatched to confer with his British opposite number and put together a joint draft Covenant. This draft, known as the Hurst-Miller Plan, was jammed through the committee at its first meeting as "the basis for the Commission's deliberations."[47]

To the French and the Italians, who had appeared at the meeting with their own drafts, the adoption of the Anglo-American draft was a serious defeat. Any changes they wanted to make would have to come as amendments, and they could be sure that the Anglo-Saxons would make this as difficult as possible. To the French in particular the Hurst-Miller Plan was infuriating. There had not even been a French translation of the draft document at the time it was adopted.

This was not the end of the French humiliations. The senior French member of the commission was Léon Bourgeois, a garrulous elderly lawyer who had for many years been prominent in the world peace movement. The other members of the commission were generally unaware of Bourgeois's previous experience in this work. "Is there really a Permanent Court of Justice at The Hague?" someone innocently inquired.

"I have the honor to be one of its members," was Bourgeois's stiff reply.[48]

Bourgeois was again mortally offended when the commission declined his request to include in the Covenant some sort of flattering reference to the work of the Hague Peace Conferences of 1899 and 1907, to which Bourgeois had been a delegate. "That was noble pioneer work," the Frenchman protested, "and it should not be forgotten."[49]

During the first week of the commission's sittings Wilson managed to keep the group moving forward. He had established an atmosphere of urgency by advising the committee that the Congress of the United States was about to adjourn and that it was absolutely necessary for him to return temporarily to Washington to sign legislation. He intended to leave Paris in mid-February and would be gone for a month. It was urgent, the President announced, that the commission complete the Covenant in time for the next plenary session, on February 14. Having given the warning, the scholar prophet drove the commission at a rapid pace. Wilson drove himself just as hard. His mornings were devoted to private conferences, his afternoons to the Council of Ten, and his evenings—frequently until well past midnight—to the commission drafting the Covenant.

At first the commission issued laconic daily progress reports to the press—that "the preface and the first two articles had been discussed" or (a later announcement) that "appreciable progress had been made."[50] In fact there was agreement only on the more general sections of the Covenant. When it came to specifics, the French were digging in their heels to fight for the international army or, at the very least, the international general staff, neither of which Great Britain and the United States would accept. The fight was becoming bitter.

The French press erupted in a wave of government-inspired anti-

Wilson articles which infuriated the President. Inevitably compromises were made in the framing of the Covenant: the sticky question of "freedom of the seas" was put aside on the grounds that the League of Nations would make the issue obsolete; the victors were permitted to keep their German colonial spoils by a complex system of "mandates" from the League. But the French would not give up their demand for an international army. They were not willing to accept Wilson's unwritten promise, "When danger comes we will be there."[51] Even the usually acquiescent Japanese were creating a problem. One of the articles in the Hurst-Miller draft of the Covenant was a Wilsonian phrase calling for equal treatment (including equal immigration rights) for religious minorities. It had been designed to protect the Jews, but now the Japanese proposed that racial minorities be included in the article. This drew a furious objection from the "yellow peril"–conscious Australians, and even Wilson suddenly realized how ill this amendment would sit with the Western states at home.

Soon the commission was deadlocked. Not even morning, afternoon and evening sessions on February 10 could start it moving again. The harried Wilson had no choice but to declare a two-day suspension of the meetings. It now appeared almost certain that there would be no Covenant completed before Wilson's departure. He would have nothing to present to the plenary session on February 14. Nor would he have a Covenant to take back on his trip to the United States. Everyone would know that he had been defeated in the thing he cared about most.

There was one more session of the commission. It began on the morning of February 13, with Wilson in the chair. By one in the afternoon the wrangling was still intense and only six of the projected twenty-seven articles had been agreed upon. Thoroughly dejected, Wilson quit the commission to appear at a Council of Ten meeting, leaving Colonel House as his personal representative. The commission was now at the precise point where the little Texan could work most effectively. Compromises had to be made—everyone knew it—and House was just the man to suggest them in the most palatable manner. During the previous nine meetings he had scarcely uttered a word, but now he opened up. He cut short the garrulous M. Bourgeois, forced the French amendments to a vote, and got them defeated one by one. Next House dealt with the Japanese. He made it easy for them to withdraw their insistence upon a racial-equality amendment by offering to delete the entire religious-freedom article. There could be no amendment if there was nothing to amend. The Japanese were agreeable. The commission was now making rapid headway. House glossed over objections from the overruled nations with the suggestion that they vote for the Covenant now and bring up their reservations at the plenary session the next day.

Over all of this there still hangs a certain obscurity, an aroma of quiet, private anteroom conferences between the tactful Colonel and the French, the Japanese and the Italians. There is more than a hint of promises of sympathy and support for later demands. At any rate, the draft Covenant was suddenly and unanimously approved by the commission. At seven in the evening, House was telephoning the overjoyed Wilson that the Covenant would be ready for presentation at the plenary session.

The next day, February 14, the President stood before the plenary session and read the Covenant. Quite probably he regarded this hour as the pinnacle of his life's achievement. "A living thing is born," he declared.[52] From the chair, Clemenceau abruptly announced that the report was now accepted "for examination and study by all the interested powers."[53] The session was then adjourned. House scrawled a note to Wilson: "Dear Governor, your speech was as great as the occasion. I am very happy." Wilson passed back the reply, "Bless your heart—thank you from the bottom of my heart."[54] But in fact congratulations were premature. The conference had not yet officially adopted the Covenant. It had listened to Wilson's speech, but the delegates had not approved the Covenant. And the Senate of the United States had not ratified it.

That evening Woodrow Wilson left Paris for his brief trip back to the United States. The successful drafting of the Covenant had put him in a jubilant frame of mind—but he knew well the problems which would face him in Washington, just as he suspected the difficulties which would accumulate in Paris during his absence. House had suggested that Wilson call together the members of the Senate Foreign Relations Committee for a dinner at the White House to explain the Covenant to them and ask for their support. Wilson had appointed the quiet Colonel as his alter ego at the conference. At the Paris railroad station he warned him, "Heavy work before you, House."[55] And, almost certainly for the last time, he put his arm around the shoulders of his little disciple. With this, the President departed Paris.

*   *   *

With Wilson temporarily absent, the peace conference entered a new phase during which the leaders of the great European powers devoted their time to quashing incipient political revolts at home. While it is true that the European members were firmly in control of their respective governments, it must not be supposed that they lacked political enemies. Lloyd George rushed off to London for a series of cabinet meetings, and Orlando vanished to Rome on the same mission.

The Council of Ten continued to hold its daily meetings, but, now that three of the principals were gone, lassitude quickly set in. Even though the various subcommittees were still deliberating, and even though a vast amount of behind-the-scenes work was being accomplished, nothing *seemed* to be getting done. With the exception of the League of Nations draft Covenant, almost nothing had been completed which the delegates could take to their people. A month had passed and the Kaiser had not been hanged, the conquered nations were not paying the victors billions in reparations, even the spoils of the secret treaties had not been divided. The delegates were beginning to hear distinct rumbles of dissatisfaction from home.

Much of the world's disappointment could be traced to wretched press relations. More than five hundred newspaper correspondents were in the city, and they were being told almost nothing of the progress of the conference. The official interviews were so sparse, the official press announcements so vague, that there was virtually nothing left for the newspapermen to do but file copy criticizing "the dawdlers of Paris."

Clemenceau, more than any other principal, was in serious trouble over the question of reparations for France's wartime sufferings. In the course of the war, the French Army had sustained over six million casualties—more than the losses of the British Commonwealth, Italy, Japan and the United States put together. The war had been fought largely on French soil, and French farms, villages, towns and cities had been devastated. France had fought the Germans almost alone for more than two years while the other Allies raised their armies. When the war had been won, the French were promised a peace of justice. But to them "justice" meant compensation to France for the hideous suffering which she had endured;

justice demanded that the other Allies display their gratitude toward France in some tangible manner. Again and again they claimed that the case of France was "unique." The Allies were expected to understand that no other nation had made comparable sacrifices, and it was assumed that they would act accordingly. The French anticipated that France's grateful friends would make it their first order of business to compensate her for her losses, and it was thought only right that the second order of business would be to take such steps as were necessary to protect France against a future German onslaught.

As the weeks went by, it became evident that a sense of obligation toward France was *not* the dominating concern of such figures as Lloyd George and Woodrow Wilson. The French were astounded at this. A famous cartoon by Forain showed a mutilated French veteran banging with the stump of his leg on the door of a room marked "Conferences" and crying, "I have come to find out whether or not I conquered." The French delegation made endless attempts to inveigle Wilson into a tour of the devastated areas of France and took offense at his repeated refusals. Wilson knew why they wanted him to make the trip: "They want me to see red."[56]

The French could think only of one reason for the failure of the Allies to acknowledge their debt to France. It must be that Georges Clemenceau was not representing the French case properly. Certain prominent Frenchmen, enemies of Clemenceau, began to fear that the old man was not making France's claims clear to the Allies. One could not fail to remark it. His spine must be stiffened. The Allies *must* be made to recognize their responsibilities to France.

Among the foes of Clemenceau none was more implacable than the President of the French Republic, Raymond Poincaré. Clemenceau hated Poincaré, who, in return, detested the Tiger. Normally the Presidency of the French Republic was a figurehead position. ("There are two useless organs," Clemenceau had once observed, "the prostate and the Presidency of the Republic."[57]) Poincaré was an exception. A lawyer with a conservative, excruciatingly legalistic mind, he had created for himself a position of greater influence than had his predecessors in the office. He was quite prepared to lead the opposition to Clemenceau. Poincaré believed, as did most of the French right and center, that the nation had been saved from defeat only by a providential miracle. He could not forget the three days in August of 1914 when it had not been certain that Great Britain would declare war against Germany. He could not forget how long it had taken the United States to come into the war; or that Italy had initially been allied to Germany; or how whisper-thin had been the defense against the German attack in March, 1918. Germany had almost won the war, and Poincaré was convinced that she would try it again. The French Parliament, which contained so many former soldiers that it was called "the Horizon-Blue Parliament," supported the President of the Republic. France's only salvation was a divided and weakened Germany. France must bleed her enemy's economy with enormous reparations, surround her with armed and hostile client states, reduce her Army to impotence. And this must be done while Germany was exhausted and blockaded, and while France could still claim an obligation from the "Anglo-Saxons." To be sure, France was now victorious, but this was only temporary. Poincaré's supporters were fond of quoting Madame Letizia Bonaparte, who, when asked her opinion of her Emperor son's achievements, would reply, "It's all right as long as it lasts."

Poincaré and his friends were not Clemenceau's only enemies. More formidable still was the French Army, in the person of the "General in Chief of the Allied Armies in France," Marshal Ferdinand Foch.

The desires of Foch and the Army could not be ignored by Clemenceau. The French Army had gone to war encumbered with faulty doctrine and faulty armament, it had lost the opening battles and had been driven out of a sixth of France, but somehow it had recovered and gone on to bear the brunt of the fighting for year after hideous year. Now that the war had been won, there was no question in the minds of Frenchmen as to where the credit for the victory lay: with the Army of the French Republic. Each Sunday, in the towns and villages of France, scores of memorial tablets and statues were unveiled, all dedicated to the Army which had saved France. Forgiven was the Army's old antirepublicanism, forgotten the Army's innate conservatism; the awful suffering of the French Army gave it an overwhelming claim to the nation's sympathy. Not in a hundred years, not since Napoleon, had the Army's prestige been so high.

The prestige of Marshal Ferdinand Foch was no less high. At first glance he seemed improbable as a military officer. Short, bearded, dynamic and sixty-seven years old, Foch looked much like an energetic and well-preserved professor in a provincial university. But his appearance was deceptive. Foch was generally regarded as the world's greatest living military genius. Even as a young officer he had been haloed with the aura of great things to come. His early writings on the theory of war became textbooks in military schools throughout the world; his lectures at the War College exerted a decided influence on French military doctrine. And, unlike many theorists, he proved personally able to implement his ideas. When war came Foch acquitted himself admirably, first as a corps commander and then as the commander of an army group. He suffered reverses and spent six months of 1917 in disfavor, but quickly recovered from this. Clemenceau appointed him chief of the French General Staff and later, in the desperate days of March, 1918, when the Germans nearly broke the Allied front, he obtained for Foch the position of commander in chief of all the Allied armies in France.

Foch was far from being Clemenceau's protégé, however. The Tiger had appointed him only because he was the best man for the job, and they had several sharp disputes. The Tiger terrified most men; Foch was an exception. On the day Foch was given command of the Allied armies, Clemenceau tactlessly remarked, "Now you have got the position you wanted so much." Foch whirled around and spat out, "What do you mean? You give me a lost battle and you ask me to win it. I accept, and you think you are making me a present."[58] Even Clemenceau was silenced by this. But he remained suspicious of the Army's constant attempt to encroach upon political decisions which were the responsibility of the civil government. There was nothing very new about this. The French Army had traditionally attempted to pursue its own goals and policies, independent of the government. It had always distrusted the civil government, and in turn the civilians had learned to regard the Army with a certain suspicion. From time to time Clemenceau rebuked Foch for intruding into the sphere of policy; harsh words were exchanged between the men.

In October, 1918, Foch wrote to Clemenceau asking to be informed of the government's exact postwar objectives, particularly regarding the acquisition of German territory adjoining the French frontier. Foch requested that a Foreign Ministry official be assigned to Army headquarters to keep him *au courant* with respect to the government's diplomatic intentions. Clemenceau decided that this was as good an opportunity as any to put Foch in his place. His reply was blunt and intentionally offensive. He reminded the Marshal that he was a technical adviser to the Government, nothing more. The government would apprise the military of its intentions only if the government found it convenient or desirable to do so. In the meantime, diplomatic and economic questions were outside the Army's purview and Foch would not be consulted regarding them.

It appeared at first that this reprimand had gone home. On November 11 the Marshal handed the signed armistice to Clemenceau with the punctiliously correct statement, "My work is finished. Your work begins."[59] However, the French Army had retired from the political scene with several reservations. It hoped, for instance, that some serious attempt would be made to eradicate the Bolshevik government in Russia. Foch had developed a whole series of schemes for this; the most promising of them involved the creation of a huge inter-Allied army which, under French officers, would invade Russia and crush the Red Army.

This Russian adventure was only a fond wish. It was as nothing compared to the Army's resolute determination to advance the military frontiers of France to the Rhine. The broad and swiftly flowing Rhine, with its bridges blown and its west bank fortified, provided the ideal military barrier against Germany. The French Army was obsessed with the vision of it.

There was only one problem. To advance her frontiers to the line of the Rhine, France would have to annex or occupy ten thousand square miles of German territory which lay to the west of the river. This area, the Rhineland, contained five million persons and had been German since 1814. Before that, but only for twenty years, it had been a French conquest; before *that* it had been a welter of duchies and petty kingdoms of Germanic persuasion. France had no convincing title to the Rhineland.

The Army cared nothing for these legal niceties. The permanent occupation of the Rhineland and the fortification of the left bank of the Rhine were the only diplomatic objectives which the Army had demanded of its government, objectives which the Army thought the French government had positively agreed to obtain. In fact, a treaty of sorts had already been negotiated. Early in 1917 the French had exchanged a series of secret notes with the tottering imperial Russian government in which the French recognized Russia's "complete liberty in establishing her western frontiers" with Germany, while the Russians in return offered their support to a proposal that "the German areas on the left bank of the Rhine . . . be entirely separated from Germany."[60] When the armistice terms were formulated, Foch demanded that the Rhineland be occupied by the Allied armies, and the other Allies all agreed, assuming it was a temporary measure to enforce the armistice provisions.

No sooner had the armistice been signed than the French moved to secure permanent possession of the left bank of the Rhine. When in December of 1918, Foch and Clemenceau visited London, it was judged an opportune occasion to make certain concessions and then to apprise the British of French desires. The concessions were made and an evening conference was scheduled, from which Clemenceau purposefully absented himself, pleading a "social engagement."[61] It was a deftly calculated move. The French assumed that the British could refuse Foch nothing. Thus it was left to him to spring the Rhineland proposal upon the British. With the utmost delicacy the Marshal described France's fear of a resurgent Germany and announced that "the natural barrier against such an invasion" was the Rhine.[62] Foch referred to the German territory west of the Rhine as "the Rhenish *provinces*."[63] With a start, the British suddenly realized where Foch was directing the discussion. Lloyd George asked how Foch reconciled his proposals with President Wilson's Fourteen Points. Foch replied airily that somehow "it could be arranged,"[64] and the meeting adjourned, Lloyd George having taken good care to make no commitment.

In a matter of days the British indicated that they would not support the French plans for the annexation of the Rhineland. Lloyd George's reasons were intensely practical. A French Rhineland was bound to be a source of future European conflict, like the German seizure of the French provinces of Alsace and Lorraine. Lloyd George had little confidence in the ability of the French to deal with a restive German population suddenly made French citizens against their wishes; with Ireland blazing in rebellion, the British were acutely aware of the difficulty of suppressing a national uprising.

Moreover, the whole idea of territorial annexation ran counter to various of the Fourteen Points, and there could be no doubt that Wilson would veto the French plan. So far as the British were concerned, a French annexation of the west bank of the Rhine or even the establishment of a farcical "independent Rhenish republic" with close French ties was out of the question.

Clemenceau accepted the British rejection with a certain degree of resignation. The old man had foreseen it and was prepared to devise some alternative method for securing the left bank of the Rhine without outright annexation. He carefully avoided any direct confrontation with Lloyd George or Wilson on the matter; time, he hoped, would work in France's favor. But to Foch, who had no conception of the diplomatic difficulties which Clemenceau had to face, the attitude of the French Premier was incomprehensible and bordered on treason. The Allies must not be allowed to fail in their duty toward France. Clemenceau must *demand* that the Allies allow France the left bank of the Rhine! Foch consistently complained that he was being kept in the dark on matters at the peace confer-ence—"One could say without exaggeration that the Government and principals concerned took care not to inform me at all."[65]

Clemenceau now found himself in a difficult position. The fact that Foch had been, and still was, the commander in chief of the Allied armies gave him a special relationship to the Allied heads of state. If Foch was determined to meddle in political affairs it would be difficult to stop him. Various attempts were made to placate the Marshal. Ray Stannard Baker, the American press chief, was witness to one of these. In early January Baker was waiting in an anteroom of Étienne Pinchon, Clemenceau's Foreign Minister. Suddenly the thick double doors of Pinchon's private offices burst open "and out strode a short, stocky, gray-haired man, very erect, . . . who wore the uniform of a marshal of France. Behind him came flying the little agile figure of Pinchon, pleading for him to return. 'Never, Never!' said Marshal Foch angrily. . . . He was through with the Peace Conference. He would never go back. . . . But in a moment he was suddenly persuaded and he did go back."[66]

If these private quarrels were embarrassing to Clemenceau, they were nothing compared to the scenes which Foch staged from time to time before the principal Allied plenipotentiaries. (Whatever their other problems might be, the Anglo-Saxons could at least claim to have their own generals firmly in hand.) One such scene took place at a meeting of the Council of Ten to which several military men, Foch included, had been summoned. In short order the mili-tary matters were concluded, and, as was the custom, the soldiers immediately withdrew. Only Foch remained, much to the embar-rassment of all. Clemenceau, irritated, loudly announced, "The military men and naval experts will please retire," a statement which could hardly have been more direct, since Foch was the only soldier left in the room. The Marshal chose to pretend that he had not heard his Premier. Clemenceau repeated himself, and still Foch made no move. There was an embarrassed silence. Clemenceau climbed to his feet, walked over to Wilson and muttered, "I don't know what to do; he won't leave."[67] In strained perplexity, it was suggested by the ever tactful Arthur Balfour that the Council recess for tea. Self-invited, Foch stayed on—until finally the exasperated

Clemenceau walked over to the Marshal and spoke a few words into his ear. What they were no one heard, but suddenly Foch jumped up and left the room.

This was the formidable coalition which faced Clemenceau—Poincaré and the archnationalists, Foch and the Army. They were powerful, but Clemenceau controlled most of Parliament and a good part of the French press. He had fought opposition before, and he could do so again—especially since his objectives at the conference did not really differ greatly from those of his enemies. There would be many opportunities for France in the course of the drafting of the peace treaty. For now, Wilson seemed unassailable. But Clemenceau was sure that this would not endure indefinitely. One had only to be patient.

Chapter Three

The Russian Dilemma

IF the major concern of the peace conference was the defeated enemy, Germany, the most perplexing was an ally—Russia.

Technically Russia was still one of the principal Allied powers, though she was in no position to press this claim at Paris—nor did her government, intent upon world revolution, have any interest in doing so. In March, 1918, the Bolsheviks had signed the Treaty of Brest-Litovsk, by which Russia abandoned the Allied cause and made a separate peace with Germany. Thereupon the Allies, considering themselves betrayed, had, on one pretext or another, landed troops at various points on the Russian perimeter; the British now occupied Murmansk and Archangel in the north, a French force had been landed at Odessa in the south, and the Americans, with the greatest reluctance, were maintaining a small force at Vladivostok in the east and another at Archangel. Chiefly these troops had been landed to protect the huge dumps of military supplies which the Allies had delivered at the seaports for use against the Germans by the Imperial Russian Army and, later, by the forces of the Kerensky government which succeeded the czarist regime—supplies which might fall into the hands of the Germans now that the Bolsheviks had seized power and made peace with them. Almost inevitably, the Allies had soon begun to encourage and support the "White" armies which had sprung up to counter the Lenin revolution. The original motive for this was the Allies' desire to replace the Red government with one which would resume the war against Germany, but as the months passed this objective became somewhat obscured. The Allies found themselves caught up in a vast civil war which was being fought with the utmost ferocity and which showed no sign whatever of slackening when Germany collapsed in 1918.

The attitude of the Allies toward Russia now had to be reassessed. The position which the United States took was that, while Bolshevism was certainly unattractive, the White forces (practically all of which were monarchist) were scarcely less so. There was no prospect that the American people would support the sending of additional troops or money to Russia to assist in the restoration of the Russian monarchy. Moreover, Wilson believed that Allied intervention would only serve to increase Russian popular support for the Red forces. As for the United States, Wilson announced that he did not fear the attraction of Bolshevism, because "considerable progress had [already] been made in checking the control of capital over the lives of men."[1] Regarding Russia the United States was fairly well committed to a three-point program: she would not recognize a Bolshevik government; she had guaranteed the territorial integrity of Russia; and she was attempting to pursue a policy of nonintervention. When all these were put together they amounted to a program which permitted very little latitude.

Lloyd George announced that Great Britain, however much she abhorred Bolshevism, could not afford the men and the immense amounts of money that a prolonged interventionary struggle would require. There was in fact a serious question as to the reliability of the British Army should large numbers of men be ordered to Russia. On January 4 there had been a major riot of British troops at Folkestone, who had carried banners proclaiming "We will not fight in Russia" and had demanded immediate demobilization.[2]

France's position was that Bolshevism was an archenemy and that she would do anything to strangle it anywhere in Europe. However, like Great Britain, France could not afford to embark on any vast anti-Bolshevik undertaking. In fact, signs of Red-inspired mutiny had already appeared among the French forces at Odessa, which would soon have to be withdrawn. The Italian government confessed its mortal terror of Bolshevism, but Italy had no money to spare and did not dare to send troops to Russia, where they too might become infected with Bolshevism.

The French and the Italians did, however, have a suggestion. Why should not a huge anti-Bolshevik army be raised, perhaps as many as 400,000 men, from among the Poles, Czechs, Finns, and

Rumanians? Such an army, paid for by the Allies and stiffened by divisions from one of the Allied nations (presumably the United States or Great Britain), could invade Russia outright and overthrow the Bolsheviks. The French Army indicated that it would be happy to provide the officer corps for such a crusade. Lloyd George swiftly demolished this idea. Which among the Allies, he asked, was prepared to contribute the money or the men? Wilson replied that the United States would not. The other Allies said that they could not.

The Allies did not really understand what Bolshevism was—aside from the fact that it was manifestly hostile to the forms of government which the Allies represented. They used the words "Bolshevism" and "anarchism" as if they were interchangeable. None of them maintained formal diplomatic relations with the Soviet government; they had long since withdrawn their diplomatic missions to remote cities like Archangel, where they could be protected by the Allied expeditionary forces. The only contact they maintained with the Lenin government in Moscow was through certain isolated "agents," the substance and reliability of whose reports varied widely. Nobody seemed equipped to give the Council of Ten any sound and unbiased advice. On January 17 the French brought before the Council their former ambassador to Russia, M. Noulens, introducing him as a Russian expert who could give firsthand knowledge of developments within that nation. Noulens proceeded to paint a horrendous picture of Bolshevik depravities, contrasting it with a glowing exposition on the White armies (all of whom were depicted as possessing every virtue and being on the way to victory over the Reds), and reported with horror how the godless Bolsheviks had proclaimed, "He who does not work, neither shall he eat."[3] The Noulens report failed to impress the American and the British. Lloyd George observed that the Bolsheviks' ultimatum was not original to them—it was actually an excerpt from Saint Paul. And it quickly became apparent that M. Noulens was scarcely equipped to provide up-to-date facts; he had left Bolshevik Russia a full twelve months before and, in fact, had been in France since July. Even the French were disgusted at the poor showing their witness had made.

The Russian Bolsheviks, for their part, knew equally little about the intentions and objectives of the Allies in Paris. To Lenin and his government the Allies were all implacable enemies dedicated to the destruction of the Russian Revolution. The Bolsheviks at first determined to waste little time quibbling with what they regarded as the decadent leadership of the decaying capitalist regimes of Western Europe. They were busy putting together a Red Army to fight the White counterrevolutionary armies which the Allies were supporting. Besides, as early as January, 1919, even before the Paris Peace Conference had started, a full-scale revolutionary insurrection was taking place in Berlin; and on the Baltic a Red Russian army had chased German occupation forces out of Estonia and most of Latvia and was now preparing to invade Lithuania and East Prussia. The Russians thus had reason to believe that Germany would shortly establish a Communist government; after that, surely France and Italy would quickly succumb. What was the point, the Bolshevik leaders asked themselves, of entering into negotiations with capitalist governments soon to be swept into the dustbin of history?

But then, as they considered the matter more carefully, the Bolsheviks realized that there was an advantage, possibly a very substantial one, in opening discussions with the Allies. Perhaps the capitalists could be persuaded to withdraw their support from the White armies—surely a very welcome concession. For this reason, Lenin determined to adopt a guarded but generally receptive attitude toward Allied attempts to negotiate with the revolutionary government in Moscow.

Meanwhile, in Paris, the British and the Americans had come to somewhat the same conclusion. From the very first, Lloyd George and Woodrow Wilson had recognized the importance of Russian representation at the Paris Peace Conference. It did not take great genius to realize that the making of a general European peace would be considerably hampered if Germany's mightiest neighbor were not somehow represented. In fact, Lloyd George was convinced that "world peace was unattainable as long as that immense country was left outside the Covenant of Nations."[4] There were additional reasons for coming to some kind of agreement with Russia. Simple humanity required the Allies to make some effort to stop the appalling butchery of the Russian civil war. Self-interest demanded that they somehow extricate themselves from the morass of the war—although the Allies could not help but feel some sense of obligation toward the White forces whom they had encouraged and to whom various promises had been made.

The first idea of Lloyd George and Woodrow Wilson, expressed shortly after the peace conference began, was to bring the conflicting Russian factions to a meeting table in Paris and, by exhibiting a spirit of goodwill to both sides, to inspire them to a compro-

mise of their differences. Essentially, the object was to negotiate an
armistice in the civil war and then to create a bipartisan Russian
government. The fact that this Anglo-American plan displayed an
exceedingly naïve view of the Russian political situation is almost
beside the point, because the French, backed by the Italians, refused to tolerate the presence of the Bolsheviks in Paris. Clemenceau announced to the Council of Ten that rather than receive those
monsters in Paris he would resign, and the French Foreign Minister
stated, "The French government, so far as it is concerned, will make
no contract with crime."[5]

The British and the Americans consulted again and came up with
a variation on the original plan, proposing that the conference with
the Russians be held on the island of Prinkipo in the Sea of Mar-
mara, the Turkish sea which is connected with the Black Sea
through the Bosporus. The island had little in its favor as a conference site. Prinkipo was accessible only at the end of a two-hour
steamer trip from Constantinople, and its facilities were primitive.
It was known only for having once been a place of imprisonment for
unsuccessful rivals for the Byzantine throne. Its sole advantage was
that the Bolsheviks could reach it by ship without having to cross
the territory of any other nation.

In the last week of January the Council of Ten agreed to send a
message to all Russian factions inviting them to a conference at
Prinkipo on February 15. The Allies—France and Italy agreeing
reluctantly and with reservations—would moderate the meeting,
the objective of which would be the termination of the Russian civil
war, an amnesty for all the forces which the Allies were supporting,
and the graceful withdrawal of the Allies' own armies. It was even
hoped that it might be possible to secure the establishment of a
coalition government to bring peace and order to Russia. However,
as a condition to their sponsoring the conference at Prinkipo, the
Allies demanded that both the White and the Red forces cease fire
at once and observe a truce.

This last requirement displayed a serious failure to understand
Russian realities. The Bolsheviks had already murdered the Czar
and his entire family, together with such other nobility as it had
seemed convenient or prudent to dispatch. Leon Trotsky, at the
head of the growing Red Army, was directing a series of furious
battles against a miscellany of White armies supported by the Allies.
There was no central command for the various anti-Bolshevik

forces, and the Reds themselves were then not much better off in this regard. From week to week the battlefronts might fluctuate by scores or hundreds of miles. Each side gave no quarter, and wholesale butchery of possible opponents was the rule rather than the exception. Roaming about in all this savagery was the "Czech Legion," consisting of Czech former war prisoners who had formed their own little pro-Allied army; this army now found itself perhaps the strongest single military force in Russia and was able, for a time at least, to wrest control of most of the Trans-Siberian Railway from the Bolsheviks. The possibility of a cease-fire between these diverse forces, each of which regarded the others with indescribable hatred, simply did not exist. And it is illustrative of the confusion which prevailed that the Allies, having no representation with the Bolsheviks, did not even have the means of delivering to them an invitation to Prinkipo. The best that could be done was to broadcast it toward Russia by radio and hope that Moscow would pick it up.

The result of the Prinkipo invitation was unexpected, at least by the Americans and the British. The various White forces all flatly declined the Allied offer—encouraged, it appears, by private French assurances that the Allies would not cease to support them if they refused to come to Prinkipo. One of the White leaders summed it up with the observation, "Moral considerations do not permit us to confer on an equal basis with traitors, murderers and robbers."[6] The Bolsheviks accepted the invitation, but in very conditional and insulting terms; it never occurred to them that the Allies might be acting in good faith. There was no attempt by either side to declare a truce in the civil war, and the entire Prinkipo project died before it was born.

The third attempt to deal with the Russian problem began on the evening of February 14. Immediately following the conclusion of the third plenary session of the conference (which had been devoted almost exclusively to the report on the draft of the Covenant of the League of Nations), Georges Clemenceau announced that he had been requested by the British delegation to convene an immediate meeting of the Council of Ten in order to discuss a matter of pressing importance. The moment was surely unpropitious. Lloyd George had returned to London six days before. Orlando had gone back to Italy temporarily, and Woodrow Wilson was to leave that very evening for his hurried trip to the United States. The meeting began just before seven in the evening. No one had dined, and Wilson's train was scheduled to leave at eight-thirty. It could not very well be delayed, since the President of the French Republic was to attend Wilson's departure at the railroad station.

Under the circumstances, there was no time to waste. Arthur Balfour, the senior British delegate in the absence of Lloyd George, at once introduced to the Council a round-faced man of forty-five who had just come to Paris that day. It was Winston Churchill, the Secretary of State for War and Air in the Lloyd George Cabinet. Churchill announced that he wished to inform the Council of the thinking of the British Cabinet regarding Russia. The Cabinet, he said, had met only the day before and was at a loss to understand what its Russian policy should be. There were British forces in Russia, and by one means or another they had contracted obligations toward the White Russian armies which they were supporting. Millions of pounds had already been invested in supplies for Russian operations, and many millions more would obviously be required in the future. Churchill observed that the present Russian policies of the Allies seemed to be leading nowhere. The Allies had all been put into an absurd position by the Prinkipo fiasco, and he trusted that there would be no more invitations of that type. He went on to suggest that the time had come for the Council to reconsider its policy toward Russia.

Churchill's speech *seemed* most reasonable; there was no doubt among the Allies that they must develop a new Russian policy, and nobody could take exception to Churchill's request that they do so. There were those present, however, who questioned the motives behind this demarche. They knew Churchill well, or at least they knew of him; his reputation was not one to inspire confidence. He was considered impulsive, intensely ambitious and very frequently wrong. His judgment in the matter of Russia was open to serious question because his hatred of Bolshevism was known to be almost pathological. Cynics observed that Churchill, himself the descendant of dukes, regarded the execution of the Romanov grand dukes as a crime without parallel in history. In any event, his presence in Paris was suspicious. Perhaps he had come with the permission of the British Cabinet, but had he come with Lloyd George's full knowledge and blessings? What did he really want?

There was no time for speculation. President Wilson glanced at his watch and announced that he must be off. Clemenceau observed that "a matter of such importance could not be settled at a short and unexpected meeting."[7] Wilson rose to his feet and leaned against the back of his chair. If a new Russian policy must be created, he said, he was in favor of resolving this "cruel dilemma" by withdrawing all Allied forces from Russia and letting events there take their course. Perhaps the Allies could negotiate some agreement with the Bolsheviks through informal channels. But, Churchill asked, what about the White armies? This would be condemning them to destruction and an "interminable vista of violence and misery."[8] The President said that he could not help this. Everyone agreed that the only way Bolshevism in Russia could be beaten was to launch a huge invasion stiffened by Allied armies—and even this offered no guarantee of success. Anyway, not a single one of the Allies was prepared to contribute men to such an invasion. On this inconclusive note, Wilson rushed off and the Council of Ten adjourned.

The next day the Council met again. The situation had now changed. Clemenceau alone of the heads of delegations was present. The French Army's Chief of Staff, General Alby, presented a very optimistic picture of possibilities in Russia. Allied regular forces, he claimed, could easily defeat the Reds, and it would not take too many divisions to do so. Churchill then took over and began to castigate the whole conception of the Prinkipo Conference. His arguments were so cogently presented that it was soon difficult to find anyone who would admit to having ever been in favor of a conference with the Bolsheviks. Clemenceau said that he had always "been completely opposed." Balfour allowed that he had "never been in favor of the Prinkipo proposal." And Sonnino announced that he had been "opposed to it from the commencement."[9]

Having gone this far, the Council now found itself presented a Churchill proposal calling for the immediate establishment of an "Allied Council for Russian Affairs," whose principal task would be to draw up a plan for "concerted action against the Bolsheviks." This plan, as Churchill sketched it out, was to be "a definite war scheme."[10] Everyone seemed to think this a good idea, and the Council adjourned, intending to take up the matter more fully at its next session.

It took no time at all for this Churchillian proposal to be quashed. Lloyd George and Wilson learned of the scheme and sent categorical instructions to their delegations that no plan for Allied military intervention was even to be considered. Wilson cabled House to make it plain that the United States was "not at war with Russia" and would in no foreseeable circumstances "take part in military

operations there against the Russians."[11] Lloyd George fired off a
blistering telegram to Churchill charging him with grossly exceeding his authority in the whole affair. Simultaneously, Balfour was
instructed to withdraw all support for an armed invasion. "Who,"
Lloyd George demanded to know, "is going to pay for these [pro-
posed] mercenary armies? How much will France give? I am sure
that she cannot afford to pay: I am sure that we cannot. Will America bear the expense?"[12]

The whole interventionary scheme thus collapsed. Churchill returned to London, the French Army retired to lick its wounds, and
the Russian civil war continued. But this did not mean the end of
plans to conclude an arrangement with Bolshevik Russia.

William C. Bullitt of Philadelphia was an unusual young man.
Although he was only twenty-eight in 1919, he had had a great deal
of experience abroad and had come to occupy a reasonably influential position within the American contingent at Paris. The scion of
a wealthy family, a Democrat, and a graduate of Yale, Bullitt had
been a foreign correspondent for the Philadelphia *Public Ledger*
and a member of the Ford peace mission of 1915. Following this he
had met Colonel House, upon whom he had made a very favorable
impression. House had brought him into government service and
then taken him to Paris with the peace delegation. Practically
everyone agreed that Bullitt was a brilliant man—but he was also
excitable, brash, and very, very forward.

Just before Wilson's departure from Paris, the President had mentioned the possibility of an informal exploratory mission to the Russian Bolsheviks. With military intervention now out of the question,
Colonel House summoned Bullitt and dispatched the young Phila-
delphian to Moscow, to find out the terms on which the Russian
civil war might be ended. The British were apprised of the affair
and evidently approved. The French were told nothing about it,
because it was suspected that they had sabotaged the Prinkipo Conference plan. For reasons of his own, House did not tell any of the
other American plenipotentiaries of Bullitt's mission. The first that
they were to learn of it was when Bullitt returned with a direct
proposal from the Bolsheviks, but this was when the Paris Peace
Conference had entered a completely different phase—in fact, when
it had nearly broken up.

Chapter Four

"I don't give a damn for logic!"

THE Council of Four had its real beginning at 8:40 A.M. on Wednesday, February 19, 1919, when Georges Clemenceau left his home on the Rue Franklin to be driven off to a meeting. The automobile had only just started up and turned the corner onto the Boulevard Delessert when a young man named Pierre Cottin, who was hiding in a public urinal, darted out. Shouting "I am a Frenchman and an anarchist!,"[1] he began to shoot a pistol at Clemenceau's car. The chauffeur accelerated frantically and the automobile sped away, leaving Cottin standing on the sidewalk, firing after the diminishing target. One of his shots struck home: Clemenceau was hit in the back with a bullet that lodged next to his lung cavity. The would-be assassin was seized by a mob, whereupon Clemenceau's automobile doubled back and the old man, gasping and cursing, was supported into his home.

This wound would surely have been fatal to almost any other seventy-seven-year-old man. Clemenceau was an exception. Within a matter of hours he was sitting up in a chair (the wound was especially painful when he lay down), arguing with his doctors and discussing conference matters with two visitors, House and Balfour. (Balfour had greeted the news of the shooting with a characteristically restrained comment: "Dear, dear, I wonder what that portends."[2])

The result of the attempted assassination was the eventual formation of a new group, nicknamed the Council of Four, consisting of the chief delegates of Italy, France, Great Britain and the United States. It came about by accident. The British, American and Italian delegates came to the Rue Franklin to pay calls on the recuperating Clemenceau, and in a day or two they were staying to try to get the peace conference moving. In truth, the Council of Four would probably have come about ultimately in any event. Its creation was almost inevitable. The Council of Ten, with its attendant experts, its secretariat, its endless delegations from smaller nations, had become a council of thirty or forty persons, hopelessly large to cope with the delicate questions which were now coming forward.

The first weeks of these informal meetings, the forerunners of the sessions of the Council of Four, were to mark a crisis in the relationship between the President of the United States and his devoted deputy, House. Before Wilson left Paris, House had suggested to him that in the President's absence the peace conference should draft a plan for a "preliminary peace" with Germany to outline the new German frontiers, fix a reparations sum and demobilize the German army and navy. The conference "could button up everything the next four weeks," House told Wilson. At this, House noticed, the President seemed "alarmed and even startled," and House hurriedly assured him that he had no intention of usurping any of Wilson's prerogatives; he would only attempt to bring matters to some sort of solution for the President's approval when he returned in mid-March. Finally, House warned Wilson that certain compromises—"not a compromise of principle but a compromise of detail"—might have to be made.[3]

House believed that he had received carte blanche in most matters from the President, and he fell to with a will. It soon became evident that in his dealings with the other Allies it was impossible for him to limit himself to the matters he had outlined to Wilson. Other issues kept intruding; even the League of Nations draft Covenant was brought up, and there was no way for House to avoid it. If he was to be Wilson's personal representative and the chief American delegate, he could hardly refuse to discuss the matters raised by the other principals. He could not announce that he possessed only power to negotiate certain terms pertaining to Germany, and that his authority did not extend to other related matters; this would have made him ridiculous. Thus House was forced to discuss everything.

As a boy in Texas Edward House had swapped jackknives endlessly, as a young businessman he had made it a special point always to maintain a cordial relationship with those with whom he dealt in order that they would deal again, and as a politician he had built his reputation on the tactful reconciliation of opposing positions. With him, the urge to negotiate and to compromise was compulsive. This was the man whom Wilson, unbending and stern, had left to represent him in Paris, without specific instructions, with little guidance and with only the sporadic and inconvenient contact of the long-distance cable—and at a time when House had become convinced that some sort of German peace treaty must be drafted quickly lest Europe collapse in chaos.

The *George Washington*, bearing the Presidential party, arrived at Boston on February 23. The next day Wilson spoke on the League of Nations before a vast crowd of well-wishers at Mechanics Hall. Speaking of the League's foes, Wilson cried, "Any man who resists the present tides that run in the world will find himself thrown upon a shore so high and barren that it will seem as if he had been separated from his human kind forever."[4] This did not frighten Wilson's principal foe, Senator Henry Cabot Lodge of Massachusetts. Lodge had respected the President's request that the League of Nations not be discussed until he had returned to present it to the Senators for their comment. Now Wilson had taken advantage of Lodge's silence to attack Lodge in his own state! "Very characteristic," was the only comment the Senator would make.[5]

Back in Washington by February 26, Wilson, at House's suggestion, invited the members of the Senate Foreign Relations Committee to dinner at the White House, in order to advise them of what he had done in Paris and to answer any questions they might have regarding the draft Covenant of the League. But the dinner did not go well. Two Senators, Fall and Borah, had flatly refused to come. Mrs. Wilson was seated next to Lodge at dinner and tactlessly gave him a glowing description of Wilson's speech in Boston. And later, in the East Room, when the President outlined the Covenant to the Senators, he was hectored by Senator Brandegee. The principal line of attack was that the Covenant was a clear invitation to the United States to involve itself in foreign entanglements, that it invalidated the Monroe Doctrine, and that it would have to be substantially amended before the Senate would consent to it or to any peace treaty in which it was found. Senator Lodge did not even deign to take part in the discussion. After a few questions by others, Lodge rose and coolly but politely announced that he would retire.

The next morning the Republican Senators made public horrifying comments on the White House dinner. "I feel as if I had been wandering with Alice in Wonderland and had had tea with the Mad Hatter" was Senator Brandegee's statement.[6] A few days later Lodge brought forward a round-robin resolution which advised that it was "the sense of the Senate" that the energies of the peace conference negotiations in Paris should be directed toward the conclusion of a peace treaty with Germany and that the League of Nations should be created separately later. This resolution obviously constituted a condemnation of the Covenant and a threat that the Senate would not ratify any treaty which contained it; it was signed by thirty-seven Senators and Senators-elect—more than enough to prevent ratification.

To Wilson this was the most bitter draught. It did not occur to the scholar prophet that many of the Senators whose names appeared on Lodge's round robin were only lukewarm in their opposition to the League. House had suggested that Wilson invite a few of these men, such as Senator Hoke Smith of Georgia, to the White House and appeal to them privately for their help. But Wilson would not do this. Smith had started as a lawyer in Atlanta at the same time as he and had succeeded where Wilson had failed; now, forty years later, the thought of the man still enraged Wilson. "That man is an ambulance chaser. I scorn to have any relations with him whatsoever."[7] The thought of conciliation was anathema to the President. If the Republican Senators hated him, he returned their hate in full measure. He had fought the forces of reaction before, and now he would fight them again, only harder, more pitilessly, more unbendingly. He would crush them between the hammer of his words and the anvil of world opinion. As for separating the Covenant from the treaty, "When that treaty comes back, gentlemen on this side will find the Covenant not only in it but so many threads of the treaty tied to the Covenant that you cannot dissect the Covenant from the treaty without destroying the whole vital structure."[8] And with the gage thrown down, the President, suffering from an abscessed tooth, a cold and the return of his old nervous indigestion, boarded the *George Washington* to return to Paris.

These were not the end of his afflictions. He had begun to think about the implications of the dispatches he had received from House in Paris. All of them seemed to smack of compromise, of European attempts to jam through a "settlement" in Wilson's absence. House, it appeared to Wilson, had considerably exceeded his brief. He had allowed himself to become the friend and intimate of the Europeans. In fact, there were rumors that House had even listened to a European proposal that the hallowed Covenant of the League of Nations be separated from the treaty. Enemies of Edward House told Wilson that the Colonel's son-in-law and aide, Gordon Auchincloss, had told certain British sources that it was only through House's effort that progress was being made at the peace conference. Wilson learned that Arthur Balfour had called for all peace conference subcommittees to submit their reports by March 8, and this appeared suspicious to the President. Were the Europeans trying to jam through the peace treaty in his absence?

Wilson finally concluded, as he told his secretary, that there was a definite "conspiracy"[9] against him. "I gather," he told his entourage aboard the *George Washington,* "that these men have agreed upon a definite program. Apparently they are determined to get everything out of Germany that they can, now that she is helpless . . . If they insist on this sort of program, I shall be compelled to withdraw my commissioners and return home and in due course to take up the details of a separate peace."[10]

The worst of the Presidential fears seemed borne out when, on the *George Washington's* arrival in Brest on the afternoon of March 13, he heard House's report. The quiet little Colonel had journeyed up from Paris, to be greeted with the bitter comment, "Your dinner to the Senate Foreign Relations Committee was a failure."[11] Then, according to Mrs. Wilson, the two men closeted themselves in the President's stateroom to discuss what had occurred in Wilson's absence, and House did not leave until after midnight. Mrs. Wilson wrote in her memoirs:

> *I opened the door connecting our rooms. Woodrow was standing. The change in his appearance shocked me. He seemed to have aged ten years . . . "House [Wilson said] has given away everything I had won before we left Paris. He has compromised on every side . . . Well, thank God, I can still fight and I'll win them back or never look those boys I sent over here in the face again.*[12]

The bitter President journeyed on to Paris, where his first act was to repudiate any concessions which House might have made in his absence. His press secretary was instructed to issue a categorical statement that the Covenant of the League of Nations would remain an integral part of the treaty of peace and that there was "no basis

whatever for the reports that a change in this decision was anticipated."[13]

With Wilson's return to Paris, and with the return of Lloyd
George and Orlando, the first real sessions of the Council of Four
began. To everyone's relief, the Japanese did not seem to be
offended by their exclusion from this group—not as offended, at
any rate, as the various foreign ministers, who found themselves cast
out and instructed to form a group of their own. This sullen group,
which became known as the Council of Five, met infrequently. The
Council of Four, on the other hand, was to hold 145 meetings by the
end of the peace conference, most of them taking place in the afternoons at Wilson's residence. It was here in the Council of Four that
the greatest conflicts of the peace conference were joined, that the
map of Europe was finally redrawn, and that the treaty of peace was
hammered out.

The Paris Peace Conference was now entering its third and final
phase. The first had been the inconclusive sparring which marked
the opening six weeks, when the Covenant had been drafted and the
questions requiring expert appraisal had been shunted off to the
committees. The second period had seen the departure of the principals, during whose absence much of the detail work had been done.
Now the principal figures had returned to Paris, to find that the mass
of the committee reports had been turned in and that there remained four intractable items over which there was violent contention and which only the Council of Four could settle: the question of reparations payments from Germany, the renewed French
demands for control of the Rhineland, the Italian claim to the important Adriatic seaport of Fiume, and the Japanese claim to the old
German concessions in China. To these Wilson now added a fifth:
the revision of the draft Covenant of the League of Nations.

It must not be supposed that Wilson himself desired to revise the
Covenant. He found it entirely acceptable as it stood. Indeed, more
than anyone else's it was his own creation. But he had just received
an important cable from ex-President William Howard Taft, who
was working hard in the United States to promote Senate acceptance of the League. Taft had outlined six changes to the Covenant
which would, in his opinion, guarantee its passage. Most important
among them was a provision that the Monroe Doctrine be exempted
from interference by the League of Nations. Wilson well recognized
the difficulties which he faced in explaining to the Europeans that

the Covenant must now be revised. It would mean admitting that he had lost control over political affairs in his own nation, and it would mean asking the Europeans to make just the sort of special concession to one nation which Wilson had fought against when the Covenant was first drafted. Nevertheless, he decided to appeal for the revisions.

It was this decision which mortally weakened Wilson's position in the crucial struggles that were to follow. Wilson needed the agreement of the Allies to the revision of the Covenant. He had to have the changes which Taft had suggested. Without them, the Senate would certainly veto the treaty. None of this could be concealed fom Lloyd George, Clemenceau and Orlando. Doubtless the President's predicament was viewed by them in a spirit of wry amusement. This sanctimonious prophet who had journeyed across the ocean to redeem the sins of the Old World had first demanded of them the creation of a Covenant for a League of Nations which they did not particularly want, and now, after having himself been the chairman of the committee which drafted his Covenant, was returning to admit that it would have to be revised to satisfy his Senate at home. Very well, it would be done—eventually. The drafting committee for the Covenant would be reconvened and Wilson's revisions would be made, but in return Wilson would have to take cognizance of *their* political problems. Henceforth their demands would be blunt and there would be no need to cloak them with righteous protestations.

Betrayed by his own political weakness, his reputation rapidly declining, Woodrow Wilson quickly found the daily meetings of the Council of Four becoming an ordeal. The Allies no longer troubled to pay much more than lip service to his Fourteen Points. Only when it suited their own interests were the Points brought up—as when the Italians, to whom the British and the French had promised large sections of the Austro-Hungarian Empire under the terms of the secret Treaty of London, now extended their demands to include Fiume, the only good seaport available to the new Yugoslav nation.

The reparations problem was even more complicated. During the course of the war Wilson had made the famous announcement that at the end of the conflict there would be "no annexations, no contributions, no punitive damages." It was an historic statement. Then, in the pre-armistice exchange of notes between Wilson and the German government, the President had stated that Allied demands for reparations would include "damage done to civilian population of the Allies and to their property." What Wilson—and the Germans—had assumed was that this meant principally the damage done to the farms, villages and factories in the invaded portion of France. But Lloyd George had gone to Paris propelled by the popular demand to "squeeze the German lemon until the pips squeak." And as for France, Clemenceau's Minister of Finance, Klotz ("the only Jew I have ever known who does not understand finance," the Tiger mused[14]), appearing before the Horizon-Blue Parliament, had only one answer to every question regarding the French budget: "The Germans will pay."[15] The Allies had now broadened their definition of "civilian damages" to cover demobilization allowances, interest charges on wartime loans and shipping taxes, together with the most grossly inflated costs of reconstruction. On top of this, they proposed to add the future costs of pensions to widows, disabled soldiers and orphans. Wilson realized that Germany could not possibly pay what Britain and France would demand. He wanted to establish some sort of lump-sum figure which Germany could pay relatively quickly, even if it did not cover all of the costs that Britain and France claimed. But the French would have none of this. They demanded everything and would accept no time limit. The Germans would be made to pay, even if it took generation after generation.

The Rhineland was a never-ending source of conflict. Marshal Foch had not given up his attempts to force through an "independent" Rhineland state under French protection. The French generals in the Rhineland were displaying considerable imagination in encouraging separatist activity. The territory seethed with rumors of coups and offers of support and recognition by the French Army. More than this, Clemenceau suddenly announced to the Council of Four that France demanded possession of the Saar Basin with its valuable coal mines. This was startling news to the British and the Americans. The Saar was almost completely German, and its acquisition by France had never been considered before.

In the face of these conflicts, which were becoming deeper and more serious by the day, only the Japanese were maintaining their customary calm. The Japanese diplomats, Makino and Chinda, had accepted their exclusion from the Council of Four with only a cursory protest to House. They seemed to have no particular interest in the various European imbroglios. In fact, they were so uniformly polite and so generally deferential that it was difficult to believe they were paying attention to the subject under discussion.

It had been noted that at the Council of Ten the Japanese frequently held upside down the European maps and documents under discussion. They usually voted with the majority; on one occasion the Council of Ten was evenly split on an issue by the time it was the turn of the Japanese to vote, but still they announced inscrutably, "We vote with the majority."[16]

There was, however, nothing Orientally inscrutable about the Japanese attitude toward the former German possessions in the Pacific. Two years before, when the German submarine campaign had been at its height, the Allied merchant shipping losses in the Mediterranean had mounted to frightening levels. Neither the British nor the French could spare destroyers to patrol the Mediterranean, and it had been decided to appeal to Japan for escort vessels. The Japanese were willing to help, but there was one condition: after the war, Japan wanted all the German possessions in the Pacific north of the equator, together with the extensive German railroad, port and mining concessions in China's Shantung province. The British and the French, desperate to get the Japanese destroyers into the Mediterranean, quickly concluded a secret agreement to support these Japanese claims. Now the time had come for the bargain to be consummated. The Japanese had already been given mandates for the islands; now they were insisting upon the Germans' Shantung concessions, which could be transferred to Japan only at the expense of friendly China. Wilson was violently opposed to the deal, but the Japanese were determined and the Europeans were committed to support their claim.

Against all these violations of the Fourteen Points Wilson found himself forced to struggle almost alone, although it must not be supposed that the Europeans were in complete agreement among themselves on all the issues. Each of the various plenipotentiaries found it easy to be rational when his own nation's interests were not involved or when there was no secret-treaty commitment. Lloyd George, for example, was always quick to point out the awful potential danger involved in creating a buffer state on the Rhine, which, he said, would inevitably become another Alsace-Lorraine. And both the French and the British were privately opposed to the Italian demand for Fiume; they thought it unreasonable and unjustified—and exceeding the territory promised Italy under their secret treaty. But all the Europeans found themselves forced into a sort of ragged alliance by the various entanglements of their secret treaties, as well as by the intransigence of Wilson, whose nation had signed none of the secret treaties—treaties made in moments of desperation far greater than any that the United States had known —and who kept reminding the Europeans of their pre-armistice promise to make peace under the terms of his Fourteen Points; whose country neither wanted nor needed reparations money, and who opposed their demands for a huge German indemnity.

The Council of Four generally met in the little study of Wilson's residence, the members occupying brocaded armchairs that were drawn into a small semicircle facing the fireplace. Clemenceau appeared old and tired now, with a hacking, gurgling cough which was the result of the bullet still lodged in his chest. Lloyd George, on the other hand, seemed even quicker, more mercurial and more flexible than before. Orlando, with his white hair, his genial pudgy, dimpled face, gave the impression of a none-too-bright cupid. Wilson looked gray-faced and haggard, but still he fought earnestly his cause and his belief. Each day they took the same seats and began again the same sullen wrangles. Usually no one else was present except for a secretary, Sir Maurice Hankey (who compiled a *procès-verbal* of the sessions) and an interpreter (whose presence was necessitated by the fact that Orlando could master only three English phrases—"goodbye," "eleven o'clock" and "I do not agree"[17]), although from time to time the various principals would bring in a couple of their experts.

The privacy was all to the good, because the exchanges between these world leaders frequently became unseemly and sometimes degenerated into bitter conflict. The day when Wilson could intimidate the Europeans had passed. They had had enough of "beating around the Wilsonian bush."[18] To his face Clemenceau bluntly charged Wilson with being a "pro-German" who was "seeking to destroy France."[19] And later, when, during an argument over the Saar, Wilson attempted to face down Clemenceau with the question "Do you wish me to return home?," Clemenceau snapped back, "I do not wish you to go home, but I intend to do so myself," and walked out of the meeting.[20] The French press instantly launched into a violent attack on Wilson which deeply distressed the thin-skinned President, as Clemenceau had expected it would.

On instructions from their governments, the French and British members of the League of Nations Commission dragged their feet in the matter of revising the draft Covenant to satisfy Wilson's domestic pressures. Obviously the other Allies intended to bargain off the revision of the Covenant against certain American concessions.

Under this sort of pressure, the President's health began to fail. He was squandering his energy at a prodigious rate. In addition to the Council of Four meetings, he had permitted practically every other waking moment of his time to be scheduled. Delegation after delegation of special pleaders, would-be nationalities, and petitioners from small countries were ushered into his presence, mostly without the benefit of preliminary staff screening. Sometimes he saw twenty different groups a day, each asking something from him and each placing upon him another burden of responsibility. He granted interviews to Greek priests, Albanian peasants, Armenian and Irish nationalists, Galicians who wanted to be annexed by Poland, and Lithuanians who wanted independence from Poland. He met with representatives of labor, farmers, Negroes, and women's suffrage groups.

Wilson even attempted to do much of his own secretarial work. Each evening he personally locked in his own metal strongbox the minutes of the day's Council of Four sessions. Important letters were mislaid and never found. Colonel House pleaded with him to make use of his own large personal secretariat. Wilson refused the offer. House urged him to have an American secretary present at the Council meetings and not rely on the British to produce the minutes. Wilson did nothing about it.

By the end of March the American President was absolutely exhausted. In the space of only a few weeks he had aged visibly. Around Wilson's left eye a muscle began a constant twitching which he was unable to control. Day-and-night labor had exhausted him, yet he would leave almost nothing of importance to others. He had virtually cut himself off from the other American commissioners; he did not even send them copies of Hankey's minutes, much less consult with them. When they were needed for anything, usually only to sign a document, they were summoned to House's office for the purpose and then abruptly dismissed.

Wilson even deprived himself of the personal relationship with Edward House which had been so necessary to him in the past. Although House was still sometimes given important tasks, the President had definitely cooled toward the little Colonel. They no longer met privately for the long, intimate discussions which had helped Wilson, more than he realized, to coalesce his own thinking. There were very few of the scribbled notes of admiration beginning "Dear Governor" and ending "Affectionately." And now there was no one left to give him the private encouragement which he secretly

craved. Moreover, Wilson attached the most sinister meanings to
certain editorials appearing in British newspapers which applauded
the work House had done while the President was in Washington.
House was reported as saying that it was possible for peace to be
made in only a few days, because everyone knew what concessions
had to be made. Wilson also drew ominous conclusions from Clemenceau's obvious affection for House. "I suppose I shall have to
stand alone," Wilson ruminated bitterly to his press secretary.[21]

On April 2, at luncheon with his wife, Woodrow Wilson burst into
a violent fit of temper as he described the French demands in the
Council of Four, crying out that Clemenceau was trying to break
him physically. Since Wilson was practically always calm in the
presence of his family, the scene was notable—and ominous.

The next day he collapsed. He showed symptoms of what seemed
to be a sudden cold, and as the day went on he developed a constant
rasping cough. In the late afternoon, members of the American
reparations committee came before him to announce that the British
and the French were more determined than ever in their demands.
By nightfall the President had been put to bed. During the night the
fits of coughing alternated with severe diarrhea and vomiting, and
the President's physician, Admiral Cary Greyson, found that his
temperature had suddenly risen to 103 degrees. Wilson could not
sleep. He could keep nothing in his stomach. He had trouble breathing. Despite the President's history of arteriosclerosis, Greyson diag-
nosed the illness as influenza. °

During the next few days Wilson was almost fatally sick. But then
he rallied, and on the fourth day he summoned Greyson to his bedside and instructed him to cable the Navy Department and ask how
soon the *George Washington* could be brought to Brest to embark
the American delegation. The news of Wilson's inquiry was immediately given to the press, but it failed to have the desired effect
upon the Europeans and the Japanese. Wilson had made an empty
threat and his adversaries knew it.[22] He could not go home now. If
he deserted the peace conference, the Europeans would force their
own peace on Germany. An open indictment by him of their designs

° A number of close observers of Woodrow Wilson at the time, among them Herbert
Hoover and John B. Davies, have indicated that they believed the President had
actually suffered a stroke. Subsequently, experts on cerebral arteriosclerosis have
suggested that Greyson's diagnosis was incorrect and that Wilson's affliction was a
vascular occlusion caused by prolonged tension and extreme exhaustion; see notes
in Walworth, Arthur, *Woodrow Wilson: World Prophet*, Vol. II, p. 297.

might cause one or more of the Europeans to be flung from office—but would this be an advantage? If Lloyd George or Clemenceau or Orlando was turned out, who would take his place? Certainly no one more moderate or any easier to deal with. A new French premier, for example, would have to be named by Raymond Poincaré—and Clemenceau would be sweet reason itself by comparison with any-one whom Poincaré might designate.

No, the peace had to be made now and with the personalities on hand. If only the League of Nations could be kept in it, then per-haps the League could ultimately modify some of the more cancer-ous features of the treaty. Bitter and revolted, Woodrow Wilson rose from his sickbed and prepared to make compromise with his prin-ciples.

The first of the agonizing Wilson compromises concerned the reparations question. To the direct costs of actual wartime civilian damages Wilson permitted his allies to add the cost of pensions, thus vastly inflating the bill. And when his experts remonstrated that this was illogical, he flared back, "Logic! Logic! I don't give a damn for logic. I am going to include pensions!"[23]

The result was that the reparations problem was disposed of in a particularly ominous and shabby manner. A "Reparations Commis-sion" was established which would calculate the amount Germany was to owe the Allies (and it was certain that the claims for damages would be grossly inflated). The Reparations Commission would announce its findings in 1921, and Germany would be forced to accept this figure and pay it—no matter how long it took. In the interim, Germany was to acknowledge her guilt for the war and for its damages, and to hand over twenty million gold marks as an advance payment against an unknown total.

This compromise filled the American delegation with horror. It had already been decided to strip Germany of her colonies, to seize her merchant marine, and to remove valuable territory along her frontiers. It now seemed that Germany would be reduced to a per-manent slave state, shackled to the Allies by her debts. The only alter-native was that she might refuse to pay. Then the Allies would be compelled to collect from her by force. Even some of the British were appalled by what had been done. Curiously, they blamed Wilson for it. John Maynard Keynes, the brilliant young chief British Treasury delegate, proposed to give up his position and flee Paris in disgust.

The fact that the Rhineland and Saar settlements were somewhat more moderate was due mainly to the fact that the French were compelled to fight both the British and Wilson on these issues. They did, however, nearly destroy the peace conference. Poincaré and Foch allowed Clemenceau little room for maneuver. Press attacks on Wilson were stepped up to a point where the most tough-minded public figure, much less the now haggard and distraught Wilson, could not have ignored them.

Even Lloyd George had become intensely disturbed at the way things were going. It had been decided that the German Army should be reduced to a bare police force of 100,000 men, and the Poles were already taking advantage of this future German weakness. They had persuaded the Allies to equip a Polish army—"Haller's Army," which had been raised in France—and send it to Poland. There the Poles had immediately set about enlarging their territory at the expense of both Russia and Germany, and were refusing to obey Allied orders to cease firing. The power of Wilson, Lloyd George and Clemenceau to control the affairs of Europe was on the wane. To a man as acutely perceptive as Lloyd George, the Polish affair was a portent of things to come. As a result, the Prime Minister had called a meeting with his senior advisers at Fontainebleau in March. The outcome of this British conference was a memorandum entitled "Some Considerations for the Peace Conference Before They Finally Draft Their Terms." It was a lengthy document and typical of Lloyd George. It did not concern itself at all with what was right, only with what was practical, and it was based on his substantial knowledge of men and affairs. "The greatest danger in the present situation," Lloyd George felt, "is that Germany may throw her lot in with Bolshevism and place her resources, her brains, and her vast organising power at the disposal of the revolutionary fanatics whose dream it is to conquer the world for Bolshevism."[24] It would, he wrote, be "comparatively easy to patch up a peace" which would "last for thirty years."[25] He warned that it was impossible to make Germany so weak that she would never be able to strike back. "You may strip Germany of her colonies, reduce her armaments to a mere police force and her navy to that of a fifth-rate power; all the same in the end if she feels that she has been unjustly treated in the peace of 1919 she will find means of exacting retribution on her conquerors."[26] Finally, he warned that Britain would not under any circumstances be party to the severance of the Rhineland from Germany.

The French reaction to the Lloyd George memorandum was

quick and bitter. The Quai d'Orsay saw in the British note merely another instance of the eternal perfidy of Albion. Shrewdly the French pointed out that if it was Britain's desire to placate German wrath, there were many other paths available. Archly they suggested that the German colonies, most of which were now held by British dominions, could be returned; or perhaps Germany could be given certain naval concessions or offered opportunities for expanding her world trade.

The final compromise, while it represented definite concessions on the part of the British and the Americans, nevertheless left the French right wing far from content. In the Saar Basin, administration of the German coal mines was to be transferred to France, and sovereignty over the Saar region was given to a League of Nations commission. After fifteen years there was to be a plebiscite in the Saar to determine whether the territory would revert to Germany or be annexed by France. The Rhineland settlement was even less to France's liking. The German side of the Rhine was to be demilitarized to a depth of fifty kilometers; in this belt the Germans were not to build fortifications, assemble troops or conduct military exercises. The left bank of the Rhine was to be occupied by the Allies for a period of fifteen years, with a series of gradual withdrawals from German territory at five-year intervals. France was, however, left with one assurance: Wilson and Lloyd George agreed to give her a treaty which would guarantee Anglo-American aid in the event of "unprovoked" German aggression. This was only partly helpful to Clemenceau. It was questionable whether the United States Senate would pass the peace treaty itself, let alone a joint Anglo-American treaty of assistance to France.

Most of the Saar and Rhineland settlements were negotiated by House, in what was probably his last major assignment from Wilson. On April 15 he was sent to Clemenceau with Wilson's final offer on the Rhineland controversy. House was just the man for this. He burst into the Tiger's office with a glad shout: "I am the bearer of good news. The President has consented to all that you asked of me yesterday!"[27] Clemenceau rose to the occasion. After embracing House, he called for his *chef de cabinet* and instructed him, in House's presence, to inform the French press forthwith that "relations with the United States were of the very best."[28] The effect next day was, as House described it, "magical."[29] The entire "heavy press" suddenly burst forth with praise for Wilson and the United States. The effect in the League of Nations Commission was equally magical. The French representatives at once withdrew their objections to the revision of the draft Covenant, and the Wilson amendments were adopted.

In the midst of these sweeping compromises, the whole matter of Bolshevik Russia, once viewed as so crucial, was thrust to one side. At the end of March young William Bullitt returned all agog from his flying visit to the Bolsheviks. The Russians had spared no effort to impress him and his traveling companion, the journalist Lincoln Steffens, with the discipline and determination of war Communism, and they had succeeded. (On Steffens' return he made his famous remark "I have been over into the future, and it works!"*) Bullitt had been accorded a series of interviews with Soviet Foreign Minister Chicherin and had even been received by Lenin himself. The Bolsheviks had made a serious offer and committed it to writing: if the Allies lifted their blockade of Russia, withdrew their troops, and ended their support of the White armies, the Bolsheviks would agree to stop the civil war, leave the Whites in possession of whatever territory they now controlled, proclaim a general amnesty, and even pay off certain of the imperial Russian debts to foreign nations (which, of course, they had previously repudiated). There were only two conditions: the offer must come from the Allies, and it must be made before April 10. Neither of these stipulations seemed to Bullitt to pose any particular problem.

When he arrived back in Paris he expected, perhaps not unreasonably, to be received instantly by Wilson. He found that the President was not interested in seeing him. Wilson sent word that he had a headache and could spare neither the time nor the energy to deal with the Russian problem. The President referred Bullitt to House, who in turn, passed him down to members of his own staff. It became evident that House's staff did not think much of the news which this excited young man had brought to them. They had evolved another idea. Herbert Hoover had proposed a plan for feeding starving Russia, on condition that the civil war be terminated. House's entourage liked this scheme better than Bullitt's deal with the Bolsheviks. And if Hoover's plan did not work out, the White army under the command of Admiral Kolchak now seemed to be doing quite well against the Reds, while the newly created inde-

---

* Bullitt later confessed that Steffens composed this ringing phrase on the train on his way to Stockholm, long before he ever entered Russia. See Thompson, John M., *Russia, Bolshevism, and the Versailles Treaty*, p. 176.

pendent Czechoslovak and Polish nations were beginning to stabilize themselves and were expected to serve as a barrier to the expansion of the Russian Bolsheviks. Perhaps there was no need for the Allies to make any concessions at all to Soviet Russia.

This indifference to his proposal drove Bullitt frantic. He was under the impression that he had been sent to Lenin with sweeping powers, and he rather fancied that he had handled the Communists in superior fashion and had driven a marvelous bargain. (As it transpired, he probably had.) Clutching his agreement with the Russians, Bullitt ran desperately around Paris as the April 10 deadline grew closer. The American commissioners, whom House had told nothing of Bullitt's mission, declined to involve themselves. The French, whom House and the British had taken care to keep in the dark, took gleeful pleasure in refusing to discuss the proposition. Lloyd George, finding himself under attack at home by the Conservative members of Parliament for negotiating with the Bolsheviks, refused to receive Bullitt and went so far as to imply that the British government had never even heard of him and his mission.

Thus the April 10 deadline passed, and with it the peace conference's last serious opportunity to come to terms with Communist Russia.

The settlements involving the Saar reparations and the Rhineland had not exhausted the compromises which had to be made in order to complete a draft treaty for presentation to Germany. There still remained the Italian demand for Fiume and the Japanese claims in Shantung. These promised to be serious problems, but there was one which seemed even more crucial. World opinion had become jaded with regard to the peace conference. The conference had been in session for three months and practically nothing, it appeared, had been resolved. The vast hopes which had been held for this congress of the world had yet to be realized. No wrongs had been righted. No Germans had been punished. The Allied armies were not yet completely demobilized. The world was no longer at war—but it was not yet at peace either. The peoples of the various nations had not been officially informed of what progress, if any, had been made in Paris. All that could be learned were vague reports of huge compromises with which every nation was dissatisfied. It did not seem that the Fourteen Points which Wilson had promised to the world had come to pass.

The pressure for peace became more intense every day, until at length the principal Allies succumbed to the demand. They had passed through so many difficulties and compromised so many disputes that it seemed certain they would be able to resolve those which remained. Obviously the peace treaty with Germany should be signed as soon as possible, and this could only be done by bringing the Germans to Paris. Accordingly, on April 18, without having resolved the Fiume and Shantung questions, the Allies notified the Germans that they must appear at Versailles in a week's time to receive the treaty. It was thought that this *fait accompli* would force the Italians and the Japanese to moderate their demands. It does not seem to have occurred to the French, the British and the Americans that the result might be quite the opposite.

The Italians objected furiously to the invitation which had been extended to Germany. They knew it meant that the big powers regarded the important work as being done—and to this the Italians would not agree. During the time when all the major compromises were being made, the Italians had made it their business to be as genial as possible to the French, British and American delegates. Carefully avoiding controversy, Orlando had steered the middle course, going out of his way to be courteous and accommodating to Wilson and House. The Italians had purchased the support of several French newspapers and had achieved distinction as the hosts of the best dinner parties given in Paris. They did their best to maintain a drawing account of goodwill—a difficult and demeaning task, because France and England were only reluctantly abiding by their Treaty of London obligations to Italy. The French and the British could not forget the circumstances under which the London Treaty had been signed. Italy had been neutral in the war until the spring of 1915, when, after shopping between the Allies and the Central Powers, she had found the most generous bargain to lie in joining the Allies. The secret Treaty of London had thereupon been concluded, but Italy had then declared war on Austria-Hungary only; not until more than a year later had she declared war on Germany. The British could not help but regard the Italian entry into the war as being more than a trifle cynical. At the time of the signing of the secret treaty the Italian ambassador had reproached the British, "You speak as if you were purchasing our support." "Well, and so we are," was the offhand and contemptuous British retort.[30] Moreover, France and Britain had soon begun to repent their generosity. They thought that the Italians had not fought particularly well and had required too much in the way of encouragement and support. The French and the British were candid in saying that as far as they were concerned the secret treaty had turned out to be a poor bargain.

It was especially so because what the Italians were now demanding was the territory, not of a defeated enemy, but of the new "Kingdom of the Serbs, Croats and Slovenes"—as Yugoslavia was then called—whose Regent, Prince Alexander Karageorgevich (later King Alexander I), had been the wartime leader of Serbia, an ally. No nation in the Allied cause could claim to have outdone Serbia in devotion, determination and fighting spirit. When the Serbian Army had been driven from its homeland after awful suffering, Alexander had rebuilt his forces abroad and tenaciously continued the struggle. The Allies owed an immense debt to this people and their Regent, and it was exceedingly unpleasant to have Italy demand compensation at their expense. But if France and Britain failed to honor their agreement, what nation would ever again trust a French or British treaty?

Lloyd George and Clemenceau did try to push the matter aside, on the technical grounds that Italy's claims were really against the old Austro-Hungarian Empire and had no place in a German treaty. The Italians instantly answered that unless their demands were satisfied now they would not agree to the establishment of the Yugoslav nation and would not sign the treaty with Germany. Next the three major Allies attempted to set up an impartial commission to recommend a proper line of demarcation between Italy and Yugoslavia. The Italians refused to permit such a commission to be established. The French and the British had some success in urging the Italians to drop their treaty claims to the islands along the Yugoslavian coast and to the province of Dalmatia, without which there could scarcely be a sovereign Yugoslav nation. The Italians finally agreed, but only on condition that they receive the port city of Fiume, which had been specifically denied them under the Treaty of London. This was too much to ask, the others said. Italy had already been given the Adriatic port of Trieste, as well as the South Tyrol with its 200,000 German Austrians; and France and Britain were willing to make substantial territorial concessions in the Near East, in the Dodecanese islands. The Italians had no legitimate use for Fiume, whereas it was the only port Yugoslavia could use. The only possible reason for Italy to want Fiume was so that she might cripple the overseas trade of the Yugoslav nation. The Italians conceded that this was so; perhaps it was selfish of them, but it was "*sacro egoismo*"—sacred selfishness. Either give us Fiume, they said, or give us the Adriatic islands and Dalmatia, both of which you promised us under the Treaty of London.

This put the French and the British in an untenable position. Either they had to support Italy's "legitimate" treaty claims or they had to agree that she should be given Fiume. Both prospects were intensely disagreeable; they were made even more so by the Italians' attitude. Orlando frankly admitted that he must have Fiume because Italy had been made substantial territorial offers by the Central Powers before she entered the war; if he did not get a good settlement now, his people would ask "why Italy had troubled to join the Allied side."[31] Even the French found this cynicism appalling.

By mid-April they were all disgusted with the Italians. They were sick of Orlando's emotionality in the Council of Four—his alternating outbursts of weeping and storms of Sicilian rage; they were disgusted with *sacro egoismo;* and they were surfeited with the Italian threats to abandon the peace conference and conclude a separate treaty with the Germans.

To the discredit of the French and the British, the brunt of the repudiation of the Italian claims was left to Woodrow Wilson.

By now the President was an utterly spent man. His face was gray and lined. The only way his doctor could bring color to Wilson's cheeks was to stand him by an open window and, grasping his hands, pull his arms back and forth in an approximation of a golfer's swing. The President's household servants noticed that he was developing strange little idiosyncracies. He convinced himself that the French servants were spies; he was suspicious that United States government vehicles were being used by peace conference delegates for private junkets; he would decide that the furniture in his residence was wrongly arranged and worry that some of it had been stolen.[32] Herbert Hoover also found Wilson much changed by his brief illness.

> *He sometimes groped for ideas. His mind constantly strove for previous decisions and precedents even in minor matters. He clung to them. Prior to that time [Wilson's illness] he was incisive, quick to grasp essentials, unhesitating in conclusions. [Afterward] I found that we had to push against an unwilling mind. And at times, when I just had to get decisions, our constant resort was to find "a precedent."*[33]

*   *   *

More than ever Wilson was alone and unadvised. Colonel House had been cast into outer darkness. Lloyd George thought that House's dismissal from Presidential favor came when he made the mistake of inviting the Prime Minister and Clemenceau to his rooms at the Hotel Crillon for a private conference a half hour before a Council of Four meeting, without informing Wilson. The President, coming unexpectedly into the room, demanded in a suspicious and bitter tone, "Hello, what is this about?" and the atmosphere was decidedly strained and embarrassed. "House was never forgiven," Lloyd George wrote. "I saw little of him after this unpleasant interview. He was not charged with any more errands by Wilson."[34]

The other American commissioners fared no better. They were almost completely in the dark about what was going on. At a reception Secretary of State Lansing approached Christian Herter, then a junior staff member, and inquired, "Have you heard what 'the Four' decided about Fiume?" Herter said that he had not, and Lansing instructed him, "Snoop around a bit and see if you can find out."[35]

By April 22, with the Germans due to arrive at Versailles in a week, the Fiume crisis had reached a stalemate. Every possible compromise had been considered and rejected. The only hope for a solution was for one side or the other to give way. But if there was to be surrender on the matter of Fiume, Wilson was determined that it would not be on his part. Exhausted as he was, the President rallied himself for one more battle. Wilson was certain that he held a trump card. Still with him were the glorious memories of the vast popular reception given him in Italy during his visit in January: the huge crowds crying *"Viva Wilson!,"* the accounts of Italian peasants burning candles before his picture, the delegation of a thousand village mayors who met him in Turin and, weeping with emotion, crowded about to shake his hand—many to stoop and kiss it. So Wilson, gladly assuming the role of an avenging angel, determined to confront these Italian politicians and their "old diplomacy" with the power of the new. He would go over Orlando's head and appeal directly to the Italian people. Since the support of Clemenceau and Lloyd George was faint and qualified, he would ignore them.

On the evening of April 23 Wilson published his personal manifesto to the Italian people. This unprecedented message from the head of one nation to the people of another was, as might be expected from Wilson, an eloquent and coherent statement of the American position regarding Italian claims. He explained to the Italian people that much had changed since the Treaty of London had been signed. He outlined the immense territorial acquisitions which Italy had already obtained and appealed to them to be content with these. Regarding Fiume, Wilson pleaded that it was the only port for the new Yugoslav nation and he appealed to the Italians to display in this matter "that noblest quality of greatness, magnanimity, friendly generosity, the preference of justice over interests."[36]

The effect of the Wilsonian manifesto was sensational—and the complete opposite of what Wilson had expected. The next day Orlando appeared at the Council of Four to announce that he and his delegation would return at once to Rome, where his people could "choose between Wilson and me."[37] Orlando would not predict when or if he would return to Paris. It was a stunning maneuver. The Italians were sure that the peace treaty could not be signed without them, yet it was not until Wilson's manifesto that they had been given an opportunity to quit the conference without blame being attached to them. Now they could do what only a few weeks before they would never have dared—leave Paris and not return until the Allies agreed to give them Fiume.

The most surprising—to Wilson—result of the Wilson manifesto was the attitude of the Italian people themselves. When, on April 25, Orlando's train arrived in Rome, he was met by a tremendous mob shrieking, "Down with Wilson!" Throughout Italy the portraits of the President were torn down. Nowhere in the country was a voice raised in the President's behalf. The American embassy in Rome warned Wilson that if the Orlando government wavered for a moment on Fiume it would be flung from office and replaced by a government which would probably be pro-German! Nor did Wilson receive much support for his "new diplomacy" even in the United States. Such enemies as Henry Cabot Lodge professed to favor the Italian claims, and, while it was ironically observed that Lodge's Massachusetts constituency doubtless contained a great many more voters of Italian than of South Slav ancestry, there was no question but that Wilson had suffered domestically from his manifesto.

The decay of Wilson's prestige had now been revealed in pitiless detail. He had played his trump card, an appeal to the common people, and it had been a disaster. Even the Europeans at the peace conference were astonished at the extent of the President's failure.

They had not dared to hope that the prophet's powers had so receded from their high-water mark of only twelve weeks before. And the dreary tale did not end with the Italian departure. On April 24, the day Orlando left Paris, the Japanese shrewdly presented to the Council—now shaken and shrunken into a Council of Three—their claims to the old German rights in China. Coupled with their demands was the threat that if they were refused the Japanese too would leave Paris.

The peace conference had reached its most desperate moment. Although the French, British and American delegates felt that they could sign the treaty without the Italians, they recognized that if the Japanese also were to quit Paris there might be a general exodus of smaller nations, and the force and authority of the conference and its treaty would be fatally damaged. Even the Belgians were threatening to abandon the conference.

The French and the British were bound by secret treaty to support the Japanese claims. The United States was the historic friend of China and her traditional protector against foreign greed; for more than a generation America had championed the "Open Door" and had supported the principle of Chinese national integrity. Wilson, the proponent of the self-determination principle which the Japanese claims so obviously contradicted, had fought to protect the Chinese. But now the Japanese had to be conciliated and kept in Paris.

Once again it was Wilson's frail shoulders that carried the crushing weight of compromise. On April 30 he gave in to the Japanese demands.

Exactly one week later, the treaty of peace was presented to the German delegation. By this time not one of the Allies was satisfied with it.

PART 2

Experience teaches us that, generally speaking, the most perilous moment for a bad government is one when it seeks to mend its ways. Only consummate statecraft can enable a king to save his throne when after a long spell of oppressive rule he sets to improving the lot of his subjects. Patiently endured so long as it seemed beyond redress, a grievance comes to appear intolerable once the possibility of removing it crosses men's minds.
—ALEXIS DE TOCQUEVILLE

Chapter Five

Prelude to Revolution

SHORTLY before midnight on November 9, 1918, Berlin was so quiet that it was difficult to believe a revolution had actually taken place that day. Only in a few places, on the Friedrichstrasse and before the library and the university on Unter den Linden, was any fighting taking place, and that was only a desultory exchange of shots between a few sailors of the "People's Naval Division" who had come out of the Schloss Berlin, the imperial palace, and some officers whom they could not see in the darkness. Otherwise all was quiet. The streetcars were even beginning to run again, and there was almost the usual number of Saturday-night strollers in the streets. From the big windows of the reading room in the Reichstag building—at one of which the Socialist Philipp Scheidemann had stood that day and casually proclaimed the birth of a German republic—one could see the Schloss clearly. The Spartacist revolutionaries under Karl Liebknecht had occupied it early in the day, and a flag made out of a red blanket now floated over it, illuminated by the lights of the neighboring cathedral.

It had been a remarkable day for Berlin—indeed, for all Germany. So much had happened that it was all difficult to grasp.

In a French railroad car near Rethondes, in the Forest of Compiègne, a confused German delegation had spent the day waiting for whomever might represent the German government to approve an armistice which, for all practical purposes, was a complete surrender. It appeared that the only concession the Allies were pre-

pared to make was in the number of machine guns which the
German Army was to surrender. Originally they had demanded that
thirty thousand be given up. The German delegation protested that
if that were done "there would not be enough left to fire on the
German people, should this become necessary."[1] It seemed that
Marshal Foch would permit the Army to keep an extra five thousand
machine guns for this eventuality.

Until the armistice was formally signed—and it could not be
signed until there was an officially constituted German government—the war was still going on. The German field army beyond
the borders, still under the control of its officers, was retreating to
new positions. It was very different with the armed forces stationed
in Germany. The red flag flew over almost every vessel of the
Imperial Navy, and the port of Kiel was under the command of a
Socialist ex-basketweaver who was attempting to restore the Navy's
sailors to some sort of discipline. In Berlin, as in every other large
German city, the military government had evaporated. Overnight
the officers had found that not even the most famous and supposedly
best-disciplined regiments would obey them. "Workers' and soldiers'
councils" on the Russian Bolshevik pattern were springing up everywhere.

That very evening in Moscow, the deliberations of the All-Russia
Congress of Soviets were interrupted twice to permit the latest
telegrams from Germany to be read, and when it was evident that a
revolution had taken place the Kremlin was put *en fête*. Lenin appeared at a balcony window and addressed a huge throng below. A
prominent Bolshevik, Karl Radek, was overjoyed at the size and
enthusiasm of the crowd: "Tens of thousands of workers burst into
wild cheering. Never have I seen anything like it again. Until late
evening workers and Red Army soldiers were filing past. The world
revolution had come. The mass of the people heard its iron tramp.
Our isolation was over."[2]

The first day of the German Revolution had been full of surprises,
not the least of them being the astonishing ease with which the
monarchies that in theory ruled Germany had been overthrown.
Two days before, King Ludwig III of Bavaria had been walking in
his gardens in Munich when someone came up to him with the
request that he return to his palace. There he found his Cabinet
ministers assembled to announce to him that a Bavarian republic
was about to be proclaimed by a Jewish revolutionary Socialist,
Kurt Eisner. The Cabinet could not guarantee the King's safety.

Without further ado the old King and his family packed together a few belongings, jammed themselves into an automobile and fled the city. It had been almost the same with the King of Württemberg, whose only serious objection to his forced abdication was that he would not allow the new Socialist government to fly the red flag over his palace, on the highly technical grounds that the palace was his personal property. So too it had gone (or would go within hours) with the kingdom of Saxony and the miscellaneous other kingdoms, duchies and principalities—Brunswick, Oldenburg, Hesse, etc.—which had made up the German Empire.

It had been a little more difficult to depose Wilhelm II, King of Prussia and German Emperor. But on this day even his abdication had been announced. Suddenly and incredibly the power of imperial Germany, with its disciplined and superbly efficient bureaucracy, its regiments of the guards and its satrapy of titled nobility, had completely evaporated. Even the Imperial Chancellor, Prince Max of Baden, had disappeared from Berlin, leaving in the Chancellery a successor of sorts: a pudgy forty-seven-year-old ex-saddle-maker, the "Majority Socialist" leader Friedrich Ebert. No one, it seemed, had been willing to fight for the continuation of the monarchy. Its adherents, confused, vacillating, and exhausted by a succession of catastrophes, were completely unable to resist the collapse of a system to which they had devoted their lives and careers. In fact, it seemed almost that they had given it up with a sense of relief.

By nightfall of November 9, Germany was in the flimsy grasp of the Social Democratic Party—the so-called Majority Socialists—Germany's largest political *Fraktion*. These men had suddenly been handed the power for which their party had struggled fifty years. In theory this night should have been an occasion of great rejoicing for them. Instead, a pall of apprehension hung over the Social Democrats. Ebert, pacing the floor of his office in the Imperial Chancellery, his jacket off, his shirt sweat-stained, knew that the quiet in the streets was deceptive and that the German Revolution was far from complete. Powerful conservative elements still remained in Germany; if they were now scattered and confused, this would not last long. At the moment, however, the threats of resurgent monarchism and reactionary militarism were the least of Ebert's worries. It was the far left which frightened him and his friends—for they were revolutionaries who were horrified at the thought of revolution, Socialists who hesitated to socialize the means of production, and democrats who, until a few days earlier, would gladly have permitted a German Emperor to remain on the throne.

This was the party which found itself responsible for Germany's destiny at its moment of defeat and revolution. It would attempt to guide Germany through months of awful crisis. There would be mobs and countermobs, private armies and Bolshevik militia. There would be insurrections, political assassinations, separatist rebellions and undeclared border wars. The Social Democrats could foresee none of this; they could only be sure that Germany itself was a vast unguarded arms dump and that their enemies on both the right and the left would soon be helping themselves to the weapons. Unless the Majority Socialists moved with exceptional caution and cunning, they would surely be the first victims of either a Red or a White terror.

In the years before the war, the Social Democratic Party had been the "official" voice of German socialism. It was this party which represented Germany at international socialist meetings, and its leaders regarded themselves as the legitimate heirs of Marx, Engels and Lassalle. The declared position of the Social Democrats was that Marxism was "the official position of the Social Democratic Party."[3] The party's announced attitude toward capitalism was that under it the proletariat could expect only "mounting insecurity, misery, pressure, subordination, debasement and exploitation." The result of this was expected to be "an ever more bitter class struggle."[4]

The establishment and the early years of the Social Democratic Party had been far from easy. At first there was a terrible struggle to reconcile the views of various socialist groups and weld them into one party. This was finally accomplished in 1875 at the famous Gotha congress. Next came the struggle against government repression. With its theories of class conflict, revolutionary republicanism and antimilitarism, the Social Democratic Party had won for itself the cordial hostility of the dominant monarchial and bourgeois elements in Wilhelmine Germany. Bismarck had been the party's active enemy. He passed anti-Socialist legislation under which (until its lapse in 1890) 150 Socialist newspapers had been suppressed and 1,500 Socialists imprisoned. Even after the official anti-Socialist legislation had expired, the Social Democrats had every reason to complain that they were denied many of the privileges freely granted to politically more conservative citizens of the Second Reich. They found themselves, for example, rigidly excluded from the Army's officer corps—if, indeed, it was conceivable that any Socialist would care to serve with the Junker aristocracy—and totally divorced from the favor of the Kaiser (who, when someone was presented to him as a member of the middle-of-the-road National Liberal Party, commented that that was "acceptable," but only just[5]). Never in his life had the Kaiser received a Social Democrat into his presence.

Germany's ruling elements did not content themselves with vocal disapproval of the Socialists. Social Democrats were constantly being arrested and sentenced for such crimes as *lèse majesté* and breach of the peace. The police would frequently stop a Socialist funeral procession and remove red streamers from the coffin on the grounds that the procession constituted an unauthorized political parade. A police officer with the power to suspend a meeting was present at every Social Democratic rally. The Kaiser himself had warned the German people that if the Social Democrats shall gain a majority they would "at once proceed to plunder the citizens"; in that event, he promised, "I shall have loopholes cut in the palace walls and we'll see how much plundering will take place."[6] The voting districts for members of the German parliament, the Reichstag, were purposely left predominantly rural in order to cripple the Social Democrats, whose votes came largely from the industrial workers of the growing cities. The lower house of the Prussian Landtag, the parliament of the state which dominated the German Empire, was elected by the notorious "three-class" system in which representation was split into thirds on the basis of amount of taxes paid. The workers and the peasantry, who, of course, together comprised the vast majority of the electorate, received only a third of the seats. The newspapers of the Social Democratic Party were not sold at newsstands in stations of the state-owned railways, and Social Democratic literature was banned from Army barracks. No employee of the German federal, state or municipal government was permitted to belong to the Social Democratic Party or to subscribe to its publications.

Paradoxically, the Social Democrats seemed to thrive on this opposition. Despite the aggressive hatred of the right and the center, the party made phenomenal political gains, especially in the years just before the war. When the German Reichstag was formed in 1871 there had been only two Socialists among its 397 members. By 1912 the Social Democratic representation had grown to 110 and it was the largest single *Fraktion* in the Reichstag. And while it was

true that the Reichstag did not wield much actual power in monarchial Germany, the Socialists had become a political force to be
reckoned with in the Second Reich. This was in large measure
because their voting discipline in the Reichstag was far better than
that of any of their conservative rivals. Before any queston came up
for vote in the Reichstag, the Social Democratic deputies invariably
met in secret caucus and decided by majority ballot how the party
should vote; when the question came up, every member of the bloc
either voted accordingly or withdrew unobtrusively from the
Reichstag chamber without voting. It was well known that there
were bitter differences in the Party—there were a left wing, a center
and a right wing—but before the eyes of their political enemies the
ranks of the Socialists were always closed. It was with considerable
justice that in 1907 the Social Democrat deputy Gustav Noske,
replying to the charge that the Socialists were subverting discipline
in the Army, answered, "Where in Germany is there a greater
measure of discipline than in the Social Democratic Party and in the
modern trade unions?"[7]

All this had been accomplished by a party whose revered theorists—Marx, Engels, August Bebel, Wilhelm Liebknecht—were
dead; their places had been filled by men of lesser talents. Unlike
the leaders of the Socialist parties in other European countries, the
German Socialist leaders were not generally intellectuals. But they
were forceful and dedicated men, most of them graduates of the
German trade-union movement and superb organizers. They had
built a staff of paid professional organizers which ultimately
reached fifteen thousand persons. By 1914 the party's financial
worth exceeded twenty million gold marks, all prudently invested.
Under the direction of these ex-workers, the German who was
himself a worker and a Social Democrat could lead a truly distinc-
tive way of life. The Social Democrats had given him his own
fraternal and sports organization, his own singing groups, and clubs
for his wife and his children. He could read any of more than ninety
Social Democratic newspapers, led by the vigorous Berlin daily
Vorwärts. The political and organizational success of the Social
Democrats had enabled them to demand and obtain a respectable
body of legislation incorporating social reform, outlawing child
labor and improving working conditions and wages, to the point
where the German Social Democratic Party was the model for
socialist parties in every other nation, and the German worker the

most envied in Continental Europe. What did he care if the capitalists, the militarists or the bourgeoisie hated him?

But by now the very success of the Social Democratic Party had brought with it serious contradictions. Marx had preached the inevitability of the socialist revolution as the middle class was ruined by ever-growing concentrations of wealth in the hands of the very rich at the same time as the proletariat was increasingly impoverished. This was not happening, however—certainly not in Germany. The middle class was clearly growing in size and wealth, and the Socialist proletariat found its own lot substantially improving. Around the turn of the century the dogma of the German Social Democrats began to change as they realized that their future did not in fact lie on the bloody barricades of violent revolution.

There were several strong arguments to support this "revisionist" position. Friedrich Engels, the protector of Marxist purity and the military expert of the Second Socialist International, had died in 1895. Soon after his death there appeared a collection of writings attributed to Engels and known as his "Testament." In these Engels seemed to be saying that, with the emergence of new firearms, and given the wider, straighter streets of the growing industrial cities, the conception of the proletariat defending a revolution from behind cobblestone barricades was obsolete. Then, in 1899, the prominent German Social Democrat Eduard Bernstein published an appeal to his comrades. It seemed, Bernstein announced, that capitalism had developed a flexibility and adaptability which Marx had not foreseen. In fact, it might well be that capitalism would turn out to be a very enduring system indeed. If this proved to be the case, the Social Democrats must develop some means of persuading the masses of the superiority of the Socialist system. Germany would then evolve into Marxism. In effect, Bernstein urged the party to substitute evolution for revolution; it should, he said, "emancipate itself from outworn phraseology [and] come out in its true colors as a democratic socialist reform party."[8]

Revisionism had an immediate and special appeal to the German Social Democrats. Violent revolution was not an objective which really suited them. Their movement had no terrorist section; German Socialists had no experience in directing street riots or assassinating crowned heads of state. Terror and insurrection were simply not their style. Like other Germans, they secretly prided themselves on being more honest and upright than foreigners. When they heard of disturbances in other countries, they would say to themselves, "Such things do not happen here. We have law and order."[9] So it was probably with a very real sense of relief that the Social Democrats allowed themselves to be persuaded that the ultimate victory of socialism would take the form of a gradual evolution, a "slow revolution," during which they would ultimately obtain a majority in the Reichstag and then convert it from an impotent "talking shop" into a truly democratic parliament, with the Kaiser either deposed or, more likely, converted into a constitutional figurehead. Thus the German workers were to be emancipated from capitalist exploitation legally and by majority vote. Among German Socialists the concept of an inevitable violent revolution was gradually thrust into the background, except for ceremonial occasions when it was given cursory lip service by Social Democrat orators.

This comfortable German revisionism did not go unobserved by Socialist comrades in other European nations; nor were the German Social Democrats free from a certain embarrassing sense of guilt. With a pang they heard Jean Jaurès, the giant of French socialism, attack them at the Amsterdam congress of the Second International as a party grown fat and passive. Jaurès said:

> Certainly you are a great and admirable party which had given to international socialism not all its thinkers, as is sometimes said, but some of its most powerful and precise thinkers . . . you have an admirable machine for propaganda, for recruiting and enrolling, but neither the traditions of your proletariat nor the mechanism of your constitution permit you to cast that apparent colossal force of three million votes into useful and real action of political life Why? . . . [You] have neither revolutionary action nor parliamentary action. . . . You do not know yet, in practice, what road you shall take, whether you shall be revolutionary or parliamentary, [or] how you will institute democracy in your own country.[10]

There was, however, one hallowed Socialist theorem which not even the German Social Democrats thought of revising. This was the matter of the stand to be taken by Europe's Socialists should a general war break out between nations. The Second International had foreseen such a war and resolved that it would amount only to the workers "shooting one another for the sake of capitalist profits, for the sake of ambitions of dynasties, for the accomplishment of the aims of secret diplomatic treaties."[11] To block a declaration of war, the European Socialists had agreed upon a plan. Even in peacetime the Socialist party of each nation was expected always to vote against conscription laws and against military appropriations. August Bebel had announced the policy for the Germans—"Not a man, not a farthing for this system." But the crushing blow would come at the time when any European government was about to mobilize its army preparatory to war. The Socialist party of every nation would refuse to vote for the special budgetary appropriations—the "war credits"—which the government would have to obtain from its legislature in order to finance military mobilization. Simultaneously, all European Socialist parties were obliged to "do all in their power," by a general strike or other means, "to utilize the economic and political crisis caused by the war to rouse the people and thereby to hasten the abolition of capitalist class rule."[12]*

On August 2, 1914, the First World War began, with almost simultaneous declarations of war by France, Germany and Russia. And on August 4 Count von Bethmann-Hollweg, the German Imperial Chancellor, appeared before the Reichstag and asked it to appropriate special war credits of five million marks.

The leaders of the German Social Democratic Party were now faced with a terrible dilemma. It was clearly their duty as Socialists to act as members of the international proletariat and to take advantage of the outbreak of war in order to wreck the capitalist structure. Now was the hour to display the might which years of organization and discipline had brought to German socialism.

But these Social Democrats were Germans as well as Socialists. In a furious caucus the party leadership debated the question of the war credits—a question on which there should, theoretically, have

---

* The attitude of the German Social Democratic Party toward the matter of a general strike in the event of the outbreak of war was never precisely defined. At the Stuttgart congress of the Second International in 1907 a resolution was proposed by the Socialist parties of several nations, led by the Russians and the French, that a general strike be obligatory at the time of military mobilization. Their motto was, "Better insurrection than war." Although the German Social Democrats conceded that the general strike was clearly the workers' most powerful weapon, the majority of the German delegates refused to accept any resolution which specifically required a general strike. They claimed that if they voted for the resolution the German government would probably suppress the party as potentially insurrectionist. The Socialists who sponsored the general-strike resolution scoffed at this excuse. They intimated that the Germans simply wanted to preserve their own personal safety and to leave themselves a way out in the event of a war which might be supported by the German workers.

been no debate. Finally they arrived at an astonishing decision. By a majority vote, with only fourteen deputies opposed, the Social Democratic members of the Reichstag decided to vote *for* the war credits. "In the hour of danger," announced Hugo Haase, the leader of the Social Democrats in the Reichstag (and one of those who had voted in caucus *against* the war credits), "we will not desert our own Fatherland."[13] All save one of the Socialists stayed in the Reichstag chamber and voted for the credits.

The German Socialists quickly advanced a number of explanations for this stunning reversal of position: the war had already started, and, with press censorship and martial law (officially called the "state of siege") in effect, there was really nothing they could do to stop it; although they were, it was true, the largest single *Fraktion* in the Reichstag, they controlled less than a third of the total vote, and even if they had opposed the war credits the appropriation would still have been carried by the majority; and they further pointed out that the French Socialists were supporting *their* government in the war. These were all rationalizations. The true reason why the Social Democrats voted for the war credits was that they were Germans and their nation, they thought, was in danger. For this same reason their rank-and-file adherents among the German proletariat cheerfully mobilized for war. The Kaiser and the German government had announced that this was a defensive war which had been forced upon Germany, and the Social Democrats chose to accept this. Together with most other Germans, they believed that their nation had been surrounded by envious enemies who, led by Russia, had now attacked. What would happen if Germany lost to Russia? The nation would then be occupied by the most reactionary ruler in Europe, and German socialism would quickly be suppressed under the knouts of the Czar's Cossacks.

In a special issue of their Berlin newspaper, *Vorwärts*, the Social Democratic leaders explained their position, bearing down heavily on the need to defend the Fatherland against Russia.

> *We are face to face with destiny . . . the inexorable fact of war. We are threatened by the horror of hostile invasion. Today it is not for us to decide for or against war but to consider the means necessary for the defense of our country . . . We demand that as soon as the aim of security has been achieved and our opponents are disposed to make peace this*

*war shall be brought to an end . . . With these principles in
mind we vote for the desired war credits.*[14]

The impact of this reversal of position by the German Socialists
was awesome. Lenin, for example, refused at first to believe that it
had happened. He could not conceive that socialism's largest, best-
disciplined and best-organized national party had become "rene-
gades," "chauvinists" and "opportunists." Even when he was shown
a copy of *Vorwärts* carrying the Social Democrats' statement, he
was sure that it must be a government forgery. Later, in Switzerland, Lenin refused to shake hands with Karl Kautsky, a prominent
German Social Democrat, or to call him "comrade"; instead he
shrieked insults at Kautsky and called him to his face a coward, a
hypocrite and a prostitute.

It was with a queasy sense of guilt that the German Socialists
heard "the spirit of August 4" warmly commended by the parties of
the right, who patronizingly called them "good *Sozi.*" There were,
on the other hand, certain tangible rewards for their fidelity to the
Fatherland. Social Democratic literature was allowed to be circulated in the barracks of the Army. The Social Democratic leaders,
who were to have been arrested at the outbreak of the war, were left
at liberty. *Vorwärts,* which had been suppressed shortly after the
outbreak of the war, was allowed to resume publication, on the basis
of an understanding with the military governor of Berlin that "the
topic 'class hatred and class struggle,'" would "be in the future
avoided in *Vorwärts.*"[15] Along with the Reichstag deputies from
other parties, the Social Democrats were ushered into the presence
of Wilhelm II, who smiled upon them and announced, "I no longer
know any parties—I only know Germans."

During the first year or so of the war, the left-wing German
politicians faithfully observed the *Burgfriede,** the party truce,
during which all political controversy was put aside in the interest
of winning the war. The Social Democratic Party put no obstacle
whatever in the way of more effective mobilization of workers for
war production or service at the front. By September, 1914, more
than thirty per cent of the party's members had been mobilized and

---

* Literally, the "peace of the castle." In medieval Germany a traveling knight could
enter any castle or town and obtain food and shelter if he swore to observe the
Burgfriede.

were serving in the Imperial Army. With their mottoes "The fight is against Russia" and "Down with czarism,"[16] there was nothing lukewarm about the Social Democrats' wartime spirit. In December, 1914, an official delegation of German Social Democratic leaders was sent to Italy to plead with that nation's Socialists to exert their influence so that Italy would enter the war on the German side or, at the very least, remain neutral. And when from time to time the Reichstag was asked to vote additional war credits, the Social Democrats invariably supported the government's request.

But as the months dragged on, the Social Democratic Party, or at least a sizable part of it, began to suffer a disquieting sense of doubt. The Russian invasion had been decisively repelled, and there was little further danger that the Cossacks of the Czar would ever be found sabering down German workers on the streets of the industrial cities. It had also become apparent that the German General Staff had never really regarded Russia as the principal enemy. The main thrust of the German Army had been directed toward the conquest of neutral Belgium and the invasion of France, on whose soil the major battles of the war were now being fought. No one spoke much about it, but it had begun to be very difficult to believe that Germany was fighting the defensive war on which "the spirit of August 4" had been predicated. Nor were such influential conservative groups as the Pan-Germans or the Landowners' League troubling themselves to allay the gnawing Socialist fear that this war was and always had been an aggressive, expansionist conflict. Leaders of the Catholic Center Party spoke disquietingly of huge reparations payments which were to be extorted from Germany's enemies when they were defeated. The Progressive Party leadership came out candidly for a postwar partition of Belgium, with Germany getting the lion's share. "Where a drop of German blood has flowed, *we remain*," announced the leader of the National Liberal Party.[17] And a spokesman for the Pan-German League was frank to say, "only force is of avail. Whoever teaches that Germany can assert itself among the nations in any other way than by the accretion of its force sins against his Fatherland."[18]

Gradually, painfully, many of the Social Democrats came to the conclusion that they had been deceived. Their own prewar warnings that Europe's capitalist rulers intended to foment an expansionist war in order to stave off the inevitable collapse of their society seemed now to have been borne out in practice. The autocrats and capitalists of France, Germany and Russia had contrived to fill the trenches with mobilized workers, who were now engaged in killing off multitudes of fellow workers. To certain of the German Socialists, the most shameful aspect of the whole business was that the Socialists, who had themselves foreseen this conflict and had sworn to have nothing to do with it, had done nothing to oppose it. They had voted for the war credits, had cooperated with the Junker militarists to eliminate strikes and to squeeze more war-goods production out of the workers, and were faithfully observing the *Burgfriede,* while parties to the right were announcing Germany's intention to extract vast indemnities and territorial annexations from the nations she defeated. What had the Social Democrats gotten for this renunciation of their principles? Only a few condescending crumbs from autocracy's table—the right to publish Socialist newspapers and the personal liberty of the Social Democratic leadership. It was questionable whether they had ever been dealt with in good faith. On an inspection tour of the front a group of Social Democratic deputies were given lunch at a restaurant at Zeebrugge which had been commandeered as an officers' club. As they left the restaurant, an Army photographer took a picture of them with the officers'-club sign over their heads. To the embarrassment of the Socialists, the photograph was widely distributed by the Army. It became a matter of grave concern to many Socialist leaders that their party was "in danger of losing its soul"—if, indeed, it had not already done so.

In December, 1915, the German government announced that it would soon ask the Reichstag to approve additional war credits of ten billion marks. It would be the fifth such bill to be voted on since August, 1914. When the Social Democratic deputies met in caucus to decide how their *Fraktion* would vote, the balloting was much closer than it had ever been before: sixty-six in favor of supporting the government request, forty-four against. And when, on December 21, the measure was voted on in the Reichstag, for the first time a group of Socialists, twenty of them, stayed in the chamber to cast their votes in opposition to the majority of the Social Democratic *Fraktion*—that is, *against* the credits—while another twenty-two abstained from voting. The vaunted discipline of the Socialists had finally broken.

By the spring of 1916 the Social Democratic Party had actually split.° A sizable group of Socialists, including eighteen Reichstag deputies, had formed what became known as the "Independent Social Democratic Party," as opposed to the parent Social Democratic Party, whose members were now called the "Majority Socialists." The controversy between the two groups rapidly became bitter. Within the ranks of the Independent Socialists were the bulk of German socialism's theoreticians, among them Eduard Bernstein, Karl Kautsky and Hugo Haase, the former chairman of the Social Democratic Party and once its leader in the Reichstag. Remaining with the Majority Socialists were such old stalwarts and party officials as Friedrich Ebert, Philipp Scheidemann, Eduard David and Gustav Noske, who, if they were not quite up to the others as social theorists, possessed a good deal of practical political knowledge and ability, and had a strong following in the trade unions from whose ranks they had come. More important, they were able to retain control over most of the Socialist newspapers and the trade unions. Nevertheless, the Independent Socialists, representing themselves as the only true believers and the sole apostles of legitimate Marxist dogma, touched on a raw nerve when they attacked the Majority Socialists as opportunists, revisionists and traitors to socialism. To this abuse the Majority Socialists could only reply with fumbling and wordy defenses of their cooperation with the monarchist-militarist elements which ruled Germany. "Only by obtaining the unity of our people and assuring thereby its military power of action"—so ran their defense—"did it become possible to stop the invasion of the Empire by the Russian war power and to defeat it."[19] In vain the Majority implored the minority, "Comrades! We again appeal to you! The danger which threatens the party is great! . . . Defend the party! Close the ranks!"[20]

To all these blandishments the Independent Socialists responded with the disdain of the pure and the holy. They renounced their sins of August 4 and, while admitting that they represented only a small segment of the German electorate, demanded that the Kaiser's government immediately state its real war aims and enter into negotiations for peace. They insisted that the peace should be one in which there would be "neither victors nor vanquished," and that there should be no indemnities or territorial annexations. The Independents also demanded that the government revoke the press

---

° The Independent Social Democratic Party (U.S.P.D.) was formed in January, 1916. It was not until April, however, that the parent organization (S.P.D.) read the rebels out of the party and thus formalized the split.

censorship and lift the repressive "state of siege" which had been imposed at the beginning of the war.

If they served no other purpose, these developments at least hastened the breakup of the *Burgfriede* within the Reichstag. It became evident that most of the Independent Socialists, reverting to Marxist dogma, had abandoned the revisionism of the prewar years and were, however secretly, anticipating the ultimate victory of socialism by violent revolution. This being the case, they could no longer support the German war effort—for if Germany won the war the prestige of the Kaiser, the Army and the capitalists would probably be heightened to such an extent that the system would be unassailable.

Extreme as the views of most of the Independent Socialists might seem, they were almost conservative in comparison to the demands of a small, secret, militantly revolutionary organization which had attached itself to the ranks of the Independents. For the first months of its existence, the identity of the leaders of this "Gruppe Internationale," as it was then called, was closely concealed from the police, who would have given much to be able to arrest them. One of them was a lawyer in his early forties, a short, slender man with close-cut curly hair and a fuzzy little mustache, whose steel-rimmed pince-nez contributed to his characteristic compressed, intense expression. His name was Karl Liebknecht.

Liebknecht came from a revolutionary background. The son of Wilhelm Liebknecht, a hallowed figure in German socialism and an intimate friend of Karl Marx, he had grown up in the traditions of his father. Before the war he had led a militantly leftist section within the Social Democratic Party, fighting revisionism tooth and nail. His fight had not made him popular among the party's leaders, who regarded him as an intellectual troublemaker, a sort of *enfant terrible,* possibly brilliant but lacking the balance and common sense of his father. The trade-union leaders, in particular, distrusted Liebknecht. The passionate intensity of his opinions frightened these middle-of-the-road Social Democrats. They thought of him as a potential menace, and many of them refused to have anything to do with him. Liebknecht, in his turn, had consistently attacked them as former revolutionaries who had degenerated into nothing more than "officials" and "social reformers"—a scathing condemnation in left-wing Socialist circles.

Nobody could deny Liebknecht's dedication to the cause. He had become a lawyer in order to defend fellow Socialists in the courts. He had led the Socialist attack on militarism—indeed, he had dedicated his life to the overthrow of German militarism. Liebknecht hated the Army and all it stood for. To him it was the principal bulwark of capitalism; he was sure that without the Army both the monarchy and the German economy would collapse into Marxist hands. Before the war he had developed a number of ingenious ideas for combating the Army's influence. One was an extensive training program for Social Democratic youth so that by the time they came of military age they would no longer be pliable conscripts but intractable enemies of the entire military system. The scheme had achieved some significant successes, a fact which had earned Liebknecht the enduring hatred of Germany's ruling circles. When he published a deliberately provocative antimilitarist pamphlet in 1907, the authorities acted. Liebknecht was brought to trial for high treason. It was rumored (and never denied) that the Kaiser personally followed the trial by means of day-to-day transcripts. In the end Liebknecht was sentenced to eighteen months in a Silesian prison.

His trial and imprisonment served him well. They attained for him a popularity and fame which he had never enjoyed as a free man. While he was still in prison the workers of Berlin elected him to the Prussian Landtag as one of the tiny group of Social Democrats which the repressive three-class electoral system permitted. In 1912, after his prison sentence was served, Liebknecht was also elected a Reichstag deputy.

More than to anything else, Liebknecht owed these election victories to his reputation as a jailed antimilitarist. Certainly they were not due to personal popularity with his fellow Social Democrats, for Liebknecht had never had any personal following. His overweening revolutionary evangelism made that impossible. He was frequently arrogant, domineering and vain, always boundlessly enthusiastic, nervous, constantly in motion. At his home he would interrupt meetings with Socialist comrades when his children ran into the room and, while his astonished associates looked on, would roll on the rug with the children and turn somersaults with them, all the while laughing frantically. Sometimes he seemed, even to his friends, to be living at a level just below hysteria.

In August, 1914, Liebknecht reluctantly obeyed the demand for Socialist discipline and voted for the August 4 war credits. It was the last service he was to render the Social Democratic leadership.

Shortly afterward he traveled to occupied Belgium and convinced himself that the Reichstag deputies were being lied to. Earlier than any of the other Social Democrats he came to the conclusion that this was not a war of defense for Germany, and upon his return to Berlin he became the first Socialist deputy to remain in his Reichstag seat and refuse to vote for any additional war credits. He ignored party discipline again by revealing to the uncensored Swiss newspapers that there existed a secret division of opinion among the Social Democrats about the war credits. And from his seat in the Landtag and the Reichstag he exercised his parliamentary privilege with constant questions which the government found impossible to answer: How many Belgian civilian hostages had been shot by the Army in acts of reprisal? Was the Army prepared to abolish secret diplomacy after the war? When would the government make available the foreign documents relating to the responsibility for the outbreak of the war? These questions became known as "Liebknecht's Little Interpellations" and were immensely irritating to the government.

Liebknecht's rebellion brought him worldwide notoriety. He suddenly became famous as a man who voted solely according to his conscience against overwhelming pressure. In the United States, *Harper's Weekly* printed a poem commending his moral courage. The German authorities could not fail to react. They could not arrest him, because of his parliamentary immunity, but they could and did call him up to active Army duty as a private in a Landwehr—militia—regiment. Even there he could not be silenced. Under the law he was entitled to return to Berlin whenever the Reichstag was in session. And there his "interpellations" continued. No one could stop him—not the Independent Socialists, with whom Liebknecht had made an alliance of sorts, and certainly not the Majority Socialists, whom he utterly despised. It was only a formality when, in January, 1916, the Majority Socialists threw him out of the Social Democratic Party.

Now Liebknecht found himself virtually an outcast. But this did not last for long. He began secretly to recruit a small number of like-minded followers. Most of them had been part of the far-left wing of the Social Democratic Party before the war and had left the party in disgust and joined the Independents, whom they now found to be too conservative for their views. They were incorrigibly theoretical. Liebknecht named his tiny organization the Gruppe Internationale, and his followers all agreed to subscribe to a set of "Guiding Principles" written in prison by a woman who was called by the police "the Red Rose."

Rosa Luxemburg, then forty-five years old, was a dainty, slender, fastidious little person who was fussy about the furnishings of her apartment and who tended her flower garden carefully. She walked with a pronounced limp, the result of a childhood hip disease. Generally she wore a large hat and carried a parasol, looking rather like a period photograph of someone's maiden aunt. The appearance was deceptive: Luxemburg was an acknowledged giant of Socialist theoretics, with an international reputation as an antirevisionist revolutionary.

She had been born in Russian Poland, the daughter of a middle-class Jewish merchant. From her earliest years Rosa Luxemburg had been recognized as brilliant. She had been admitted to the best girls' high school in Warsaw—an astonishing accomplishment, since most of the places were reserved for Russian children; very few Poles and still fewer Jews were admitted. Attracted by socialism even as a schoolgirl, Luxemburg joined a revolutionary cell and narrowly escaped being arrested by the Russian secret police. At the age of eighteen she was smuggled out of Poland, concealed under a load of hay in a peasant's cart, and went to Zurich, where she entered the university and won a doctorate in law. In Switzerland she became, for a time, a leading figure in the emigré section of the Polish Social Democratic Party. Then she rebelled against the nationalism of the party and led in the formation of a new Polish Socialist group. The Socialists of other nations, France and Germany, laughed at the disarray of the Polish Socialists, whose party meetings were bedlams of factional feud. Luxemburg herself grew discouraged and decided to leave Zurich.

In 1898 Luxemburg came to Berlin, where she joined the Social Democratic Party. To prevent being deported by the German police (a very serious danger for an alien Socialist), she became a German national by entering into an arranged marriage with a party comrade's son, from whom she parted company on the steps of the registry office after the wedding. It did not take her long to become prominent within the German Social Democratic Party. She was made one of its delegates to the congresses of the Second International, where she did not hesitate to debate even the most august figures in international socialism. Her oratory was brilliant, and she was a popular speaker. She was recognized as being one of the best writers in the German Social Democratic Party. By 1914 Rosa

Luxemburg was certainly as well known as Lenin—with whom she had several bitter disputes. Luxemburg admired the nerve and determination of the Russian Socialist, but she was frankly suspicious of the authoritarianism of Lenin's Bolshevik faction; she found herself more sympathetic toward Trotsky, at that time a member of the Mensheviks. Certainly Rosa Luxemburg was better liked than Lenin. She possessed a human warmth and a friendly wit, and she rarely descended to the character defamation which Lenin habitually employed.

The Red Rose was not, however, particularly popular with the prewar leaders of the German Social Democratic Party, who tended to regard her as an impractical dreamer and a likable crank who was out of touch with day-to-day realities. When the war came, Luxemburg had little difficulty coming to the conclusion that the Social Democratic leadership had made a terrible mistake. At the time the war credits were first passed she nearly committed suicide in despair at her party's acquiescence. She attempted to publish a clandestine protest newspaper, *Die Internationale,* but in February, 1915, the authorities found out about her plans. She was arrested and held in prison without trial under "military protective custody."

The German authorities made one serious mistake in the handling of this little woman—they permitted her to correspond with her friends. And in short order Luxemburg was in contact with Liebknecht and drafted the "Guiding Principles" which served as the blueprint for the formation of the Gruppe Internationale.

These "Guiding Principles" dealt primarily with the attitude of the Gruppe Internationale toward Socialists in Germany and, indeed, in other European nations. The war was seen to have "destroyed the result of forty years of work of European socialism." By voting for the war credits and agreeing to the *Burgfriede* the German Social Democrats "committed treason against the most elementary lessons of international socialism." They were charged with having given up the class struggle and thus having "given the ruling class in each country the chance to strengthen itself enormously." Nationalism in any form was pitilessly attacked. "The fatherland of all proletarians is the Socialist International, and defense of this must take priority over everything else."[21]

The "Guiding Principles" committed their adherents to a definite course of action. Foremost was the establishment of a new international to take the place of the existing Second International organization, which had failed in its duty toward the proletariat. Once this was done, Luxemburg proposed, the Socialist party in every nation should place itself under the new international's control. The international would have the power to determine each party's tactics with regard to militarism, colonial policy, national economic policy—even May Day celebrations. Each national party must obey the dictates of the international, and no discretion would be permitted them—for by their attitude at the time of the war-credits voting the national Socialist parties had proved their unreliability. As a matter of course, the Gruppe Internationale called for the dissolution of the *Burgfriede*, for immediate resumption of class war, for trade-union activity against the war, and for revolutionary action on the part of the international proletariat.

These demands were more extreme than even the Independent Socialists were prepared to accept. Although the Liebknechtians found a shelter of sorts in the ranks of the Independents, they were a group apart—alone, uninfluential, hating and hated, without even a working-class following. The only reason Liebknecht and his friends even bothered to remain among the Independents was, as Liebknecht himself said, "in order to drive them forward, to have them within reach of our whip."[22] Few people understood the subtle but very real differences in Socialist theory between Liebknecht and both the Independent and the Majority Socialists. Fewer still cared. But Lenin did. At the time of the Zimmerwald Conference in Switzerland he announced himself appalled at the "social chauvinism" and "opportunism" of the Majority and Independent Socialists. "For us," Lenin said, speaking for the Bolsheviks, "there exists the Liebknecht group only."[23]

On January 22, 1916, the German police authorities, knowing nothing of Rosa Luxemburg's involvement with the Gruppe Internationale, decided that she was relatively harmless and released her from prison.

January 27, 1916, was the fifty-seventh birthday of Kaiser Wilhelm II. All over Germany there appeared the ritual greetings to the All Highest in the form of placards and posters. But there also appeared an unlooked-for handbill, crudely mimeographed, which greeted the Kaiser's birthday with unflattering comments and attacked both the Majority and the Independent Socialists, whose professed opposition to the war was described as nothing more than a "beautiful gesture." This openly revolutionary handbill was in the form of an open letter and was signed "Spartacus."

Probably few of the Germans who had the opportunity to read this leaflet knew that the original Spartacus was a first-century gladiator who led an uprising of Roman slaves and obtained such popular support that he came close to overthrowing the Roman Empire. Nevertheless, the name had an impressive ring to it, and the pamphlet, like those that followed it, was so violent in its attacks that Spartacus instantly became a force to be reckoned with among German Socialists. As the months passed these pseudonymous letters appeared with increasing frequency and became increasingly inflammatory. They called for an immediate end to "the vile crime of nation murdering" and urged the soldiers of every nation to turn their weapons against the exploiting classes. They attacked the Majority Socialists, and quite frequently the Independents too, as bankrupt and soulless. No one knew where the letters came from or how, but, passed from hand to hand, they found their way to the trade-union leadership, to the left wing of the Independents, to the Swiss Socialist leaders, and from them to the outside world. Inevitably a few were picked up by the police. But only a small circle knew that Spartacus was Karl Liebknecht and that Liebknecht's followers, gradually discarding the name "Gruppe Internationale," now called themselves the Spartakusbund (Spartacus Union).*

The circulation of the Spartacus Letters did not, however, bring immediate influence to the Spartakusbund. Only five hundred copies of each were issued until September, 1916, when Liebknecht's supporters began to print the letters on presses and increased the number to about five thousand copies. To Liebknecht this clandestine publication was unsatisfactory. He had not even dented the strength of the Majority Socialists, who continued to vote for the war credits and to support the national war effort. Moreover, he was beginning to be popularly regarded as an eccentric. "Liebknecht's little interpellations" were now greeted by a storm of catcalls, ridicule and outright laughter from Reichstag deputies of every complexion. Many even believed that Liebknecht had gone out of his mind. While he was speaking, various deputies would shout, "Nonsense!," "Madness!" and "Lunatic!"[24] Liebknecht could not stand this. He did not mind in the least being called a traitor to his country, but he could not tolerate being laughed at.

* The principal early Spartacists included, apart from Liebknecht and Luxemburg, a number of well-known left-wing figures such as Leo Jogiches, Clara Zetkin, August Thalheimer, Paul Levi, Wilhelm Pieck, Ernst Mayer, Hugo Eberlein, and Hermann and Kate Duncker.

In April, 1916, Liebknecht resolved to make a bold move to attract a popular following to the Spartakusbund. From its secret press the group published leaflets announcing a mass meeting in the Potsdamer Platz in Berlin at 8 P.M. on May 1. At the time set, there were nearly ten thousand people in the square; Liebknecht's appeal for peace, bread and freedom had a drawing power which even the Majority Socialists could not deny. Around the edges of the crowd swarmed police and mounted troopers from the Berlin garrison. Liebknecht rose and began to speak. They let him get as far as "Down with the war! Down with the government!"[25] Then they whipped their horses into the mob, dragged Liebknecht down and arrested him.

His trial for "attempted treason," "aggravated disobedience" and "contumacy to the authority of the state" caused just the kind of sensation that Liebknecht had always wanted. He was found guilty, stripped of his Reichstag seat, dishonorably discharged from the Army and given a two-and-a-half-year prison sentence. He appealed to a higher court, and made such violent and inflammatory statements that his sentence was increased to four years. Workers' demonstrations protesting the sentence were held in various German cities. These resulted in the jailing of a number of known pacifists—among them Rosa Luxemburg, who, on July 10, was flung into prison without trial and on no specific charges.

Now, serving his sentence as a shoemaker in Luckau Prison, Liebknecht was at last an authentically influential figure: he had become a martyr. Both he and Rosa Luxemburg contrived to smuggle letters, appeals and manifestos from their prisons. The Spartacus Letters were kept going. And although the Spartakusbund was still only a tiny organization, Liebknecht now had a broad sympathy which might someday be worth much more. Certainly he had put the Majority Socialists in an uncomfortable position. They had denounced Liebknecht's May Day demonstration: "How grotesque was this enterprise. . . . This is a war for our very homes. . . . Contrast this [Liebknecht's] pathological instability with our clear-headed and methodical calm."[26] But they found that this approach did not go down well with their membership. Increasing numbers of workers were deserting to the Independents, compared with whom the Majority Socialist leadership seemed confused, indecisive and impotent. The latter began to wonder whether they were making a mistake by attempting to operate as "loyal Germans" within the legitimate framework of the German political structure.

* * *

Germany's system of government was an anachronism for an industrialized nation in the twentieth century. It was a federation of twenty-seven kingdoms, duchies, principalities and "free and imperial cities." By far the largest of these components was Prussia, whose Hohenzollern King, under the terms of the imperial Constitution of 1871, also bore the title of German emperor. The various states which comprised the federal German Empire had managed to retain a certain amount of autonomy in administrative matters, and most of them had their own individual parliaments of sorts. But the more important questions—foreign affairs, the Navy, the direction of the Army in wartime, imperial finance, and foreign trade—were all under the control of the Empire. In practice, this meant that they were under the personal control of the Emperor himself, who, without let or hindrance, appointed his own Imperial Chancellor, who in turn appointed his own "secretaries of state," who were the administrative department heads of the imperial government. The Prussian Army swore an oath of fealty to the Emperor personally, not to the German nation. The only voice which the German people had in the direction of the affairs of the Empire was through their popularly elected deputies in the Reichstag, the lower house of the German imperial parliament. But Bismarck, who had framed the constitution, had taken great care to make the Reichstag almost powerless. The Reichstag could not initiate legislation, it could only approve it. It could not amend the constitution. It had no control over the Imperial Chancellor or the various secretaries of state. The Kaiser did not require the Reichstag's approval to declare war, make peace or conclude treaties. In fact, the only power which the Reichstag possessed was the right to approve legislation and the military budget. Should the deputies prove obstinate in these matters, the Emperor was constitutionally empowered to dissolve the Reichstag and call for new elections.

It was an immature political system, which had worked well only once—when Wilhelm I was emperor and Bismarck his chancellor. Now the Kaiser was Wilhelm II, a fifty-seven-year-old spoiled boy whose arrogance, bombast and dilettante direction of Germany's foreign and military affairs had been responsible as much as anything for the outbreak of the war. Until 1914 Wilhelm II had been perhaps the most powerful monarch in the world. Not only was his power almost absolute, but even his most intimate advisers dared not disagree with him, for he was capable of furious outbursts of temper and could provoke the most humiliating scenes with those who displeased him. But when the war came, the Kaiser's influence began to wane rapidly. Although he bore the title "Supreme War-lord" and prided himself on his military abilities, even he could see that he was incapable of directing the German Army in the field. Because he had never troubled to understand his subjects or to undertake the role which he could have played in coordinating his nation's wartime aims and policies, the Kaiser contented himself with aimless and erratic journeys and inspections. From his military headquarters to his palace in Potsdam, to Homburg for the cure, to Kiel for a look at the fleet and back to Berlin the imperial train traveled endlessly. He was always surrounded by obsequious and devoted courtiers, and his people rarely saw him. Thus the Em-peror's influence had withered and atrophied. There is no evidence that this decline seriously disturbed him. He was not emotionally equipped to withstand severe stress, anyway. His retinue of syco-phants had long since observed that the All Highest hated to hear bad news, so they never told him any. He was now free to indulge himself in the sort of Byzantine existence he liked best—military inspections, tours, wildly optimistic predictions of colossal victories to come, and a few threatening speeches. He took less and less interest in politics; the Reichstag to him was "that monkey house."[27]

As the war entered its third year Germany was a political vacuum. The Kaiser had submerged himself among his entourage, the Reichstag was without any real measure of power, and the Ger-man people were helpless bystanders as the direction of every phase of their lives came to be usurped by what was, in essence, a military dictatorship.

By the summer of 1916 it had become evident to many Germans that their nation was approaching a period of crisis. The Russians had broken the Austrian front in Galicia, and Rumania, with 750,-000 fresh troops, had entered the war against Germany. For all their initial successes, the Central Powers had begun to take on the aspect of defenders of a beleaguered fortress.

The Chief of the German General Staff, Erich von Falkenhayn, seemed incapable of bringing Germany closer to victory. He had planned the February offensive in which the French Army was to be hammered to death on the anvil of Verdun—instead of which both armies had been almost destroyed in a four-month battle. On the Somme, the British were mounting a series of elephantine attacks which were remorselessly breaking into the German trench system. True, more British than Germans were being killed, but not very many more. And the never-ending, day-by-day loss of small fragments of the defensive line was exerting an eroding effect on the German Army's morale. The conviction had grown within influential German circles—the prominent industrialists, the conservative politicians, even some members of the General Staff—that the colorless and unlucky Falkenhayn must go. The Kaiser was gradually converted to this thinking, though reluctantly, for he liked Falkenhayn. On August 28, 1916, Falkenhayn was tactfully informed that the Emperor had decided to seek the military advice of others. As was expected, Falkenhayn instantly submitted his resignation.

There was no question as to who would replace him. The team of Field Marshal Paul von Hindenburg and his chief of staff, General Erich Ludendorff, had a compelling record of victories on the eastern front. They had been sent there in August, 1914, when disaster threatened. Almost at once they had smashed the invading Russian armies at the battles of Tannenberg and the Masurian Lakes. These victories, and those which followed, had flung the Russians back into their own territory and brought an almost god-like fame to the name of Hindenburg.

The Field Marshal was a simple man, really. He was good to his subordinates, devoted to his duty, and gripped by an almost feudal loyalty to his Emperor. Ludendorff was the brains of the team.

On August 29 Hindenburg and Ludendorff were ushered into the imperial presence and the Field Marshal was appointed chief of the General Staff—which, in practice, meant principal strategist and commander in chief of the German Army, since the Kaiser, notwithstanding his title "Supreme Warlord," had become little more than an observer. It was proposed that Ludendorff be given the title "second chief of the General Staff," but he felt that the word "second" was insulting and asked that his abilities be recognized in some more suitable form. In the end he was given the title "first quartermaster general," with Hindenburg's approval and with the specific understanding that he would share equally with the Field Marshal in any decisions affecting the operations of the Army. In this manner a wholly novel situation arose. There were in reality, from August of 1916 on, two chiefs of the General Staff. Although Hindenburg might reap the laurels of popular acclaim, it was

Ludendorff who actually made the plans, wrote the memoranda and directed strategy. It is doubtful that he wanted more.

To his new position Ludendorff brought a personality which was the antithesis of the General Staff tradition of quiet anonymity. He did not even look like the common conception of the German officer. His legs were short and he had a pronounced girth. The top of his head was sparsely covered with a close-cropped fuzz of white hair, he had a double chin, and his mustache was straggly and coarse. In almost every photograph his eyes are veiled by drooping lids and he stares at the camera with an expression that is almost ridiculously truculent. But there was nothing laughable about this Prussian general. Ludendorff was an aggressive, domineering, overbearingly self-confident man who had risen to his present eminence by his tremendous energy, power of concentration and capacity for work. As a military strategist he was undoubtedly first-rate, as an organizer he was virtually without peer.

From his first day at Army Supreme Headquarters (Oberste Heeresleitung) Ludendorff found time to survey all of German life—domestic, political, economic—and to develop plans for its reorganization, while simultaneously directing German military strategy on every front and handling such details as drafting the official military communiqués twice a day. Nothing was safe from him. He bombarded the Imperial Chancellor in Berlin with demands, plans and observations concerning every detail of German life—on raising the birth rate, fighting venereal disease, battling subversives, redistributing population, improving housing, planning postwar rural resettlement. Apparently it meant nothing to Ludendorff—and to Hindenburg, who invariably put his stamp of approval on Ludendorff's ideas—that many of these highhanded plans were well outside the scope of military responsibility. When this was called to his attention, Ludendorff had a quick reply: Germany was engaged in a total war, was she not? And he, Ludendorff, had been given coequal responsibility for the strategic direction of the war, had he not? Then obviously his "responsibilities" extended into every sphere of German life, since everything must be subordinated to the crushing of the enemy and the winning of the war. With this "doctrine of responsibility" the Supreme Command acquired the right to be consulted by the civil government on an ever-increasing number of political decisions. Moreover, Ludendorff made no secret of the fact that in the opinion of the Supreme Command the civilian government, from Chancellor von Bethmann-Hollweg down, was failing to perform its duty with sufficient vigor. Decisions in the fields of domestic politics and foreign affairs ought to be easy enough to make, Ludendorff clearly felt—doubtless because he had no experience in either. He had not the slightest knowledge of diplomacy or of the role of the politician. His impatience overrode everything and everyone. His method was to shout and bang the table. "That Ludendorff is no politician, this we all know," said one of his generals. "He is too impulsive. With him something must always happen at once, whereas a politician must wait and see."[28]

Pose any problem to Ludendorff and one received an immediate answer, set down in meticulous detail and pursued with amazing tenacity. One had only to do exactly what Ludendorff suggested—or demanded—in order to deal with strikers (shoot them), to increase production (put all factories under government control) or to weaken the recalcitrant Independent Social Democrats (brand them as traitors). Regarding the troublesome question of Germany's war aims Ludendorff was even more explicit. He saw no point whatsoever in diplomatic maneuvering. There was only one way to achieve peace: by crushing Germany's enemies militarily. And there was only one peace worth having: the "Hindenburg Peace," as the General Staff named it—the imposition of treaties, Napoleonic in their grandeur, whereby Germany would annex broad belts of Russian and French territory and would incorporate Belgium into the German Empire. Germany would then be ready for the next war. It was all so simple; it needed only firm, disciplined direction from the top. And Ludendorff despaired of getting this. The more he saw of civilians and politicians, the more worthless he thought them. He found it "quite striking to see how the officer class, the members of which were always thought to be the most narrow-minded, had produced men of decision, while the civil official class, on the contrary, had, unfortunately, so conspicuously failed in this respect."[29] The spectacle of Imperial Chancellor von Bethmann-Hollweg scurrying about consulting various political leaders struck Ludendorff and Hindenburg as grotesque, inefficient and unnecessary. They could only view the Reichstag members and the leaders of the political parties as a group of subordinates to whom the Chancellor, their superior officer, must give explicit orders, which should then be instantly obeyed.

This being their outlook, it was only a matter of months before the new Supreme Commanders arrived at the conclusion that Chancellor von Bethmann-Hollweg was totally unfit for his post. They had been unfavorably impressed with his "slowness" in compelling the Reichstag to pass the universal-war-service bill demanded by them, under which every German male between seventeen and sixty not already in uniform was drafted into "auxiliary service" under the direction of the Ministry of War. They had been distressed by the reluctance of the Foreign Office ("the *Idiotenhaus*," they called it)[30] to reinstitute unrestricted submarine warfare, a policy which, it said, would surely drag the United States into the war. In fact, Bethmann-Hollweg had proved so unwilling to embark on this adventure that Hindenburg and Ludendorff had bypassed him and gone directly to the Kaiser (whom normally they scarcely troubled to consult) with the veiled threat that if unrestricted warfare was not begun before February 1, 1917, they could no longer be responsible for the outcome of the war. With the Kaiser thoroughly intimidated, the two generals summoned Bethmann-Hollweg and demanded that the U boats be released, no matter what the consequences regarding the United States. They brushed aside his arguments that there were not and never would be enough U boats to sink the British merchant navy, and that the inevitable entry of the United States into the war would be cataclysmic to Germany. The generals had other information. The British *would* be starved out, and a United States army would never reach France—and even if one did, the Supreme Command would accept the responsibility for dealing with it. Under pressure from both the Kaiser and the generals, Bethmann-Hollweg accepted their decision.

But the generals were not willing much longer to put up with Bethmann-Hollweg and his tiresome forebodings about the consequences of their actions. In July of 1917 a crisis in the civil government gave them the opportunity they had been waiting for. By then the effect of the Allied blockade was reaching its height and all Germany was suffering acutely. There had been no great German victories for six months or more; the submarine campaign was proving a disappointment; the United States had entered the war. Meanwhile in Russia the Czar had been overthrown—an event which gave the German socialist parties new encouragement; in particular, the following of the Independent Socialists and the Spartakusbund was growing. This combination of events served to convince the Reichstag deputies that their influence must be brought to bear on German wartime policy. Almost spontaneously they determined to demand a real role in the German political system.

Their demands took different forms, depending upon the parties involved. Both of the Socialist parties called upon the Imperial Chancellor to adopt the peace formula of the International Socialist Committee, which called for "peace without annexations or indemnities." On this broad basis, they proposed, a negotiated peace could be arranged with Germany's enemies. The parties of the center, led by Matthias Erzberger of the Catholic Center Party, put more stress on parliamentary liberalization; most importantly, they demanded that the appointment of the Imperial Chancellor and the secretaries of state be subject to the Reichstag's approval. As for the Conservatives, they went along reluctantly with demands for certain political reforms—even they conceded, for example, that reform of the Prussian electoral system was long overdue—but they opposed the Socialist peace formula and demanded that Chancellor von Bethmann-Hollweg make a flat declaration against it.

Against these conflicting demands, all of which reflected a general want of confidence in the government and a growing fear that the war was being lost, Bethmann-Hollweg could do little. The uncomfortable situation in which the Imperial Chancellor found himself did not particularly displease Hindenburg and Ludendorff. For some months they had been quietly laying the groundwork for the dismissal of Bethmann-Hollweg and the appointment of a more tractable Chancellor. Officers of the Supreme Command staff had been dispatched to inform the Crown Prince, the influential industrialists and even certain members of the Reichstag that Hindenburg and Ludendorff were opposed to the prolongation of the Bethmann-Hollweg chancellorship. The approval of the Crown Prince—a personality whose arrogance was fully equal to Ludendorff's—was quickly obtained. ("Throw him out, then," was his comment.[31]) But the Kaiser himself proved unexpectedly obstinate, and he was the only person who could dismiss the Chancellor. He rather liked Bethmann-Hollweg; moreover, he had come vaguely to realize the tremendous inroads which Ludendorff had already made into the constitutional government of imperial Germany. He went so far as to refuse to discuss this political question with Hindenburg and Ludendorff. But the Kaiser was not allowed to indulge his own opinions in this matter. On July 12 he received a telephone call from the Supreme Command. Unless Bethmann-Hollweg was dismissed, Hindenburg and Ludendorff announced, they would resign; they

could no longer collaborate with the Chancellor. With this ultimatum, the Kaiser was forced to choose between his generals and his
Chancellor.

Had Wilhelm II been a stronger and more perceptive man, like
his grandfather, he could have solved the dilemma by summoning
Hindenburg and Ludendorff to Potsdam and bluntly informing
them that it was their duty to serve in the posts to which he had
assigned them. But the Kaiser vacillated, unable or unwilling to
confront the generals and demand obedience. The future consequences of military domination over every phase of German life
eluded him, and Wilhelm could think only of the impossibility of
explaining to the nation the resignation of the deified Hindenburg
and the brilliant Ludendorff. As the Kaiser agonized, Bethmann-
Hollweg, who did not wish to see his Emperor in this dilemma any
longer, resigned.

There now came about a situation which was not without over-
tones of grotesque humor. Because Wilhelm's capitulation to the
generals' threat was so complete that it amounted to a virtual
abdication, it was obvious that Hindenburg and Ludendorff must be
consulted about the naming of a new Chancellor. Accordingly, von
Valentini, the chief of the Kaiser's civil secretariat, was dispatched
to Hindenburg and Ludendorff to find out who it was that they had
in mind. It is a testimony to the generals' political incapacity that
the thought of a successor to the man they had overthrown had
never occurred to them. Finally Valentini asked if the generals
would be agreeable to the appointment of a man he knew, a certain
Dr. Georg Michaelis, a totally obscure bureaucrat who was in
charge of food distribution in Prussia. At first no one could recollect
having met or even heard of the man. But then it was recalled that
Michaelis had visited Supreme Headquarters some months before,
and those few officers who could remember him seemed to feel that
he had made a favorable—or, at any rate, not an unfavorable—impression. Hindenburg allowed that Michaelis was undoubtedly "a
decent, God-fearing man"[32]—apparently the most that could be
found to say about this insignificant official.

The approval of the Supreme Command having been solicited
and obtained, the Kaiser proceeded to summon into his presence and
to appoint as his Imperial Chancellor a man he had never even met
before! With this the victory of Ludendorff and the corresponding
capitulation of the Emperor were complete. The Kaiser was now a
crowned cipher over whom Hindenburg and Ludendorff held the

tested whip of threatened resignation. The Chancellor was Ludendorff's fig leaf, and he knew well to whom he owed his dazzling and abrupt elevation.

The Reichstag, never a real power, became still weaker under the military's domination. Its last attempt to gain some measure of power was the famous Reichstag Peace Resolution, which was passed by a coalition of Socialists and center parties shortly after Michaelis was appointed chancellor. In it they attempted to restate the war aims which had been professed in August, 1914. "The object of the Reichstag," the resolution declared, "is to obtain a peace of understanding and lasting reconciliation between nations. With such a peace forced concessions of territory and political, economic and financial oppression are incompatible."[33] It was a sincere statement, and by issuing it the deputies sought to force Michaelis and the Supreme Command to seek a negotiated peace. But the resolution failed in its purpose. To Hindenburg and Ludendorff such a declaration amounted to treason. Their Chancellor, Michaelis, could not prevent its being passed in the Reichstag, but he could and did strip it of all meaning by stating that he would be guided by the resolution only as he interpreted it. In a letter to the Crown Prince he wrote: "The hateful resolution has been passed by 212 votes to 126. . . . I have deprived it of its greatest danger by my interpretation. One can, in fact, make any peace one likes and still be in accord with the resolution."[34]

The Supreme Command could now operate in almost perfect freedom. General Staff officers supervised the press, forbade public meetings at their whim, ordered preventive arrests, fixed the wages of Germany's workers and set the prices of foodstuffs. The Supreme Command completely dominated foreign policy—which was nothing new. Ludendorff had earlier engineered the fall of Foreign Secretary Gottlieb von Jagow, who, he said, was "an intelligent man, but not one who can bang his fist on the table."[35] And later when Richard von Kuhlmann, a successor in the post, made a speech before the Reichstag which the generals disliked, the Supreme Commanders summoned the Chancellor to their headquarters to make an explanation—like "a teacher excusing a pupil's bad essay to a school inspector."[36] It did not save Kuhlmann. The Supreme Commanders declared that they could not work with him, and out he went.

The Kaiser now found that he was not even to be allowed the freedom of taking his own counsel. Once when Wilhelm spoke to

General Max Hoffmann, an expert on Poland, he was promptly
rebuked by Ludendorff, who wrote to him that this situation was
intolerable, "for General Hoffmann is my subordinate and bears no
responsibility in the Polish Question."[37] Firmly in the grip of a full-
blown megalomania, Ludendorff so far forgot himself as to whisper
to Hindenburg while the Kaiser was speaking to them and then
slammed the door in disgust as they took their leave of the imperial
presence. Ludendorff even demanded that the Kaiser dismiss certain
members of his immediate entourage, who were promptly replaced
by his own nominees. A German Foreign Office official in Geneva
described the Kaiser as "having practically ceased to exist. He is not
even formally consulted in Berlin . . . he is treated as an annoying
child who gets under foot or in the way. The only function he has
left is that of making his speech about Germany and God, which the
Germans themselves have come to regard as the harmless absurdi-
ties of a religious maniac."[38]

War is the supreme test of any political system. This test had
been applied to imperial Germany, and the system had broken. The
German nation had become a *de facto* military dictatorship. At its
head was Ludendorff, a man who was probably paranoid and certainly beyond reasoning with others. Hindenburg had neither the
desire nor the ability to control his nominal subordinate. The First
Quartermaster General was free to demand instant obedience from
everyone. He would tolerate no interference. His supremacy must
always be unquestioned.

At first he was able to produce successes. Ludendorff transported
Lenin from Switzerland to Russia, thus injecting Bolshevism into
the veins of the weakened enemy. The result was all that could be
hoped for. Bolshevik Russia sued for peace, and the rapacious
Treaty of Brest-Litovsk was imposed on her. With a skillful hand
the Supreme Command extracted from the territories held by German arms enough foodstuffs and livestock to feed Germany for yet
another winter of war. The entire economy of the German nation
was placed under the control of a set of military officers, coordinated and directed by a brilliant General Staff officer, General
Wilhelm Groener, whose efficiency and common sense were of such
high order that he even won the respect and willing cooperation of
the Majority Socialist leaders. On the western front Ludendorff kept
the German armies on the defensive during the winter of 1916–17
and the following spring. It proved to be a profitable strategy: the

French and the British mounted huge offensives, and their losses were enormous against the skillful German defense. As always, no detail of organization was too small for Ludendorff to concern himself with. Skillful memoranda poured out from Supreme Headquarters at Kreuznach, bearing the most explicit orders, instructions and tactical advice. It was all very sound; the German "elastic" defense, the skillful strategic withdrawals, the employment of machine guns and the direction of artillery were all vastly successful.

But inevitably there came a day of reckoning. The victories had been won, but they had been paid for by bills drawn on the future. In 1918 these bills were coming due. The political maneuvers of the Supreme Command were gradually revealed to be a series of short-term improvisations. Lenin had done all that had been hoped of him: Russia had abandoned the war—but at the price of the establishment of an internationalist revolutionary regime, with a Soviet ambassador in Berlin. Nor had the ruthless submarine campaign produced the results which Ludendorff had predicted. The Supreme Command had calculated that it would take only six months of unrestricted torpedoings to bring England to the point of collapse, but six months passed, then another six months, and still the British gave no sign of being starved out of the war. Now the submarine offensive had brought the United States into the war, and, contrary to the German Navy's optimistic promises, the U boats were unable to prevent American troops from arriving in Europe in ever-increasing numbers. The Fourteen Points proposed by the American President as a basis for peace had aroused great interest both within Germany and among her allies. If peace could be obtained on this basis, the common people of the Central Powers could see no reason for continuing the war. In Germany Wilson's name was rapidly becoming a symbol for honesty, moderation and, above all, peace.

The suffering which the German people had already undergone was enormous. The Allied blockade had nearly succeeded in starving Germany out of the war. The nation had barely gotten through the winter of 1916–17, known as the "Kohlrübenwinter" (Turnip Winter), when for weeks at a time there were no potatoes available and the turnips normally used for cattle fodder were substituted. By the following winter the German population would have been glad to have even the turnips; the weekly bread ration was only seventy ounces per person, fats were rationed at the weekly rate of two ounces per person, and even this was not always available. The mortality rate among German children had increased by fifty per cent over 1913. In early 1918 the average adult ration was reduced to one thousand calories a day.

The result was a sudden strike and food riot at the end of January, 1918, by 400,000 of Berlin's munitions workers, who demanded not only food but also "the speedy bringing about of peace without annexations and indemnities in accordance with the principles formulated by the Russian People's Commissioners in Brest-Litovsk."[39] The strike came as a tremendous surprise, even to the Majority Socialist leaders, some of whom were asked to serve on the strike committee after the strike had started, and could hardly refuse. It ended after a few days, but not before the Berlin garrison had been called out, the state of siege had been made even more repressive than before, and the workers had been threatened with mobilization and service in the trenches.

It was at this point that Ludendorff came to the conclusion that he must go over to the offensive in France before so many Americans arrived that the German Army would be overwhelmed. In the spring of 1918 the "Ludendorff Offensive," Germany's last great attack, was launched. Beginning in March, the Army, reinforced by hundreds of thousands of troops released from the east by the Russian peace, blasted through the Allied front to a point on the Marne River only fifty-six miles from Paris and came close to cutting the Allied armies apart and driving the British up against the Channel ports.

By early June, however, the Ludendorff attacks had ground to a halt. The Germans could bombard Paris with long-range guns, but they could advance no farther. Then, in July, Foch began his counteroffensive. Gradually, irresistibly, inevitably, the Allies, now superior in both manpower and equipment, beat back the German front. By August 8 the Australian Army Corps succeeded in breaking a wide gap through the German lines, a gap which was patched up only at the last moment. Suddenly even Ludendorff was struck with a chill of horror. Another gap in the lines might bring instant disaster. The Allies had tanks, the Germans had none. And American troops were pouring into France. In March there had been only 300,000 of them; in July there were 1,200,000; by November there would be two million.

Under the overwhelming Allied attack the morale of the German soldiers began to drop abruptly. The troops brought back from

Russia had turned out to be almost a liability. Too many of them had been exposed to Bolshevist propaganda, and subtly, imperceptibly, they had been warped by it. Nor was the western-front army the same staunch, unquestioningly obedient force it had been only a few months before. The compliant young soldiers of conservative peasant stock and the prewar noncommissioned officers were in the minority now. Their places had been taken by older men from the big cities, where the socialists of every complexion were powerful. This problem had been made more acute by the decision to mobilize and send to the front a number of the workers who had taken part in the January strikes. And now the Spartacus Letters were entering the trenches. Some of them reached the soldiers by mail; Liebknecht's followers in the post offices had compiled mailing lists by copying the names and addresses of thousands of fighting men from mail that had been posted in the working-class districts of big cities. Other Spartacus Letters were hidden in loads of empty sandbags sent to the front. This propaganda had a slow but cumulative effect. Most of the German divisions would still fight stubbornly, but their tenacity was not what it had once been and the rear areas were beginning to fill up with deserters and malingerers. Starvation was becoming a problem even at the front; the soldiers were so hungry that they were stealing the barley issued for horse fodder, grinding it up in their coffee mills and baking crude pancakes from it. As reserve divisions marched forward to the front they could hear shouts of "You are prolonging the war!" or "Strikebreakers!" from the demoralized troops being replaced.

The Ludendorff dictatorship could have survived all these stresses in only one way: through an overwhelming military victory that would compel the Allies to seek peace. Nothing less. After the failed offensive of March and April, 1918, there was, of course, no further hope of this, but Ludendorff and Hindenburg were as yet unprepared to admit it. In July the Secretary of State for Foreign Affairs, Paul von Hintze, asked Ludendorff bluntly whether he was "certain of finally and decisively beating the enemy." "I can reply to that with a decided yes," was Ludendorff's answer. It must be emphasized that this was not a statement made for the public, but a private conversation on the basis of which Hintze was expected to develop German foreign policy. A month later the furthest that Ludendorff would go was to admit that the German Army was no longer capable of a "great offensive," although he claimed that by a skillful defensive policy he could break the Allies' morale so that they would sue for peace. All that Ludendorff demanded was that the home front be subjected to "more severe internal dicipline."[40]

But the time came, only a few weeks later, when this reassuring charade could no longer be maintained. Suddenly it was necessary to face the fact that the mounting Allied pressure could not be withstood much longer. Ludendorff's personal equilibrium deteriorated remarkably. His ability to deal with crises left him, and he became almost hysterically concerned with details.

On September 26 the French launched a massive attack west of the Argonne. A major American attack was already in progress between the Argonne and the Meuse. On the next day the British Army began an offensive, and the day following that the Belgian Army attacked. This series of crises was more than Ludendorff could stand. On the afternoon of September 28 his self-control snapped and he went raging around his office cursing the Kaiser, the Reichstag, the home front and the politicians. His aides were appalled at the scene. All they could do was shut the door to his office and wait for the fit to pass.

By evening he had brought himself under control. But there was no respite. The next day, September 29, Germany's ally Bulgaria sued for peace, leaving a wide gap in Germany's southern flank. The army on the western front was tottering under an Allied onslaught of unprecedented violence. Hindenburg and Ludendorff summoned the aged current Chancellor, Count Georg von Hertling (the woefully inept Michaelis had been jettisoned after a few months), Foreign Secretary von Hintze and the Kaiser himself to Supreme Headquarters at Spa in Belgium. To this audience Ludendorff revealed that the war was lost. The situation was desperate. An armistice must be negotiated immediately. Moreover, it was the suggestion of the generals that the Emperor take immediate steps to liberalize the German government and bring into it influential members of the Reichstag. Then, almost as a casual afterthought, Hindenburg instructed Hintze that he must take care that in the final peace settlement Germany would be awarded the rich French mining districts of Longwy and Briey!

Their audience was aghast. Apparently no one had the courage to ask how it was that they had not been informed earlier of this desperate state of affairs. They had not dreamed that things had gone this far so suddenly. In fact, they could not quite believe it now. "I get the impression that they have all lost their nerve here," a

Foreign Office official wired Berlin from Spa.[41] Only a few weeks before, the generals had demanded the ouster of a secretary of state for discussing the possibility of a negotiated peace. And now they were announcing that the war was already lost.

The next night, in Berlin, the leaders of Germany's political parties were informed of the Supreme Command's wishes. The politicians were even more astounded than the government had been. Ebert, the leader of the Majority Socialists, "went white as death and could not utter a word." Only one man, the Independent Socialist Hugo Haase, could find words. He appeared overjoyed at the development. "Now we have got them!" he exclaimed to a colleague.[42]

The German government found itself in a terrible dilemma. The Supreme Command, having demanded an armistice, abruptly washed its hands of all further responsibility. Ludendorff chose to represent himself as little more than a simple soldier. "The Supreme Command does not regard itself as being a power in politics," he wrote the government; "is therefore without political responsibility."[43] The Supreme Command announced itself willing to make certain sacrifices in the west. It would release Belgium (as if the Allies would conceivably have allowed Germany to keep it), and it was prepared to give up certain sections of Alsace-Lorraine (as if France would have settled for this). Such was the generals' ignorance that they believed the Allies could be persuaded to compensate Germany for these "concessions" with Polish territory and two of France's richest industrial districts.

With an open hand the once tight-fisted Ludendorff distributed the responsibility for disaster upon the civilians. He professed to be astonished at the profoundly demoralizing effect his demands had on his hearers, and he criticized the Chancellor for having failed to warn the Reichstag that the Army was in desperate straits. The Majority Socialist leaders of the Reichstag, formerly regarded by him as little better than traitors, were brought into conference and asked what *they* intended to do about the collapse. Ludendorff indignantly reproached them for failing to lift German morale. "Capture the imagination of the people! Cannot Herr Ebert do that?" he complained.[44]

And now the government which had been lied to, intimidated, threatened and scorned was suddenly bombarded with demands to speed up negotiations. From the Supreme Command at Spa there came a deluge of telephone calls, telegrams and emissaries. Every

day during the first week in October another officer was sent to
inform the government that all was lost, an armistice must be concluded immediately. Nobody could quite believe it—especially the
Conservatives, whose leader, Ernst von Heydebrand, lost all control
and screamed, "We have been deceived and cheated!"[45] On October 3 there was a note from Hindenburg himself: "The Supreme
Command adheres to its demand made on Sunday, 29 September,
for the immediate dispatch of the peace offer to our enemies."[46]
The generals had made an astonishing discovery: "Every day lost
costs thousands of brave soldiers' lives."

During the days which followed, Ludendorff recovered his courage somewhat. When confronted by a civilian government which
demanded to know precisely what the situation was, he managed to
confuse the issue. He now complained of the burden of the tremendous responsibility which lay on him, "where it has rested for
four long and difficult years."[47] From day to day he was unclear as
to whether Germany was defeated or not. He demanded more reinforcements for the Army, and the government promised to scrape
them up even if this cut drastically into the faltering German industrial and agricultural production. But, Ludendorff was asked, what
did all this signify? If the war was totally lost, why continue rein-
forcing the Army? What was the Supreme Commanders' real objective? Did they hope that an armistice would constitute a breathing
space during which the German Army and its equipment could
retire to defend the Rhine? To all this Ludendorff replied, "Every
exertion of our strength that is made at the present moment will
improve our situation,"[48] and then he went on to claim that enemy
morale was weak. The Secretary of State for Foreign Affairs complained that this was not very helpful. Ludendorff had demanded
an armistice, and now he seemed to be saying that an armistice was
not necessary. At this Ludendorff flared up. It was all the civilians'
fault. He had only asked the government for more men. "Why I was
unable to get them earlier I will not discuss,"[49] he said, conveniently forgetting that for nearly two years *he* had been the government.

But now there was a significant alteration in Ludendorff's position vis-à-vis the German government. His demands, requests and
entreaties were addressed to a Chancellor and a Cabinet far different from the browbeaten nonentities with whom the Supreme Command had dealt in the past.

* * *

On October 3 a new personality had entered upon the scene.

The equilibrium of the aged incumbent Imperial Chancellor, Count von Hertling, had been derailed by Ludendorff's dumbfounding espousal of governmental liberalization. Hertling had faithfully done the bidding of the Supreme Command, and in so doing had won the enmity of the Reichstag. Now, with the Kaiser (still in the trance of the Ludendorff dictatorship) suddenly announcing that "men enjoying the confidence of the people would partake to a greater extent in the rights and duties of government,"[50] Hertling had no choice but to resign.

The choice of his successor was a perfect example of a brilliant decision made too late. Prince Max of Baden, fifty-one years old, was a highly intelligent, extremely able, intensely patriotic man who had won a deserved reputation as the liberal heir to the throne of the grand duchy of Baden.° It was widely known that he had long favored the conclusion of an honorable peace and had consistently opposed the strident annexationism of the Supreme Command. For at least a year, Max had been discussed as a possible chancellor in the event that the Supreme Command would permit a negotiated peace. A little slogan about him, "Max equals Pax," had even sprung up. It was noted that the Prince spoke perfect English and was the son-in-law of the English Duke of Cumberland. He had been an Army officer during the first part of the war, but his health had failed and he had retired to devote the remainder of the war to working with the Red Cross. In this capacity he had done a great deal to improve the lot of foreign soldiers in German prison camps. It was widely assumed that all this would serve to make him acceptable to the Allies despite the fact that Max was also the Kaiser's first cousin. Moreover his reputation as an advocate of German constitutional reform was such that he had even won the respect of the Social Democrats.

Summoned to Berlin, Prince Max arrived on the afternoon of October 1, to be met by a General Staff officer who disclosed to him Ludendorff's demand for an immediate armistice. Max was

---

° Baden itself was a traditionally liberal state. Its rulers had freed their peasantry before any other German state. Politically it was a stronghold of the Social Democrats and the moderate center parties.

astounded. He had come to Berlin with no illusions about the war—
he knew it was lost—but he had enough common sense and diplomatic experience to realize that to appoint a new chancellor who
must immediately ask the Allies for an armistice was equivalent to
surrendering. Max wanted time, a breathing space in which to
establish his government and announce certain reforms, before
opening negotiations with the Allies. In the past he had never believed that things were as good as Ludendorff had said they were;
now he did not think the German Army's situation was as desperate
as Ludendorff claimed it was. He pleaded with the Supreme Command for "ten, eight or even four days before I have to appeal to the
enemy."[51] In response the Kaiser snapped, "The Supreme Command requests it, and you have not been brought here to make
difficulties for the Supreme Command."[52]

The Prince realized, as the generals should have, that the German
Army would not continue to fight and die for long once its government had appealed for an armistice. Moreover, he had actually read
Wilson's Fourteen Points (it is questionable whether Ludendorff
had ever done so), and he sensed that the Points were not matters to
be negotiated but demands which would have to be accepted in
their entirety. It was apparent to him that Wilson, as the world's
foremost spokesman for peace, was the Allied leader to whom he
must appeal for an armistice. The Fourteen Points had greatly
impressed Max. He regarded Wilson as one of the truly great men in
the history of the world, and he was eager for the opportunity to
restructure Germany along the democratic lines of which Wilson
was the prophet. But, at the same time, the Prince suspected that
the Supreme Command might not permit him to deal with Wilson in
good faith. He believed that the generals were thinking of an armistice along the lines of those concluded during the Napoleonic Wars,
when a defeated nation sued for a truce and then went away to
recover, make new alliances, recruit fresh armies and resume the
war in the spring.

Prince Max's first impulse was to refuse the chancellorship. Hindenburg himself then rushed to Berlin to entreat him to accept—
and told him that the Supreme Command had already taken it upon
itself to inform Germany's allies that she was requesting armistice
terms. Max instantly realized that the secret was out—too many
people knew. Neither he nor any other Imperial Chancellor was
going to be permitted a breathing space before appealing for an

armistice. Nevertheless, he felt it his duty to accept the chancellorship.

Thus, doubtless dreading the weeks to come, Max of Baden became Germany's trustee in bankruptcy and dispatched the first German note to Wilson. At the same time, he was shrewd enough to demand and get a written statement from Hindenburg to the effect that the war was lost, that there was "no further chance of forcing a peace on the enemy,"[53] and flatly demanding an immediate armistice.

Max proceeded to form a government to conduct negotiations leading to the "honest peace" he hoped to get. It was the first truly parliamentary and democratic German government. The various secretaries of state who made up the new Cabinet were the leaders of the four largest political parties—Grober, Trimborn and Erzberger from the Catholic Center Party, Hausmann from the Progressives, Friedberg from the National Liberals, and Bauer and Scheidemann from the Majority Socialists. There was no representation from the once dominant right wing.

The Majority Socialists had entered this government after considerable soul-searching. Again, as with their other compromises with Socialist theory, they found themselves forced to ignore their own beliefs. Now they were lending themselves to what seemed like a last-minute attempt to save the monarchy, by joining in a government headed by a royal prince. Moreover, there were a number of solid and strictly practical arguments against entering the government at this point. One was the suspicion that the presence of the Socialists in the government was tolerated only in order to tar them with the odium of general defeat. Another was the fact that in the weeks preceding Max's appointment the influence of the Independent Socialists and the Spartacists had increased perceptibly. They were issuing continual doctrinaire appeals demanding the complete and immediate realization of traditional Socialist aims; by comparison, the Majority Socialists appeared decidedly bourgeois. Against these arguments was the fact, as Majority Socialist chairman Friedrich Ebert pointed out, that they had the higher duty of saving Germany from general ruin. Overriding all arguments to the contrary, a Majority Socialist caucus determined to support the government. Scheidemann and Bauer entered the Cabinet, explaining to their restive followers that only by taking an active part in the government could they have an authoritative influence on the peace negotiations as well as on constitutional reform.

The Independent Socialists were not asked to join the government, nor would they have agreed to. They saw with perfect clarity
that the German Empire was on the edge of collapse, a prospect
that did not dismay them. As the Empire foundered, the German
Revolution would inevitably take place. All they had to do was
stand aside and wait.

At five-fifteen on the afternoon of October 5, in a Reichstag
chamber so crowded that there was only standing room, Prince Max
announced the aims of his new government. With considerable difficulty it had been agreed that there would be no debate following
the Chancellor's speech. Of necessity a certain amount had to be left
unsaid in order to conceal from the Allies the desperation of Germany's position. Prince Max announced that from now on the
Chancellor would serve only with the approval of the Reichstag—
not, as heretofore, at the pleasure of the Emperor. He promised that
the eternally rankling question of Prussian electoral reform would
be dealt with speedily. To a volley of cheers from the left he announced that the dominance of the Army over German life, secured
by its control of the mechanism of the state of siege, would be
relaxed. Finally, he officially informed the Reichstag of his note to
Wilson designed to secure for the German people "a speedy and
honorable peace of justice and reconciliation."[54]

The speech generally satisfied the Reichstag, particularly the
announcement that Prince Max had made his armistice appeal to
Woodrow Wilson, whom the Reichstag deputies, like most Germans, did not regard as an enemy. The proscription against debate
prevented embarrassing attacks from both the sullen Conservatives
and the Independent Socialists on the far left—although at the end
of Max's speech the Independents had shouted, "Amnesty!," which
everyone knew was a demand for the release of Karl Liebknecht,
Rosa Luxemburg and all the others imprisoned for pacifism under
the Ludendorff regime.

If the Reichstag was generally satisfied, the German people were
less so. As Max had foreseen, the mere request for armistice discussions was sufficient to bring about the swift collapse of the German
economy. In Berlin banks had begun to fail. People were selling war-
savings certificates on the streets for whatever they would bring.
The food ration, already at starvation level, was reduced still further, and influenza had found many victims; in one day, October 18,
there were seventeen hundred influenza deaths in Berlin alone. The
Majority Socialist Philipp Scheidemann told the Cabinet that it was

hopeless to attempt to shore up civilian morale. "It is a question of potatoes, We no longer have any meat. . . . [The] misery is so great that it is like asking a complete riddle when one asks oneself, What does North Berlin live on and how does East Berlin exist?"[55]

Against this background there now began an exchange of notes between the German government and the President of the United States, who sought to make the Germans accept each and every one of the Fourteen Points, as well as the amplifying statements which Wilson had made subsequently. As Max had predicted, Wilson had no intention of allowing Germany a breathing space or of permitting the Fourteen Points to be made items subject to negotiation. He would tolerate no ambiguities, evasions or half-promises from the German government. Every German statement was examined for the faintest evidence of Prussian duplicity. Max himself was highly suspect to the Allies. Everything about him seemed almost too good. They were more than half convinced that he was nothing more than a dummy for the monarchists or the soldiers who had trundled him out onto the stage at a convenient time. Meanwhile, the Allied armies mercilessly assaulted the exhausted Germans. And with every exchange of notes the German bargaining position eroded still further—in particular on October 16, with the receipt in Berlin of Wilson's note calling to the Germans' attention his statement of July 4, 1918, in which he had sworn the United States to "the destruction of every arbitrary power anywhere" that could "separately, secretly and of its own single choice disturb the peace of the world," and had added, "The power which has hitherto controlled the German Nation is of the sort here described."[56] This reference, wordy and obscure, was not clear to Prince Max and his Cabinet. The implication was that Wilson was demanding nothing less than the abdication of the Kaiser and the dismissal of Ludendorff as his price for granting an armistice. The note surprised and angered Max by its harshness. Quite naturally it infuriated the Kaiser. "Read it!" Wilhelm II shouted to an aide. "It aims directly at the overthrow of my house, at the complete overthrow of monarchy!"[57]

Prince Max now found himself in a perplexing situation. He was prepared to do almost anything to liberalize the German government; indeed, he felt that he had proved that Germany was now a parliamentary democracy. It was, after all, Max himself who had proposed the constitutional changes which were now nearly ready to become law. But it was too much to ask him to dismiss his cousin the Kaiser and abolish the monarchy. He temporized, considered resigning, and even thought of breaking off negotiations with Wilson altogether. Max summoned Ludendorff to a conference in Berlin to study this last possibility. A number of questions were put to the General, but they could all be reduced to one: Was there any possibility that the German Army could hold the front long enough to improve Germany's bargaining position? The First Quartermaster General's replies were evasive; there was no sign of his previous panic. Ludendorff was flatly opposed to the acceptance of Wilson's terms, or any others which did away with the monarchial system or with Germany's power to resume fighting after the period of the armistice. The General seemed to be telling the government that there was quite a good possibility that the Army could hang on. At this the civilians could not resist pointing out acidly that the impasse in which Germany now found herself was essentially the result of Ludendorff's frantic demands of only a few weeks before.

The conference left Max far from reassured. He had no confidence in Ludendorff, whom he personally disliked and distrusted. Max agreed with the Majority Socialist Philipp Scheidemann, who observed, "Better a terrible end than terror without end."[58] The Prince Chancellor feared that the Supreme Command had now decided to fight to the last German rather than admit to final defeat. He recalled an ominous statement that Ludendorff had made to him months before, when Max had asked what would happen if the German front were broken. "Then Germany will just have to suffer annihilation," had been Ludendorff's chilling reply.[59]

With all this in mind, Max and his Cabinet decided to continue negotiations. They tried to explain in their notes to Wilson the many changes which had taken place in Germany in the past few weeks. To buttress this argument, Max convened the Reichstag on October 22 and announced a series of new constitutional amendments. Henceforth members of the Reichstag could serve in Cabinet posts without losing their Reichstag seats.* Another constitutional amendment gave to the Reichstag the sole power to declare war or make peace. The officers of the Army would now be appointed by a minister of war responsible to the Reichstag, instead of by the Kaiser alone. Finally, as a concession to the Independent Socialists, he announced that a widespread amnesty would be given to prisoners convicted for wartime strikes, pacifism or street demon-

---

* Although not too specific on this point, Article 9 of the German Constitution of 1871 had been interpreted as prohibiting a member of the Reichstag from serving as one of the secretaries of state.

strations. Immediately after Max's announcement a debate took place, and Hugo Haase, leader of the Independent Socialists, got up to sneer at the amendments. "All around us republics are being set up" he said. "Crowns are rolling about the floor. . . . And shall Germany alone, surrounded by Republics, still keep a crowned head, or, rather, a whole lot of heads all wearing their little crowns and coronets?"[60]

Wilson too found Max's constitutional reforms unimpressive. The American government retained its suspicions of this new German democracy. In his note of October 23 Wilson made clear his refusal to discuss an armistice if the United States and the Allies "must deal with the military masters and monarchial autocrats of Germany." Max was unable to decide how far he must go to satisfy Wilson. Obviously the President was not content with what had been done so far. Would he insist on the abolishment of the monarchy, or would he be satisfied with the dismissal of Ludendorff? What did he want? It seemed to Max that Wilson was demanding far more than his Fourteen Points, and he began to feel personally betrayed.

The blunt tone of Wilson's note had excited the Supreme Command, the Conservatives and the Pan-Germans, who were now demanding that the government cease negotiations and continue the war. Ludendorff and Hindenburg obviously had not dreamed of the consequences of their earlier demands. They were astonished at the sweeping character of Wilson's terms, and it had suddenly become clear to them that the Allies had no intention of granting an armistice which would permit Germany to resume the war at a later date. The price for an armistice was going to be the demobilization of the German Army and handing over of the German fleet. As Wilson had warned in one of his notes, the Allies intended to insure themselves of absolute superiority over Germany for as long as the armistice lasted. Militarily the armistice would amount to a German surrender. The generals suddenly began to reassert their old political claims. They announced that it was their right to review and amend the notes which were being sent to Wilson. Hindenburg wrote to Max that the Army's morale was shattered by the failure of the Imperial Chancellor to give the troops the "conviction that it is necessary to fight." Bitterly the old Field Marshal reproached Max for his "failure to rise to the height of this holy task."[61]

On the same day, October 24, an officer of the Supreme Command drafted a proclamation to the Army which was signed by Ludendorff for dispatch under Hindenburg's name. The proclama-

tion warned that the Allies were demanding an unconditional surrender which was "unacceptable to us soldiers" and was thus a
"challenge to continue our resistance with all our strength."[62] This
proclamation was, of course, a direct defiance of the German government's authority. After it had been reread even Ludendorff
decided that it went too far, and he issued orders that it was not to
be released to the troops. As an alternative he and Hindenburg left
Supreme Headquarters for Berlin (against Prince Max's orders) to
inform the Kaiser in person that Germany must continue the war.

The Army's proclamation, however, quickly became common
knowledge. A draft had been telegraphed to the headquarters of the
German Army in the east, where a soldier telegraphist who was an
Independent Socialist copied it down. Instantly appreciating its
significance, he redispatched the draft proclamation to the Independent Socialists' headquarters in Berlin. Within hours an Independent deputy read it out to the Reichstag, where the proclamation's insubordinate statements created a sensation.

In a fury, Prince Max telephoned Supreme Headquarters and
learned that Hindenburg and Ludendorff had defied his orders and
entrained for Berlin. Swearing that "this insubordinate journey
could only end in General Ludendorff's dismissal,"[63] Max fired off
to the Kaiser the ultimatum that the Emperor must make a choice
between the First Quartermaster General and the Imperial Chancellor. He hoped that Hindenburg could be persuaded to stay on for
his value as a figurehead, but even a threat of resignation from
Hindenburg must not be allowed to stand in the way of Ludendorff's dismissal—which would, of course, have the supplementary
value of making a favorable impression upon Woodrow Wilson.

This was the situation when Ludendorff and Hindenburg appeared before Wilhelm on October 25 in the Schloss Bellevue to
demand that Max break off negotiations with Wilson. The generals
had thought up an ingenious excuse to explain their panicky armistice demands of only four weeks before. They claimed that the
demand had been necessary in order to show the German people
that Wilson and the Allies meant to extort a ruinous price for peace.
Now that this had been proved, the German people would fight
with renewed vigor. The Kaiser, hedging, referred the two generals
to the government. Late in the evening of October 25 they were
received by Vice-Chancellor von Payer in the absence of Max, who
had been taken ill. Payer was in the enviable position of being the

first government official in two years to treat with Ludendorff on distinctly superior terms.

The First Quartermaster General angrily attacked him: "in the name of the Fatherland, I throw the shame of it [the impending armistice] on you and your colleagues. And I warn you, if you let things go on like this, in a few weeks you'll have Bolshevism in the country."

"I'm not afraid of that," was Payer's cool reply—an answer which was rather less than candid, but which sufficed for the moment. "Furthermore," he said in dismissal, "you'll have to leave the interpretation of such matters to me. I understand them better."[64]

The numerous accounts of what followed vary widely on certain points. Ludendorff later claimed that he had intended to resign anyway; Max that he, the Chancellor, had finally forced the Kaiser's hand. At any rate, on the morning of October 26 Ludendorff and Hindenburg were summoned into the imperial presence at the Schloss Bellevue. Wilhelm opened the interview by criticizing the Supreme Command's October 24 proclamation to the troops. The civil government, he said, should have been consulted before any such proclamation had been made. There was then an awkward pause. Wilhelm stared at a wall, avoiding Ludendorff's eyes. The General did not wait for more. In these, "the bitterest moments of my life,"[65] he offered his resignation to the Emperor. It was accepted with a nod. There was no word of regret or appreciation.

Thus ended the military dictatorship which had lasted since the summer of 1916. Ludendorff was furious and embittered that Hindenburg did not insist upon submitting his own resignation. He believed that he had been made the scapegoat. When the two men left the Schloss Bellevue Ludendorff would not even get into the same automobile with Hindenburg. The latter asked why. "Because you treat me so shabbily."[66]

Alone, Ludendorff trailed off to observe the finish of the war in a dreary Berlin boardinghouse. Within weeks he would have to flee to Sweden, his face disguised with false whiskers and dark glasses.

The dismissal of Ludendorff seemed like a signal victory for the embryo parliamentary government. With the military dictatorship smashed, the right of a duly constituted government to direct the foreign policy of its nation had been established in Germany for the first time. But this had been true only in a narrow sense. For obvious reasons, Max and his government had not been able to announce publicly that the reason they were exchanging notes with Wilson was that the German Army was in desperate straits. They had not made public the frantic demands of the Supreme Command. They had tried to preserve at least a shred of a bargaining position. Accordingly, the majority of the Army's officers believed that the civil government alone was responsible for the armistice appeal. It was a mistake for which both Max and those who followed him were to pay a heavy price. Most of the nation and the Army were sincerely convinced that Max (whom they called "the pacifist Prince") had taken the chancellorship in order to make peace and had then maneuvered Ludendorff out of office when the General protested against the demands of the vindictive Allies. By a narrow margin, in the midst of defeat and dismissal, Ludendorff had been successful in transferring the responsibility for the defeat to the civil government.

If the responsibility for the armistice appeal was a matter of concern to the Army (or, more precisely, to the Army's officers), it was an incidental question to the majority of the German people, so great was their shock and disillusion over Germany's defeat. Until the beginning of October most Germans had been deluded into the belief that if only they could hold out a little longer Germany would be victorious; at the very least she would not be defeated. Now the truth could no longer be hidden; too many men had returned on furlough from the front. Suddenly the German people realized that the war was lost. It was a shattering realization.

The wrath of the people turned abruptly on those who had led them into war, especially on the conservative "war societies"—the Landowners' League, the Central Organization of German Industry, the League of Industrialists, the Pan-German League—and even the once impeccably honest bureaucracy of the German Empire, whose starving and demoralized officials were now reduced to widespread bribe-taking. Overnight there developed a violent hatred of Germany's military leaders. They had been given unquestioning obedience, they had been permitted to assume dictatorial control over the government, but now they had failed. From this point on the German people could not be convinced that there was any point in fighting. In the once docile Reichstag the representatives of the minority nationalities within the German Empire began to talk openly of the dismemberment of the Reich, the creation of an independent Poland, the return of Schleswig-Holstein to Denmark. Censorship broke down, and such questions as "What is the Kaiser going to do? When will he do it?"[67] were openly reported in the press.

In Berlin, especially among the workers, the reaction against militarism and the monarchy was intense. The reaction was all the more violent for its suddenness. The people saw that they had been deceived all along. The appointment of Prince Max of Baden to the chancellorship had come too late. The constitutional reforms had been too late. The Kaiser's dismissal of Ludendorff was too late.

The only people who did not yet understand that time had run out for the German Empire were those who were directing it. Neither Max (who was still under the illusion that the monarchy could be preserved) nor the Majority Socialists nor the Kaiser himself realized that they were dealing with an enraged and totally warsick populace. The experiences of only a few weeks before, when it had been sufficient to read a soothing imperial proclamation or display a few bayonets, were now totally irrelevant. The German people had become a mob whose only aim was to end the war.

Chapter Six

The Kiel Mutiny

I N Germany the first mutiny took place not among the exhausted and retreating troops at the front but in the German force which had suffered least—the battleships and battle cruisers of the High Seas Fleet.

For two and a half years, ever since the Battle of Jutland, the High Seas Fleet had been virtually immured in the big naval harbors which opened out into the North Sea or the Baltic. The submarines, the destroyers and the light cruisers had all made contact with the enemy, but except for a few quick raids into the Baltic, the capital ships had lain alongside the piers at Kiel, Wilhelmshaven and Hamburg for month after weary month. No one knew what to do with these ships. There were twenty-four of them, too few to give battle to the British, too many to sacrifice in a hopeless sea fight. For all these months, while the submarines and destroyers slipped out of the harbor to seek battle with the enemy, the big ships had lain in port.

Inactivity had been corrosive for the High Seas Fleet. Not, of course, in terms of actual rust—there was nothing much to do but scrape and paint—but in terms of the morale of these sailors, who were not, in any case, the best elements in the Imperial Navy. The most ardent and the best-disposed of the Navy's enlisted men had long since volunteered for service aboard the submarines or in the destroyer flotillas, and among these craft morale remained fairly good. Aboard the bigger vessels were left the discontented, the con-scripted workers from the big cities, and sullen sailors who had been court-martialed for various offenses and sent to penal service in the naval brigade at the front in Flanders, and who were now returned to duty afloat.

Nor was the situation made any better by the glory-thirsty officers of this embalmed fleet, who felt their personal honor to have been tarnished by their failure to meet the British Navy in battle. They bitterly resented the scarcely concealed sneers of the Army officers. Colonel Bauer, Ludendorff's chief political officer, had declared, "In the war itself the High Seas Fleet has only cost men and money. I can see no military use for it."[1] There were rumors that the Supreme Command had once considered giving the Imperial Navy to England in exchange for a negotiated peace. As the war drew into its last year the embittered officers of the fleet came to believe that all was lost, including honor. They were short-tempered and increasingly savage in their discipline over the sullen battleship crews.

During July of 1917 there had been a mutiny of sorts in one squadron. The principal cause had been the miserable and scanty rations of the enlisted men as compared to the food served in the officers' messes. It had not been a violent mutiny: on several ships the sailors refused to load stores, and a few hundred men walked off the battleship *Prinzregent Luitpold* and, ignoring the commands of their officers, marched in protest through the port city of Wilhelmshaven. They returned to their ship, but were arrested and court-martialed. A number of the ringleaders were sentenced to long prison terms, and two sailors, Reichpietsch and Köbis, were taken to Cologne and shot by a firing squad drawn from the trustworthy Army garrison.

The Navy claimed that the mutiny had been instigated by Independent Socialist politicians, and there was a wild scene in the Reichstag when this was announced. If there was any truth to the charge, it could not be proved. The outcome of the food protest was that the Navy High Command authorized the formation of "food committees" aboard the ships, elected by the sailors themselves and charged with the distribution of rations. Ironically, these committees became fronts for Socialist cells which began secret agitation aimed at setting up "sailors' councils" on the pattern of those already established in the Russian Navy. Reichpietsch and Köbis became legendary martyrs, and the imprisoned Karl Liebknecht was regarded with great sympathy. As a clandestine recognition signal among themselves, many of the sailors sewed a thin red thread inconspicuously on the collar of their jumpers.

This agitation went on in front of a group of officers whose lack of perception was truly astonishing. They do not appear to have realized the extent of their crews' disaffection; if they did, they chose to regard it as a manifestation of incipient Bolshevism. In point of fact, the political views of the High Seas Fleet sailors were startlingly unformed. The men were not revolutionaries, nor had the Spartacus Letters made any perceptible headway among them. They were sympathetic to the Independent Socialists only because the Independent Socialists stood for ending the war. The sailors would probably have responded well to a simple appeal to patriotism had their officers possessed the intelligence to make it. Instead, there was a constant repetition of such scenes as that which took place on board the *Helgoland* in 1917, when the captain summoned his crew to hear a speech in which he defined the aim of Germany's enemies as the overthrow of the Kaiser. "Then, when the Hohenzollerns have been driven out," he said, "a parliamentary regime like that in England and France is to be forced on us. Then shopkeepers, lawyers and journalists will rule here as they do there."[2]

By October of 1918 it seemed that the disciplinary troubles in the High Seas Fleet were finally at an end. The first German armistice note had been dispatched to Wilson, and, in response to his demand that submarine attacks on merchant shipping cease before negotiations started, all German submarines were recalled to port. The Navy High Command was incensed and embittered, but it was obviously only a matter of days before the war would end.

Then, in the last days of October, rumors began to reach the High Seas Fleet that the war was not yet over for them. There was, it was said, something special still in store for these massive gray ships, their sullen crews and their proud officers. It was rumored that the most conservative and diehard elements in Germany were pointing to the Navy as the perfect instrument for a last blow at the English. After all, it was certain that Britain would not allow Germany to keep her Navy after the war, so why not sacrifice it now? Let the High Seas Fleet put to sea and challenge the British Grand Fleet in a gigantic sea battle. Given luck, the British might even be dealt such a blow that the peace terms could be improved. And if all went badly, at least the Navy's honor was saved. "Better an honorable death than a shameful peace,"[3] the naval officers were reported to be saying.

The sailors did not view the prospect in quite the same manner. For one thing, they could see no point in dying a senseless death. For another, they read into these rumors another, deeper intention. In the Cabinet of Prince Max's newly formed government there were two Social Democrats. The sailors suspected that the naval officers and the conservative elements within the Second Reich were anxious to discredit this government and sabotage the peace negotiations. They were convinced (and in this they were correct) that Max and his government had been told nothing of the battle plans for the High Seas Fleet.[4] The sailors were willing to defend the German seacoasts, but not willing to launch a suicidal attack which had as its object the prolongation of the war.

There is a certain confusion about what the plan of battle was when, on October 28, the fleet received orders from its commanders to raise steam and rendezvous at the fleet anchorage in the Schillig Roadstead, halfway up the Jade from Wilhelmshaven to the sea. Probably the intention was to have the light vessels attack the Thames estuary and draw out the British fleet to a point off the Frisian Islands where it would be trapped by German mine fields and submarines; following this the High Seas Fleet would appear on the scene to complete the destruction of the British.[5] Perhaps the plan had some chance of success, but it was most difficult to persuade the German sailors that this sortie was anything but a "death ride." They would believe nothing that their officers told them. Wild rumors swept through the big ships: that the British Navy had challenged the German fleet to a final duel and the officers had accepted the challenge; that old Admiral von Tirpitz had come out of retirement to join the fleet and witness the destruction of the Navy he had created; that the Kaiser was personally leading the fleet aboard the battleship *Baden*.

By nightfall of October 29 the ships of the High Seas Fleet had all made their rendezvous and were riding at anchor in blustery Jade estuary. The force consisted of nineteen battleships, five battle cruisers and assorted light cruisers and destroyers; the submarines had been sent out earlier to rendezvous at sea. The main fleet was scheduled to sail at midnight. But now the sailors knew what the orders were, and from the shaded portholes of the big ships there was a constant winking of signal lights. By midnight the big ships were in rebellion—*Kronprinz Wilhelm, Grosser Kurfürst, König, Markgraf* and, in particular, the old battleships *Thüringen* and *Helgoland* of the First Squadron. The frantic captains of these vessels signaled to the fleet commander, Admiral von Hipper, that their stokers were threatening to put out the boiler fires if the ships raised anchor. Reluctantly Hipper postponed the sortie for a day to give the officers time to get their men in hand. But the next day, October 30, the mutinies continued. Early in the morning the officers of the *Thüringen* piped all hands to sea details—only to have several hundred sailors instantly rush belowdecks and gather in a huge compartment through which the anchor cables ran. Through spokesmen the sailors made it clear they would not go to sea to fight the last battle of a war already lost. When the officers piped quarters for inspection the men obeyed. But they would not raise anchor.

At four in the afternoon Hipper once more attempted to put his vessels to sea. Again the fleet would not move. In the boiler rooms of *Thüringen* and *Helgoland* the stokers put their slicer bars into the fires, drew the coals out onto the floor plates and wet them down with hoses. From forward came the noise of sledgehammers as other sailors smashed the anchor windlass. On the afternoon of October 30 Hipper canceled the sortie; the fleet would not be sent to sea. The mutineers had won. Now they must be punished.

The first move in the suppression of the mutiny was made against the *Thüringen*, whose crew had been by far the most violent in their refusal to go to sea. On the morning of October 31 a submarine, the *U-135*, was sent to lie abeam *Thüringen* and menace her with its torpedo tubes. To insure obedience aboard the *U-135*, one officer was stationed in the torpedo room, another in the conning tower and another at the deck gun. At noon two loyal destroyers came alongside the anchored *Thüringen* and tied up to her. Another destroyer lay off a little way with her torpedo tubes trained out. Immediately afterward, a steamer came alongside *Thüringen*'s port quarter and disembarked two hundred marines.

The situation as it now developed would have been almost humorous had it not been potentially so deadly. The mutineers had fled to the forward compartments of the *Thüringen*, and the marines were forming ranks on deck to march forward, when the mutinous *Helgoland* crew, anchored a short way off, trained their gun turrets around to point at the *U-135* and the destroyers. Instantly the *Helgoland*'s crew found themselves menaced in return by the after gun turrets of *Thüringen,* which were manned by officers and loyal enlisted men. While this standoff was taking place, the mutineers aboard *Thüringen* were given two minutes to surrender; if they refused, the officers warned, the marines would fire on them. Nothing more had to be done. Three hundred and fifty mutineers were marched off onto the steamer, which then pulled alongside *Helgoland* and took aboard another 150 prisoners.

In this manner the majority of the mutineers were taken from the two most rebellious vessels. The suppression had gone rather easily this time. It was never to go so easily again, but Hipper and his officers could not know this. They, assuming that the answer to the problem of restoring discipline had been found, ordered the High Seas Fleet to disperse to various ports and arrest the remaining mutineers aboard its ships. The Third Squadron, consisting of the battleships *König, Grosser Kurfürst, Kronprinz Wilhelm* and the mutinous *Markgraf,* was ordered to Kiel, where it arrived on November 1.

Kiel, an old Hanseatic port, lies on the Baltic Sea and is connected by canal with the German naval ports on the North Sea. In 1918 it was regarded as the principal port of the Imperial German Navy. Set in among the quaint houses and crooked streets of the old town were bigger, newer buildings—the Naval Academy, the Royal Yacht Club, a big dockyard and shipbuilding works, and huge barracks for recruits and for the naval schools ashore. The nominal commander of this port, as well as of the entire High Seas Fleet, was the Kaiser's brother, Prince Henry of Prussia, who flew his flag from an old castle overlooking the city. But the actual port commander was the military governor of Kiel, the famous Admiral Souchon of *Goeben* and *Breslau* fame, who had just assumed his post on October 30, two days before the Third Squadron arrived.

Souchon was no novice at handling mutinous sailors. Following the food protest of July, 1917, he had been given command of the Navy's most restive squadron, and, by means of intelligent discipline coupled with a series of small but successful operations against the Russian Navy, he had restored its morale. It was inevitable that when the Third Squadron tied up at the Kiel piers its commander, Admiral Kraft, would seek Souchon's advice. He found Souchon to be full of ideas, one of which was that marines be sent aboard the *Markgraf* to arrest the mutineers. This was promptly done, and 180 men were taken ashore and locked up in the naval prison.

But removing the mutineers from one ship was no solution to the problem. There were plenty of rebellious sailors aboard the other vessels in the Third Squadron, and when they heard of the *Markgraf* arrests they determined to free their comrades. At the inspiration of a group of socialist sailors, a protest meeting was called for the afternoon of Saturday, November 2, to be held at the trade-union headquarters in Kiel. Admiral Souchon was not without a certain resourcefulness of his own. He heard about the proposed meeting and quickly gave orders that the trade-union building was to be closed and a police guard placed around it. When the sailors arrived, they could only mill around outside. Then, under the leadership of a stoker named Karl Altelt, they marched out to the huge Exerzier Platz, a park on the outskirts of the city.

There, in the dusk, some five hundred sailors and a few civilian dockyard workers listened to inflammatory speeches from Altelt and Arthur Popp, the leader of the Independent Socialist Party at Kiel. They decided to call another meeting at the Exercise Field on the following afternoon, at which both workers and sailors would be present. With this the meeting broke up and the sailors made their way back to their ships, easily avoiding a dispirited company of marines marching out to the Exercise Field to arrest them.

That night Admirals Souchon and Kraft met. It was agreed that they lacked the power to keep all the sailors on the ships or in their barracks and thus prevent the meeting, but they hoped that they could do something else. The streets of Kiel would be heavily policed by shore patrols from the destroyers. When the meeting was scheduled to begin, the emergency recall signals would be blown. Every sailor with even a spark of discipline remaining in him would return to his barracks or his ship, the admiral hoped. This would leave in the streets only the hard-core mutineers, who would be arrested by the patrols.

Sunday, November 3, deserves to be called the first day of the German Revolution. The streets of Kiel rapidly filled with sailors and dockyard workers, and by five in the afternoon the Exercise Field was jammed with nearly twenty thousand men. The emergency recall signals were sounded, hooting and racketing down the streets—but in vain. No one paid any attention.

At the Exercise Field, Altelt and Popp addressed the crowd. They said they did not regard themselves as mutineers any more than they did their imprisoned comrades. The sailors were being punished simply for being loyal to the intentions of the present German government. They must free the *Markgraf* prisoners. They must restrict the power of their officers. They must form a "workers' and sailors' council." With a roar the crowd agreed. Then, forming a huge column, the men marched off for the Feldstrasse and the naval prison. Carrying torches and singing the "Internationale," they thundered through the narrow streets.

At the sight of the vast crowd, Souchon's patrols stepped back into darkened side streets. But there was one patrol which stood undaunted. On a rise in the street in front of the naval prison was a company of rifle-bearing sailors from the destroyers, under the command of a determined lieutenant named Steinhauser. As the rioting column drew closer these sailors could hear a noise like a huge train advancing toward them. When the torchlight column burst up the hill, the lieutenant ordered his men to fire a volley over the rioters' heads. The crowd slowed, but still it came on. At their lieutenant's command the sailors lowered their rifles and fired a volley directly into the mob. There was a sudden silence, and then the sound of running feet. In a moment there was no one left in the Feldstrasse except the rifle-carrying patrol, its lieutenant, and a score of dead or wounded men lying before them on the cobblestones. For the first time in this last autumn of the war, Germans had fired upon Germans.

The next day Kiel was swept with violence. The mutineers now realized that they must arm themselves, and aboard the big ships and in the barracks ashore the sailors broke into armories and small-arms lockers. Only rarely could they be held off. In the training barracks the officers armed recruit companies, and these eighteen-year-old sailors proved reliable enough. But there were not many of them, and in the huge Wik Barracks, the headquarters of the Baltic "Torpedo School," stoker Altelt formed the Kiel Sailors' Soviet—the first soviet to be proclaimed on German soil.

In huge mobs the sailors descended into the streets, but now that they were armed there was no one left for them to fight. The destroyer flotillas had fled the harbor. No officers were to be seen on the streets, and Souchon's patrols had disappeared. By 2 P.M. the sailors, joined by the striking dockyard workers, were virtually in command of Kiel, and Admiral Souchon had invited Altelt to come to his headquarters and present the sailors' demands.

In retrospect the demands of the Kiel Soviet seem somewhat curious—a sort of testimony to the often hesitant and undecided nature of the German Revolution. Some of them were serious, others almost comic in their insignificance. Altelt demanded of Souchon that the *Markgraf* prisoners be freed and that the sailors themselves have the right to approve the operation plans for any future sorties of the High Seas Fleet (as if a fleet in full-scale mutiny could launch an attack). Then, in a series of lesser demands, he insisted upon such requirements as better food and freedom from the obligation to salute retired officers. Point nine of the sailors' demands stipulated that an officer was to be addressed by his title at the beginning of an interview only—not, as in the past, in the third person throughout ("Herr Leutnant, would it be permitted to advise the Leutnant that the Leutnant's boat is alongside?").

Souchon seems to have received these demands with good grace. Pointing out that some of them were political in character and must be referred to Berlin, he agreed to others, such as the release of the *Markgraf* sailors. In the meantime he telegraphed to Berlin, asking that a representative be dispatched to assure the sailors that the government had no intention of ordering the fleet to sea. It would be best if the representative be from a party acceptable to the sailors— a Majority Socialist, preferably.

It is doubtful whether Souchon could have done anything to stem the mutiny. By November 4 the sailors had almost complete control of the city. All the loyal elements had fled the port or were under arrest. The battleships, with the exception of the *König*, which was in drydock, had gotten steam up and, still flying the black imperial ensign and manned by their officers and such sailors as were still loyal, had left port. Of the ships still in port, only the *König* did not fly the red flag of revolution. Her officers, who had armed them- selves, had set a watch on the flag halyards and would not allow the crew to approach. Then snipers began to fire at them from the dock. Within moments a lieutenant was killed, and as the ship's captain bent over the body he was wounded by three shots. In the rush of sailors which followed, the dying captain shot one mutineer, and then it was over. Now the red flag flew over every vessel in Kiel.

Ashore, the sailors turned to hunting down their officers. From building to building they searched them out, stripped them of swords, decorations or insignia and threw them into the cells of the naval prison. On foot, by car or on bicycle every officer who could get out was fleeing the city. Prince Henry, wearing civilian clothes, escaped in a motorcar, and soon a red flag flew over his castle. In the center of town a huge sailor directed traffic wearing a red sash around his waist, into which he had stuck eight officers' dirks and two pistols. He carried a rifle and around his neck he wore the Pour le Mérite, Germany's highest military decoration, which he had snatched from a famous submarine captain.

This whole wild scene was enacted to the accompaniment of fantastic rumors: the British Navy had mutinied and was flying the red flag, the Kaiser was dead, Army troops were marching on Kiel from the garrison at Altona. This last rumor was a dread one, for the sailors were in great fear of Army intervention, so a detachment of sailors was stationed in the railroad yards. As trains pulled in carrying troops sent to aid Souchon, the sailors swarmed aboard and disarmed the startled troops, who had not been prepared for this. But one infantry company commander was more clever than the others. He detrained his troops just outside the city, and on November 4 he marched them into Kiel. In tight field-gray ranks the soldiers paraded to Souchon's headquarters, where they took up guard duty. The disorganized sailors did nothing about it. They were overawed by these veteran infantrymen who stared straight ahead as they marched and whose hobnailed boots struck sparks from the pavement.

For the moment these were the only disciplined and loyal troops in Kiel and the sailors were safe from attack. Delegations of workers and sailors were on their way to the other ports—Hamburg, Wilhelmshaven, Lübeck, Brunsbüttel, Cuxhaven, Rundsberg, Warnemünde, Rostock, Bremerhaven and Geestemünde. In a day or two all of these would be in revolt, flying the red flag, under the control of workers' and sailors' councils. None of the ships at sea would be allowed to return to port or enter the Kiel Canal unless they flew red flags. The Army could not interfere—the mutiny was too widespread to put down by force, and by now imperial Germany was in its death throes.

The arrival of Gustav Noske at the railroad station in Kiel on the evening of November 4 was an intensely dramatic scene strikingly similar to the famous arrival of Lenin at the Finland Station in Leningrad in April, 1917. There was the same sort of railroad station jammed with revolutionaries seeking leadership from the prominent Socialist whose arrival was expected. There were the shouting sailors, the automobiles waiting outside to speed the new arrival to address a public meeting. There was an almost identical sense of revolutionary expectancy. And, like Lenin, the man on the train from

Berlin was apprehensive over the reception he would get. Like Lenin, he was not sure what the actual situation was in the city. He might be imprisoned, perhaps shot, immediately on his arrival. To his horror, he found that someone had even put a company of infantrymen on the same train and that it was too late to get them off before they arrived at Kiel.

Finally the train pulled up to the station platform and Noske stepped out. He was not hard to recognize, even though few in the mob at the station had ever seen him before. Gustav Noske was a tall ugly beetle-browed man with a straggling mustache and small gold-rimmed glasses. He walked with a slight stoop. Now fifty years old, he was a former basketweaver in a baby-carriage factory who became a Social Democrat early in life, then an editor of Socialist newspapers, and finally a Reichstag deputy. Over the years he had applied himself to the study of military matters, until he became the Social Democrats' "expert" in the field. He had acquired the reputation of being a "rightist" and a nationalist among Socialists. He had warmly defended the vote for the war credits and, of course, remained in the parent party at the time of the Independents' breakaway. As early as 1907 he had attacked Rosa Luxemburg for her internationalism, and in response he had received a bitter rebuke from August Bebel: "There was a time when I hoped that you would develop. Now I must say that this hope was in vain."[6]

There is no evidence that attacks such as this disturbed Noske. He made no claim to being an intellectual. He regarded himself as a patriot, a man of action, a rough-speaking proletarian who had no time for theories. During the war he spent a great deal of time as an observer at the front, for he was one of the few Socialists whom the Supreme Command trusted. They let him see everything. He visited the trenches in France, in Poland, in Lithuania and even on the Italian front. He spent a great deal of time talking to the troops, whom he came to know and understand better than almost any other politician. But it was frequently observed that he seemed to have a fondness for military discipline, and he was severely criticized for it by antimilitarist Socialists.

So now, as he alighted from the railroad carriage at Kiel, Noske had good reason to be apprehensive. He had been sent by the government to bring a leaflet from *Vorwärts,* an appeal for calm among the sailors, and he realized that he might be the least appropriate person for the mission. But with outward bravado he faced the mob.

One man recognized him and shouted, "Noske!" And suddenly the whole crowd of sailors charged down the platform, screaming, "Noske! Noske!" In the crush, the company of soldiers aboard Noske's train went unnoticed.

The sailors hoisted the dumfounded but relieved deputy to their shoulders, carried him to a waiting automobile and dumped him into a seat next to the stoker Karl Altelt, who at once advised Noske that the officers were deposed and powerless and that the German Revolution had begun. Altelt interrupted himself from time to time to wave a red flag from the automobile and cry out, "Long live freedom!"[7] Through lines of cheering sailors Noske was driven to a mass meeting in the Wilhelmplatz, where Altelt leaped up onto the speakers' platform, flung his arms wide to the vast crowd and shouted, "Noske is here!" There was an immense roar of revolutionary applause. Red flags waved everywhere. From the buildings surrounding the *Platz* there was an occasional ominous shot, but the noise was lost in the roars of the crowd. Noske was pushed up onto the platform; a sword was thrust into his hands. Hastily he gave it back and, turning to the crowd, began to speak.

It is here that any similarity to Lenin's arrival evaporates. For this ex-basketweaver had not come to Kiel to infuse the sailors with increased revolutionary fervor. Noske was actually an imperial commissioner who was supposed to investigate the situation for the government and then return to Berlin. But within a few hours he decided to stay in Kiel and suppress the mutinies if it was possible.

Chapter Seven

November Ninth

Germany's defenses against the Allied attack were now at the point of being breached. In these last weeks the Supreme Command had been forced to disband twenty-two divisions and distribute their manpower among other divisions. Even so the infantry battalions were down to only 450 men. On the western front the shrunken divisions were buying time by sacrificing successive screens of machine-gunners who slowed up the Allied advance as the German Army stepped back. Strategically the Army was *in extremis*—unable to give battle, unable to move fast enough to avoid it. Germany's own allies were almost all out of the war now. On October 31 the Turks signed an armistice. On the same day the Austrians sent an officer across the Italian lines to request armistice terms. An Allied army was moving up the Danube against an almost undefended German frontier.

Within Germany itself, the munitions workers were threatening a general strike and the troops at home were beginning to form soldiers' councils on the Russian pattern. Even the Bavarian kingdom was rumored to be contemplating a separate peace plea, to be made in conjunction with German Austria.

In these last stages of the decay of imperial Germany, Prince Max could only try to keep the German Empire together until he received the answer to his October 26 note to Wilson. Day after day the German government tottered along, waiting for a reply which would finally grant them an armistice. There were reasons for the delay. The Allies could scarcely be blamed for doubting the sincerity of Germany's eleventh-hour espousal of the Fourteen Points. Even in the United States Wilson was being urged to break off negotiations with Berlin. "There is no German government in existence with which I would discuss anything," thundered Senator Lodge. "I deplore at this stage, when we are advancing steadily to a complete victory, any discussion or exchange of notes with the German government."[1]

The Allied military commanders were uncertain and divided about an armistice. The opinions of all the commanding generals were solicited, and Pershing wrote to Foch: "We should take full advantage of the situation and continue the offensive until we compel her unconditional surrender." Pershing stressed that the German Army was ready to collapse (a view which none of the other Allied Commanders held) and cautioned: "It is the experience of history that victorious armies are prone to overestimate the enemies' strength and too eagerly seek an opportunity for peace."[2] Foch was not so sure. The decay of the German Army was not so apparent to him. He feared that the Germans might make good a retreat to the Rhine, rest and regroup behind this natural barrier, and then continue the war into 1919. He foresaw the possibility that the Allies might lose another 100,000 dead and still not extract better armistice terms than those which he had already drafted. He urged an armistice on the grounds that the conditions which the Allies would demand were equal to a German surrender. "Once this object is attained," he wrote, "nobody has the right to shed one more drop of blood."[3]

Prince Max and his government could not know of this. They could only assume that Wilson (whom Max now hated) was waiting for the abdication of the Kaiser and the resignation of the government. But at the same time they noted that in none of his messages had Wilson actually and specifically demanded the overthrow of the German monarchy. This puzzled them. They desperately hoped that the assurance in their note of October 26, "The President knows the far-reaching changes which have taken place and are being carried out in the German constitutional structure," would be enough. But as the days passed and they did not hear from Wilson they became convinced that the Allies were determined upon the dissolution of the Hohenzollern monarchy. The Majority Socialists were the first to broach the matter in the Cabinet. As Philipp Scheidemann put it, "We [the government] have always tried to interpret Wilson's notes in such a way that the President did not actually insist on the Kaiser's abdication. But the Foreign Office will agree with me that the rest of the world does not share this interpretation. People believe what Wilson implies—that we will get a better peace if the Kaiser is removed." But even the Majority Socialists were not prepared to demand that the Kaiser be forcibly deposed. Scheidemann urged that Wilhelm be asked to "take this step voluntarily."[4] The abdication of their Emperor seemed such an enormous step that the Cabinet members could not bring themselves to speak directly of the matter, but made oblique references to the Kaiser's failure "to do the right thing at the right time."[5]

When it became apparent that Wilhelm had no intention of doing the "right thing," Prince Max decided that he must approach the Kaiser and explain what was required of him. Perhaps, if the step was taken in time, Wilhelm could abdicate in favor of one of his sons or grandsons; then at least the Hohenzollern monarchy would be preserved. But on the very night Max made his decision, October 29, he received startling news. The Kaiser was preparing to leave Potsdam without notice, to join the Supreme Command at Spa in Belgium. Max, able only to speak to him on the telephone, pleaded with the Kaiser to remain near Berlin. His leaving would be another "flight to Varennes," and Max was sure that it would have the same outcome. Wilhelm knew, however, that if he stayed in Potsdam he would be subject to constant pressures for his abdication. He cut Max short with the assurance "If you do what I have advised you to do, everything can still turn out well."[6] That night the Kaiser left for Spa.

His flight was not the only anxiety which was to torment Max on October 29. Almost simultaneously with the Kaiser's departure, Philipp Scheidemann, the senior of the two Majority Socialists in the Cabinet, presented Max a letter demanding Wilhelm's abdication. Only with great difficulty was Max able to persuade Scheidemann to withdraw the letter, which had every overtone of a Majority Socialist ultimatum. Max knew what it portended: the Majority Socialists were beginning to feel the ground slipping from beneath their feet. And he knew that he must satisfy them at almost any cost; they were the only party in his government which could exert any influence on the increasingly restive workers, the only party which could deal with the new soldiers' councils.

But the Majority Socialists were subject to pressures of their own. On October 23 Karl Liebknecht had been released from jail in a general amnesty. The scene of popular rejoicing which followed was a frightening experience for the Majority Socialists. There were huge demonstrations in Berlin and other cities, with crowds far larger than anything the Spartacists or the Independent Socialists had been able to produce until now. Liebknecht, the man who had once had no popular following, rode through the streets of Berlin in a flower-filled carriage pulled by workers. When the news of his release reached Russia the streetcars stopped running and the factories closed for a holiday. The Soviet government instantly dispatched ecstatic congratulations signed "Lenin, Sverdlov, Stalin": "Immediately convey to Karl Liebknecht our very warm greetings. The release from prison of the representative of the revolutionary workers of Germany is a visible sign of the new epoch, the epoch of triumphant socialism now being revealed for Germany and for the whole world."[7]

With a chill, the Majority Socialists began to realize how much ground they had lost to the Independent Socialists and especially to the extreme-left-wing factions, which they had ignored in the past. Only a few weeks before, the Majority Socialists had been absolutely confident of their authority within the working class. But now they were not so sure. Philipp Scheidemann, who had advocated Liebknecht's release on the grounds that he was much less dangerous outside prison than inside, was frankly dumfounded—"Liebknecht has been carried shoulder high by soldiers who have been decorated with the Iron Cross. Who could have dreamt of such a thing happening three weeks ago!"[8]

This landslide to the left was due in no small part to influence exerted by the Russian Bolsheviks. Lenin himself consistently declared that revolution in Germany was the logical sequel to the Russian Revolution. In his "Farewell Letter to the Swiss Workers" he had stated flatly: "The revolution will not stop at Russia. The German proletariat is the most faithful and reliable ally of the Russian and worldwide proletarian revolution."[9] Lenin had made no secret of who it was that he supported among the German proletarians. In his speech at the Finland Station he had gone out of his way to say, "The hour is not far off when, at the summons of our comrade Karl Liebknecht, the people will turn their weapons against their capitalist exploiters."[10] As for the Majority Socialists, he detested even their name. The very phrase "Social Democracy" he castigated as "a soiled shirt."[11] Only the Liebknecht Spartacists and certain other left-wing sections of the Independent Socialists were acceptable to Lenin. And because he had always believed that the world revolution could not take place until a German revolution had taken place, Lenin was prepared to make any sacrifice to promote it. Even if "it were necessary for us to go under to assure the success of the German revolution," he told Trotsky, "we should have to do it."[12] In March of 1918 Lenin made a long speech at a Russian party conference declaring, "It is an absolute truth that we shall go under without the German revolution, . . . [but] Liebknecht will rescue us from this."[13] The Spartacist's were the first to agree. In the September, 1918, Spartacus Letter Rosa Luxemburg had written: "Without a German Revolution there can be no salvation for the Russian Revolution, no hope for socialism after this world war. There remains only one solution—mass rising of the German proletariat."[14]

A major reason for Lenin's acceptance of the ruinous Brest-Litovsk Treaty with imperial Germany was that it gave Russia an embassy in Berlin. Since April, 1918, the Soviet Embassy on Unter den Linden had been a sort of headquarters for the promotion of German revolution. Lenin had sent an able young man named Adolf Yoffe as the Soviet ambassador. He was a well-educated Jew from the Crimea who had inherited a good deal of money, all of which he gave to the Russian Socialist Party in the prewar years. Yoffe had suffered from a serious neurosis and had lived in Vienna for some time under the care of the psychoanalyst Alfred Adler. But the Russian Revolution seemed to have cured him of all his complexes "better than the psychoanalysis," Trotsky observed.[15] Yoffe had been part of the Bolshevik delegation at Brest-Litovsk and then had been sent on to establish the Soviet Embassy in Berlin. He brought with him an enormous staff—more than three hundred persons— and moved into the palace which had formerly been the Imperial Russian Embassy. Over the building Yoffe hoisted an enormous red banner on which was written "Workers of all countries, unite!" From this headquarters he began an extensive agitation among the Independent Socialists and particularly among Liebknecht's Spartacists. He gave them money; tons of diplomatically immune revolutionary literature was imported from Russia for distribution in Berlin; almost every night Yoffe conferred with Independent Socialist leaders on questions of tactics; he brought in a number of famous and skilled agitators from Russia, who, as members of the embassy, were dispatched to major German cities to promote revolutionary activity. When Liebknecht told Yoffe that he did not believe the moment to be quite ripe for the German Revolution, the Soviet ambassador recalled the experiences of the Russian Bolsheviks in Leningrad only a year before, when the political situation had been much the same. "Within a week," Yoffe predicted, "the red flag will be flying over the Berliner Schloss."[16]

On October 7, with the then imprisoned Liebknecht's blessing, the Russians had even managed to hold what they called a "national conference of the Spartacus Union" in Berlin. They had brought together from all over Germany a mixture of extreme Socialist splinter groups, which came to be regarded as part of the Spartacus Union; their program was frankly revolutionary and Leninist. As days passed and Liebknecht himself was freed from jail, the strength of the Spartacus Union increased. Close alliances were made with the Revolutionary Shop Stewards* and with Georg Ledebour, the leader of the left wing of the Independent Socialists. None of them particularly liked Liebknecht, nor did they really trust him. Nevertheless, they had to concede that Spartacus was building up a sizable following. Liebknecht spent his days racing from meeting to meeting and from factory to factory. The bewildered government could not keep up with his activities. Much of the time the police did not know where he was. To confuse them, in the event that the government should decide to rearrest him, Liebknecht had taken to spending every night at a different address, even going too far as to sleep under the trees in the nearby Treptow Forest.

The only way the Majority Socialists could halt this slide to the left would be to behave in an increasingly militant manner themselves. At this point they were still willing to accept some form of constitutional monarchy. When it had been proposed that Wilhelm II might abdicate in favor of a regency for one of his grandsons, the

---

* The Revolutionary Shop Stewards (Revolutionäre Obleute) was a small organization of leaders in certain trade unions (mostly the metalworkers' unions in Berlin) who broke away from the Social Democratic Party at about the time the Independent Socialists were forming. Like the Spartacist Union, the Revolutionary Shop Stewards took cover under the Independent label. And like the Spartacists its members were intensely revolutionary and determined to retain their own individuality from the Independents, even though several of the shop stewards were also important figures holding office in the Independent Social Democratic Party. Although small, the group was very influential, by reason of the union support it could turn out. Its leaders were successively Richard Müller, Emil Barth and Ernst Däumig. All of its members regarded themselves as revolutionary activists; they differed from the Spartacists only in that they considered the latter too theoretical.

Majority Socialists had acquiesced. But now they began to have
second thoughts.

They found the Russians' connection with Liebknecht particularly ominous. At a Cabinet meeting Scheidemann suggested that a
railway porter be instructed to abuse one of the incoming Soviet
diplomatic boxes so that it would spill open in the station and reveal
the revolutionary propaganda which Ambassador Yoffe was importing. For the time being the idea was shelved as being incommen-
surate with the gravity of the situation.

The appointment of General Wilhelm Groener in the place of the
fallen Ludendorff was yet another instance of an excellent appointment made too late. Groener had been called from the post of chief
of staff of the army of occupation in Russia. His appearance was
unprepossessing—he was short and stocky, with a face so round and
an expression so mild that he appeared almost childish—but he had
every other qualification needed at that hour. He was a Württemberger, a South German, not a Prussian; he was the son of a noncommissioned officer; and he was capable of projecting an aura of
personal warmth and understanding which few Prussian officers
possessed or cared to cultivate, least of all Ludendorff (who had
been his professional rival on the General Staff in the years before
the war). More important, he had a background of experience in the
fields of railway transport and economics, a knowledge of which,
Prince Max suspected, would be crucial in the days to come. In the
early years of the war Groener had served in the vital post of chief
of field-railway transport, with every German railway, road and
waterway under his direct control, and he had performed brilliantly.
Next he had been the military officer in charge of the "Hindenburg
Program" for the economic mobilization of the German war effort.
In this too he had been startlingly successful—particularly in his
frequent dealings with the Majority Socialist leaders. The latter had
been astounded to find themselves growing almost fond of this fifty-
year-old general who listened tactfully to their own ideas; it was
then a wholly novel experience for a Socialist to be regarded by an
officer as anything but a disguised enemy of the state.

For all his successes, Groener had not gotten on well with Ludendorff. He had not agreed with the First Quartermaster General's
strategy for the conduct of the war. As early as 1917 Groener had
warned, "We should be satisfied with a draw. . . . The important

thing is to prepare our strategy and our politics in good time."[17] Word of this had gotten back to Ludendorff, who promptly exiled him to the Russian front.

Groener, then, was much more than a technician; he was a clear-sighted, highly intelligent officer with none of the unreasoning hatred of Socialists or democracy which characterized the officer corps. But he was still a subordinate to Hindenburg, and, like every other soldier, he had sworn an oath of fealty to the Kaiser. In addition, he had only just returned from a year in Russia and was somewhat out of tune with the temper of the times. So, when he arrived in Berlin on November 5 to confer with the Cabinet, Groener attempted at first to uphold the monarchy and even expressed the opinion that Germany might be able to defend herself long enough to extract more favorable terms from the Allies. But by the following day he had learned enough to persuade him that he had been wrong—at least concerning Germany's ability to defend herself for more than a few days. Noske was reporting from Kiel the full dimensions of the Navy mutinies, and the Cabinet had made Groener aware of the true situation among the workers of Berlin. He now realized that if the government did not hear from Wilson within a day or so the Germans "must cross the lines with a White flag" and beseech the Allied armies for an armistice. He named Saturday, November 9, as the very last day that Germany could hold out. "It must be Saturday at the latest," he told Max.[18]

But Groener would not agree to support the movement for the Kaiser's abdication. At noon on November 6 Max arranged a meeting between Groener and the Majority Socialist leaders, headed by Friedrich Ebert, the party's chairman. They all knew and liked Groener, and they told him frankly that unless the Kaiser abdicated they would no longer be able to control the workers. Ebert stressed that the abdication of Wilhelm II need not mean the end of the monarchy, which could be preserved in some form of regency. Groener took refuge behind his instructions from Hindenburg. He revealed that each of the Kaiser's six sons had sworn an oath not to succeed their father as regent. The meeting broke up with the Majority Socialists in despair. "Under the circumstances any further discussion is superfluous," Ebert said. "We have reached a parting of the ways. . . . [But] we will always remember with pleasure our work with you during the war. From now on we go separate ways and who knows whether we shall ever see each other again."[19]

❊ ❊ ❊

At the very moment this meeting was breaking up, Prince Max was at last taking decisive action. Two days with Groener had completely convinced him that an armistice had to be obtained at once, under any circumstances, with or without Wilson's approval. He immediately set about appointing an armistice commission—but in an unusual manner.

If historical precedent had been observed, the Armistice Commission would have consisted entirely of military officers drawn from the General Staff; it would have been these officers who crossed the lines under a flag of truce and signed the protocols. But Max did not trust the Supreme Command in this matter. He suspected that if he appointed a commission of Army officers they might find some way to sabotage the armistice, especially if one of its terms was the abdication of the Kaiser. There was another reason why Max did not want the Armistice Commission to consist solely of Army officers. Despite his distrust of the Supreme Command, he retained to the end a certain vestigial worship of the Army and its place in German life, and he did not wish to saddle it with the complete blame for the armistice. For these reasons, Max appointed to the German Armistice Commission two civilians, Cabinet member Matthias Erzberger of the Catholic Center Party and Count Alfred von Oberndorff, a Foreign Office dignitary. The Army was to be represented only by an elderly major general named von Winterfeldt, who was not a member of the General Staff but merely a former military attaché in Paris, and who had to be called hastily from retirement for the mission. The fact that the Supreme Command was not to be represented at the armistice negotiations and could later disclaim responsibility for them seems to have eluded the Chancellor. In fact, Max himself reports the prevailing feeling of his Cabinet as being "one of relief that at least the Army would not have to wait upon Foch."[20]

There then ensued a frantic search for credentials of plenipotentiary power. A special train was obtained, and at 5 P.M. on November 6 the two civilians set out for Spa. Minutes prior to their departure the long-awaited note from Wilson arrived, telling the German government that Marshal Foch had been authorized "to receive properly accredited representatives of the German Government, and to communicate to them the terms of an Armistice."

The Armistice Commission having been dispatched, Max and his Cabinet sat down to review developments within Germany. The first item was the reports from Noske in Kiel. All things considered, the news was surprisingly good.

Noske had swiftly perceived that there were really only two courses of action open to him. One was to suppress the mutiny by force; the other, to join it. After being in Kiel only a few hours he could see that a policy of repression would be futile. There were at least forty thousand well armed mutineers; even if all the Army garrisons in Germany could somehow be marched against Kiel, they would probably not be enough, and in any event they would not arrive fast enough to save Noske from retaliation by the sailors. So he decided to seize control of the rebellion and to make himself the sailors' spokesman, protector and mentor. Instead of suppressing the rebellion, he would stimulate and encourage it—but only along a path of "moderate" revolution. He had read with great care the demands which the sailors had presented to Admiral Souchon. He saw that they were not really revolutionary in nature, but were merely the protests of war-sick, hungry and overdisciplined men badly frightened by the prospect of a "death ride" with the High Seas Fleet. Noske believed he could deal with these men. But there was also in Kiel a leavening of ardently left-wing sailors and workers who, if Noske overplayed his hand, would quickly expose him. Every move he made must be shrewd, calculated—and successful.

Noske began his work on November 4, the very night he arrived in Kiel. Having addressed the mass meeting in the Wilhelmplatz, he drove to the trade-union headquarters for a meeting with representatives of the sailors and workers. After this conference he dispatched a telegram to Berlin asking permission to free any mutineers still in prison, requesting that the ships which had fled Kiel be ordered to return and embark the mutineers, and urging that any Army troops then on their way to Kiel be recalled instantly. Then he drove to the railroad station, where he found the company of soldiers (now disarmed) who had arrived on his train that morning; he ordered them aboard the first train out of Kiel. At the station Noske also met with the military governor, Admiral Souchon and cautioned him not to attempt a counterrevolution under any circumstances. It was a superfluous warning—and wryly humorous, since Souchon and his staff were actually the prisoners of the sailors. They were shut up in the second-class waiting room as hostages against the feared arrival of a cavalry regiment, the Wandsbeck Hussars, which the sailors had heard was on the way from Altona. The next day it was established that the rumor was false, and Souchon was released. The sailors had nothing to fear from him. Souchon was a military governor who governed nothing, and no one would accept his orders. He and what remained of his staff were exhausted, bewildered and defeated by the events of the past days.

Noske's energy, by contrast, was inexhaustible. After having been up all night, he appeared on the morning of November 5 at a meeting of a thousand trade-union delegates. He reported to them his activities of the night before and urged them to designate a small committee of representatives to assume control over events in Kiel, and then he dashed off to attend another huge meeting of sailors in the Wilhelmplatz. Here too he stressed the need for a committee—in this case, of delegates who would meet with him and present the sailors' demands so that he could pass them on to Berlin.

Within a few hours Noske had the delegates he had asked for. Into a room at the trade-union headquarters crowded some fifty sailors. Every one of the various sailors' councils in Kiel had sent a delegate. Noske was horrified. He pointed out that this unwieldy mob was scarcely what he had had in mind when he spoke of a committee. Looking around the room, he selected from among the more intelligent-looking of these strange faces a group of nine men. This, he announced, would be known as the "Supreme Sailors' Council."

Thus Noske had his committee. All he needed now was the authority to act. He got it that same day, November 5, when a group of sailors and workers proposed that he assume the post of military governor of Kiel. It is not hard to imagine how this offer came about. Noske's consistent message to the sailors was the need to maintain order. He carefully avoided any suggestion of reproach for the excesses of the past few days, but he constantly reiterated that the only way the sailors could protect themselves and protect what they had won was to reestablish *Ruhe und Ordnung*. Obviously there had to be someone in charge at Kiel, but who? It would have to be a man with influential contacts in the government, one who had had experience in political negotiations, and one who was a recognized leader within the Socialist camp. It was quickly realized that the only man with these qualifications was Noske himself. Would he accept the post of military governor? Graciously and modestly Noske acquiesced, contriving to give the impression of accepting an unexpected and unwanted duty. When he announced to the sailors that he had assumed the governorship of Kiel, he carefully added, "At my side is the Supreme Sailors' Council of the region."[21] And he made sure to obtain the countersignature of these nine bewildered sailors on every order he issued.

By the afternoon of November 5, Noske was able to telephone the government in Berlin and tell them, "I have been obliged to accept the post of governor and have already had some successes."[22]

In point of fact, Noske had already accomplished miracles—and within a few days he was to accomplish more. It was not that he did anything unusual or spectacular. It was only that he provided in Kiel an infusion of common sense, determination, and moderation which made a return to order certain. He did not sleep for days. And as he hurried from ship to ship and from barracks to dockyard, sometimes attracting as many as ten thousand men to hear him speak, Noske swiftly discovered that the sailors were frightened men. The mutineers had lived a disciplined life for so long that they could not bring themselves to believe in their own success. Noske was constantly being sought out by groups of sailors bearing frantic reports that the officers were massing in a forest outside Kiel for an attack on the city, or that Army regiments were on their way from one direction or another, or that the officers still remaining aboard some of the ships in port were preparing to bombard the city. There were constant bursts of small-arms fire in the streets of Kiel from sailors who were convinced that officers concealed behind upper-story windows were sniping at them.

Each of these reports had to be investigated by Noske. He established that, far from planning to bombard the town, the officers had actually put most of the ships' guns out of commission. Again and again Noske trotted out Admiral Souchon to swear to the sailors' councils that there were no counterrevolutionary armies forming in the forests. Every day he called Berlin to repeat his warning that under no circumstances should an attempt be made to send the Army against the Kiel mutineers. And he conducted an inquiry into the alleged sniping by officers which established that the nervous sailors had probably been shooting at each other.

Gradually the firing in the streets died down. The armed sailors were persuaded to turn their weapons over to Noske's Supreme Sailors' Council, and within a day or two the only armed men on the streets were the patrols which reported directly to the new military governor. The prisons and the detention barracks were combed through, and any man still in jail as the result of either the food riots of 1917 or the current mutinies was released.

As the ships of the Third Squadron returned to port Noske ordered them manned again, and he raised no objection when the crews insisted upon flying the red flag. He asked only that they resume regular patrols of the Baltic to guard against a surprise attack by the British Navy. Miraculously the sailors agreed, and the patrols resumed.

Noske studied the demands the sailors had made at the height of the rebellion and put into effect as many as he could. He granted furloughs in wholesale lots, and when he learned that there was not enough money in Kiel to pay the sailors he dispatched a plane to Berlin to bring back a load of cash. The Social Democrat even managed to win the good will of the officers. He went so far as to apologize to Souchon for taking over the Admiral's post as military governor. More important, he stopped the firing in the streets, put armed sentries in front of the officers' quarters, and virtually brought to an end the personal attacks on officers in Kiel. Within only a few days after his arrival, Noske was beginning to receive letters of thanks and pledges of future cooperation from various officers.

If the news from Kiel was fairly reassuring to the government, the same could not be said for the rest of Germany. Reports were reaching Berlin that in almost every Army regiment behind the front the men were electing "barracks councils" which in turn combined with other regiments in the same city to elect a "garrison council." The officers could do nothing about it. Behind the front in France the railroad stations were jammed with half-mutinous deserters. The Second Guards Division, which had been ordered from the front to Spa, practically had to fight its way to the rear. Only by commandeering trains from the striking railwaymen and clearing the station platform by setting up machine guns could the division make its way to Supreme Headquarters. All the seaports too were in rebellion.

At the Cabinet meeting on November 7 the Majority Socialists, now frankly frightened, reported that the Independents were planning five huge meetings in Berlin that night to hail the mutinies at Kiel. The police and the Berlin garrison were ordered to suppress these meetings. Press censorship had almost completely lapsed, and every left-wing newspaper was full of demands for the Kaiser's abdication. Philipp Scheidemann warned the Cabinet that the Majority Socialists could do nothing more to insure order: "You gentlemen and the Reich Chancellor must understand that we have done all within our power to keep the masses in check."[23] He was frankly critical of Prince Max's failure to obtain the Kaiser's abdication: "He did not display the necessary determination. . . . We are convinced that the Reich will collapse unless the Emperor abdicates."[24]

There was little that the government could do to contain the tide of revolution; it could only hope that both the armistice and the abdication would come in time to save it. A few regiments that were thought to be particularly reliable were ordered into Berlin. The only action which the Cabinet took against the Bolshevik menace was to adopt Scheidemann's suggestion that some of the Russian ambassador's incoming baggage be "accidentally" smashed open. This was promptly done, and, even though it seems to have been necessary to plant a set of revolutionary tracts in the smashed box, a cordon of troops was placed around the Russian Embassy and Yoffe was ordered to leave Berlin that day.

On November 7 Max finally decided that if the Kaiser would not come to him, he must go to the Kaiser. It had become a footrace between abdication and revolution. The emissaries he had sent, the letters, telegrams and telephone calls, had all been in vain. Now he must confront Wilhelm with his plan for saving the Hohenzollern monarchy. But first he wanted to assure himself of the support of the Majority Socialists. He called in their leader, Ebert, and asked him point-blank, "If I should succeed in persuading the Kaiser, do I have you on my side in the struggle against the social revolution?"[25] Without hesitation Ebert replied, "If the Kaiser does not abdicate, the social revolution is inevitable. I do not want it—in fact, I hate it like sin."[26]

With this assurance, Prince Max prepared to depart that evening for Spa. His preparations were interrupted at 5 P.M. when an official dashed into his Chancellery office with the news that Ebert and Scheidemann requested him to receive them at once and hear a series of demands which had just been formulated by a caucus of the Majority Socialists. The Chancellor had no choice but to see them. The two men, who, Max could see, were "overwhelmed by a sudden panic,"[27] delivered a five-point ultimatum which demanded, among other things, that the prohibition against mass meetings be lifted, that the Majority Socialist representation in the government be increased, and, most important, that by noon of the following day, November 8, the Kaiser abdicate and the Crown Prince renounce his rights of succession. "The Kaiser must abdicate," said the frightened Socialists; "otherwise we shall have the revolution."[28] If their demands were not met, the Majority Socialists would resign from the government; this, they well knew, would mean its immediate collapse.

Their message delivered, the two Socialists departed, leaving Prince Max in a quandary. He knew what had brought them to him with this ultimatum. The Majority Socialists were scheduling twenty-six mass meetings in Berlin for that night, and they felt it imperative to announce that it was they who had forced the Kaiser's abdication—"Otherwise the whole lot will desert to the Independents."[29] He knew that the Majority Socialists were not truly opposed to the monarchy. In fact, the editor of *Vorwärts* said, "We wanted to save the monarchy, but if someone called 'Long live the Republic!' there was nothing left for us to do but call with them."[30] But Max also knew that he could not get to Spa and secure the abdication by noon of the next day. The exhausted Prince canceled his trip to Spa and turned his flagging energies toward convincing the Majority Socialists that they must stay on, while simultaneously trying to persuade the Kaiser by telephone that he must go. In a Cabinet meeting next day Max announced that he himself intended to resign, and this threat wrung a reluctant half-promise from the Socialists to continue in the government a little while longer—at least until the armistice had been concluded.

It was almost at that exact moment that Erzberger and his companions were crossing the front lines to treat with Foch. A radio message sent *en clair* from Spa to the Allied headquarters had secured a cease-fire along a road bisecting the front. With considerable difficulty the armistice delegates had made their way through the wretched jumble of the German lines. The German divisions in the area, two of which were reduced to fewer than five hundred men, were retreating and had planted the roadway with mines and blocked it with felled trees. Finally a track had been cleared and the delegation's automobiles had churned their way through. In an anachronistic touch, a trumpeter had stood on the runningboard of the white-flagged first car, blowing sharp blasts from his horn. At the French outposts they were transferred into other cars and thence into a special train. By 7 A.M. of November 8 they had reached the artillery siding in the Forest of Compiègne, near Rethondes, where Foch's train awaited them.

Within two hours the exhausted and disheveled Germans were granted an audience with Foch, who handed them the Allied terms. The conditions of armistice were tantamount to complete surrender. All occupied territory, including Alsace-Lorraine, was to be evacuated by Germany within fifteen days; the Allies were to be given three bridgeheads on the east bank of the Rhine; huge amounts of military equipment were to be surrendered; the most modern elements of the German fleet were to be interned by the Allies. Nobody made any secret of the fact that this armistice would make it impossible for Germany to resume the war in the event that the final peace terms were unacceptable to her. Moreover, Foch demanded that the Germans accept these armistice terms within seventy-two hours. In the meantime he denied the plea of the German delegation for a temporary cease-fire while the terms were referred to their government. With apparent unconcern the Allied generalissimo rejected Erzberger's claim that the German Army must be kept strong enough to suppress Bolshevism, which, should it seize power in Germany, would spread to France. "Western Europe," Foch assured the Germans, "will find means of defending itself against the danger."[31]

Had Foch known the exact situation within Germany, he might have found it difficult to maintain so complete an air of assurance. But the Allies could not know of the position in which the German government found itself on November 8. All was chaos and confusion in the Chancellery. News had been received that Ludwig III, King of Bavaria, had been deposed and that a revolutionary Bavarian government, known as the "Council of Workers and Soldiers" and dominated by Independent Socialists, had been proclaimed. Now word came in that Düsseldorf, Frankfurt-am-Main, Stuttgart, Leipzig and Magdeburg had all come under the control of quasi-revolutionary regimes; the imperial flag had been pulled down in those cities and the red flag hoisted. Communications had deteriorated to the point where nobody knew precisely what was going on outside Berlin, but the Ministry of War forwarded a horrifyingly laconic report to the government:

9 A.M.: Serious riots at Magdeburg.

1 P.M.: In Seventh Army Corps Reserve District rioting threatened.

5 P.M.: Halle and Leipzig Red. Evening: Düsseldorf, Halstein, Osnabrück, Lauenburg Red; Magdeburg, Stuttgart, Oldenburg, Brunswick and Cologne all Red.

7:10 P.M.: General officer commanding Eighteenth Army Corps Reserve at Frankfurt deposed.[32]

Berlin itself was now almost a besieged fortress. There were well-founded rumors that huge gangs of sailors from the ports had escaped Noske and, calling themselves the People's Naval Division, had entrained for the capital. Already a few small groups of sailors and marines had been arrested and jailed in the Moabit Prison. A few others had gotten away and were roaming loose in the city. The frantic Cabinet sent for General Scheüch, the Minister of War, and instructed him to rip up sections of the railroad tracks' between Berlin, Hamburg and Hanover. The Army was also instructed to set up machine guns to cover the tracks in the Lehrter Station in Berlin. The gas and electric works were occupied by troops. Three Jäger (sharpshooter) battalions brought in from Finland were stationed in a few of the large restaurants and in various government buildings on the Wilhelmstrasse. Armored cars patrolled the center of the city, and pickets of helmeted troops were at all the main street crossings.

Such was the confusion on November 8 that no one really knew whether these measures would be effective. The Majority Socialists had found out that the militant factions of the Independents had secretly armed themselves out of funds supplied by the Soviet ambassador and had adopted the slogan "all or nothing."[33] It was learned that they had planned the revolution for November 4 but had postponed it for a few days. Karl Liebknecht had suggested that it take place on November 8 or 9, but the Revolutionary Shop Stewards had pointed out that these were paydays and that it might be difficult to get the workers out of the factories, so the revolution had been put off for a few more days. On November 8 the police arrested Ernst Däumig, the Revolutionary Shop Stewards' leader, and found in his briefcase detailed plans for a revolution which was to take place on November 11.

The government planned to put down any revolutionary attempt with quick brutality, but its plans were curiously ambiguous and confused. To avoid provoking the workers, the troops and police were instructed to use their weapons only if they were actually attacked. The military governor of Berlin, General von Linsingen, sent fighter planes aloft to bomb the trainloads of sailors supposedly hurrying toward Berlin. The Minister of War canceled the order, and Linsingen immediately resigned. All officers on leave in Berlin were ordered to report to the Ministry of War at noon on November 8. Hundreds arrived as ordered, bearing field packs and side arms. Thereupon it dawned on the government that this sort of thing gave the unfortunate impression of a White counterrevolution in the process of organization. The officers were left to mill around without instructions; gradually they drifted away. At the Schloss Berlin the garrison was reinforced by several armored cars, and the troops were given orders to shoot any revolutionaries who attempted to storm the castle. Then the orders were changed: the soldiers were not to shoot at any unarmed civilians.

The chief reason for the government's confusion was that all of the Chancellor's energies were being devoted to engineering the Kaiser's abdication. On the night of November 8 Prince Max pleaded with the Kaiser over the telephone. "I must speak to you as a relative," he told Wilhelm. "Your abdication has become necessary to save Germany from civil war. The great majority of the people believe you to be responsible for the present situation. . . . The troops are not to be depended upon. . . . Nowhere have the military been of any value. . . . This is the last possible moment. . . . Unless the abdication takes place today, I can do no more."[34]

The Kaiser rejected Max's argument in its entirety. He declared that if necessary he would put down the revolution by using his army from the front. As for Prince Max, Wilhelm refused again to accept his·resignation as chancellor and made the grossly unfair charge that it was Max who was responsible for the situation. "You sent out the armistice offer, you will also have to accept the conditions,"[35] he said, and with that he hung up.

By nightfall on November 9 all was over. Wilhelm II, Emperor of Germany, had made the final political mistake of his reign. He had thought that the Army would protect him. He had been wrong. This erratic, bombastic personality whose incautious pronouncements had once terrified the foreign ministries of a dozen European nations was now, at fifty-nine, a broken and indecisive old man as he sat eating dinner aboard his private train at a railroad siding in Belgium.

He had fled his palace at Potsdam to appear unannounced—and unwanted—at the Supreme Headquarters of the Imperial Army in Spa. Certainly Wilhelm had not come there "in response to the request of the Army," as he had told Max.[36] It was, of course, his right to be with the Army. He was the King of Prussia, the German Emperor and the All-Highest Warlord, and every soldier and officer in his armies had sworn a solemn oath of personal obedience to him. A few years earlier he had publicly told a Prussian guards regiment that it must always stand ready "to risk its life and its blood for the King and his house; and if ever again the city [of Berlin] should presume to rise up against its master," he had said, "then I have no doubt that the regiment will repress with the bayonet the impertinence of the people toward their King."[37]

But now the Army had failed him. Since about four-thirty in the afternoon, most of the five thousand soldiers on duty at Spa had ceased to salute their officers. A soldiers' council had even been formed at Supreme Headquarters. The Emperor's bodyguard had dwindled to his aides-de-camp and a single company of the Rohr Battalion. In Berlin the Independent Socialists had called a general strike for 9 A.M.; by noon the Wilhelmstrasse in front of the Chancellery had been filled with a torrent of shouting workers waving red flags—and the Army had done absolutely nothing to stop them. The fourteen regiments in the capital had refused to fire on the workers. The Jägers brought in from Finland had deposed their officers and actually disbanded. The First Guards Reserve Regiment had handed its weapons to the workers. The Imperial Army's Berlin garrison seemed to have evaporated.

November 9 had been the final act of a dreary and prolonged drama in which, at the last, the Kaiser had degenerated into a minor player in whom no one had any interest other than somehow to get him off the stage. He had arrived at Spa on October 30 and set up Imperial Headquarters at the Château de La Fraineuse, a handsome white-colonnaded villa set in a huge park. The grounds had been beautiful then, but soon the weather had turned cold and foggy. By November 9 the flowers were blackened and rotted by frost and the trees dripped from a cold autumnal rain. The Emperor had come to Spa in order to be with the one force he felt able to rely on—his Army, with its sworn fealty. But he had been pursued by the telephone line from Berlin. On November 9 the phone in the little first-floor office of the aide-de-camp on duty rang incessantly. That morning the Majority Socialists had quit the government of Prince Max and declared their own sponsorship of the general strike. "When will the Kaiser abdicate?" was the frantic question from the remnants of the government in Berlin.

Simultaneously, from Supreme Headquarters at the Hotel Britannique in Spa there came a steady stream of officers to be ushered into the Presence, most notably the ponderous and silent old Field Marshal von Hindenburg and his new First Quartermaster General, Wilhelm Groener.

It is not hard to imagine how the Kaiser was regarded by these officers. The German army on the western front was in its final retreat. Practically the only limit to the speed of the Allied advance was the problem of moving men forward along the shattered roads. The front-line German divisions—what was left of them—were utterly exhausted and on the verge of mutiny. In the *Etappe*, the rear, the troops were completely unreliable. The vast supply dumps which had been established on the east bank of the Rhine had fallen into the hands of rebellious soldiers, as had the bridgehead cities. At any time the rebels could cut off transport, leaving the front without food or ammunition. The only hope was for the armistice to be concluded as quickly as possible—but the armistice delegation was still with Foch in the Forest of Compiègne, and so far nothing had been heard from them at Supreme Headquarters.

By November 9 the burden of having the once hallowed figure of the All Highest in their midst must have become almost unbearable to the officers at Supreme Headquarters. They were shackled to the Kaiser by their oath of obedience, which the German officer corps had always regarded with feudal awe. If they were to be *Kaisertreu*, it was their duty to defend the person and the dynasty of the Emperor even if it meant that Germany and her Army would be destroyed. But if they were to be left with at least a remnant of the Army, and if the officer corps was to survive, they must cast aside their oath.

On the night of November 8 Hindenburg and Groener had finally come to the conclusion that the monarchy was doomed. They were now positive that the Army would not fight for the Emperor. Someone must convince him that he had to abdicate, and only the Army could do this. Prince Max had tried and failed. The Emperor simply would not believe how desperate the situation was. For too many years the courtiers of his personal entourage had conspired to present a happy picture of events. "His Majesty must hear nothing but good news,"[38] was always their caution to visitors. They were as incapable of telling the blunt truth as the Kaiser was of listening to it. So it was up to the Army to put the case for abdication to him.

Hindenburg began by offering his resignation, which the Kaiser refused to accept. The old Field Marshal could not go on; he lapsed into silence, and Groener had to take over. Gradually, in a series of conferences which lasted nearly all day, punctuated by a crescendo of telephone calls from Berlin, the Kaiser was made to understand that the war was truly lost and that the interior of Germany was in rebellion. In little groups the conferences wandered back and forth, from the foggy and depressing garden into the villa, where the Kaiser warmed himself at the fireplace, then out into the garden again as the Kaiser fled Prince Max's pleas to speak with him on the telephone.

Silently Groener and Hindenburg heard out a mad plan proposed by the Emperor's entourage for reconquering the rebellious German cities by sending "picked troops to Verviers, Aix-la-Chapelle and Cologne, all with the most modern equipment, smoke bombs, gas, bombing squadrons and flamethrowers. . . . They would be able to restore order."[39] Hindenburg, numb with misery, would say nothing, but Groener answered flatly that it was impossible. Troops could not be found who would do it. "Sire," he said, "you no longer have an Army." But this the Kaiser would not believe. His courtiers had assured him of the undying loyalty of his soldiers. Crown Prince Wilhelm arrived and, after making his usual unfortunate impression on everyone, assured his father of the Army's support. The emboldened Kaiser challenged Groener to ask the corps commanders for their opinion. "If they tell me the Army is no longer with me I am ready to go," he said, "but not before."

To deal with this, a staff officer, Colonel Heye, was introduced into the conference. Groener was a realist. He no longer trusted the *couleur de rose* reports which reached him from certain of the army-group commanders. Anticipating that he would have to prove his case, he had ordered to Spa some fifty field officers, most of them regimental commanders. Only thirty-nine of them had arrived by that morning, but Groener decided that this number would do. Colonel Heye had then interviewed each of the officers privately and under a pledge of secrecy, had asked him to answer two questions: first, could the Emperor at the head of his troops "reconquer the Fatherland by force of arms"?; second, would the troops "fight the Bolshevists on the home front"?[41]

In a voice a little too loud and perhaps a trifle too harsh, Colonel Heye now read out the results of this poll. Only one officer had given a definite yes to both questions. The remainder either had said that their men would not fight or had given only a qualified or ambiguous answer. To sum up, the troops were "tired and indifferent" and wanted "nothing except rest and peace," Heye reported. "They want only one thing—an armistice at the earliest possible moment."[42]

A silence followed. Then Hindenburg and Groener were asked if this report could possibly be true; had not the troops sworn an oath to the colors and to their Warlord? Hindenburg could not bring himself to answer. He inclined his head and remained mute. Finally it was Groener who said what had to be said and what Hindenburg would not. With an exasperated shrug of his shoulders, he stepped forward and made his historic reply, "Oath to the colors? Warlord? Today these are only words."[43]

It was then about 1:15 P.M. At last the shaken Kaiser agreed to abdicate as German emperor but not as king of Prussia (a patently ridiculous idea, because under the German constitution the King of Prussia was always the German Emperor). He announced that he would sign over to Hindenburg his rights of command over the Army. Aides were set to work drafting a proclamation to this effect, and the Kaiser and his retinue went in for lunch. "After a good lunch and a good cigar, things will look better," the Crown Prince had reassured them. But even this was not to be permitted the Emperor. They had barely sat down when over the telephone came word that Prince Max had already announced Wilhelm's abdication both as emperor and as king of Prussia. It was useless for Wilhelm to shout, "Treason, gentlemen, barefaced, outrageous treason!"[44] and to send aides running for telegraph forms on which to write protests and manifestos. Aides-de-camp ran over to Supreme Headquarters and brought Hindenburg and Groener back to the villa. The distraught Kaiser was obviously not pleased to see them—particularly Groener. "My God, you back already?" he snapped.[45]

The generals told him that the Army no longer controlled Berlin. In fact, they revealed, even the Rohr Battalion which guarded the Kaiser was no longer sound. The Kaiser's aides asked how the safety of the Emperor's person was to be insured. Hindenburg gave the oblique answer that "the course of events could no longer be controlled."[46] The Army could no longer guarantee the Emperor's personal safety, even for the night. Word had just been received that a division which had been thought to be especially reliable and which had been chosen to cover the rear of Supreme Headquarters had now melted away. There were no troops left who could be depended upon to honor their oath. The Emperor was told that he must flee to Holland for refuge.

The last day of imperial Germany began in Berlin late on the night of November 8, when the Majority Socialists learned that the Independents (and especially the Spartacists) had called a general strike for 9 A.M. on November 9. The purpose of the strike was to demand the abdication of the Kaiser and the dissolution of the monarchy. The Majority Socialist leaders met that night and came to the conclusion that they must somehow seize control of this strike. They knew that they could do nothing to prevent it, and they had good reason to suspect that it was the first act of the Bolshevik revolution. The only thing they could do was quit the government and try to represent the general strike as being theirs.

Accordingly, early on November 9 Philipp Scheidemann telephoned the Chancellery and demanded to know whether or not the Kaiser had abdicated. Not yet, he was told by Arnold Wahnschaffe, an undersecretary of state. Scheidemann said he would wait only one more hour—"If he has not gone, then I will go."

An hour later, at precisely 9 A.M., he phoned again. The Kaiser still had not abdicated, Wahnschaffe told him. "I must ask you," Scheidemann said, "to announce my resignation to the Chancellor."[47] And with this the Majority Socialists withdrew their support from the government.

Simultaneously, the government became aware that the general strike had started in earnest. Telephone reports from the police stations and from a few Army outposts told of huge mobs of workers leaving the factories to march on the Chancellery. The strikers carried big placards with the words "Brothers, don't shoot" for display to the troops. Unresisted, a ring of marching men was closing in on the government. Both the police and the Army had deserted the streets. The Jäger regiments would do nothing—even the officers, who, overwhelmed by the size of the crowds and confused by the succession of ambiguous orders from the War Ministry, followed their men back to the barracks. It quickly became evident that this situation was not confined to Berlin. In Hanover the authorities had attempted to use troops against a crowd of strikers, with the result that the troops simply joined the strike. In Cologne the soldiers had hoisted a red flag over their barracks. It was the same in Kassel and Frankfurt-am-Main.

Within the Chancellery in Berlin there was a scene of awful confusion. An informal and incoherent meeting of the remaining members of the Cabinet was in constant session. And in another room Wahnschaffe was on the telephone to Spa. He could not always get through to the aide-de-camp's office at La Fraineuse. There were two telephones there, and the Kaiser's entourage, to shield themselves against the unrelenting pressure, had taken one off the hook and were trying to keep the other constantly in use to avoid calls from Berlin.

The Reich Chancellery was located at the intersection of the Wilhelmstrasse and the Leipziger Strasse—almost the exact center of Berlin. Facing the building on two sides was a broad cobblestone esplanade which, together with the side streets adjoining it, provided a huge plaza for demonstrations. By midmorning it was beginning to fill up with the vanguard of the strikers, shouting slogans and carrying red flags.

It was natural that the telephoned entreaties from Berlin to Spa should take on an increasingly desperate character. Whenever he could get through to La Fraineuse, Wahnschaffe summoned other members of the government to take the phone and describe the situation. There is some evidence that he attempted to stampede the abdication with the false statement "The streets of Berlin are running with blood."[48] In vain he implored the Emperor's staff to summon the Kaiser himself to the telephone so that Prince Max could speak to him. The harried and distraught staff at La Fraineuse began to put Berlin off with evasive assurances like "Events are taking their course" and "The decision is about to be made."[49] Prince Max ordered a draft announcement of the Kaiser's abdication and the Crown Prince's renunciation to be prepared.

Meanwhile the crowds outside the Chancellery grew thicker and louder. All Berlin was obviously on strike. Karl Liebknecht was known to be touring the city in an automobile, speaking to the excited workers. At any moment he or some other Spartacist might arrive to proclaim the revolution. The crowd might even storm the undefended Chancellery; the memory of the attack on the Winter Palace in Petrograd was still fresh in everyone's memory. Max had clung to the hope that the house of Hohenzollern might be preserved in the form of a regency, but now he was ready to settle for anything short of a Bolshevik revolution. He did not know whether or not the Kaiser had already abdicated; if he had not, Max had the impression that he would soon.

At 11:30 A.M., consulting no one, Prince Max gave the draft abdication announcement to an aide for release to the principal German news bureau, the Wolff Telegraph Agency. Within minutes it was known on the streets of Berlin. The announcement said: "The Emperor and King has decided to renounce the throne. The Imperial Chancellor will remain in office until the questions connected with the abdication of the Emperor, the renunciation of the throne of Germany and of Prussia by the Crown Prince, and the setting up of a regency have been settled. . . ."[50]

Max's proclamation was, of course, completely false. The Kaiser was still wandering about the foggy garden at La Fraineuse, explaining to the glum generals his plan for returning to Germany at the head of his troops. In fact, as yet no one at Spa had so much as mentioned abdication to Wilhelm. He did not learn of Max's announcement until some two hours later. Everyone had forgotten poor Wahnschaffe, tied to the telephone in the Chancellery. No one in Berlin was interested in Spa any more.

At noon a delegation of five Majority Socialists made its way through the densely crowded streets and into the Chancellery. It was led by Friedrich Ebert, the forty-seven-year-old head of the Social Democratic Party. Ebert's background was similar to that of the other Majority Socialist leaders. He had risen from the workbench, in his case a saddlemaker's. After being attracted into the Social Democratic Party's organization, he had operated a tavern for a while in order to provide his fellow Socialists with a place to meet. Being a tavernkeeper was difficult for him, because he was not gregarious by nature and, in fact, did not even like to drink. His wife chided him, "As a host you should not look like a vinegar merchant who has to drink his own vinegar."[51]

Ebert had been one of the earliest advocates of a strong paid bureaucracy for the Social Democratic Party, and in 1906 he had been given the post of executive secretary of the Berlin organization. When he took office he found that there were no files, no membership lists, no accounts. His predecessors had all been elderly volunteers who operated in a semiconspiratorial manner which was their legacy from the early days of German socialism; they had burned all their mail as soon as it was read, and they had never kept copies of any letters they sent out. A compulsion toward methodical organization is a trait not unknown among Germans, and in Ebert it was particularly intense. In short order he had his office running like clockwork. The party membership grew enormously, and Fritz Ebert's Berlin organization was copied by Social Democratic offices in every other German city.

Ebert's reputation was therefore that of a highly competent administrator whose honesty was above question. Like most of those who remained with the parent party at the time of the Independent Socialist split-off, he was not particularly interested in social theoretics. He was known for his clear-sightedness and common sense. Prince Max had consulted him frequently within the past few days. It was Ebert, for example, who had suggested Noske as the man to send to Kiel.

Now, as Ebert led the Majority Socialist delegation into the Chancellery, Max knew why he was there: he had come to demand that the government be turned over to him. The Chancellor, in company with several members of his Cabinet, received the Social Democrats in the Reich Chancellery library. All remained standing during the brief interview.

Ebert, in a calm, almost pleasant tone, told the Prince, "For the preservation of peace and order . . . we regard it as indispensable that the office of imperial chancellor and the Brandenburg command be held by members of our party."[52] He went on to say that perhaps a few selected Independent Socialists might also be invited into the new government, although this was not certain. There was, however, no question as to who the new Chancellor must be. It must be Ebert himself.

In an equally pleasant tone, Max asked if the Majority Socialists could guarantee that order would be maintained. The response was that the troops were already on the side of the Socialists. Should the Chancellor care to verify this, the Socialists would be happy to escort him on a quick tour of the barracks. Max declined the offer. He then asked if it was Ebert's intention to summon a constituent assembly to determine Germany's future. Ebert said that it was. After one or two other questions, Max and his followers withdrew to discuss the matter.

There was nothing really to discuss. The crowd around the Chancellery had swollen to a mob swirling about the building in a sort of parade. To a roar of approval, an Army truck mounting a machine gun and a red flag was driving down the Wilhelmstrasse. Merely by looking out the Chancellery windows Max could see that his government was finished. By this time he was anxious only to get out of Berlin and back to Baden. He quickly returned to the library and told Ebert that he was ready to hand the government over. Max had only a few further questions. Was Ebert prepared to assume office "within a monarchial constitution"?

"Yesterday I would have answered yes, absolutely," Ebert answered. "Today I must first consult my friends."

"Now," said Max, "we must solve the question of the regency."

"It's too late for that," responded Ebert, and behind him his friends all chorused, "Too late! Too late!"[53]

With no further promises or formalities, the office of imperial chancellor was simply handed over to Ebert.

It was a day characterized by confusion and haste. While Philipp Scheidemann rushed off to the Reichstag to tell his comrades that there was a new Imperial Chancellor, the occupant of the office conducted a cold and bitter interview with three Independent Socialists, Cohn, Dittmann and Vogtherr. Ebert—whom everyone was addressing as "Chancellor"—offered his enemies a few seats in the new government, but he did it in an imperious manner, with the warning that his offer would hold good for only a few hours. They departed for consultations, and Ebert then left for the Reichstag. He arrived there to find a scene of incredible uproar. Scheidemann, who had preceded him, had stopped in at the restaurant of the Reichstag to have his lunch—a bowl of potato soup. While he was eating, several deputies had come up to tell him that a large crowd had assembled in the *Platz* in front of the Reichstag. Scheidemann had put down his spoon and run upstairs to the Reichstag reading room. Flinging open the French windows, he had leaned out and announced to the crowd that Ebert had taken over as chancellor. Then, to great applause and almost as an afterthought, he had cried, "Long live the great German *Republic!*" Having thus proclaimed a republic, he had returned to his soup.

Ebert, unaware of all this, arrived at the Reichstag soon afterward and sat down at the table with Scheidemann. A few moments later some people came into the room shouting the news of the republic. Ebert's face turned livid. He turned to Scheidemann and asked if this was true. Scheidemann casually allowed that it was. Ebert banged on the table with his fist. He was furious at Scheidemann's presumption. The proclamation of a republic invalidated the existing constitution; Germany was now technically without a government. The accreditations of her Armistice Commission, still waiting in the Forest of Compiègne for Berlin's permission to accept the Allies' terms, were now technically void. The Army, even if its discipline could survive the Kaiser's abdication, no longer had a legal basis. "You have no right to proclaim a republic!" Ebert stormed at Scheidemann. "What Germany is to be—a republic or anything else—is for the Constituent Assembly to decide!"[54] He rushed back to the Chancellery in a rage.

The revolutionary fervor in Berlin had not slackened with the proclamation of a republic or the takeover of the government by Ebert. The far-left organizations sheltered within the Independent Socialists had no intention of letting the revolution stop there. In the late afternoon the center of Berlin was jammed with strikers. One of the few Americans in Berlin, the wife of Prince von Blücher, wrote in her diary:

> *Across the compact masses of the moving crowd big military lorries urged their way, full to overflowing with soldiers and sailors, who waved red flags and uttered ferocious cries. They were evidently trying to excite the strikers to violence. These cars, crowded with young fellows in uniform or mufti, carrying loaded rifles or little red flags, seemed to me characteristic. These young men constantly left their places to force officers or soldiers to tear off their [imperial] badges and took the task upon themselves if they refused. . . . About two hundred of these big lorries must have passed beneath our windows in two hours.*[55]

The soldiers who had not simply given their rifles away were now selling them on the streets for a couple of marks. Even Army trucks and automobiles could be bought from their drivers for a few hundred marks. Whenever the crowds found an Army officer, they tore off his epaulettes and medals.

At about 4 P.M. Liebknecht himself appeared at the Schloss Berlin, where a large crowd had gathered. Most of the palace guard had wandered off; the remainder were standing around looking apathetically at the crowd. No one even attempted to stop Liebknecht as he entered the palace and walked upstairs to the historic corner window from which Wilhelm II had made several famous speeches. A red flag already flew over the Schloss. Made out of a blanket taken from a servant's bedroom, it had been raised an hour ago by a man named Schlesinger, who had implored the crowd not to harm the palace since it was now public property. From the corner window Liebknecht began a passionate harangue to the crowd below: "The day of liberty had dawned. A Hohenzollern will never again stand at this place. . . . I proclaim the free Socialist republic of Germany, which shall comprise all Germans. . . . We extend our hands to them and call on them to complete the world revolution. Those among you who want the world revolution, raise your hands to an oath."[56] There came a great roar of applause and a sea of raised hands. Liebknecht hurried off to another meeting. A few people from the crowd came into the Schloss and began to pilfer small articles from the rooms.

While this was going on, a soldiers' council occupied the Army district barracks, and Emil Eichhorn, a member of the extreme left wing of the Independents and recent telegraph chief at the Soviet Embassy, took over the Berlin police headquarters on the Alexanderplatz. When Eichhorn arrived on the scene, workers were demonstrating outside the building and the besieged police within seemed anxious only to discard their uniforms and disappear. He walked in, announced, "I am the new police president," [57] and was promptly given the job. The demonstrators let into the building, by Eichhorn, went through the cell blocks freeing 650 prisoners who had been arrested in the last few days. In the courtyard they found a heap of pistols, sabers and rifles dropped by the disbanding police.

A little later in the afternoon Liebknecht, backed by a party of armed soldiers, took over the offices of a Conservative newspaper, the *Lokal-Anzeiger*. All the paper's editorial staff were thrown out of the building and a Spartacist group began to print a new newspaper, *Die rote Fahne* (*The Red Flag*). Rosa Luxemburg, who had just been released from prison in Breslau, arrived in Berlin and went straight to the newspaper's offices to take charge.

In only a few spots in Berlin was there any real resistance to the revolution. Here and there a little firing took place and about a dozen people were killed.

Toward evening Prince Max appeared at the Chancellery to say goodbye to Ebert. And it is testimony to the frantic nature of the moment that Ebert, now beginning desperately to reach for support, asked the astonished Max to stay on in Berlin as "administrator" (presumably regent) for the Hohenzollern monarchy. Max refused flatly. The game was obviously over. He said goodbye with the observation "Herr Ebert, I commit the German Empire to your keeping."

Ebert answered, "I have lost two sons for this Empire."[58]

It was late at night. Fritz Ebert was chancellor—but it was a position which was simultaneously illegitimate, ludicrous and frightening. Illegitimate because he had been made chancellor without the sanction of monarch or Reichstag; he had simply been handed the office by its incumbent. Ludicrous because, now that Scheidemann had proclaimed a republic, Ebert was the "Imperial Chancellor" of an empire which had ceased to exist. And frightening because his position was so similar to that of Kerensky exactly one year before. At any moment the Spartacists occupying the Schloss might emulate the Bolsheviks in the Smolny Institute, and Lieb-knecht—or perhaps Barth or Müller or Ledebour—would be the German Lenin. It did not seem that there would be much to stop them. Ebert's "government" could hardly claim to rule over Germany's largest cities. Munich, Hamburg, Cologne, Frankfurt were in full revolution. Not even Berlin could be considered under the government's control. The police had disappeared from the streets, and no one could tell whom the Army and the officer corps would obey—if anyone.

Ebert was alone in the Chancellor's private office on the second floor of the Chancellery pacing the floor, his coat off and his shirt sweat-stained. Suddenly one of the telephones on his desk began to buzz. It bore the number 988. This was not an ordinary telephone; it was a direct wire to the Supreme Command at Spa and had originally been installed to provide instant and totally secret communication between Ludendorff and his Chancellor.[59] So it is almost certain that when it rang in this quiet office Ebert did not know what it was. Nevertheless, he picked up the phone.

"Groener speaking," said the voice of the First Quartermaster General of the Army.

The two men exchanged a few brief amenities. Then Ebert cautiously asked Groener what the Army's intentions were. Groener replied that the Kaiser, who was now asleep in his private train, had decided to go into exile in Holland and had ordered Field Marshal von Hindenburg to take complete charge of the field army. Hindenburg had done so, and he intended to march it back to Germany upon the conclusion of the Armistice. It was evident that the Su-

preme Command did not intend to begin a civil war or an insurrection against the Ebert government. Without actually saying it,
Groener indicated that he and Hindenburg would recognize the
new government as legitimate. They had even given instructions
that the new soldiers' councils were to be dealt with in "a friendly
spirit." Then Groener paused.

There was an awkward silence, which was cautiously broken by
Ebert. "And what do you expect from us?" the Chancellor asked.

"The Field Marshal expects the government to support the officer
corps in maintaining discipline and strict order in the Army. He
expects that the Army's food supplies will be safeguarded and that
any disruption of rail traffic will be prevented."

"What else?"

"The officer corps expects that the imperial government will fight
against Bolshevism and places itself at the disposal of the government for such a purpose."

So great was Ebert's relief that he could only ask Groener to
"convey the thanks of the government to the Field Marshal."[57]

And then the conversation was over. The ultimate compromise
had been secretly concluded.

PART 3

The imperialist capitalist class, as the last offspring of the caste of exploiters, surpasses all its predecessors as far as brutality, open cynicism, and rascality are concerned.

It will defend its "holy of holies," its profits and privileges of exploitation, tooth and nail. . . . It will get its officers to commit massacres. It will attempt to nullify Socialist measures by a hundred and one methods of passive resistance. It will put in the way of the revolution twenty uprisings à la Vendée. To save itself it will invoke the assistance of the foreign enemy, the murderous armed force of a Clemenceau, a Lloyd George or a Wilson. It will sooner turn the country into a smoking heap of ruins than relinquish its power to exploit the working class.

—Die rote Fahne, December 14, 1918

Chapter Eight

"Someone must become the bloodhound"

The evacuation of the German field army from France, Belgium, Luxembourg, Alsace-Lorraine and the German Rhineland in only thirty-one days was a triumph of military organization. In that short time two million men, their supplies, and such weapons as the armistice permitted them to keep were marched back from a front which was 360 miles wide. For, according to the armistice terms, any German troops remaining in the area after one month would be taken prisoner by the advancing Allies.

Hindenburg had violently protested against this provision of the armistice. When the Supreme Command had received word of the Allies' terms he had sent a message beseeching Erzberger to obtain a two-month extension of the time for evacuation—"otherwise the Army will collapse, as the technical execution of the terms is impossible."[1] But the Allies had been adamant. And so, at two o'clock on the morning of November 11, after struggling through a welter of confusing telegrams, the German delegation in the Forest of Compiègne had accepted all of the armistice terms. Even the Allies had been perplexed and concerned at the series of messages, some coded and some *en clair,* which the Germans had received. One of them had been signed "REICHSKANZLER SCHLUSS," and it had been necessary for the Germans to explain that *Schluss* was not the name of a new German political figure but merely the German word for "full stop" at the end of the telegram.

The Supreme Command was now confronted with a military

operation of stupendous complexity. The rear was in chaos, the entire railroad system was nearly worn out, the civilian workers were on strike. The field-army troops were sullen, hungry and totally exhausted. Yet only hours after the armistice went into effect the two million German soldiers on the western front began to move. Every road heading east was suddenly filled with unending gray-clad columns trudging back toward the Rhine. Simultaneously the Supreme Command itself moved from Spa in Belgium to an old hotel in the Hessian city of Kassel, firing out orders as it retreated to its new position.

The field army was no disorganized mob. The troops marched in strict order, perfectly under the control of their officers. The left-hand side of each road was filled with troops and trucks; the right-hand side was reserved for streams of French and Belgian civilians who had been brought to Germany and now had to be repatriated. The German columns did not even stop at night. There were billets assigned for every regiment, and while they were resting other regiments were marching. Even the field army's officers were astounded at the precision of the staff work. "For each of these troops the time is computed, the place is designated where he rests, where he eats, where he sleeps. . . . Never has a human clockwork functioned so ingeniously, so precisely."[2] As the marching troops reached the railheads, some of the regiments were shunted aside to board whatever trains could be scraped together. With a thrill of pride the company-grade officers saw how everything fitted precisely into place. The marching columns swelled as they were joined by rear-echelon troops, then marked time as they waited to funnel across the Rhine bridges, but still everything remained in perfect order. When each marching regiment, after toiling up the last hills before the Rhine, topped the rise and saw the ancient cathedrals of the cities on the eastern bank, the troops gave out hoarse cheers.

Such Allied officers as were able to witness their evacuation were frankly impressed. To the senior American member of the Armistice Control Commission the German field army did not look like a defeated force; the regiments which passed him were in good order, singing, their bands playing. The German retreat was so rapid that Allied advance parties frequently could not make contact with their enemy to accept the various weapons which were to be surrendered under the armistice provisions. When this happened, the Germans simply left the equipment piled in neat stacks along the road.[3]

Doubtless this phenomenal efficiency was due in part to the

perfect weather—there was no rain and no mud—but a major share of the credit must be given to the First Quartermaster General Wilhelm Groener, the expert in military transport and economics, and to the meticulous staff work of the Supreme Command. The war may have been lost, but complicated operations like this were still the specialty of the German General Staff. Everything had been thought of—including a plan for dealing with the soldiers' councils.

On the evening of November 10, when the Supreme Command was still at Spa, a group of seven enlisted men presented themselves at headquarters. They were the "Executive Committee" of the Supreme Headquarters Soldiers' Council. Their demands were somewhat unclear, but obviously they expected to play a role in the command of the Army during its retreat. At the very least they wanted the right to countersign the Supreme Command's orders and to insure that the field army was not used for any counterrevolutionary purpose.

The seven soldiers were courteously received by a Lieutenant Colonel Wilhelm von Faupel, who had been carefully rehearsed for the occasion. Faupel did not fail to play upon the camaraderie which was thought to exist between these soldiers and field-army officers like himself. He invoked the hallowed name of Hindenburg. There could be no question of the officer corps opposing the government—in fact, the Field Marshal had placed himself at the service of the government. Then Faupel led the delegates into the Supreme Command's map room. Everything was laid out on a gigantic map which occupied one wall: the huge complex of roads, railway lines, bridges, switching points, pipelines, command posts and supply dumps—the whole an intricate lace of red, green, blue and black lines converging into narrow bottlenecks at the crucial Rhine bridges.

Faupel pointed to and discussed the details of the map with calculated and easy familiarity. The seven soldiers were stupefied; they had never dreamed of such complexity. Faupel then turned to them. The Supreme Command had no objection to the soldiers' councils, he said, but did his hearers feel competent to direct the general evacuation of the German Army along these lines of communication? Orders had to be issued quickly since any delay—for example, to obtain countersignatures from the soldiers' council—might unhinge the complex operation and reduce the field army to a disorganized mob jammed up against the Rhine. It would be every man for himself, and most of the troops would not be able to escape before the Allies' time limit expired, so they would become prisoners of war. Would the soldiers' council accept the responsibility for this?

The disconcerted soldiers stared uneasily at the immense map. One of them allowed that this was not what they had really had in mind—"This work can well be left to the officers."[4] In the end, the seven soldiers willingly gave the officers their support. More than this, they practically begged the officers to retain command. Faupel even stampeded them into drafting a manifesto calling upon the troops to maintain discipline and obedience. The proclamation was printed immediately at Spa and distributed to the entire field army.

As the November days went by, and as the field army poured to the rear in perfect order, the confidence of the officer corps in itself and its power of command began to return. Whenever a soldiers'-council delegation appeared at Supreme Headquarters, Colonel Faupel was trotted out to repeat his earlier performance; it always worked. The field army had not disintegrated on the departure of the Kaiser, as had been feared. Its loyalty had been transferred smoothly to the aged Hindenburg, who sat in now somnolent splendor behind the protective screen of his staff. As in the past, the Field Marshal did not interfere with the activities of his First Quartermaster General. He had intruded only once. The Supreme Command had gone to Kassel expecting to install itself in the castle at Wilhelmshöhe, but when they arrived Hindenburg announced that the castle was the personal property of Wilhelm II and must not be used without Wilhelm's permission. The Supreme Command was obliged to move into an old and inconvenient hotel.

It is doubtful whether the officers of the Supreme Command even noticed their discomfort. Their minds were concentrated upon the soldiers of the field army. It was observed that the troops, gaunt and tired though they might be, were beginning to render military courtesies with something like the snap and *élan* of a few years before.

True, there were fearful rumors from the cities in the interior of Germany. In Munich, for example, the railroad stations were patrolled by soldiers wearing red cockades who seized arriving officers and ripped the decorations and insignia of rank off their uniforms. Any officer who attempted to resist was badly beaten. Even a few of the advance parties of the field army itself had suffered indignities from the population in cities of the interior. They had been regarded as the advance columns of a counterrevolutionary force, and as these little units paraded along the streets they were insulted, spat upon and sometimes actually attacked by civilians. Berlin was said to be a madhouse. The troops of the garrison were completely out of hand and had virtually ceased to function as a military force. On payday and at mealtime the Berlin barracks were jammed with troops, to whom the government did not dare refuse money and food, but when patrols had to be made up or any other military task assigned there was no one to be found. The officers had practically given up. Within Berlin there were now a half-dozen competing paramilitary organizations. Some were armed civilians, some were mutinous sailors who had fled Kiel, others amounted to little more than organized gangs of thieves, and still others were obviously the nucleus of a Red Guard on the Russian pattern.

The officers of the field army, marching east across the Rhine, made their plans. With their regiments of battle-hardened troops back in Germany, it could be only a matter of days, a few weeks at most, before order had been restored to the cities. They would suppress Bolshevism and disarm the population. The privilege and duty of bearing arms had always been the sole prerogative of the Army. The officer corps intended to recapture its heritage. They foresaw no real difficulties with the ill-armed rabble of the cities. The troops of the field army understood how to clear a street, force a line of defenders, site a machine gun; they were the veterans of a thousand battles in a hundred ruined towns.

On November 25 the first phase of the Army's evacuation was complete: practically every German soldier had returned from France and Belgium. The Supreme Command, emboldened by the success of this operation, now determined to take certain steps which would strengthen its position as the field army moved back within Germany itself. The soldiers' council at Supreme Headquarters had proved so suppliant that Groener decided to convene a "Congress of Soldiers' Councils of the Field Army" on December 1, at Ems, and devised a resolution which he intended to have the soldiers pass. In brief, the resolution called for the suppression of the workers' and soldiers' councils, the dissolution of all armed forces in Germany other than the Army, and firm establishment of the authority of the officer corps.

This congress was a serious miscalculation. Groener's resolution went much too far—as he was warned by Chancellor Ebert. Nearly every night, at some time between eleven and one, Groener spoke with Ebert over the secret telephone line connecting the Chancellor's office with Kassel. Ebert, who had not told any of his associates about these conversations, had gone to great lengths to mollify and support the Supreme Command. He had even sent Hindenburg a message to be passed on to the field army, stating, "The officer's superiority in rank remains . . . The soldiers' councils have an advisory voice in . . . questions of food, leave [and] the infliction of disciplinary punishments, [but] their highest duty is to try to prevent disorder and mutiny."[5] The Congress of Ems and the resolution which Groener intended to force through were another matter. Ebert warned the First Quartermaster General that he was greatly overplaying his hand in this; the soldiers' councils of the field army might appear cooperative, but they were still intensely suspicious.

Disregarding this advice, Groener pushed ahead. He intended to play heavily upon the Army's supposed devotion to Hindenburg. At this point he seems to have believed that the German Revolution was a surface phenomenon, a passing hysteria. He had been told that the red cockades which vendors were selling in the streets of Berlin were only the old wartime Hindenburg cockades. "Hindenburg's face has been painted over red, but the paint comes off quite easily and Hindenburg's face appears once more," a Berlin newspaper reported.[6]

The Congress of Ems opened at the appointed time, and at first everything seemed to go in accordance with the Supreme Command's plans. Speeches were made condemning the excesses of the workers' and soldiers' councils of Berlin. The resolution which the Supreme Command had drafted was introduced and nearly adopted. But then events slipped from Groener's hands. Emil Barth, the influential head of the Revolutionary Shop Stewards, arrived from Berlin and proceeded to make an incendiary speech. Berlin, he said, was not the scene, of wild disorder which the officers had pictured to the men. If they wished to see for themselves, the field-army soldiers were welcome to send a delegation to the capital. Barth went even further: he told them that they were being duped by the officer corps, and he scoffed at their naïveté. The field army, he claimed, was becoming the tool of resurgent monarchism and counterrevolution. Its officers had even denied the men the right to fly the red flag!

The angry soldiers at Ems approved Barth's speech with a roar. Groener's resolution was voted down.

It was a severe setback for the Supreme Command. Their maneuvers exposed, the generals were forced to make certain concessions: they granted the men the right to fly the red flag over billets, and they issued a statement that the soldiers' councils were "the immediate and unquestioned representatives of the will of the people and the vehicle of political power."[7] Nevertheless, the officer corps did not regard the situation as hopeless. The divisions of *Feldtruppen* were still marching across the bridges of the Rhine in good order. The officers still counted on the deep-seated hatred which the front-line veteran was generally thought to bear toward the rear. The diaries of German officers at the time were full of such comments as "Yes, and then we have the rear! The rear lies far, far behind the front and there is plenty of everything there: plenty of comfort, food, conveniences, peace . . . the rear! . . . . Front and rear— between them lies a chasm between action and words!"[8]

By December 5 the return of the field army was so nearly complete that there were nine infantry divisions in the outskirts of Berlin. They had been selected from among the best of the field-army divisions and had entrained at the east bank of the Rhine. Now they were in barracks south, east and west of the capital, in good order. There was no doubt in the minds of the officers that they had plenty of men to handle the operation they had in mind. In addition to these divisions, there were five "centuries" of troops specially trained in street fighting, who had been organized under the direct command of a Major Meyn of the General Staff. There was to be a parade of the returning field army into Berlin, followed immediately by the "disarming of the population," the "elimination of deserters and of unreliable elements in the barracks," and the restoration of the authority of the officers.[9]

But this plan was unacceptable to the Chancellor. When Ebert made his pact with Groener on November 9, he needed the support of the Army desperately. A month later he needed it still more desperately, but there was a line beyond which he was not prepared to go—indeed, beyond which the members of his government and the Berlin workers' and soldiers' councils would not let him go. Ebert trusted the Supreme Command, but only up to a point; the members of his government did not trust the Supreme Command at all. The intentions of the Army were now only too obvious, and, however much Ebert would have welcomed a return to order in the capital, he was not prepared to let loose nine field-army divisions against the Berlin population.

For the first time Ebert demanded obedience from the Army to

the orders of the government. He absolutely forbade the field army
to march on Berlin. Only those regiments which had been raised in
Berlin and which had their home depots in the capital could enter
the city, and even then they were to parade in over a period of days.
The troops could carry arms, but no ammunition. The marching
regiments were to be interspersed with columns of workers. Ebert
promised that the miscellaneous armed organizations in Berlin
would be disarmed, but this, he said, would be done by the civil
government, not by the Army.

These orders, in turn, were unacceptable to the Army. The Supreme Command now played its trump card. Field Marshal von
Hindenburg was shaken out of the stupor into which he had fallen
since the Kaiser's flight to sign a phenomenally condescending letter
to Ebert. "If I address the following lines to you," he wrote, "I do so
because I am informed that you too, as a true German, love your
fatherland above all else. . . . In this spirit I allied myself with you
to rescue our people from the threatening collapse." Hindenburg
went on to demand the abolishment of the workers' and soldiers'
councils, the reinstitution of the salute to officers ("which is a
matter of critical importance"), and recognition that the "appalling" lack of order could be ended only by the Army—"an army in
which the sharpest discipline is kept." He demanded that the
government issue a decree stating clearly that "the power of military
command" was solely the "prerogative of military authorities."[10]

Ebert recognized this for what it was—another attempt by the
Army to restore its dominance over the government. He was willing
to make almost any other concession to the Army, but he could not
give way on this point.

Finally a compromise was reached. The civil government would
supervise the disarmament of the population. In return, most of the
nine field-army divisions outside Berlin would be allowed into the
capital, apparently on the grounds that they had at least some claim
to being Berlin-raised units. The troops were allowed to keep their
ammunition, but were forbidden to bring either tanks or machine
guns into the city. It was a compromise which pleased the Supreme
Command. A tough general named von Lequis had been designated
to command the entry into Berlin, and once the troops were in the
capital much could safely be left to his discretion. In the meantime
the Supreme Command would wait offstage in Kassel. Ignoring the
advice of officers already in Berlin, the Supreme Command issued
secret orders to Lequis that once in the city he was to "act inde-

pendently, even against the orders of the government or of military authorities, including the Minister of War."[11]

The field army began its march into Berlin on the morning of December 11—exactly one month after the signing of the armistice. The period of good weather had ended and the sky was heavily overcast. Along the line of march—Unter den Linden leading to the Brandenburg Gate—there were only modest crowds on the sidewalks. Among them stood groups of sailors belonging to the People's Naval Division, their rifles slung muzzle down in the style which had been the historic trademark of a revolutionary armed force since the Paris Commune.

Leading the marching column of troops were Lequis and his staff, all on horseback, and all wearing their decorations. Their steel helmets were circled with wreaths of oak leaves, a traditional German symbol of courage and loyalty. Behind the officers tramped the regiments of infantry, many of them units of the old imperial guards. But they no longer carried the imperial flags; instead they bore plain brown flags which the Army chose to believe were the temporary banners of the German Republic.

From the sidewalks a faint cheer broke out, but it was only faint. The troops, sensing the indifference of the crowd, stared straight ahead. Despite the fact that their equipment was freshly refurbished, they appeared suddenly old and tired. Only the cavalry contrived to make a brave show. The horses were perfectly groomed and the riders perfectly erect, and the pennons on their lances fluttered and snapped. The kettledrums of the cavalry band filled the streets with sound, temporarily concealing the absence of applause from the watchers. And when the band crashed into "Deutschland über Alles" there was even a burst of cheering from the curb—but not from the armed sailors, who simply stared impassively.

At the Brandenburger Tor the troops were greeted by Ebert with a phrase which he would live to regret: "As you return unvanquished from the field of battle . . ."[12]

For three days Lequis' divisions marched into Berlin. Their reception became increasingly cool, until only the relatives of the Berlin soldiers appeared to welcome them—joined always by the silent clusters of armed sailors, who did not fail to observe the machine guns concealed on carts beneath mounds of oak leaves.

Then, suddenly, the field army evaporated. The troops which

marched into Berlin (and into the various other German cities) went to their assigned barracks, met with the soldiers' councils of the rear and, in a matter of hours, became nothing but a mob of men dressed in field gray. The officers could not believe what had happened—that their cherished field army was a sword which had disintegrated in their hands. Soldiers who were close to their homes did not wait for leave or demobilization, they just walked out of the barracks and went home; there was no one to stop them—certainly not the gaping and helpless officers. Soldiers who were far from home milled around the barracks while their soldiers' councils demanded that the officers provide transportation to their home cities in time for Christmas. There were no more salutes, no more patrols, no cooks, no clerks. The guards at the military stockades walked away—as did their prisoners. In a flash of belated perception, the officer corps realized that the "discipline" which had sustained the field army in its evacuation from France and Belgium was nothing more than recognition by the soldiers that that was the easiest and quickest way to get home.

Any thoughts of using the field army to disarm the population became utterly ridiculous. Instead of the soldiers disarming the civilians, it was the civilians who were disarming the soldiers; the troops were handing over their weapons to anyone who wanted them. When officers in uniform appeared on the city streets they were attacked by old "comrades" of the field army wearing red badges, who ripped off the officers' insignia and tore out of their hands any weapons that they happened to be carrying.

Supreme Headquarters in Kassel was in a panic. At a conference of division commanders it was even proposed that the Supreme Command dissolve itself and that its officers go home to protect their families as best they could. Except for the mutiny-riddled divisions strung out in defense of the eastern frontier, and some remnants of a few other divisions, which had shut themselves up in their barracks, the Imperial Army had disappeared overnight.

In the midst of all this military turmoil, there were similar convulsions within the political embryo which was the German Republic.

The secret mutual-assistance pact that Fritz Ebert made with the officer corps late on November 9—at the end of the day on which the Kaiser's abdication had been announced and the republic proclaimed—was of no help to him as he tried to meet the immediate problems facing him. In squalid procession these tormenting problems paraded themselves before him—the concluding of a treaty of peace, the feeding of a starving nation, Bavarian separatism, White terror and Red Guards. Above all, there was the fact that Liebknecht's Spartacists had become the pivotal force of the German left. Liebknecht had entered into an increasingly close alliance with the left wing of the Independent Socialists and by this means had begun to absorb much of that party into his camp. The People's Naval Division, allied to him, had been formed from sailors who had fled the seaports. They had entered Berlin amid the confusion of November 9 and the days immediately following and had barracked themselves in the Schloss Berlin and the Marstall, the huge stone stables which adjoined the palace. Ebert and his adherents did not want them in Berlin, but there was little they could do about it; the sailors said they had come to "defend the revolution," a theoretically praiseworthy aim, and, moreover, they were well armed and had put their headquarters in a state of defense. Soon there were more than three thousand of them, the largest single armed force in the city. The sailors were ominously sympathetic to Liebknecht, who had given them a warm welcome to Berlin and who appeared frequently at the Schloss to address them.

To be sure, it was not all clear sailing for the Spartacists. When, on November 9, they had occupied the premises of the conservative newspaper *Lokal-Anzeiger* and begun to print their own journal, *Die rote Fahne,* Liebknecht and Luxemburg had at once denounced any compromise with the "bourgeois" Majority Socialists. "The flag of the German Republic," the new journal proclaimed, "is not the black, red and gold flag of the bourgeois republic of 1848, but the red flag of the Commune of 1871 and the Russian revolutions of 1905 and 1917."[13] But it was found that the printers of the *Lokal-Anzeiger* were almost as conservative as their employers—they were not opposed to a bourgeois republic. They refused to put out any more issues of *Die rote Fahne* and demanded that the newspaper be restored to its former owners. A rousing appeal for proletarian solidarity delivered by Rosa Luxemburg failed to have any effect on them, and the Spartacists were forced to search for a week before they could find a printing plant for *Die rote Fahne.*

There were a few other setbacks for the far left, mostly due to the revolutionary euphoria of the first days following the ninth of November. For example, on November 10 the chief burgomaster of Berlin received a scrawled note summoning him and several of his assistants to a meeting. It was signed "Müller, Chief of the War

Food Department." At the appointed hour the bureaucrats arrived, to find that the new "Chief" was an Army private in a worn gray uniform. He proceeded to berate the nervous civil servants, "The Revolution has appointed me to take charge of the Food Department. I'll soon get rid of its rotten disorder." It was not until some time had passed that a Food Ministry official summoned up enough courage to ask Müller who had authorized his appointment. The reply was startling: "My mates at Spandau said I'd better come here and run things." The relieved bureaucrats laughed him out of the building.[14]

Unfortunately for the Majority Socialists, there were not many occasions like this. The left-wing Independent Emil Eichhorn had not relinquished the post of Berlin police president which he had seized on November 9. There was no one to make him do so. Indeed, this was the very heart of Ebert's dilemma. His government had no legitimate authority to compel anyone to do anything. Obviously he could not continue as "imperial chancellor" in a republic. He had not been elected to his office; he had not even been confirmed in it by any sovereign authority. Germany was literally in a state of anarchy. The Independents, the Spartacists, a group of Army officers or any group at all could force their way into the Chancellery and depose or murder Ebert without worrying much about the legitimacy of their coup. Any one person or party in Germany had about as clear a title to the direction of the German Republic as did Fritz Ebert.

For this reason Ebert determined finally to make a bargain with the Independents. He knew that it was ridiculous to appeal to the Reichstag for confirmation of his government. The present Reichstag deputies had been elected to their seats in 1912; many were conservative monarchists whose competence no one was prepared to concede. On the other hand, almost no one in Germany could deny the legitimacy of a coalition of the Majority and the Independent Socialists, if such a coalition could be put together. Moreover, Ebert suspected that it might even be rather advantageous to have the Independents in his government. It was safer to give them a share of the responsibility for what had to be done than to let them attack the government from without.

Early in the evening of November 9 Scheidemann was dispatched to see what terms the Independents would require if they were to enter the government. They gave him a list of six conditions, among them that Germany was to be "a social republic," that members of the bourgeoisie were to be excluded from ministerial posts, and that all governmental authority must derive exclusively from the workers' and soldiers' councils. The Independents also demanded equal representation with the Majority Socialists in the formation of any government. These requirements, at first, seemed too steep to Ebert, particularly the demand that the workers' and soldiers' councils have supreme authority for an indefinite period. This, he pointed out, would amount to a dictatorship of the proletariat, which was "contrary to the democratic principles" of his party.[15]

But, as the night wore on, Ebert had second thoughts. Scheidemann was sent back to the Independents to see whether some sort of compromise could not be worked out. Ebert was even willing to accept Liebknecht as a member of the government in deference to the explosive increase in Spartacus' influence. Scheidemann found that Liebknecht was now sitting in with the inner council of the Independent leadership. In fact, as Scheidemann and the Independents talked on into the night it was Liebknecht who did practically all the speaking. Scheidemann was surprised. It was the first open indication of the rising Spartacist influence among the Independents. What had Liebknecht to do with the Independents? Scheidemann asked. "He is now a member of us," the Independents told him.[16]

Finally, after a session which lasted all night, Scheidemann and the Independents struck a bargain. A six-man "Council of People's Commissioners [*Volksbeauftragte*]" would replace the Imperial Cabinet. These Commissioners would supervise the work of the various secretaries of state who would head the separate government ministries. In deference to the demands of the Independents, all the Commissioners and secretaries of state would be Socialists. The only exceptions permitted were the secretaries of those ministries where special technical knowledge was required, such as the Ministry of War and the Ministry of the Navy, and in these cases their orders were to be countersigned by two Socialists, one a Majority Socialist, the other an Independent. The six Commissioners were to be selected on the basis of equal representation from the Majority Socialists (Ebert, Landsberg and Scheidemann) and the Independents (Haase, Dittmann and Barth). It was agreed that they were all to be equals in rank and authority. This was a big concession on the part of Ebert, whose party was far larger than the

Independents'. But Liebknecht did not agree at all; he demanded that the government be completely turned over to the Independents, and he flatly refused to become a Commissioner in a mixed government. Making no attempt to hide his disgust with his Independent allies, he left the meeting. ("I was urged to compromise," he reported to his Spartacists, "but I refused to make any concession."[17]) The meeting closed with the final agreement that the Commissioners would draw their authority from the workers' and soldiers' councils. There was not enough time to convene a nationwide assembly of delegates, so it was agreed that for the time being the Berlin workers' and soldiers' councils would represent the nation.

Early on the morning of Sunday, November 10, instructions went out to the Berlin proletariat. At 10 A.M. they were to meet in their factories or barracks to select representatives on the basis of one for every thousand workers or one per battalion of soldiers. By five that afternoon three thousand delegates were assembled in the Zirkus Busch, a huge hall which housed a famous circus. The meeting was long and rather disorderly. It began on a radical note, with the delegates voting to "send the Russian Workmen's and Soldiers' government . . . fraternal greetings," to proclaim their conviction that a revolution of proletarians was "being prepared throughout the world,"[18] and to demand the immediate socialization of German industry. Then events began to take a more satisfactory turn for Ebert and his Majority Socialists. The proposed Majority-Independent coalition of the six People's Commissioners was discussed, and, despite angry protests from left-wing radicals, it was ratified by acclamation. Liebknecht, Haase and Ebert had all spoken, and it was apparent that Ebert's call for Socialist "unity" had been far better received than Liebknecht's attack on Ebert for obstructing the revolution. For the present the subtleties of the Spartacist's dialectic seemed obscure to the worker and soldier delegates, and Ebert, playing his hand cleverly, contrived to push Liebknecht into the role of a niggling theoretician.

In the end, the Zirkus Busch delegates elected a twenty-eight-member "Executive Council [*Vollzugsrat*] of the Berlin Workers' and Soldiers' Councils." The membership of the *Vollzugsrat*, which declared itself the sovereign representative of the German people, was divided equally between workers and soldiers, and almost equally between Majority and Independent Socialists. Neither Karl Liebknecht nor Rosa Luxemburg nor any other Spartacist was elected to it, but its members did include a number of Independents, like Richard Müller and Emil Barth, who were closely allied to the Spartacists by doctrine.

Ultimate power was now nominally in the hands of the Berlin *Vollzugsrat*. This council, however, recognized the obviously legitimate demands of the rest of Germany to representation in governmental affairs and was about to call a National Congress of Workers' and Soldiers' Councils. In the meantime the *Vollzugsrat* had confirmed the "provisional government" consisting of the six Commissioners, with Ebert as chairman and the Independent Socialist Hugo Haase as vice-chairman. It was this provisional government which was, in practice, conducting the nation's affairs.

Politically, the situation in Berlin was somewhat more complex. Ebert and the other two Majority Socialist Commissioners, although careful always to pay lip service to the idea of a worldwide proletarian revolution, were in fact terrified of the prospect. Their view of the German Revolution was that it was complete—it had cleared the way for widespread social reforms and the establishment of a parliamentary and truly democratic political system. Unlike the Independents, the Majority Socialists saw no need for more revolutionary activity. The democratic system they proposed to establish, in which the rights of all classes would be protected, would be dominated by the workers in the natural course of events, because of the weight of their numbers. As for the socialization of German industry, they did not believe that it could be accomplished immediately or that it would be desirable to attempt it. With all that must be done within the next few years, the imposition of widespread economic nationalization would, they felt, only invite disaster.

The Majority Socialists completely repudiated Lenin's doctrine of the dictatorship of the proletariat, which they considered morally untenable. They regarded the Russian Bolshevik Revolution, with its terrorism and its suppression of contending strains of Socialist thought, as a depraved and Asiatic form of Marxism. They could not believe that it was anything more than a stupendous historical accident that had taken place in a backward nation, and they did not for a minute believe that the Lenin government would be able to maintain itself. A revolution on the Bolshevik pattern, they felt, would be an invitation to swift counterrevolution and certain disaster.

From the very beginning, the relations of revolutionary Germany with revolutionary Russia had posed an awful problem to the

Majority Socialists. On November 9, as soon as the news of the German Revolution had arrived in Moscow, Lenin had dispatched the Polish Bolshevik Karl Radek to the German Embassy to telegraph over the embassy's direct line to Berlin an offer of two carloads of Russian wheat for the German people, as a gesture of international Socialist solidarity. Almost immediately an answer from Ebert had gone back over the wires: "Knowing that there is famine in Russia, we request the bread you wish to contribute to the German Revolution be given to the starving in Russia . . ."[19] This German refusal had been fraught with meaning for the Bolsheviks. "Judas Iscariot has completed his betrayal," Radek snorted.[20]

Soviet Russia wasted no further time on the Majority Socialists or even on the Independents. On November 11 the Russians broadcast a radio message urging the German people to continue the revolution and establish a government of workers' councils under Liebknecht. A few weeks later Adolf Yoffe revealed publicly the details of his interrupted embassy in Berlin and told of having given money to the Independents to fund the revolution. The Independent Socialist Commissioners were furious at this embarrassing admission, which, of course, made them appear like foreign agents. They issued a categorical denial of Yoffe's allegation—a denial which the Majority Socialists accepted with tongue in cheek.

Although the Russians did not expect very much of the Majority Socialists, they did expect that, at the very least, Yoffe would be permitted to return to Berlin. They sent him back to Germany as part of a delegation of five senior Bolshevik officials—the others were Bukharin, Rakovsky, Ignatov and Radek—who were to be Moscow's self-invited representatives at the National Congress of German Workers' and Soldiers' Councils. Over the violent opposition of Emil Barth, the *Vollzugsrat* sent a message to the Bolsheviks that their delegation "would do well to cancel its trip in view of the German situation," and that entry was not granted.[22] The Russian delegation came anyhow. At the frontier it was stopped by German troops who—in the words of the Russians—"pointed a machine gun at our delegation, compelled it to turn back and in the most undignified conditions conducted it back across the demarcation line."[22] One of the Bolsheviks, Karl Radek, refused to accept this rejection as final. Disguised as a wounded German who had been a prisoner of war in Russia, he attached himself to a little group of authentic prisoners being repatriated° and in short order found himself in Berlin. Because of the political situation in the capital, the Majority Socialists could no nothing about it.

The picture one gets of Ebert and his followers in this period is a depressing one. These were not triumphant warriors exulting in the success of their cause. Their victory offered them no happiness— only a wide range of unpleasant possibilities. A close friend of Ebert's was once asked, "Did not Ebert and Scheidemann experience a secret pleasure on this day [November 9] at the outbreak of the revolution?" "Oh, no," was the answer, "not at all. They were seized with deathly fear."[23]

If these Majority Socialists seem to have lacked color, fire and inspiration, it is because they were anxious and tormented personalities, oppressed with a sense of responsibility. One cannot avoid the suspicion that almost the last thing they wanted was to actually run the government of Germany. A lifetime in the Socialist movement had conditioned them only for a role of opposition. They had been neither trained nor emotionally prepared for a Socialist victory; in truth, they had not really expected that it would come in their lifetime. Then they had pushed at the imperial edifice—given it only a slight shove, really—and found it more rotted and fragile than they had ever dreamed. Now they had the power, and it astounded and frightened them. It had come too soon.

During the first few days following November 9, the six Commissioners enacted sweeping social legislation which only a few months before had been utopian dreams to them. They passed laws establishing the eight-hour day and guaranteeing the unrestricted right of labor to organize into unions; they increased workers' old-age, sick and unemployment benefits; they abolished censorship of the press; and they released all prisoners convicted of political crimes during the war. Then the imaginations of the Majority Socialists suddenly ran out. After the first heady days, they found themselves faced with the sort of task they did not like and did not really want to do: running a government bureaucracy, handling foreign affairs, making peace with the Allies. One almost gets the impression that if Ebert and his friends had been able to find someone else to govern Germany, they would have been secretly delighted to step down.

° Among the group was Ernst Reuter-Friesland, who after World War II, as Ernst Reuter, was to become the first mayor of West Berlin.

Indeed, they regarded themselves as a sort of interim government pending the convening of a constituent assembly and the holding of general elections. In the meantime they would not give Germany back to the monarchists, and they were grimly determined never to turn it over to the only other force prepared to wield power, a coalition of the Independents and Liebknecht's Spartacists.

The Spartacists were confident that the true German Revolution had not yet taken place—or, if it had, that it was only in its beginning stages. The nation was still in its "Kerensky period." Fundamentally the Spartacists were Leninist in their conception of revolution and socialism, although the Spartacists' chief theoretician, Rosa Luxemburg, differed from Lenin in that she denied the right of any one small group of conspirators to seize all power in the name of the revolution. Luxemburg believed that the masses must be educated to the point where a majority of the proletariat would take part in the making of the revolution; the whole basis of Socialism was a belief in the workers' class instinct and in their capacity to understand their revolutionary mission. She was skeptical of the theoretical correctness of what Lenin had done in Russia, and she made no secret of it. "The Spartacist League is not a party which wants to come to power over the heads of or by means of the toiling masses," Luxemburg claimed in the pages of *Die rote Fahne*. "The Spartacus League is only the most determined segment of the proletariat . . . and will never assume the power of government unless it be by the clear, unequivocal will of the vast majority of the proletarian masses throughout Germany."[24]

But this was only Rosa Luxemburg's view. Most of the Spartacists, Liebknecht in particular, were impatient activists. They saw a perfect parallel between their present situation and the position of the Bolsheviks in Russia shortly after the March, 1917, revolution which had resulted in the Czar's abdication and brought the liberal Kerensky to power. The Leninists too had been regarded as no more than a tiny gang of extremists, but they had persevered, agitating ceaselessly, provoking strikes, riots and demonstrations, until, in the October Revolution, they had prevailed.

Because the Spartacists' program in the following weeks is difficult to follow, it is important to understand that their aim was the dissolution of the German nation in order that they might take power and rebuild it. This being their objective, it was clearly the duty of the Spartacists to accept an alliance with any group or faction which could help them create chaos and hasten the disintegration. The Spartacists fully recognized that their party was small and that if a German election were to be held at that time (November, 1918) Ebert and his friends would almost certainly win a majority. But the Russian Bolsheviks had been few in number, too, and they had conquered. So the Spartacists studied what they believed had been the lessons of the Russian Revolution and began to put their studies to use.

Each day they would shake Berlin with a new crisis, and every crisis not of their making would be made to serve the Spartacist cause. The political and economic crisis in which Germany now found herself would be worsened until calamity followed catastrophe in seemingly endless succession, buffeting the sham-Socialist government and displaying to the proletariat the total incompetence of Ebert and his friends. Strikes, famine, armed bands in the streets and encouragement of outright anarchy were all necessary weapons in the fight. The workers must be torn from their factories, led into the streets, sent to neighboring workshops to persuade other workers to put down their tools. Thus in a growing torrent the proletariat would push through the city, sweeping aside all obstacles, seizing public buildings for continuous revolutionary meetings with a shifting audience. Agitators would be dispatched to the barracks and to the meetings of opposition parties, whose membership they would win over to the revolution. Arms would be distributed to the workers, and finally a general strike would be proclaimed. Then, when Germany was racked with civil war, the climate would be right and the Spartacists would take over.

Between the Majority Socialists and the Spartacists were the Independents, who were torn now one way and now the other. They had never been a particularly cohesive group anyhow. The principal *raison d'être* of the party had been opposition to the war; now that the war had ended, the party was beginning to crumble into little bands, some of them tending to re-ally themselves with their old Majority Socialist comrades, others—the left wing of the Independents—leaning abruptly toward the Spartacists. Some of the left-wingers, such as Emil Barth, one of the six People's Commissioners, and Emil Eichhorn, the new police president of Berlin, seemed more Leninist than Liebknecht. "Our party presented a grotesque appearance," was the way one of its most prominent members, Karl Kautsky, later described the situation. "Its right wing was in the government and its left wing worked for the downfall of that very government. . . . What kept it together was only a common hatred of the Majority Socialists which had been inherited from war-time."[25]

If anything more was needed to confuse the political scene, it was provided by the astounding collapse of almost all the parties to the right of the Majority Socialists. All of them, in particular the old Conservative Party and the German Reich Party, were contaminated to a greater or lesser degree by their prewar chauvinism and monarchism. The end of the war and the flight of the Kaiser had left their plans and reputations in tatters. In these early weeks following November 9, they were completely crushed. The old Reichstag, most of whose deputies were of the right, made a couple of half-hearted attempts to reconvene, but gave up when Ebert told them bluntly that the government regarded the Reichstag as having lost the confidence of the people. The right-wing parties raised no outcry at being wholly excluded from the government, nor did they have a program for combating the Socialists. (As yet they had not thought of the "stab in the back" as an excuse for Germany's losing the war.)

The great Junker landowners of East Prussia, once immensely powerful, now found that their formerly docile Lutheran peasantry was sullen and restive. The great industrialists were frantically making concessions to their employees, half expecting that almost any day a workers' committee would walk into their offices to announce that henceforth the factories belonged to the people.

The abdication of Wilhelm II had been a terrible blow to the German parties of the old right and center. Although in their hearts his subjects had always known that the Emperor was vain and bombastic, no one had ever thought him lacking in courage. His flight to Holland had ruined even this last shred of his reputation. It was now common knowledge that on the day before his flight he had been urged to go to the front to seek a hero's death in the trenches and had refused, with the excuse that this sort of semi-suicide was incompatible with his position as titular head of the Lutheran Church in Germany. When, on November 28, he signed his formal abdication in his Dutch exile, the debacle of the right was complete.

For the time being the various non-Socialist parties presented a ludicrous and impotent spectacle as they tried to unstick themselves from the flypaper of their old imperial loyalty. A few of the particularly able centrist politicians, such as Gustav Stresemann and Matthias Erzberger, found an opportunity to be of some service to the government. The rest of the politicians and their parties were reduced to searching for party names which would be more palatable to the electorate in the present climate; the Conservatives renamed themselves the "German National People's Party," the Catholic Center Party changed to the "Christian People's Party." But at this moment few people believed in them or in their glum and perfunctory professions of loyalty to the Republic.

The day-to-day governing of Germany was entirely in the hands of the six Socialist Commissioners. It was not a very effective government. Though Ebert bore the title of chairman, it was mostly an honorific. With the Majority Socialists and the Independents evenly split, the government was almost immobilized by any dispute. The only work that could be accomplished without difficulty was the enactment of the social legislation upon which the two parties agreed, but after this the meetings of the six Commissioners degenerated into a series of endless wrangles. Neither Socialist faction trusted the other, and every decree, message or announcement was subject to the most suspicious inspection by the other side. The Majority Socialists feared that the Independents were betraying the government to the Spartacists; the Independents suspected the Majority of secret agreements with the capitalists and the Army. Each faction was busily engaged in secretly opening the other's mail, monitoring its phone conversations and checking up on the visitors to its offices.

This hostility played into the hands of Liebknecht's Spartacists. Throughout November they seized every opportunity to harass the government and foment civil war. Out of the sixty thousand or so soldiers wandering about Berlin in mid-November Liebknecht created a "Council of Deserters, Stragglers and Furloughed Soldiers," which began to serve as a sort of Spartacist shock force. From time to time the armed sailors of the People's Naval Division would sortie out of their strongholds in the palace and the adjoining stables to commandeer food supplies and haul them off in captured automobiles or trucks flying the red flag. Any shop sign which bore the words *kaiserlich* (imperial) or *königlich* (royal) was sure to be ripped down.

On November 21 Liebknecht harangued a Berlin crowd with the claim that the government was arresting Spartacist revolutionaries and throwing them into prison. Then, collecting an excited mob of soldiers and accompanied by a unit of the People's Naval Division, he marched on the Berlin police headquarters—an unusual destination inasmuch as Liebknecht's supporter Emil Eichhorn was the police president. The march was stopped by a truckload of soldiers dispatched by Otto Wels, the Majority Socialist military governor of Berlin. There was some firing, and a few people were killed on each side—giving Liebknecht the opportunity to make a funeral oration in which he accused the government of counterrevolutionary and White-Guardist activity.

On another occasion the Spartacists shepherded hundreds of school-age youths in a march on the Prussian Landtag building, where the *Vollzugsrat* of the Berlin workers' and soldiers' councils was in session. The children marched into the hall bearing red flags, and a seventeen-year-old boy delivered a speech which contained a series of demands: the vote for all persons eighteen years old, the abolition of corporal punishment in schools, and the immediate removal of Ebert and Scheidemann from the government. Unless these demands were met, he threatened there would be a general strike of German youth. Meanwhile strange rumors, stimulated by the Spartacists, spread through Berlin. It was claimed that Marshal Foch had been assassinated, that the French Army had mutinied and was now flying the red flag, that the President of the French Republic had fled Paris.

This type of Spartacist activity was all carried on under Liebknecht's direction. While Rosa Luxemburg edited *Die rote Fahne* and handled most of the problems connected with theory and dogma, and while Leo Jogiches dealt with the Spartacus Union's day-to-day organizational problems, Liebknecht supervised agitation. He was absolutely tireless at it. He seemed to appear at every barracks, seemed to be leading every strike and every one of the endless Spartacist marches, protests and demonstrations. This was his element. Liebknecht was a poor organizer and had a careless contempt for routine matters, but when it came to agitation in the streets he was a virtuoso performer. He had an innate sense which told him when a crowd had been talked to long enough and when it was ready to march. As an ex-soldier and a former political prisoner, he was always sure of an eager audience in the various barracks of the Berlin garrison. Liebknecht's only problem in this regard was that his demonstrations tended to get out of hand. He was so effective at whipping up the enthusiasm of crowds that when he was through they would not disperse and frequently became uncontrollable. This worried some of the Spartacist leaders, most notably Rosa Luxemburg, who feared that it might lead to excesses for which the proletariat was not ready.

But none of their differences prevented the Spartacists from taking quick advantage of any opportunity which presented itself. They were soon handed a particularly choice occasion. The bureaucracy of the German government was still largely staffed with civil servants who had been trained and appointed in the years of the Hohenzollern Empire. These functionaries were generally conservative in outlook. The six Commissioners knew this, but were helpless to do much about it. There were few qualified persons in the Socialist factions who could be appointed to take the place of the trained officials, and Ebert and his Majority Socialists did not feel that the time was right for wholesale dismissals even if replacements had been available.

On the evening of December 6, three of these officials who occupied positions in the Foreign Office, a certain Count Matuschka and two subordinates named von Rheinbaden and von Stumm, attempted a *coup d'état,* the object of which was to eliminate all Independent Socialist influences from the government. Scraping together several hundred soldiers from the various Army barracks, they marched them to the square outside the Chancellery and proclaimed the stupefied Ebert to be Germany's "President"—in effect, her dictator. Ebert lost his presence of mind, mumbled something about "consulting his friends"[26] and retreated to his office. A little earlier a group of about thirty soldiers invaded the Prussian Landtag building and placed the *Vollzugsrat* of the Berlin workers' and soldiers' councils under arrest. At the same time, and possibly quite by coincidence, another group of soldiers took over the offices of *Die rote Fahne,* while others fired upon a Spartacist demonstration in north Berlin, killing sixteen and wounding twelve.

It is hard to imagine how the rightists in the Foreign Office could have placed Ebert in a more dangerous position. Their counterrevolutionary *Putsch* in favor of the Majority Socialists drove the Independents into the arms of the Spartacists and gave Liebknecht's followers the excuse they needed to arm themselves. Ebert attempted desperately to disentangle himself from the *Putsch.* He refused the proffered title of "President," ordered the *Rote Fahne* offices cleared of counterrevolutionary troops, and freed the *Vollzugsrat;* the rightist leaders of the attempted coup fled the country. But no matter what he did, Ebert could not erase the widespread impression that the Majority Socialists had actually stimulated the coup and had deserted when it failed to gain popular support.

Liebknecht called a protest meeting in the Siegesallee for December 7, and the response was tremendous. With a ring of trucks, each mounting a machine gun, guarding the meeting, Liebknecht demanded the ouster of Ebert, Scheidemann and Otto Wels. On the evening of the following day, a Sunday, he appeared before the Chancellery with an enormous crowd of followers that jammed the Wilhelmplatz. Many of the Spartacists were armed. Standing on the top of an automobile, Liebknecht whipped the crowd to a frenzy with references to the workers and soldiers killed on December 6. Within the building, the lights of which had been prudently extinguished, the six Commissioners stood in darkness and silence, watching the scene below. They saw Liebknecht point at the Chancellery and shout, "There they sit, the traitors, the *Scheidemänner,* the social patriots. We have shown that we have the power to take the whole nest of them, but I demand for tonight only the cry 'Long live the social revolution! Long live the world revolution!'"[27] The apprehensive Commissioners, feeling that they could not permit this attack to go unopposed, sent out onto a balcony their most left-wing colleague, the Independent Emil Barth. He had been regarded as so far to the left that he was practically a Spartacist, but now he was hissed and hooted down by the crowd. The Independents among the Commissioners stirred uneasily. It was apparent that they had been tarred with the Ebert brush. They now began to wonder whether they should ever have entered his government.

In the following days the left wing of the Independents began a wholesale desertion to the Spartacist camp.

It was at this point that the field army returned to Germany and the Supreme Command demanded entry to the capital.

The situation was parlous in the extreme. Ingenious though Ebert and his Majority Socialists might be at political infighting, their government could not claim to control the streets of Berlin, much less those of Munich or of Hamburg, Halle, Düsseldorf, Dortmund and Schwerin, all of which had been the scenes of intensive Spartacist rioting in the last few days. The People's Naval Division in the Marstall had flatly refused the government's order to either disband or reduce its forces. In theory, this group should have responded to the government's commands. Shortly after the armistice, when the police had deserted and the Imperial Army garrison had practically disappeared the government had announced the formation of a fourteen-battalion "Republican Soldiers' Army" (Republikanische Soldatenwehr). There had not been an overabundance of volunteers, and Otto Wels, the military governor of Berlin, had been obliged to use whatever he could get. This "army" was sketchily disciplined and shabbily uniformed, and it scarcely constituted an imposing military force. Wearing red armbands, the troops stood guard around the public buildings and patrolled the streets in a cautious manner. Not only were they ineffectual, but a number of the battalions were so heavily infiltrated with left-wing Independents and Spartacists that they were also unreliable. To augment the fourteen authorized battalions, the three-thousand-man People's Naval Division had announced that henceforth it would consider itself the fifteenth battalion of the Republikanische Soldatenwehr.

It turned out to be a very different kind of battalion. The sailors did not trouble to ask for orders from Wels or to perform such duties as he chose to give them. They did not even bother to ask for supplies; they just sallied forth from the Schloss and the Marstall to take whatever they needed. One of their former leaders had admitted, "My men are an organized band of robbers."[28] The sailors were so heavily armed and under such vigorous leadership that they were beyond persuasion or control. The government, recognizing this, had entered into an agreement which was actually little more than a bribe for good behavior. They had appointed the People's Naval Division the "guards" for the palace and the stables, and had promised to pay the sailors for this service. But even this had not weaned the sailors away from the Spartacists.

The miscellany of armed forces in Berlin did not end with Wels's Republikanische Soldatenwehr or the People's Naval Division. Emil Eichhorn, the Independent police president, had created his own military force. It was called the Sicherheitswehr (Security Force), and it enlisted Spartacists and Independents almost exclusively. To counter this, a group of Majority Socialists was trying to put together its own little army, the Republikanische Schutztruppe, whose members wore red-and-black armbands and had their headquarters in a Berlin high school. And roaming about the streets were little groups from the Imperial Army, some monarchist, some calling themselves "Red Guards," some little more than armed looters.

On December 16 the National Congress of Workers' and Soldiers' Councils began in Berlin. Its purpose was to transfer sovereignty

over Germany to a national group, as distinguished from the collection of Berlin workers' and soldiers' councils which had met at the
Zirkus Busch on November 10.

The bulk of the delegates, nearly three hundred out of 488, were
Majority Socialists—as was to be expected, for the organizational
superiority of the Majority's political apparatus was unquestioned.
Using their voting preponderance like a blunt weapon, the Majority
Socialists forced through the congress a crucial resolution calling for
a general election, on January 19, of delegates to a National Assembly which would draft a constitution and, while doing so, would
conduct the affairs of the German Republic.

To Ebert and his Majority Socialists, the forthcoming general
election and the resulting National Assembly were the goal toward
which every political effort was now bent. If they could survive
until the Assembly had done its work, all might yet be saved. There
would be a legitimate Republic with a constitution and a parliament, and with an Army pledged to defend it. Conversely, it became
the major objective of the Spartacists to prevent the election and the
convening of a constituent assembly. They foresaw very clearly that
a successful election would anchor the Ebert government to the
bedrock of the German bourgeoisie, and the prospect stirred them
to a frenzy of agitation.

They attempted to break up the National Congress of Workers'
and Soldiers' Councils, which, they said, the Majority Socialist
machine had fraudulently packed with its own members ("Ebert's
Mamelukes," *Die rote Fahne* called them[29]), and which therefore
did not truly represent the thinking of the workers' and soldiers'
councils. For the five disheveled days (December 16–20) that the
congress met, Liebknecht and his followers turned it into a bedlam.
Some seven thousand Spartacists gathered outside the Prussian
Landtag building, where the sessions were held, and the noise of
their catcalls and hoots could clearly be heard inside. From time to
time Spartacists burst into the meeting, shouted slogans, exhortations and threats, then dashed out the exits. Others paraded up and
down the aisles carrying placards. When it was discovered that
there were thirteen former Army officers among the congress delegates, the Spartacists in the spectators' gallery kept up steady shouts
of *"Raus die Offiziere!* Out with the officers!"[30] No sooner had the
chairman hammered the meeting back to order than groups of
armed sailors of the People's Naval Division charged into the hall.
They had daubed their faces with mud, and the effect was as start-

ling as they could have wished. Waving their rifles, they demanded that a true Red Guard be formed immediately, that plans for the National Assembly be abandoned, and that the system of government by the workers' and soldiers' councils be perpetuated. They succeeded in intimidating the congress delegates to such an extent that the meeting was suspended for a day.

As a result of the agitation, a few vital matters at the congress went the Spartacists' way: Ebert was violently attacked by the Independent Socialist Georg Ledebour, and a multipoint resolution regarding the Army, introduced by an Independent delegate from Hamburg, was passed. This resolution, which became known as "the Hamburg Points," triggered a very serious situation. It called for the abolition of all insignia of rank, for the election of all officers by vote of the soldiers, for matters of discipline and punishment to be handled by the soldiers' councils, and for the speedy replacement of the regular Army by a new "People's Army" (Volkswehr). The Hamburg Points put Ebert in an intensely awkward position. He dared not openly oppose the resolution, but he was well aware of how Groener and Hindenburg would regard it—and Ebert still needed their support; in fact, he needed it more than ever, because on the last day of the congress the Independent Socialists walked out in protest against the dominance of the Majority. Despite the fact that the old Imperial Army had almost evaporated, the influence of the Supreme Command and the officer corps was still a force. In the days to come it might provide just enough weight to tip the scales against the Spartacist coup which Ebert knew would soon be launched. But the Hamburg Points, if enforced, would mean the end of the officer corps.

Over the secret telephone line Ebert tried to assure Groener that the government would delay implementation of the resolution, but he found the Supreme Command intransigent on this matter. Groener telegraphed all his division commanders to disregard the Hamburg Points, and Hindenburg made the flat statement "I do not recognize the resolution of the Congress . . . I shall oppose it by every means in my power. . . . I shall not allow my epaulettes to be taken from me." When Ebert pleaded with Groener to understand the position in which the government had been placed, the First Quartermaster General snapped back, "It is not we who began the quarrel, and it is not our business to end it."[31]

On December 20 Groener traveled to Berlin to bring the matter to a head before the six Commissioners. He was accompanied by the

Supreme Command's political expert, Major Kurt von Schleicher. The two officers arrived in Berlin wearing full-dress uniform—heavy epaulettes, the claret trouser stripes of the General Staff, crimson overcoat lapels and all their medals. Emboldened by the fact that they had made their way across Berlin without being attacked, the officers stated their case plainly. The Hamburg Points were completely unacceptable. Groener said flat out, "My task is difficult enough—it is the hardest with which I have ever been faced. If you complicate it by nonsense of this sort, I must say that this is the end!"[32]

Ebert attempted to placate the First Quartermaster General. He said that of course "the Army must be given a certain amount of leeway" in the matter and that surely the Hamburg Points did not apply to the field army.[33] The Independent Socialist Commissioners objected violently. Barth wanted to arrest the two officers on the spot.[34] Finally Ebert succeeded in sweeping the matter under the carpet by stating positively that the resolution did not apply to the field army. Everyone present knew what that meant. The Supreme Command was obviously free to designate every unit in the Army to be a part of the field army. The Hamburg Points would never be carried out.

The Independents were infuriated at this. Barth shouted, "The congress reached a very definite decision yesterday, and now you are planning to throw it overboard!"[35] Wilhelm Dittmann warned Ebert, "If the Central Committee° agrees to General Groener's proposals, it will sign its own death warrant, and so will the government. The workers' and soldiers' councils will not tolerate it that the Central Committee should go back upon [its] most important decisions."[36] The two flung themselves out of the room and began a rapid tour of the various Berlin workers' and soldiers' councils, to each of which they told the same simple story: Ebert had betrayed the revolution to the officer corps.

Within forty-eight hours Berlin was in arms. On December 23 the People's Naval Division marched against the government.

This development was the outgrowth of a series of weird and

° The National Congress of Workers' and Soldiers' Councils had established a Central Committee (Zentralrat) to replace the earlier Vollzugsrat in its duties of review and general supervision of the government. The Independent Socialists eventually decided not to participate in the Central Committee, and, as a result, all its members were Majority Socialists.

complex events. On December 13 the government had given a bribe of 125,000 marks to the sailors under the pretext that it was payment for their services in guarding the Schloss. In return for this, it had been agreed, the People's Naval Division would move out of the palace and into the Marstall, and its "commanders," two sailors named Dorrenbach and Radtke, would reduce their force to six hundred men, which was about the size of the other battalions of the Republikanische Soldatenwehr.

On December 20 the government was informed that the sailors had spent the 125,000 marks and now wanted an additional eighty thousand marks as a "Christmas bonus." They had not yet cleared the Schloss, nor had the division been reduced to six hundred men. The government agreed to the supplementary payment, but said that it would not turn over the money until the palace was evacuated and the keys were given to Otto Wels.

On the morning of December 23 a delegation of sailors appeared at the Chancellery, carrying the keys to the palace in a leather key case. They told Hugo Haase, one of the Independent Commissioners, that they would not deal with the Majority Socialist Wels. Haase, who was leaving the building, told them that he was sure it would be all right if they turned the keys over to any of the Commissioners. He suggested Emil Barth. Barth was in conference, but sent word out to the sailors to take them to Ebert. But Ebert had gone out for lunch.

At this point another group of sailors appeared in Wels's office and demanded the eighty thousand marks. Wels refused to give up the money unless he was given the keys. The sailors told him to call Emil Barth, who said that he had not seen the keys, but was sure they were somewhere in the Chancellery. This was not good enough, Wels said, whereupon the enraged sailors tore apart his office and took him and two of his subordinates back to the palace— which, it turned out, they had not evacuated. After beating Wels with rifle butts, they threw him into a rat-infested coal cellar, where he was to remain as hostage for the payment of the eighty thousand marks. At the same time a contingent of sailors marched on the Chancellery, surrounded it, took over its switchboard, locked the gates, and refused to permit anyone to enter or leave the building.

Ebert, who by this time had returned to the Chancellery, bargained with the leaders of the sailors' contingent for the release of Wels and his subordinates. They told him, "Might is right. We have the men under arrest and will not release them."[37] At that moment

Wels was being pushed against a cellar wall and told, "Now your time has come. You'll be finished off now."[38] There was a momentary reprieve while Dorrenbach telephoned to Ebert, now barricaded in his Chancellery office, to announce that he could not control his enraged sailors any longer; unless Ebert paid the eighty thousand marks at once, the military governor of Berlin would be shot.

Ebert replied in soothing tones. The government was willing to negotiate the matter of the eighty thousand marks. He persuaded the sailors to agree not to shoot Wels until the government could meet to bargain with them.

In the meantime—and, of course, unknown to the sailors who had taken over the Chancellery switchboard—Ebert had called the Supreme Command over his secret line. At the other end was Major von Schleicher.

"The government is made prisoner, Major," said Ebert. "You have always said that if such an event took place you would come to our assistance. Now is the time to act."

Back from Kassel came the crisp reply: "I will take the necessary measures at once. General von Lequis' trusted troops, who are in barracks at Potsdam, shall march on Berlin to set you free."[39]

It was then still the evening of December 23. By midnight the situation had begun to take a slightly more favorable turn for the government. The sailors had been persuaded to leave the Chancellery by Ebert's promise that they would get the eighty thousand marks. Flushed with the assurance of success, doubly certain because they still held Wels as "security" for the payment, they began to straggle back to the palace.

At about the same time, several squadrons of the Imperial Horse Guards, about eight hundred men, left the garrison town of Potsdam fifteen miles to the southwest and moved on Berlin. There they were joined by the only trustworthy remnants of the field army, a thousand or so troops under the personal command of Lequis. Within the hour the Spartacists and the People's Naval Division were aware of the Imperial Horse Guards' presence in Berlin. Dorrenbach raced back to the Chancellery and, bursting into Ebert's office, demanded the immediate withdrawal of the troops, who at that moment were proceeding toward the Schloss and the adjacent Marstall.

Ebert saw before him the almost certain prospect of civil war. He telephoned Groener that an agreement had been reached with the sailors and that the crisis was over; the army must withdraw from

Berlin. The Supreme Command, however, did not see the situation in that light. They now had an opportunity to destroy the reddest of the Red Guards; it might not occur again. Only a few hours before, Ebert had frantically beseeched the Supreme Command to set the government free—proof in itself of the desperate character of the situation in Berlin. "The Field Marshal and I are at the end of our patience," Groener told Ebert. "Your persistence in this eternal negotiation is breaking down the fighting spirit of the last troops faithful to the officers." He flatly refused to stop the Horse Guards' march into Berlin. "The Field Marshal and I are determined to hold to the plan of liquidation of the Naval Division, and we shall see to it that it is carried out."[40]

At that very moment the Army was setting up machine guns and artillery in the square before the palace.

Although the People's Naval Division was numerically superior to the Horse Guards in the square below, the sailors were terrified. The Horse Guards were a famous unit of the Imperial Army. Though they were less than a thousand strong, there were another thousand supporting troops bivouacked in the nearby Tiergarten. The sailors had no artillery, and their discipline was ragged. It was apparent that their leaders within the Marstall and the Schloss had no very clear conception of how to put these two immense buildings, with all their gates and windows, into a state of defense. It was a frightening experience to look out and see the ominous expertise with which the professional soldiers of the Horse Guards went about their preparations.

All through the pre-dawn hours of December 24 the opposing forces silently eyed each other, watched at a distance by little groups of civilians. A series of negotiations, all initiated by the sailors, began to take place. Ebert arrived on the scene, stood on an automobile and tried to convince the soldiers to withdraw a little way and give him a chance to meet with the People's Naval Division. But he was ignored by the Army, and the sailors would discuss nothing with him. Finally, at 5 A.M., Georg Ledebour came to the square, entered the palace and persuaded the sailors to relieve the tension by releasing Wels and his two assistants. Ledebour thought that perhaps this would satisfy the Imperial Horse Guards and provide a basis for some sort of *détente*. Accordingly, the three hostages were set free. Wels's clothes were torn and his nerves completely shaken. Three times the sailors had pushed him against a wall and almost shot him down. But the release of the hostages had no effect upon the Army. The Horse Guards' officers cared nothing for the Majority Socialist military governor of Berlin. The ring of machine guns remained in place.

At seven-thirty in the morning of December 24 an officer of the Horse Guards, one Rittmeister Waldemar Pabst, strode briskly across the cobblestone *Platz*. He demanded complete surrender within ten minutes, failing which the Army would attack. There was no answer from the People's Naval Division. Its leaders had telegraphed the Baltic ports and were promised that a thousand sailors would entrain immediately to assist them. It was only a matter of hours before they would be reinforced to such a degree that they could drive off the Horse Guards.

At seven the Army began firing. Within minutes the front of the building was pierced in a dozen places. Return fire from the palace was confined to rifle shots—and not many of these, for the machine guns of the Horse Guards had driven the sailors away from the windows. Shortly a few hundred soldiers dashed across the *Platz* and burst into the palace. They found it practically empty, the sailors having fled to the stables through an underground passage. The artillery fire now turned to the Marstall.

At nine-thirty a white flag waved from the front of the stables. A delegation of sailors appeared before the attackers and requested a twenty-minute truce in order to conclude arrangements for their surrender. What was left of the People's Naval Division was totally demoralized and could not continue the battle. They were almost out of ammunition and had eaten nothing since noon of December 23, and the stables were full of wounded sailors for whom no medical attention was available. Nearly thirty sailors were dead. There was no longer any hope of help from the seaports. Noske had persuaded the sailors' councils to take a neutral position in this fight. The reinforcements which the People's Naval Division had expected were not going to arrive.

However, the twenty-minute truce made a crucial difference to the fortunes of the division. Since early morning the Spartacist street agitators had been active. They had been driving around Berlin shouting, "Monarchist counterrevolution! Imperial officers are seizing the Schloss! The republic is in danger! Come to the Schloss and save the republic!"[41]

A large crowd had gathered on the streets leading into the square before the palace. Some of the civilians were armed. Most of them were not. So long as the firing was going on they had not dared to come too close, but now that the shooting had suddenly ceased the civilians began to pour into the square. The startled officers of the Horse Guards ordered the machine-gunners to swing their weapons around, but it was too late—the civilians were already among the troops, pleading with the soldiers to give up this attack on the People's Naval Division. The soldiers were suddenly helpless. There were far more civilians among them than they could handle without actually shooting into the crowd—and to machine-gun civilians, women and children among them, was at this point still unthinkable. Some of the Horse Guards troops threw their rifles down onto the cobblestone *Platz*. Others slung theirs over their shoulders and, in sullen silence, listened to exhortations from the civilians.

The sailors of the People's Naval Division took instant advantage of this startling situation. They retreated into the Marstall, hauled down their white flag, and began sniping at any Army officer who offered a clear target.

It was all too much for the troops. The Horse Guards melted away. Within a few minutes the huge square was littered with abandoned weapons, wagons and ammunition crates. By sticking together in little groups, the officers and those few enlisted men who still accepted their orders escaped from the square. Had they not been heavily armed and resolute, the crowd would probably have lynched them.

This fiasco, the "Christmas Eve Battle," was the final defeat of the Imperial German Army. The Horse Guards, only two months earlier the flower of the German Army, had been defeated by a crowd of civilians, mostly unarmed. The news was received with horror by the Supreme Command at Kassel. Lequis was immediately relieved of his command, but it was a hollow punishment. On Christmas Day the Army garrison in Berlin consisted, apart from its officers, of not more than 150 men.

The defeat of the Army in front of the Marstall almost brought the Ebert government to its knees. Berlin was in a state of anarchy. The government could not even control its own streets. There was no Army to defend it, and even the Berlin police were controlled by the Majority Socialists' enemies. Both the Independents and the Spartacists were attacking Ebert with violent accusations of false dealing in the negotiations with the People's Naval Division, and of having attempted a counterrevolutionary *Putsch*. On Christmas Day a crowd collected before the *Vorwärts* offices, listened to Spartacist harangues, then rushed the building. Within minutes the Majority Socialist Party did not even have a Berlin newspaper.

On December 29 the Independent Socialists quit the government on the grounds that they could not sanction the "bloodbath" of Christmas Eve. On the same day a national conference of the Spartacist Union was convened in the chambers of the Prussian Landtag. It was not a very large meeting—eighty-seven delegates and about sixteen special guests. But there were some ominous figures among these delegates and guests. In particular there was Karl Radek, who had arrived from Russia the week before as Lenin's personal representative.

Like Luxemburg, Karl Radek was a Polish Jew. For a time the two had been associated in the formation of the Polish Socialist Party, but then they had had a bitter falling out. Radek had gone on to become an intimate of Lenin, whom he accompanied on the famous "sealed-train" ride across Germany in 1917. He was a short man with thick, curly black hair which he let grow down his cheeks in sideburns. His nearsighted eyes were magnified by thick glasses. Radek was noted for his searing wit and his facility as a speaker and writer, and for his phenomenal nerve. He had been part of the Russian peace delegation at Brest-Litovsk; as the train pulled into the Brest-Litovsk station, Radek had leaned out a window and thrown propaganda leaflets to the German sentries lining the tracks.

Now, as the only one of the five Bolshevik plenipotentiaries who had managed to get into Germany, Radek created a sensation. He himself was delighted with his reception, his initial impression was that "nine tenths of the workers were taking part in the struggle against the government."[42] Radek instantly became a major drawing card at Spartacist rallies. The Berlin workers were captivated by his brilliant accounts of the Bolshevik successes in Russia. It flattered his German listeners when Radek declared, "What we are now carrying out in Russia is nothing but the great *unperverted teaching* of German Communism, which Marx represented for the working class of the whole world."[43] They did not even mind when Radek castigated the Berlin proletariat for its delay in carrying out the "real" revolution. He is said to have sneered that the German worker, when exhorted to action, would reply, "Excuse me for a little while. I'd like to go home and put the tablecloth that I inherited from my grandmother in a safe place."[44]

Rosa Luxemburg was much less enthusiastic over Radek's arrival than were the rank-and-file Spartacists. Her hatred of the man went back a long time. As early as 1912 she had told her German friends, "Radek belongs in the whore category. Anything can happen with him around, and it is therefore much better to keep him at a safe distance."[45]

On December 20, when Radek arrived in Berlin, he went directly to the offices of *Die rote Fahne*. Luxemburg, Liebknecht and Jogiches were all there. They were all astounded to see Radek in Germany. Their astonishment quickly gave way to dismay when they found that he elected to behave toward them in the manner of a Leninist apostle to the heathen. They all went out to eat dinner together, and Rosa Luxemburg made it quite clear that the German Spartacists were not prepared to concede the primacy of the Russians within international Socialism. Dinner was almost forgotten as she condemned Lenin's undemocratic suppression of other parties. Then she attacked the Russian Bolsheviks' use of terror, which Luxemburg believed was both inhuman and theoretically incorrect.

Radek told her that she did not know what she was talking about, that she had no conception of how isolated the Bolsheviks were. They must use terror in order to complete the world revolution. "How can you deny the need for terror under these circumstances?" he demanded. After all, it was being applied only against "classes whom history has sentenced to death."

Luxemburg still could not accept it. She could not even understand how the Leninists could find sufficient people to run a program of revolutionary terror. She had known Dzerzhinsky, the current head of the Cheka, from her Polish Socialist days. He had been a kindly man. "How can Josef be so cruel?" she asked.[46]*

The relations between Luxemburg and Radek did not improve in the following days. Luxemburg and certain other Spartacists felt that Radek was pushing them too hard, that he believed they lacked courage. But they could scarcely deny his influence with the masses. By the time the national Spartacist conference opened on December 29, Radek had secured a position just after Liebknecht and Luxemburg as a principal speaker, and he had assumed the leadership of a small group of quasi-Spartacists from northern Germany who called themselves the "Left Radicals" and whom he had invited to the conference.

* Dzerzhinsky's first name was Felix, but Polish Socialists always referred to him as "Josef."

At Radek's urging, the conference voted to boycott the forthcoming elections, even though Rosa Luxemburg had come to the conclusion that the Spartacists should take part in them. She termed the elections and the resultant National Assembly "a counterrevolutionary fortress which has been erected against the revolutionary proletariat. It is our task to storm this fortress and tear it to the ground." This could not be done by staying outside. "We must utilize the election and the floor of the Assembly properly to mobilize the masses against the Assembly."[47]

The conference also took up the matter of bringing the Revolutionary Shop Stewards into the Spartacists' ranks, just as they had absorbed the Left Radicals. But the Shop Stewards were suspicious. They were, in their own way, just as ardent as the Spartacists, but they distrusted the impulsiveness of Liebknecht. They decided to retain their independence.

The conference adjourned on January 1, after a momentous announcement. The Spartacist Union had changed its name. Henceforth it would be known as the "Kommunistische Partei Deutschlands"—the German Communist Party.

By this time the Majority Socialist government had practically collapsed. Alone and isolated, without an armed force to protect his government, Ebert considered resorting to the only device left to prevent the Communist *Putsch* which was expected any day. He told Groener over the telephone that he intended to forestall a Communist takeover by simply evacuating the Reich Chancellery. "I shall go away," the exhausted Majority Socialist leader said. "I shall disappear utterly from the Chancellor's palace and go to sleep. . . . Only a porter will be left. If the Liebknecht crowd takes this opportunity to seize power, there will be nobody here. . . . And then we shall be in a position to set up our government somewhere else in a few days' time, possibly in Potsdam."[48]

Groener did not think this a very good idea. He had a much better one. He suggested that Gustav Noske be called back from Kiel; surely Noske would have some advice to give on the subject of thwarting a leftist coup. Ebert acted on the suggestion at once.

Noske came to Berlin and arrived at the Chancellery to find a crowd of soldiers outside the building, yelling for arms. In Ebert's office a noisy meeting was going on—everyone standing, loudly debating the question of who was to be named minister of defense. Obviously whoever was given the job would have to be given carte blanche to deal with any situation as he saw fit. (At this stage the Majority Socialists were willing to forget about conciliation and to dismiss proletarian solidarity from their minds; when all was so nearly lost, there were no more rules in the game.) The job of defense minister would be a nasty, dangerous, perhaps impossible one. It had almost been given to Colonel Walther Reinhardt, a career Army officer from Württemberg. A letter of appointment had already been drawn up, but Reinhardt protested. The officer corps might not accept him, he said; he was too junior and not a Prussian.

Noske was exasperated. He demanded that a decision be made— whereupon someone asked if he would take the post. "Of course!" he replied. "Someone must become the bloodhound. I won't shirk the responsibility!"[49]

Reinhardt seized the letter of appointment, drew a line through his own name, filled in the name "Gustav Noske" and handed it to the new Minister of Defense.

Chapter Nine

"Volunteers to the front"

As the new year of 1919 began, there was little reason to believe that the German Republic would long survive. In fact, it seemed likely that the nation itself would starve during the coming months. There had been too few farm workers to plant or bring in the harvest of 1918, and the general disorganization caused by the repatriation of French and Belgian forced laborers had completed the agricultural ruin.

In Article 26 of the armistice the Allies had stated in somewhat general terms that they contemplated "the provisioning of Germany during the time of the Armistice as shall be found necessary." Thus the German government had cause to expect that it would be able to purchase food supplies from other parts of the world. This was not proving to be the case. The Allies—the French in particular—were adamant that Germany's gold reserves must be kept for reparations payments; she must not be allowed to squander her gold on food. Until this matter could be settled, the Allied naval blockade remained in force: no German vessels were permitted to sail, and no food ships of any nationality were permitted to call at German ports.

Herbert Hoover, the chairman of the Allied Council of Supply and Relief, repeatedly demanded that the shipping of food supplies, especially pork products, into Germany be permitted. But, with some justice, the French saw this as an attempt by Hoover to dump onto the German market a tremendous glut of pork which the U. S.

Food Administration had bought at high prices from American farmers. The European Allies insisted that Germany must turn her merchant fleet over to a world shipping pool before being permitted to import food, and there was endless wrangling over how this pool should be constituted. Meanwhile the German government, still unable to have food brought in either on its own ships or on foreign vessels, was forced to cut the already pitiful bread ration by two thirds.

Finding jobs for all those Germans who wanted work was almost as desperate a problem as food supply. One reason why so many workers were rioting in the Berlin streets was that they had nothing else to do. It was pointless for the war industries to continue to operate, so most of them had been closed. Thousands of German refugees from Posen, East Prussia and Alsace-Lorraine had flocked into the German cities, and they too were looking for jobs. Compounding this unemployment were the millions of demobilized soldiers who crowded the streets and the hospitals, selling bits of their old uniforms or begging from passers-by. By January there were 250,000 unemployed workers in Berlin alone. Each of them had to be given ten marks a day by the government.

Another desperate need of the German nation was for shoes, clothing, tools, agricultural implements—manufactured articles of almost every kind. Her mines should have been producing coal, iron and potash for export, but there were too few raw materials to supply the factories, there was nowhere to send the exports, and there was too little food to feed the workers who still had jobs. For the proletariat, the bright promise of revolution had not materialized. A sense of sullen apathy hung everywhere.

It was not even possible to view Germany as a political or economic entity. Bavaria, the second largest of the separate kingdoms which had made up imperial Germany, was now ruled by a government headed by Kurt Eisner, an Independent Socialist of the far left. Eisner had published in the Munich press certain memoranda from the files of the old Bavarian Foreign Ministry which suggested that the Prussian government had been directly responsible for the war. This was readily accepted by the Bavarians, who had long chafed under Prussia's dominance. With popular support, Eisner officially broke off relations with certain of the German Republic's ministries, including the Foreign Office. It was not impossible that Bavaria would secede from the hapless republic.

In the Rhineland, now occupied by the Allies, the German government's sovereignty had ceased to exist. Vague accounts reaching Berlin indicated that French political officers were agitating for the creation of an independent "Rhenish Republic" closely tied to France. The new year found the remainder of Germany in equally sordid disarray. In Düsseldorf the Communists had seized the municipal government and imprisoned the mayor. In Bremen and Hamburg a Communist insurrection was expected at any moment.

What were the victorious Allies doing about Germany? Presumably they had the power to compel their defeated and prostrate enemy to do whatever they desired. Obviously it was in their interest to prevent Germany from becoming a Bolshevik nation allied to Russia. But at this period the Allies were not greatly concerned about political and economic developments within Germany, and such matters as they did find worth considering they misinterpreted. One reason for this state of affairs was that none of the victors had as yet devoted much time to studying the Ebert government's dilemma. On New Year's Day, 1919, the Prime Minister of Great Britain, having won an overwhelming electoral victory three days before, was savoring his triumph on a five-day vacation in Criccieth, Wales. Lloyd George had given little thought to the troubles of prostrate Germany. The war had been over for only some seven weeks, and during this period the Prime Minister and his Cabinet had led their coalition in a national election, had spent endless hours in negotiations and state visits from Britain's allies and had set in motion the demobilization of the nation's Army, Navy and wartime economic system. With all this to do, Lloyd George could scarcely be blamed for not directing his attention toward Germany's internal difficulties.

On the same day the President of the United States was on his way from Great Britain to Rome for yet another triumphal reception. He had been in Europe for several weeks, but the Paris Peace Conference was not ready to begin. The intervening days had been passed agreeably enough in official visits to the Allied capitals. But the mere acknowledgment of the awesome popular adulation of Wilson was full-time work in itself. The remainder of the President's energy was being husbanded for the peace conference, which would not open for another eighteen days. He had had no time for and no particular interest in German political troubles. In the Wilsonian view these matters were part of the travails of an emerging democracy and it would be wrong for the victors to meddle in them.

The New Year found France's *président du Conseil*, Georges

Clemenceau, at his home on the Rue Franklin in Paris. More than any other major Allied figure, Clemenceau should have been in a position to understand the consequences of an overthrow of the German Majority Socialist government, but Clemenceau elected to ignore them. He and his nation cared nothing for Germany's troubles; the more she had, the better. The loser in any war must expect some difficult moments. Let the Germans suffer the consequences of the war that they had started. Many advantages to France might well accrue amid the general German chaos.

In sum, the Allies were indifferent to Germany's internal crisis— many of the principals did not even believe that Germany was in fact ruled by a Socialist government. Four years of wartime propaganda had conditioned them to doubt that the Army, the Conservatives and the monarchists could fall from power so abruptly, and to suspect that it was all a sham. In London the *Times* commented: "Ebert is suspected of being a mere tool of the old regime whose difficult task it is to pave the first stages of the road to the restoration of the Hohenzollerns."[1] Three days later the *Times* advanced the widely held theory that the German Army chiefs proposed "to let the Spartacans upset the Government so that they· can summon Hindenburg to save the day and re-establish the Monarchy."[2]

Many of the Allies did not even believe the German accounts of starvation. Appeals for food might well be another instance of the Hun trickery. In London's *Morning Post*, articles dealing with German starvation appeared under such headlines as "Feeding the Beast" or "German Whines—Limit of Endurance Reached."[3]

Much of the indifference and incomprehension stemmed from the fact that the Allies, by design, had practically no diplomatic contact with Germany except at Spa, where the Armistice Commission was sitting. The French delegation had taken over the Château de La Fraineuse, the Kaiser's former residence. The Americans made their headquarters in what had once been Hindenburg's residence. The German armistice delegation stayed in the old Supreme Headquarters at the Hotel Brittanique. Every morning at ten the commission met in a large room at the Brittanique. The victors sat on one side of a large table, the vanquished on the other. There was very little conversation. The Allies would pass formal notes to the Germans, who would hand back written replies. Although the meetings rarely lasted more than an hour, sometimes more than a hundred notes would be exchanged. Practically all of the delegates were military officers; there was no real diplomatic exchange. A couple of small

Allied military delegations were in Berlin, but their activities were confined to such details as prisoner-of-war exchanges, and these groups were scarcely staffed with the sort of personnel who could provide their governments with accurate political analyses of the German situation. The United States tried to compensate for this by dispatching an intelligence officer, Colonel Arthur L. Conger, to visit the Supreme Command and talk with Groener and Hindenburg. But Conger's visits were intermittent and dealt largely with military affairs. Only the French had made an effort to learn more. In mid-December they had sent to Berlin two "diplomatic observers," Professors Haguenin and Hesnard, both of whom were students of German history and were trusted by Clemenceau, but their efforts were largely confined to appraisals of positions likely to be taken by the Germans at the forthcoming peace conference. These scatterings of heterogeneous missions, together with a few newspaper reporters, comprised the Allied surveillance of Germany at the beginning of 1919. Under these circumstances, it is not surprising that their picture of their principal adversary was completely distorted. They did not foresee any serious possibility that Germany would become Bolshevik. They were sure that she would be able to protect herself. That was Germany's business. Let her only agree to the treaty of peace when it was presented, and Germany's enemies would be content.

Apart from appealing for food, there was nothing the German government could do to obtain support from the conquerors who viewed her civil torment with disdain and unconcern. The Ebert government was reduced to pitiful pleas for support from the German people.

> If you burden us with the responsibility you must do more: You must create power for us! There can be no government without power! Without power we cannot carry out your mandate! Do you want the German Socialist Republic? . . . Then help us create a people's force for the government that will be able to protect its dignity, its freedom of decision and its activity against assaults and putsches.[4]

These appeals had no perceptible effect. At this juncture the Majority Socialists ceased any government functions which might antagonize the proletariat. They only marked time. They lived from day to day, awaiting a *Putsch* from the left or, hopefully, the successful conclusion of the elections of January 19 and the convening of the National Constituent Assembly. The Majority Socialists were now caretakers of the most pitiful and powerless type. Only one figure seemed capable of vigorous action—the "policeman" the government had appointed to protect itself, the new Minister of Defense, Gustav Noske.

The Army chiefs, of course, welcomed Noske's appointment, for they had followed the events in Kiel with the greatest interest. They had seen how Noske succeeded in restoring order among the sailors when the professional officers had failed. They had seen how he prevented the sailors from sending reinforcements to the People's Naval Division, and they had noted with great interest his establishment of an "Iron Guard" of Kiel sailors which functioned as Noske's personal shock force dedicated to the suppression of antigovernment tendencies.

The parties of the left had watched Noske carefully, too, though not with the same emotions as the officer corps. What the Communists, the Revolutionary Shop Stewards and the left wing of the Independent Socialists saw in the government's new Minister of Defense was a man who for years had cherished a curious love of the officer corps. They recalled clearly his prewar fascination with military affairs. They reprinted the savage poem written about Noske in 1907, which ended:

> *Noske straps his saber on,*
> *Noske is fire and vim;*
> *Noske shoots, bang, bang, bang, bang,*
> *He storms the bulwark grim.*
>
> *Noske shouts, "Hurrah! Hurrah!"*
> *He guards us in the night;*
> *Noske will bring victory,*
> *He'll fix things up all right.*[5]

The Communists were scarcely oblivious to the implications of Noske's appointment. They knew him to be ruthless, implacable, energetic and utterly opposed to the further extension of the proletarian revolution.

In Kiel Noske had gained experience and confidence. It did not bother him in the least when *Die rote Fahne* called him "the Butcher," "the Bloodhound" or *"Mörder Noske"* (Murderer Noske). He wasted no time in getting down to work. His first move was to visit the Marstall, where, alone and unarmed, he spent several hours with the sailors. They were sullen and unfriendly, although obviously impressed by Noske's nerve. The cool reception did not depress the new Minister of Defense, who breezily assured his fellow Cabinet members that the sailors were "good fellows who had simply taken the wrong road."[6]

Then, between visits to the Army barracks in Berlin, Noske vigorously reshuffled his own ministerial staff. He seemed to care nothing for proletarian background; he asked only for efficiency. The Supreme Command sent Noske the cream of the officer corps, and these men made a point of behaving in an agreeable and respectful manner toward the new Minister of Defense. Noske's personal chief of staff was Major Erich von Gilsa, a shrewd young nobleman whose forebears had been Army officers for generations. Within a few days after his appointment to the ministerial post, Noske had filled out the balance of his staff with such experienced officers as the small, slender Freiherr Walther von Lüttwitz, an unreconstructed monarchist, who was appointed commandant of the military forces in Berlin. Other clever and ambitious young officers such as von Stockhausen, von Hammerstein and von Stephani were given various commands in the Berlin area.

These appointments seemed at first to be superfluous. Surely there was no object in handing out commands over forces which did not exist. After the Christmas Eve fiasco in Berlin, the old Imperial Army had, for all practical purposes, disappeared. Noske knew this as well as anyone else, however, and he had no intention of making merely honorary appointments. For upon the ashes of the old Imperial Army a new sort of military force was being built. On January 4, while Berlin was racked with Communist-led strikes and riots, Noske and Ebert drove out of the capital to the little garrison town of Zossen, thirty-five miles southwest of Berlin. The two Socialists had been invited to Zossen by a certain General von Maercker. At the close of the war Maercker, a very experienced but otherwise not particularly distinguished officer, had commanded the 214th Infantry Division. His division had marched home together with the rest of the field army, and, like the rest of the field army, once home it had dissolved. But there the similarity ended. Now, on the afternoon of January 4, on the snow-covered parade ground at Zossen,

Maercker displayed to Germany's government what he had since accomplished.

As the two shivering Socialists waited at the edge of the parade ground they heard the blare of a military band, and then across the field there began a review of four thousand fully armed and perfectly disciplined troops. Ebert was astounded. Even Noske was amazed at the precision and bearing of these soldiers. Included among the parading troops were artillerymen and machine-gunners. This was obviously no sketchily armed and scantily disciplined "Republican Soldiers' Army." These men were, as Ebert commented, "real soldiers"—just like the prewar Imperial Army. And as each company drew abreast of the two civilians the commanding officer executed a crisp military salute. It was not lost on either Noske or Ebert that this was the first time in the history of the Prussian Army that a military review had been staged for civilians. The commander, General von Maercker, informed the two Socialists that every soldier in this amazing force was a volunteer, and that each one had signed a statement pledging loyalty to "the provisional government of Chancellor Ebert."

Surrounded by the ramrod-straight officers of his staff, his hand at rigid salute, the deferential Maercker saw the two civilians off in their automobile. His unit was ready for any service which the government might command, he said. And as Noske and Ebert drove away, the joyful Minister of Defense turned to Ebert, clapped the ex-saddlemaker on the back and exulted, "Don't worry. Everything's going to turn out all right now."[7]

They had seen the first of the *Freikorps.*

Because the *Freikorps* were to play such an important role in the period of German history which followed these early-January days, it is worthwhile to study their background.

In their formation, the *Freikorps* owed much to two concepts which were legacies from the old Imperial Army. One of these was the status of the Army officer in Germany; the other was the techniques of the *Sturmtruppen*—storm troops—which the Army had developed during the war.

The officer of the Imperial Army had occupied a unique place in the German social scheme. In a nation where it seemed that almost everyone wore some type of uniform, where many persons, whether of noble birth or not, bore some sort of official title or had been awarded some type of medal or decoration, the Army officer was supreme. He was frequently a member of the nobility; failing this, he was certainly from the upper reaches of the bourgeoisie. He was usually the product of one of the famous cadet schools. Although he was given his commission by his King, not even the Kaiser would have dared to award it until the candidate's acceptance had been approved by every single officer in his prospective regiment. The Imperial Army officer was outside the jurisdiction of civil law and responsible only to the military code, which, incidentally, obliged him to punish on the spot any display of insolence or disrespect by a civilian. Everyone deferred to the military officer. Prior to 1914 it was said that "the young lieutenant went through life as a god, the lieutenant of reserves as a demigod."

Much had changed during the few wartime years. The tremendous growth of the Imperial Army and the casualties which the relatively small (fifty thousand men) officer corps sustained had resulted in an explosive increase in its size. By the end of the war there were some 270,000 German officers. It had not been possible to maintain the same exalted social standards as before in selecting the new officers. But they thought themselves fully the equals of the prewar officers, whom they regarded with awe and whose manners they aped.

Given these circumstances, it is not surprising that when peace came the officer corps of the German Army comprised a caste apart, a large percentage of which was unprepared for a return to civilian life. Sullen and bitter, these suddenly declassed men found themselves stripped of everything they cared about: they had lost a war, lost an Emperor, lost their prestige, and lost their profession. The breakup of the Imperial Army left the bulk of the officer corps wandering purposelessly about the cities and the old garrison towns. "I find," was the typical reflection of one of the officers, "that I no longer belong to this nation. All I can remember is that I once belonged to the German Army."[8]

Another influence on the character of the *Freikorps* was the development of a special type of attack-troop formation within the Imperial German Army. By 1916 it had been discovered that there was a need for a number of small units, generally of battalion size, consisting of specially trained, equipped and conditioned shock troops. These elite formations, the *Sturmbataillone*, were carefully husbanded far behind the front line until it was time for a major raid or an assault. Then the *Sturmbataillone* were raced to the front by truck to lead the attack. They did not look like ordinary infantry. The German Army regarded them as "the perfected form of the front-line fighter."

> *He did not march with shouldered rifle, but with unslung carbine. His knees and elbows are protected with leather patches. He no longer wears a cartridge belt, but sticks his cartridges in his pockets. Crossed over his shoulder are two sacks for his hand grenades. . . . Thus he moves from shell-hole to shellhole through searing fire, shot and attack, creep-ing, crawling like a robber, hugging the ground like an animal, never daunted, never surprised, . . . always shifting, cunning, always full of confidence in himself and his ability to handle any situation . . ."*[9]

An array of special equipment had been created for these *Sturm-truppen:* carbines, lightweight machine guns, small flamethrowers, all designed to be brought forward with breakneck speed during an action. To supplement their special training and superb equipment, the storm troops were given extra privileges. The enlisted men were issued pistols, worn only by officers in the rest of the Army. Their food was the best the German Army had to offer. They got more leave than the rest of the Army. They were allowed to choose their own special unit insignia, for which they generally picked the silver death's head reserved in the past for the cavalry. Nothing was spared to reward these superb troops for the bravery, the blood lust and the merciless efficiency which were demanded of them.

The elite among this elite were the officers of the storm-troop battalions—the *Stosstruppführer.* They were a meticulously se-lected group—unmarried, never older than twenty-five, and perfect physical specimens. A special intimacy grew up between the en-listed men and their officers. They spoke to one another using the familiar *du,* a manner of address which was utterly unthinkable in the rest of the Army. The storm battalion itself was called by the name of its commander. When the storm battalion attacked, the officers went forward ahead of their men. They were even braver, tougher and more merciless than their men. "The turmoil of our feelings," wrote a young *Stosstruppführer,* "was called forth by rage, alcohol and the thirst for blood. As we advanced heavily but irresistibly toward the enemy lines, I was boiling over with a fury which gripped me. . . . The overpowering desire to kill gave me wings. Rage squeezed bitter tears from my eyes. . . . Only the spell of primeval instinct remained."[10]

In response to their successes, a whole body of legend grew up about the famous storm troops and their officers. They were called "the New Man, the storm soldier, the elite of Mittel Europa," a "completely new race, cunning, strong and packed with purpose."[11]

But when the war ended it was the storm trooper and the storm-troop officers who were the most lost and bewildered members of the disintegrating German Army. They were later described by Herman Goering as "fighters who could not come debrutalized."[12] They had no particular ideological convictions and no special political outlook. All they knew was fighting and the tradition of the "front-line soldier."

These were the elements which, mixed together, made up the various little armies that were soon to be called the *"Freikorps"**: the officer who could not conceive of returning to civilian life; the restless young soldier yearning for some sort of new German life; and the storm trooper tradition of ruthless efficiency.

The first *Freikorps* had its origin on December 12, 1918, when, in the horror of the general dissolution of the field army, Maercker had appealed to his corps commander, General von Morgen, for permission to form a "Corps of Volunteer Rifles." Morgen instructed Maercker to draft and submit to him a scheme of organization for the volunteer group. This was immediately done. It bore the title "Organizational Directive [*Grundlegender Befehl*] for the Volunteer Rifle Corps." The directive and the subsequent "Conditions for Admission to the Corps of Volunteer Rifles" were instantly approved by Morgen and the Supreme Command.

These documents make interesting reading. It is a common supposition that the *Freikorps* were ultrareactionary gangs formed of White-Guardist types under the iron control of the most monarchial elements of the General Staff. This was not the case. The events of the German Revolution had convinced the more perceptive members of the officer corps, particularly the levelheaded Groener, that if the Army was to survive it must make certain concessions to the rank and file. Nor did the office corps think that this was necessarily

---

* The original title for these forces was *Freiwillige Landesjägerkorps*, but it was quickly shortened in common use to *Freikorps*.

bad. Maercker intended to recruit only the very best fighting elements of the old field army and to organize them on the lines of the storm troops. Each infantry company would be practically self-sufficient, like a miniature division in the old field army; it would have its own trench-mortar section, its own transport and its own heavy mortars. Obviously a high degree of initiative, flexibility and imagination would be required of the enlisted men who made up these rifle companies. The *Kadaverdisziplin* of the old Imperial Army had no place here. A different sort of relationship between officers and privates must be developed, somewhat similar to that which had grown up in the *Sturmbataillone*.

In any event, Maercker's organizational directive, while insisting that "iron discipline was absolutely necessary," also conceded that "discipline should be founded upon ready and consenting obedience."[13] The order dwelt at length on the newly created post of *Vertrauensleute*—"trusted men." These men, who were to be elected by the privates in each company, were given unprecedented privileges. The officers were required to consult with them on such matters as food and leave. The "trusted men" had the right to bring complaints against any officer or noncommissioned officer, and these charges had to be investigated by a senior officer.

On December 22, Maercker's directive having been approved, he published the "Conditions for Admission to the Corps of Volunteer Rifles," which spelled out the terms under which men would be enlisted. Only soldiers who had completed their military training in the old Imperial Army were acceptable to Maercker. Each man enlisted for a period of thirty days, which was renewable every month. He could leave by giving fifteen days' notice. A generous scale of pay and allowances was published, and service in the Volunteer Rifle Corps counted for retirement and pensions just as did service in the Imperial Army. As to the matter of an oath of loyalty, both the Supreme Command and Maercker gave considerable thought to the form this should take. Obviously *some* form of pledge of allegiance had to be given. To swear loyalty to the old monarchy was out of the question. To pledge fealty to the "Ebert-Haase government" was also impossible. Haase was an Independent Socialist and could be counted upon to condemn the formation of this corps once he heard about it. As Maercker said, "No one could ask me to swear loyalty to the person of Herr Haase, who in 1914 had declared he wanted to undermine the Army in order to set the world revolution in motion."[14] In the end each volunteer was required to sign a statement pledging only, "I will loyally serve the provisional government of Chancellor Ebert until the National Assembly has created the new constitution."[15]

The Majority Socialists could have asked for nothing more. But it is significant of the confusion of the times that they knew little or perhaps nothing about the Volunteer Rifle Corps. No doubt distance had something to do with this. Maercker's Volunteer Rifles had set up their headquarters in a secluded Franciscan convent at Salzkotlen in the province of Westphalia; shrewdly, Maercker was not calling attention to his corps in its early days. Despite this seclusion, he had no difficulty in obtaining volunteers. His old infantry division, the 214th, like every other division in the Imperial Army, had broken up, but in it there had been a nucleus of hardy souls willing to remain with Maercker as volunteers. It is difficult to assess their motives with any exactitude. Doubtless this first *Freikorps* had its share of professional soldiers who knew no trade, had no family and could not conceive of life outside the barracks. Other volunteers were motivated by patriotism and sincerely believed that they were Germany's salvation against a wave of Bolshevism. Still others were motivated by a brutal hatred for the *Etappe,* the rear, which they had begun to see as the source of their wartime defeat and suffering.

Whatever their motives, it is significant that out of a single infantry division a sufficient number of tough veteran soldiers could be found to form, within a few days after the publication of the organizational directive, a "section" consisting of three infantry companies and a battery of artillery. Getting enough volunteers, however, was not the end of Maercker's organizational problems. The men had to be fed, paid, armed and clothed. The Supreme Command could supply only the money; the rest was Maercker's responsibility, and it proved to be a tremendous burden. He and his staff officers visited depot after depot in frantic succession, hearing the same story in practically every case: the troops guarding the supply dumps had disappeared, and whatever was stored had been looted. It was ominous that Maercker had great difficulty in finding small arms and ammunition for his men. In the few supply depots where any sort of order still existed, the local soldiers' councils had taken over, and they refused to give him any of the stores. Neither the Supreme Command nor the staff of Maercker's own army corps could provide him with transport. They referred him to the Seventeenth Corps motor park, but there he again found himself too late.

As Maercker described it, everything was in "Russian conditions."[*] "A sad spectacle met my eyes—lorries, guns, munitions wagons, artillery, lay scattered about. . . . Everything was rusted, broken, beyond use; the axle trees were twisted, the copper plates wrenched off and sold."[16] Maercker could not even find enough winter coats for his men. He appealed to the Supreme Command and then to the War Ministry in Berlin. No one could help him. Bitterly he reflected that the situation was truly desperate when neither the German government nor the Supreme Command of the German Army could find enough overcoats for a few companies of infantry.

Eventually some unpillaged supply dumps were found, and enough equipment was scraped together to outfit Maercker's troops. The Supreme Command had sent three popular generals to help with recruiting, and by late December the Volunteer Rifles had nearly four thousand men. A staff of the officers began work devising doctrine for clearing streets, defending public buildings and controlling mobs. As fast as these tactics were worked out, the troops were trained in them. On December 28, following the fiasco before the Marstall, Maercker's corps was ordered to move east to Zossen, where, on January 4, they appeared—almost miraculously, it seemed—before Noske and Ebert, stepping smartly across the snow-covered paradeground.

By January 4 Maercker's Volunteer Rifles were not the only *Freikorps* in Germany. In Kiel the Navy had put together several brigades composed of officers, petty officers and naval cadets. Each of the young company commanders was a former U-boat captain who had been decorated with the Pour le Mérite, the most coveted of Germany's military awards. The various naval brigades took the names of their commanders—the Ehrhardt Free Corps, the Löwenfeld Corps. In Berlin in mid-December a *Freikorps* had even been formed by a sergeant named Suppe, who had called together a group of his men from the Second Guards Regiment and appealed to their sense of honor; thus the Suppe Free Corps was born. Another *Freikorps*, known as the "Guard Cavalry Rifle Division" (Garde-Kavallerie-Schützen Division), was being put together out of the wreckage of several divisions of the old Imperial Guards.

As yet, in early January of 1919, there were not many of these volunteer corps—probably no more than a dozen—and each was still quite small. But they were proliferating, and some common

---

[*] The German phrase *russische Zustände* is used to describe any situation which is ramshackle and disorganized.

threads ran through them. Most of them, for example, were copying Maercker's organizational directive. And most of them, even though they were "free" corps, were quite willing to accept orders from the Supreme Command or from the Ebert government, which, after all, was paying them. They were neither monarchist nor Socialist. They were merely tough, determined and anti-Bolshevik.

The "Spartacist Revolution" began in Berlin on January 6, 1919. It came as no surprise to the citizens of Berlin, who had seen huge strikes and riots become daily occurrences during the first week of the new year. In fact, the only people who were really caught un-awares was the leadership of the new Communist Party.

During the first week in January the Ebert government, aware that its power was rapidly deteriorating, had finally abandoned all restraint in attacking the opposition to the left. The Majority Social-ists had, after some fighting, managed to recapture the *Vorwärts* printing office which the Spartacists had seized on Christmas Day. Now they used their presses to publish a series of violent newspaper and pamphlet attacks on the left wing of the Independents, the Revolutionary Shop Stewards and the Communists—all of whom they lumped together as "Spartacists."

> *The despicable actions of Liebknecht and Rosa Luxemburg soil the revolution and endanger all its achievements* [Vor-wärts *charged*]. *The masses must not sit by quietly for one minute longer while these brutal beasts and their followers paralyze the activities of the republican governmental offices, incite the people more and more to civil war and strangle with their dirty fists the right of free expression* . . .[17]

The Majority Socialists ridiculed the Communists' announced inten-tion of taking over the government only when they had obtained the support of the majority of the proletariat. They did not believe Rosa Luxemburg's claim that the left would never stage a *Putsch*. As it turned out, they knew the Communists' intentions better than the Communists did themselves.

The tension came to a head over the left-wing Independent Emil Eichhorn, who had held on to the Berlin police presidency ever since November 9. It was common knowledge that Eichhorn was filling up the police ranks with Spartacist sympathizers who, with their chief's approval, took only the most perfunctory notice of rioters against the Ebert government. He had declared his police to be "neutral" at the time of the Christmas Eve fighting in front of the Marstall, and he was outspoken in his opposition to the forthcoming elections for the National Assembly. All of this Ebert had felt constrained to accept as long as the Independents had remained in the government. When the Independents quit, the Majority Socialist newspapers let loose a volley of attacks on Eichhorn until, on Saturday, January 4, he was given notice of dismissal by the Prussian state government.

Eichhorn refused to be fired. Upon receiving the news, he reported directly to the headquarters of the Independent Socialists. The Independent leaders quickly met in turn with the Revolutionary Shop Stewards and the Communists, and a joint manifesto demanding Eichhorn's retention and appealing to the proletariat for a mass demonstration in his support was drafted and rushed onto the Berlin streets. At a meeting of the three left-wing parties it was agreed also to demand that the government give arms to the Berlin proletariat and disarm the *Freikorps*, about which the left had begun to hear rumors.

The mass demonstration took place on Sunday, January 5, in front of the police headquarters on the Alexanderplatz. The crowd filled the big square and extended for blocks east and west along the Königstrasse. Its size and vehemence astounded even the organizers of the protest, who had never seen a crowd like this before. Many of the demonstrators were armed. When the workers were addressed from the police-headquarters balcony by various prominent revolutionary figures, such as Ledebour of the Independent Socialists, Däumig of the Revolutionary Shop Stewards and, of course, Liebknecht, they responded with a deafening clamor.

In the midst of this demonstration Eugen Ernst, the new police president designated by the government, had the ill fortune to appear. He was roughly handled by the crowd, which would not even allow him to get near the headquarters building. Prudently he drove back to the Reich Chancellery. Then, in a scene of great enthusiasm, Eichhorn appeared on the balcony and proclaimed his determination to remain in office no matter what the government might do. The crowd cheered wildly and, even as night fell, remained in the *Platz* to listen to speeches.

Meanwhile the officials of the left wing of the Independents, the Revolutionary Shop Stewards and the Communists all gathered within the building. There were seventy-one persons present, of whom only two, Liebknecht and Wilhelm Pieck, were Communists. This coalition made a momentous decision: to call a general strike, to support an armed attack upon the government and "to place Germany in the vanguard of the international proletarian revolution."

The decision was by no means unanimous. The leaders of the three parties had not originally come there with the intention of declaring the revolution. They had been aware that their respective organizations were far from perfected and that a good deal of agitation remained to be done. They must have realized that a declaration of revolution would be tantamount to civil war, and that this would be a bloody affair which would have to be repeated in almost every major German city. It would not be enough to capture Berlin. If the other great cities were not won over, the Berlin proletariat could be cut off and starved out.

Nevertheless, the majority of the left-wing leaders at the meeting in police headquarters suddenly became absolutely certain that the revolution's hour had struck. They were overwhelmed by the enthusiasm of the unbelievably huge mass demonstration which was cheering outside on the Alexanderplatz. As they met, messengers came dashing in from all over Berlin to report that revolutionary workers had begun to occupy the newspaper offices in the Belle-Alliance-Platz, that the proletariat was attacking the railway stations, that an entire issue of *Vorwärts* had been seized at revolver point and dumped into a canal; and Dorrenbach rushed over to announce that his People's Naval Division was ready to go into action in support of the uprising. To those who gathered at the meeting it must have seemed that the revolution was actually taking place while they talked. Surely the mere fact that they were discussing it while sitting in the Berlin police headquarters, of all places, was proof that the Ebert government had collapsed. Obviously the workers were ready. They wanted only to be led. Glorious comparisons with the Smolny Institute in Petrograd came to every mind.

Practically everyone present was later to claim that, although it was the Revolutionary Shop Stewards who proposed the revolution, it was Liebknecht who carried the decision. Probably an element of competition entered into his motivation; it would have been intolerable to Liebknecht if the Revolutionary Shop Stewards had been permitted to lead this "second revolution." And he is said to have feared that if there was no revolution soon, the sailors of the People's Naval Division would feel he was betraying them.[18] Be that as it may, his eyes shone, his face glowed and he radiated absolute

certainty of revolutionary victory. Away from the moderating coun-
sels of his party associates, Liebknecht was free to commit the Communist Party to the ultimate move. No one was there to remind him
that the official Communist policy was still relentless agitation
among the workers until, without the need for a *Putsch,* the party
was summoned to power by the masses.

It is easy to see how under Liebknecht's exhortations, delivered to
the accompaniment of the intoxicating clamor of the armed masses
outside, the group at police headquarters was stampeded into a
decision. The leaders of the masses could scarcely afford to be found
timidly trailing in the wake of the masses. By a vote of sixty-five to
six, the leaders of the left decided to summon the Berlin proletariat
to revolution.

The next step of the combined group of Independents, Revolutionary Shop Stewards and Communists was to draft and send out
into the nighttime streets a manifesto calling for that final revolutionary combination, the arming of the workers and the launching
of a general strike. On the following day, Monday, January 6, the
Ebert government would have to fall: there would be no electricity,
no streetcars, no factories operating, no shops open; nothing would
move on the streets of Berlin except an armed mass of workers. As
the police-headquarters meeting continued into the night, the
seventy-one men present approved the formation of a fifty-three-
member "Revolutionary Committee." This committee immediately
prepared another manifesto, to be published as soon as the general
strike had taken effect, declaring that the "Ebert-Scheidemann government" was "deposed" and that the Revolutionary Committee had
temporarily taken over governmental affairs.[19] The second manifesto was set in type at once and held in readiness for the takeover.

That night and the next morning the Revolutionary Committee
distributed arms to the workers. The general strike of January 6
began on schedule. A mammoth demonstration of some 200,000
workers paraded through the Berlin streets. Groups of workers succeeded in capturing the bourgeois newspaper offices and the Wolff
Telegraph Agency. By the morning of January 7 the revolutionaries
had seized the Brandenburg Gate and placed riflemen among the
statuary at its top. From there they could now fire east down Unter
den Linden, west across the Charlottenburger Chaussee, and north
and south along the Königstrasse. The Government Printing Office
had been seized, as had the most important of the railroad stations.
The revolutionaries took over and fortified the huge Bötzow Brew-

ery. The Reichstag building was under attack and defended only by a scratch force of government bureaucrats hastily armed for the occasion.

News spread through the city that several of the remaining Army regiments were about to march on Berlin in support of the revolution. The garrison in Frankfurt was said to have gone over to the revolutionaries also and to have entrained for the capital. In other cities of Germany—Brunswick, Düsseldorf, Dortmund, Nuremberg and Hamburg—revolutionary workers seized the bourgeois newspapers. In Bremen a soviet republic was declared. Lenin, overjoyed at the news from Germany, was preparing an "Open Letter to the Workers of Europe and America" which lauded "the German Spartakusbund with its world-famous leaders" for its attack on the "imperialist robber bourgeoisie of Germany."[20]

By Wednesday the Majority Socialist government controlled only a few of the major public buildings in Berlin; it had managed to hold on to the Reich Chancellery only by crowding the Wilhelmstrasse in front of the building with a couple of thousand Majority Socialist supporters. It could not issue appeals to the workers—the revolutionaries had taken over the *Vorwärts* office. Walled up behind their barricade of human flesh, Ebert and his government sat, depressed and practically helpless, wondering if they should flee Berlin. They did not dare go home, for fear they would be arrested. The general strike even made it impossible for them to go to a restaurant for dinner; finally a friend of one of the Majority Socialists, after being appealed to by telephone, made his way to the Chancellery with a hamper of food for the government.

Gustav Noske, the newly appointed Minister of Defense, had been forced to flee from inner Berlin on January 6. He had found it impossible to work in the Chancellery and had made his way on foot to the Army General Staff building, the famous old red house on the Königplatz. When he arrived, he found a huge revolutionary crowd preparing to storm the building. Clearly this was no place to stay. Telling Ebert that he was leaving the city to rally support—"Perhaps we'll have luck"—Noske summoned an automobile and fled the heart of Berlin along the road which led to Dahlem, a quiet section in the southwest suburbs of the city. Someone knew of a girls' boarding school there which was empty because of the holidays. At 3 P.M. on January 6 Noske arrived at the school and established his headquarters there, with an empty classroom as an office, a couple of tables shoved together as a desk, and a telephone screwed onto a plank.

The city of Berlin was, and still remains, one of the newest of the major cities of Europe. Before the Hohenzollern kings of Prussia erupted into prominence, it was little more than a glorified fishing and trading village on one bank of the River Spree. Then, as Prussia grew and prospered, the home city of its kings grew simultaneously. Between 1820 and 1918 Berlin expanded its population by more than ten times, and after 1871, when it became the capital of Germany, the growth had been particularly rapid. Government buildings, mostly constructed in the massive stone style ironically known as "Berlin Renaissance," were built everywhere. The city was laid out along a series of broad avenues which converged, spoke fashion, in a number of central squares. Inner Berlin, the city's center, was dominated by the main thoroughfares, the massive government buildings, large parks such as the Tiergarten, and the fashionable residential districts. The industrial districts, consisting principally of huge metalworking and electrical-equipment factories, dominated the northern, eastern and southern outskirts of the city. In the suburbs to the west lay the arsenals and munitions factories of Spandau. The eastern quarter of Berlin consisted of a sea of low brick working-class residences.

More than two million persons lived in Berlin, and most of them were industrial workers and their families. There were few ties to the soil among the city's proletariat; when they came from the farms to Berlin the workers quickly shook off their rural docility. Before the war most of the Berlin workers had been Social Democrats, a fact which the old Imperial Army had noted and because of which the Army had preferred to take its conscripts from the farming regions. Although the Berlin worker was disciplined, efficient and hard-working, he was also very class-conscious and was convinced that he and his children were the victims of glaring social injustice. His experiences during the war had deepened this conviction. True, not every Berliner felt this way. But a very great many, perhaps the majority of the industrial workers, did, and these were the supporters of the three revolutionary parties—the left wing of the Independents, the Revolutionary Shop Stewards and the Communists, all of whom were now lumped together by the Ebert government under the collective term "Spartacist."

This was the city which the Ebert government had to defend and the populace against which it had to defend itself.

January 7 was the low point of the Majority Socialist government's fortunes. The first two days of this "Spartacist Week" had proved to Ebert and his colleagues that there was no hope of reaching any sort of compromise with the revolutionary parties. At a meeting in the Chancellery Commissioner Landsberg had reported, "The Spartacists have taken over the Railroad Administration Building, the Ministry of War is next in line in a few hours and then it will be our turn."[21] Ebert had come to the conclusion that the first duty of any government is to survive, and this realization made decisions easier. The Majority Socialists now gathered unto themselves every party or faction which could possibly support them in this crisis. Ebert and his fellow government members kept their heads. There was no more talk of abandoning the Reich Chancellery or of fleeing Berlin. Noske was in Dahlem organizing an army to reinvade the city. The Cabinet had decided to give him carte blanche—"We must not interfere with his decisions."[22]

Within the capital the government sought the support of the bourgeoisie, the monarchists, the conservatives, even the frankly counterrevolutionary elements which it had gone to great pains to hold at arm's length only a few weeks before. It issued a proclamation, addressed this time to "Fellow Citizens" (*Mitbürger*), not to the customary "Comrades" (*Genossen*), appealing for the support of every class. A constant vigil of Majority Socialists was maintained outside the Reich Chancellery. (They crowded the streets and paths around the building, but carefully refrained from standing on the grass, for there were signs which forbade this.) A corps of five thousand men was recruited from among the civil servants, armed, and given the task of defending the major public buildings still left in government hands. These volunteers managed to drive the revolutionaries off the Brandenburg Gate and to set up machine guns atop it.

From the outset the government managed to rupture the revolutionaries' main potential source of armed power, the People's Naval Division. A Majority Socialist official, Anton Fischer, visited the Marstall and harangued the sailors, making promises of payment for their neutrality. For a little while the issue was in doubt. Dorrenbach, the sailors' leader, who on the wild night of January 5 had

promised the support of the division against the government, ordered Fischer arrested. But the sailors, apprehensive over the future
consequences of a government victory, arrested Dorrenbach himself, freed Fischer and declared their neutrality. Liebknecht, who
had made the Marstall a sort of operational headquarters, was
evicted from the building.

Prominent Majority Socialists were dispatched to the garrisons at
Spandau and Frankfurt and came back with assurances of the
soldiers' neutrality. But other soldiers were not neutral. The government, caring nothing at this point for the political implications of its
action, summoned Colonel Wilhelm Reinhard,* who was in the
process of forming a *Freikorps* in Berlin, and ordered him to recapture the various newspaper offices located in the Belle-Alliance-
Platz. Reinhard's corps had only nine hundred men, and with this
pitiful force he had been lucky to hang on to the Moabit barracks in
northern Berlin. But he quickly gathered a stronger force made up
of other embryo *Freikorps*—General von Röder's Volunteer Scouts,
General von Hoffmann's Horse Guards Division, and other little
groups then forming under Generals Held, von Wissel and von Hülsen. Another *Freikorps* called the "Potsdam Regiment" was scraped
together from the First Infantry Guards Regiment and various noncommissioned officers' schools at the Potsdam barracks. These were
for the moment tiny organizations, but many of their "privates" still
wore their old Army tunics, on which officers' shoulder tabs were
plainly visible. Some companies consisted entirely of noncommissioned officers, and a large number of all ranks had been members
of the wartime storm troops. All of them, with the exception of a
couple of hastily put together bourgeois companies composed of
very young students and older professional men, were veteran front-
line soldiers.

On the night of January 9–10, the twelve hundred troops of the
Potsdam Regiment, under the immediate command of Major von
Stephani, occupied the Belle-Alliance-Platz in front of the *Vorwärts*
building. Stephani had not forgotten the lesson of Christmas Eve at
the Marstall. All the streets leading into the *Platz* were blocked off.
No one was allowed to approach the troops which were being assembled. Anyone who did was greeted with an extended bayonet
and the old Prussian sentry's warning cry, *"Zehn Schritte vom Leib!*

---

* Not to be confused with Colonel (later General) Walther Reinhardt, mentioned
earlier.

Ten steps from my body!" Anyone who came closer was automatically considered an enemy and fired upon.

Stephani had a good idea of what he was up against. On the previous night he had dressed himself in worker's clothing and presented himself at the *Vorwärts* building as a revolutionary who had come to offer his services. This had given him a opportunity to inspect the building's defenses and prepare his plans for assaulting it. He gave the Spartacists defending the *Vorwärts* building only one opportunity to surrender. Then his trench mortars opened up. A large hole was immediately blasted in the front of the four-story masonry structure. Machine guns were carried across the rooftops, and they began to fire into the *Vorwärts* offices. Two howitzers were towed into the *Platz* directly in front of the building, and the gun crews shot point-blank at the building. A tank rumbled across the square and smashed in the front doors. It was followed by armored cars which drove up onto the front sidewalks and fired into the windows.

The defenders of the *Vorwärts*, who numbered only about 350, had barricaded themselves behind upturned rolls of newsprint. Their only weapons were small arms, and against the explosions of the artillery they could do nothing more than take cover behind these barricades. A few of the more intrepid revolutionaries sniped at the gunners in the square below, but when the building's entrance was blasted in the defenders knew the battle was lost. From the upstairs windows they began to wave white flags and handkerchiefs. The *Freikorps* soldiers paid no attention. Two huge mortar shells practically blew in the roof of the building, and then, covered by the smoke and the debris, squads of riflemen sprinted across the cobblestone *Platz*, hugged the walls of the building for a moment, tossed hand grenades through the windows and then dashed through the blown-in doors and up the stairs. Simultaneously, a company of *Freikorps* soldiers with a flamethrower burned down a high board fence at the back of the building and broke through the rear doors. They took about three hundred prisoners, marched them to a nearby barracks and shot a number of them down.[23]

By eight-fifteen on the morning of January 10 the *Freikorps* had cleared out all the newspaper offices adjoining the *Vorwärts* on the Belle-Alliance-Platz. Some of the defenders had scrambled across the roofs to safety. The rest were prisoners. Reinhard's troops now turned to the reduction of other Spartacist strongpoints.

* * *

Noske had not been wasting his time at the girls' school in Dahlem. A scant five days had passed since he had fled the center of Berlin, but he and his staff had made every moment count. They had alerted Maercker's Volunteer Rifles at Zossen to prepare to march on the capital, and a *Freikorps* company had been brought to Dahlem to fortify the school against any possible attack. This was hardly necessary. The mere news that Noske was putting together a force to crush the revolution brought thousands of officers and soldiers to Dahlem, where his large and skillful staff quickly organized and armed them. Dahlem was a wealthy residential suburb consisting mostly of villas with large landscaped grounds. The area surrounding Noske's headquarters provided plenty of room. Troops were encamped and motor pools set up. A signal detachment was put together and telephone switchboards were installed; a radio station was erected and went on the air. Troop commanders and their staffs were appointed, and a map room was established. At the center of it all was Noske, working for days without sleeping. It is difficult to avoid the impression that he enjoyed all this. He was in his element, and he made no apology for the conservative character of his military staff.

> *It was our great misfortune that no incomparable leader appeared in the ranks of the privates or the noncommissioned officers. . . . I was obliged, therefore, to fall back on the officers. It is quite true that many of them are monarchists, but when you want to reconstruct you must fall back on the men whose profession it is. An undisciplined army is a hollow mockery. . . . I sought out, one by one, the former officers and former officials, beaten and spat upon as they were, and it is with their help that I averted the worst.*[24]

The worst was indeed being averted. The revolutionary groups were showing themselves to be far weaker than had been suspected on January 5. On that fateful Sunday evening when the Revolutionary Committee had met at police headquarters, its supporters had seemed to be in control of the streets of Berlin. But after the initial successes of Monday and Tuesday the revolution had begun to falter. The Revolutionary Committee of fifty-three persons from three parties had proved grotesquely inefficient. The committee even had three coequal presidents, one from each of the sponsoring parties. The objectives of the groups varied just enough to make rapid decisions impossible. It was a far cry from the tightly knit Military Revolutionary Committee over which Lenin and Trotsky had presided at Petrograd in 1917. There was no small, cohesive revolutionary group in Berlin which could give instant orders to trained cadres leading the Red Guards in the streets. It was not that there was any shortage of armed workers. *Die rote Fahne* later wrote:

> *What was seen on Monday in Berlin was probably the greatest proletarian manifestation in history . . . From the statue of Roland [in front of the City Hall] to the statue of Victory [at that time in the Königplatz] proletarians were standing shoulder to shoulder . . . They had brought along their weapons, they had their red flags. They were ready to do anything, to give everything, even their lives. There was an army of 200,000 such as Ludendorff had never seen.*
>
> *Then the inconceivable happened. The masses were standing from nine in the morning in the cold and fog. Somewhere their leaders were sitting and conferring. The fog lifted and the masses were still standing. Their leaders conferred. Noon came and, in addition to the cold, hunger came. And the leaders conferred. The masses were feverish with excitement. They wanted one deed, even one word to calm their excitement. But nobody knew what to say, because the leaders were conferring. The fog came again and with it the dusk. The masses went home sad. They wanted great things, but they had done nothing. Because their leaders conferred. They conferred in the Marstall, then they went to the police headquarters and continued to confer . . . They sat the entire evening and the entire night and conferred; they sat during the next morning. When dawn came, they either were still conferring or were conferring again.*[25]

There was no direction or coordination from the Revolutionary Committee. Where the armed workers had taken over a railroad station, a government office or a newspaper plant there was nothing left for them to do but entrench themselves and await a government counterattack. No one sent them instructions, no one gave them reinforcements, no one encouraged them to seize other buildings. After January 10 the Revolutionary Committee even ceased to meet.

As the days passed, even the general strike began to lose its effectiveness. It was a complete success in the metalworking factories and the other major industries where the Revolutionary Shop Stewards or the Communists were strong. But the movement had failed to achieve the principal objective of a general strike, the abrupt and total cessation of normal life. The workers in the electrical generating plants remained at their jobs as did the Berlin fire department, whose engines now toured the city picking up the dead and wounded. The telephones still worked. A young American Army lieutenant, part of a small prisoner-of-war repatriation contingent in Berlin, noted in his diary the bizarre situation on January 7: "Firing can be heard all over the city . . . [but] theaters are wide open and crowded. The city is mad, and without the slightest hesitation men wipe their bloodstained hands and come in from the street battles to the cabarets to dance and drink and dine with women."[26]

Almost visibly the uprising was losing its momentum. Some of the right-wing members of the Independent Socialists, horrified at the bloodshed, returned to the Majority Socialists. Even the most revolutionary of the Independents were privately attempting to negotiate some sort of compromise agreement with the government. They had not bargained on Ebert's actually resisting their revolution, and they had no stomach for fighting in the streets. They did not seem to understand that they could not attack the Reichstag building while simultaneously negotiating for a return to their old seats on the Council of People's Commissioners. The Independents could not bring themselves to the realization that revolutionaries must burn every bridge behind them.

Nor did the revolution proceed with the kind of ruthless energy that marked the October Revolution in Petrograd. When, on January 7, the Ebert government announced that no demonstrations or parades would be permitted on the Wilhelmstrasse in the vicinity of the Chancellery, the revolutionaries made only a tentative probe down this avenue which led to the citadel of German power, had a few shots fired over their heads by the handful of troops which were then guarding the Chancellery, and turned away.

On January 6, before the People's Naval Division declared its neutrality, a section of sailors was sent by Liebknecht to occupy the Ministry of War. There was practically no one to defend the ministry, since most of its staff had gone to Dahlem with Noske. To the

officer left in charge the sailors displayed a written warrant author-
izing their seizure of the building. Thinking quickly, the officer
examined the paper and pointed out that it was not properly signed.
The sailors took the document back, looked at it and saw that in fact
there was no signature. Back they trooped to the Marstall, where
they hunted up Liebknecht and got him to sign the paper. On their
return to the ministry it seems to have dawned on the sailors that
this was not the way to conduct a revolution. Musing on this, their
leader threw away the warrant and drifted back to the Marstall.

The most confused spectacle of all was provided by the Communist Party itself. Rosa Luxemburg, Leo Jogiches and Karl Radek
had been appalled when they learned that the January 5 conference
of the parties of the left had decided to proclaim the revolution.
They were not alone. The majority of the party's *Zentrale* was
similarly horrified. They saw quite clearly that the proletarian
movement was not yet ready for a real revolution, and they cursed
the luck which had permitted Liebknecht to go almost alone to the
meeting at police headquarters. The masses were not yet properly
educated. The thing which Rosa Luxemburg had most feared, a premature uprising of the proletariat, had occurred. When Liebknecht
came back to the *Rote Fahne* offices with the news of the revolution,
Luxemburg cried out, "But Karl, how could you? What about our
program?"[27] Only the week before she had written: "It would be a
criminal error to seize power now. The German working class is not
ready for such an act. . . . It is useless, it is childish to overthrow it
[the Ebert government] and replace it by another if the masses are
not ready and able to organize Germany."[28] Agitation and propaganda were both well short of their goals. Even if this uprising succeeded—and Luxemburg was sure it would not—it could be sustained
only by Leninist policies of terror.

Radek was equally opposed to the uprising, but for somewhat
different reasons. He certainly had no compunction about using
terror, but as a highly experienced revolutionary, he was convinced
that the German Communist Party was not ready for the revolution.
The Bolsheviks in Petrograd had possessed much greater force in
terms of revolutionary cadres and Red Guards, and still their revolution had been a close-run thing. He urged the party's leaders to
withdraw from the Revolutionary Committee at once. If necessary,
they should disarm the workers. It was what Lenin would do.
Mistakes must be liquidated at once, however brutal that might
seem.

Luxemburg and the other German Communist leaders could not bring themselves to do this. They realized that they themselves had aroused the workers. The party could not now abandon them. As doomed as this revolutionary attempt might be, they must share the workers' fate. It was "a matter of revolutionary honor."[29] For this reason, *Die rote Fahne* was forced to give the revolution its support. Luxemburg wrote:

> *The masses followed the call of their leaders with impetuos-ity. . . . They are waiting for further directing and actions from their leaders. . . . No time must be wasted. Thorough measures must be taken immediately. Clear and urgent direc-tives must be given to the masses and to the soldiers who re-mained faithful to the cause of the revolution. . . . Act! Act! Courageously, decisively and constantly . . . Disarm the counterrevolution, arm the masses, occupy all positions of power. Act quickly!*[30]

Radek refused to go even this far. It was all madness. "A govern-ment of workers," he wrote to the Communist *Zentrale* on January 9,

> *"is unthinkable without an existing proletarian mass organiza-tion. At present the only mass organizations to be considered, the workers' and soldiers' councils, are of only nominal strength. . . . If the government should fall into your hands as the result of a* coup d'état, *within a few days it would be cut off from the rest of the country and would be strangled.*

He went on to attack those who in their enthusiasm "transformed the protest demonstration [of January 5] into a struggle for political power. This," he said, "enables Ebert and Scheidemann to strike a blow against the Berlin movement which can weaken the entire movement for months." He pleaded with the *Zentrale* to abandon the fight. "The only force which can prevent this disaster is you, the Communist Party. You have sufficient insight to know that the fight is hopeless. . . . Nothing can prevent a weaker power from retreat-ing before a superior force."[31]

Radek was right. On the rainy evening of January 11, the various *Freikorps* of Gustav Noske began to march on inner Berlin.

A careful plan for the reconquest of Berlin had been worked out by Noske's staff. The first step involved a march of infantry, artillery, cavalry and armored cars into the heart of Berlin. This was completed by nightfall of January 11. Noske himself led these troops, perhaps only three thousand men in all, in a march which crossed Berlin from south to north. With Noske marching on foot at the head of a column made up of sections of Maercker's Volunteer Rifles and his own Iron Brigade from Kiel, the troops proceeded in ranks up the Potsdamer Strasse and turned east onto the Leipziger Strasse, then north again up the Wilhelmstrasse. They had now reached the center of Berlin and had not been fired upon. The city was wrapped in a dead silence except for occasional shots from the direction of the Belle-Alliance-Platz, several blocks east of the line of march, where Stephani's Potsdam Regiment was cleaning out the last of the revolutionaries hidden in the newspaper offices. A few civilians came to cheer the marching columns, and in response the soldiers began to sing some of the old Army marching songs—"Die Wacht am Rhein" and "O Deutschland hoch in Ehren." After the troops had crossed Berlin, they dispersed into the Moabit barracks, which were still held by Reinhard's *Freikorps.*

That night a detachment of Reinhard's command was dispatched to the Alexanderplatz to recapture the police headquarters, where Emil Eichhorn and his supporters were still barricaded. It attacked viciously. The artillery practically blew in the front of the building; then the assault section, under the command of a sergeant major named Schulze, charged the building and rapidly cleared it. Little quarter was given to its defenders, who were shot down where they were found. Only a few of them escaped over the roofs.

The next day Noske's plan developed according to schedule. Coming from the south, a blunt wedge of *Freikorps* pierced the center of Berlin and spread out to the east and west. They held a pie-shaped piece of the city comprising about a third of its area. From left to right the various contingents consisted of Hülsen's *Freikorps,* with headquarters at the Charlottenburg Palace; the Horse Guards Division under General von Hoffmann, with headquarters in the Eden Hotel; in the center of Berlin, Maercker's Volunteer Rifles, with headquarters in the palace of the Crown Prince, directly across from the imperial palace itself and commanding a full view of the Marstall, still held by the People's Naval Division; on Maercker's right, Röder's Volunteer Scouts, with headquarters in the Victoria School on the Neanderstrasse; then Wissel's *Freikorps* from the Thirty-first Infantry Division, with headquarters in the barracks of the old Telephone Corps near Treptower Park; and General von

Held's Seventeenth Division Volunteers, who took over the town hall of Neukölln, on the extreme right. They were all under the command of General von Lüttwitz, who accepted his orders from Noske and the officers of Noske's staff. A network of communications between the various headquarters was insured by the immediate occupation of all the most important telephone exchanges.

By January 13 the *Freikorps* began operations. Working out from their wedge, they successively expanded the areas under their control. The troops deployed into skirmish formation and, working a few blocks at a time, searched the buildings, flushed out any Spartacist defenders and stationed machine guns and armored cars in the central squares. There were not enough men to throw a continuous cordon around the cleared areas, but there were enough to maintain general control over the sections of the city which the *Freikorps* occupied. It proved impossible for the revolutionaries to recapture a building which the soldiers had taken over. Demonstrations were equally impossible. Whenever even a small group of civilians gathered in a street an armored car appeared almost instantly, and under the threat of its machine guns the crowd would disperse. Anyone attempting to cross one of the bridges over the Spree was searched and interrogated. At night searchlight beams from the patrolling armored cars were flung down various streets to detect any demonstrations being organized. On January 13 the Revolutionary Shop Stewards called off the general strike, and by midnight of January 15 the city of Berlin was securely in the hands of the *Freikorps*. The "Spartacist Week" was over.

The leaders of the revolution were now hunted men. The conquest of the police headquarters had enabled the government to install at last its own police president, who instantly dissolved Eichhorn's "Security Force" and summoned back to duty the old prerevolutionary police. These men now began to scour Berlin for the various members of the Revolutionary Committee. They quickly caught Georg Ledebour and Ernst Meyer of the Independent Socialists. Leo Jogiches and Hugo Eberlein were captured in a raid on the Communist Party headquarters. Some of the party's leadership escaped arrest by fleeing to the relative safety of Frankfurt-am-Main, where a strong Communist organization existed. A reward of ten thousand marks was offered by the "Association for Combating Bolshevism" for the arrest of Karl Radek. But Radek, accompanied by Eichhorn, had fled the city.

The real prizes, Luxemburg and Liebknecht, remained uncaught.

The *Freikorps*, knowing little of the Revolutionary Snop Stewards, were under the impression that the uprising had been inspired by the Communists. The Majority Socialists did nothing to correct this opinion. In the pages of *Vorwärts* they published a poem:

> *Many hundred dead are lying in a row,*
> *Proletarians!*
> *Karl, Rosa, Radek and company don't care.*
> *None of them lies there, none of them lies there,*
> *Proletarians!*[32]

Toward the end of the uprising, *Die rote Fahne* (which was suppressed on January 16) ran a bitter editorial by Luxemburg entitled "Order Rules in Berlin." In it she admitted the failure of the current revolution, but was optimistic about the eventual victory of the revolutionary movement. Addressing herself to the Ebert government, she wrote, "Your 'order' is built on sand. Tomorrow the revolution will 'rise again with clattering noise' and, to your horror, will proclaim to the sound of trumpets: I was, I am, I shall be."[33]

As the *Freikorps* tightened their hold on the city, the search for Liebknecht became more and more intense. But he was not easily found. He had spent the last days of the uprising visiting each of the Spartacist strongpoints, attempting to encourage his followers. In company with the other Communist leaders, Liebknecht even went out for dinner at various small restaurants. Then the mortal danger which they were in finally dawned on them. Liebknecht made his way in disguise through the *Freikorps* lines and took refuge in the home of a working-class family in the Neukölln district.

Now, for once in his life, Liebknecht seems to have found a certain tranquility. There was nothing that he could do to stem the overwhelming *Freikorps* victory. There were no demonstrations to lead, no frantic speeches to make, no plans to lay, no articles to write. He passed hours reading fairy tales to the small daughter of the family who sheltered him. Liebknecht, who in Rosa Luxemburg's words had always lived "in a gallop, in eternal haste, hurrying to appointments with all the world, to meetings, committees, forever surrounded by packages, newspapers, all the pockets full of writing pads and slips of paper, jumping from auto into the electric and from the electric into the steam tram, his body and soul covered with street dust,"[34] had nothing to do. He knew that he was being searched for everywhere in Berlin and that the search was getting hotter every day, but he took comfort in the thought of the ultimate Communist victory: "The Calvary of the German working class is not yet over, but the day of salvation nears."[35] Even the news that his wife and son had been captured did not upset his calm. They would all suffer, but the proletarian victory would come, of that he was certain.

On the night of January 14 Liebknecht left Neukölln, where the search was getting intense, for another hiding place, the apartment of a relative, a Frau Markussohn, at 53 Mannheimer Strasse in the Wilmersdorf district. Rosa Luxemburg and Wilhelm Pieck joined him there. The Red Rose was in a pitiable condition. She suffered from constant headaches. Her biographer says that she had become "taciturn and reserved." In the past "she had risen above her physical infirmities. But now it seemed . . . even her will could no longer triumph."[36] At first thought it would seem that Wilmersdorf was a poor place for the Communist leaders to hide. It was an upper-middle-class area only a few blocks from the headquarters of the Horse Guards Division at the Eden Hotel. But doubtless Liebknecht hoped that this very proximity would save him from discovery.

He was wrong. At 9 P.M. on January 15 a patrol from the Horse Guards Division broke into the apartment and seized the three Communist leaders, who apparently had been betrayed by a neighbor of Frau Markussohn's. They were taken to headquarters in the Eden Hotel for questioning, in the course of which they were beaten. Later in the night automobiles were brought around to the back entrance of the hotel, and Liebknecht and Luxemburg were brought out separately. As Liebknecht emerged through the doorway, a *Freikorps* soldier, an enormously built private named Runge, raised his rifle and smashed it down on Liebknecht's head. More dead than alive, "Spartakus" was flung into a car. Six *Freikorps* officers climbed in, and the automobile drove off toward Moabit Prison.

A few moments later Rosa Luxemburg hobbled out through the same hotel doorway. She too was clubbed with Runge's rifle. She too, almost lifeless, was thrown into an automobile, which drove off under the command of a Lieutenant Vogel.

Meanwhile, the car bearing Liebknecht had stopped in the wooded Tiergarten a few blocks north of the hotel. Liebknecht was taken out of the car by the six officers, who later claimed that the vehicle had broken down. He was asked if he could walk and replied that he could. According to the *Freikorps* officers, he broke loose and was shot twice and killed while "attempting to escape."

No one knows whether Rosa Luxemburg was still alive when Lieutenant Vogel blew her brains out with a single shot. Her automobile was stopped and the body was thrown off the Lichtenstein Bridge into the ice-covered Landwehr Canal, from which it was not recovered until May 31. Leo Jogiches, who had once been Rosa Luxemburg's lover, dispatched a one-sentence telegram to tell Lenin of the murders: "Rosa Luxemburg and Karl Liebknecht have carried out their ultimate revolutionary duty."[37]

When Friedrich Ebert learned of these murders he was, by every account, sincerely horrified and angrier than he had ever been seen before. He had not even been informed of the arrest of Liebknecht and Luxemburg. Only that day in a Cabinet meeting he had issued instructions that Liebknecht's wife was to be released. He told his government, "We have kept warning the troops to proceed with caution."[38] Many of his followers were upset, too—but not necessarily on moral or humanitarian grounds. They felt that Liebknecht and Luxemburg were only two of the many victims of a *Putsch* which they more than anyone else had been responsible for starting; Scheidemann, for example, observed that "they had now become the victims of their own bloody terroristic tactics."[39] It was generally agreed that the murder of the Communist leaders would inevitably result in their martyrdom and quite possibly in future Communist uprisings.

Ebert ordered an investigation of the affair, which the *Freikorps* commanders were able to frustrate. Lieutenant Vogel was convicted of failing to report a death and of illegally disposing of a corpse. He had no difficulty in obtaining a false passport and crossing the Dutch border. After waiting in Holland for a few months, he returned to Germany. He was never imprisoned. Private Runge served a sentence of several months for "attempted manslaughter."

It was now time for the election of delegates to the National Assembly. On the face of it, it would appear that the Majority Socialists had been successful. They had managed to defend their government against Bolshevism, and the elections for which they had struggled would take place on schedule. Germany would probably have a democratically elected government to draft a constitution and make peace with the victors. Ebert realized, of course, that there were other grave matters still to be dealt with: the Bavarian situation; Poland, where border warfare was already breaking out; and the Baltic States, where German troops were stemming the Russian Army's advance into Europe. Nor was the "Spartacist" menace yet dead, as the government would find out when it sent troops to the little town of Weimar. There was still a significant danger on the left.

What the government did not fully realize was that there was an equally great danger on the right. The moderate German labor movement was now irrevocably fractionalized, and its largest element, the Majority Socialist, had allowed itself to become thoroughly compromised by the armed and resurgent right. Recruiting advertisements for scores upon scores of new *Freikorps* were beginning to appear in the Berlin papers. Within a few weeks the frustrated and vengeful Ludendorff would return from Sweden saying to his wife, "It would be the greatest stupidity for the revolutionaries to allow us all to remain alive. Why, if ever I come to power again, there will be no pardon. Then, with an easy conscience, I would have Ebert, Scheidemann and company hanged and watch them dangle."[40]

The German kings had departed. The captains had not.

Chapter Ten

Weimar and Munich

THE city of Weimar, sitting astride the River Ilm 150 miles south-west of Berlin, was in the geographical center of Germany. Until November, 1918, it had been the capital of the grand duchy of Saxe-Weimar-Eisenach, which had been a sovereign member state of the German Empire, part of the Thuringian district of the province of Saxony.

Weimar was—outwardly, at least—a rather insignificant place. In 1919 it had fewer than fifty thousand inhabitants and retained a somewhat medieval appearance, with its narrow cobblestone streets, its central marketplace surrounded by a confusion of old houses with high-pitched gables, and its grand-ducal palace—the residence of an enlightened line of rulers who as early as 1817 had bestowed a liberal constitution upon their subjects. Practically the only modern structure in the city was the "New" National Theater, built in 1907 over the moldering ruins of an older opera house.

Weimar was a city which lived very much in the past, and for good reason. It had been the home of Goethe, Schiller and Herder. Many of the first performances of Wagner's operas had been given at the old National Theater. Weimar had become synonymous throughout Germany with culture and the humanities.

It was chiefly because of what the city stood for in the minds of most Germans that it had been selected as the site for the National Constituent Assembly which was to convene on February 6, 1919. Berlin and Potsdam had been considered, but it had soon been realized that these cities had unfortunate associations with militarism and the Prussian monarchy. Weimar, symbolizing as it did the spirit of liberalism, was felt to be a more auspicious birthplace for a new German constitution.

The city was thought to have another advantage: because it was small, it could be occupied and made secure by a *Freikorps* detachment. But this proved to be not as easy as had been hoped. An advance unit of Maercker's Volunteer Rifles which was sent to Weimar on January 30 was overwhelmed and disarmed by a hostile crowd of workers. To establish security, it was necessary to move the entire corps of Volunteer Rifles into the town and to threaten pitiless reprisals for any subsequent uprising. The corps, now grown to seven thousand men, dug a defensive perimeter seven miles outside Weimar and secured the heart of the town with strong contingents in the railway station, the post office and the National Theater itself.

The elections which had chosen the deputies to meet at Weimar had been held on January 19, a day of perfect winter weather throughout Germany—cold and clear. Thirty million Germans, out of an electorate of thirty-five million, had voted that day. All citizens over twenty years of age, including women for the first time, were eligible voters. They went to the polls to elect 423 deputies to the National Assembly, with the understanding that this body would then be charged with three duties: to appoint a sovereign government to replace the one which had been formed under the authority of the National Congress of Workers' and Soldiers' Councils; to make peace with Germany's enemies; and to draft a new German constitution.

The elections of January 19 constituted a double success for the Majority Socialists. First, there was the remarkable fact that the elections had been held at all; the still-smoldering wreckage of the Spartacist Week uprising was evidence that a sizable body of Germans believed the National Assembly was merely a device for smothering the revolutionary proletariat. Second and more important, the Majority Socialists had obtained thirty-nine per cent of the popular vote, winning 163 out of the 423 seats, and were by far the largest single party in the Assembly. The Independent Socialists had received only seven per cent of the votes. The Communists, of course, had boycotted the elections.

The most surprising result of the elections was the resilience shown by the bourgeois—even the conservative—parties, which had managed to stage a remarkable recovery. The old Conservative Party reappeared under the title "German National People's Party." Its leaders were willing to admit that their party included the majority of Germany's monarchists, but they claimed that their program was not really monarchist or restorationist—they desired only to take advantage "of old and proven ideals," upon which, they said, "we intend to build our new superstructure, but with strict regard to the requirements of present days."[1] This ambivalence fooled no one. The German National People's Party was firmly antirepublican, and clearly it looked forward to a Hohenzollern restoration. It was the party of the industrialists and the large landowners. Under the circumstances, it had done well to poll ten per cent of the popular vote.

The old National Liberal Party had had an even more difficult task. Its prewar platform had combined a fainthearted liberalism with an ardent nationalism; during the war its principal leader, Gustav Stresemann, had functioned as the chief apologist in the Reichstag for the Supreme Command. Now the party rechristened itself the German People's Party and, together with the German National People's Party, comprised the reactionary right in the National Assembly. The party had done badly in the elections. Despite the political dexterity of Stresemann, many of the old National Liberals had drifted off to the center parties; those who remained rallied around a program of recrudescent nationalism, stressing a cultural kinship with Germans living overseas, the importance of retaining German colonies, and an eventual union with Austria. It was not a program which had great popular appeal at the moment, and the party had been lucky to win five per cent of the National Assembly's seats.

The former Catholic Center Party, now temporarily renamed the Christian People's Party, had survived a Bavarian schism and won ninety seats in the Assembly. Under the aggressive leadership of Matthias Erzberger, the party managed to convince everyone of its sincere republicanism, and it had actually benefited from Catholic concern over the possible anticlericalism of a Socialist government. It won nearly twenty per cent of the popular vote.

The new German Democratic Party was equally successful. Before November of 1918 it had been known as the Progressive Party; its loyalty to the monarch had been lukewarm, its attitude antimilitarist and in favor of a democratic constitution. Its members could legitimately campaign as proven liberals with credentials almost as good as those of the Majority Socialists. Even Ebert acknowledged this; as early as November 15 he had appointed a prominent Democrat, Hugo Preuss, to the task of preparing a draft constitution for consideration by the National Assembly. The Democratic Party appealed to those political liberals who found Socialism distasteful, and there were enough of these to give the party eighteen per cent of the popular vote—almost double what the Progressives had won in 1912.

The final outcome of the voting was that two rightist parties which were considered reactionary and antirepublican, the National People's Party and the German People's Party, controlled a total of about fifteen per cent of the Assembly seats; two which were centrist and republican in their outlook, the Christian People's Party and the Democratic Party, controlled almost forty per cent; one party of the left, the Majority Socialists, had thirty-nine per cent; and one far-left party, the Independent Socialists, had seven per cent.

No Cabinet could be formed without domination by the Majority Socialists, but they would have to accept the support of at least one of the bourgeois center parties in order to have a working majority. This became especially important when, one day before the Assembly was to open, the Independents rejected the terms which the Majority Socialists stipulated for the Independents' admission into the new government. The Majority demanded that the Independents agree to the principles of parliamentary democracy and that they renounce any plans for another *coup d'état*. The Independents refused, and Ebert immediately proceeded to make an alliance with the Democrats and with Erzberger's Christian People's Party. Since these three parties together possessed a huge majority—331 out of the 423 seats—it was now certain that the Assembly would draft a democratic constitution. But this coalition with the bourgeois center parties also meant that an avowedly socialist economic program was now out of the question. In this fashion, the Majority Socialists found themselves clasped firmly to the bosom of the bourgeoisie.

The National Assembly began its deliberations on Thursday, February 6, in Weimar's New National Theater. A valiant attempt had been made to turn the opening session into a spectacle which would be dignified and impressive to the German people. But somehow it did not quite come off. Compared to the imposing public events staged by the Hohenzollern monarchs, the first meeting of the National Assembly seemed drab and dull. There were none of the cavalry escorts, the bands or the swarms of spectacularly uniformed personages that the German people had come to associate with a great affair of state. Indeed, the only uniforms to be seen were worn by the section of Maercker's Volunteer Rifles on guard duty outside the theater. Inside, the deputies elected to the National Assembly were ushered to seats temporarily set up in the orchestra pit. Friedrich Ebert and the other five Commissioners sat behind tables placed on the stage, surrounded by tubs of tulips and carnations.

At the opening session Ebert, dressed in a black frock coat, formally turned over the powers of the government—based on its franchise from the National Congress of Workers' and Soldiers' Councils—to the Assembly. His speech, an earnest one, was marred by frequent catcalls and other interruptions from right-wing and Independent deputies.

It took five days for the National Assembly to organize a working government. The first step was to name a presiding officer for the Assembly itself. Dr. Eduard David, a Majority Socialist, was elected to this post. Then, in order to provide a legal structure for a provisional government, the Assembly adopted a temporary constitution. Under its provisions, there was to be a President of the German Reich, who would be empowered to appoint a German Chancellor, who, in turn, would select a Cabinet to serve under him. By a vote of 277 out of 379 ballots, Friedrich Ebert was elected President. He at once appointed Philipp Scheidemann as chancellor. As his Cabinet Scheidemann chose four members of the German Democratic Party (three to serve as the ministers of finance, foreign affairs, and the interior, and one to serve without portfolio), three Christian People's Party members (the ministers of colonies and the post office, and a minister without portfolio), and five Majority Socialists. The latter were the ministers of economics, food, justice, and defense, and a minister without portfolio, Eduard David. The Minister of Defense was Gustav Noske.

The dominant figures in the new German government were Ebert and Noske. Both of them overshadowed Scheidemann, who resented this and from time to time told petty little stories about the two men. He could not, however, damage the increasing respect in which Ebert was held by the members of the center and the left at Weimar. Unsmiling and unemotional, Fritz Ebert trudged through his duties with quiet competence. All his life he had worked long hours and done his duty; there was no reason to stop now. He saw to it that the National Assembly proceeded at an orderly pace in the drafting of a permanent constitution.

Gradually Germany was being fed. On March 12 the first American food ship arrived at Hamburg with six thousand tons of flour, described in the Berlin papers as being "of faultless quality and snow white."[2] Ebert was the man who had been the Social Democratic Party's first paid administrator and the man who had built up the party's investment portfolio. Prudent administration and the conservation of assets was nothing new to him. Nor was it new to Democrat Eugen Schiffer, the Minister of Finance, who worked out an involved plan to pay Germany's internal war debt and restore the value of the mark. To the fury of the Independents, none of Germany's wartime financial obligations were to be repudiated, a budget calling for the most rigorous economy was drawn up, and there was no plan for the confiscation of private property, for the seizure of bank accounts or for a tax on capital. To the relief of the bureaucrats, there was no plan for wholesale firings of present officials and their supersession by Socialist functionaries; their morale revived and they began to function again. The old police forces were nurtured back to life, and some attempt was made to see that the ragged ex-soldiers wandering the streets possessed valid demobilization papers. Under Ebert's direction the modest social advances made under the legislation passed in November were gradually consolidated.

Second only to Ebert in the German government was Gustav Noske, as minister of defense. Unlike the careworn Ebert, Noske obviously relished his job. While Ebert felt obliged to dress to his position and frequently appeared attired uneasily in *Zylinder und Spatzen,* Noske made a point of clothing himself in a roughhewn manner—baggy pants which frequently failed to match his coarse-textured suit jacket, and a rumpled broad-brimmed hat. The constant abuse which was showered upon him from the far left did not seem to bother him at all, nor did the fact that he was called "the Bloodhound." In fact, one gets the impression that he rather liked the sobriquet and had begun to see himself in the role of a sort of superpoliceman rather than as a politician or a Socialist.

Noske, a vigilant, clever and exceptionally hard-working man, was at his best when dealing with workers, but he was frequently less than honest with them. It would almost seem that he had come to dislike the proletariat. In Noske's memoirs workers are usually portrayed as being either slightly oafish or corrupt. No chapter is without a dainty little anecdote to show his contempt for them. There is, for example, his account of his dealings with a Berlin soldiers' organization before and after the January Spartacist uprising in Berlin. At this first meeting with them the soldiers made various demands on him, such as more mustering-out pay and free suits of civilian clothes for demobilized troops, and, when Noske put them off, told him that they would not wait much longer, because—according to Noske—they were "the power." Then the Spartacist insurrection came and Noske fled Berlin. When he marched back at the head of his *Freikorps*, he hunted up the soldiers' leader and told him that he was rejecting their demands. "Now I am the power," he said.[3] Then, with obvious relish, Noske goes on to tell how the soldiers' leader asked him for a bribe of a thousand marks—which Noske gave him because of the man's nuisance value.

When it came to the officer corps, it was a different matter. In Noske's memoirs one is encouraged to believe that the officers who comprised his staff stood about openmouthed with admiration for the intuitive military genius of this ex-basketweaver. The officers always come through as efficient, loyal and patriotic. Noske returned their loyalty and was solicitous of their morale. He notes that after the suppression of an uprising in Bremen "the confidence of the officer corps . . . revitalized as they realized how much they were needed." He never criticized the officers. He was almost pathetically grateful for their support, and he got it. On March 18 Groener wrote Noske, "The Supreme Command has confidence in the government, limited confidence in the Ministry of War and unlimited confidence only in the Minister of Defense."[4]

Noske served as an admirable front for the Supreme Command. The astute Groener admitted that his principal concern was "keeping our weapons clean and the General Staff unburdened for the future"[5]—and, of course, suppressing German Bolshevism. For these purposes Noske was everything that the Supreme Command could have hoped for: a *Socialist* who was willing to participate in the raising of *Freikorps*, who issued orders which suppressed the soldiers' councils, and who marched at the head of the troops entering Berlin to suppress a proletarian uprising. When Noske's staff officers explained to him the difficulty of maintaining discipline in a military force where soldiers' councils were active, Noske obliged them, on January 19, with a decree which reduced the councils to a consultative capacity. For the Supreme Command and the officer corps, Gustav Noske was a windfall.

It is not surprising that during the early months of the German Revolution the Ebert government had exercised only a vague and sporadic control over events in Bavaria, particularly in the Bavarian capital, Munich. Even in the prewar years the Hohenzollern emperors had been careful to treat Bavaria with a light touch. The Empire, for all its successes, had never quite succeeded in overcoming the lingering nationalism of these stolid, phlegmatic Bavarians. This was partly due to the general Bavarian distaste for Prussia and all things Prussian. Some 150 years earlier Bavaria had been indisputably the most important of the German states; her people regarded Prussia as a crude Johnny-come-lately. The blue-and-white flag of the house of Wittelsbach had flown over Munich for more than 750 years; by comparison, the Prussians had only recently risen from their bleak farms east of the Elbe in a clatter of weapons. Their capital of Berlin lacked the patina and warmth of Munich. The events of 1871, in which Bavaria had been forced to accept Prussian hegemony, had never ceased to rankle. Bismarck, the Prussian Chancellor, had managed to inveigle the Bavarian King Ludwig II into making the formal offer of the German Imperial crown to Wilhelm I of Prussia. The idea was that this gesture would indicate the desire of Bavaria for incorporation in the Reich. The maneuver fooled no one—least of all Ludwig, who at first wanted to decline the dubious honor. "Do you think it's pleasant to be swallowed up?" he asked his counselors.

In return for this grudging fealty, Bismarck's German Constitution of 1871 granted Bavaria certain special privileges within the imperial federation. They were known as the "reserved rights" (*Reservatrechte*) and made Bavaria semiautonomous in many respects. Bavaria was permitted to maintain a separate diplomatic service, with its own ambassadors at Vienna, St. Petersburg and the Vatican. The Bavarian kingdom controlled its own postal, telegraphic and railway systems. Like Saxony and Württemberg, Bavaria retained her own Army; unlike them, she possessed a General Staff, and her generals were appointed by the King of Bavaria, not by the Emperor. The Prussian Army was not permitted to enter Bavarian territory, and the Bavarian Army came under the command of the German Emperor only at the outbreak of war.

These concessions did not completely satisfy Bavaria, for there were many basic differences between the Prussian and the Bavarian. Seventy per cent of the Wittelsbach subjects were Catholic, while the Prussians were mainly Protestant. There was a far greater percentage of small proprietors and landowning peasants in Bavaria than in Prussia. Temperamentally, the easygoing Bavarians felt themselves closer to the Austrians than to the Prussians, whose aggressiveness and militarism seemed to them artificial and pompous. All in all, the Bavarians were not enthusiastic members of the German Empire. But they were not disloyal either. As the years passed, they grew to accept their situation. No one could deny the economic benefits which the Empire had made possible; Munich and Nuremberg expanded rapidly with new industries which brought general prosperity to Bavaria.

When the war began, the Bavarian Army mobilized as swiftly as the Prussian Army. The Bavarian Crown Prince, Rupprecht, took command of two corps of the Bavarian Army and proved to be more efficient and far more popular with his troops than the Prussian princes with theirs. The Bavarian officers were the equals of the Prussian, and the Bavarian enlisted men won as many decorations for valor as their Prussian counterparts.

For the first two or three years of war the common cause drove Bavaria closer into the Empire, but as the war dragged on, with no perceptible end in sight, the Bavarian attitude began to change. The war sickness which manifested itself in Prussia had its Bavarian counterpart in a progressive disenchantment with the Kaiser. Bavarians began to think that the war was really Prussia's and recalled that Berlin had not consulted Bavaria about the declaration of war. It began to appear that the Wittelsbachs' kingdom had been dragged into the conflict behind the war chariots of their Hohenzollern masters. This seemed to be borne out by the fact that Allied propaganda was generally aimed at "Prussian militarism," and this, in turn, gave rise to speculation that it might be possible for Bavaria to secure lenient peace terms if she denounced her masters in Berlin.

By November, 1918, the Bavarians were sick of war, were more than faintly anti-Prussian and had all lost confidence in their King, the placid and uninspiring Ludwig III. As a result, the Independent Socialists had done rather well in Bavaria. Indeed, the term "Majority Socialist" was practically a misnomer here; because of their yearning for peace and their distrust of Prussia, more Socialists had defected to the Independent camp than had remained "Majority" adherents.

* * *

About a half mile west of the very center of Munich, but still well within the limits of the city, is the Theresienwiese, the huge grass-covered field which is the site of the annual Oktoberfest. On the west side of this field is Bavaria Park, which faces an immense statue, the figure of Bavaria. On Thursday, November 7, 1918, at two in the afternoon, the Theresienwiese was jammed with people. It was a perfect day for an open-air meeting—sunny and unseasonably warm. An enormous crowd had turned out for a peace demonstration. Although most of the throng was made up of workers from the Munich war plants, there was also a sprinkling of soldiers—remarkable because the military governor had ordered all troops confined to their barracks. Some twenty Socialist orators of various opinions had set up a platform and were speaking to the throng. The leader of the Majority Socialists in Munich, Erhard Auer, had established himself directly beneath the statue of Bavaria and was proposing that a peace-demonstration march should be made through the city. With typical Majority Socialist thoroughness, Auer had hired a band to lead his march.

But one man, an Independent Socialist, outdrew the others by far. His name was Kurt Eisner, and he was the most inflammatory of all the speakers. "Scatter throughout the city," he urged the soldiers, "occupy the barracks, seize weapons and ammunitions, win over the rest of the troops, and make yourselves masters of the government!"[6]

This was precisely what most of the crowd did. While Auer, his brass band and a few thousand adherents made their way eastward through the center of the city and dispersed harmlessly at the other side, Eisner and his larger group of excited followers marched west. They walked as far as the Guldein School, a temporary munitions depot for the Bavarian Army. There they pushed aside a few officers and helped themselves to an assortment of rifles. Then, turning north, Eisner led them over the railroad tracks to the big Maximilian Kaserne and the other barracks which adjoined it. In a few hours they had made a clean sweep of the Munich garrison. Red flags hung from every barracks.

In the midst of this, Eisner went off to the Mathäser Brauhaus, Munich's largest beerhall, and met with Munich's first workers' and soldiers' council, which authorized him to form a "Bavarian Republic" and place himself at its head. It was as simple as that. Within a few hours, Eisner named a Cabinet of three reluctant Majority Socialists, three Independent Socialists, one unaligned member and Eisner himself, who took the portfolio of foreign minister as well as that of prime minister.

By the next morning, November 8, Eisner's government controlled the central railroad station, the newspaper offices, the Bavarian Army headquarters and practically every other building of importance. Eisner proclaimed Bavaria a republic and announced that sovereign power had passed into the hands of the Council of Workers, Soldiers and Peasants.

The Wittelsbach dynasty evaporated. The palace guard had gone over to the revolutionaries, and the royal Residenz was invaded by groups of curious Müncheners who wandered about, hooting in the huge galleries and ballrooms to hear the echoes. King Ludwig III had no stomach for counterrevolutionary attempts. His ministers put it to him bluntly that he ought to abdicate. Even the general who was the royal Minister of War was no help. Stunned, he could only mutter apprehensively, "The revolution—and here am I in my uniform!"[7] Ludwig and his family took an automobile and fled the city, leaving Bavaria in the undisputed control of a Jewish intellectual who had been a drama critic for most of his adult life.

It is indeed astounding that Kurt Eisner, who was an exotic personality for Catholic and conservative Bavaria, should have succeeded in so tremendous a feat. Eisner was not even a native Bavarian. He had been born in Berlin some fifty-one years before, the son of a prosperous Jewish shopowner dealing in military insignia and ornaments. After graduating from one of the best *Gymnasien* in Berlin, Eisner attended the Friedrich Wilhelm University, which he left to become a journalist. In 1897 he wrote a magazine article satirizing the Kaiser; arrested and convicted of *lèse majesté*, he served a nine-month sentence in a Prussian penitentiary. This brought him to the attention of the elder Liebknecht, who recruited Eisner into the Social Democratic Party and later made him an editor of *Vorwärts*. In the controversy between the party's revisionists and the revolutionaries, Eisner aligned himself with the former, which resulted in his being thrown out as a *Vorwärts* editor. He had made many enemies among the party's intellectuals. Rosa Luxemburg, for one, abominated Eisner. She thought him an insincere student of economics and social theoretics (which he surely was), too concerned with literature to be a Social Democratic functionary. "May you drown in the moral absolutes of your be-loved *Critique of Pure Reason,*" she wrote Eisner.[8]

In 1907, unable to make a living in Prussia, Eisner abandoned his wife and five children and fled to Bavaria, first to Nuremberg and then, in 1910, to Munich. His personal needs were very small. He lived in a small cottage on the outskirts of Munich with the daugh-ter of an old socialist. Every day he took the trolley into Munich, where he managed to make a slender living as a drama critic, essayist and poet. The fact that he was an idealistic dreamer and a bohemian intellectual of the most outré sort did not single him out for any special attention in the Bavarian capital. Munich was full of artists and political theorists.

During the war Eisner emerged from obscurity. He established the Independent Socialist Party in Bavaria and took a leading role in the January, 1918, food and peace strikes in Munich. The authori-ties broke the strike and flung its leaders, Eisner included, into prison, where they remained without charge, trial or conviction.[*] Eisner was not released until October, 1918, when Prince Max's government declared its amnesty. Eisner's imprisonment, like Lieb-knecht's, brought him to the attention of the proletariat. But there were others whose revolutionary activities had made them fully as well-known, and this makes Eisner's success seem all the more amazing, for he was a Jew in overwhelmingly Catholic Bavaria, he had no particular personal following, and his physical appearance was distinctly unimpressive. He was short and thin, with a sallow complexion; a large gray beard obscured most of his face, and he wore tiny steel-rimmed pince-nez. The only thing that was striking about his appearance was the immense *vie de bohème* black hat he affected.

Because it seemed so incredible that this little intellectual should have taken over all of Bavaria, it was immediately rumored that he was an agent of the Russian Bolsheviks and had been provided with vast sums to bribe officials and pay his followers. This Eisner denied with laughter. The entire revolution had cost him only eighteen marks—the small change he had in his pocket on November 7 which he had spent in the following days. Nor was he the Bolshevik type.

---

[*] Eisner served most of his imprisonment in Cell 70 of the Bavarian state prison at Stadelheim. This same cell was subsequently occupied by Count Arco-Valley, Eisner's assassin, and by Adolf Hitler in 1923 following the failure of the "Beerhall Putsch." In 1934 Ernst Röhm was shot in the same cell.

A French journalist who witnessed the early days of Eisner's regime found him an attractive personality. His speeches were always witty, shrewd, caustic and controversial; his range was enormous, and no one could forecast what he would say. "Poetry, drama, criticism, philosophy—there is no domain into which his restless and inquisitive thought does not venture, always attracted to excess by a taste for new formulae," the Frenchman wrote. "This last characteristic is found even in his politics, where his ideas are always excessively bold, sometimes fantastic and paradoxical as well, often bordering on anarchy."[9]

Eisner's personal work habits were equally extravagant. Convinced that a new age of open diplomacy and exposed government had dawned, he conducted Bavaria's affairs in public. The doors to his office—formerly the sumptuous apartments of Count von Hertling, who had been the Bavarian Minister President before he became the German Imperial Chancellor—were left wide open. Visitors found Eisner's desk strewn with proclamations, telegrams and memoranda. He made no particular effort to hide even the most confidential documents. Would the visitor care to see a copy of a telegram only just sent off to Ebert in Berlin? Here it was. Would the journalist like to read the minutes of the Cabinet meetings of the Bavarian Socialist Republic? They were available in full for the journalist's immediate inspection.

Surrounding Eisner were a clutter of desks behind which worked typists, clerks and miscellaneous functionaries, who from time to time interrupted their labors to smoke a cigarette or munch a sandwich. Unused chairs had been dragged up to the desks and their seats stacked high with documents. Outside the once beautiful office suite, lounging on the huge sofas of the old regime, waited various workers and peasants who had come to ask for Eisner's help in some matter or other. Occasionally one of them, bored with waiting, would burst unannounced into the *Ministerpräsident's* office, and Eisner, looking frail and seedy and wearing a black skullcap, would look up from his work and deal with the worker's request on the spot.

"There seems to be no method, no organization and no order in this curious government," observed a journalist.

> *Every function seems to be concentrated in the head and heart of this man. Nevertheless, despite the fantasy which seems to*

characterize his decisions, his personality is so forceful that it makes a tremendous impression on us. His power lies in the depth of his convictions, in his sincerity, and in his utter frankness. . . . He is for the Bavarian people the living symbol of their revolution.[10]

In these November and December days the military situation in Munich closely paralleled that in Berlin. There was a contingent of revolutionary sailors who had been on their way to Kiel from the shipyards at Pola at the time the mutinies began. They had been ordered to remain in Munich and had subsequently set themselves up on the same lines as the People's Naval Division in Berlin. When the Bavarian Army divisions returned to Munich there was the same wholesale mutiny—although a great many of the soldiers still hung around the barracks because the soldiers' councils had insisted that the government feed any demobilized enlisted men.* Only a few small Army units managed to remain intact. There were still some dedicated and warlike spirits who persisted in clinging together in their barracks and preserving the shambles of their regiment. The Eisner government made no serious effort to disband them or control their activities. As in Berlin, there were occasional weak attempts at a counterrevolutionary *Putsch* which were beaten back with ease.

Politically the major difference between the two regimes was that in Bavaria the government was controlled by the Independent Socialists; the Majority Socialists were actually in the minority. This was only partially offset by the fact that the Majority Socialist Erhard Auer held the important post of minister of the interior. The dominant position of Eisner and his group allowed them to remake Bavaria according to their own conception of democratic progress.

Eisner's plans for the Bavarian economy were somewhat incoherent. He did not understand economics, and he was not much interested in the subject. He made no effort to socialize industry, because, he said, "it seems to us impossible, at a time when the production power of the land is nearly exhausted, to transfer industry immediately to the possession of society. There can be no

---

* Adolf Hitler returned to Munich in late November. For a few days he stayed in the barracks of the List Regiment, until the activities of the regiment's soldiers' council became "so repellent to me that I decided at once to leave again as soon as possible." He went to serve as a guard at a prisoner-of-war camp for Russians at Traunstein, near the Austrian border. Hitler did not return to Munich until March, 1919.

socialization when there is scarcely anything to be socialized."[11] It was almost with a sense of relief that he postponed this matter until some vague future date when socialization could be accomplished on an international scale. The only activity in Munich which was socialized was the theater; Eisner felt this to be crucially important in the revolutionary struggle, and he summoned representatives of the actors to his office and encouraged them to distribute the principal dramatic roles more equitably.

But if Eisner had no desire to become involved with economics, he was enthusiastically at home in the world of abstract ideas. The Munich workers' and soldiers' councils included a "Council of Intellectual Workers," formed from among Eisner's old friends in the newspapers, the coffeehouses and the University of Munich. Eisner threw himself into the labors of this council, which was soon busily turning out proposals of a praiseworthy but highly theoretical nature. The Bavarian government was urged by this council to "encourage man's moral improvement as a means to prepare him for a fuller political life"; to develop within the workers an "international spirit"; to "imbue everyone with a sense of personal responsibility"; and to recognize the government's obligation to "extend to youth all possibilities of intellectual and moral development."[12] Mixed with these proposals were more concrete ideas: the abolition of military service, the reduction of working hours and the reform of women's education.

These being the objectives of the Bavarian government, it was at first difficult for even the most archreactionary faction to find much fault with it. There was absolutely no Red terror, no trace of Bolshevism and little anarchy or disorder. There had never been much class hatred among the tolerant Bavarians, and there seemed no particular reason for it to begin now. Despite the popularity of Crown Prince Rupprecht, there was no significant sympathy for the restoration of the Wittelsbachs. Whatever enmity existed seemed directed against Prussia. In the streets, demobilized soldiers sold hand-painted satirical postcards showing cartoons of Kaiser Wilhelm boating on a Dutch canal, with his crown and scepter floating in the wake of his vessel. Other drawings showed a shabby gravestone with the inscription "Herr Militarismus, born in Berlin, died in Munich, and buried with all the honors of his rank."[13]

Eisner was not immune to this anti-Prussianism. He was convinced that Prussia must bear the responsibility for losing the war—indeed, for having started the war in the first place. He had come to believe that the Allies, especially the French, could be persuaded to make a separate peace with Bavaria, and in this he was quite possibly right. Eisner conceived of a new Germany which would allow wide individual latitude to its various federal republics. He thought of himself as a brilliant diplomat and dreamed of occupying a commanding role in German foreign affairs. He thirsted for recognition by the Allies (particularly by Woodrow Wilson, whom he admired enormously) as the man who symbolized the new Germany.

On November 24, 1918, the Bavarian government published a series of documents taken from the 1914 files of the old royal Foreign Ministry. These documents were intended to establish that Bavaria had been innocent of all hostile intent and that the outbreak of war had been exclusively a Prussian responsibility.

The following day Eisner journeyed to Berlin for a meeting with Ebert. It was a stormy session. Apart from the usual doctrinal differences between an Independent and a Majority Socialist, the publication of the diplomatic correspondence had infuriated Ebert. He claimed that the documents were not authentic, that they had been deliberately excerpted from the originals to make the anti-Prussian case more damning. Moreover, by publishing these diplomatic exchanges, Eisner had provided the Allies with additional data with which to "prove" the culpability of Germany as the instigator of the war. Eisner would see, Ebert charged, just how much Germany would pay for Bavaria's anti-Prussianism. Eisner's naïve attempt to obtain more lenient terms for Bavaria by means of this "true and loyal confession" directed at the sympathies of Wilson and the intrigues of the French would come to nothing. Ebert assured Eisner that the new constitution would provide for a more centralized authority over the various German states rather than less. The elections for the National Assembly would take place as swiftly as possible, whether Eisner liked it or not. As an Independent Socialist fully committed to the perpetuation of the workers' and soldiers' councils, Eisner did not.

Frustrated and angry, Eisner hurried back to Munich. He had no intention of permitting the Prussian Majority Socialists to dictate the foreign policy of Bavaria. On November 26 he announced that the Bavarian government was severing diplomatic relations with the Ebert government in Berlin. Henceforth Bavaria would conduct its own foreign affairs.

But Eisner now found himself in almost the same situation as Ebert in Berlin—only in reverse. Three members of his Cabinet were Majority Socialists, and they could scarcely be considered loyal opposition. In particular, Erhard Auer, the Minister of the Interior, was determined that the German nation must not be fractionalized. He demanded that an election be held to select members for the Bavarian Landtag, which would then become the sovereign power in Bavaria, replacing Eisner's workers' and soldiers' councils. Ultimately Auer won, and the elections were scheduled for January 12.

In the meantime, the Munich equivalent of the People's Naval Division, supported by the Bavarian wing of the Spartacists, staged an attempted *Putsch* from the left. They were far from satisfied with Eisner. The Bavarian far left believed that Eisner lacked the ruthlessness necessary to consolidate the Bavarian revolution. They could not understand why he had failed to use terror as a revolutionary weapon and why he permitted the Majority Socialists to remain in the Bavarian government. The answer was simple: Eisner was not a Bolshevik. He distrusted Lenin and Trotsky, and he believed that Germany had nothing to learn from Russia, a nation which he regarded as culturally inferior. "We have neither used Russian methods nor pursued Russian obectives," he said. "There is no Russian Bolshevism in Germany, perhaps with the exception of a few visionaries."[14] The more radical elements in Munich thereupon decided to act on their own.

On the night of December 7, a band of four hundred sailors and Spartacists surrounded Auer's offices and, putting a pistol against his head, demanded and got his resignation as minister of the interior—which Auer later retracted. With considerable difficulty Eisner suppressed this extension of the revolution. Then he suddenly found himself faced with counterrevolution from the right.

Eisner had made a serious mistake. He had failed to appreciate the actual feelings of the mass of the Bavarians about separatism. The average Münchener rather liked Eisner as a person. He was the sort of eccentric idealist whom the Bavarians—perhaps *only* the Bavarians—could understand. The accounts of Eisner talking endlessly to foreign journalists as he served them tea and stale cookies in his shabby little home had a quaint ring which the Bavarian proletariat liked. Eisner thought that when the crowds in the Munich streets chanted "Bavaria for the Bavarians!" they meant exactly that, but he misunderstood their true sentiments. What they wanted when they spoke of Bavarian "independence" was simply a relaxation of the old Prussian domination over the German nation.

Another point which worked to Eisner's disadvantage was the rapidly deteriorating economy of Bavaria. The state was on the edge of financial ruin. The railroad system had run down during the war, and more than half its remaining locomotives had been turned over to the Allies as required under the armistice. There were twenty thousand unemployed workers in Bavaria by the beginning of the second week in January, and the figure was spiraling upward. Tens of thousands of soldiers were drawing demobilization pay, which the government felt obliged to continue indefinitely because there were no jobs for them to go to. The state was bankrupting itself with unemployment-compensation payments. There was no housing for the masses of ex-soldiers who wanted to leave their barracks. There were no more vegetables in the Munich markets, and none were expected until late spring.

By mid-December, demonstrations against Eisner and his government were taking place daily. Students assembled in the Max-Joseph-Platz in front of the Residenz, the former Wittelsbach winter palace and now the seat of the government. They came to revile Eisner with cries of "Out with the Israelite devil!" and "We want a Bavarian!"[15] Rumors spread that Eisner's real name was Salomon Kuchinsky and that he was actually a Russian and an agent of Lenin. It did no good for Eisner to reply, "I am a member of an old Berlin family,"[16] and to offer his birth certificate for inspection. The various Catholic newspapers began to attack the government with the rallying cry "Religion is in danger!"

To stem the tide, Eisner elected to explain his position at a special "Fete of the Bavarian Revolution" in the opera house. The leaders of the workers' and soldiers' councils were all invited, as were Munich's artists, poets and writers. The orchestra, under the direction of Bruno Walter, played one of Beethoven's Leonore Overtures and a Handel aria, and a chorus sang a hymn composed for the occasion by Eisner himself; entitled "The Song of the People," it ended with the exhortation "O world, rejoice!" Then Eisner appeared on the stage to try to explain his policies to a restive and unsympathetic audience. For a half hour he was unable to make himself heard over the whistles and the shouts of "Rascal!" "Bandit!" "Slacker!"[17] Finally the crowd let him speak. He addressed them on the theme "Education and Democracy," which struck his audience as not particularly to the point. The revered leader of the Bavarian revolution was now revealed as an ineffectual and impractical theorist whose interests and abilities were wholly inconsonant with the requirements of the time.

By January Eisner found himself deprived of support from all quarters except for a small coterie of still-loyal followers. On the left the Communists were preparing for a coup. On the right the bourgeoisie and the Majority Socialists were his enemies. Within the government itself Eisner had lost his influence. Cabinet meetings produced the most awful scenes. Even the one supposedly unaligned member of the Cabinet, Heinrich von Frauendorfer, was willing to blurt out to Eisner, "You are no statesman, you commit blunders, you are an anarchist . . . You are no statesman, you are a fool. . . . We are being ruined by bad management."[18] The Majority Socialist members had begun to make decisions without consulting the Prime Minister.

On Friday, January 12, a special election was held to choose the members of the Bavarian Landtag. Eisner and his Independent Socialists were utterly humiliated at the polls: they received a mere 86,000 votes to the Majority Socialists' 1,124,000, and won only three seats in the Landtag. Nevertheless, by dint of endless compromises with every possible faction, Eisner was able to cling to his office for a few more weeks, but only as a figurehead. Finally even this pitiful charade could not be maintained; the forces on the left and the right had grown too powerful. On February 21, just before ten in the morning, the despairing Eisner set out from his office in the Foreign Ministry for the Landtag, to tender his government's resignation. He never got there.

In the street outside the ministry his assassin was waiting: the twenty-two-year-old Count Anton Arco-Valley. The young Count, who had been a student at the University of Munich and then, toward the end of the war, a lieutenant in a guards infantry regiment of the Bavarian Army, had recently tried to enter a local racist group called the Thule Society. This society was ostensibly a literary club devoted to the study of Germanic culture (it took its name from that of the legendary Nordic kingdom where the German race had supposedly first appeared), but in practice its members devoted themselves to anti-Semitic literature. The Thule Society and a companion organization called the Schutz und Trutz Bund (League for Protection and Resistance) had grown rapidly in the months since the armistice. It had recruited writers and intellectuals such as Dietrich Eckart and young officers such as Rudolph Hess, and its charter members included an outspoken racist from the

Baltic, Alfred Rosenberg, who had brought with him to Munich an early copy of *The Protocols of the Elders of Zion*. As a symbol of their anti-Semitism its members chose the Hakenkreuz, which was also known as the swastika. They greeted one another with the cry "Heil!"[19]

Arco-Valley had longed to become part of this organization, but, to his despair, his application had been rejected—probably because the society discovered that his mother was of Jewish descent. It can only be supposed that he thirsted to prove to those who had rejected him that he was braver than they were.

The young man had followed Eisner to the Foreign Ministry earlier that morning, but there had been no opportunity for a clear shot. So Arco-Valley waited in the Promenadestrasse, the street which ran between the Landtag building and the Foreign Ministry. He knew that the Landtag session would begin at ten and that Eisner would walk across to attend it.

At nine forty-five, Eisner, accompanied by two secretaries and two guards, came out of the Foreign Ministry and, walking rapidly, turned left on the Promenade Platz and left again into the Promenadestrasse. When the stubby little man, wearing his usual huge black hat, drew abreast of the waiting Arco-Valley, the young Count pulled out his pistol and fired two shots at him point-blank. Both bullets hit Eisner in the head, and he died instantly. A second later the bleeding Arco-Valley, shot in the neck, mouth and chest by one of Eisner's guards, was lying on the pavement. It was practically a miracle that Felix Fechenbach, Eisner's devoted secretary, was able to keep a crowd from lynching the Count. The young man was dragged into the courtyard of the Foreign Ministry, and from there the police carried him away to a famous Munich surgeon, who saved his life.

The popular reaction to Eisner's assassination was instantaneous and frightening. The Munich workers would not believe that Arco-Valley had acted alone; the murder must be part of a counterrevolutionary plot by officers and students. Infuriated, the proletariat embarked upon a program of immediate revenge.

Exactly one hour later a nondescript butcher's apprentice named Alois Lindner walked into the chamber of the Landtag, where Eisner's enemy Erhard Auer had just finished orating upon the death of the Prime Minister. Unnoticed, Lindner walked down the aisle and leaned against a railing directly in front of Auer. Pulling out a pistol, he rested it on the railing to steady his aim and, in a moment of absolute silence and in full view of the horrified members of the Landtag, shot Auer out of his chair. Then, leaving the Minister horribly wounded and writhing on the floor, he calmly walked back up the aisle. An Army officer who flung himself at Lindner was killed with a single shot. Pushing his way through the doors, the butcher's apprentice walked outside and disappeared in the crowd.

By now the Munich church bells were all tolling for the death of Kurt Eisner; flags were already flying at half mast. A Red guard quickly gathered to protect and enshrine the spot where Eisner had been murdered. The Munich proletariat, unwilling only a few hours before to support Eisner, now remembered only his services at the time of the revolution and mourned his memory. Workers set up framed copies of his portrait in the streets, and all who passed by were forced by rifle-carrying soldiers to remove their hats. Members of the nobility were arrested and thrown into prison as hostages.

Eisner's funeral took place on February 26, which was declared a day of mourning throughout Bavaria; the Munich workers improved on this by declaring a three-day general strike which practically paralyzed the city. The funeral procession was enormous. Vast delegations of workers and peasants marched behind the hearse. All the city officials and most of the Landtag deputies joined the procession. Some of the people in the parade carried signs demanding "Vengeance for Eisner!"[20] The Munich church bells rang incessantly; where necessary, the priests were forced to the task at gunpoint. Crowds assembled around the offices of the bourgeois newspapers, broke down their doors, piled stacks of newspapers in the streets and set fire to them.

Meanwhile the Bavarian government became a shambles. It was obviously impossible for the Landtag to function in an atmosphere so bizarre that one of its members had been shot down in its chamber. Accordingly, its sittings were discontinued. In the vacuum the Majority Socialists claimed the right to direct the Bavarian government. A coalition Cabinet headed by Johannes Hoffmann announced itself and was almost immediately forced to flee Munich for Nuremberg, at the northern edge of Bavaria, where a slender force from one of Noske's *Freikorps* could protect it.

This left Munich itself in a state of anarchy. A group of Independent Socialists, led by the poet Ernst Toller and including various other personalities such as the playwright Erich Mühsam and the anarchist Gustav Landauer, formed a government which was supposed to carry on the tradition of the martyred Eisner. But by now the Communists had joined the melee. Two Russian-born Bolsheviks sent south from Berlin managed to reach Munich, where they denounced Toller and his Independents, assumed the leadership of the old Spartacist organization, and started a Munich edition of *Die rote Fahne*. The fact that these two Russians were named respectively Levien and Leviné added to the wild confusion of the situation.

Munich had become a city in which gun battles in the street were a daily occurrence. The German government in Weimar did not even pretend to control the situation. The upper bourgeoisie and the Bavarian nobility armed themselves and began fighting both the Independent Socialists and the Communists. Members of the Thule Society mixed the scent of bitches in heat into bags of flour which they then scattered on the site of Eisner's assassination; the dogs which gathered quickly made this shrine into a foul-smelling spot.

It must not be thought that the German government was indifferent to what was going on in Munich. Ebert and his associates were appalled at this Bavarian anarchy, and it is certain that they would have done anything in their power to prevent Bavaria from separating herself from the rest of Germany. But the government's powers were still very limited, and such armed forces as it controlled were already stretched paper thin. In addition, the Eisner government had prohibited the recruitment of *Freikorps* within its borders. Thus there were no native forces available for a Bavarian adventure.

The principal burden of defending the German Republic still lay on the shoulders of Gustav Noske. In December and early January he had, with the blessing and significant support of the Supreme Command, managed to raise a number of strong *Freikorps*—enough to put down the Spartacist uprising in Berlin during the second week of January. But after this there was a lull in the formation of new combat-ready *Freikorps*. Many new *Freikorps* were being recruited, but they were of a very different character from Maercker's Volunteer Rifles. The very nature of the recruitment method made this almost inevitable. So desperate was the government's need for troops that practically anyone who wanted to raise a *Freikorps* could be sure of obtaining money and recognition from Noske and his officers. All that was required was a few posters, an office and some sort of barracks for the recruits. It helped if the organizers of a *Freikorps* could establish some sort of bond with a regiment of the old Imperial Army, so that it could be claimed that the new corps carried on the old traditions. A typical recruiting poster read: "The

Brown Hussars require volunteers for the defense of our frontiers. . . . Anyone who loves horses and prefers the strictest discipline and justice to anarchy should at once enlist."[21] But as time went on it became less necessary to appeal to the old Imperial Army bonds. It was not even mandatory that the Supreme Command or the Ministry of Defense recognize a new *Freikorps*. A group of German industrialists, among them Krupp, Kirdorff and Stinnes, had set up an "Anti-Bolshevik League" to which they contributed millions of marks for the private financing of *Freikorps*.

These new *Freikorps* varied greatly. Some had two hundred men, others fifteen hundred. More important, they differed markedly in leadership and political outlook. The six *Korps* which had invaded Berlin during Spartacist Week had all come from the immediate wreckage of old regiments, so the command of each *Freikorps* usually remained in the hands of the regiment's old commanding officer; the troops of these formations thought of themselves, with good reason, as still being in "the Army." The new *Freikorps*—and there were vast numbers of them—had to start from scratch. They were generally the product of the enthusiasm of a few young captains or, at most, majors. These company-grade officers obviously did not welcome the recruitment of officers senior to them, and so, increasingly, they elected to preserve their independence by accepting financing from the Anti-Bolshevik League.

The problem of recruiting enlisted men was becoming somewhat difficult. The best of the old Army privates and noncommissioned officers either had joined the early *Freikorps* or had gone home after being demobilized. The result was that the new *Freikorps* could no longer recruit enough experienced front-line soldiers with the call for a "return to order and discipline." Instead they began to accept very young men—the conservative schoolboy sons of the bourgeoisie, for example—and offered an ideological appeal such as the defense of the homeland, the suppression of Bolshevism, disguised monarchism, open anti-Semitism, or German "folkishness."

The new *Freikorps* were filling out slowly during the first months of 1919. Each of their young commanding officers, acutely aware of his own modest military rank, was careful to preserve the independence of the troop he was forming, lest it be absorbed into a larger formation. Thus great stress was laid on the personal loyalty of the *Freikorps* member toward the *Führer* of his group. And, as an aid to recruitment and an indication of the type of spirit desired, most of the new *Freikorps* began to liken themselves to the glamorous *Sturmtruppen,* the storm troops of the war.

This was the position in which the German government found itself late in January, 1919. Bavaria was, for all practical purposes, not under the control of the German Republic. The National Constituent Assembly was about to convene in Weimar, defended by the guns of the *Freikorps.* The suppression of the Spartacist rising in Berlin and the murder of Liebknecht and Luxemburg had not had the discouraging effect upon the German revolutionary elements that had been hoped for; the Communists and the Independent Socialists of the far left, together with other organizations which might loosely be described as "Spartacist," had not lost their conviction that victory was still possible. The events in Berlin had been a defeat, but there was much to suggest that this was only temporary. Munich was in the hands of the revolutionaries, and in other parts of Germany the workers' and soldiers' councils were still powerful and progressively more revolutionary. In Berlin itself the government was experiencing a setback: it was actually forced to withdraw most of its victorious *Freikorps* from the capital. The experience of firing on German workers, of searching their flats for arms and of facing the hate-filled glances of the workers on the Berlin streets was too much even for the *Freikorps.* Their officers became alarmed at the change in the attitude of the troops and abruptly pulled them out of the capital.

On January 24 the Moscow radio broadcast an invitation to revolutionary parties throughout the world to send delegates to a congress for the purpose of forming a new Communist International in place of the discredited Second Socialist International. The new organization would duly be created by the Moscow congress in March; it would become known as the Third International and, later, as the Comintern. Within Prussia the *Rote Fahne,* which had been suppressed by the Ebert government, was preparing to resume publication on a clandestine basis.

All of these signs brought renewed encouragement to the revolutionary elements in the cities outside Berlin, especially in those industrial areas which had never experienced occupation by one of the bigger *Freikorps* equipped with armored cars, cavalry and artillery. As they looked about them, the local Communist or Independent Socialist leaders in the provincial cities saw only the little re-

cruiting centers in which a few young officers were signing up a
handful of old soldiers and the young sons of the bourgeoisie. These
recruiting centers, generally housed in small shops or residences,
were surrounded with barbed wire and placarded with posters, and
a machine gun or two might be visible in the upper-story windows,
but there was nothing to suggest that they could do more than
defend themselves. So in the North Sea ports, in the mines and
factories of the Ruhr and among the industrial cities of central
Germany revolutionary activity increased in tempo.

The insurrection in Bremen actually began in early January at the
same time as the Spartacist uprising in Berlin. Red revolution came
naturally in this port city. Even before the end of the war, the group
known as the Bremen Left Radicals had outdone the Spartacists in
revolutionary zeal. It was therefore not difficult to put together a
Communist-Independent coalition, which, backed by the Bremen
Workers' and Soldiers' Council, seized the municipal government. In
a manner now routine, the Majority Socialist newspaper offices were
taken over and an autonomous "Republic of Oldenburg" was proclaimed. The local bank accounts of the Majority Socialist organization were pillaged, weapons were distributed to the revolutionary workers, and a general strike was proclaimed. Within a few
days the other ports on the North Sea—Hamburg, Cuxhaven and
Wilhelmshaven—were also in revolution.

There was nothing the government could do to suppress this rebellion. The task of raising the initial *Freikorps* contingents and
reconquering Berlin absorbed all of Noske's resources. But when
these tasks were completed, the problem of subduing the ports
became crucial. These cities, in which the general strike was now
total, were practically the only avenue through which food shipments from abroad could enter Germany. In late January the food
ships from the United States began to arrive, but the ports were
blocked and the docks sealed off by Red Guards.

Clearly the matter was urgent. The number of revolutionaries was
unknown; rumor put it at forty thousand armed men, although it
might well be more. To recapture the North Sea ports Noske had
only the men from the *Freikorps* in Berlin, and not all of these could
be spared from defending Weimar and keeping a vigil on Berlin. On
January 21 he told the Cabinet that so far he had total forces of
22,000 men. "In two or three weeks we hope to have fifty thousand
men at our disposal. . . . For Berlin we require ten thousand men.
We have sent off a thousand men today to Upper Silesia. Eight

hundred men belonging to the Baumeister Regiment took off today for the east. Maercker's corps will be used to protect Weimar, and it will reestablish order in Halle and Brunswick in passing."[22] This did not leave very many men for the port cities. Nonetheless, the case was urgent, and in the very last days of January Noske put "Gerstenburg's Division" in motion toward Bremen. Despite its impressive title, this "division" was merely one of the three sections of Röder's Volunteer Scouts. The total number of *Freikorps* fighters who were dispatched to reconquer the port cities was only 3,500 men. There was no help for it. "We arrived at the conclusion," Noske wrote, "that if order was not restored in Bremen, the government might consider itself lost, for no one in the country would respect it. Any risk was preferable."[23]

When this *Freikorps* left for Bremen, Noske was bombarded with threats. Workers and soldiers' councils in other parts of Germany telegraphed that they would go out on strike if the troops fired on German workers. The revolutionaries in Bremen announced that they would sink the ships in the harbor. Noske ignored them all.

The attack on Bremen was a repetition of the Berlin story. Gerstenburg's *Freikorps* troops began their attack on February 2. In numbers they were vastly inferior to the revolutionaries, but their superiority in equipment, determination and organization more than made up for this. The *Freikorps* had armored cars and artillery. At the price of a few hundred dead and wounded on both sides, the *Freikorps* drove into Bremen, smashed the centers of resistance, occupied the city and reopened the port. The Bremen Workers' and Soldiers' Council was dispersed and a Majority Socialist city administration installed. As revolutionary reinforcements marched in from Hamburg, they were met on the road by *Freikorps* columns, which scattered them and chased them in disorder into the countryside. Within the next few days Wilhelmshaven, Cuxhaven, Bremerhaven and Hamburg were all occupied. It was, for a time, a tenuous occupation. The most that the tiny *Freikorps* forces could do was leave a cadre within each town, arm the bourgeoisie and stimulate the recruitment of new *Freikorps* forces. But they left something else: the memory of a ruthless and seemingly irresistible shock force which could shatter any sketchily armed Red militia. The "Spartacist" elements would consider this before they attempted another revolution.

Sometimes a city had to experience a *Freikorps* suppression for itself. Only a few days after the North Sea ports had been occupied, the miners and steelworkers of the Ruhr district of Westphalia threw down their tools and proclaimed a general strike, announcing that they would not return to work until the government socialized the mining and steelmaking industries.

The Ruhr was a conspicuously fertile field for agitation by the Independents and the Communists. The population had a high percentage of industrial workers who had suffered badly during the war. Now they had learned that part of the money with which Noske was financing the *Freikorps* operations came from the Ruhr magnates. The various workers' and soldiers' councils in the Ruhr proclaimed their support of the strike, and a Red Guard began to arm. They proceeded to authorize the expropriation of some of the mines and to sabotage others.

The forceful suppression of a strike of this magnitude was a task almost too great for the available *Freikorps* forces. But without the coal and steel of the Ruhr the German economy would collapse, and at Spa the Allies made no secret of the fact that they would refuse to continue food shipments if the German government allowed the strikes to continue.

Noske's first move was to cut the rail lines supplying food to the region. Next he ordered the *Freikorps* from the North Sea ports to move south into the Ruhr.

The *Freikorps* which moved on the Ruhr in the second week of February was only a scratch force. Bits and pieces of newly recruited *Freikorps* were added to some two thousand civilian volunteers with no previous military experience. Fortunately for Noske, these troops were never put to the test. A clever Supreme Command representative, General von Watter, seized the opportunity to open negotiations with the strikers. All that he asked of them was that they hand over their arms and return to work. There would be no reprisals against the workers, but there was to be no socialization of the mines and the factories. The workers were sullen—but starving. They went back to work.

As the blast furnaces and the mines of the Ruhr started up again, the rebellion moved to central Germany. The most violent outbreak took place in Halle, a major river port and manufacturing center in Saxony. Halle was not the only Saxon city which was in revolution, but it was the most important; it had a population of 200,000 and was a principal rail switching point. In late February the workers proclaimed a strike and issued proclamations demanding that the workers' and soldiers' councils have control over governmental affairs. To emphasize this demand, the strikers stopped traffic along the railway line which ran between Weimar, fifty miles to the south-west, and Berlin, one hundred miles to the northeast. The workers of Halle formed a revolutionary council under an Independent Social-ist leader, disarmed the police and distributed their weapons among the proletariat.

This was a challenge which Noske was compelled to meet. Halle was so close to Weimar that the National Assembly was in constant danger. Moreover, no government could be considered sovereign which could not control rail traffic from its capital to the point where its legislators were sitting.

From the ring of defenders protecting the National Assembly at Weimar, Noske detached such experienced *Freikorps* as Maercker's Volunteer Rifles. Even so hardened a force as this did not find Halle an easy task. The city was in chaos. The bourgeois elements in the city had declared a counterstrike in response to the strike of the proletariat. Schools and doctors' offices were closed, electricity was shut off, no streetcars were running.

In the early morning of March 1 a brigade of Maercker's troops arrived outside Halle and pushed an advance guard into the city. This proved to be a serious mistake. The little column of soldiers was surrounded by shouting workers who wrestled with the troops for possession of their rifles and cut the traces of wagons carrying the machine guns. Within a few minutes the melee was general. Some of the *Freikorps* officers were beaten to death and their bodies were thrown into the Saale River. The remnants of the patrol fought their way to the post office, where they barricaded themselves, ex-changing rifle fire with the Red militia in the buildings around them. It was not until noon of the next day that Maercker was able to push another section of his Volunteer Rifles into the town.

Maercker himself took command of the forces in the town and was almost lynched in the process. A certain Lieutenant Colonel von Klüwer, a liaison officer from the Supreme Command to General von Maercker, had the audacity to leave the post office wearing civilian clothes in an attempt to reconnoiter the Red positions. To Klüwer's misfortune, he was recognized, arrested and dragged be-fore the Halle Soldiers' Council, which ordered his imprisonment. On his way to jail a crowd seized him and beat him horribly. Twice Klüwer broke free and stumbled into nearby houses, and both times the crowd pulled him out. Then, their patience at an end, they threw him off a bridge into the Saale. To their astonishment, the broken Klüwer began to swim. A crowd ran along each bank, and whenever the unfortunate officer drew close to the shore they pushed him back into the stream. As he drowned, a Red Guardsman bent down and killed him with a pistol shot in the head.

This event brought swift vengeance. Maercker, who had previously been reluctant to fire directly into masses of workers, now ordered his troops into the street to kill anyone caught with a firearm. The next day the general strike began to end. The bourgeois stopped their counterstrike, and the following day the workers trudged back to their jobs. By March 5 Halle was peaceful. Maercker even began to recruit a "Halle Freikorps," using officers from his own Volunteer Rifles as a cadre. Only four days later this new *Freikorps* boasted three companies of infantry and an artillery section. It was hoped that these troops would be able to keep order in Halle and might even provide reinforcements to suppress an insurrection in Leipzig, some twenty-five miles to the southeast.

In the midst of this incessant revolutionary turmoil, the discussions among the victors in Paris went largely unheeded in Germany. The draft Covenant of the League of Nations had been prepared, and Wilson made his hasty visit back to Washington to confront the Senate Foreign Relations Committee. Clemenceau had been shot and the Council of Four had been established at his bedside. But for all the impact that these events had on Germany, they might as well have happened on the moon. The newspaper accounts from Paris were sketchy and, in the case of the government-controlled French press, frequently misleading. The Allies, with the example of Talleyrand at the Congress of Vienna ever in mind, continued to refuse to permit a German mission of any type into Paris. Thus no one in Germany could make out what the demands of the victors would be. There was a general impression that Wilson possessed great power over the other Allies and that he was Germany's advocate against the vengeful French. Aside from this, practically all of Germany's attention was riveted on her own awful disarray.

It is one of the anomalies of the German Revolution that although spontaneous revolts were breaking out all over the nation the leaders of the German Communist Party had nearly given up hope that their kind of revolution could ever be successful in Germany. In March of 1919, with insurrections flaring up everywhere, the Communist leadership itself was thoroughly disorganized.

With Liebknecht and Luxemburg dead, the party's *Zentrale* had appointed Leo Jogiches as chairman. Jogiches had been an intimate friend of Rosa Luxemburg. He had been in Berlin during the January Spartacist Week and had been arrested by Noske's troops, but they had not identified him and had let him go. In the succeeding weeks Jogiches found that he had little to work with. The Russians were of no help. The Comintern, only just forming in Moscow, would for many weeks consist of a two-man staff stuck away in a back room at the Smolny Institute in Petrograd, trying to edit a magazine called *The Communist International.* The Moscow radio poured out propaganda, but it could be heard only in a few neighboring countries, whose press would scarcely publish what Moscow said. Communications were so unreliable that the accounts of the first meeting of the Communist International did not reach France, for example, until eleven days after the meeting had ended. In turn, Lenin and his followers were reduced to scavenging their news of the outside world from Western newspapers that reached them in circuitous fashion.[24] Lenin's principal emissary to Germany, Karl Radek, was picked up by the government and flung into jail, where for the time being he languished in solitary confinement.

Within Germany also the intraparty relationships were tenuous. The *Rote Fahne* appeared only intermittently and, usually, on a clandestine basis. The Communist *Zentrale* had no real control over its party members in the cities outside Berlin. When revolutions occurred, the surprised Communist leadership read about them in the newspapers along with everyone else. It was even difficult for the German Communists to put forward a clear-cut program of their own. Against Radek's advice, they had become so entangled with the left wing of the Independent Socialists and with the various splinters of other revolutionary parties (which, in many cases, had not joined the Communist *Zentrale*) that nobody knew who was directing whom. There was no shortage of proletarian enthusiasm, but there was a great shortage of disciplined Communist leadership, especially in the outlying cities.

As Jogiches viewed this tangled situation, certain facts became clear to him. The proletariat, however well armed, had never succeeded in defending itself against Noske's *Freikorps,* and it was obvious that these *Freikorps* were becoming more efficient every day. At Bremen, for instance, the government had employed only thirty-five hundred men, at Halle a mere three thousand. What could be expected when the government forces grew? It was also obvious to Jogiches that the German revolutionary movement was dissipating its strength in a series of isolated insurrections. What good was it that Brunswick announced itself a Red state or that Leipzig was in revolt? The *Freikorps* would soon deal with them, and another local revolution would be put down. It was apparent that the government and the bourgeoisie were gathering strength.

The Communist *Zentrale* found itself forced to the conclusion that if there was to be a revolution in the Communist sense of the term it must take place quickly. With every day that passed, the National Assembly came closer to completing a constitution. The revolution must not attempt to defeat the government by military action, there must be no Red Guard to fire on the soldiers, because the infinitely better-armed and better-trained *Freikorps* would simply massacre the workers. The Communists could only use the working class's most effective weapon, the general strike. They felt that Ebert would never allow government forces to fire upon unarmed workers.

Accordingly, on March 3 the front page of *Die rote Fahne* was entirely devoted to this announcement:

WORKERS! PROLETARIANS!

The hour has come again. The dead arise once more. Again the downtrodden ride through the land. The followers of Ebert and Scheidemann believed that they had ridden you down . . . The "Socialist" government of Ebert-Scheidemann-Noske has become the mass executioner of the German proletariat. They are only waiting the chance to bring "peace and order." Wherever the proletariat rules, Noske sends in his bloodhounds.

Berlin, Bremen, Wilhelmshaven, Cuxhaven, . . . Gotha, Erfurt, Halle, Düsseldorf—these are the bloody stations of the cross of Noske's crusade against the German proletariat. . . .

WORKERS! PARTY COMRADES!

Let all work cease. Remain quietly in the factories. Don't let them take the factories away from you. Gather in the factories! Explain things to those who want to hesitate and hang back. Don't let yourselves be drawn into pointless shooting. Noske is only waiting for you to do that as an excuse for spilling more blood. . . .

> *The fate of the world is in your hands! . . . On to the general strike!*[25]

The preparations for this general strike had been much more thorough than the hasty arrangements on the eve of the January Spartacist Week. Now, for the first time, the Communists and their allies controlled the central association of the Berlin workers' and soldiers' councils. On March 4 some fifteen hundred delegates, each representing a workers' council of about a thousand men, met in the Berlin Gewerkschaftshaus, and more than ninety per cent of them voted in favor of the general strike. They also approved the Communists' list of demands which were to be the conditions for ending the strike: the government must dissolve the *Freikorps*, must resume trade and full diplomatic relations with Soviet Russia, and must agree to a vastly increased governmental role for the workers' councils. These demands were, of course, only a prelude. If they were accepted, there would be others which the government, stripped of its military forces, would be unable to resist.

By March 5 it was apparent that the strike was effective: all industrial activity in Berlin had halted, the streetcars and railroad trains had stopped running, and there was no electricity. But it was vital that the strikers should not under any circumstances give the government an excuse to fire upon them; once the strike became an armed insurrection, all would be lost.

It quickly became evident, however, that the Communist Party had so little control over its followers that it was unable to prevent the proletariat from taking up arms. No sooner had the strike been proclaimed than armed revolutionaries attacked and captured some thirty-two Berlin police stations. The sailors of the People's Naval Division, remorseful and humiliated by their own neutrality during the January uprising, now determined to avenge their revolutionary honor. They marched into the streets and laid siege to the main police headquarters on the Alexanderplatz. The building was resolutely defended by several companies of *Freikorps* infantry, and the firing became intense.

The armed revolutionaries, now joined by the Red Soldiers' League and the remnants of the various "republican" military forces which had been set up by Emil Eichhorn in November, concentrated in the eastern part of the city. They began to throw barbed-wire entanglements across the streets and set up machine guns in the subway entrances, which, with their heavy concrete construction and the access they afforded to communications below, made perfect gun positions. Bands of thieves put on red armbands and broke into the houses and apartments in the Tiergarten district.

As early as March 4 the horrified Communist "leaders" of the strike were running about Berlin trying to persuade their followers to lay down their weapons. The Communist *Zentrale* pleaded with the workers for discipline and denounced many of the armed revolutionaries as "hyenas of the revolution."[26] But its entreaties were ignored. For too long the revolutionary-minded proletariat had been told that the first principle of revolution was to take arms and seize power.

The government had now been given every excuse to intervene. There was no hesitation, none of the extemporized organization that had taken place in early January. On the night of March 3 the Ebert Cabinet had given Noske dictatorial powers over all of Berlin. Within the hour the Minister of Defense had declared martial law and *Freikorps* had begun to mobilize in the capital's suburbs. On the morning of March 4 they seized the munitions works at Spandau, where, without hesitation, they fired upon any workers who defied them. By the next day, columns of infantry led by tanks were pouring into Berlin. At least thirty thousand *Freikorps* troops entered the city on this day alone. There was no attempt to overawe the revolutionaries merely by a show of force. The *Freikorps* opened fire at the sight of an armed worker. When a few shots were fired at them from the Marstall the *Freikorps* blasted huge holes in it with their cannon, stormed the building and carried it at bayonet point.

The center of the revolution was in the immediate neighborhood of the Alexanderplatz, and the *Freikorps*, again under the command of General von Lüttwitz, made this the focal point of their attack. Lüttwitz had plenty of troops now. Mixed in with the experienced formations which had fought in January were dozens of other groups: the Ehrhardt Brigade, the Augusta Regiment Freikorps, the Reinhard Brigade, Röder's Scouts, the Horse Guards Division, Hülsen's *Freikorps*, and various "iron brigades" created from newly recruited university students. They lacked nothing in the way of equipment. To recapture the main police headquarters, which the revolutionaries had taken on March 3, the attackers called in aircraft to bomb the building. Other buildings were carried with flamethrowers.

By March 6 the Alexanderplatz had been captured by the *Freikorps* and the subway seized. The revolutionaries were retreating eastward, building by building, down the Frankfurter Strasse. The machine guns they placed on the rooftops and the barbed-wire barricades they strung across the streets only served to delay the advance of the troops.

The general strike was now useless. On March 9 the workers' and soldiers' councils declared it to be at an end. This made no difference to Noske and his *Freikorps*. They continued to drive the armed rebels east toward the suburb of Lichtenberg, upon which separate *Freikorps* columns were converging. Noske then issued an order which was perhaps the turning point of the German Revolution. On March 9 he announced, "Any person who bears arms against government troops will be shot on the spot."[27] Subsequently (and apparently without protest from the government) the Guard Cavalry Rifle Division broadened this order to include anyone who possessed a firearm, whether in rebellion or not. The Majority Socialists had dropped any pretense of being a revolutionary government. Many German workers had weapons which they had come by more or less legitimately during the days following the end of the war. From now on they were liable to be shot without trial by the *Freikorps*, who had claimed what amounted to an unrestricted hunting license. The government had made its choice. It placed its trust and its defense solely in the hands of Noske and the *Freikorps*. Henceforth even those workers who supported the Majority Socialists would be unable to defend their government from attack.

Noske went even further. On the morning of March 10 several Berlin newspapers carried an account, which had been telephoned to them by a member of Noske's staff, that the Lichtenberg police station had been "taken by assault by the revolutionaries" and that "all the occupants—to the number of seventy—[had] been savagely massacred."[28] This report was not true, and Noske knew it. But it was convenient that there should be an "atrocity" to avenge; it provided an excuse for reprisals.

The survivors of the People's Naval Division were the first to go. They were ordered to report to a building on the Französische Strasse on March 11, to be paid off and to receive demobilization papers. It was a trap. As the sailors appeared they were to be seized and herded at gunpoint into the basements of the building by soldiers from the Reinhard Brigade. The trap worked only too well. So many sailors responded to the lure that they rapidly exceeded the size of the Reinhard Brigade detachment, and more sailors were arriving all the time. The lieutenant in charge, a one-armed front-

line veteran named Marloh, telegraphed his headquarters for help.
"Bullets are the best help,"[29] he was told by Reinhard; Marloh should
"remember Lichtenberg, where seventy police were shot."[30] The
lieutenant at once picked out twenty-nine sailors, marched them
into the yard behind the building and had them shot down by
machine guns fired at point-blank range. Marloh later admitted that
he had intended to shoot 150 sailors but had been stopped by
another officer.*

The fighting ended on March 13. The rebels had been pushed into
Lichtenberg and trapped by the converging *Freikorps*. When they
asked for terms of surrender Noske replied, "Yield unconditionally
or I will not be responsible."[31] Some of the revolutionaries surrendered—a mixed bag of workers, sailors, Communists and Independents. The rest died on the spot as the troops closed in.

When it was over, the ten days of fighting had cut a gulley several
blocks wide and extending from the Alexanderplatz in the center of
Berlin eastward to Lichtenberg. Between fifteen hundred and two
thousand revolutionaries were dead and ten thousand were
wounded. Among the dead was Leo Jogiches, the chairman of the
Communist Party. He had been shot down in a police station by a
detective named Tamschik. A few days later in another police
station, Tamschik killed Dorrenbach, the leader of the shattered
People's Naval Division.[32]

The suppression of the second Berlin revolt was a turning point in
many ways. To begin with, the strength of the *Freikorps* was now
overwhelming. During the March rebellion the issue was never
really in doubt. The various *Freikorps* had become bigger, more
numerous and more efficient. Their leadership had been taken over
by hardened front-line veterans, junior officers imbued with the
spirit of the *Stosstruppführer*. These officers were thoroughly professional—and thoroughly callous. Their string of successes was
growing, and they had come to delight in their fierceness and
efficiency.

A large number of these free-corps fighters no longer knew, or
cared, what they were fighting for, and as they grew more powerful
they became more independent. They would go wherever and
whenever they were ordered, but what they did when they got there
was no longer controlled by the government. When, at a Cabinet
meeting on March 19, several members of the government protested

---

* Nine months later Marloh was tried and acquitted.

the excesses of the *Freikorps,* Noske responded that there had been some unfortunate incidents but that the troops had been under "extreme tension."[33] He promised to investigate such incidents and report on them to the Cabinet. But there was no investigation and no report. After the March uprising in Berlin, it was understood that a Red insurrection in any German city was an invitation to a counterattack by savage semiautonomous armies over which the government had little control. From now on only fools would test the *Freikorps.*

The second Berlin suppression was also a turning point for the German Communist Party. Its rebellions had twice been put down in blood, and it had lost two successions of leadership. The Communists attributed this to the fact that they had attempted to cooperate with other revolutionary groups and had thus lost control over their rebellions. From mid-March on, the Communist *Zentrale* was determined to isolate itself. Actually, it had no other choice. Harried out of its offices, with the *Rote Fahne* outlawed in Prussia, the party existed on a hand-to-mouth, semi-illegal basis. Many of its leaders were forced to go underground or else flee the country. By this time they had lost most of their proletarian support; even the most revolutionary-minded workers turned away from futile terrorism and deserted to the Independent Socialists.

With most of the older Communist leaders dead or imprisoned, the chairmanship of the Communist Party fell into the hands of a thirty-six-year-old intellectual, Paul Levi. He was not a good choice, especially since the party's immediate objective was to regain the confidence of the proletariat. Levi did not enjoy contact with the laboring masses; he had neither the contagious enthusiasm of Liebknecht nor the humanity of Rosa Luxemburg. But he was a competent strategist and he perceived that the Communist Party must begin to rebuild itself from scratch. It must become a mass party and it must purge itself of any persons or factions that might attempt another abortive *Putsch.* He cut the party's membership from 107,000 to a hard core of 50,000 better-disciplined followers and put them to work reestablishing Communist influence within the trade unions. Thus the German Communist Party, reluctantly putting aside any thought of immediate revolution, devoted its energies for many months to its own reconstruction.

Meanwhile, in an island of calm within a protective ring of *Freikorps* bayonets, the National Assembly continued to meet in the

New National Theater at Weimar. Its principal task, at this particular point, was to prepare a permanent constitution.

By February 24, when debate began on the form of the German constitution, the delegates had the advantage of having a complete draft to consider. Hugo Preuss, the Minister of the Interior in the Ebert-Scheidemann government, had been a university professor of political science and was an acknowledged authority on constitutional law. He had been working on a draft constitution since November, and it was now ready for consideration. It was presented to the complete Assembly, which for three days debated it in a businesslike but curiously lethargic manner. Then the Assembly referred the whole matter to a twenty-eight-member committee, which began months of discussion and revision.

Even at an early stage, it was possible to see the ultimate form which this "Weimar Constitution" would take. Preuss's first draft, as well as those which followed it, was a combination of what seemed to be the best features of European parliamentarianism with graftings from the American Constitution. At the base of this political system would be the Reichstag, the German parliament's major house, which was to contain one representative for every sixty thousand Germans voting and the members of which were to be elected through a system of proportional representation. All German men and women twenty years old or over were eligible to vote in the elections. The German Chancellor and his Cabinet ministers had to have the approval of the Reichstag before they could take office, and they were required to resign in the event that the Reichstag withdrew its approval.

In some ways the constitution was influenced by American example: the President of the German Republic (who functioned as the commander in chief of the armed forces and who appointed the Chancellor subject to the Reichstag's approval) was given more power than a parliamentary chief of state and was to be elected directly by the German voters; there was a high court modeled on the Supreme Court of the United States, and an "upper" house, the Reichsrat, consisting of the appointed representatives of the various German states.

The Reichsrat, however, had little actual power. It could protest any legislation, but the Reichstag could override its protest. The authority of the Reichsrat had been curtailed by design. In the opinion of Preuss and many other Germans, one of the faults of the old Bismarck constitution had been that Germany was nothing more than a confederation of semi-sovereign states, held together by the dominance of Prussia and her King, who was also the German Emperor. Now there was no German Emperor—and no apparent substitute. The only solution was to create a centralized government, with the various states—to be known now as *Länder*—reduced to relative impotence. In order to overcome the dominant position of Prussia, Preuss even proposed that she be subdivided into various *Länder*, which would approximate the size of Bavaria or Saxony. On these points the National Assembly became obstinate. Bavaria, in particular, was adamant in refusing to relinquish her cherished semi-independent status to a unified central government controlled by a Reichstag in which four sevenths of the deputies would be Prussians. Prussia, on the other hand, refused to be dismembered.

So a laborious compromise was evolved: the central government would control a single, unified German Army, would handle all foreign affairs, raise its own funds by direct taxation, and assume ownership of all German railways. The bulk of Germany's civil servants were to be transferred from the old state governments to the central government. The *Länder*, however, would be allowed their own representation in the Reichsrat. To offset Prussia's domination it was agreed that every *Land*, no matter how small, would have at least one Reichsrat seat, while Prussia herself would have no more than two fifths of the Reichsrat seats. The individual *Länder* were permitted authority over their own strictly internal affairs; to direct these, they were allowed their own miniature parliaments, which, like the Reichstag, had to be elected by proportional representation. In the event that one of the *Länder* defied the authority of the central government, the President of the German Republic had the power to supersede the state government with special commissioners or, if this failed, to take military action against the *Land*.

There were certain points in the successive constitutional drafts which were destined to cause endless difficulties. One was the question of Germany's name. Was she to be called the German Republic, for instance, or the German Nation? The National Assembly decided upon the word *Reich*, the literal meaning of which is "reach"; "the German Reich" meant, therefore, the German reach or extent. It was a polarized and traditional term which reflected a yearning for national unity and a sort of pan-Germanism which would encompass Germans everywhere.

The matter of the German flag was not so easily resolved. The old black-white-red colors of the Hohenzollern Empire had to go, and the center parties proposed that they be replaced by black-red-gold, which brought back memories of the liberal democratic days of 1848. The Independent Socialists argued for the red flag of international Socialism. The conservative factions declared that any change in the old imperial colors was an insult to the memory of the German soldiers who had died defending the flag.

The black-red-gold faction won, on the grounds that these colors represented "Greater Germany" and provided a flag under which Austria could unite with her—for at this point it was generally assumed that an *Anschluss* with Austria was an imminent event. Nor was this an unwarranted presumption on Germany's part. The Austro-Hungarian Empire had dissolved, with its component nationalities going their independent ways. Having been abandoned, German Austria had, in November of 1918, been reduced to making its own declaration of independence, or, more correctly, its own declaration of dependence. This was made in a document which, for brevity at least, must surely be historic. In its entirety, it read:

ARTICLE 1
German Austria is a democratic republic. All power emanates from the people.

ARTICLE 2
The German-Austrian Republic is an integral part of the German Republic.[34]

The Austrians had dispatched delegates to Weimar, where they were given a consultative voice in the proceedings. Article 61 of the final German draft constitution began with the words "German Austria after its union with the German Reich will receive the right of participation in the Reichsrat . . ."

A separate section of the constitution guaranteed the individual rights of citizens, on the pattern of the American Bill of Rights. Another, the "economic section," was a conglomeration of Socialist principles and some liberal views of the center parties with which the Majority Socialists now shared power. Property rights were guaranteed, but property owners were obligated to serve the public good. Under the constitution, "private economic enterprises suitable for socialization" could be taken over by the state or have their activities closely regulated by government officials; in addition, the state reserved the right to compel private firms to combine with others in the same industry. The only requirement which must be met was that the industry must be "ripe for this socialization." The result was that the threat of expropriation remained suspended over German industry. Nobody really knew when, if or how land or other property would be seized by the government. The conservative interests denounced the constitution as a Socialist document, while the far left condemned it as a betrayal of Socialist principles.°

It was inevitable that the subsequently famous Article 48 would appear in any German constitution drafted at this time. This ominous proviso made it possible for the President of the Reich to intervene whenever "the public safety and order in the German Reich" were "seriously disturbed or endangered." In such emergencies, by simple decree, the President was empowered to suspend the various rights of the citizen (freedom of assembly, freedom of opinion and expression, etc.) and to use the German armed forces in any manner he saw fit. The only restrictions to this were that the President's decree must be countersigned by a Cabinet member, and that the suspension of civil rights must be revoked upon the demand of the Reichstag. But these were very slender controls over what amounted to provision for constitutional dictatorship. Just what constituted a "serious disturbance" was not defined. How and when Article 48 was to be used was left to the discretion of the President of the Reich. It was assumed that it would be applied in the event of a war or, more probably, a Communist insurrection. No one foresaw how often it was to be used, and the Independent Socialists, who attacked Article 48, were howled down when they pointed out that it was possible that the President of the German Reich might someday be a man who would betray the cause of democracy.

The Independents were right to attack Article 48. It symbolized the lack of confidence among those assembled at Weimar in the very constitution they were creating—a lack of confidence characteristic of the popular mood. There was curiously little public concern over the form of the constitution. This worried the more perceptive of the delegates at Weimar; it frankly frightened Preuss. He asked, "Do you hope to give a parliamentary system to a nation like this, one that resists it with every sinew of its body? . . . Germans cannot

---

° The government had, in November, 1918, established a "Committee on Socialization" to investigate possibilities for industrial nationalization. But when months went by with practically all of its recommendations being ignored, the committee came to the conclusion that the government had no intention of socializing anything of consequence. On April 7 it resigned in a body.

shake off their old political timidity and their deference to an authoritarian state."[35] And later a delegate to the National Assembly wrote, "I believe that the proletariat was not yet ready for this democratic responsibility, and certainly we went about our business with the constitution in an all too theoretical and lifeless way."[36]

The history of the world's democratic constitutions had, up to this point, been largely a story of people searching for a rational political document under which they could live. The constitution now being drafted at Weimar was different. Written in an isolated town at a nervous and uncertain hour in German history, it began and would end as a document in search of a people.

Almost simultaneously with the introduction of the draft constitution, the Assembly was asked to consider the matter of a new German Army.

It was early recognized that a key factor in the consolidation of the German Republic would be the creation of an Army responsible solely to the central government. Before the war there had never really been a "German Army." Actually, the Army of Germany had consisted of four separate contingents. The largest, by far, was the Prussian Army, which was administered by the Prussian state Minister of War and in which were incorporated the forces raised in twenty-two other German states. The separate armies of Saxony and Württemberg were administered by their own state ministers of war, although the Emperor appointed their senior officers. The Bavarian Army was a case in itself. Not only did it have its own Ministry of War, but the German Emperor did not have the right of appointing any of its officers. The Bavarian Army came under the emperor's command only at the time of mobilization for war. This organization of separate contingents was recognized as having been cumbersome and complicated and as having preserved dangerous sectionalism. The National Assembly was determined not to perpetuate the system.

At first it was generally thought that there was no point in creating a new German Army until the Allied peace terms had been revealed. Obviously the Allies would put some kind of restriction on the size of the German armed forces, and it seemed wisest to await developments. But, as the weeks passed, Noske and the Supreme Command convinced the Assembly's members that they could not postpone the creation of a new Army, even if it was somewhat premature. At this point, the old Imperial Army having crumbled away, the German armed forces consisted almost exclusively of *Freikorps*. Although it was thankful for their existence, the Supreme Command had never regarded the *Freikorps* as anything more than a stopgap measure. The longer the creation of a formal Army was delayed, the more difficult it would be, for the salvageable traditions and organization of the officer corps and the old Imperial Army would be dissipated. The Supreme Command was anxious to commence rebuilding at once. Even if the Allies subsequently demanded changes, there would still be a nucleus for a posttreaty Army. Thus the "Law for the Creation of a Provisional Reichswehr" was proposed, and, after certain difficulties, it was adopted by the National Assembly on March 6, 1919.

The Supreme Command did not, to be sure, get all that it wanted in the creation of the "Provisional Reichswehr." The National Assembly refused to permit conscription and insisted that every soldier be a volunteer—a wrench from the traditional Prussian system. As a concession to the spirit of the times, the law of March 6 greatly modified and liberalized the code of military justice. It also stipulated that the Provisional Reichswehr was to be "formed on a democratic basis," a suitably vague statement which was reassuring to certain suspicious members of the National Assembly. In practically every other respect the Supreme Command had little cause to be dissatisfied. Over the objections of the Independent Socialists, the soldiers' councils were declared eliminated and were replaced by a system of *Vertrauensmänner* ("trusted men") who were elected by their comrades on the basis of three per company. They were a shadow of the old soldiers' councils and possessed only vague consultative functions. They could, for example, transmit complaints and suggestions from the enlisted men to the officers, but they were permitted absolutely no powers of command, nor, of course, did they have a voice in the selection of officers.

The whole method of recruitment of both officers and enlisted men was obviously considered a crucial matter by the Ministry of Defense and the Supreme Command. There was a wealth of officers available and there seemed no point in not selecting the very best. All Provisional Reichswehr officers were to be selected from among those who had "proved themselves apt and experienced in their relations with the troops during the war" and who had "fought valiantly at the front."[37] Subsequently this requirement was broadened to permit the commissioning of junior officers with only *Freikorps* experience.

The enlisted men were equally hand-picked. Battalion commanders enjoyed wide latitude in the selection of their troops and were required to refuse enlistment to any man who was suspected of having left-wing sympathies or who had an unsatisfactory record in the old Imperial Army.

Organizationally, the Provisional Reichswehr was divided into three area commands—Gruppenkommando I (north and east Germany), Gruppenkommando II (south and west Germany) and Gruppenkommando III (a special force for operations in the Baltic and on the Polish frontier). Within these area commands, the Provisional Reichswehr was organized into units of brigade strength. There were twenty-four of these, corresponding to the twenty-four army corps of the old Imperial Army. Also, as in the old army corps, each brigade was assigned a particular city as its depot and a surrounding territory as its area for recruiting.

For months, however, the organization of the Provisional Reichswehr was only on paper. Germany was in such chaos that many of the brigades could not be recruited because their garrison cities were actually unsafe. In Bavaria the regional authorities refused to allow the Minister of Defense to send in any troops whatever. There was a problem, for a while, in finding enough suitable soldiers who were not already members of the *Freikorps*—a problem which was solved by simply absorbing the best *Freikorps* into the Provisional Reichswehr en masse. Thus Maercker's Volunteer Rifles became the Sixteenth Brigade of the Provisional Reichswehr, Reinhard's *Freikorps* became the Fifteenth Brigade, Hülsen's *Freikorps* was made the Third Brigade, etc. But all this took a long time to accomplish. In the meantime, the principal military forces in Germany were the various *Freikorps* which the Ministry of Defense was busily recruiting and arming.

Chapter Eleven

The Second Bavarian Revolution

T HE most violent of the insurrections in revolutionary Germany was set off as the direct consequence of an event which, peculiarly, did not take place in Germany at all. It was the example of the Hungarian Bolshevik Revolution which suddenly gave hope to the Bavarian Comunists. The apparent success of the Hungarian Communists gave their Bavarian counterparts the impression that there was conveniently at hand in Central Europe a sizable Red Army which could support and defend a "second" Bavarian revolution.

From 1867 to November of 1918, Hungary had been a partner in the Dual Monarchy of Austria-Hungary under the Hapsburg Emperor-King in Vienna. The empire controlled by this joint monarchy consisted of a horde of separate nationalities—Germans, Magyars, Poles, Czechs, Slovaks, Croats and others—and had always been a ramshackle affair. By the fall of 1918, when an Allied army under a French general, Franchet d'Esperey, was fighting its way up the Danube from Bulgaria, the empire had pretty well collapsed. The various nationalities were declaring their independence, and the Hapsburg Emperor Karl had fled his capital. One of his last official acts was to appoint as prime minister of Hungary one of the richest men in that kingdom of rich landowners, Count Mihály Károlyi.

It was an unusual appointment, but then Károlyi was an unusual man. Forty-three years old in 1918, he had been brought up in the Magyar aristocratic tradition. In an agricultural nation where a tiny percentage of the population owned most of the land, Károlyi's family was among the wealthiest. His childhood had been spent on the family's vast estates, in the Károlyis' huge home in Budapest or in their residence in Paris. As a young man he had enjoyed all the semifeudal pleasures reserved to the Magyar aristocracy—gambling at the National Casino, traveling the world, or hunting with friends on his estates, with every man finding in his bed at night a peasant girl who had been brought in from the village.[1] But Károlyi tired of this sort of life. Elected to the Hungarian Parliament, he founded his own political party and began to advocate a program of Hungarian independence and democratic reforms. To the utter incomprehension of his family and friends, Károlyi became a liberal. When the war began he joined a cavalry regiment and saw a little active service. Then, perceiving how things were going, he began to advocate a separate Hungarian peace with the Allies.

On October 31, 1918, Count Károlyi found himself the Prime Minister of Hungary. His appointment was approved by General Franchet d'Esperey, whose troops were occupying Belgrade. Károlyi's government was not a strong one; it could not be. He was forced into a coalition with the Hungarian Social Democratic Party and then had to devise a program to restore a defeated nation in which were ranged against him on one side the influential land owners and on the other the small industrial working class.

At first Károlyi had the support of the French, but after the first months of truce the French attitude began to change. At the Paris Peace Conference the separate interests of the victors were beginning to manifest themselves. The British were interested in colonial and maritime affairs. The Italians were concerned with Trieste and the newly emerging Yugoslav nation. The United States was devoting her attention to the League of Nations and to the development of "Succession States"—Poland and Czechoslovakia in particular— from national groups which had large immigrant populations in the United States, and the leaders of which had interested Woodrow Wilson in their cause. This left vast areas of Central Europe more or less available for the attentions of any major power which chose to concern itself with them—a situation which France found most fortuitous.

The first objective of France at the peace conference was security against a resurgent Germany; first security, then reparations. In Germany's west she was attempting to foment a movement for an independent Rhenish state. In Germany's south the French military leaders were letting it be known that they would not be averse to the concluding of a separate treaty with Bavaria. On Germany's eastern frontiers a different game was to be played. The objective of French policy was the creation of a cordon of well-armed nations which would offer a constant threat to Germany's eastern frontiers and at the same time contain Russian Bolshevik expansion. It was France's plan to tie these nations to her with a web of alliances, with gifts of munitions and with loans. Their armies would be French-trained and would use French weapons. Their foreign policy would be built around their French alliances, which would protect them against a hostile Germany, while simultaneously France would be protected by the threat to Germany of a war on two fronts.

This amounted to a disaster for Hungary. On her northern frontiers the Czechs pressed their claims for important areas of Hungarian territory—and backed them up by an armed invasion. To the east, the Rumanians were invading Transylvania, a Hungarian province to which Rumania had certain valid ethnic claims. From the south the Serbs were marching into Hungary to "liberate" the Croats, who for hundreds of years had been closely bound to Hungary. Each of Hungary's invaders justified its actions by claiming large ethnic populations within the old borders of Hungary. Many of these claims were valid, but further territorial demands which could be explained only by greed were also pressed by the Czechs, the Rumanians and the Serbs. Soon three-fifths of the old Hungarian kingdom was occupied by its neighbors.

The Rumanians had the most convincing claim. In 1916 it had been important for the European Allies to have Rumania declare war on the Central Powers, and as an enticement they had promised, in a secret treaty concluded in August of that year, that Rumania would be given a major part of Transylvania after the war. With this inducement and others, Rumania entered the war, but her armies were speedily crushed and she asked for an armistice. In May of 1918 she was forced to sign a harsh peace treaty with Germany and Austria-Hungary. The Hungarians were particularly rapacious in their demands: Rumania lost to Hungary an additional seven thousand square miles of Transylvania, together with nearly 150,000 Rumanian nationals.

This was the situation in which the French found themselves in the early spring of 1919. France recognized that the claims of Hungary's neighbors upon the defeated Magyars were extreme and unfair, but this was not really the point. France was supreme in

Central Europe. The Allied Supreme War Council had delegated to her the task of policing Central Europe on its behalf. No other major Allied power had troops in the region, and no other major Allied power knew or cared what was going on there. France wanted to become recognized as the powerful protector of at least three nations which had claims against Hungary, and, for the sake of future alliances, she intended to make good her secret-treaty commitments to Rumania. With a swiftness that would have done credit to the Borgias, France threw Hungary to the wolves.

Obtaining the permission of the powers assembled at the Paris Peace Conference to reduce Hungary's boundaries proved to be no problem. On February 21—when, significantly, neither Wilson nor Clemenceau was present—André Tardieu of France presented to the Council of Ten the recommendation that the Hungarians be ordered to withdraw such armed forces as they had left from an additional section of Transylvania, which would then become a neutral zone. This innocent-sounding proposal was quickly adopted. No notice was taken of the fact that the new Hungarian boundary was almost identical to the one promised Rumania in the treaty of August, 1916.

France, the only nation with substantial representation on the scene in Budapest, could scarcely have been unaware of the effect this would have on Károlyi and his liberal government. Hungary was already an economic ruin. The railroad system had collapsed. The large landowners, who hated Károlyi, had succeeded in frustrating a plan he had developed for distributing land to the peasants. It was questionable whether a viable economy could ever be created in this shrinking nation which lost more and more territory every day to her neighbors. There was only one common interest which united all Hungarians, from the most conservative magnate to the most impoverished peasant: Hungary's historic frontiers. To the Hungarians it was obvious that they had been cheated by the Allies and by the greedy Succession States. Any Hungarian government that yielded to their demands could not last a minute.

On March 20 Lieutenant Colonel Vyx, the haughty and supercilious French chief of the Allied mission in Hungary, who had already succeeded in arousing the hatred and distrust of Károlyi and his Cabinet, appeared before them and, in imperious tones, laid down the Allied ultimatum: the Hungarians must withdraw to the new line within ten days; if they did not, the Allies would consider the armistice to have lapsed and would treat Hungary as an enemy at war. When Károlyi began to protest, Vyx cut him off with the words "I declare the discussion to be ended."[2]

The Allied ultimatum was all it took to bring Károlyi's government to an end. He was not a personality of great strength, and he certainly could not fight a war with the Allies, nor could he find support from any side within his own nation. The members of the old aristocracy, stupid and spiteful, could not conceal their delight at the humiliation being forced on him. "Now the end has come," they rejoiced.[3]

On the day that Vyx delivered his ultimatum, Károlyi resigned in favor of the Social Democrats, who in turn abandoned the government the next day to a thirty-three-year-old Russian-trained Communist named Béla Kun. Thus, to the consternation of the Allies and to the particular horror of the French, Central Europe now had an authentic Bolshevik nation.

There have been few figures in modern history who have experienced such a startling change of fortune as did Béla Kun. On March 20 he had been a prisoner in Budapest's Marko utca jail, where, in the Hungarian fashion, he had been beaten by the police. On March 21 he was released, to be deferentially greeted at the prison door by his former captor, the now servile public prosecutor. By March 22 he had assumed the title "Commissar of Foreign Affairs of the Hungarian Soviet Republic" and was the actual head of this Communist government. His first act was to radio the news to Soviet Russia, asking for a treaty of alliance and requesting Lenin's instructions for the furtherance of worldwide revolution. His next steps were to reject the French ultimatum, to organize a Red army and to launch a series of successful attacks on the encroaching Rumanian and Czechoslovakian armies.

For the Russians the creation of the Soviet Hungarian Republic was a vast triumph. Coming on the heels of the series of defeats in Germany, the Hungarian Revolution seemed the first positive indication that Europe might be ready for the proletarian revolution. In the pages of the magazine *Communist International,* Lenin himself applauded the Hungarian achievement, "which fills us with joy and triumph."[4] In many ways Béla Kun was everything the Russians could hope for. He was no quasi-bourgeois revisionist like the Majority Socialists who were proving to be bitter enemies in Germany. Kun, a Jew from Transylvania who had been mobilized into the Austro-Hungarian Army, had been taken prisoner by the Russians in 1916 and had been converted to Bolshevism in a prison camp in Tomsk. After the Russian Revolution he had been put in charge of agitation among Magyar prisoners. He had been quite successful. Lenin. knew him well and was much impressed with Kun's ability. Within a few months his active organization had grown to over a hundred men.

As soon as the war ended, Kun and his cadre of agitators were dispatched to Hungary in the guise of representatives of the Russian Red Cross. But his activities, and particularly the vast sums of money he had brought with him, swiftly identified him as a Russian agent. He put together a Hungarian Communist Party, organized a newspaper, and began to attack the Károlyi government, which arrested him only a month before its downfall. Now that he was in power, Kun wasted no time. Almost daily he received radioed advice from Lenin. Hungarian Communist agitators were dispatched to Bulgaria, Austria, Rumania and even as far as Munich. Kun knew that the power of the Czechs, the Rumanians, and the Yugoslavs was growing daily and that his Red Army could not hold them off indefinitely. Salvation for Soviet Hungary lay in the immediate Communization of other European nations.

In sudden alarm, the members of the Council of Four in Paris began to interest themselves in Hungary. They now regretted deeply their cavalier treatment of the moderate Károlyi. House wrote in his diary: "Bolshevism is gaining ground everywhere. Hungary has just succumbed. We are sitting upon an open powder magazine . . ."[5] The Allied experts told them that it was quite possible for Bolshevism to take over in Austria and Czechoslovakia. The principal American specialist for the area, Charles Seymour, wrote to his wife: "If no prompt action is taken it looks as if Vienna would be the next to go Bolshevik and after that probably Prague."[6] The Italians in particular were terrified by the quiet ease with which the Communists had taken charge in Hungary.

On March 27 Marshal Foch was summoned before the Council of Four and his opinion solicited. His proposal was merely another version of the anti-Bolshevik campaign he had proposed more than a month before: a vast army would be created, using Finns, Poles, Czechs, Rumanians, Greeks and various Baltic nationalities; financed by the United States and presumably led by a French staff headed by the Marshal himself, it would clear Bolshevism from Eastern Europe. This proposal failed to convince the Council. The European Allies could afford neither the money nor the men. As for the United States, General Bliss told Wilson: "If we send troops to assist . . . against the Hungarians we have made the first step in involving the American army into a series of European wars which would rapidly stretch from the Atlantic to the Ural Mountains."[7]

Thus, bereft of the means and the will to enforce its dictates by means of military power, the Council of Four resorted to an age-old device of diplomats in a dilemma: in early April it dispatched a fact-finding mission to Budapest. This Allied mission was, however, different from those that had gone before. The Council of Four was no longer disposed to continue French exclusivity in Central Europe. A definite suspicion had grown within the British and American delegations that the Hungarian crisis might not have occurred but for the French. General Bliss wrote to Wilson: *"The United States is being dragged into war through the fact that all negotiations or dealings with the enemy are in the hands of the French."*[8]*

Moreover, the British and American delegates believed that French military circles now found certain advantages in the presence of Hungarian Bolshevism. Many opportunities for France could arise out of general fear of a Communist success in Eastern Europe. The astute representatives of the Succession States—Poland, Czechoslovakia and the Baltic States—instantly picked up this theme and began to play variations upon it. Their requests were now couched in the form of veiled threats: unless this or that territorial concession was granted, they could not (they claimed) hold back their people, who would turn to Communism in despair at such injustice.

The head of the mission which the Council of Four sent to Hungary was a British nominee, General Jan Christiaan Smuts, a South African. He took with him a sizable staff composed principally of British and American diplomatic specialists. No Allied diplomat had met Béla Kun, and Smuts did not know quite what to expect. The Hungarian Soviet government had placed some of the members of the Allied missions in Budapest under arrest, so it was anticipated that Kun would be arrogant and threatening. However, Smuts found the head of the Hungarian government anxious to please. Kun was quite conscious of the fact that the Allies had sent a senior diplomat to treat with him. It was, indeed, quite a triumph for a young Bolshevik. The members of the Smuts mission were well aware of this and behaved frigidly. They observed that Kun was not a physically attractive man. He was short and had a huge head, the

* The emphasis is Bliss's.

most noticeable features of which were his pointed ears. An American Army colonel who was a member of the Allied mission thought that Kun "looked like a lizard."[9] The British diplomat Harold Nicolson described him as having a "puffy white face and loose wet lips: shaven head, impression of red hair: shifty, suspicious eyes."[10] The Allies' opinion of Kun's government was no better. They cannot be criticized for disliking Bolshevism, and, at that time and in those circumstances, it would have been too much to expect that they would refrain from noting the predominantly Jewish character of the Kun government. Eight of the eleven Hungarian commissars were Jewish.

From the very beginning of the discussions, Smuts was able to establish a certain ascendancy over Kun. When the special Allied train pulled into the Budapest station, it had been met by Kun and a delegation waiting to escort Smuts to quarters which had been prepared for him at a luxury hotel. Smuts firmly declined this offer to become the guest of the Hungarian Soviets and declared that he and his staff would remain aboard their own train. As Kun descended from the train it was observed that none of the sloppily dressed Red guards standing about knew how to present arms. As he walked down the station platform, a locomotive engineer walked up to him and said something in Magyar. Kun said, "Of course, comrade," and held out the stump of his cigarette, with which the locomotive engineer lighted up. The watching British could scarcely conceal their contempt.[11]

There ensued two days of staff discussions, all conducted aboard the train. The objective of the Hungarians was to obtain Allied diplomatic recognition and a favorable modification of the Allied demands regarding the Rumanian frontier. Smuts made an offer which, in effect, reduced the size of the territory from which Hungary would have to withdraw. Kun chose to regard this concession as the opening offer in an extended round of haggling. At once, and with great courtesy, Smuts rose to his feet. "Well, gentlemen," he said, "I must bid you goodbye."[12] He escorted Kun and his three companions to the station platform, waved to the locomotive engineer and raised his hand in salute. To the astonishment of the four Hungarians, the train immediately glided out of the station, bound for Paris.

The opinion which Smuts brought back to the Council of Four was that the Allies need not concern themselves about Hungary. From what he had observed of Kun and Hungarian Bolshevism,

Smuts could not believe that they were a serious threat. Kun himself had failed to impress Smuts as a ruthless man of action. Leave Hungary alone, Smuts advised, and Communism would collapse of itself. He did not think that Austria would succumb.

This was exactly what the members of the Council of Four wanted to hear. They set the question of Hungarian Bolshevism aside, and in due course Smuts's assessment proved correct. The only problem was that their decision took no account of the effect which the example of Hungarian Communism would have in Germany. And this effect was considerable.

The assassination of Kurt Eisner on February 21 left Munich and, indeed, most of Bavaria in a condition of near-anarchy. The Ebert-Scheidemann government of Germany, preoccupied with affairs at Weimar and with insurrection in Berlin, had been able to devote little time or military resources to reducing Bavaria to order. Three competing factions claimed to be the government of the former Wittelsbach kingdom: the Majority Socialists, under Adolf Hoffmann; the Independents, led by the twenty-five-year-old poet and playwright Ernst Toller; and a Communist faction led by three Bolsheviks known as "the Russians," Eugen Leviné, Max Levien and Towia Axelrod.

Until Béla Kun achieved power in Hungary, the Majority Socialists managed to exert a shaky influence over Bavaria, although they were constantly obliged to defer to the wishes of the workers' and soldiers' councils, which were quite powerful in Munich. At this point the task of governing Bavaria was close to impossible. Munich was in constant turmoil. Every evening there were Independent or Communist political rallies in the enormous Munich beerhalls. An unprecedented cold wave struck the city. On April 1 there were twenty inches of snow on the ground; by mid-March the city had run out of coal. There were 45,000 unemployed, and the bankrupt city government had begun to print its own currency to pay them unemployment compensation. After Eisner's death arms had been distributed to the workers; now the police had no idea who possessed them.

When word of the Hungarian Soviet Republic reached Munich, the game was up for the Majority Socialists. On the night of April 6 Ernst Toller and his friends met in the former palace bedroom of the Wittelsbach Queen and proclaimed a "Republic of Councils" which was to join with Hungary and Austria in a Danubian revolutionary confederation. The support of the workers' and soldiers' councils for this plan was so immediate and widespread that Hoffmann and his Majority Socialists fled north to the city of Bamberg in Upper Franconia, where, pledging loyalty to the central government in Berlin, they established a sort of Bavarian government-in-exile.

In Munich the rule of the "Coffeehouse Anarchists" now began. Toller and his friends displayed a degree of eccentricity which swiftly outstripped even that which had been exhibited by Kurt Eisner. Toller began his rule with a lengthy plea for new art forms in sculpture, drama, painting and architecture which would permit the liberation of the spirit of mankind. The Commissar for Public Instruction announced that admission to the University of Munich (which was regarded as a hotbed of monarchist sympathizers) was now free to everyone, that no special courses of study need be pursued and that "the instruction of history, that enemy of civilization," was suppressed.[13] The Commissar for Finances experimented with his own pet theory involving free money. The Commissar for Housing declared that from now on no home could contain more than three rooms and that the living room must always be placed above the kitchen and the bedroom.

With a group of this sort in power, it went unnoticed for a time that the Commissar for Foreign Affairs, Dr. Franz Lipp, was an outright madman. Lipp was a little man with a beard so immense that it seemed to cover his whole face. Each day he brought a bunch of red carnations to his office and decorated the desks with them. He dispatched a telegram to Moscow complaining, "The fugitive Hoffmann has taken with him the keys to my ministry toilet,"[14] and followed this up with a letter to Lenin commending to his attention two theses of Immanuel Kant. Next Lipp circulated an announcement to his fellow commissars: "I have declared war on Württemberg and Switzerland, because these dogs have not at once loaned me sixty locomotives. I am certain that we will be victorious. Furthermore, I will ask the Pope, with whom I am well acquainted, to grant his blessing for this victory."[15]

With this sort of personnel, the Coffeehouse Anarchists did well to last six days. Then they collapsed into the arms of authentic Communists. What had begun as a farce was to end as a tragedy.

At this point it is necessary to explain just who these Communists were. They were not authorized representatives of the K.P.D., the German Communist Party, which was still trying to reconstruct itself from the wreckage of the March uprising in Berlin, and whose Central Committee had given categorical orders that its followers were to avoid armed action "even when a local or momentary success might be possible."[16] The leaders of the K.P.D. chose to ignore the events in Munich.

Nor were the Communists who headed this Munich Commune the direct representatives of Lenin, as was commonly supposed. Only Towia Axelrod, who had been with Lenin in Petrograd, was anything like a delegate of international Communism. He had come to Germany before the war ended, as part of the immense staff of Adolf Yoffe, the Soviet ambassador to imperial Germany. When Yoffe had been thrown out of the country, Axelrod had made his way to Munich, which, under Kurt Eisner, was far safer for him than Berlin.

The other two "Russians" who led the Munich Commune were as much German as Russian. Max Levien was a tall blond man thirty-four years old, the scion of a rich Jewish merchant family which was part Russian and part German. Until he was twenty-one he had lived in Moscow. Then, fleeing Russian anti-Semitism, he had come to Germany to study. Subsequently he had gone back to Russia, had been arrested for revolutionary activity and had been sentenced to work in a Siberian lead mine. He had escaped from this and made his way to Zurich (where he met Lenin) and then finally back to Germany. The war had caught him there and he had been drafted into the German Army. Levien could scarcely be described as a good soldier. He became a Spartacist and consistently agitated for an Allied victory over Germany, declaring, "It is necessary that Germany be humiliated, that the colonial troops of France and England march through the Brandenburg Gate, that Helgoland become the property of the English, that the (German) fleet be taken away . . ."[17] There was nothing timid or halfway about Levien. He became a staunch international revolutionary, and in mid-December of 1918 he was sent south to Munich to organize the Spartacists in Bavaria. Upon the death of Kurt Eisner, and in the revolutionary fervor which followed it, Levien proposed that the Roman Catholic cathedral in Munich be transformed into a "revolutionary temple." This was done, with the "Goddess Reason" presiding over the ceremony.

Levien was regarded as the flame of the Munich Commune. Among the three men known as "the Russians," Axelrod and Eugen Leviné were more effective as publicists and propagandizers than anything else, but Max Levien was an organizer and a man of action. During the last days of the Eisner regime a group of counter-revolutionaries arrested Levien and locked him in the Stadelheim Prison, but a band of soldiers marched out to the prison, released him and escorted him in triumph back to Munich. The event made him famous among the Munich proletariat. He had studied what Lenin had done in the months following the Russian Revolution and was prepared to copy him exactly. Levien did not shrink from employing terror or the murder of hostages. It did not bother him that "the young doctor," as he was called, was accused of being a sadist.

Eugen Leviné, who was thirty-six and the oldest of the three "Russians," had been born in St. Petersburg of a Russian Jewish family. Like Levien, Leviné had come to Germany to study. The Russian uprisings of 1905 had taken him back to his homeland, but he had fled in 1909 to return to Germany. Like Levien, he was a highly educated man, and like Levien he had been drafted into the Germany Army, where he had become a Spartacist. Just before her death Rosa Luxemburg had dispatched Leviné to Moscow to represent the German Communist Party at the first meeting of the Comintern, but he had been unable to cross the German border. Returning to Berlin, he had been redispatched by Paul Levi to head the Communist Party in Bavaria.

Leviné arrived in Munich on March 5 and began a drastic reorganization. He purged the party's executive committee and took over the editorship of the Munich edition of *Die rote Fahne*. He called in all party membership cards for review and reissued fewer than three thousand of them. Although Leviné was no less fanatical than either Axelrod or Levien, the use of terror repelled him. He was the least practical of the three and incontestably the least violent. The influence of these three men was, of course, enormously enhanced by their Russian connections. A Bavarian Communist observed, "The great feat of the Russian Revolution lends to these men a magic luster. Experienced German Communists stare at them as if dazzled. Because Lenin is a Russian, they are assumed to have his ability."[18]

The only native German among the upper echelons of the Munich Commune was Rudolf Egelhofer, a twenty-six-year-old sailor who had taken part in the Kiel Mutiny. The "Russians" admired Egelhofer's ruthlessness and daring and made him the military commander of the Republic of Councils. He was not a polished revolutionary theoretician, but he had the common touch and succeeded in creating a Bavarian Red Army which contained a very large number of dedicated and determined revolutionaries. On April 16 Egelhofer issued a call to arms.

> *Proletarians of all lands, unite! You will and must conquer! Discipline yourselves! Choose for yourselves able leaders! Obey them implicitly, but remove them from office if they fail in battle! Form companies and battalions! Assemble daily at the designated places in your factories for military training. . . . Practice close-order drill daily. . . . March through the city in close formation as a demonstration of your material strength. Keep your arms and ammunition and do not let them be taken from you.*[19]

Egelhofer's army was certainly one of the best-paid in history. Privates were paid twenty-five marks a day, non-commissioned officers received 130 marks, and the pay of officers was practically beyond calculation. The Bavarian Red Army also offered free food, free liquor and free prostitutes. The soldiers broke into the safe-deposit boxes in the Munich banks and were allowed to keep a portion of the loot. A nearby camp filled with Russian prisoners of war awaiting repatriation was opened up and the prisoners were recruited into Egelhofer's army. The barracks of the old Bavarian Army were ransacked to provide arms; when these proved to be insufficient, Egelhofer published a simple decree: "Citizens must deliver all firearms to the City Commandant within twelve hours. Anyone failing to do so will be shot."[20]

In less than two weeks, this Red Army probably grew to twenty thousand men.* They were kept busy preparing the defenses of Munich and arresting known antirevolutionaries. One of these was a lance corporal serving in what remained of the old Bavarian Army. Adolf Hitler had just returned to Munich from duty as a guard in a Russian prisoner-of-war camp at Traunstein. When the camp was broken up, he returned to the barracks of the Second Bavarian Infantry Regiment. On the morning of April 27, three members of the Red Army came to arrest Hitler, who had apparently already achieved a local reputation as a diehard nationalist. The arrest was never made. As Hitler described it, "Faced with my leveled carbine,

---

* It has never been possible to state with certainty how large the Bavarian Red Army was. Estimates range up to 30,000 men. It is generally supposed, however, that no more than 20,000 rifles were handed out. Because each man who got a rifle was given ten days' pay in advance, it is quite probable that the desertion rate was high.

the three scoundrels lacked the necessary courage and marched off as they had come."[21]

Hitler's experience, if it is true, probably typifies the Bavarian Red Army. It was too much to expect that an army which was thrown together from nothing in a matter of only a few days could become a tough fighting force. Only the example of the martyred Kurt Eisner sustained the revolutionary spirit of the Bavarian proletarians; they were persuaded to believe that a mighty Russian army was moving toward their relief and that the Hungarian Red Army would shortly be moving up the Danube from Budapest. This sort of encouragement was certainly necessary. Any Münchener could see that the Bavarian Republic of Councils would collapse soon without support. The first few days of the Munich Commune, following the fall of Ernst Toller's Coffeehouse Anarchists, were a bedlam. The "Russians" proclaimed a dictatorship of the proletariat and a program of Red terror. The Stadelheim Prison was filled with hostages taken from among the families of the bourgeoisie and the nobility. Schools were closed. Opposition newspapers were banned. The Majority Socialists attempted an anti-Bolshevik coup, which was quickly quashed by Egelhofer's army. There were at least three political groups in Munich which could be described as "revolutionary" to a greater or lesser degree, and it was almost impossible to differentiate among them—or even for them to differentiate among themselves. The experience of Ernst Toller typifies the situation. He was arrested by the "Russians" on April 9, released a few hours later by a force of "White" counterrevolutionaries, arrested by the "Russians" again on April 13, and soon released by them because of his popularity. A day or two later his former captors, who had announced that Toller had been stripped of all public offices, put him in command of the most important sector of the Bavarian defenses.

The combination of this confusion and the cost of supporting the Red Army, which grew to 500,000 marks a day, rapidly completed the ruin of the Bavarian economy. Munich was now cut off from the rest of Germany. Hoffmann and his Majority Socialist government-in-exile at Bamberg had declared a blockade of foodstuff deliveries into Munich. The blockade was being observed by the peasants, if for no other reason than that they did not trust the new money which the Republic of Councils had printed. The Commissar for Finance, a twenty-five-year-old bank clerk named Emil Männer, was running the bank-note printing presses night and day to pay the army. There was plenty of manpower available for such revolutionary duties—most of the industries had stopped operating for lack of raw materials or markets—and the Communist directorate had succeeded in arousing a good deal of revolutionary enthusiasm among these unemployed workers by telling them of the vast Red armies advancing into Germany from the east and the south. The Bavarian Communists had only to hang on for a short time and they would be relieved and become part of a larger Bavarian-Austrian-Hungarian soviet nation.

But Levien, Leviné and Axelrod had no more knowledge of what Communists in other parts of the world were doing than Lenin had of what was happening in Munich. In fact, Moscow seems to have learned about the Communist takeover in Munich several days after the event—and even then only by monitoring radio stations in other parts of Germany. In early April, when the Coffeehouse Anarchists had first announced the creation of a Republic of Councils, the Russian government had praised it. Then, finding that Toller and his friends did not conform to Comintern specifications, they had attacked it. When the actual Communists took over on April 13, Moscow thought at first that theirs was a White counterrevolution and shifted over to praising Toller and attacking his successors. By the time it was apparent that this latest Bavarian government was completely acceptable, the Bolsheviks in Moscow were so confused that they could not trust themselves to dispatch even vague expressions of good wishes until April 27. These were picked up, translated and rebroadcast to Munich by the Béla Kun government in Hungary. At no time did Lenin send instructions, promises of aid, or special envoys to Munich. The Comintern confined itself to cautious cheering from the sidelines. The "Russians" in Bavaria, distressed at this lack of recognition, dispatched Axelrod to attempt to reach Russia or Hungary by airplane and explain their adherence to international Communism, but bad luck continued to haunt the Munich Commune. The airplane, flown by a student pilot, developed engine trouble and was forced to come down inside Bavaria.

In truth, this Communist government had little time to spare from its preparations to defend itself. It was obvious that the Hoffmann government was going to attempt a reoccupation of Munich. And if it did not, the central government would. But as the days passed and no anti-Communist army appeared at the gates of Munich, it became apparent that the Majority Socialists in Bamberg were experiencing certain difficulties. The Bavarian anti-Prussian tradition, combined with the pacifist legacy of Kurt Eisner, had prevented the

Majority Socialists from building up *Freikorps* of their own. There had been some *Freikorps* recruitment on Bavarian soil, but only on the condition that these recruits be taken out of Bavaria for training. This left Hoffmann and his government in a quandary. Either they could invite Noske to send in forces—which would be composed principally of Prussians—or they could attempt to raise their own army and march on Munich themselves. In the end, the Bavarian Majority Socialists consulted Noske and were told that the central government would help them on one condition only: that it be permitted to march upon Munich with a large body of *Freikorps*. Noske pointed out that the Munich Communists had, in a very short time, managed to put together a large army. To subdue them might well require a force of thirty thousand men or more. As the core of this army, Noske offered to send the large newly formed *Freikorps* of Colonel Franz Ritter von Epp, a former officer of the Royal Bavarian Army, whose men had just completed their training at Ohrdruf in Thuringia, just north of the Bavarian border. It was a corps which had enough Bavarians in it to be passed off as a Bavarian army for propaganda purposes.

The Bavarian Majority Socialists were hesitant. They calculated the effect which a predominantly Prussian invasion of Munich would have, and the prospect seemed horrifying. They decided, "Bavaria needs no outside help,"[22] scraped together a force of their own and within a couple of days were marching on Munich.

They got only as far as a small city named Dachau, located some twenty-five miles to the north of Munich. There they were met on April 20 by a force of several thousand Red troops under Ernst Toller. The fighting did not last long. The Majority Socialists, greatly outnumbered, broke and ran, and the workers of Dachau chased them, throwing stones. The Munich Communards had astounded even themselves by the ease with which they had beaten these Majority Socialists whom they accused of being "White counterrevolutionaries"—a charge which was made easier to sustain by the fact that Majority Socialist troops wore armbands of blue and white, which were not only the Bavarian colors but, unhappily, also the colors of the Wittelsbach dynasty.

By nightfall of April 20 the Majority Socialist army was streaming north, its commander had seized a railway locomotive to expedite his own flight, and the Communist forces had captured five Majority Socialist officers and thirty-six enlisted men. Egelhofer ordered them shot, but Toller refused to obey. Hoffmann and his Majority Socialist government at Bamberg now had no choice left in the matter of reconquering Munich. They traveled to Weimar, prostrated themselves before the central government and relinquished all influence over the events which were to follow. Noske, as an official of the central government, made it quite clear that he would make no concessions to Bavarian separatist sentiments. The invasion of Bavaria was to be handled as a strictly military operation.

The speed with which the central government's forces were deployed makes it evident that Noske's staff had anticipated the Bavarian Majority Socialists' defeat. Only a day or two after the Dachau debacle the *Freikorps* columns were ready to march. The preparation of the operation plan had been delegated to General von Lüttwitz' staff, who had prepared the plans for the Berlin suppression in March and were thoroughly experienced. The entire force was under the command of General von Oven, who, in turn, received his orders directly from Noske's staff. ("The operational objective is Munich. In Munich the power of the legally constituted Bavarian regime is to be restored. . . . As soon as Munich is occupied and the resistance is extinguished, the Bavarian General von Möhl is to assume command in Munich."[23] Von Oven was given strict instructions that during the course of the operation he was not to accept orders from the Hoffmann government, which, it was suspected, might panic when it came to serious bloodshed.

The *Freikorps* forces involved were very large. Many of the older units were employed elsewhere, but still there were plenty of men available. Although the Provisional Reichswehr was as yet barely organized, the *Freikorps* had come a long way since January 4, when there had been only Maercker's four thousand Volunteer Rifles. Now there were nearly 400,000 *Freikorpskämpfer* under arms, and more than thirty thousand of them had been concentrated on the Bavarian borders. They included the toughest and most professional of the private armies. Among them were detachments from the Horse Guards Division, von Epp's *Freikorps,* von Görlitz' *Freikorps* (just returned from the suppression of an insurrection at Magdeburg), and an unusual brigade composed of naval officers and students and commanded by a Navy captain named Hermann Ehrhardt. This last was one of the fiercest of all the *Freikorps.* It had started out as one of the little units which Noske had raised while he was in Kiel and, under Ehrhardt's leadership, had performed so well that Noske authorized its enlargement. Ehrhardt had taken over the "Thousand-Man Barracks" in Wilhelmshaven and issued a call for recruits. His reputation was such that he was flooded with applicants and was able to pick and choose, principally from among former naval officers and the conservative students from the port cities. Without question Ehrhardt was a remarkable leader, and his men were utterly devoted to him. They marched to a song they had composed, the "Ehrhardt Lied" ("Comrade, give me your hand / Steadfast we'll stand together / Let those fight us who will / Our spirit marches forever"). Throughout its service this brigade retained a nautical flavor. The men's cry of greeting was "Ahoy!"

Supporting these *Freikorps* fighters, most of whom were Prussians, were an aviation detachment and an armored train. In addition, there were sizable contingents from Württemberg and Bavaria itself.

After a brief pause to assemble on the borders of Bavaria, the *Freikorps* units crossed her frontiers. Easily conquering the smaller north-Bavarian cities on their way, the principal forces came directly south in a two-pronged attack directed at Munich through Dachau and Freising. Other units, principally the Bavarian and Württemberg contingents, drove toward Munich from the west. Detachments of von Epp's *Freikorps* circled around to cut off the city from the south, while a smaller force swung in from the east through Mühldorf. Moving by truck or rail, these forces quickly conquered practically all of Bavaria, and it was not until they reached the ring of towns which comprised the outer suburbs of Munich that Communist resistance became significant. On April 29 there was sharp fighting from Freising, Erding and Starnberg, all of which fell to the *Freikorps*. Only Dachau held out, until Görlitz' troops conquered and subdued its Red Guards on April 29. The *Freikorps* encirclement plan was now essentially complete: Munich was surrounded on all sides at a distance of ten miles. By April 30 the government's forces were gathering their strength for the attack on the city itself. Not wishing to provide Communist martyrs on May Day, they deferred the attack until May 2.

Meanwhile, within the city the Republic of Councils was frantically attempting to stem the enemy onrush. Certain sections of the Bavarian Red Army had fought very well, but others were not fighting at all. On April 29 Egelhofer issued a plea to the Munich proletariat:

* * *

> *Workers! Soldiers of the Red Army!*
> *The enemy is at the gates of Munich. The officers, students, sons of the bourgeoisie, and White Guard mercenaries are already in Schleissheim. There is not an hour to be lost. . . . Protect the Revolution! Protect yourselves! Every man to arms! . . . Everything is at stake! At Starnberg the White Guard dogs murdered our hospital attendants. . . . Forward into combat for the proletarian cause!*[24]

The appeal did little good. The *Freikorps* circle was closing with machinelike contractions. The Communist organization, discipline and communications were all rapidly decaying. There was awful dissension among the Communist leadership as the Germans berated the "Russians." Ernst Toller and Emil Männer formally accused Leviné and Levien of having perpetrated "a calamity for the people of Bavaria."[25] They charged that the "Russians" approached every matter caring nothing for "the views of the great mass of our working people, the cares for our present and future, but only whether it conforms to the teachings of Russian Bolshevism, whether Lenin and Trotsky in a similar circumstance would react thus or thus . . . *we Bavarians are not Russians!*"[26] Levien and Leviné resigned, but it was too late. Large contingents of the Red Army began to throw away their rifles, hide their red armbands and desert.

On the afternoon of April 30 there was one last meeting of the government of the Republic of Councils. Everyone was clearly terrified. Toller had contacted the Hoffmann government in Bamberg and had been told that the terms of a Communist surrender were out of its hands; the only thing the Red leaders could do was give themselves up to the *Freikorps*. Levien and Leviné were the victims of general recrimination, following which the defense of the city was discussed. Every defensive line which Egelhofer had set up had been broken by the *Freikorps;* the Red Army was shrinking hourly. That evening Toller met with Egelhofer in the crowded Ministry of War. As they talked, a man came running through the office crying, "The Whites have taken the railway station!" It was a false alarm, but in a panic the Red forces abandoned their headquarters. Within a few minutes only three persons were left in the enormous building

—Toller, Egelhofer and a twenty-year-old sailor, one of Egelhofer's hand-picked bodyguards, who approached his commander and said, "I shall stay with you, Rudolf." This was practically all that was left of the Red Army.[27]

The city's bourgeoisie, emboldened at the obvious decay of the Communist armed force, had meanwhile seized the Residenz in the center of the city, and now the blue-and-white flag flew over this palace, which was occupied by a company of armed students. Church bells rang incessantly in an unnerving clangor. In the outskirts the *Freikorps* armored train was firing upon such Red strongpoints as remained, and *Freikorps* patrols were already feeling their way down some of the city streets. The best the Communists could hope for was to gather some armed workers and fortify the railroad station, the Palace of Justice and the huge Mathäser Brauhaus in the city's center and prepare to sell their lives dearly. They could not expect mercy from the *Freikorps*. Max Levien made his way out of the city and fled across the border to Austria. Leviné and Axelrod went into hiding within the city.

The murders of the hostages in the Luitpold Gymnasium began that night.

For some weeks the Red Army, under Egelhofer's instructions, had been arresting prominent royalists and conservatives and imprisoning them in a large school building, the Luitpold Gymnasium. Among these prisoners were a number of members of the Thule Society, which the Communists held to be indirectly responsible for the assassination of Kurt Eisner. The warden in charge of these hostages was a Bavarian named Seidel, who had the unusual distinction of being a recently demobilized officer of the Bavarian Army. Some of his guards seem to have been former Russian prisoners of war. On the night of April 30 Seidel, acting upon orders from Egelhofer, began to kill his prisoners. Two by two they were pushed against a wall and either shot or bludgeoned to death with rifle butts. Before Ernst Toller stopped the massacre, some twenty of Munich's most prominent citizens had been murdered and their bodies so mutilated that they were unrecognizable. Seidel reported to Egelhofer that he had killed off "the gentlemen of the Thule society."[28]

The *Freikorps* waiting on the outskirts of the city quickly heard of this atrocity. The rumor spread that the sex organs of those killed had been cut off and thrown in a dustbin. The murders were described as having been performed "by Russians," which may have been true. In any event, it was all that was needed. The pace of the attack was stepped up, and, by a gruesome irony, the *Freikorps* burst into the city from all sides on the first of May. In Moscow on that day Lenin was telling an immense crowd in Red Square, "The liberal working class is celebrating its anniversary freely and openly not only in Soviet Russia but also in Soviet Hungary and Soviet Bavaria."[29] In point of fact, the streets of Munich had been deserted by the Red Army, and the *Freikorps* forces experienced no difficulty in capturing the major part of the city. In columns they marched down the broad Ludwigstrasse, goose-stepping as they passed the Feldherrnhalle, and tramped into the Marienplatz at the very center of the city. A Te Deum was sung, and there was an open-air Mass for the troops. The red flag was pulled down everywhere and replaced by the blue-and-white. The only real resistance they encountered was in the complex of buildings surrounding the railroad station, and even here it did not take long to kill off the defenders—among them Rudolf Egelhofer, who was pulled from hiding in an automobile in which he was trying to escape the city and was shot on the spot. Artillery and flamethrowers were used freely, and the Mathäser Brauhaus was gutted.

By May 3 Munich had been entirely secured. Now the *Freikorps* began to give the city "a thorough cleansing."[30]

The white terror which followed was vastly more savage than anything the Communists had undertaken. Indeed, in defense of the Republic of Councils it must be said that its revolutionary courts had seldom handed down a death sentence. With the exception of the massacre in the Luitpold Gymnasium, the orders to shoot prisoners which had come from Egelhofer, a terrified psychopath at the end, were generally circumvented. The Munich revolutionaries had talked about terror a great deal more than they practiced it. Not so the *Freikorps*.

By now the character of the typical *Freikorpskämpfer* had undergone a great change from the early days when order-loving footloose professional soldiers had comprised most of these forces. By May of 1919 the *Freikorps* ranks had begun to fill up with young students and adventurous bourgeois who thought of themselves as "freebooters," in the tradition of the "free companies" who roamed Germany during the Thirty Years' War. Their political philosophy was undefined; indeed, it was undefinable. They could not exactly describe why they marched, but it was all bound up somehow with the

joy of crushing underfoot the "rotten" elements of German life—
proletarianism, Judaism and the "November criminals" who had
stabbed Germany in the back and caused her to lose the war.

Men such as these did not much care what they did. They rejoiced in the thrill of tramping through the Reich heavily armed,
remorseless and hard, of smashing the rifle butt or the hobnailed
boot into the soft face of an enemy, and of seeing the terror which
their coming aroused.

Although they had sworn allegiance to Ebert and his government,
they regarded this as only a casual formality. They were loyal only
to their own individual leader, their *Führer*, whom they would
follow anywhere. The *Freikorps* leaders, in turn, felt no particular
devotion toward the government. Many of them had been refused
appointments in the Provisional Reichswehr. Others did not even
want to join it, preferring the status of leader of a *Freikorps* to the
obscurity of service as a junior officer in the Army. By May of 1919
the government had begun to lose control of the *Freikorps*. The
Munich Terror is an example of the result.

About seventy *Freikorps* soldiers had been killed in the attack on
the city, in addition to the twenty-odd hostages murdered in the
Luitpold Gymnasium. As an excuse for revenge it would have been
hard to find an improvement upon this. "Gentlemen," Major Schulz
of the Lützow Freikorps announced in an address to his officers on
May 4, "Anyone who doesn't now understand that there is a lot of
hard work to be done here or whose conscience bothers him had
better get out. It's a lot better to kill a few innocent people than to
let one guilty person escape. . . . You know how to handle it . . .
shoot them and report that they attacked you or tried to escape."[31]

The first thing to do was to comb Munich for the leaders of the
Republic of Councils. Eugen Leviné was soon found, was tried for
high treason before a court-martial and was shot as he cried. "Long
live the world revolution!" Gustav Landauer, the anarchist philosopher who had been the Commissar for Public Education during the
rule of the Coffeehouse Anarchists, was picked up at Kurt Eisner's
former home. A *Freikorps* patrol brought him to the Stadelheim
Prison courtyard and played with him as a cat plays with a bird. His
face was beaten in with rifle butts, and then, as he lay snuffling in
his own blood, a sergeant major shot him in the head. Still he lived.
"This putrid thing has two lives," the sergeant exclaimed.[32] They
turned him over and shot him in the stomach. Landauer was still
breathing. Because the bullets were ricocheting off the courtyard

pavement, they contented themselves with kicking him to death, after which they stole his ring and left his body to lie in the court-yard for two days.

Most of the Communist leaders were dealt with similarly. The editor of the Munich edition of *Die rote Fahne,* a peasant leader named Gandorfer, a professor named Horn and scores of others were shot after being "tried" by impromptu *Freikorps* courts-mar-tial. Only a few leaders escaped. Axelrod was one. He was arrested, but he had diplomatic status, and when the Russians heard of his arrest they immediately broadcast a threat of reprisals on German diplomats if he was harmed.

With the leaders out of the way, the *Freikorps* next turned to Munich's workers—in particular, those who were suspected of hav-ing been Red Guards. Notices were put up throughout the city that, on pain of death, anyone possessing arms must surrender them, and that anyone bearing arms would be shot on the spot. When it was pointed out that a citizen carrying a weapon to a collection point would probably be shot down by a passing patrol, an adjutant in the Ehrhardt Brigade agreed that this would quite probably happen. He offered a suggestion which he found quite amusing: citizens should tie their rifles to long strings and drag them through the streets to the collection points.[33]

In the courtyard of the Stadelheim Prison the corpses piled up as former Red Guards, or often persons simply suspected of having been Red Guards, were shot down. In an effort to keep down the number of witnesses, the troops shot any prisoner who put his face to the window of a cell looking out on the courtyard. The *Freikorps* soldiers were politically so naïve, or were so bloodthirsty, that they were incapable of distinguishing between the various working-class groups. On the evening of May 6, thirty Catholic workingmen, members of the Society of St. Joseph, were gathered at a tavern on the Augustusstrasse. They met frequently to discuss religious mat-ters and could not be considered in any way revolutionaries. Never-theless, their meeting was broken into by a patrol looking for "Spar-tacists," and they were marched off to the former palace of a Wit-telsbach prince which was serving as a *Freikorps* headquarters. It was useless for the terrified workingmen to try to explain that they had never been revolutionaries. They were herded into the cellar of the palace and made to lie on their stomachs, and then twenty-one of them were shot or bayoneted to death.

This massacre of the members of the St. Joseph's Society was too much. The Munich bourgeoisie, which only a week before had welcomed the entry of the *Freikorps* with joy, was now thoroughly frightened at the promiscuous savagery of its deliverers. The proletariat was both terrified and hostile. Even General von Oven, the military commander, realized that things had gone too far. Well over a thousand persons had been killed by the *Freikorps* in a six-day period.[34] Secretly printed posters were going up all over Munich denouncing the savagery of "the Prussians."

To counter this hostility, von Oven's headquarters issued a series of proclamations signed "The Bavarian Commander." They were clumsy attempts to blame the Communists for spreading false rumors with the intention of making the citizens forget "the eminent services rendered by the troops of the Reich."[35] Finally, on May 13, the Bavarian government was permitted to return from Bamberg to Munich, and, almost as suddenly as they had come, the Prussian *Freikorps* regiments departed Bavaria.

They left behind them a peculiar legacy. Munich was a city which in the course of only six months had lived successively under monarchy, revolutionary Socialism, moderate Socialism, anarchy, Communism and, finally, brutal counterrevolutionary suppression. It was inevitable that in the course of these successive regimes practically every Bavarian class and faction would be left with some grievous suffering to brood over—and to avenge. Munich, once the city of easygoing tolerance, was now racked with hate and suspicion. Every social element had its own hatreds to cherish and advocate. Much more than any other German city, Munich seethed with intrigue. General Ludendorff, finding the political climate promising, moved to Munich. Dozens and dozens of political parties sprang up in this fertile soil. There were Communists, anti-Semites, royalists, nationalists, separatists. The right was resolute, armed, ruthless and dominant. The left knew that it could expect neither justice nor mercy in Munich. Each group behaved accordingly and set up its own "defense leagues" to protect its members, attack each other's meetings and carry out political assassinations.

Within weeks of the departure of the *Freikorps*, Munich swarmed with spies and informers. The Bavarian Army was then in the process of reconstitution into brigades of the German Reichswehr,° and some of the veteran soldiers from the old Bavarian regiments

---

° Bavaria became District VII of the Provisional Reichswehr. Its commander was General Franz Ritter von Epp. Rudolph Hess and Ernst Röhm were officers on his staff.

who had demonstrated a staunch anti-Communism were recruited, put through a hasty schooling, given the title *Bildungsoffizier* and sent out to conduct indoctrination lectures among the newer troops. Adolf Hitler was one of these Army political agents. He lived with the Second Infantry Regiment in a room which was bullet-marked from the fighting in the first weeks of May. He spent his days talking to the troops of the Forty-first Rifle Regiment. In the evening this strange, friendless thirty-year-old man toured Munich's taverns and coffeehouses, checking on the latest political developments. On September 12, 1919, he visited a shabby beerhall, the Sternecker, in the Herrenstrasse. On instructions from his superior officer, a Major Giehrl, Hitler was to look into the program of a tiny group with an interesting name for an openly nationalistic organization—"the German Workers' Party."

Chapter Twelve

The East

Iт is difficult to explain the German people's intense attraction to the land to the east. It is perhaps a primeval urging—a desire to return to lands thought once to have been inhabited by Germans or their antecedents, who were forced from them by the irresistible westward migrations of the Slavs. But there may be a simpler and more practical explanation. The east has consistently offered tempting opportunities to Germany. As early as the tenth century, sizable German colonies were established in Russia, Poland and what was to become Czechoslovakia. In the thirteenth century the Teutonic Knights conquered and Christianized the lands on the eastern Baltic. German emigrés occupied a large percentage of the senior positions in the czarist Russian bureaucracy, especially in the Ministry of War and the Ministry of Foreign Affairs, both of which they dominated for a time.

There was more than fame and honor to be won in the east. German merchants achieved spectacular successes on the Baltic, where they had a virtual monopoly on all commerce. In Germany's Polish provinces an aggressive policy of industrialization brought vast returns to German investors. And to the militarists the east offered endless potential, both as maneuvering space for the inevitable "next war" and as a limitless supply of patient, disciplined soldiers who needed only the German sergeant to beat them into troops able to withstand any hardship or suffering.

Ludendorff had seen great military possibilities in an eastward

German expansion. Observations of Polish soldiers had especially excited his interest. All during the war plans had been developed—indeed, they had practically matured—for members of miscellaneous German royal houses to be called to newly established thrones in German-conquered eastern territories. In castles all over Germany, princes of the blood found it prudent to study strange eastern tongues and to examine family trees for convenient connections with antique eastern royal houses.

The armistice put an end to this, but it was noted that, although the agreement was most explicit as to the surrender of arms and withdrawal of German troops on the western front, it was vague concerning the east. Only five articles out of the thirty-five in the armistice document dealt with Eastern Europe, and all five were brief. As these articles were studied and restudied, the hope began to grow that perhaps this was actually a covert message from the Allies. Were the victors, by inference or omission, permitting Germany a free hand in the east? If this was the case it would, of course, have to be skillfully handled by Germany. Among Wilson's Fourteen Points, to which Germany had agreed, there was a pledge to create "an independent Polish state." But what did that really mean? Wilson had not specified the borders of this resurrected Poland, and no one had mentioned Russia's former provinces on the Baltic. Surely Germany was uncommitted there? And Bolshevik Russia was a case in itself. The Allies themselves, now in the process of landing troops and supplies to support White Russian armies, would surely welcome German anti-Bolshevik forces. In fact, under the provisions of Article 12 of the armistice, German troops were required to remain in place until "the Allies shall think the moment suitable, having regard to the internal situation of these territories." Could anything be more obvious? Seemingly, the Allies were confirming Germany in her historic role as the defender of the eastern marches against the Slavic horde.

For those Germans who found this view too sanguine, there was a thought almost equally comforting: perhaps the Allies had no resolute position on the east, other than the establishment of an independent Poland and Czechoslovakia. Everything pointed to a certain flexibility of Allied policy. Germany need only adopt an aggressive course of action in the east to reap benefits which could surely be used for bargaining purposes at the time when the peace treaty was finally negotiated. General Groener assured the Cabinet, "I am firmly convinced that Wilson does not have in mind a decisive alteration of our eastern border. We are certainly able to maintain our present border. I am convinced that it is child's play to preserve our eastern border at the peace conference."[1]

No matter which view was taken, it appeared that much could be gained. All that had been lost in the west—honor, land, wealth, glory—might yet be redeemed in the east. Prince Max, during his brief chancellorship, had recognized the opportunities of this situation. Germany already had a foothold and more in the Russian Ukraine, where an army of 400,000 Germans supported an "independent" Ukrainian government with which Germany had advantageous treaties. Even before the armistice, Max had sent special emissaries to negotiate with the most prominent figure among the Poles, General Józef Pilsudski, and a German high commissioner had been sent to the Baltic with wide powers to conclude treaties. After the armistice, however, Fritz Ebert's government, wholly absorbed in internal affairs, found no time for adventures in the east. Such abstractions as the *Drang nach Osten* ("Drive to the East") and Germany's historic "mission" to civilize the Slavs had no interest for these harassed Socialist politicians.

But if the government did not find time for eastern intrigues, there were many Germans who did. In late February the Army's Supreme Command moved east to establish itself in the city of Kolberg on the Baltic. Special military commands were set up to supervise military affairs on Germany's eastern frontiers—and beyond them. German refugees from the east poured back into the homeland. Most of them had in the past enjoyed special privileges of one type or another in the Polish provinces, in Russia or in the Baltic Provinces. Now they had been compelled to flee, abandoning their homes, businesses, estates and positions. They formed a solid nucleus of discontent. The east also attracted a host of discharged and declassed Army officers, the *Freikorps* and the suddenly deposed nobility. To all these groups seeking an outlet for their frustration the east offered an opportunity for wealth and glory.

In the ten centuries during which a Polish national life, language and culture can confidently be said to have existed, the boundaries of the nation had fluctuated to an almost unbelievable extent. There had been times, most recently in the mid-eighteenth century, when Poland was an enormous nation. Her northern frontier had stretched from what would later become Latvia south and west along the

Baltic seacoast, skirting only the East Prussia enclave, to west of Danzig. To the south the Polish kingdom had bordered on Hungary and Moldavia. To the east it had extended deeply into Russia—farther, in fact, than Vitebsk and Kiev. Supported by a brave and docile peasantry, the aggressive Polish kings and nobles fought Prussians, Swedes, Austrians, Hungarians, Russians and Turks. When victorious, the Poles annexed huge territories. When defeated, they were dealt with in equal fashion, for the featureless Polish plains offered no natural barriers either to invasion or to colonization.

In the second half of the eighteenth century, Poland's neighbors began to accumulate a strength which her rulers could not resist. Beginning in 1772, there were three successive "partitions" by which Austria, Prussia and Russia divided Poland among themselves. By 1795 the dismemberment was complete. Poland, as an independent nation, ceased to exist.

For more than one hundred years the Polish people suffered the rule of the partitioning monarchies. They refused to accept their subject status as permanent and yearned for the day when Poles would again be free and united. From time to time, almost always in Russian Poland, popular insurrections broke out. There was sporadic guerrilla warfare. Polish heroes arose and were crushed. Their successors arose and were crushed again.

The rulers of the Poles were equally determined. They knew that until the Polish people were assimilated into their respective ruler nations they would constitute a discontented and rebellious minority; accordingly, vast programs were undertaken by both Russia and Prussia to "de-Polonize" their subjects. In Russian Poland various programs of conciliation alternated with brutal repression. The Germans went about the task more systematically. A German "Imperial Colonization Commission" spent billions of marks purchasing land in the Polish provinces and moving 100,000 German settlers into it in an effort to create German enclaves among the Poles. To encourage additional German colonization of predominantly Polish West Prussia and the province of Posen, all posts in the governmental services were reserved for German settlers. The Poles were forbidden to operate their own schools, and German teachers were brought in, speaking only German as the language of instruction.

With amazing tenacity, the Poles resisted these attempts to denationalize them. Despite the steady increase of Germans in the largely Polish provinces, they managed to preserve their language, customs and religion. Their priests helped by conducting secret instruction in Polish history for the children. For those Poles who could not tolerate German rule there was always the outlet of emigration. By the millions they fled to settle in France, Great Britain and, principally, the United States. But even from overseas they continued to plan and dream of the day when Poland would again be free and united.

If the Imperial Colonization Commission's attempt to assimilate the Poles was not as successful as it could wish, it had at least certain achievements to its credit. In West Prussia, for example, where a Polish population had settled along the Vistula River from Warsaw to the port city of Danzig on the Baltic Sea, Germany made considerable progress in creating a continuous ethnographic belt from Germany proper through to the East Prussian homeland. And under German rule the port of Danzig had been vastly improved and was almost completely resettled with Germans.

Nor was German rule an undiluted calamity for the Polish minority. The purchases of the Colonization Commission had driven up the price of land to the point where its sale made rich men of many Polish peasants. And under the impetus of Germany's forced industrialization the standard of living in her Polish provinces had risen greatly—far higher than in Russian Poland, where most of the population consisted of peasant laborers who worked for the repressive Russian and Polish landowners. The German Poles rarely rebelled against their masters. The closest thing to a popular insurrection was a brief educational strike of Polish children in 1906. In such provinces as Posen, once thought of as the cradle of the Polish nation, the Germans invested vast sums. The province's capital, the old Polish city of Poznań, tripled in size. Even though the territory's population became forty per cent German in the process, it was difficult to deny the prosperity which German rule had brought. It had, in fact, attracted Poles from Russia to Germany; whereas in 1861 there were 800,000 Poles in Posen, by 1911 there were one and a half million. Upper Silesia was a similar case. It had not really been Polish for seven hundred years, and much of the original Polish influences had long since vanished, yet, with German development of important coal, lead, zinc and iron mines, so many jobs had been created that Poles had flocked into the area. By the turn of the twentieth century, parts of Upper Silesia which had once been principally German or Bohemian had become predominantly Polish.

* * *

Over the years the cause of Polish unification and independence had aroused much sympathy in the great democracies—particularly in France and in the United States, where the opinions of four million Polish immigrants could not be ignored. From time to time, various foreign governments had appealed to Germany or Russia to permit the formation of an independent Poland. Nothing had ever come of this, and at the turn of the twentieth century it was obvious to most of the twenty million Poles in Europe that they would never be able to achieve independence and unification by revolutionary means, much less through the ineffectual good wishes of the democracies abroad. They could only pray that some apocalyptic event would destroy the partitioning monarchies. The beginning of World War I was therefore greeted with joyous anticipation. Although it was certain that much of the war would be fought across the Polish provinces of Russia, Germany and Austria, and even though Poles would obviously be conscripted into each of the conflicting armies and thus forced to fight against their brothers, the war might be the cataclysm for which Poland was waiting. It was a desperate hope, and it called for leaders prepared to take instant advantage of any fugitive opportunity which might present itself. No one was better prepared than Józef Pilsudski.

At the outbreak of World War I Pilsudski was forty-seven years old and the most dashing revolutionary figure of a people among whom glamorous insurrectionaries proliferated. He had been born a Russian subject, in Wilno, a city which was predominantly Lithuanian but which had once been part of Poland. Pilsudski's parents were impoverished gentry who, like most of the Lithuanian nobility, preferred to consider themselves Polish by virtue of the dynastic union which had existed between the Lithuanian and Polish kingdoms. From his earliest youth, Pilsudski was a determined Polish patriot. As a boy of nineteen he was sentenced to five years in Siberia for his part in an anti-czarist plot. As soon as he returned he helped to form the secret Polish Socialist Party and dedicated himself to a revolutionary life.

In 1894 Pilsudski founded a clandestine Socialist newspaper, *Robotnik* (*The Workingman*), which came to be widely circulated among Poles in Russia, Austria and even Germany. Under the pseudonym "Wiktor," Pilsudski crossed and recrossed the frontiers, recruiting agents everywhere. He was a man of medium height, gray-eyed, slender, strong and handsome. His education and birth, superior to that of his Socialist comrades, served further to set him apart. While there were other Polish leaders, most notably Roman Dmowski of the conservative Polish Nationalist Party, none was so daring or resolute as Pilsudski.

As time passed, several things became apparent about the character and convictions of Józef Pilsudski. To begin with, his Socialism was hardly more than skin deep. It was only a means to an end. Pilsudski lived for only one thing—the restoration of a free and independent Poland.* He was not even a democrat; debate, dispute and compromise were all abhorrent to him. He developed a passion for military affairs and an authoritarian personality to match it. Proud, vain, taking counsel of no man, Pilsudski began to organize disciplined terrorist groups whom he directed in "expropriations"— armed attacks on Russian banks and post offices. His agents were principally employed in purchasing weapons abroad and smuggling them into the Polish provinces.

Pilsudski quickly came to be regarded by the Russians as the most dangerous of the Polish revolutionaries. In 1900 the Russian secret police succeeded in capturing him and locked him into Cell 39 of the infamous "Tenth Pavilion" in the Warsaw Citadel. This prison had absolute security. No one ever escaped from it.

Pilsudski was never brought to trial. In the months which followed his arrest, his Russian warders saw his mind collapse. He began to mumble strange words and phrases. Then he began to scream and sob at night. When the prison doctor appeared at Cell 39, Pilsudski became frantic at the sight of his uniform. Foam came to his lips. His appearance deteriorated shockingly. He cried out that the Russians were trying to poison him, and eventually he would eat nothing but raw eggs, which he swallowed shells and all, to avoid poison. Finally the Russians transferred the madman to a prison for the criminally insane in St. Petersburg. From this much less well-guarded institution Pilsudski immediately escaped. His lunacy had been an act.

After a period of exile in London, Pilsudski returned to Poland. He set up his headquarters in Galicia, the Austrian-held Polish prov-

---

* Rosa Luxemburg, in exile in Zurich, had tried to establish a "real" Polish socialist party with the emphasis on internationalism, but her group had been unable to compete with the dynamic nationalism which Pilsudski espoused.

ince, a safe haven where the police were more than tolerant. From this base he formed an "Association of Secret Conspiracy and Combat" to conduct terrorist activity in Russian Poland. It was nearly impossible to run a terrorist organization within German Poland; the German police were far too efficient, and the German Poles lacked the burning sense of grievance which animated their brothers in Russia. To supplement his association, he formed secret "riflemen's clubs," which trained Poles in the use of weapons. From the best of these recruits he created a "Polish Legion" which was designed to be the core of a Polish Army at the day of independence. Pilsudski even established an "officers' school" in Lwow and drew candidates from among Poles of every class and nation. Little attention was paid to the question of whether these men were Socialists; Pilsudski did not really care. He formed a military staff, and he and his followers began to wear their gray military uniforms openly in their travels throughout Galicia; they conducted lectures in military tactics and exercised their "soldiers" on fifty-mile forced marches.

The outbreak of the war did not catch Pilsudski completely unprepared. He had long ago made his plans. Since two thirds of the Poles in Europe lived in Russian Poland, it was obvious that Russia was the major enemy. If Germany and Austria could beat Russia, and then if France and Britain could beat Germany, the way would be free for Polish independence. To take advantage of this opportunity, Poland must have an army of her own. This could come about only with the permission of the Germans and the Austrians, and obviously such permission would be given only if the army was fighting on their side. As it turned out, the Central Powers were glad to aid in the creation of any difficulties which could be fomented in Russian Poland. Thus, at 3 A.M. on August 6, 1914, Pilsudski was permitted to lead his Polish Legion across the border into Russian territory, where he occupied the town of Kielce, smeared black paint over the Russian signposts, raised the crimson-and-white flag of a free Poland and called for Polish volunteers to join his legion.

At first this Polish army was a rather pitiful thing. The "legion" with which Pilsudski had attacked the Russian Empire consisted of 163 foot soldiers and eight cavalrymen, five of whom had no horses and had to carry their own saddles across the frontier. But in the following weeks the men from Pilsudski's "riflemen's clubs" and the graduates of his officers' school flocked to his standard. By September his men numbered five thousand, split into two brigades. The

Austrians, seeing in this Polish Legion a source of extra manpower, permitted its members to serve under the Polish banner, although, to reduce Pilsudski's personal influence, they detached the Second Brigade of the legion and sent it to another part of the front.

Within the inefficient Austro-Hungarian Army, Pilsudski's First Brigade quickly became a legend. Though they had no artillery and few machine guns, the soldiers of the Polish Legion were renowned as fierce fighters. They could take any position or defend any front. They were fanatically loyal to Pilsudski.

It would have been even better for the cause of Polish independence if Pilsudski had been able to coordinate his activities with other Polish leaders. There was, however, startlingly little unanimity of effort among them. In Russian Poland, Roman Dmowski formed a "Polish National Committee." Dmowski believed that Russia and her allies would win the war and that an independent Poland depended upon their future gratitude. Dmowski recruited his own "Polish Legion" to serve on the Russian side. Meanwhile, in Cracow, the Austrians formed *their* own "Polish National Committee," with the objective of establishing a unified Austrian Poland after the Central Powers had won the war.

By the end of 1915 the Germans and the Austrians had driven the Russian Army from most of the territory inhabited by Poles. Pilsudski now lost all interest in fighting Russia. He foresaw her eventual defeat and determined to devote no more of Poland's energies to aiding the Central Powers. Secretly he let it be known that recruiting for his Polish Legion should be slowed down. Young Poles who desired to enlist in the legion were diverted to a newly formed group, the "Polska Organizacja Wojskowa" (Polish Military Organization), or P.O.W., a clandestine force of Poles who worked in all parts of what Pilsudski regarded as Poland. Members of the P.O.W. acted as spies or messengers or propagandists for Polish independence. Pilsudski regarded them as the secret reserve of the Polish Army on the day of liberation.

In the fall of 1916, with the Germans in full control of all of Russian Poland and with a German garrison occupying Warsaw, General Ludendorff became convinced that the time was ripe for Germany to declare Poland's "independence." It was hoped that nearly a million Poles of military age would be recruited to fight for the Central Powers. The proven fighting qualities of Pilsudski's Polish Legion made these men tempting prospects. "My eye turns again to the Poles," Ludendorff wrote. "The Pole is a good soldier.

. . . Let us create a Grand Duchy of Poland and immediately after [this] a Polish Army under German command."[2] On November 5, 1916, a group of Polish officials were summoned to the Castle of Zamek, the historic Warsaw residence of the Polish Kings. There, amid appropriate fanfare, the German military governor announced that the Kaiser had decided to grant independence to Poland as soon as the war was won. There was a catch, however: "Independent" Poland was to consist of only *Russian* Poland, not the Polish provinces of Germany.

The Germans named a "Polish Regency Council" to be set up in Warsaw and began to recruit a Polish army. The first step in the recruitment was to enlist the Polish Legion, but the Germans demanded that its members take an oath of loyalty to the Kaiser. For a full six months there was constant argument over the form which this oath was to take. Pilsudski, through the P.O.W., let it be known that no Poles were to enlist in the new army. As a result, only thirty-nine men were recruited. On July 9, when it came time for the fourteen thousand men of the Polish Legion to take the German oath, they refused almost to a man. The exasperated and infuriated Germans disbanded the Legion, arrested Pilsudski and shipped him off to prison in the fortress at Magdeburg. For more than a year he was in complete isolation, and it was during this time that what he had hoped for came to pass: the three partitioning monarchies collapsed.

Meanwhile the policy of the Allies toward Polish independence underwent several confusing alterations. Initially it had been impossible for France or Britain to propose freedom for Poland, since two thirds of the Polish people were subjects of Russia, an ally. It was even difficult to decide whether the Poles should be regarded as friends or enemies; the Allies had in their prisoner-of-war stockades a large collection of Poles who had been captured while serving in the armies of the Central Powers. For the United States the problem was easier. She had no commitments to czarist Russia and was scarcely likely to make any. The Polish immigrant population in America comprised more than four million persons. Their various fraternal organizations had composed their differences and accepted the leadership of Ignace Paderewski, who had given up a brilliant musical career to head the movement for Polish independence. This was an attractive cause for Woodrow Wilson—indeed, for any American President. The freedom of Poland was identified with the righting of perhaps the greatest wrong ever perpetrated under the "old diplomacy." It was, in fact, an historic American cause; Thomas Jefferson himself had attacked the Polish partitioning as "a crime . . . , an atrocity . . . [and] a baneful precedent."[3] The Catholic Church, anxious to preserve Poland as a bastion of Roman Catholicism, lent its not inconsiderable efforts to the cause of a free Poland, and it did no harm to the Polish cause that Paderewski made himself especially agreeable to Woodrow Wilson and Edward House. Until the spring of 1917, however, it did not much matter what the position of the United States was. Then came a series of events which made Polish independence inevitable. In March Czar Nicholas II abdicated, thus releasing the French and the British from their commitments. In April the United States entered the war. And in January of 1918 Woodrow Wilson announced his Fourteen Points, the thirteenth of which demanded the establishment of "an independent Polish state . . . inhabited by indisputably Polish populations, which should be assured a free and secure access to the sea." France and Britain swiftly endorsed this pledge.

The Poles themselves hastened to cooperate. Roman Dmowski moved to Paris with his Polish National Committee, which was recognized by the Allies as the quasi-official voice of Poland. A part of the Polish Legion, under the command of General Józef Haller, fought its way to the Baltic seacoast, where it was picked up by Allied naval vessels and brought to Paris. Using Haller's force as a nucleus, the French quickly set about recruiting and arming a force of Poles for service on the western front. They scoured the Allied prison stockades for Polish volunteers and they advertised for Polish emigrants abroad. In a short time "Haller's Army" had 100,000 men.

The Allies were now firmly committed to Polish independence. Only one problem arose, and it was a problem which was to plague the Allies for months to come: where, exactly, *was* Poland? The first organization to face this question was the Inquiry, the American group set up during the war to chart United States plans for the peace conference. From the very outset the Inquiry reported the Polish frontiers to be "by far the most complex of all problems to be considered."[4] To begin with, what standards should be used to establish Poland's boundaries? Obviously they could not be historical. To re-create the frontiers of 1772, before the First Partition, would establish a Poland of phenomenal size and work a gross injustice upon millions of Balts, Ukrainians, Czechs and Germans. Moreover, the legitimacy of the 1772 Polish borders was in itself suspect. After all, the Poles had conquered much of this territory from others, and no indications existed that the Poles at that time had worried much about the national aspirations of their foreign subjects. The criterion of geography for the establishment of Poland's borders was an equal failure. Poland had no suitable "natural" borders. Even the test of language had awesome limitations. In this country which had not existed as a nation for more than one hundred years, the language frontiers defied definition. No line could possibly be drawn which would not work injustice upon millions of persons.

The question of the "free and secure access to the sea" which Wilson had pledged was fully as complex. Without a seaport Poland was doomed to landlocked impotence. But the only seaport available to be given her was Danzig, whose population was ninety per cent German. And if Danzig were given to Poland, how should she get to it? A Polish "corridor" would have to be cut through West Prussia. This would give to the Poles the two German railroads connecting Danzig to Warsaw, as well as a waterway on the Vistula River, but it would also sever East Prussia from Germany proper. The probable consequences of this gave pause to even the most violent Polonophiles on the Inquiry's staff. The Inquiry's Polish section split apart on the question. The pro-Polish members leaked the dilemma to the attentive Paderewski, and the United States delegation sailed for Paris without having completed a policy on Poland.

Józef Pilsudski learned that Germany was in revolution and the war practically over when two German officers appeared in his cell at Magdeburg on November 8, 1918. They were Count Harry von Kessler of the imperial guards, now attached as an aide to Chancellor Max of Baden, and a Dr. Schulze, political aide to the German military governor in Warsaw. Pilsudski knew them well. But he had never seen Kessler dressed in civilian clothes, as now. In an extraordinarily deferential manner they asked Pilsudski to pack his personal effects and come with them. Then the two Germans, obviously nervous and distraught, hurried Pilsudski into an automobile and drove with him into Berlin. On the way their car stopped at a railway crossing, and a train from the northwest came by. It was filled with sailors from Kiel, who waved red flags and brandished rifles. It now became obvious to Pilsudski why Kessler was wearing civilian clothes.

Pilsudski and his escort spent the night at the Hotel Continental in Berlin. The next morning, November 9, they went to Hiller's

Restaurant on Unter den Linden. A private dining room had been prepared, and waiting in it were representatives of the German Foreign Office. Everyone sat down to a lavish luncheon, during which the Germans made certain proposals. Germany had committed herself to Wilson's thirteenth point. Since it seemed apparent that Pilsudski would be the dominant figure in an independent Poland, the Germans hoped to get him to reach an early agreement on frontiers. Could not some sort of arrangement be made now? Much could be gained. Need there be a German-Polish dispute? Various borders were proposed, but Pilsudski would have none of them. He flatly refused to commit himself. Why should Poland make any commitments to the Germans at a time like this? In the streets outside a fearful clamor had begun. A nervous Foreign Office official kept leaving the table to go to the telephone. Finally Pilsudski's hosts admitted to him that Berlin was in revolution. None of the officials present even knew whether Prince Max was still the Imperial Chancellor.

Pilsudski broke up the luncheon. Rising from the table, he demanded that the Germans furnish him a train to Warsaw. After great exertions a train was made ready. In the early afternoon Pilsudski forced his way through the revolutionary masses now streaming into the center of the city and boarded his train. By six the next morning, November 10, he was again in Warsaw, where he was greeted by vast crowds. Shortly afterward he was given the title of chief of state by the Regency Council, which thereupon resigned.

The situation which Pilsudski inherited was scarcely enviable. Eighty-five per cent of what might be considered Polish territory had been fought over. The country was devastated. Four separate currencies circulated. The laws of three different nations were still in force. There were at least three other Polish "governments"—one in Lublin, one in Posen and one in Paris. No one knew where Poland's boundaries were. The Germans had set up an independent Ukrainian nation in territories which Poland would probably claim. Lithuania was about to announce her own independence, even though many of her citizens, particularly the nobility, had traditionally preferred to regard themselves as Poles. Indeed, Pilsudski himself was technically a Lithuanian.

Typically, Pilsudski first turned his attention to military matters. Within the territory which was destined to be Poland there were eighty thousand German troops; the Warsaw garrison alone consisted of thirty thousand men. To the east, in the Ukraine, there were nearly 400,000 German troops. Against this vast army Pilsudski could dispose only the remnants of his old Polish Legion and the poorly trained P.O.W.—a total of 35,000 men who were not organized into any coherent force. Before Poland could be master in her own house the German troops must be evacuated to Germany. In the armistice agreement, the Allies had been of little service in this matter. They had required that Germany withdraw all her troops "within the frontiers of Germany as they existed on the first of August, 1914," but in formerly Russian territories this evacuation was to take place only "as soon as the Allies . . . think the moment suitable, having regard to the internal situation of these territories." The purpose of this afterthought was to compel Germany to defend Eastern Europe against Bolshevism, but most of the German forces which remained in the Ukraine and Poland were second-class troops, with none of the "front-line fighter" *esprit* that animated the western-front army. In fact, the commander of the Warsaw garrison had abandoned his command and fled the city in disguise on the night of November 9. The only concern of these largely demoralized troops was to return to their homeland. Pilsudski was more than willing to help them do so.

On November 11, Pilsudski summoned before him a group of delegates from the soldiers' councils which had formed among the German garrison in Warsaw and announced that they would be evacuated from Poland immediately. The railroads used for this purpose would be operated by Poles. For their personal protection the German troops would be permitted to keep their rifles and machine guns, but all heavier weapons were to be left behind. When the trains crossed the Polish "frontier," the Germans were to give up all weapons to representatives of the P.O.W. The German soldier delegates at once accepted this proposal, and on the very next day the first trainloads of German soldiers left Warsaw.

But it was quickly discovered that the soldiers' councils, while they might enter into an agreement, lacked the means to enforce it. Some of the German units in Poland still obeyed the orders of their officers, who did not consider themselves bound by the agreement with Pilsudski. In some cases the officers refused to accept transportation on Polish-operated railways and elected to march out of Poland on their own. And, as a matter of pride and discipline, they would not hand over their arms at the border. In the city of Seriadz a company of German dragoons was fired on by Polish snipers. In

retaliation, the dragoons seized Polish hostages and threatened to
burn down the town. In other cities German cavalrymen charged
threatening crowds of Poles. Pilsudski thereupon announced that he
would not permit the German troops from the Ukraine to cross
Poland. They would have to take a roundabout northern route
through the Baltic states. A burst of intense hatred toward Germans
swiftly rose among the Polish population, and the final evacuation
of German troops was marked by a series of Polish ambushes and by
counterattacks by the retreating Germans. The intensive fighting in
the province of Posen was, however, of a different character.

Posen, with the historic Polish city of Poznań as its capital, was a
hallowed place to every Pole. It was also part of the German Empire
and had been since the Second Partition. Even the Germans conceded that most of its population was ethnically and linguistically
Polish, but there was a good case for its remaining German. A large
part of the population *was* German, even if they had gotten there as
the result of artificial colonization. Wilson had said that a Polish
state would be created in territories inhabited by "indisputably
Polish populations," and there was ample room for dispute about
the character of the population of Posen. There were tremendous
German investments in Posen. Many famous Germans, including
Hindenburg and Ludendorff, had been born in Poznań. Moreover,
the Poles in the province had accepted de-Polonization to a far
greater degree than had their countrymen in Russia or Austria.
They were noticeably better educated, more efficient and more
prosperous than were Poles anywhere else. It seemed to most Germans a gross injustice for Posen to be transferred to Poland. What
would happen to the 700,000 Germans who lived in the province? It
was unthinkable that they should become subjects of this new Slav
nation.

At first the Allies seemed to agree. At the time of the armistice
they shied from drawing up specific Polish frontiers. They required
only that the Germans withdraw within their frontiers of August 1,
1914. The only mention of Polish access to the sea in the armistice
was in a clause which said that "the Allies" were to "have free access
to the territories evacuated by the Germans on their eastern frontier, either through Danzig or by the Vistula." In fact, the word
"Poland" was not once mentioned in the armistice document. The
Germans reasoned that this was a secret message from the Allies,
who probably realized that German Poland had been completely
Germanized. Or perhaps Wilson's thirteenth point had merely been

a wartime propaganda sop thrown to the Poles. When Woodrow Wilson spoke of a "free and independent Poland," he was doubtless, the Germans thought, referring to *Russian* Poland. When he spoke of Polish access to the sea, Wilson surely meant no more than a German guarantee of unrestricted passage between Danzig and Warsaw. When Wilson said that Poland was to be created out of territories with "indisputably Polish population," it could well be inferred that any area where there *was* a dispute would not become Polish.

The first direct territorial confrontation with the Poles took place in December, 1919, in the city of Poznań. It was almost inevitable that this should have occurred. The German Supreme Command, in the temporary euphoria accompanying the disciplined evacuation of the field army from France and the Rhineland, had come to the conclusion that nothing was beyond its capabilities—certainly not the defense of Germany's eastern frontiers. Thus they swiftly determined that Germany must not give up an inch of its eastern soil. A separate Army command, "Grenzschutz Ost" (Frontier Defense Force East), was organized to deal with the matter of the eastern borders. A special effort was made to send to the east some particularly well-disciplined veteran regiments which had been evacuated from France. The Supreme Command, ignoring the provisions of the armistice agreement, did everything possible to speed up the withdrawal of German troops from Russia so as to expose Poland's eastern borders to the Russian Bolsheviks and engage her energies there. A certain degree of care was taken that the Ebert government should not learn too much of these activities of the Supreme Command in the east.

On December 24 Ignace Paderewski arrived in Danzig aboard the British cruiser *Concord*. The German port authorities furiously protested against his disembarkation. They pointed out that Germany had agreed to give "the Allies" free access through Danzig; but this, they said, did not extend to Poles, whom they did not consider to be among the Allies. Anxious to avoid dispute on such a fine point, the British made Paderewski a more or less official member of their military mission to Poland and successfully demanded that he be allowed to accompany them to Warsaw. Actually, Paderewski went first to Poznań. He arrived on Christmas Day to find the streets filled with delirious Poles waiting to welcome him. The crimson-and-white flag of Poland waved from buildings all over the city, in combination with the flags of Britain, France and the United States.

A unit of the P.O.W., uniformed and carrying rifles, provided a guard of honor at the railroad station.

The officers of the German Army witnessed this spectacle with unconcealed rage. Posen was a German province. Poznán was the headquarters of the Prussian Fifth Army Corps. It was unthinkable, and surely contrary to their orders, that foreign flags should be raised over the city and a gang of Slavic irregulars paraded under arms. This was civil insurrection among German citizens! It constituted a provocation which was unbearable. The officers of the Sixth Regiment of Grenadiers, a crack unit recently returned from the western front, descended upon the police headquarters and demanded that the foreign flags be torn down. When the chief of police protested that he had not the force to do this, the enraged grenadiers marched across the city, tearing down the flags themselves.

This could only lead to bloodshed. The Polish militia began to fire on German troops. The next day the Germans opened fire on a procession consisting mostly of Polish children who had come to welcome Paderewski. Polish irregulars began to attack police stations and isolated German Army outposts. Using the arms they seized, the Poles widened the conflict. One by one they took over smaller villages and towns throughout Posen. The German troops found themselves increasingly hemmed into the few positions they could dominate with their machine guns, and even these were not secure. Poles, led by P.O.W. officers, stormed and captured the military airfields outside Poznań. In retaliation, aircraft from Germany bombed the airfield's barracks. In the center of Poznań the Poles were victorious, and after several days of sustained fighting they managed to capture the headquarters of the Fifth Army Corps. The Polish flag was now raised everywhere in the city.

The German officers were stunned. No support had been given them by the Supreme Command or by Grenzschutz Ost. The fighting in Poznań had coincided with the Christmas Eve Battle in Berlin between the People's Naval Division and the remnant of the Imperial Army, which had thereupon disintegrated. If there were no troops available to reconquer the capital of Germany, there could be none to send to Posen, and as this became apparent the German garrison in Poznań melted away. By New Year's Day half of the three thousand troops of the Sixth Regiment of Grenadiers had thrown down their arms and fled to the west. The rest were disarmed and evacuated. General von Bock und Polach, the commander of the Fifth Army Corps, was taken prisoner in a state of nervous exhaustion. The principal cities of Posen were in Polish hands, and there was nothing the German Army could do about it.

In the meantime the Polish leaders in Warsaw wasted little time. The problems and opportunities posed by the vagueness of the Allied positions regarding Poland's boundaries had not gone unobserved by the Poles. They recognized that, whatever divisions might split them in the future, for the present they must get together and act with speed and ruthlessness to seize what could be seized. Haste was their friend, time their enemy. Territory claimed and occupied by Poland in the days following the armistice would be exceedingly difficult for either the Allies or Poland's neighbors to recover later.

Within two months after the armistice the Poles held a national election for a parliament, the parliament had its first sitting, and an official Polish delegation appeared before the Allies in Paris, where Poland was formally recognized as an independent nation. Despite the awesome differences between such personalities as Dmowski, Paderewski and Pilsudski, they managed to reach a settlement for the time being. Paderewski was given the posts of prime minister and minister of foreign affairs, while Pilsudski continued as chief of state, with special responsibility for the Army. As an American diplomat observed, "To Paderewski the words 'Chief of State' meant the equivalent of a constitutional monarch who reigned but did not govern and who was bound by the advice of his ministers. To Pilsudski the words 'Prime Minister' meant the Western equivalent of a Grand Vizier who took orders from the Chief of State and, by assuming nominal responsibilities, protected him from the consequences of his mistakes."[5]

Pilsudski was furiously expanding the Polish Army. By mid-January he had one hundred infantry battalions, seventy cavalry squadrons and eighty batteries of artillery. By March his infantry alone was 170,000 men, of whom eighty thousand were actually on the fighting fronts.

For by now Poland was fighting a whole series of small wars. To the southeast a Polish force was forcing its way into the old Austrian province of Eastern Galicia, driving back a Ukrainian army. Polish troops, pushing east, had made contact with the Red Army, and a general conflict had begun. To the west they were moving in Posen against a German *Freikorps* offensive. To the south the Poles were

fighting the Czechs for the valuable province of Teschen, while to
the north Pilsudski was invading Lithuania.

The Polish delegates to the Paris Peace Conference were blessed
with three distinct advantages. One was the trust and the support of
Woodrow Wilson—a confidence which the Poles were shortly to
forfeit. Another was the aggressive expansionism which, by February of 1919, had gained them most of Galicia and important sections of Lithuania, Posen and Upper Silesia. The last, and most
important, was the support of the French government for the establishment of a Poland which was to be, as Pinchon put it, "big and
strong—very, very strong."[6]

This attitude was not based on sentiment. For years the keystone
of France's foreign policy had been her alliance with imperial
Russia. Now this alliance was gone, and Russia was Bolshevik. For
France the next move was obvious. A bristling hedge of Succession
States must be created to act both as a barrier against Bolshevism
and to take Russia's place as a threat against Germany. The principal Succession States would certainly be Poland and Czechoslovakia.
By herself, France, with a population of forty million, would always
be militarily inferior to Germany with her sixty-five millions. But if
twelve million Czechoslovaks and possibly thirty million Poles were
added to the forty million French, the scales would be more than
tipped back. Thus France was prepared to devote almost any effort
to the support of these new nations. She would give them alliances,
money, weapons and instructors for their armies. A Frenchman,
General Paul Henrys, was already in Poland serving as Pilsudski's
chief of staff. More to the point, France would not hesitate to support Polish claims to territory which was predominantly inhabited
by Germans. A certain amount of Polish greed would be of double
benefit to France. It would cut into Germany's population, while
simultaneously creating a permanent and dependable source of tension between Germany and Poland.

Toward this end French policy had been nothing if not consistent.
As early as October 31, 1918, when the Allied Supreme War Council
first discussed the terms of armistice, the French proposed that the
Poles be assured of all those lands which had formed the kingdom of
Poland in 1772, before the First Partition. This was too much for the
Americans and the British. Those frontiers would be grossly exces-
sive. The French proposal was voted down. In the following weeks,
the Poles learned who their friends were. The Americans would

soon be gone from Europe, and no one knew if they would ever return. The same was true of the British. But with the French they found a community of interest that transcended all other considerations.

The first appearance of the Polish delegates before the Paris Peace Conference took place on January 29, 1919, when Roman Dmowski came forward to plead the case of the Polish boundaries. His hearers were the members, attendants and advisers of the Council of Ten, a group of thirty-five persons in all, seated in the large hall at the Quai d'Orsay. The Polish delegate's address was a tour de force. Dmowski first spoke in perfect and idiomatic French and then immediately made his own translation in perfect English. His audience broke into spontaneous applause at this performance.

The gist of his discourse was that the boundaries of Poland should be approximately those of 1772. But even these frontiers might well be enlarged. Upper Silesia was a good example: while it was true that this province had not belonged to Poland for nearly seven hundred years, the conference should remember that Upper Silesia was now inhabited by a population ninety per cent Polish. Blandly Dmowski went on to caution his listeners against relying upon German population statistics, which, he assured the Council of Ten, were notoriously misleading. Very large areas of what might be thought of by some as eastern Germany (and by this Dmowski implied West Prussia, Posen and very substantial sections of East Prussia) were not really German at all. They had been unlawfully seized from Poland many years ago, and if it seemed that the inhabitants of these areas were largely German, it was only because the statistics had been falsified or because the area had been artificially colonized. Dmowski put forward Danzig as an example. Obviously this city was an integral part of "historic Poland" as well as its essential port on the Baltic. The Germans claimed that only three per cent of the population of Danzig was Polish. Dmowski was delighted to reveal that his estimate of the Polish population was forty per cent.

As Dmowski's argument unfolded it became disturbingly apparent to his listeners that he was talking about a Poland which would contain more than thirty million people, less than two thirds of whom could possibly be Poles. Urbane and superbly confident, Dmowski continued in this vein for five hours. He sketched out the Polish position regarding the province of Teschen. In most of this territory, Dmowski said, Poles comprised the great majority, yet

Czech soldiers had recently entered the Polish areas and fighting had begun. It was all the Czechs' fault, and Dmowski was confident that the conference would order them to withdraw.

Indeed, Dmowski saw only one real problem in drawing the Polish borders, and that was the very center of East Prussia. He generously conceded that here Germans *were* perhaps in the majority, but he had a suggestion: since Poland would surely surround East Prussia on three sides (the other side being the Baltic), the conference might find it easier to detach East Prussia from Germany and make it into a separate republic under Polish supervision. Here was a concept well calculated to appeal to the French. Clemenceau was frank in admitting that "the more separate and independent republics were established in Germany, the better he would like it."[7]

At length Dmowski concluded his oration. The French Foreign Minister instantly pronounced himself to be in perfect accord with Dmowski's views. Clemenceau, from his seat behind the Louis XV desk, rose to congratulate Dmowski on a "masterful statement."[8] The Italians and the Japanese were obviously indifferent and prepared to vote as expediency might dictate. But the Polish case left several of the Allied figures, notably Lloyd George and Woodrow Wilson, in a state of acute apprehension. Neither the United States nor Great Britain had anticipated the creation of a Poland remotely resembling the one that Dmowski was talking about. This new Poland would incorporate nearly three million Germans, a predictable source of trouble. The frontiers which Poland claimed did conflict with Wilson's thirteenth point, under which, according to the Cobb-Lippmann interpretation of October 30, Poland was to receive "no territory in which Lithuanians or Ukrainians predominate."

In the face of this deadlock, the Council of Ten referred the matter of Poland's western frontiers to a subcommittee, the Commission on Polish Affairs. It is possible that neither Lloyd George nor Wilson noted that the chairman of this commission was a Frenchman, Jules Cambon. The military adviser was also a Frenchman, General Le Rond, and the senior American member was Professor Robert Lord, a violent Polonophile.*

The first report of the Commission on Polish Affairs was delivered

---

* When the commission was first constituted, the U. S. member was Isaiah Bowman, but on April 9 he was replaced by Lord.

on March 19, when M. Cambon appeared before the Council of Four. He began by explaining that a Polish-German frontier on a strictly ethnological basis had proven to be not only impossible but undesirable. After this preface, a map was unveiled and the commission's proposed boundaries for western Poland were displayed to the Allied leaders.

The Poles were still left with little cause for dissatisfaction. Practically the entire province of Posen was given to Poland, as was all of Upper Silesia and many sections of East Prussia, where Poland's claims were tenuous at best. But the major award was reserved for the last part of the commission's report. It was proposed that a "Polish Corridor" be driven through West Prussia, thus dismembering East Prussia from Germany proper. Within this corridor lay the Vistula River and the two main railway lines from the Baltic to the Polish interior. East Prussia was to be demilitarized. Finally, the port of Danzig, despite its indisputably German population, was to be awarded to Poland. When the boundary had been drawn General Le Rond had, with practiced eye, paid great care to its strategic implications; wherever possible it followed a chain of lakes or some other natural barrier. All told, slightly more than two million Germans would be brought into the Polish state.

The British Prime Minister listened to this report with profound distaste, for the alliance which Great Britain would sign with France (and the alliance which France would surely sign with Poland) would mean that Great Britain might find herself the unwilling warden of the Polish border. If this was to be so, Lloyd George determined to intervene forcefully in the matter of this border. There would be no eastern Alsace-Lorraines if Lloyd George could help it.

Lloyd George was prejudiced against Poles, whom he thought a shabby and greedy lot, and against Poland, the British view of whom was that she "was an historic failure and always would be a failure."[9] But, prejudices apart, the Prime Minister was beginning to wonder if the terms of the treaty might not be so severe that no responsible German government would agree to sign it. The Polish-German border would be a crucial point. He dare not let the Poles and the French go too far. Even before the conference had begun the British Foreign Office had warned that the award to Poland of Danzig and a corridor to it "would create an unstable position which would probably render the Polish position untenable if, and

when, Germany recovers. . . . For the sake of Poland's own interests, we must firmly oppose exaggerated claims."[10]

Lloyd George turned to the commission members assembled before the Council of Four and began to make a series of pointed
observations. Why could they not find some alternative answer to
the Danzig question than to hand the port, with its 400,000 Germans, to Poland? Why must sections of East Prussia be cut off from
Germany just because a railroad happened to run through them?
Why not simply move the railroad? The British attitude was contagious, and Woodrow Wilson moved that the commission withdraw to redraft its report in the light of the discussion. The French
protested, but the motion carried.

During the weeks that followed, the Polish question was a constant source of anxiety to the Allies. It intruded into everything; it
worried everyone. The Poles, their armed strength growing daily,
began what amounted to an invasion of the old Austrian provinces
of Eastern Galicia, where the population was predominantly Ruthe-
nian, and which wanted to join a separate Ukrainian republic.
Serious fighting broke out between Ukrainian forces and the Poles.
The Allies managed to put a halt to it, but after only three days of
truce fighting began again. At Teschen the Poles and the Czechs
were exchanging fire. To the north, Polish forces were moving into
Lithuania, which had recently declared its independence.

By the beginning of February a general conflict between German
and Polish forces had begun in the province of Posen. Since November, following the collapse of the German Imperial Army, much of
Posen had been under the control of Polish irregular troops. The
German Supreme Command now determined to restore its authority
with *Freikorps* forces. The Supreme Command moved to Kolberg,
on the Baltic coast, where it could direct the operation at close
hand. Hindenburg issued a personal appeal to the forces, and the
Supreme Command busied itself with raising additional troops.

The German strategic plan consisted of a two-pronged offensive
into Posen. One force, under General Otto von Below, struck down
from West Prussia. The other army, commanded by General von
dem Borne, moved north from Upper Silesia. They were to advance
slowly, clearing the province of armed Polish forces as they went
and finally effecting a junction in the principal city of Poznań.

No sooner had the operation started than the Poles succeeded in
persuading the Allies to stop it. The armistice was due for its
periodic renewal. Marshal Foch summoned the German Armistice

Commission before him and traced a line corresponding roughly to the frontiers of Posen, over which German troops were forbidden to cross. Unless the Germans agreed to this, Foch warned, the Allies would consider the armistice at an end and advance into Germany from the west. Sullenly the Germans complied and signed the agreement.

The Poles were overjoyed. Even though Posen was technically German territory, they now had a free hand within it. They resolved to carry this victory a step further. There were still nearly 100,000 men of Haller's Army in France. Pilsudski demanded that they be returned to Poland to defend Posen. The French pressed the point, and the British reluctantly agreed after extracting from Paderewski a promise that this force was to be used only for the maintenance of internal security.

President Wilson himself now had serious misgivings about the Poles. The new nation no longer seemed a land of sturdy democrats demanding nothing more than the right to dwell peacefully within their own borders, wherever those might be. They seemed to lack any conception of democracy, and they refused every political compromise. In order to produce a delegation to represent Poland at the peace conference, it had been necessary for Colonel House to lock thirty of their leaders in an office; only after they had been warned that if they could not agree upon two names Poland would not be represented—and after they had screamed at one another for three hours—had they elected Dmowski and Paderewski. Disturbing news was reaching Paris from within Poland. The landed Polish aristocracy, intensely conservative and accustomed to holding their peasantry in virtual serfdom, had seen no reason to dispense with their usual practices, nor did the peasantry seem to want them to. There were rumors, in many cases substantiated, of pogroms against the Polish Jews, and when Roman Dmowski was questioned about this he cheerfully asserted that Jews were "grasping storekeepers and avaricious moneylenders," adding, "They form ten per cent of our population and this is at least eight per cent too much."[11] Apparently an agreement to protect their minorities must be extracted from the Poles.

The greatest disappointment was the evidence of Polish expansionism (although the Czechs seemed equally greedy). Granted, the territories into which Polish forces were moving or which were claimed by the Polish delegates had once been taken away from

Poland, but it generally transpired that the Poles had earlier taken them away from somebody else.

Even Paderewski was proving to be difficult. He no longer cut the same delightful, deferential and distinguished figure that he had in the United States. His communications to the American delegation all bore a suspicious and vaguely irritating sameness. In them Poland's enemies were invariably described as treacherously attacking peaceful crowds of Polish women and children, at whom they fired explosive or dum-dum bullets.[12] Polish attacks were always defensive measures, in which the youth of Poland, hardly more than children, came to the rescue of their countrymen. It was generally mentioned for good measure that the American flag had been insulted by Poland's enemies.

It became apparent even to the friends of Poland among the United States delegation that the Poles had no sense of proportion. They tried to make every world issue revolve around Poland. General Tasker Bliss was frankly disgusted with them. He told an apocryphal story in which an Englishman, a German and a Pole were all required to prepare a monograph on the subject of the elephant. The Englishman told how to hunt an elephant. The German described the elephant's biological details. The Pole began his monograph with the words *"L'éléphant, c'est une question polonaise!"*[13]

To Wilson the final discouragement was the transparent French determination to support Polish claims, however unreasonable. When the peace conference reached a deadlock in early April, the President ruminated bitterly, "The only real interest of France in Poland is in weakening Germany by giving Poland territory to which she has no right."[14]

The British, at least, were not disappointed in Poland. They had never expected much. They had deliberately delayed the dispatch of Haller's Army to Poland, and on various Allied missions to Poland it was invariably the British delegates who fought with the French. Thus it was no surprise to Lloyd George when he found that Haller's Army was being used for a full-scale invasion of Eastern Galicia in early May. The Czechs cried out in alarm that Polish troops were crossing the eastern borders of Czechoslovakia. The Poles replied that this was only an attempt to join with Rumania to present a continuous front against Communist Russia—and, anyhow, the Ruthenians and the Ukrainians were backward peoples and incapable of self-government. As always, the French supported the Poles. Paderewski appeared before the Council of Four to explain that the Polish incursion was "not an offensive but a defensive advance," which was being conducted by a group of Polish boys whom "we could not keep back."[15] Lloyd George would have none of this. Haller's Army must be withdrawn from offensive operations, he said. At the insistence of the British and the Americans, a peremptory telegram was dispatched to Pilsudski and to Haller directly, ordering him to withdraw. No reply was received, and Lloyd George was told that the Allies' order had evidently gone astray. The disgusted British Prime Minister made no secret of his suspicion that the French had seen to it that the telegram was mislaid in Warsaw.

At meetings of the Council of Four Lloyd George contrasted the territorial claims of the Czechs with those of the Poles. The Czechs had, during the war, created their own Czech Legion, which had fought on the Allied side without (as the Czechs pointed out) "asking for guarantees or weighing the possibilities of success."[16] It was a telling argument. Compared to the real sacrifices of the Czechs, the Poles appeared merely to have taken a last-minute dive into the Allied camp. The fact that the Czechs asked for the incorporation of somewhat more than a million German Austrians into their nation in order to establish a good defensive frontier seemed, when backed by the valid claims of the Czechs to Allied loyalties, to be thoroughly reasonable.

Finally the Committee on Polish Affairs reappeared before the Council of Four, bearing its new recommendations on the Polish-German border. With minor exceptions, the commission had made no changes in its original recommendations. Lloyd George was enraged. He considered that the Poles' demands, supported by their partisans on the commission, were wholly irrational. He asked whether the Poles understood that they were going to have to live as Germany's neighbors. And it would be a far stronger Germany in times to come, when there were no Allies in Paris to protect Poland. The demands of Poland were clearly excessive and must be moderated. Lloyd George refused to meet again with this commission whose partisanship for Poland had, the British Prime Minister believed, rendered it worthless.

Woodrow Wilson had been reluctantly won over to Lloyd George's views on Poland. Torn between the violent Polonophilia of several of his experts and the logic of Lloyd George, Wilson retreated into an equivocating posture which was generally interpreted as discreet support for the British Prime Minister. Since the Italians took no position on Polish matters, the French thus found themselves in a minority. The consequence was that the peace treaty which was submitted to the Germans on May 7 called for Danzig to be a "free city" under the administration of the League of Nations. The Polish Corridor remained, but its borders were redrawn to exclude many of the predominantly German areas which the commission had promised Poland. Most of the province of Posen was given to Poland, as was most of Upper Silesia.* A series of plebiscites was called for in other border areas to determine whether the population chose to belong to Poland or to Germany.

Both the Poles and the French took this settlement as a severe defeat. Clemenceau, protesting the denial of Danzig to Poland outright, threatened that this might cost him his office. "If you don't give me what I want," he cried, "I can't meet my people. I shall have to resign."[17] Raymond Poincaré told the French Parliament that it should have thrown out the Tiger over this issue. In the Chamber of Deputies it was charged, "The affair of Danzig is a scandal which covers us with ridicule."[18]

In the final scene with the Poles an exasperated Lloyd George showed himself at his most ruthless. Paderewski, appearing before the Council of Four, complained bitterly of the treatment which his nation was receiving from the Allies. He made the threat (by now a ritual for small nations appearing before the Allies) that if the Polish people did not get what they wanted they would succumb in despair to Bolshevism. "My people," Paderewski declared, "have belief in no one now, because they were told by me, and most emphatically, that these things promised to them would be given to them. Well, now if something is taken away from them they will lose all faith in my leadership. They will lose faith in your leadership of humanity and there will be revolution."[19]

To this reproach Lloyd George instantly responded in kind. It was time for plain speaking. Who were the Poles to castigate the Allies? During the war, the Poles were fighting ("insofar as they were fighting at all") mostly on the German side. In any case, the British Prime Minister pointed out, no wartime promises of specific frontiers had ever been made to Poland by the Allies. Nor was there

* The Allies later agreed to a plebiscite in Upper Silesia.

any reason why there should have been. Only five years earlier the Poles had been a subject nation

> with no human prospect of recovering its liberty: certainly without the slightest chance of recovering it by its own exertions. . . . [They] have only got their freedom because there are a million and a half dead Frenchmen, very nearly a million British, half a million Italians, and I forget how many Americans. . . . Poland has won her freedom, not by her own exertions, but by the blood of others; and not only has she no gratitude, but she says she loses faith in the people who have won her freedom!

Lloyd George then alluded to the matter of Polish greed. This nation which had always claimed to want only independence was now "claiming three millions and a half of Galicians," and this led him to the acid complaint that Poland, like the other new Central Europe states, was treating the Allies to the sorry spectacle of "annexing the territory of other nations and imposing on them the very tyranny which they have themselves endured for years. . . . It fills me with despair," he cried.[20]

There was nothing left for the flustered Paderewski to do but accept the Allies' decision and withdraw "with profound respect but with deep sorrow."[21]

Unfortunately for the Allies, they had not heard the last of problems on Germany's eastern borders.

The lands bordering the eastern edges of the Baltic Sea—the area which was to become Latvia, Lithuania and Estonia—are low and flat. Somber marshes and morains alternate with thick forests. Along the coastline, where high sand dunes meet the sea, there is an almost constant fog. Except for a brief period around the time of the birth of Christ, when the region was an important source of amber, the Baltic lands never produced much except timber.

In the early Middle Ages this wild and unappealing land was populated by a conglomeration of pagan tribes and races which subdivided themselves into incoherent rustic kingdoms. These tribes —Kurs, Livs, Esths, Letts and Prussians—fought constantly against seaborne invaders from Denmark and Sweden. Then, beginning in the tenth century, they were threatened from the interior by the rising power of Poland. But, despite their backwardness, they were

almost unassailable in their dense forests. (The word *Latvian,*
which comes from the old Livic tongue, means "man who clears
forests.") The result of these invasions by sea and land was an inconclusive series of struggles in which no single power was strong
enough to conquer and rule.

In the midst of this primitive turmoil, the more sophisticated
forces of the Hanse, the German North Sea trading league, now
introduced themselves. From time to time they landed on the Baltic
coast to barter. In their wake followed German bishops and missionaries who, seeking to convert the native tribes, constructed churches
and fortified places as bases from which to spread the faith. They
were not successful. The local tribes rose in arms, leveled the
churches and slew the missionaries. Nor could the Germans do
much about it, for at this time the energies of Christendom were
devoted to the Crusades, to which the Hanse had contributed a
floating hospital off Acre. It was this hospital, or, more exactly, the
hospitalers who served aboard it, which evolved into the Teutonic
Order, a knightly group recruited only in Germany and dedicated to
the spreading of Christianity and Germanic civilization.

In the early thirteenth century the Teutonic Order, now grown
into a rich and illustrious military congregation which had close
connections with Rome, transferred the bulk of its operations to
Europe. At the same time, another, smaller Germanic military-reli-
gious order, known as the Knights of the Sword, was established in
Livonia (Estonia and Latvia) and began the conquest of the pagan
tribes in that region. It soon became apparent, however, that a
much larger effort would have to be mounted if all the Baltic tribes
were to be Christianized. A call went out to the Teutonic Order,
which was awarded what amounted to a franchise for the conversion and colonization of the eastern Baltic. The Teutonic Knights—
who later absorbed the Knights of the Sword—soon flung their considerable forces and talents onto the Baltic Coast.

In this period the knights of the Teutonic Order were an austere
and ascetic group. Each of the order's recruits was required to take
the triple vow of poverty, chastity and obedience. In return, the
knight received a symbolic crust of bread, a threadbare garment
and, of course, a sword. He was forbidden to wear his family's coat
of arms and could not travel alone. He was not permitted to frequent cities, with their manifold occasions for sin. The Teutonic
Knights always slept clad for combat, with their swords beside
them. They were subject to a discipline the smallest infraction of

which drew a terrible punishment. Their military abilities, tested and refined in the Crusades, were of the very highest caliber.

From Acre, where the Grand Master of the Teutonic Order made his headquarters, instructions were sent out to establish two "chapters" on the Baltic—one for the conquest of the heathen Prussians and the other, the Livonian chapter, for the subjugation of the lands to the northeast. Both drives were quickly successful. After the style of the times, the knights regarded it as their mission to kill whomever they could not convert, and they did not waste much time in proselytizing. The Prussian tribes were swiftly massacred or driven from their lands, which the knights repopulated with German peasants brought by sea from the Hanse ports. This German Baltic enclave was to become known as East Prussia. To the northeast, the Livonian chapter speedily conquered the Kurs and established a Baltic base which the knights called Kurland. From this they spread farther out. Most of the native kings were unable to withstand them. Some, like the King of the Esths—who sold his land and all its people to the order—did not even try. In what was to become Latvia, the knights seized the holdings of the Livs and slaughtered the Letts in a series of battles.

In the fourteenth century the fortunes of the Teutonic Order began to wane. East Prussia was securely German, but to the east the Liths had formed a strong united state, the grand duchy of Lithuania, which resisted the knights' incursions; and in the conquered lands there were constant revolts by unruly and intractable native tribes who, although they could not storm the fortified castles of the order, could and did hold out in the vast forests. Then, in 1386, Lithuania and Poland combined in a dynastic union, and together they put into the field a force capable of fighting the knights.

This accretion of native power coincided with a gradual ebbing of the forces of the order. The Teutonic Knights had, in their conversions and conquests, always followed a policy of rigid exclusivity. They had made it a point never to admit the conquered nobility into their order; nor did they really acknowledge the native nobles to be of noble birth. When the order required knights or armed retainers, it always obtained them from the German homeland. This resulted in its being constantly regarded as a "foreign" body by the natives, peasantry and gentry alike, with all the hatreds which this was bound to engender. At the same time, the character of the Teutonic Order was itself changing. After they invaded these Baltic lands, the knights settled them in the only way they knew—by parceling out

fiefs to members of the order, who, after building a castle, proceeded to capture as many native peasants as possible and to treat
them as slaves. Many of these holdings were vast, and they were
easier to come by than an equivalent piece of property in Germany
itself. The result was that the order attracted a large group of
knights who were prone to disregard the triple vows in favor of
creating estates for themselves in these virgin lands. The battles
against the Polish-Lithuanian coalition, as well as those against the
more warlike of the local tribes, began to become a defense of individual baronies rather than the conversion of pagans. Indeed, most
of the knights' enemies were now Christians themselves. The climax
came in 1410 on the battlefield of Tannenberg, where a combined
Polish-Lithuanian army practically wiped out the 83,000-man army
of the Teutonic Order.

From the fifteenth century on, the German hold on the eastern
Baltic lands waned rapidly. In the following century the Teutonic
Order was secularized and its members, now Lutherans, divided the
properties of the order among them and became vassals of the
Polish kings. With this the power of the Teutonic Order came to an
end. Its former members devoted themselves to the operation of
their individual estates and took no real part in the subsequent
northern wars, in the course of which the Baltic states were conquered first by Sweden and then, in the time of Catherine the Great,
by Russia.

But the Teutonic Order had left its legacy. The descendants of
the knights were now well established in these Baltic lands. They
were the owners of huge estates. In the port cities such as Riga and
Tallinn, the mercantile class was overwhelmingly German and the
architecture was indistinguishable from that of any city in Germany. In these impoverished lands the Germans controlled the bulk
of all wealth and constituted the majority of the educated population. Like the old Teutonic Knights, the Baltic Germans jealously
preserved their racial strain. They would enter the service of the
Russian czars, and they eagerly accepted Russian titles of nobility,
but they regarded the native Baltic peoples with disdain. The Germans married among themselves, spoke their own language and
created what amounted to their own university at Tartu in Estonia.
In every way they rejected assimilation into the native population.
They regarded various attempts at Russification as efforts "to replace our clean, well-fitting coat with their shabby and lice-infested

sheepskin,"[22] and they treated the native Balts with such haughty disdain that the Estonian word meaning a German, *Sakslane,* came to mean a snob as well. The German landowners, known as the "Baltic barons," viewed their peasants as nothing more than a race of stupid and fundamentally lazy beasts from whom only the landlord's knout could extract work. The barons held their peasantry in ravenous bondage, extracting whatever they wished of their crops or labor; peasants were even rented out to work off their landlords' debts. Nowhere else in all of Europe were peasants so oppressed as on the Baltic. It was only after several peasant rebellions that some restrictions were imposed by the Russian government on the ruthless greed of the barons.

The turn of the twentieth century brought fresh unrest to the Baltic lands. Like the Poles, the native populations of this area had traditionally resisted Russification. Finding themselves caught between the Germanic barons and Russian repression, they realized that the only solution was national independence. In Lithuania a small native middle class spread the yearning for independence to the common people. The Russians found that they could do little to halt this. Even the most rigorous military suppression, which made it a crime for anyone to own a book published in the Lithuanian alphabet, failed to halt the agitation for independence. Simultaneously, the Lettish people began a program of "national self-study," led by a clandestine press which agitated for the creation of a free Latvia. In an effort to free themselves from the economic domination of both the Baltic Germans and the Russians, the people established farm cooperatives and native Latvian banks. In Estonia too the native population began to stir. By 1900 the mercantile population of Riga was as much Estonian as German.

In 1905, following the Russian defeat in the war with Japan, the movements for Baltic independence came to a climax. Vast strikes brought the port cities to a standstill. In the agricultural areas the peasantry began to burn the manor houses of the landlords, paying special attention to those of the German barons. Marxist political parties sprang up in each of the Baltic Provinces and soon achieved a respectable following.

All this enraged and frightened the propertied classes, especially the Germans, who decided that their best interests lay in helping the Russians restore order and authority. With Russian blessing, the Germans formed little "self-defense" forces of their own and joined in the tracking down and arrest of native revolutionaries. They wrung payment from the peasants for German property which had been damaged, and they saw to it that the voting franchise was restricted to persons who held substantial amounts of property. Fearing the native populations, these Baltic Germans now wrapped themselves tightly in their national cloak and became, if possible, more German than before. It is hard to see how they could have done more to arouse the hatred of the masses in the Baltic Provinces.

The war was a disaster for the Baltic Provinces. The Russian mobilization plan called for a two-pronged attack against East Prussia, with the northern advance starting from the Baltic region. Because the Baltic Provinces bordered on East Prussia, it was convenient to use the divisions mobilized in these provinces as part of the spearhead of the Russian invading force. The Latvian, Lithuanian and Estonian divisions comprising the Russian Twentieth Corps marched into East Prussia and were crushed in the Battle of the Masurian Lakes, with a terrible loss of life. Simultaneously, the provinces themselves suffered badly when Russian Siberian troops arrived as reinforcements and, deceived by the German architecture of the Baltic cities, began to loot as if they were in enemy territory. This, at least, did not last for long. In 1915 the German Eighth Army invaded and captured all of Lithuania and most of Latvia. By 1917 a succession of additional offensives had resulted in the extension of the German Baltic conquests to include Estonia.

The attitude of the German government toward the Baltic Provinces was curiously indecisive at first. The region was devastated. The Germans entered a fog-shrouded and demolished land. Such industry as had existed had been either destroyed or evacuated to the Russian interior. In Latvia, for example, over half the farms and estates were destroyed or abandoned. Forty per cent of the population had been killed or had fled. There must surely have been some doubts in the Germans' minds as to the value of these impoverished provinces. Nonetheless, the age-old Baltic attraction was still potent. The German government decided that these incipient nations would be of value as grand duchies ruled by German nobles. Thus the Treaty of Brest-Litovsk provided that Russia give up Latvia, Lithuania and Estonia, reflecting the Germans' confident assumption that these "freed" nations would shortly establish thrones to which German princes would be called.

Events did not, of course, work out that way.

* * *

The armistice finally brought political independence to the new Baltic States of Latvia, Lithuania and Estonia. Native governments declared themselves and were quickly recognized by the Allies. Delegations were dispatched to the Paris Peace Conference, and plans were made for the calling of national elections. Each nation began to raise its own national army, generally using as a base the old regiments of the Imperial Russian Army which had been recruited within its borders.

But in fact the new nations had not ceased to be a battleground for foreign powers. The Red Army, striking southwest from Petrograd, had started to invade these former Russian provinces. The only force immediately available to stem the Bolshevik attack was the German Eighth Army, which, under the provisions of the armistice, was required to remain in position on the Baltic and defend the new nations. But, like the German Imperial Army in every other place, the Eighth Army disintegrated rapidly. Soldiers' councils were created and refused to obey the orders of the officers. Whole regiments demobilized themselves and departed for Germany. The German forces did not make even a pretense of defense against the invading Red Army. In November the German Army vanished from Estonia. By December most of Latvia had been abandoned to the Bolsheviks, and the port of Riga had fallen. On January 8 the Germans blew up the arsenal in the principal Latvian city of Mitau and withdrew farther southwest into Lithuania.

Retreating with the Eighth Army were many of the Baltic Germans—especially the wealthier landowners and the conservative students, who suspected that the Red Army would show them little mercy and knew all too well that they could not rely on the native populations to protect them. In the major cities of Germany, particularly in Munich, organizations were established to receive and assist the refugees. Many young Baltic-German students, such as Alfred Rosenberg and Max von Scheubner-Richter, fled there and were sheltered by sympathetic conservatives. These embittered refugees swiftly set themselves up as experts on the "Judaeo-Bolshevik menace" from the east.[*]

---

[*] Scheubner-Richter, like Rosenberg, was an early and prominent member of the Nazi Party. The legitimacy of his "von" was highly suspect and his background rather mysterious, but he was a man of undoubted ability and great personal charm. Scheubner-Richter was the principal organizer of the Munich "Beerhall Putsch" of

The time had come when the German Army could retreat no further. The Poles were refusing to allow the German forces in the Ukraine to pass through their nation, and consequently these troops were being shipped north to cut across Lithuania and the southwest tip of Latvia into East Prussia. If more of the Baltic territory was lost, the Germans in the Ukraine would be cut off. And if the German Army retreated any further it would be driven into East Prussia itself, with the Bolsheviks in hot pursuit.

This was a situation which concerned the Allies almost as much as it did the Germans, but they were powerless to do much about it. The only way to check the advance of the Red forces was to land an Allied army at one of the Baltic ports. This was plainly impossible, for public opinion would never tolerate the expenditure of Allied lives (or money) in an attempt to defend the borders of Germany. And where would such an expedition end? It would involve the debarkation of troops on Russia's doorstep, and no one could foretell how many Allied divisions would eventually be drawn into the fighting.

So the Allies sent to the Baltic only a group of military advisers, supported by a small British naval force known as the Baltic Squadron. This little fleet arrived on December 12, 1918, and could do little more than steam up and down the coastline offering encouragement to the native governments. In the case of Estonia, this proved sufficient. Estonia's eastern border was protected by a chain of lakes. The major weight of the Red Army attack was deflected by this natural obstacle, Estonia was bypassed to be dealt with later, and the Bolshevik forces continued south into Latvia.

The arrival of the British Baltic Squadron upset the Russian plans for Estonia. The Royal Navy landed supplies and a few thousand volunteers from Sweden and Denmark. Other ships from the Baltic Squadron swept up the coast and captured two Russian destroyers, which were immediately turned over to the Estonians. Nearly two thousand Latvians, a part of the embryonic Latvian Army, which

---

November, 1923. As the Nazi column tramped down the Residenzstrasse toward the cordon of "Green Police" blocking entry to the Odeonsplatz, the man marching on Scheubner-Richter's right linked arms with him. When the police fired, Scheubner-Richter was mortally wounded. As he fell to the pavement, he pulled his companion with him, dislocating his fellow marcher's arm and saving his life. The fellow marcher was Adolf Hitler. *Mein Kampf* is dedicated to Scheubner-Richter, among others. Hitler regarded him so highly that after Scheubner-Richter's death he mourned, "All are replaceable—all save he."

had been cut off in the Bolshevik advance and had retreated into Estonia, were armed and supplied by the British on condition that they assist in the fighting. The tiny Estonian Army now had supplies, reinforcements and command of the sea. It went over to the offensive and, within a few weeks, managed to drive the weak Bolshevik forces from Estonian territory.

But the task was not so easy in Latvia. There the native government was headed by Karlis Ulmanis, a forty-one-year-old former teacher of agronomy in the United States. He had come to America when he was ten years old to live with an uncle in Nebraska, had attended the University of Nebraska and had become a high-school teacher. Shortly before the war broke out he had returned to Latvia to visit his elderly mother. The war had caught him, and Ulmanis had been compelled to remain in his homeland. He had organized a Latvian National Committee which had named him the nation's Prime Minister. Before the Bolshevik invasion, and despite obstruction by the German landlords, Ulmanis attempted to form a Latvian Army with little success. A great many of the Latvians with military training had been part of the old Russian Imperial Army, where they had been formed into nine sharpshooter regiments known as the Lettish Rifles. After the Russian Revolution, the Bolsheviks noted that this force maintained its discipline and seemed remarkably free from embroilment with the contending Russian revolutionary camps. The Russian Communist leadership decided that these regiments could be used as a sort of praetorian guard, especially when it was found that they could be hired for duty. These mercenaries—for such they had become—were still in Moscow.

Both time and resources thus conspired against the formation of an authentically native Latvian Army. Before the German Eighth Army retreated out of Latvia, Ulmanis had managed to recruit only a single battalion of native Latvians, under the command of a Latvian officer, Colonel Francis Ballodis. To this was joined a company of White Russians under the command of a Russian, Prince Liéven. The German Baltic barons declined to serve under native command and created their own military force. They called it the "Baltic Landeswehr" and recruited troops from among the German Latvians and the peasantry on their holdings.

As the German Eighth Army retreated through Latvia, the Ulmanis government, its Army, the Baltic Landeswehr and the German Latvians all had no choice but to retreat with it. Ulmanis himself hoped that the Allies would defend Latvia, but, in a conference aboard the British flagship *Princess Margaret* at Riga in late December, it was made clear to him that this was wishful thinking. The British candidly confessed that they could do nothing to help Ulmanis. They suggested that he make whatever deal he could with the Germans for their assistance in repelling the Red Army's attack. With this, the Baltic Squadron raised steam and cleared Riga, which shortly afterward fell to the Reds.

The desperate Ulmanis then went to the Germans and, on December 29, signed a treaty. It was not a favorable agreement from the Latvian standpoint. Ulmanis had, in the words of the German plenipotentiary, arrived "with beads of perspiration on his forehead."[23] The Germans extracted from him exactly the sort of concessions which this anxiety invited. Under the terms of the treaty the Ulmanis government, in effect, let a contract with certain German elements for the recapture and subsequent defense of Latvia. German armed volunteers were invited into Latvia for the purpose of clearing out Bolshevism. These Germans were to serve under their own officers or, if they chose, might enlist in either the Baltic Landeswehr or the Latvian Army. Ulmanis agreed not to increase the number of native troops in the Latvian Army without first permitting a corresponding increase in the German forces, upon whose size no limit was set. A German soldier who served in Latvia for a period of four weeks was automatically entitled to Latvian citizenship. An attractive rumor 'as spread to the effect that this Latvian citizenship would also entitle the German soldier to an additional bounty, his own Baltic estate in the form of ninety acres of free land.[24]

The conclusion of the German-Latvian treaty had come at a particularly fortunate moment for the German Army, which had no intention whatever of leaving the Baltic. Its back was to East Prussia, and it had definite plans for the future of the Baltic States, which in a subsequent war would provide a convenient German sally port into either Russia or Poland.

It was also convenient that this Baltic adventure was proceeding without interference from the German government—indeed, almost without the government's knowledge. At the very beginning of 1919, the government was distracted by such internal affairs as the suppression of the January Spartacist uprising and Eisner's Bavarian separatism. Faced with domestic revolution, the Ebert government found no time to devote to military operations in the remote Baltic States. Noske himself complained:

> *Alas, the poor government was expected to have perfect control of everything in Germany, while large parts of the country were like a madhouse. How could we be expected to manage our business affairs in the Baltic properly when machine guns were being fired all around us? While I was absorbed with my work at Dahlem [organizing the recapture of Berlin from the Spartacists], I could not concern myself with all the little Wallensteins* who recruited men and led them to the east. So it went on for months.*[25]

As time went on, even the Supreme Command found its hold on these Baltic adventures to be shaky. The war in the Baltic was fought by more or less private armies, privately recruited, secretly financed, and commanded by a mixed bag of adventurers, mercenaries, regular-Army officers and fanatical anti-Bolsheviks.

To fill out what the Supreme Command designated as "Grenzschutz Ost," a vigorous German recruitment campaign was begun. In the competition for *Freikorps* volunteers, Grenzschutz Ost clearly had the lead. The age-old lure of the Baltic was reinforced by the tale of free "estates" to be had for the taking. And for those to whom this did not appeal there was the role of a modern-day Teutonic Knight forcing back the pagan forces of Slavic Bolshevism which menaced Germany's borders. Recruiting posters showed a pack of ravaging wolves, their jowls dripping blood, racing across a map of Germany's eastern frontiers. The message beneath read, "Germans, defend the Fatherland from Russian Bolshevism."

The recruits poured in—an uneven lot. There were the more conventional "early" *Freikorps,* mostly reenlisted units of the old Imperial Army; the First Regiment of Uhlans and another regiment created out of the Guards Reserve Division arrived at the Latvian port of Libau, having been transported by sea to free the single railway leading northeast from East Prussia. Some Baltic *Freikorps* were recruited and took the names of their commanders—the Freikorps Yorck, the Freikorps von Rieckhoff and the Freikorps Diebitsch. Others were less formal; for example, the Hamburg Freikorps had been self-recruited for Baltic service from among the most rowdy and predatory elements of its home city. This Hamburg contingent was utterly lawless and marched under the flag of the ancient Hanseatic League, upon which they superimposed pirate

---

* Wallenstein was an adventurer and commander in the Thirty Years' War.

insignia. "They had let their hair and beards grow long," wrote a fellow *Freikorpskämpfer*, "and saluted only the officers they knew and liked. And it was a great honor to be saluted by the men of Hamburg. For this crazy outfit recognized none of the usual military regulations. They had been formed by no particular authority and they recognized none save their own. The only thing that counted was the will of their own *Führer*."[26]

Probably the best-organized of this ill-assorted collection of units was that originally formed from the debris of the German Eighth Army. One of its officers, Major Joseph Bischoff, recruited six hundred disciplined troops and put them together into a formation which he named the "Brigade of Iron." This tiny group formed the rear guard covering the Eighth Army's retreat, and it was Bischoff who blew up the arsenal at Mitau. Though only a major, Bischoff was already a legendary figure. He did everything with superb style. When complimented on the ease with which he lit his cigarette in a strong wind, Bischoff shrugged and said, "Oh, you learn that . . . This is my twelfth year of warmaking—eight years in Africa, then the World War. I'm an old freebooter."[27] Impressed with Bischoff's experience and ability, the Supreme Command built up his Iron Brigade. Within a few weeks the brigade had received so many volunteers that it was renamed the "Iron Division." Unlike the smaller *Freikorps*, which were organized on a storm-troop basis, the Iron Division was set up along conventional military lines: it had three infantry regiments, a division staff, field artillery, and balloon and aircraft sections. By the early spring of 1919 Bischoff's Iron Division consisted of nearly fifteen thousand men.

The Baltic Landeswehr was similarly reconstituted. Representatives of the refugee Baltic barons visited Königsberg in East Prussia, where they persuaded a certain Major Fletscher, an experienced Baltic hand, to take command of their force. Fletscher accepted and brought with him, as his chief of staff, Captain Waldemar Pabst. The latter, an experienced *Freikorps* officer, had organized the forces at Potsdam which had taken a prominent part in the Christmas Eve fighting with the People's Naval Division before the Marstall. With the combined experience of these officers and the influence of the Baltic barons, the Baltic Landeswehr rapidly increased until it was second only to the Iron Division.

It was this assortment of forces, assembled with remarkable speed, which awaited Major General Count Rüdiger von der Goltz when, on February 1, 1919, he arrived in Mitau to assume general command of the forces in the Baltic. His instructions from the Supreme Command gave him wide latitude, but charged him specifically with "defending the frontiers of East Prussia against a Bolshevik invasion."[28]

Goltz was not the least of the flamboyant military personalities in the Baltic region. One of his most recent commands had been a special twelve-thousand-man German army which landed in Finland in the early spring of 1918. The German force had been sent in response to an appeal by the Finnish government to assist the newly independent nation against Russian Bolsheviks and domestic Red Guards. Goltz and his German troops had proved most effective. They had quickly recaptured Helsinki from the Communist militia which had seized the city, and then, operating in conjunction with the Finnish Commander in Chief, Baron Mannerheim, they had driven the Russians back over their own border. A quick but extensive program of White terror had followed and practically eliminated Communist influence from Finland. But the Finns had not been as grateful to Goltz as they might have. It was noted that the German troops tended to regard themselves as occupation troops rather than allies. They claimed sole credit for the suppression of Bolshevism in Finland and even suggested to the Finns that they create a kingdom and call to its throne a German, Prince Friedrich Karl of Hesse. The Finns evaded this on the grounds that the Allies would surely object, and it was with scarcely concealed relief that Mannerheim had finally seen Goltz's troops leave Finland.

With such experience as this, Rüdiger von der Goltz was the logical selection for command in the Baltic. Above him was an extensive staff created by the Supreme Command to exert a general supervision over operations. To this special command, known first as "Armee Oberkommando Nord" and later as "Gruppenkommando III," the Supreme Command sent some of its most talented officers. The chief of staff was General Hans von Seeckt, while the staff officer for operations (G.S.O. 1) was Major Werner von Fritsch.[*]

In February a strong defensive line was established, running roughly north and south from a strongpoint on the Latvian coast through Lithuania and resting on Kovno in the south. Access to the sea was secured by garrisoning the port of Libau with Bischoff's Iron Division. The Baltic Landeswehr and the various *Freikorps*

---

[*] Both of these officers were subsequently to hold the post of chief of the Army Command, or military commander of the German Army.

were spread out along the front. In the rear areas German officers were designated as area commanders to clean out any incipient Bolshevism and secure the lines of communication. A number of Baltic Germans, among them Max von Scheubner-Richter, were brought back from Munich to form a press and propaganda bureau.

Goltz had come to the Baltic prepared to do battle on a number of fronts. "I had four enemies," he wrote, "the Bolshevik Army, the soldiers' councils [of the old Eighth Army], the Germanophobe Latvian government, and the Allies. Following sound strategic principles, I determined not to fight them all at once, but instead to fight them one after the other, starting first with the Bolsheviks."[29] On March 3 his troops launched a drive east on a broad front and caught the Red Army off balance. The German buildup had been incredibly rapid, and the Red Army was a rather makeshift force which was badly overextended. Moreover, the German troops were an elite fighting force. They cut through the Red Army with speed and efficiency. It was quite like old times. In the face of the German onslaught the Bolsheviks quickly retired, shooting their hostages as they went. By March 13, pivoting on Kovno in the south, Goltz's troops had cleared most of Lithuania and, along the Baltic Coast, had taken the Latvian port of Windau.

As each of the Baltic cities was recaptured, the German area commanders took ruthless action to eliminate Communist elements. Proclamations were posted offering a cash reward to anyone turning in the name of a Bolshevik. Upon the capture of the city of Mitau, more than five hundred persons suspected of Red leanings were shot out of hand. Every day for two weeks an even dozen suspects were shot by firing squads on the public plaza at Tukkum. The German military commander at Windau published a proclamation requiring all persons to register with his police if they had "during the Bolshevist occupation been members of the government, members of committees, members of the Red Army, or had ever fought against the Landeswehr."[30] Failure to register was punishable by execution, and anyone who did register was usually shot, too. Each member of a family was required, upon penalty of death, to inform upon anyone in the family who had Bolshevist leanings. Within a few days after the capture of Windau, the jails were choked with prisoners and two hundred persons had been shot.

Little effort was made to ascertain whether the persons arrested and shot were in fact Bolsheviks. It was enough to be suspected of anti-Germanism. Unlike the *Freikorps* formations marching through

Germany, the Baltic German soldiers were unrestrained by a national tie with the populace. Goltz's troops cared less than nothing for the Slavic peoples of these wild lands. They viewed the Baltic natives with undisguised contempt or open hatred. They plundered, burned and shot at will. The *Freikorps* fighters gloried in their ruthlessness and brutality.

> *The land where we had stayed* [*a famous Baltic* Freikorps *fighter wrote later*] *groaned with destruction. Where once peaceful villages stood, was only soot, ashes and burning embers after we passed. We kindled a funeral pyre, and more than dead material burned there—there burned our hopes, our longings, there burned the* bürgerlich *tablets, the laws and values of the civilized world, there burned everything. . . . And so we came back swaggering, drunken, laden with plunder.*[31]

By April the German troops were deep into Latvia, had cleared all of Kurland and were advancing on Riga. At this point, to the dismay of Goltz and his officers, political considerations intruded.

The relationship between the German forces in the Baltic and the hapless Latvian government of Karlis Ulmanis had by this time completely degenerated. The Latvian Prime Minister now bitterly regretted the desperate haste with which he had signed the treaty that brought these savage swashbuckling *Freikorps* to his land. His complaints to Goltz were ignored by the German general, who found it convenient to regard Ulmanis as pro-Bolshevik. The frantic Latvian Prime Minister then turned to the Allies. He complained that the Germans were actually driving his people to Communism. "Comparing the terrorism of the Baltic Landeswehr and the German Army to those of the Bolsheviks," he wrote, "the Latvian people have found that the Bolsheviks are less cruel."[32] The Latvian government pleaded with the Allies not to permit Goltz to capture Riga, Latvia's largest city. Anyone could foresee the mass executions which would take place upon the city's fall, and, almost as frightening, it had begun to appear that the German forces had no intention of leaving any city which they once occupied.

The ultimate designs of the German Army in the Baltic were gradually becoming clear to Ulmanis. After driving out the Red Army, the Germans would settle Latvia and Estonia as Teutonic military colonies. With the assistance of the Baltic barons, the

German *Freikorps* soldiers would become small landowners, using the natives as peasant labor. When the hour was ripe, they would re-form their battalions and march on Russia—or, more likely, upon Berlin, where they would restore the Hohenzollern monarchy. In the meantime it was convenient for the Germans to have the native governments exist. They provided a screen behind which the German designs could mature.

The various Allied military missions at first regarded Ulmanis' explanation of German intentions as farfetched. Nevertheless, they could not deny the disturbing fact that all power in the Baltic had passed into German hands. The native Latvian Army was hopelessly inferior to the constantly increasing German forces. The orders of Latvian officials were ignored by the German area commanders, who set up their own police forces, established curfews, collected taxes and issued their own orders to the "liberated" populations. The Latvian press was effectively controlled and censored by the Baltic German refugees whom Goltz had brought back from Munich to form his Press and Propaganda Bureau. Goltz himself freely admitted that the native government was a thorn in his eye and declared that someday the Germans would "kick these rascals in the teeth."[33] In preparation for that day, the Baltic barons located a pliable pro-German Lutheran pastor named Andreas Needra and held him in readiness. He did not have long to wait.

On April 15 a new *Freikorps,* under the command of Captain Franz von Pfeffer,* arrived at Libau. The Latvian government, anxious to assert its authority somehow, arrested one of Pfeffer's officers, wereupon the entire force descended upon the prison and released him. In the course of this prison break, the German troops shot a number of Latvian soldiers and arrested the entire officer corps of the Latvian Army. The next day, when Ulmanis rushed to German headquarters to protest, Goltz took good care to be out of his office on a long walk. It was a prudent move. While Ulmanis was calling, the storm-troop battalion of the Baltic Landeswehr was busy rounding up and imprisoning members of the Latvian government. It was only by luck that Ulmanis himself was able to escape to the harbor and, with a few surviving members of his Cabinet, take refuge on a ship aboard which he was protected by the British Baltic Squadron. It was here that Ulmanis learned of the establish-

---

* Pfeffer had been born Franz von Salomon and was the brother of the author and *Freikorps* historian Ernst von Salomon. He changed his name because "Salomon" sounded Hebraic. The family was not in fact a Jewish one.

ment of a new Latvian government headed by Pastor Needra and including such obviously German names as Schwartz, Smits, Kuptsches and von Brummer. He further learned that German troops were extracting signatures for pro-Needra petitions from the terrified peasantry. In Libau a *Freikorps* detachment fired on demonstrators who carried a banner inscribed "Latvia for Latvians, Not for Germans."

Goltz was careful to deny all responsibility for the affair. The *Putsch* had been provoked by the obvious Bolshevism of the Ulmanis government, he said. Moreover, it was no use protesting to him; the arrests of Ulmanis' Cabinet had been made by the Baltic Landeswehr, which was, strictly speaking, a local force and not yet properly disciplined. As for himself, Goltz protested that he had been out for a long stroll when the coup took place. He had not learned about it till afterward, when he had returned to his headquarters. He adopted a general air of amusement about the whole affair. After all, he explained, one had to preserve one's sense of humor. The people involved were only Latvians. The Allies, however, found it hard to view the matter in this jocular light.

At the same time, Goltz refused to release the imprisoned Latvians or depose the Needra government. When the Allies insisted that Pfeffer's *Freikorps* be sent back to Germany, Goltz simply broke it up and distributed its men among other Baltic *Freikorps*. And with this he dismissed the matter from his mind, for, against the orders of the Allies and even of his own government, the Count was occupied with planning the capture of Riga, the largest city on the Baltic and once the capital of the German dukes of Kurland.

The situation in the Baltic was now completely out of the Allies' control. It did them no good that the harbor at Libau was filled wih British, American and French destroyers. This meant only that they could control the sea. Ashore the *Freikorps* were so numerous and so hostile that Allied officers could travel only in groups and heavily armed. Goltz ignored Allied instructions and had even taken to demanding that any Allied officer who wished to travel across country to a Baltic city must have a "visa" from the German area commander. Drunken gangs of *Freikorpskämpfer* threw rocks at the railway carriages of the French officer in command of his nation's mission. To those Allied officers on the scene, Ulmanis' allegations that Goltz intended to make the Baltic nations into a German military colony no longer seemed wild or improbable.

Numerous complaints were made by the Allied Armistice Commission at Spa, but the Germans had a quick and disarming reply. Did the Allies wish them to evacuate the Baltic? If so, were the Allies prepared to debark an army to fill the void and prevent the area from being reoccupied by a Red army? The Allies had no ready answer. They could not deny that the Germans were in the Baltic as the result of both an armistice provision and a treaty which Latvia had concluded upon the Allies' urging.

The pressing question in the spring of 1919 was the liberation of the port city of Riga. The Allies wished to deny to the Germans both the prestige of Riga's capture and the opportunity to engage in the executions which were now their trademark. The Red Army was abandoning the Baltic, and it was hoped that the Ulmanis government could be restored. Possibly the remnants of Ulmanis' Latvian Army, operating in conjunction with the Estonian-based "North Latvian Army," could liberate Riga. Flat orders were given to the German government that Goltz's forces must not attempt to capture Riga.

Obediently the Ebert government relayed these instructions to the Supreme Command and, through them, to Gruppenkommando III and Goltz. The General was, however, unwilling to accept such an order. The capture of Riga would be of overwhelming symbolic importance, he said; furthermore, it would put German forces within easy striking distance of Petrograd, the capture of which would surely place Germany at an advantage during the peace-treaty negotiations. The German government declined to accept his arguments. The Allied orders were so peremptory that to disobey them would surely bring instant reprisal. But Goltz went to Berlin to argue his case and was successful in finding a loophole: he ascertained that the government did not regard the Baltic Landeswehr as a German force. From Berlin Goltz dispatched an immediate message to his staff: "Tax on flour [the code name for the attack on Riga] not approved. But if the Landeswehr puts a tax on flour the Iron Division can join them."[34] The Baltic Landeswehr and the Iron Division promptly went over to the offensive, and on May 22 Riga fell. By the following day *Freikorps* cavalry was cantering deep into open and undefended country beyond Riga.

The consequences were all that the Allies and the Latvians had feared. No sooner had Fletscher's Baltic Landeswehr entered the city than martial law was declared. A curfew lasting from six o'clock in the evening to six in the morning was established. Strict censorship was announced. Heavily armed German patrols scoured the streets, and machine-gun emplacements controlled every major street crossing. All arms or ammunition in the hands of citizens of Riga were required to be surrendered. The penalty for any infraction whatever was death. It was further announced that a shot fired from any building would result in the immediate execution of every occupant of that building.

The Riga prisons were swiftly filled with prisoners accused of Bolshevist leanings. Tried by drumhead courts-martial, they were shot in daily batches of fifty or more—a modest supplement to the extensive street-corner executions conducted by individual members of the Landeswehr and the Iron Division. More than three thousand persons were shot within the space of a few weeks.

The German armies in the Baltic were delirious with joy over their capture of Riga. They felt that it mitigated the defeat of German armies in the World War. Their every hope would soon be realized. There remained only Estonia to conquer, and then the task would be done.

The capture of Riga was the high-water mark of German arms in the Baltic. The determination of the furious Allies had hardened.

In Paris, the attention of the Allied principals had been drawn to this absurd chaos. On May 9 the matter had been given over the Council of Five, which had, in turn, passed it to a special subcommittee. This subcommittee made its report on May 14 at the French Ministry of Commerce. The report began with the obvious statement, "The present situation in Lithuania and Lettland, which leaves the maintenance of order entirely in the hands of the Germany army, is most regrettable and should in no case long continue." The report went on to recommend that the Allies vote a credit of ten million pounds to the three Baltic States. This fund was to be used to recruit volunteers "in the Scandinavian States, including Finland," as well as to provide native forces with food, equipment, uniforms and arms. A special military mission under British command was to be organized "to advise the Governments of Estonia, Lettland and Lithuania on all questions . . . and on the best means of defending themselves against the Bolsheviks and of keeping the Germans out of their territory."[35] The subcommittee's report was immediately approved by the Council of Five.

An experienced senior British officer, General Sir Hubert Gough, was at once dispatched to coordinate the activities of all the Allied missions in the Baltic, and the Baltic Squadron, taking advantage of its command of the sea, established a blockade which prevented German supplies and reinforcements from entering Latvia by the convenient sea route. This was a blow to Goltz. His connection with the homeland was suddenly reduced to a single, poorly maintained railroad, which could not possibly handle all the traffic.

Under Gough's direction the Allied military missions embarked upon a careful campaign to establish a moral supremacy over the Germans. Allied officers refused to apply for German "visas" to enter Baltic cities. They made it a point to tour the streets of Riga after the curfew. They visited the jails and demanded the release of the starving prisoners. The American military mission summoned Major Fletscher before them and ordered all executions ended.

Simultaneously, the British engaged themselves in building up the Latvian Army. Ignoring the Needra government, they paid, provisioned and armed the Latvians directly. A happy consequence of the fall of Riga had been that it enabled the Latvian Army to link up with the "North Latvian" force, which had been brought down from Estonia. To replace their hodgepodge collection of weapons— principally old Russian and Japanese small arms—the British landed nearly 20,000 rifles, 650 machine guns, 25 million cartridges and enough artillery to equip two divisions. British political agents arrived to deal directly with Latvian officers, who were encouraged to recruit for a war of liberation against the Germans. In a remarkably short space of time, a native Latvian Army of nearly two divisions was put into the field.

The forces of General von der Goltz, on the other hand, were suffering a gradual diminution. In reluctant response to Allied demands, the Supreme Command had evacuated a number of the Baltic Freikorps. The Baltic Landeswehr, frightened at the Allied reaction, began to weaken. It occurred to the Baltic barons who controlled the Landeswehr that it might now be wise to seek some sort of accommodation with the Latvians among whom they would have to live in the future.

In early June the unrepentant Goltz ordered the Baltic Landeswehr to march out of Riga and clear the Estonian coast. The Landeswehr got only as far as Wenden, about fifty miles east of Riga. There, in late June, it was met and defeated by a combined Latvian and Estonian army. The Landeswehr, indecisively led, retreated in confusion. A similar fate met the Iron Division and a mixed force of Freikorps when, a few days later, they too gave battle. Goltz was forced to sign a treaty which required the evacuation of all German forces from the Baltic. Bitter, frustrated and furious at this turn of events, a sizable number of *Freikorps* soldiers returned to the homeland. Others, notably the Iron Division, remained in the Baltic and took service under a semilunatic Russian adventurer named Prince Awaloff-Bermondt, who formed what he called "the Russian Army of the West."

It was a venture doomed to quick failure. German dominance in the east was at an end. Henceforth Germany's eastern frontiers would meet an aggressive Poland to the east and the mutilated and hostile Baltic States to the north. Once again *Drang nach Osten* had failed.

PART 4

In the third century before the birth of Christ, the Samnites succeeded in trapping a large Roman army in the Claudine Forks. Possessed of a glut of prisoners, the Samnite ruler asked his father, Herennius, what he should do with them. "Let them all go," replied the father. The son said that this was impossible. "Then kill them all," countered the father. This was equally impossible, said his son, and he asked for some middle course. "There is none," said the wise father, "for a middle course would neither make the Romans your friends nor deprive you of your enemies."

—Erich Eyck

Chapter Thirteen

Preparation for Versailles

ONE of the most distressing problems of the German Majority Socialist government was its parochialism of experience. Because the Socialists had never seriously anticipated that they would take over the direction of the German government, they had not troubled to develop expertise in certain fields, most notably in the area of foreign affairs.

The Socialist leaders had grown up in an age when diplomacy was the exclusive province of the titled and the wealthy. The members of the German foreign service were no different from their counterparts in other European countries. They were members of the nobility or the upper bourgeoisie. Each diplomat spoke several languages flawlessly and was expected to possess a minimum private income of fifteen thousand marks. In the prewar years, diplomacy had taken place in a glittering world of state receptions, shooting parties and weekends at country estates. And if this served to exclude from the foreign service the overwhelming majority of the population of every European nation, it at least had the advantage of facilitating diplomatic exchange by placing it in the hands of an international class of similar social station, with a definite community of interest.

Reflecting upon this, the German Majority Socialists approached foreign affairs warily. They were told that a new era in diplomatic exchange had dawned, but they were not sure. There was nothing in their working-class background to prepare them for international diplomacy. The German Foreign Office was located next door (No. 75–76 Wilhelmstrasse) to the Reich Chancellery (No. 77 Wilhelmstrasse), but to the Socialists it might as well have been a hundred miles away. Few of them could speak foreign languages, and those who could spoke them badly. The only international conferences they had ever attended were conventions of workers. With a painful sense of inadequacy, they realized that they did not know how to draft a diplomatic note, did not know personally any other European foreign-office functionaries, and had only the most sketchy knowledge of diplomatic protocol. They felt themselves utterly unequal to taking part in peace negotiations with the Allies—negotiations which, they assumed, would take place in a glittering cosmopolitan atmosphere similar to that of the Congress of Vienna.

This explains why Fritz Ebert, as early as December, 1918, had selected as his Minister for Foreign Affairs a haughty, highly strung man who was an aristocrat by birth, a monarchist turned democrat, and, for all his diplomatic brilliance, a person whom Germany's conquerors could not fail to find objectionable.

Count Ulrich von Brockdorff-Rantzau was forty-nine years old at the time of his elevation to the direction of the German Foreign Office. For a number of years he had been one of Germany's most successful diplomats. During the war he had held the important "listening-post" appointment of ambassador to Denmark. Ebert and Scheidemann had visited Denmark on an official wartime mission to enlist the aid of Danish Socialists in increasing food shipments to Germany, and they had met Brockdorff-Rantzau there and been much impressed by him. They knew that he had been one of the few German diplomats who had fought against Ludendorff's domination of wartime diplomacy, that the Supreme Command still regarded him as a defeatist and an enemy, and that the Count cordially returned the generals' dislike.

In physical appearance Brockdorff-Rantzau was almost a caricature of the Prussian diplomat—a slender man of fashion, his cold and compressed face adorned with a monocle and a thin wisp of mustache. Born Ulrich von Rantzau, a member of one of Germany's most aristocratic families, he had grown up in the world of diplomacy. His father had died when Rantzau was a small child and he had been adopted by a Danish great-uncle, Baron Brockdorff, whom he accompanied while his adopted father was Danish ambassador in Vienna and Madrid. One of Rantzau's ancestors had served two

French Bourbon kings as a general and had become a marshal of France, and there had even been tales that this ancestor was the actual father of one of the kings. When asked about this, Brockdorff-Rantzau would sometimes reply, "For years our family has regarded the Bourbons as bastard Rantzaus."[1] If it was the intention of the Majority Socialist government to prove that German policy was no longer controlled by the old aristocracy, they had picked the wrong man to represent them before the world.

Politically, Brockdorff-Rantzau was a member of the newly formed Democratic Party—an anomaly for a man whose twin brother, Count Ernst von Rantzau, was the legal administrator for the property of the exiled Wilhelm II. In December of 1918, when Ebert sounded out Brockdorff-Rantzau as to his willingness to serve as foreign minister, the Count regarded himself as being at the height of his professional powers. Supremely confident of his ability to deal successfully with the Allies, he made two stipulations in accepting the post: he wanted it understood that he supported the German Republic not by reason of any deep-seated democratic convictions, but because he believed the monarchy to be an anachronism and democracy the only alternative to Bolshevism; and he reserved the right to resign his ministry if he found himself forced to accept a treaty of peace which would "deprive the German people of a decent livelihood."[2] Doubtless these stipulations were unwelcome, but the government felt that it had no choice. The Independent Socialists (who at the time were still members of the government) protested that Brockdorff-Rantzau was too much "a diplomat of the old school." Ebert replied that he was sure the Count would collaborate with the government. "We are suffering from complete disorganization and chaos," he said. "If under these conditions a man of international repute will cast his lot with us, we can only welcome his decision."[3] Ebert forced through Brockdorff-Rantzau's appointment, and as time went by almost everyone came to agree that it had been a good one. The Foreign Minister had one curious shortcoming, however: he was an atrocious public speaker. In a small group he was witty, urbane and fluent, but when he was compelled to speak before a large group—for example, when he first addressed the National Assembly at Weimar—he became awkward and frightened, gripped the podium with white-knuckled hands and stammered, his voice sounding harsh and arrogant.

Brockdorff-Rantzau did not find his ministry totally unprepared for the peace conference which was to come. For at least a year the staff had been collecting economic data to be used in the event of either German victory or defeat, and since the armistice, the Foreign Office had created a large and thoroughly professional study group known as the Bureau for the Peace Negotiations, generally referred to simply as the "Paxkonferenz." Brockdorff-Rantzau directed the immediate enlargement of this group. A body of forty Foreign Office officials were put to work on the preparations for the peace conference. Supplementing them were well over one hundred specialists recruited from the fields of banking, agriculture, teaching and industry. They were split up into various study groups to research individual positions, and, almost oblivious to the periodic riot and revolution within Berlin, they produced position papers on almost every conceivable subject, researched with all the meticulous care customarily associated with the German race. Only at the height of the Spartacist and Communist insurrections did they stop work, and then only because Brockdorff-Rantzau did not want his subordinates divided into a group which reported for duty and a group which stayed away through fear of violence.

The difficulty of the Paxkonferenz's task cannot be overstated. Having no representatives at Paris, its members did not know exactly what would be demanded of them or when. A series of attempts to establish some sort of clandestine diplomatic contact with one or more of the Allied nations proved fruitless. Their principal source of information was a summary of press reports from Allied newspapers, and these proved unreliable and frequently misleading, mostly because the press relations of the peace conference were themselves so wretched. The only other source was the reports which filtered in from German diplomats in neutral countries relating what they had learned—a method which was fourth-hand at best.

By April 15 the Foreign Office was convinced that the Allies would not simply summon the German delegation to Paris and demand Germany's signature to a final treaty without face-to-face negotiations. Regarding the League of Nations, the Foreign Office anticipated that Germany would be granted membership as soon as the peace treaty was signed. It was assumed that Germany would be compelled to hand over Alsace-Lorraine to France, although she intended to demand a plebiscite. It was also assumed that the Rhineland would have to be demilitarized and that various limitations would be placed on the German Army and Navy. The Foreign Office anticipated a prolonged struggle over the matter of the Saar

Basin, which they knew France wanted, and it was forecast that there would be Polish territorial claims in Upper Silesia and in the region of Posen, but it was felt that these would "be dropped in [the] case of strong German resistance."[4] The questions of the loss of Danzig and the creation of a Polish Corridor through West Prussia were regarded as so improbable that they were not even discussed. However, it was feared that the Allies, at the insistence of France, might refuse to permit an *Anschluss* between Austria and Germany, although there was hope that the Italians might intercede in favor of an Austro-German union.

Concerning the matters of colonies and reparations, the Foreign Office was optimistic. It believed that the idea of annexation of German colonies had been rejected by the peace conference. The German government had made a point of naming a Minister for Colonies, and although there was nothing for him to do, since all the colonies were occupied, it was hoped that this would demonstrate Germany's determination to hang on to them. But if the Allies demanded them, they would at least be charged off against the reparations bill. Regarding reparations, the Foreign Office thought that the Allies had satisfied themselves that Germany could pay very little and that the Allied demands would thus be moderate. Perhaps the final bill would be fifty billion marks, but this would be payable over a long period of time and with many deductions, such as the value of military equipment already turned over in compliance with the provisions of the armistice.[5]

The views of the German Foreign Office were not, of course, made public. However, its air of confidence concerning the outcome of the peace conference was conveyed to the National Assembly and, through it, to the German people. The general impression given was that the situation was far from hopeless. Certain painful sacrifices would be demanded of Germany, but they would not be excessive or of long duration. And even in the unlikely event of exorbitant Allied demands, the German delegation would have at least two counterarguments to put forward during the negotiations. (It was always assumed that the Germans would be permitted to argue and negotiate.)

The first of these arguments was that Germany was not obliged to entertain any claim which was not consistent with Wilson's Fourteen Points. The diplomatic notes of late October and early November of 1918 which had led to the armistice were all restudied with the greatest care. The Foreign Office's legal experts were unanimous: Germany had not surrendered unconditionally; the exchange of notes constituted a strict "pre-armistice agreement" which was legally binding upon the victors. Without question Germany had entered into a contract with the Allies. At the insistence of Wilson, acting by and for the Allies, Germany had "accepted the terms laid down by President Wilson . . . as the foundations of a permanent peace of justice." Germany had never promised anything more. She had never been asked for anything more. On the basis of the Allied terms, Germany had ceased resistance. By any standard of international law, the Germans felt, it was unlawful for the Allies to increase their demands.

The second German defense against a Carthaginian peace was regarded as being even stronger. During the war various Allied statesmen had said repeatedly that the Allies' quarrel was not with the German people but with their military masters and monarchs. A careful index of such statements was prepared by the Paxkonferenz. Wilson himself, in his message requesting a declaration of war from Congress, had said, "We have no quarrel with the German people. We have no feeling toward them except one of sympathy and friendship." He had specifically said that the enemy was "the government of the German Empire." Germany would now point out that her people had had no effective control over their government until the final days of the war. Now the Kaiser and the monarchy were gone and Germany was a democracy. Would it be fair to punish the German people for the sins of the monarch they had deposed? Surely the German delegation could appeal to the impartial Wilson (whom they believed still to be omnipotent among the Allies) to defend them in this matter. Actually, they did not anticipate that events would deteriorate to this point. Ebert and his government believed that they had the right to expect leniency even from the French. After all, had they not, at considerable risk to themselves, saved Germany from Bolshevism? They would point out that Germany had been the living barrier protecting Western Europe from Russian Communism. For this the Allies would surely be suitably grateful.

On April 18 at the headquarters of the Armistice Commission in Spa the chief of the Allied delegation handed to the German delegates a message which read:

> *The Supreme Command of the Allied and Associated Powers has decided to invite the German delegation . . . to appear at*

Versailles the evening of April 25, for the purpose of receiving the text of the preliminaries of the treaty, as drawn up by the Allied and Associated Powers.

The German Government accordingly is asked to provide us forthwith with the number, names and titles of the delegates . . . The German delegation must confine itself strictly to its role, and must consist only of persons qualified for their special mission.[6]

This summons had been written with the greatest care. What the message had been designed to convey was that Germany was being invited to receive, not to discuss, a treaty which would be a more or less final document, not a draft. This distinction was not lost on Brockdorff-Rantzau. If Germany complied with such a summons, she would be tacitly agreeing to a dictated peace—which, of course, Brockdorff-Rantzau had no intention of doing.

The German reply to the Allied summons was particularly clever. Since Germany had been invited to appear at Versailles "for the purpose of receiving the text of the preliminaries of peace," Brockdorff-Rantzau pretended to assume that this required little more than a messenger. On April 19 he sent a pleasant note to the effect that the German government would dispatch an ambassador, two aides and four clerks to Paris "to receive the text of the Preliminary Peace Treaty and to deliver it forthwith to the German Government."[7]

As Brockdorff-Rantzau had foreseen, the flustered Allies replied that the victors could not officially receive German delegates who were authorized merely to receive the text of the treaty. "The Allied and Associated governments," they wrote, "are obliged to insist that the German government send to Versailles plenipotentiaries . . . fully authorized to deal with the whole matter of . . . peace."[8]

The German Foreign Office was well pleased with its clever riposte in this opening salvo of negotiations. It at once replied to the Allies that the complete German delegation would shortly entrain for Versailles "on the assumption that it is intended to negotiate the content of the treaty after the preliminary draft has been handed to the Germans."[9]

On April 28 two special trains bound for Versailles left Berlin. They carried in them 180 persons who constituted the German delegation to the Paris Peace Conference.

Chapter Fourteen

"The hour has struck for the weighty settlement of our account"

Judging from their various memoirs, those who were in Paris during April, 1919, were agreed upon at least one thing: the city had never been more beautiful. Warm, sunny days succeeded each other in delightful succession. The windows of the stuffy rooms in which the Council of Four, the Council of Five, the expert committees and the expert committees' subcommittees were meeting were thrown open, permitting those within to gaze out at green lawns and shimmering fountains. The noise of street traffic was muted and the buzz of the small insects flying about in the gardens was clearly audible to those within. The august representatives of the world's mightiest powers appeared serene and confident in this Paris springtime. They had summoned the vanquished Germans before them, and the presentation of the terms of peace would be made in due course and at the pleasure of the victors. But, coincidentally with the arrival of the Germans, the weather suddenly turned foul. The windows were shut up again and logs were burned in the fireplaces. It was almost like an omen.

Only a few persons knew of the near-panic which had seized the peace conferees upon the arrival of the German delegation. The Allies were completely unprepared for a confrontation with the Germans, and this fact soon became apparent to the plenipotentiaries of the defeated nation.

The Allies had not meant to be stampeded into summoning the German delegation so soon. But early in April Lloyd George had found himself under a furious attack from the *Times* of London for the alleged weakness of his defense of British interests against the idealism of Woodrow Wilson. The British Prime Minister faced a revolt of his once docile Parliament, which accused him of failing to make good on his election promises to hang the Kaiser to extract the full cost of the war from Germany and to conclude a speedy peace. On April 14 Lloyd George felt compelled to return to London to answer his critics. But he must take something with him. He asked that the Allies announce that the labors of the peace conference were practically concluded and that the Germans would shortly be called to Paris. Thus it was largely to accommodate Lloyd George that the announcement was made. The British Prime Minister returned to London, faced his Parliament and, like an avenging father, cowed it into submission.

While it was true that a compromise had been reached regarding the League of Nations, reparations and the Saar, there were still a number of major disagreements. The most important was the one involving the Italians, who had departed for Rome following Wilson's appeal to their people of April 23 and had not returned. The Belgians, dissatisfied with the reparations arrangements, threatened also to walk out, and the Chinese were announcing that the Shantung settlement was so grossly unfair that they too might leave Paris.

The arrival of the Germans found the Allies in a desperate position. The peace treaty was nowhere near ready. In scores of obscure crannies scattered in public buildings throughout Paris, the various conference subcommittees were reported to be completing their assignments, but until the major—and the minor—stumbling blocks had been eliminated the central treaty-drafting committee could not possibly complete its labors, and thus there was no treaty to hand the Germans. Indeed, it appeared quite possible that the peace conference might break up over the Italian claim to Fiume. The British, the French and the Americans might claim that the work of the conference would proceed without the Italians, but what if Italy, Belgium, China and possibly Japan refused to sign the treaty? The Allies would be placed in the ridiculous position of asking the Germans to negotiate and sign a series of individual treaties with her enemies, a humiliating prospect.

The official German plenipotentiaries to the Paris Peace Conference consisted of Foreign Minister Count von Brockdorff-Rantzau,

Dr. Otto Landsberg, a lawyer and an important member of the Reichstag; Robert Leinhart, a Majority Socialist who was president of the Prussian Landtag; the German Postmaster General, Johann Giesberts, who was a member of the Christian People's Party; Dr. Carl Melchior, a member of the Democratic Party and a brilliant financial expert; and Walter Schucking, an internationally respected professor of law.

Ranked beneath these men were various experts who bore the title of "commissioner." They represented individual departments within the German government, such as the Ministry of Finance, the Ministry for the Colonies or the Ministry of War, the commissioner of which was General Hans von Seeckt.

A careful plan had been drawn up, in accordance with which various committees specializing in such questions as the League of Nations, reparations or colonies were designated. These were the committees which were expected to meet with their Allied counterparts for the negotiation of individual questions. It was immediately apparent to the Allies that this was a first-class group. Almost a third of the members' names were preceded by the title *Geheimrat* (Privy Councilor), the highest title in the German civil service. Most of the delegation bore professorial or doctoral titles. And backing them up in Berlin was the remainder of the Paxkonferenz staff, busily engaged in supplying the latest intelligence, plans and documents.

The train carrying the principal German delegates left Berlin on April 28. It passed rapidly across Germany and Belgium, but when it came to the battlefields of northern France the train was slowed to fifteen kilometers an hour. The French intended that the Germans should be spared no opportunity to see the devastation which the war had caused, and to understand the hatred which they bore toward Germany. The train was stopped for long periods in towns where every building had been destroyed. Then it moved slowly past miles of ruined farms, across temporary bridges and past desolate villages. The only persons who could be seen were miserable German prisoners of war at work rebuilding the rail lines under the guard of French soldiers. The German delegation threw oranges and newspapers to the prisoners from the train windows and were horrified when the French guards clubbed the men back to work. The psychological effect was all that the French could have hoped for. In their letters home, the German delegates wrote of this battlefield passage as "an overwhelming experience."[1]

On the night of April 29 the German train arrived at the railroad station in Vaucresson, a town some dozen miles from Versailles. The lights of Paris were visible in the distance. The Germans were taken off the train at Vaucresson and driven to Versailles by automobile to prevent the possibility of attack by a French mob at the Versailles station. A French officer, Colonel Henri, greeted the German delegates with icy correctness and conducted them to a famous old Versailles hotel, the Hotel des Reservoirs, which had been cleared out for their occupation. The Germans quickly became aware that this was the hotel at which a French peace commission had stayed in 1871 while suing for terms from Bismarck following the Franco-Prussian War. The luggage of the German delegation was dumped helter-skelter in the courtyard and, despite the large number of French troops on guard or lounging in the courtyard at the hotel, the Germans were instructed to carry their own baggage and to find their own rooms.

In the light of morning, the Germans made an unsettling discovery. Although they had been promised "every liberty of movement," they found that this was being interpreted very narrowly. A fence of barbed wire surrounded the hotel, extending out into an adjoining park. Outside this, French sentries patrolled. The German delegates were confined to the hotel and its park. Their press representatives and clerical staff were similarly isolated in two adjoining hotels. And thus, carefully caged in from any contact with the victors, they awaited the presentation of the treaty.

The German delegation now began a succession of slow, trying days. The Allies, occupied with their own problems, completely ignored the occupants of the Hotel des Reservoirs. For several days the only exchange between the victors and the vanquished was a German demand that they be permitted greater freedom of movement. It was met by a reluctant French concession permitting them to walk a little farther out into the fenced park and allowing them daily automobile drives around Versailles, accompanied by a French officer.

The Germans settled into a chafing, quiet existence. They arose at seven-thirty, breakfasted together in the dining room of the old hotel, took a walk in the park, then read the newspapers or conferred in groups until time for a large and sumptuous luncheon, which was eaten with great gusto by these emissaries of a half-starved nation. In the afternoon the delegation met in its commit-

tees for a few hours of desultory conversation and then adjourned
for a faultlessly served dinner. In the evening the six plenipotentiaries met in the sitting room of Brockdorff-Rantzau's suite, sipped
cognac (which the Count greatly enjoyed), chatted for a while,
then trooped off to bed. The weather was unseasonably cold and
rainy. Since the hotel lacked central heating, it was necessary to
burn logs in the open fireplaces, and the smoky, drafty atmosphere
which this produced did nothing to improve the Germans' mood. As
the days passed, Brockdorff-Rantzau began to suspect that they had
been summoned to sit ignored in this cage in Versailles as a deliberate and special form of humiliation.

There was only one humorous note to these dull days. Just before
they left Berlin, the Germans had been told that there was every
possibility that the French might plant microphones throughout the
hotel. The only way to foil these sinister devices, the delegation had
been advised, was to hold all confidential conversations in a room
where music was being played. A piano was installed in Brockdorff-
Rantzau's suite, and all political matters were discussed to the constantly repeated refrains of a "Hungarian Rhapsody" or "The Pil-
grims' March" from *Tannhäuser*. With true German thoroughness,
the subordinate committees had each been provided with a phono-
graph, and during the mid-afternoon conferences the old hotel
trembled in a musical bedlam. No microphone being discovered,
however, the delegation sheepishly abandoned these nerve-racking
serenades after a few days.[2]

These were trying days for the victors as well. Far from ignoring
the Germans' presence, the Allies were acutely aware of them and of
the pressure for a treaty which their arrival placed upon the conferees.

The Council of Four, shrunk to a Council of Three by Italy's
defection, met almost constantly, usually in Woodrow Wilson's
study but sometimes in a large office at the Quai d'Orsay. The
Council of Five—the principal Allied foreign ministers—was hastily
resurrected from near-desuetude and handed a sheaf of unpleasant
questions to resolve. Meanwhile the Drafting Committee worked
practically around the clock to put the decisions into proper treaty
form. The whole procedure was complicated by the fact that the
Council of Four had sometimes met without a secretary. Now its
members were called upon to recall for the Drafting Committee the

decisions which they had taken weeks before. What, for example, *had* they decided on April 15 about the German fortifications on Helgoland? Nobody could remember, and such matters had to be taken up again.

But all these were nothing compared to the racking major decisions which could be made only by Wilson (totally exhausted), Lloyd George (now obviously experiencing grave doubts about the treaty) and Clemenceau (undergoing a wave of attacks for his alleged weakness in dealing with the other Allies). Ultimately these decisions were made. Belgium was told that she would be offered nothing more in terms of reparations; she must accept what had been allotted to her or leave the conference and negotiate a treaty of her own. Belgium elected to stay.

No secret was made of the fact that Britain, France and the United States were prepared to conclude a treaty without Italy. In anticipation that Orlando would continue to boycott the conference, the Drafting Committee tore apart the nearly completed treaty, deleting all references to Italy and Italian claims. Then, on May 5, word was received that Orlando had left Rome to return to Paris. The harassed Drafting Committee was given instructions to reinsert Italy into the treaty.

On Sunday, May 4, the German delegation, having been shut up in the Hotel des Reservoirs for nearly a week, served notice that the important members of the delegation would return to Germany, where urgent business awaited them, unless the Allies were prepared to receive them forthwith. This statement threw the victors into a final frantic convulsion of activity. They had, after all, no way to compel the Germans to remain, and it was unreasonable to expect the German Foreign Minister and a collection of the most senior German officials to remain idle at Versailles for an indefinite period. On the other hand, they could not be allowed to depart and thus proclaim to the world that the Allies were unable to agree upon a treaty.

At once the Council of Four made its decision. The treaty would be presented to the Germans on May 7 in the Trianon Palace at Versailles. In haste and inevitable confusion, the Drafting Committee flung together in one bulky volume the multitudinous work of the Conference—of the Councils of Ten, Five, Four and Three together with all their committees and subcommittees. Some of these plainly had thought they were writing preliminary drafts; some had labored under the illusion that they were merely drafting "maximum statements" to be used as initial bargaining positions; and some, yielding to pressure, had resigned themselves to the inclusion of impossibly harsh terms, with the hope that the League of Nations would shortly undo the damage.

The finished treaty, bound as a thick white-covered book comprising some two hundred pages, 440 separate articles and 75,000 words, was sent to the printers on May 5. While it was being set in type, the major Allied powers had to go through the formality of "consulting" the minor Allied powers on the form which the treaty was to take. A plenary session of the entire conference was announced for the following day, May 6. It began promptly at 3 P.M. Since the treaty was not yet printed, the conferees had to content themselves with listening to a forty-four-page summary read to them by André Tardieu of the French delegation. The majority of those present did not understand French, and the length of Tardieu's speech did not permit its translation into English, so the whole proceeding cannot have been particularly enlightening. As was his habit at the infrequent plenary sessions, Clemenceau gaveled down all discussion, but not before the Portuguese delegates had objected that never in the history of their nation had it signed a treaty which had not invoked the blessing of God upon its content; not before the Chinese had once more protested the Shantung settlement; and not before the Italians had reserved future freedom of action in the matter of Fiume.

Then Marshal Foch rose to his feet. It was impossible to deny the man who was still the commander in chief of the Allied armies the privilege of speaking. Foch began with the statement that although he had not seen the final draft of the treaty he wished to protest against what he understood the Rhineland settlement was to be, most particularly the fifteen-year limit on the Allied occupation. Foch pleaded for this question to be reopened. "The Rhine alone is important. Nothing else matters . . ." It must be held for a period of at least thirty years, while the reparations were being paid and until "the German countries" had given "evidence of unmistakable good faith."[3]

Finally Foch sat down. The spectacle of a marshal of France protesting against a treaty to which his government had agreed not only was a public humiliation for his nation but boded ill for the future. In a fury, Clemenceau announced that, the agreement of the Allies having been obtained, the plenary session was now adjourned.

The peace treaty, with the words "Conditions of Peace" printed in English and French on its cover, was assembled in its finished form late in the evening of May 6. So tight had been the secrecy and so hurried the compilation of the treaty that almost no one, neither experts nor plenipotentiaries, knew for certain what existed beyond the little watertight compartment on which he personally had worked.

Before dawn on May 7, messengers fanned out through Paris, bringing copies of the finished treaty to senior Allied officials. It came like a bombshell to many of them. Herbert Hoover, chief of the Allied food-relief services and a top American economic expert, was awakened to receive his copy at 4 A.M. Hoover immediately read it through and was horrified at its harshness. Unable to sleep, he dressed at first daylight and walked the deserted Paris streets. Within a few blocks he met others—Smuts and then John Maynard Keynes of the British delegation. "It all flashed into our minds," Hoover said, "why each was walking about at that time of the morning."[4]

A number of other Allied figures were similarly appalled, particularly at the reparations demands. To Ray Stannard Baker, the American press chief, the treaty seemed "a terrible document, a dispensation of retribution with scarcely a parallel in history."[5] Woodrow Wilson said to Baker, "If I were a German, I think I should never sign it."[6] Secretary of State Robert Lansing dictated a memorandum which said: "For the first time in these days of feverish rush of preparation there is time to consider the Treaty as a complete document. . . . The impression made by it is one of disappointment, of regret, and of depression. The terms of peace appear immeasurably harsh and humiliating, while many of them seem to me impossible of performance."[7]

But there was no help for it. The concessions had already been made. The treaty was finished. Now it must be presented to the Germans.

The treaty presentation was set in a scene which the Allies had prepared with great care. Lloyd George, Wilson and Clemenceau had taken the trouble to visit the Trianon Palace personally on May

5 to insure that all would be in readiness. The room where the confrontation was to take place was about seventy-five feet square. Along two sides of it were huge windows; a third wall was painted white, and the fourth was covered with mirrors. On a sunny day the reflected glare in the room was dazzling.

The tables at which the Allied plenipotentiaries were to sit had been arranged to form three sides of a square. A separate table had been set up on the fourth side, facing Clemenceau and the other major figures. The seating plan had been published in the Paris newspapers, which described the German table as the *"banc des accusés."* The Germans had, on May 6, been handed a copy of a document titled "Agenda for a Meeting to be Held on May 7, 1919." From this and other sources they learned that the meeting would commence at 3 P.M. and was expected to last for only five minutes. The finished treaty would be handed over and the German delegation would then be dismissed.

The Allied intentions were at last made absolutely clear to the Germans. This was to be no peace conference in the accepted sense of the term. The Germans would not be allowed to confer with the Allies. Instead they were to be haled before the court of the victors and made to sit in "the seats of the accused." Without opportunity for defense or rebuttal, they would be found guilty.

The Germans suddenly perceived that they had been living in a fool's paradise. The Allies had no intention of forgiving or forgetting. No humiliation, it seemed, was to be spared them. This was the reason they had been brought here a week early to wait caged up for the victors' pleasure. Certainly it was no accident that they would be given the treaty in the same room in which the Emperor Wilhelm I had been crowned in 1871, and on the fourth anniversary of the date of the sinking of the *Lusitania*.

How should the Germans reply? Brockdorff-Rantzau decided that they must at least protest against this monstrous injustice in words which posterity could recall. As they conferred into the night, the German delegation prepared three separate speech drafts, varying in tone, for the Foreign Minister to take with him on the morrow. Brockdorff-Rantzau would decide at the last moment which one to use, depending upon the statement which the Allies made at the time.

The confrontation between the victors and the vanquished took place promptly at three in the afternoon. The Allies had arrived early and were already in their seats when the cars containing the German delegation were driven up to the palace. The first person to alight from the automobiles was Count von Brockdorff-Rantzau. Like the rest of the delegation, he wore a black morning coat, a high wing collar, a bowler hat. From his left hand he swung a walking stick. As Brockdorff-Rantzau paused to permit his associates to gather behind him, the Allied observers who clustered about the entrance noted that he appeared ill. His complexion seemed yellow and there were distinct black circles beneath his eyes. Little beads of nervous perspiration dotted his forehead.

Then, his delegation in order and a French functionary leading the way, Brockdorff-Rantzau marched through the dark halls and the antechamber to the main meeting room. The doors were flung open to the announcement *"Messieurs les délégués allemands!"* The Germans stood squinting in the dazzling light of the room. For a moment Brockdorff-Rantzau seemed to have lost his bearings. More than two hundred persons filled the room, their numbers seeming endlessly magnified in the reflection of the mirrored wall. Collecting himself, Brockdorff-Rantzau made a formal bow to the assemblage. The occupants of the room at once rose to their feet and returned the bow. The Germans were led to their seats, which faced those of Clemenceau, Wilson and Lloyd George.

It was the prerogative of Georges Clemenceau, as president of the peace conference, to conduct the meeting. As soon as the Germans were seated, the French Premier clambered to his feet and addressed himself directly to Brockdorff-Rantzau. "Gentlemen, plenipotentiaries of the German Empire," he said, "this can be neither the time nor the place for superfluous words . . . The hour has struck for the weighty settlement of our account. You have asked us for peace. We are disposed to give it to you. The volume which the secretary general of the conference will shortly hand to you will tell you the conditions which we have fixed. . . . I am compelled to add that this second Peace of Versailles has been too dearly bought by the peoples represented here for us not to be unanimously resolved to secure by every means in our power all the legitimate satisfactions which are our due."[8]

Clemenceau concluded this brief speech with the announcement that the Germans would have a period of fifteen days to send *written* "observations" to the Allies concerning the terms of the treaty, following which the Allies would communicate their final terms together with the date upon which the treaty would be signed. Clemenceau then looked around and rattled off his usual staccato "Does anyone wish to speak?"

Brockdorff-Rantzau shot up his hand, selected a sheaf of papers from among the several speech drafts lying before him and began to speak.

He was at once interrupted by Clemenceau, who was still standing. "The translation must be made first! Translators! Where are the translators?"[9]

Two men came forward. One of them repeated Clemenceau's speech in English, the other in German. Meanwhile M. Dutasta stepped through an opening in the square of tables and handed Brockdorff-Rantzau the thick volume which was the Allies' peace conditions. Brockdorff-Rantzau pushed it to one side and fiddled nervously with the papers before him while waiting for the conclusion of the translation.

The faces of the German delegation clearly registered the horror with which they received Clemenceau's address. The phrase "The hour has struck for the weighty settlement of our account," together with the information that no oral negotiations would take place, chilled them to the bone. Of the six German plenipotentiaries, only Brockdorff-Rantzau had heard Clemenceau speak before. The rest had had no idea of how blunt and savage the Tiger could be.

At length the droning translations of Clemenceau's speech were complete. Clemenceau nodded to the German Foreign Minister, who, without standing up as Clemenceau had done, began his own speech. After a few introductory sentences, Brockdorff-Rantzau got down to cases: "We know the intensity of the hatred which meets us, and we have heard the victor's passionate demand that as vanquished we shall be made to pay and as the guilty we shall be punished. The demand is made that we shall acknowledge that we alone are guilty of having caused the war. Such a confession in my mouth would be a lie."[10] The last sentence was delivered in a voice which was practically a hiss.

As the Count continued, with an awkward pause after every sentence for a translation into French and English, there was a murmur of shocked surprise from the Allies. Brockdorff-Rantzau's failure to rise was instantly interpreted as an intentional discourtesy to the victors. Moreover, his tone of voice, his very manner, implied a suppressed rage and a calculated menace which shocked the Allies. Apparently the Germans had not changed. The German "democrats" had sent as their representative a defiant and arrogant Prussian count. Lloyd George twitched in his seat, picked up an ivory paperknife which lay before him and snapped it in two. Clemenceau, in the midst of one of the translations, shouted out indignantly, "Speak up, I can't hear a word!"[11] Wilson leaned across to whisper angrily to Lloyd George.

Meanwhile, warming to his subject, Brockdorff-Rantzau continued with such blunt observations as "The hundreds of thousands of [German] noncombatants who have perished since the eleventh of November by reason of the blockade were killed with cold deliberation, after our adversaries had conquered and victory had been assured to them."[12] At this point even the German delegates began to squirm. They began to realize how far the impression which Brockdorff-Rantzau was making differed from that which they had originally contemplated. They had forgotten just how great an ordeal public speaking was to this otherwise urbane diplomat. His sinister-sounding intonation was mainly the result of a nervous tremor in his voice. His failure to stand when speaking was due to the fact that his knees were shaking. Nor was Brockdorff-Rantzau's poise improved by the circumstance that there was only one copy of his speech, which had to be handed to the two translators after every sentence.

At 4 P.M. Brockdorff-Rantzau finished—speaking at the end into an outraged buzz of noise from the surrounding tables. Clemenceau rose to his feet at once and spat out his customary "Has anybody any more observations to make? Does no one wish to speak? If not, the meeting is closed." All the others rose and waited as the German delegation strode out of the room. Brockdorff-Rantzau, his hands trembling, lit a cigarette as he made his exit.

The Germans had made a most unfortunate impression. As the Allied dignitaries filed out of the meeting room, Marshal Foch could be seen pacing up and down a corridor. The cigar clenched in his teeth did not hide his wry smile. A British official noted that i. was as if Foch were about the tell the politicians, "I always told you that those Germans were not repentant, and now what I said has been proved."[13] Wilson said to Lord Riddell of the British delegation, "The Germans are really a stupid people. They always do the wrong thing. . . . This is the most tactless speech I have ever heard. It will set the whole world against them."[14] Lloyd George admitted, "Those insolent Germans made me very angry. . . . I don't know when I have been more angry. Their conduct showed that the old Germany is still there. Your Brockdorff-Rantzaus will ruin Germany's chances . . ."[15]

Meanwhile the German delegation had returned directly to the Hotel des Reservoirs. Brockdorff-Rantzau called an immediate meeting of the entire delegation and, when they had all crowded into the dining room, reported to them what had happened in the little more than an hour since the departure of the six principal delegates from the hotel. No word of reproach or criticism was offered by the disciplined Germans, but it was obvious that almost to a man they believed that Brockdorff-Rantzau had gone too far. The treaty was then produced, and twenty members of the delegation who were fluent in either French or English were designated as translators. The single copy of the treaty—all that the Germans had at the moment—was torn apart and a section given to each of the twenty.

By midnight a rough translation had been completed and had been mimeographed in German and copies had been dispatched to Berlin. Hardly anyone slept that night. The document which the German delegates read was worse than anything they had dreamed possible. They believed that Germany could not survive the imposition of such a treaty. Nothing had been spared them. The reparations payments would ruin Germany financially, she would be left with practically no army or navy to defend her, her principal coal mines would be distributed among the French and the Poles, her colonies were to be taken away, and she would be compelled to acknowledge her responsibility for starting the war, with the obligation to deliver up her wartime heroes to be tried as criminals by the Allies. And this was only the beginning. There was much, much more. As the stunned Germans gathered, they began for the first time to speak of the peace treaty as a *Diktat*, a dictation. They were to have the opportunity to make only written "observations," a task which could as well or better be done from Berlin. They had been lied to and swindled—and by no one more than by Woodrow Wilson. They had laid down their arms expecting mercy and understanding, as Wilson had led them to do, and now that they were defenseless against the victors Wilson had betrayed them.

Late in the night of May 7 a German plenipotentiary, Johann Giesberts, lunged into the Hotel des Reservoirs dining room and stumbled into a chair. Giesberts was a Socialist, a former worker and a man over whom the diplomatic veneer lay very thin. Obviously drunk, he shouted in fury and banged the table before him so hard that the glasses on it overturned. "This shameful treaty has broken me, for I believed in Wilson until today," Giesberts roared. ". . . I believed him to be an honest man, and now that scoundrel sends us such a treaty. . . . But I am telling you this, gentlemen, if those fellows think that the German laborers are going to work hard for that capitalist gang, they're wrong, and when they march into the mining district the few hand grenades that will be needed to flood every mine will be on hand!"[16]

Chapter Fifteen

Frontiers, Reparations and Guilt

O N May 8 the Allied peace conditions reached Berlin in the hands of the courier whom Brockdorff-Rantzau had dispatched from Versailles. The printing presses of the German Admiralty were immediately put to work. By May 10 there were several thousand copies of the treaty in print and distributed among German officials of every description. Within a few days this uncontrolled distribution had brought its inevitable result. The treaty, the precise contents of which the Allies had tried to keep secret until it was in final form, was now being hawked on the Berlin streets for the equivalent of fifty cents a copy.

The first official German consideration of the treaty took place in the Great Hall of the University of Berlin, the National Assembly having temporarily forsaken Weimar so as to receive the Allied terms in Germany's capital. The meeting began at noon on May 12 with a fiery speech from Chancellor Philipp Scheidemann. From the podium he waved a copy of the treaty. "What lies at the root of our deliberations is this thick book in which hundreds of paragraphs begin with 'Germany renounces . . . renounces . . . renounces . . .'" Then, to the applause of every member of the Assembly, Scheidemann stated firmly, "This treaty is, according to the conception of the government, unacceptable . . . What hand would not wither that binds itself and us in these fetters?"[1] He demanded a peace based exclusively on the Fourteen Points and went on to assure the Assembly that Germany would never sign the treaty until it had been vastly amended by counterproposals and negotiation.

Scheidemann was succeeded by a speaker from each political party. Each speech was practically a repetition of the one which preceded. All reflected a general horror at the terms and a determination never to accept them. "This peace is nothing more than a continuation of the war by other means," said the Majority Socialist spokesman. "It is truly a product of a half year's secret diplomacy . . . What has become of those ideals under which the Allied governments conducted their crusade against kaiserism and militarism?"[2] The Christian People's Party declared that the treaty would utterly destroy Germany, while Hausmann of the Democrats cried, "If our Army and our workmen had known on the fifth and ninth of November that the peace would look like this, the Army would not have laid down its arms and all would have held out to the end."[3] Count von Posadewsky-Wehner of the right-wing National People's Party compared the Allies' peace conditions to the "notorious" Methuen Agreement by which, he said, Britain had destroyed Portugal's industry and forever condemned her to poverty.

There was scarcely a section of the treaty which was not attacked, just as there was scarcely an Allied nation which was not attacked for perfidy and hypocrisy. The treaty was described as the product of "French revenge and English brutality,"[4] and Woodrow Wilson received almost universal condemnation. Almost all the speakers rejected Germany's war guilt.

Only Hugo Haase of the Independent Socialists broke this unanimity. He too condemned the treaty, but he also reproached the other political parties in the Assembly. Haase claimed that only his own Independent Socialists had the right to criticize this treaty, which was no more severe than the one that Germany had imposed upon Russia at Brest-Litovsk in 1917. To the discomfiture of his listeners, Haase reminded them that only the Independent Socialists had voted against the Brest-Litovsk Treaty. The Majority Socialists had contented themselves with abstaining, while the predecessors of the other parties had enthusiastically supported it. Haase observed that it was inconsistent for men who had signed the Brest-Litovsk Treaty to demand mercy and justice from the Allies, and he suggested that the negotiations with the victors should be handled by the Independents.

Galling as Haase's comment was—and it was made doubly so by

the logic of his argument—it was only a brief interruption in the unanimous attacks on the treaty. After five hours of continuous condemnation, the Assembly adjourned with its members rising defiantly to sing "Deutschland über Alles."

The mood of this historic session in the university was being duplicated in the streets. Outside the headquarters of the American military mission crowds gathered to chant, "Where are our Fourteen Points? Where is Wilson's peace? Where is your 'peace of justice'?"[5] The Prussian Ministry of War advised all Allied nationals in Germany to wear only civilian clothes "so as to avoid attacks from the indignant population."[6] A week-long period of national mourning was proclaimed and widely observed. In the sections of Silesia and West Prussia which, under the Allies' peace demands, were to be turned over to Poland, economic life virtually ceased. Only a few particularly courageous and perceptive persons pointed out that much of the shock with which the German people received the treaty was due to the fact that the government had allowed Germany to believe that the peace would be generous.

The reaction of the German people to the treaty was, if anything, more violent than that of their leaders. Even the most humble German was appalled by the severity of the treaty. Germany was to lose all her colonies, more than a third of her coal fields, three quarters of her iron-ore deposits, a third of her blast furnaces and all her merchant marine. And, beyond all this, the reparations payments were still to be fixed and paid. They would have to be paid by a Germany that was substantially smaller than it had been before the war, for on every border—north, east, south and west—she was to lose land and people. Meanwhile the Army and the Navy, reduced to pitiful proportions, would be unable to protect the nation against attack by even the weakest of Germany's neighbors.

There was one small group of Germans who had no time for either fury or self-pity. These were the German delegates in the Hotel des Reservoirs at Versailles. The shock they had experienced at the May 7 confrontation with the victors had necessarily been repressed in the urgent preparation of the notes which were their only hope of obtaining a modification of the Allied terms.

The victors had given them only fifteen days in which "to put into French and English their written observations on the entire treaty." To each of the German "observations" Clemenceau had promised a prompt Allied reply. At the end of the fifteen days the

Allies would inform the German delegation of such changes, if any, which might be made in the draft treaty, and a date for its signing would be announced.

The German delegation at once realized that fifteen days was a desperately short time. The work had to begin instantly and in a climate as free as possible from rancor. Brockdorff-Rantzau himself set the tone. He ignored his government's instructions to notify the Allies that the terms of the draft treaty were "unbearable and unfulfillable." To those of his delegation who suggested that they simply pack up, return to the Fatherland and abandon the whole affair Brockdorff-Rantzau offered cooler counsel. By now the urbane diplomat realized how unfortunate an impression he had made at the May 7 meeting with the Allies. He instructed the members of his delegation to proceed with their labors in as detached and business-like a manner as they could. Their strategy must be to adhere carefully to the original German plan: The concept of the "pre-armistice agreement" under which Germany had laid down its arms only upon the conditions of Wilson's Fourteen Points and certain "subsequent addresses." Under this interpretation, Germany came to Versailles not as an abject and vanquished nation, but as one of two "high contracting parties" who had, in the pre-armistice agreement, concluded a *pactum de contrahendo*, legally binding upon both sides.

The Germans' basic strategy in the dispatch of notes was thus clearly established. They would tread a path of narrow legalism, contesting every section of the draft treaty which did not agree with Wilson's pronouncements, and, like good lawyers, attempting to improve their position at every point.

The whole concept of the existence of a pre-armistice agreement was, of course, a shrewd line of argument. The Allies had indeed set certain conditions at the time of the armistice, and, in a legal sense, these conditions were binding upon both parties. The Germans correctly suspected that Wilson had forced his Fourteen Points on the Allies. They also suspected that the British and the French had succeeded in evading the Fourteen Points. The Germans believed that Wilson could now compel them to revise the draft treaty. In this they were wrong. They did not appreciate the extent to which Wilson had felt compelled to compromise with his allies, and the irrevocable nature of these compromises. Nor did they understand the extent to which the exhausted American President had lost his dominance over his allies.

These miscalculations were not the only defects in the German position. One misfortune was that it was they who had made the draft treaty public. The Allies had released only a vague summary; they had deliberately not made the complete draft treaty public. The French and British parliaments and the United States Senate had not even seen it. As long as it was still more or less secret, revisions, perhaps even substantial ones, could be made without embarrassment. But when the Germans published the draft treaty, the Allied leaders were at once deprived of their freedom of action. They could not possibly revise the treaty without appearing to have weakened.

The second German mistake was the form of the notes which they now began to dispatch to the Allies. In theory, these notes were all to be reviewed, redrafted and coordinated by Brockdorff-Rantzau or his principal deputy, Walter Simons, a Foreign Office professional. In practice, this proved almost impossible. The Allied deadline for the German observations was so pressing that the opportunity for a carefully calculated review of each German note did not exist. Outside the guarded gates of the Hotel des Reservoirs buses full of sightseers cruised slowly past, hoping for a look at the German delegation immured within. Representatives of the French "Ligue des Patriots" stood vigil outside the fences, waiting to hoot and jeer whenever a German delegate appeared. The Germans contrived to disregard this. The treaty was divided up among various groups of experts. Each group prepared its own notes, and after a hasty review by Simons the notes were handed over to the French liaison officer, Colonel Henri, for transmittal to the Council of Four. Many of the notes were not even seen by Brockdorff-Rantzau, much of whose time was taken up journeying to Spa to meet with representatives of the Paxkonferenz or the German Cabinet, who came halfway in order to save time.

It was the haste and confusion in which they were drafted which was largely responsible for the uneven character of the German notes. The German replies and counterproposals were drafted by small bodies of experts who could not conceive that any other subject might be more vital than their own. They did not even have sufficient knowledge of what the other expert bodies were doing. There was no time for coordination, and, as a result, the essential German thesis of the "pre-armistice agreement" became somewhat obscured. One German note even protested the restoration of Alsace-Lorraine to France, though none of the Fourteen Points was more explicit than the one which demanded the return of these provinces to France.

Nor should the Germans have protested so many articles in the draft treaty. Lengthy notes were dispatched protesting the exclusion of German missionaries from former German colonies. Other notes dealt critically and at length with the makeup of an International Labor Organization, the establishment of which was part of the treaty. Still others suggested changes in the plan for the League of Nations—a tangled subject which none of the Allies was prepared to reopen, especially at German behest. The general impression which this profusion of protests gave the victors was that Germany intended to dispute every article of the treaty, using any argument which could be produced to fit the occasion.

To respond to the German notes of observation, the Allies had set up an elaborate procedure even before the draft treaty had been handed over. This foresight was fortunate, because the first of the German notes arrived as early as May 9. As each note was received, it was referred to the conference commission or subcommittee which had originally drafted the treaty article in question. It was that group's responsibility to recommend a course of action and draft a note of reply, nearly always a rebuttal. The draft note then went up to the Council of Four, which, meeting in daily session, would either approve it or order it redrafted. To speed things up, the Council would summon Philip Kerr, Lloyd George's private secretary, from an anteroom. Kerr would receive the Council's instructions, would retire to his office and, generally before the Four had completed their meeting, would return with his draft, which was usually adopted without further discussion. Sometimes Woodrow Wilson would help by typing draft replies on his own typewriter. By nightfall the approved replies would have been typed, signed by Clemenceau and handed over to the Germans.

All of the Allied notes of reply seemed cut to the same rough pattern. A German note would be received protesting that such-and-such an article was improper, unfair and unrealistic and did not conform to the pre-armistice agreements. Somewhere in the early part of the Allied reply was usually a courteously phrased reference to "the wanton acts of devastation perpetrated by the German armies during the war" (Allied note of May 22 on economic questions), or an allusion to the obvious requirement that "a definite and exemplary retribution should be extracted" from Germany (Allied note of May 24 regarding the Saar), or a reminder to Germany that the world "recognized as well-founded . . . both her aggression and her responsibility" for the war (Allied note of May 20 on responsibility and reparations). A moral basis having now been established, the note would go on to deny that the treaty article in question violated in any respect either the Fourteen Points or the principles of international legality. Then, almost without exception, the Allied note would reject the German arguments or demands.

The spectacle of this exchange of notes would be hard to exceed as an exercise in futility. There were so many arguments to employ, so many precedents to cite, that the exchange rarely rose above the level of a tedious wrangle. The Germans would protest, say, the fact that the treaty compelled Germany to pay the costs of the Allied armies of occupation in the Rhineland. The Allies' reply was to the effect that thus it had ever been—"the cost of maintenance of armies of occupation has always been borne by the nation subject to the occupation."[7] They delighted to remind Germany that in 1871 she had collected *her* costs of occupation from France. The Germans replied that that had been done by a different German government, and had not the American President said that a new day in world affairs was dawning?

For the Germans the whole procedure was further complicated by their communication difficulties. The peace delegation was at Versailles. The German Cabinet was at Weimar. The German Armistice Commission was at Spa. The Paxkonferenz was in Berlin. Couriers could not travel between them rapidly enough. The telephone and the telegraph were susceptible to being tapped, and the Germans feared to use them overmuch. The Paxkonferenz staff in Berlin, not knowing what would be useful, deluged the Versailles delegation with torrents of undigested information. Nor did it help that Brockdorff-Rantzau disliked and distrusted Matthias Erzberger, the Cabinet member who headed the German Armistice Commission at Spa. Brockdorff-Rantzau suspected, with considerable justice, that Erzberger coveted the Foreign Minister's position and that he maintained some sort of secret personal contact with certain Allied figures.

It was partly these organizational deficiencies which led the Germans to request an extension of the period allowed for their "observations." Pleading that they were preparing a series of general counterproposals to the treaty, they wrung from the Allies a reluctant extension of seven days—until May 29.

On May 29 the German delegation handed the Allies their

counterproposals, which amounted to a small book of 119 pages and 25,000 words. To emphasize its formal character, the document had been not typed but printed—by German printers who had been rushed to Versailles aboard a special train of five cars filled with presses and type.

The first pages of the booklet consisted of a covering letter which had been written at Brockdorff-Rantzau's request by a German journalist at Versailles. It had been hoped that his popular style would make a better case in any subsequent publication to the peoples of the world.

As might be expected, this German document opened with the routine reiteration that Germany had laid down her arms only after the Allies had promised that the Fourteen Points were to be the basis of peace. Now the Allies had exceeded this agreement, and "by abandoning [it] the Allies would break an international legal agreement."[8] The book went on with page after page of quotations abstracted from the wartime speeches of Allied leaders to prove that the announced war aim of the Allies had been to punish Germany's now deposed "monarchial masters," and that there was no justification for punishing the German people themselves.

Having, they hoped, established the basis for a nonvindictive peace, the Germans proceeded to take exception to almost every article in the draft treaty. They rejected nearly all the Allied claims and offered counterproposals of so sweeping a nature as to entirely revise the treaty. Almost every page of the German document contained its own foreboding of what would happen in the event that the treaty was not revised. Phrases such as "unspeakable disaster" (for Europe) and "utter destruction of German life" were sprinkled throughout the note. But three aspects of the draft treaty came in for the bitterest attack: reparations, territorial losses and the question of war guilt.

The prospect of loss of national territory is one to which the people of every nation cannot help but respond with fury. The loss of a nation's land means more than the sacrifice of farms, mines, factories and forests. These are only economic deprivations. More important is the matter of the people whom the nation loses, the family ties which are broken and the national loyalties which are corrupted. This was a terrible prospect for the German people.

It was not simple sentimentality on their part. Fifty years of aggressive Pan-German propaganda had worked their way into the

German mind. The majority of Germans were convinced that their nation and its people had a special history and a special mission and that other nations and races were inferior. The thought of transferring German citizens to the newly created Slavic nations to the east filled Germans everywhere with special horror, for there was scarcely a German who regarded a Pole or Czech as an equal.

A disproportionate number of German "observations" regarding the draft treaty thus concerned the Polish borders. There had been little difficulty in their preparation. Much of the background material had been put together by German industrial and agricultural interests in the affected areas. They had passed it on to the Paxkonferenz staff, which had merely turned the raw material over to the delegation at Versailles. The German delegation's attacks on the Polish border question began with the acknowledgment that Germany had agreed at the time of the armistice to turn over to Poland all territories "inhabited by indisputably Polish populations." It was conceded that portions of the province of Posen met this specification, and for this reason Germany was prepared to hand them over (though since Poland now occupied practically all of Posen there was no chance that Germany could get it back).

As for the rest—the internationalization of German Danzig, the severance of East Prussia by the Polish Corridor, and particularly the proposed cession of Upper Silesia with its extensive coal and zinc mines—the Germans protested violently. They quoted Wilson's wartime statement that it was inadmissable to create "new elements of discord and antagonism or to perpetuate old elements of this kind, which probably would in the course of time disturb the peace of Europe and consequently the peace of the world."[9] The Germans claimed that a Polish Corridor would have this inevitable effect, and they offered instead a complicated scheme by which the port city and the proposed corridor would remain German and Polish access to Danzig would be guaranteed.

The case concerning Upper Silesia was even more pressing. The German notes pointed out that this territory had not had any connection with the Polish kingdom since 1163. They quoted the election results of 1907 to establish that the majority of the Upper Silesian population had voted for German candidates. They claimed that less than a quarter of the children in the territory attended Polish schools. They protested that Upper Silesia had been developed exclusively by German capital under German management and that the leaders in business, the professions and even the labor unions were all German. More important, the principal product of Upper Silesia was coal; the territory in fact produced twenty-three per cent of Germany's hard coal. In other sections of the draft treaty, the Allies were taking away the coal mines of the German Saar and extracting heavy deliveries from the Westphalian coal fields. How could German industry possibly operate without coal? For all these reasons—economic, historic, political, and moral— "Germany cannot consent to a cession of Upper Silesia."[10]

This flat statement having been made regarding their eastern frontiers, the Germans turned to the matter of the western frontier, where they made a case regarding the Rhine which was, if anything, stronger than that for the Polish borders.

For reasons of their own, the French vigorously opposed concessions to Germany in the matter of the Polish frontiers. But they absolutely refused to consider any treaty alteration in the matter of their own common frontier with Germany, now reestablished on the Rhine for the first time since the Napoleonic years. The Rhine frontier meant safety; it was a natural and easily fortified obstacle which could be made almost impassable by destroying the bridges. Nor did its advantages end there. The territory to the west of the Rhine included Alsace and Lorraine, the vast coal fields of the Saar, and five and a half million Germans in the remainder of the Rhineland area.

The recovery of Alsace and Lorraine posed, of course, no problem to France. Their case was surely legitimate. They had, it was true, once been German. Their populations spoke German as well as, perhaps even better than, they did French. But ever since the reign of Louis XIV, when the provinces had begun to come under French rule, the people of Alsace and Lorraine had become, as they themselves were proud to say, "more French than the Parisians."

In the peace which followed the Franco-Prussian War, the Germans extracted Alsace and Lorraine from France and thus pushed France completely off the Rhine. The people of the provinces had not wished to be annexed by Germany. When given the opportunity to vote for their own representatives, they immediately elected fifteen delegates who, to a man, protested their loss of French citizenship. But in that Bismarckian era, and in the Prussian kingdom, the desires of subjects carried little weight.

In the years which followed, the German government was unable to define its relationship with the people of Alsace-Lorraine. Ulti-

mately Berlin adopted the position that Alsace-Lorraine was populated by recalcitrant and potentially mutinous subjects who, by
reason of their French past, deserved nothing better than a thinly
disguised military occupation. The inevitable result of this policy
was that the people of these provinces grew rapidly to detest
Prussian rule. Although they spoke German, in their hearts they
were more than ever French. During the years 1871–1914 only
twenty-five Alsatians became officers in the Prussian Army. The
provinces' representatives in the Reichstag usually voted against
increases in the German military budgets, and in World War I the
conscripts from Alsace-Lorraine made the worst soldiers in the
German Army—disloyal, insubordinate and with a high rate of
desertion to the enemy.

The French, of course, had never given up hope for the eventual
restoration of these "plundered provinces." It was perhaps the only
political goal which united all Frenchmen. Over the years the
Alsace-Lorraine question had become much more than just a point
of dispute between two neighboring powers. It so obviously dis-
rupted the peace of Europe that it was widely recognized as an
object lesson and a constant warning for future peacemaking. Every
Allied power realized that justice demanded the restoration of
Alsace-Lorraine to France. Wilson's eighth point required that "the
wrong done to France by Prussia in 1871 in the matter of Alsace-
Lorraine . . . should be righted." There could be no doubt whatever as to what this meant, especially since Germany was compelled
to evacuate these provinces at the time of the armistice.

Thus there should have been no argument from the German
treaty delegation about the legitimacy of restoring Alsace-Lorraine
to France. Nonetheless, Germany repeatedly protested that four
fifths of the populations of Alsace and Lorraine spoke German
(which was quite true) and demanded that at least a plebiscite be
held to determine their wishes. And whatever the outcome of this
plebiscite, the German counterproposals of May 29 demanded compensation for German state property—mines and railroads in particular—which France was seizing in the provinces.

The Allies fell upon these German protests with righteous, almost
gleeful, wrath. In their replies they pointed out that Germany herself had never troubled to conduct a plebiscite when she annexed
Alsace-Lorraine in 1871. Regarding German state property in the
provinces, Germany was reminded that when she had annexed
Alsace-Lorraine in 1871 there had been no compensation to France

for mines and railroads. Now the territories were being restored to France under exactly the same terms. The Allies flatly declined to make any adjustment in the draft treaty with regard to these provinces.

The outcome of the Alsace-Lorraine question could scarcely have been more satisfactory to France. Her allies had given every support to this great goal of French policy. France's frontiers had been advanced to the Rhine, or at least to a part of the Rhine. She had the iron mines of Lorraine, and her population had been increased (and Germany's decreased) by two million persons. Despite the fact that the population of Alsace and Lorraine were tied by language and racial heritage to Germany, they obviously preferred to be citizens of France. This example was profoundly significant to the French government and particularly to the French Army. They found no difficulty in concluding that the remainder of the German Rhineland might well be seduced into accepting French citizenship. But in this maneuver they were to find many obstacles—the most formidable of which were not France's enemies but her allies.

The Saar Basin is a broad valley which lies immediately to the north of Alsace-Lorraine. Geographically it is not large, comprising about seven hundred square miles, but in terms of population it is sizable. In 1919 more than 650,000 persons lived in it. Technically the Saar Basin was only a part of the German Rhineland, but, for a compelling reason, the territory had long managed to preserve a separate identity. The reason was that the Saar Basin was a valley of coal. Its mines, estimated at seventeen billion tons, comprised nearly a quarter of the total known German coal reserves. The Saar Basin alone contained more coal than was to be found in all of France.

The Saar Basin had not always been German. Like the rest of the Rhineland, its ownership had fluctuated between Germany and France. But, unlike Alsace and Lorraine, the Saar could not be described by the French as a "plundered province." The valley had been German until the time of Louis XIV, when the French King, coveting the territory, had established several "courts" to determine whether or not the Saar was properly part of his kingdom. These French courts had returned a favorable finding in such haste that it was almost embarrassing, and Louis had felt obliged to return the verdict to the courts for a few months of additional study before the findings were reannounced.

The French had occupied the Saar for only a few years when they were forced to disgorge it. Later Napoleon seized the area, but it was subsequently given to Prussia by the Congress of Vienna. Under Prussian sovereignty the basin prospered. The ownership of the coal mines was in the hands of the Prussian state, which sent in a series of able and energetic administrators to manage them. The mine workings were extensively developed, and the miners were admitted into the extensive Prussian system of social security. Within the space of a single generation practically all the French in the basin either moved out or became thoroughly Germanicized.

By the turn of the twentieth century it was impossible to argue that the Saar was anything but German. In its entire history it had been French for only twenty-three years. Even in their wildest dreams it had not occurred to Frenchmen that the Saar would be "restored" to France. But with victory and the reestablishment of French sovereignty over Alsace and Lorraine, the prospect of French ownership of this rich valley became a distinct possibility. France had always suffered from a lack of coal, and the matter had been made more acute in the course of the war when the Germans had flooded the mine workings in the parts of France which they occupied. The French claimed that it would take many years to restore them to production, and in the meantime France's already insufficient coal production would be cut by fifty per cent.

On March 28 a special French delegation had waited upon the Council of Four in order to present France's case for the Saar. Its members bore with them a memorandum describing the background to the French demands, which were, in essence, that most or all of the Saar Basin should be turned over to France, together with its mines, factories and people. For the benefit of Woodrow Wilson a thin web of legitimacy had been spun over the demand. The French memorandum assured the Council of Four: "There exists even today in the Sarre Basin a strong middle-class and peasant element passionately attracted to French tradition."[11] For good measure, it was noted that upon the occupation of the Saar by French troops some of the population had dispatched a friendly telegram to the President of the French Republic. It was alleged that in 1865 the German Kaiser had been "very coldly received" on a visit to the Saar.[12] Since this was the best case that could be made for self-determination, the French rightly anticipated a struggle with Woodrow Wilson.

The first person to speak after the French delegation had concluded was Lloyd George, who took a vague and evasive position on the matter of the Saar. While agreeing that the French were entitled to receive coal from the area, he did not accept, nor did he really reject, the idea of actually giving the mines or the people to France.

The American President was the next to speak, and his views were more forthright. By all means, Germany should be compelled to deliver coal from the Saar to France, but as far as the land and its people were concerned Wilson was adamant. The Saar Basin was obviously German territory. Its population was certainly German and clearly wanted to remain so. The French had never mentioned the "return" of the Saar as one of their wartime aims, nor had it been one of the Fourteen Points. To bring it up now was to inflict an outrage upon prostrate Germany. It would create an eternal and justifiable point of dispute. Wilson reminded the French that the experience of Alsace-Lorraine cut both ways: it should be a warning to France as well as to Germany. He recognized only one test for the acquisition of territory by one nation from another—the "self-determination" of the people involved. And in the area in question the French had no case whatever. The United States would never assent to French annexation of the Saar Basin. With this the meeting adjourned, but Clemenceau served notice that France did not accept Wilson's pronouncement as final—"We shall soon resume this discussion."[13]

That very afternoon Clemenceau met with André Tardieu and Louis Loucheur, his principal advisers in the matter of the Saar, at his office in the Ministry of War. Faced with the opposition of Woodrow Wilson and the equivocal hostility of Lloyd George, they found that their position was, in Tardieu's words, "not promising."[14] The three Frenchmen swiftly worked out a method designed to circumvent the objections of their allies. First, as a great concession on their part, they would ask that France be given the bulk of the coal from the Saar Basin. They anticipated no argument on this; Wilson and Lloyd George had already agreed to it. Once this was settled they would move on to their next point. France would claim that in order to make sure of deliveries from the Saar in future years, the peace conference must find a way to prevent the Germans from slowing down coal production, sabotaging the mines or otherwise breaking their agreement. The only way that that could be done was by "setting aside" German sovereignty in the area in favor of a League of Nations mandate, which would be awarded to France. Thus the substance of French sovereignty over the Saar would be attained; only the form would change.

To fully appreciate the crisis into which the Saar dispute plunged the peace conference, it is necessary to recall that it was only one of a whole series of enervating questions: the Rhineland, the claims of the Poles, the reparations to be extracted from Germany and the secret treaties. All of these controversies, occurring more or less simultaneously, came at the time when the health of the American President had begun to fail and when his influence had declined enormously.

As for the French, the Saar dispute coincided with what were interpreted by the French Parliament, the French Army, Raymond Poincaré and the French right in general as a series of French defeats at the hands of Wilson, whom they thought oversolicitous of Germany's "rights" at the expense of France.

The meetings of the Council of Four which followed the March 28 introduction of the Saar question degenerated into unseemly wrangles. Wilson, while immediately agreeing to give France the coal from the Saar, refused the French demand for setting aside German sovereignty over the region. He saw clearly what this would lead to. The attacks on Wilson in the French press grew more savage daily. Clemenceau now permitted himself the use of the slashing invective which had earned him the nickname "the Tiger." He called Wilson "pro-Boche" to his face,[15] and the two men exchanged threats to quit the conference. The French would not budge from their demands. They must have the Saar coal mines, the land in which they lay and the people who worked them. Lloyd George vacillated. He too was opposed to giving the Saar to France, but he proposed nothing better than a series of complicated schemes which contributed little to the matter. Wilson called his advisers around him and announced, "I do not know whether I shall see Monsieur Clemenceau again. I do not know whether he will return to the meeting this afternoon. In fact, I do not know whether the peace conference will continue."[16] And shortly thereafter Wilson collapsed.

When the American President arose, much had altered. The poor communications within the United States delegation had resulted in House's having appointed Charles H. Haskins to work out some sort of compromise in the Saar matter. This had been done, and the outcome was a plan whereby France received *temporary* sovereignty over the Saar, subject to a plebiscite conducted at a later date. The British agreed to the arrangement. This left Wilson alone—unsupported by his own delegation, at odds with the British, enfeebled by illness and beset by a horde of other conflicts. He capitulated. The draft treaty which was presented to Gemany included this provision: "As compensation for the destruction of the coal-mines in the north of France and as part-payment towards the total reparation due from Germany for the damage resulting from the war, Germany cedes to France in full and absolute possession . . . the coal-mines situated in the Saar." Having been compelled to give away the mines, Germany was obliged to give up her sovereignty over the basin "in favor of the League of Nations, in the capacity of trustee." After a period of fifteen years, there was to be a plebiscite to determine whether or not the people of the Saar desired to remain a quasi-independent state, to return to Germany or to become citizens of France. If they decided to return to Germany, Germany would be obligated to purchase the coal mines from France at a negotiated figure, payable in gold.

The French were quite rightly elated with this "compromise." They had the mines of the Saar, and it was clear that France would be the *de facto* ruler of the Saar Basin in whatever form it might be. The only thing they had not gotten was the permanent ownership of the basin and its people, but even this was a possibility. Fifteen years was a long time. France had reserved the right to permit any person in the Saar to elect French citizenship—an attraction which was thought certain to produce a strong voting nucleus at the time of the plebiscite. And if it appeared that this was not enough, a vigorous policy of labor recruitment from within France proper should provide sufficient votes to tip the balance. Various means could surely be found to make the lives of German miners unpleasant enough so that they would tend to emigrate. And even if the plebiscite finally went against France, the treaty required that Germany must buy back the mines *at once* and with gold. If she failed to do so, the treaty stipulated, the entire Saar Basin would immediately become part of France. This was the trump card, for it was expected that the Reparations Commission would make sure that Germany had no gold to pay the price France would demand for the mines.

The implications of these treaty provisions did not escape the German peace delegation. Six days after they received the draft treaty the Germans dispatched a note which castigated the Allies' demands in the Saar as a "primitive and disproportionate form of restitution."[17] Three days later they delivered a note which proposed that Germany provide guaranteed contracts for the delivery of coal to France. They offered to insure the deliveries by turning over shares in German mining corporations to France. The rage which these proposals concealed did not have to be emphasized to the Allies. The German press itemized it all: No one had ever mentioned the Saar in the exchange of notes which preceded the armistice. Was it not the grossest injustice to separate from Germany a territory which contained 650,000 persons who by every test would prefer to remain German if they could? Was this "self-determination"? Was this a "peace of justice"?

The abashed Allies could only attempt to justify the Saar provisions on the grounds that no other arrangement "could give to France the security and certainty which she would receive from full exploitation and free ownership of the mines of the Saar."[18] With this every German counterproposal was rejected. Only one concession was made: over violent French objections, the Allies modified slightly the excessive requirement that if the plebiscite went against France, Germany must pay in gold or forfeit the Saar. Instead they agreed to permit Germany to pay in any manner acceptable to the Reparations Commission; if Germany failed to pay within one year, the Reparations Commission could sell the mines to settle the account. The French objected to this vehemently, but by this time the British and the Americans had grown adamant. France had won her case in Alsace-Lorraine and the Saar; now the position of the "Anglo-Saxons" had stiffened in its turn. In the matter of the third French prize, the remainder of the Rhineland, the French were to suffer a setback which brought the Army to the point of open revolt against the Clemenceau government.

The controversy over the German Rhineland was rooted in a major difference between France and her British and American allies. To the French nothing could be more certain than that Germany would someday attack France again. The only safety lay in preparation: France must build up her loyal alliance of Eastern European nations and reduce German power in every conceivable manner. This would weaken the next German invasion. But there was one concession which would guarantee France against the sort of devastation which the recent war had brought to her, and that was the German Rhineland. Placed on this easily defended river bank, the French could hold off a much larger German army indefinitely. And even if the Rhine was breached, the French could at least retreat through the Rhineland.

To Woodrow Wilson and to Lloyd George this was archaic and self-defeating. To give France the Rhineland, with its five and a half million Germans, would create such rancor that a permanent peace would be impossible. It would not guarantee the safety of France; instead, this monstrous Alsace-Lorraine in reverse would positively guarantee a German attack upon France. With this argument they rejected every French plan for the severance of the Rhineland from Germany. As early as December, 1918, Lloyd George had refused to discuss with Foch the incorporation of the region into France. When the peace conference opened, both Lloyd George and Wilson had declared flatly against another French scheme by which the Rhineland was to become an "independent" state linked to France under a military union. Wilson had, to be sure, greatly compromised his principles in the matter of the Saar, but in part this concession was a bargaining counter against the large issue, the Rhineland itself.

Clemenceau finally settled on the best bargain he could get: a fifteen-year Allied occupation of the Rhineland, their withdrawal to be contingent upon Germany's meeting her reparations obligations. The final settlement also compelled Germany to demilitarize the Rhineland permanently—never to station troops or build fortifications in the region—and to demilitarize the east bank of the Rhine to a depth of fifty kilometers. The British and the Americans also agreed to recommend to Parliament and the Senate that treaties of guarantee with France be concluded by which they would come to France's aid if she were the victim of an unprovoked attack. Clemenceau could wring nothing more from the Allies in the matter of the Rhineland. As it was, both Lloyd George and Wilson agreed to the fifteen-year occupation reluctantly. If France had pressed beyond this, the peace conference would surely have broken up.

But only Clemenceau and his closest associates understood this. Poincaré, the Horizon-Blue Parliament and Foch believed that Clemenceau had given way too easily to the Allies. Upon learning of the bargain which Clemenceau had struck, Foch demanded that a special Cabinet session be held to debate the matter. Poincaré, who detested Clemenceau, was glad to oblige, and so, on April 25, it was held. It opened with a warning from Clemenceau that he would permit the presence of Foch only in a consultative capacity. If the Marshal attempted to take part in the discussions of the Cabinet, Clemenceau himself would leave the room. Foch then interrupted to demand that minutes be kept of this meeting, for there would

come a time when "we shall all be accused of treason"[19] for the
government's failure to safeguard the Rhine. Clemenceau refused
and called to the Cabinet's attention the fact that the Rhineland
occupation was not to end until the Germans satisfied their reparations obligations. Clemenceau said that he did not think the Germans would be able to do so, and added, "In fifteen years, if you do
me the honor to come to my tomb, you may say to me, I am convinced, 'We are on the Rhine, and we stay there.' "[20]

This was not good enough for Foch. He stormed out of the meeting in a fury—but not before he had carefully gathered up some
sheets of paper bearing a handwritten memorandum of the session,
made by his chief of staff, General Weygand. Observing this, Jules
Cambon, a French peace-conference plenipotentiary, chided him,
"Ah, Marshal, you collect your little papers." In a rage, Foch shot
back, "I keep them, M. Ambassador, and I advise you to do the
same."[21]

He did not let it end here. In the French-occupied sector of the
Rhineland, Foch's generals, notably Charles Mangin, hastened the
completion of a plan designed to force the issue with the Allies as
well as with Clemenceau. They located an obscure German official,
Dr. Hans Adam Dorten, whom they put at the head of a plot to
conduct a political *coup d'état*, declare an independent Rhenish
republic and appeal for French protection. In the meantime Foch
did everything within his power to delay or obstruct the completion
of the treaty with this odious Rhineland settlement. In late April he
even refused to transmit the summons from the Allies for the Germans to dispatch their delegation to Versailles, an insubordination
of so gross a character that the Allies nearly dismissed him as their
commander in chief. Clemenceau intervened and extracted a half-
hearted apology from the Marshal, together with a promise of better
behavior in the future. The promise was not kept.

At the end of May news came back to Clemenceau of the Army's
plot in the Rhineland. The French Premier instantly dispatched
Jules Jeanneny, his Undersecretary of State, to the Rhineland in
order to interrogate the French commanders there. Jeanneny had
barely returned with his report when, on June 1, Dorten proclaimed
an "independent republic" with its capital in Wiesbaden, in the
French sector.

The first news of this coup received in Paris came from the
French army of occupation, which, circumventing Clemenceau,
optimistically telegraphed directly to the sympathetic President

Poincaré; "The Rhine Republic was proclaimed in all cities without difficulty. . . . This event, which ends annoying uncertainty, appears desirable to the majority of population."[22] Just who constituted this "majority of population" is uncertain, unless it was the French generals, whose troops had to be called out to suppress anti-separatist rioting and strikes by the outraged Rhinelanders. Dorten himself was of little help. Immediately after the proclamation of his government, he and his "Cabinet" took refuge in the Wiesbaden City Hall, where he could think of nothing better to do at this critical hour than dictate a long memorandum dealing with the restoration of the University of Mainz.

Within hours the dreary little charade played itself out. Clemenceau, infuriated at this near-mutiny among his generals, sent Jeanneny back to the Rhineland to demand that Dorten be turned out. Sullenly the generals obeyed. A French Army colonel strode into Dorten's headquarters, flicking his riding crop against his boots, and announced to the President of the "Rhineland Republic," "Let's go! It's all finished."[23] And finished it was. Dorten and his Cabinet disappeared into obscurity. °

Quite naturally, the German delegates at Versailles pounced at once upon this attempted coup. On June 3 they dispatched a special note to the Allies demanding that they "clarify the incidents" and "see to it that the military authorities of the occupying powers in the Rhine district should at once and very earnestly be shown the danger . . . in their ill-directed zeal."[24] The Allies could find no suitable answer, but among themselves they now viewed Foch with heightened suspicion, for they correctly suspected that there would be more plots by the forces of the French right which the Clemenceau government could not control.

As substantial as their territorial losses were in the east and the west, the Germans found that the Allied demands did not end there. Germany's northern boundary with Denmark had been disputed

° There seems to be no doubt that Konrad Adenauer, then the burgomaster of Cologne and a prominent political figure in the Rhineland, took a leading (although cautious) role in the encouragement of Rhenish separatism. He was in frequent contact with Dorten and certainly did nothing to discourage Dorten's efforts (see King, Jere Clemens, *Foch versus Clemenceau*, pp. 32–37). Clemenceau in his *Grandeur and Misery of Victory*, published in 1930, states flatly (p. 209) that "the Burgomaster of Cologne, Herr Adenauer, had become the leader of the movement." Subsequently, in 1956 Adenauer denied any connection whatever with the separatist movement (see King, p. 33).

ever since the territories of Schleswig and Holstein had been seized
from Denmark by Austria and Prussia in 1864. As part of the Treaty
of Prague in 1866, Prussia had bound herself to conduct a plebiscite
among the inhabitants of northern Schleswig to determine whether
or not they desired to be part of Prussia or to be restored, together
with their land, to Denmark. Because the overwhelmingly Danish
character of northern Schleswig's population made it certain which
way they would vote, Prussia had taken good care never to hold the
plebiscite. As time went by, the whole matter had become so complex that, as Palmerston said, only three men in Europe had really
understood it—and one of them had died, another had gone mad
and the third, Palmerston himself, had forgotten what he knew
about it. Nevertheless, at the request of Denmark the Paris Peace
Conference decided to resolve the problem.

It was a strange question to come before the peace conference.
Denmark had been a neutral during the war and had made a conspicuous, but wholly understandable, attempt to placate the German power on her borders. This same caution now manifested itself
in Denmark's attempt to regain certain parts of Schleswig. In contrast to Germany's other neighbors, now carelessly clamoring for
pieces of the defeated nation's territory, Denmark refrained from
pressing any claim which was even faintly excessive. While she was
anxious to regain the Danes she had lost fifty years before, she was
most careful not to claim any territory that was not positively and
overwhelmingly populated by Danish-speaking persons who gen-
uinely desired to regain Danish citizenship. She went so far as to
insist that for plebiscite purposes the area be divided into three
regions, descending southward from the Danish border; the northern-
most of these plebiscite regions was expected to vote overwhelmingly for reunion with Denmark, the next was thought to be questionable, and the southernmost was considered to be inhabited in
the majority by loyal Germans.

In all of the negotiations which led to these plebiscite arrangements, the Danes manifested a high degree of responsibility. They
did not want any significant German population within their borders. In fact, they began to fear that many Germans in the plebiscite
regions might vote for Danish citizenship to evade the rigorous consequences of the peace treaty. Thus, when the draft treaty was
presented and Germany protested that the plebiscite areas were too
generous, the Danes swiftly agreed. They now feared that they
would be awarded German territory through some voting fluke, and

they asked the Council of Five to eliminate the southernmost of the plebiscite regions. This amendment to the draft treaty was one of the very few concessions which were allowed.

The prospect of a union, the historic *Anschluss*, between Austria and Germany had been anticipated by the people of both nations ever since November of 1918, when the Austro-Hungarian Empire had collapsed into separate nations, leaving, in the space of a few weeks, only the remnant which was German-speaking Austria. It seemed obvious that the next and final step in the dissolution of the Hapsburg empire was for Austria to unify with Germany. Austria sent delegates to Weimar to consult on the shaping of the German constitution, and the German government even named a special Cabinet member to prepare for the *Anschluss*, which was thought to be only a few months away.

It was, of course, recognized by both governments that not every Austrian desired to become part of a greater Germany. Many Austrians feared Prussian militarism. Others pointed out that Austria had never been regarded by the victors with the hatred they exhibited toward Germany; surely an easier peace could be won by an independent Austria? Nevertheless, if a plebiscite had been taken in Austria during the spring of 1919, the nation would almost certainly have elected to become part of Germany.

The Allies had begun the peace conference with little thought of Austria. There had been some initial support given for a "Danubian Confederation" of nations, which would include Austria and would be a counterweight to Germany on the south. But then it had occurred to the Allies that Austria might ultimately lead this confederation into a union with Germany. This prospect was so alarming that the whole Danubian-Confederation idea had been abandoned. But what was to be done with Austria? The French and the Italians were found to have many proposals. The Italians claimed the South Tirol on the grounds of military necessity, and Woodrow Wilson himself, in a move which he later admitted to be ill-considered, led the movement to award this Austrian territory to Italy. Now Austria was reduced to somewhat less than seven million persons, but still the Austrian problem did not go away. The French were absolutely opposed to a union of Germany and Austria, since it would make Germany even larger than she had been before the war and would further increase the disproportion between the populations of Germany and France. The other Allies found it difficult to argue against this view. But how should this obvious violation of the Allies' own supposed principle of self-determination be disguised in a suitable manner? Finally, late in April, an indirect method was hit upon: Germany was to "acknowledge and respect strictly the independence of Austria within the frontiers which may be fixed in a Treaty between that State and the Principal Allied and Associated Powers."

It seemed like the perfect answer. It was made very clear to the Austrians that a particularly favorable treaty would await them on the basis of strict independence. Accordingly, on May 14 an Austrian peace delegation arrived at St.-Germain-en-Laye to conclude a separate peace. Their reception by the Allies was singularly cordial. The Austrians, the lesson of Brockdorff-Rantzau's denunciation of the Allies before them, went out of their way to be gracious. The head of the Austrian delegation, Chancellor Karl Renner, made a nice little speech of gratitude for the warmth of his group's reception and profusely apologized for his own regrettable inability to speak French. The French responded in kind with a notice to the inhabitants of St.-Germain to behave courteously toward the Austrians. On June 2, when the Austrian draft treaty was handed over, Chancellor Renner was described by Allied observers as having "made a very favorable impression." He received the treaty with a genial reference to the victors as "this illustrious tribunal, the world's highest authority" and continued almost obsequiously, "We came to receive peace at the hands of the victors."[25] To the fury of the Germans, the Austrians were promptly accorded the privilege of face-to-face negotiations with Allied plenipotentiaries.

This Allied strategy toward Austria was immediately successful. The Austrians, seeing the way events were leading, withdrew their delegates from Weimar and accepted without demur Allied protection of Austrian "independence." The Germans protested that they could not agree to "permanent recognition of the independence of Austria," on the grounds that Austria might desire to unite with Germany someday; this treaty requirement was "contrary to the principles expressed by President Wilson." The Allies, however, had no difficulty in drafting a rejection of this German protest, which was easily made to seem an attempt on Germany's part to acquire additional territory at the expense of a small neighbor.

Apart from the territorial losses, the sections of the treaty which most dismayed the Germans were those dealing with the matters of reparations and financial settlements. Wilson had announced in his speech of February 11, 1918, that at the conclusion of the war there would be "no annexations, no punitive damages, no contributions." The speech was one of the "subsequent addresses" to which the Germans had referred in the exchange of notes between Germany and the United States before the armistice. To be sure, this sweeping statement had been somewhat modified by two more specific Wilsonian points: that the "invaded portions" of France were to be "restored" and that Belgium was likewise to be "restored."

These limitations had not been welcome to the other Allies. The tradition of European wars had been that the loser paid an indemnity to the winner. Nobody, in the past, had seen a moral problem in this; the victor had simply taken all that could conveniently be seized. The Germans were particularly successful in the matter of indemnities. Following the Franco-Prussian War they had extracted from France an indemnity which amounted to twice the cost of the entire German wartime expenditure. This indemnity had been an attempt by Bismarck to impoverish France permanently, and it had failed only because Prussia had failed to calculate the value of France's very large overseas investments, which were sold to pay the indemnity. It was certain that Germany would not have repeated this mistake had she won the World War. From 1914 up to the Ludendorff Offensive in the spring of 1918, Germany's leaders had repeatedly promised that the defeated enemy would pay for every German suffering and sacrifice. *Vae victis*—"Woe to the conquered"—had been the German cry. Had Germany won, the consequences to France and Britain would have been ruinous; the Treaty of Brest-Litovsk had shown that.

The governments of France and Britain were only a little behind Germany in promises of indemnities to be extracted from a defeated enemy. During the war there had seemed little point in disclaiming any intention to extract whatever could be gotten from Germany. Indeed, if anyone had said that it was impossible to wring the costs of the war from a defeated foe, he would not have been believed. The British people had been allowed to imagine that Germany would be made to compensate Britain for the immense expenditures which had impoverished the world's wealthiest nation. The French had been encouraged to believe that so much would be extracted from Germany that she would be enfeebled and impotent for several generations. Neither government had seen fit to advise its constit-

uents that there was a limit to the amount which could be gotten
from Germany. Nobody wanted to hear that. Nor had the French
and British people paid much attention to Wilson's statements.

Although the French and British governments were committed to
the morally unassailable position announced by Woodrow Wilson,
there were certain ways in which the American President's Points
could be modified. At the time of the pre-armistice exchange of
notes, Lloyd George and Clemenceau insisted that Wilson warn
Germany that compensation would be expected "for all damage
done to the civilian population of the Allies." And they inserted a
vague statement in the armistice document itself that "any future
claims of the Allies and the United States remain unaffected."

With this wedge, however slender, the French and British delegations arrived at the peace conference prepared (indeed, compelled)
to do battle for all that their electorates expected in the matter of
reparations. Somehow they had to broaden the basis on which
reparations were to be charged, while at the same time avoiding the
"indemnities" or "punitive damages" which they had foresworn. One
loophole was the pre-armistice stipulation that Germany must pay
for all civilian damages. The American delegation was forthwith
treated to a spectacular course in the determination of what constituted damage done to a civilian.

The Allies found the American position stoutly defended by first-
class opponents—men such as Vance McCormick, Bernard Baruch,
Norman Davis, Thomas Lamont and John Foster Dulles were the
United States representatives on the Committee on the Reparation
of Damages—but, despite their brilliance, they were outvoted. The
stipulations and agreements which had seemed so specific before
the conference began were now found to be leaky vessels indeed.
Lord Sumner, a famous British legal authority, and Lord Cunliffe,
governor of the Bank of England, were members of the British delegation. They were savage in their demands. The British Empire
demanded reparation for all of Britain's wartime expenditures, on
the ingenious grounds that British civilians had had to pay them
and that they were thus "damages to civilians." When the appalled
Americans rejected this, the British demanded that the Germans at
least be required to pay the cost of interest on the British internal
debt which had been built up during the war. The cost of sunken
Allied merchant vessels (which were, after all, mostly civilian-
owned) was added up and included in the demands. The British

threw in the cost of pensions to disabled soldiers (who were, of course, now civilians) and to dead servicemen's widows.

The French presented their own bills. That Germany would pay for the "restoration" of devastated France was assumed to be a foregone conclusion, although the task was one of such magnitude that the French refused even to guess at its cost. But in addition they now proposed an ingenious scheme of "indirect damages" involving compensation for the financial losses of a wage earner, both to himself and to the economy, during the time in which he was mobilized in the Army. The French conceded that they could not expect to be paid this all at once. It would be acceptable for Germany to make payments over a period of thirty, forty, fifty or even a hundred years. But, of course, they would insist that the Germans pay interest on the outstanding debt—which might double or triple the original sum.

Before the incredulous American delegation, the amounts which the Allies demanded grew so fantastic that no one could really calculate them. And still the French Parliament demanded more, and the British Parliament echoed it.

But there was a practical limit. The limit was Germany's capacity to pay, though nobody could agree upon what this capacity was. A series of British financial experts had tackled the problem and had come up with estimates ranging from eight billion dollars all the way up to a fantastic 120 billion dollars—a figure which certainly exceeded the value of the entire German national wealth, which the Americans estimated at about 75 billion dollars. The French declined to consider the question seriously. It was not their problem. Let the Germans pay what was owed, no matter how long it took and no matter how Germany was impoverished.

The United States delegation kept pointing out that the maximum amount which could be gotten out of the German economy, even over a period as long as thirty years, was only a small fraction of what the French and the British (not to mention the Italians and the Belgians) were claiming. For even while the Reparations Committee was sitting other committees were busy stripping Germany of her colonies, her overseas investments, her chemicals, her transatlantic cables and every one of her merchant vessels of more than sixteen hundred tons, still others were taking away the Saar, Alsace-Lorraine and the Polish provinces, and another committee was requiring Germany to pay for all the costs of the Allied occupation of the Rhineland. With all this capital investment gone, how could Germany possibly pay the fantastic reparations bills? The only certain source of reparations was approximately five billion dollars' worth of German shipping, gold reserves and overseas investments. The Americans, joined now by certain astute Allied financial experts such as John Maynard Keynes of the British delegation, pointed out that the only way Germany could even begin to make these huge payments was for her to dump manufactured goods on the world market at ruinously low prices for as long as her raw materials held out. Then she would be bankrupt and ruined. Did the European Allies really want this? Surely the ruin of Germany would be the prologue to the collapse of the entire European economy?

As the force of this argument gradually became apparent, an element of sanity was restored. In private discussions with American delegates Lloyd George finally admitted that the real problem insofar as he was concerned was to somehow defend himself from the hysterical expectations of the British public. He confessed to House that it was now obvious to him that Germany could not possibly pay reparations even remotely approaching the size which the British Parliament anticipated.[26] House suggested that Lloyd George return to England, face his Parliament and tell them that he had discovered that Germany really could not pay very much. It was easy advice to give, but Lloyd George was sure that he would be flung from office instantly. Instead, a more subtle plan was developed. Lloyd George could not return home with a small amount in reparations; he could, however, return with nothing at all, if only he could claim that there was a prospect of large reparations to be made by Germany at some unspecified time and in unspecified amounts. He could then tell his Parliament that the reparations question had been so complex that no final determination had been possible at this time. During the many months it would take to work the reparations matter out, the British public could gradually be prepared for the sad truth.

This was the way out. The draft treaty compelled Germany to pay to the Allies five billion dollars in gold before May 1, 1921, together with sizable deliveries of coal, chemicals, river barges and practically the entire German oceangoing merchant marine. Meanwhile an Allied Reparations Commission was established. This commission was to calculate the total which was owed and, by May of 1921, was to meet with German representatives to arrange for payments, which would be spread out over a thirty-year period.

The Americans were not pleased with this compromise. To be sure, in two years' time rancor toward Germany would have cooled considerably and any payments which were required of Germany would necesarily have to take into consideration her capacity to pay. Nevertheless, they thought it preferable to set a fixed and reasonable amount at once. This would be a goal for all Germans to strive for. They would work hard and pay off the debt rapidly, and Europe would prosper in the process.

The French, of course, refused to accept this argument, with its implication that France might not get all that was coming to her. They ignored the American claims that France could not prosper if Germany was ruined economically. The French could scarcely conceive of a happier circumstance than to have Germany sunk deep into debt to France, with a French army of occupation on the Rhine to enforce payment. They declined to recognize that the treaty's reparations clauses represented a compromise. They refused to concede even privately that France might get anything less than full payment.

When the draft treaty was presented to the Germans, their reaction was all that could be expected, for they were being compelled to sign what was in essence a blank check: they were obligating themselves to accept in advance any amount which the Reparations Commission might determine. The Germans protested that when they had agreed to be responsible for "damages to civilians" they had not imagined the possibility of stupendous "indirect damages." As counterproposals they offered to restore the ruined parts of France and Belgium and to make a definite cash payment, spread out over a period of years and without interest on the unpaid balance.

The last of the three provisions that most shocked the Germans concerned the question of war guilt. As a preface to the treaty section on reparations, the Allies had attached one short paragraph, known as Article 231. To the Allies it had seemed innocent enough. All it said was: "The Allied and Associated Governments affirm and Germany accepts the responsibility of Germany and her Allies for all the loss to which the Allied and Associated Governments and their nationals have been subjected as a consequence of the war imposed upon them by the aggression of Germany and her Allies."

It is unfair to say that this section had been drafted casually, but certainly no one had foreseen its ultimate consequences. In fact, the peace conference's Committee on the Reparation of Damages had not even thought of including it until the French suggested that it might be well to introduce the whole subject of reparations with some sort of statement to establish the moral justice of the claims. The other Allies had thought this a good idea, and the clause had quickly been drafted, inserted and forgotten. Thus, when the Germans received the draft treaty, the Allies were astonished to find that this particular paragraph was the most violently disputed point in the entire treaty.

In note after note, the German delegates protested this "war guilt clause," which they found outrageous. The perplexed Allies studied the paragraph. They were sure that they had said nothing about war guilt, only war "responsibility"—although the Germans apparently regarded the two as much the same thing. And, by honest coincidence, this article was immediately preceded by Articles 227–230 in another section of the treaty. These articles dealt with "penalties" and imposed requirements upon Germany which, by the time the Germans had been given the treaty, were conceded to be mistakes. In the penalties section of the treaty the Allies announced their intention to bring the abdicated Wilhelm II to trial for "a supreme offense against international morality." This project had been a favorite of Lloyd George's who felt himself committed by his electorate to bring the Kaiser to London for trial. The other Allies had been somewhat apprehensive about the wisdom of this, but went along with the British—especially when it was clear that the Dutch government could be relied upon to refuse to surrender the exiled Emperor, and that the question was thus academic. Another article in the penalties section compelled the Germans to hand over for Allied trial any Germans whom the Allies might have "accused of having committed acts in violation of the laws and customs of war."

The Germans protested these articles, too, but they gave special attention to the refutation of Article 231, which seemed to them to be a continuation of the penalties section and thus a general indictment of the German people as criminals. There was nothing hypocritical in the German indignation over this "war guilt" article. Wartime propaganda and censorship had convinced the German people that they had been attacked by czarist Russia and that the German invasion of France had only forestalled a French invasion of the Fatherland. Most Germans believed that the war was the consequence of a monstrous conspiracy against Germany directed by her jealous enemies. The view of even the most knowledgeable German officials differed only slightly from that of the people. They regarded the war as a tragic historical accident for which Germany was no more responsible than anyone else. They granted that there had been serious defects in the German political system, but who was to say that Russia's, for example, had not been worse?

On May 10 the German delegation at Versailles handed the Allies a note announcing that Germany considered herself neither "solely nor chiefly to blame for the war."[27] They had learned that the Allies had set up a "Commission on the Responsibility of the Authors of the War and on the Enforcement of Penalties," and they asked for a copy of the report of this commission. This was, of course, just the sort of thing which the Allies were determined to avoid. They had no intention whatever of involving themselves in some tedious wrangle over wartime responsibility. Anyway, the German responsibility for the war seemed self-evident to the Allies. They replied that the commission's report was of an "internal character" and could not be transmitted. The Germans answered this on May 28 with a lengthy submission, drafted by a committee of German historians and political experts, which blamed the war on Russia and made the not altogether illogical demand that if Germany was to be compelled to acknowledge her guilt for starting the war, she should at least have the opportunity of defending herself. The Germans proposed that some sort of independent "commission of inquiry" be set up to investigate the matter and render an unbiased report regarding Germany's war guilt.

The Allies now perceived that this single treaty article had grown to an importance which no one had even remotely anticipated. Although they were themselves convinced of Germany's war guilt, they had no intention of submitting the matter to a neutral court and pleading their case like common litigants. It suddenly dawned on them that upon this unobtrusive and unregarded article the entire Allied case revolved. They had all talked so much of the "moral rightness" of their cause that were Germany to be found not guilty, or guilty under equivocal circumstances, the moral position of the victors might collapse. They would gladly have cut Article 231 out of the treaty, except that too many people now knew of its existence, thanks to the Germans. To abandon it now would imply that the Allies had agreed Germany was not responsible for the war. No Allied government could possibly return to its inflamed electorate after having made such a concession.

There being no alternative, the Allies refused to discuss the matter further. In lieu of explanations, they felt compelled to go even further, and they told the Germans that the war "was the greatest crime against humanity and the freedom of peoples that any nation calling itself civilized has ever consciously committed."[28]

For nearly three weeks the German delegates sat idly by in Versailles, waiting for a final Allied answer to their comprehensive counterproposals of May 29.

Each of the Allied notes received so far had been a categorical refusal to consider any change in the draft treaty. Sick at heart, the Germans now waited for the final note, which they were sure would be little different from those which they had received before. Like the hapless pickets of a small trade union outside a busy store, the Germans found themselves reduced to trudging in a circle crying, "Unfair! Unfair!" to indifferent passers-by.

Although the Germans could not know it, their notes had not been quite so callously received and answered as appearances seemed to indicate. The succession of German protests, observations and counterproposals had had a cumulative effect on at least one man—David Lloyd George. The German arguments had now begun to make an impact upon the British Prime Minister, whose quicksilver temperament permitted an almost instant reversal of position without apparent embarrassment or fear of self-contradiction.

He had not arrived at this pass on his own. The convictions of General Jan Christiaan Smuts, Minister of Defense and plenipotentiary of the Union of South Africa, had helped. Smuts was an unusual personality. Cold, aloof and devout, he had once been the sworn foe of Great Britain. As a young man he had led one of the famed commandos of the Boer War. But once his cause was lost and he had sworn allegiance to the British King, Smuts was superlatively true to his salt. The generosity of the British peace treaty with the Boers had made it easy for him to forget old hatreds. During the World War he had spent much of his time in London, where his advice made him greatly valued for his clarity and foresight. More than the representatives of the other British dominions, Smuts had managed to divorce himself from the parochial view. He stood for the best interests of the British Empire as a whole. Further than that, Smuts's reputation for having been right when most others were wrong had grown to the point where his counsel could not be ignored. The opinions of this highly influential man were certain to receive the immediate and considered attention of Lloyd George and the entire British cabinet.

On May 22, at the height of the exchange of notes between the Germans and their conquerors, Smuts wrote a comprehensive letter to Lloyd George. As a man who had not so long ago been an official of a defeated nation, Smuts was sensitive to the plight of the vanquished. His letter to Lloyd George was reasonable—and filled with forebodings.

He began with the somber warning that the Rhineland occupation was a certain source of future trouble. He painted a dark picture of the tensions and troubles which were sure to result. He pointed out that, because the Germans were required to pay for the costs of the Allied armies of occupation, the French could (and, Smuts thought, probably would) garrison practically their entire Army in the Rhineland, thus compelling Germany to meet most of France's military budget. Even the fifteen-year limit on the Rhineland occupation was a delusion, for under the provisions of the treaty the occupation was to end only when Germany had satisfied all the various other requirements of the treaty! And Smuts was certain that this was absolutely impossible. The reparations demands alone were ridiculous. He said that even the "short-term" payments of cash, ships, coal and chemicals were too much. The Allies would "kill the goose which is to lay the golden eggs."[29] Smuts went on to point out that, with Germany having presumably lost the coal mines of Upper Silesia to Poland and the coal of the Saar to France, and being required to make huge reparations deliveries from the Westphalian fields, it was very unlikely that German industry would have enough left to operate. This, Smuts warned, was not justice; it was not even intelligent planning. Future reparations payments could not possibly be extracted from a blighted German economy which did not have enough coal to fuel its factories.

On the matter of Germany's eastern frontiers, Smuts castigated the "enlargement of Poland beyond anything we had ever contemplated during the war." Poland was "a house of sand," and her present frontiers represented "a cardinal error in policy which history will yet avenge."[30] The penalties section of the treaty was equally unworkable, Smuts wrote. How could Germany be expected to agree to hand over for trial any German that any one of the Allies might subsequently name? It was absurd. Just as absurd were the military clauses. He warned that to reduce the German Army to 100,000 insufficiently armed men was to invite internal revolt.

Smuts's final criticism was reserved for what he stigmatized as the "pinpricks—the whims of minor officials which should not remain in the Treaty in its final form."[31] Typical of these were the various boards which the treaty established the regulate the internationalization of major rivers and railways, most of which ran principally through Germany and upon which German representation was either small or nonexistent. Smuts urged that the treaty be culled through to remove these offensive and unnecessary articles.

In sum, Smuts warned, unless the treaty was thoroughly revised the Allies would soon regret having forced Germany to sign the document at the point of a bayonet. "The final sanction of this great instrument," he wrote, "must be the approval of mankind."[32]

A week later he followed this letter with one to Woodrow Wilson. It is a curious document, for in it Smuts seems to accuse Wilson of having forgotten or abandoned the principles of "your Fourteen Points." He pleaded for the revision of the treaty, candidly conceding that the Germans did "make out a good case" in the notes to the victors. Smuts concluded with the flat statement that the present treaty was "against the letter and spirit" of Wilson's Points.[33]

Surely Woodrow Wilson must have read this gratuitous remonstrance with a certain wry amusement. It told him nothing which he had not believed all along and for which he had not fought, frequently alone, for week after weary week. But the Smuts letter was of particular interest to Wilson because it explained the anxieties which seemed suddenly to have gripped Lloyd George at the daily sessions of the Council of Four. The American President described the British Prime Minister as being in "a funk—a perfect funk."[34]

It was quite true. On Sunday, June 1, Lloyd George took the most unusual step of abruptly summoning to Paris practically the entire British Cabinet. In company with the plenipotentiaries from the British dominions, they shut themselves up in the conference room of Lloyd George's residence on the Rue Nitot, where they debated for two whole days.

The Prime Minister opened the meeting by summarizing the German notes, together with such replies as the Allies had so far made. Smuts then took the floor with a sweeping condemnation of the draft treaty. It was now apparent that the South African's warnings, together with the German arguments, had made a deep impression upon Lloyd George. He revealed himself to be suddenly shaken and apprehensive. He acknowledged that without doubt the Allies had the power to compel the Germans to sign any treaty they might present. But first there was a very practical question which had to be answered. What if the present German government refused to sign the treaty and resigned in a group, to be replaced by a government composed of either sacrificial lambs or arrant opportunists, whose signatures on the treaty would mean nothing? Such a German government would be powerless to carry out its undertakings. There would be endless crises as the French, sucking the British in by treaty obligation, sought to compel a reparations payment here, a proof of disarmament there, or an evacuation some other place. Central Europe would be in a perpetual ferment, in which Britain must constantly be involved. She would be compelled to maintain a large peacetime army, which she could not afford, in order to compel Germany to abide by treaty provisions for which she cared nothing.

And what if no German government would sign the treaty? The Allies would be forced to declare the armistice at an end, begin an immediate invasion of a prostrate Germany, and eventually either govern Germany themselves or dictate a treaty in Berlin to some sort of government scraped together for the occasion. The practical consequences of such a move were apparent to Lloyd George. For all the vengeful fury of the British people, it was doubtful that they would support the remobilization of their Army. There was even some question as to whether the British Army would permit itself to be remobilized.

In January the British detachments at Calais had mutinied, and for a period of nearly two days they had controlled the city. Two divisions of British infantry had had to be sent back from the Rhineland to surround Calais and reduce their comrades in arms to order. On February 8, in London, three thousand British soldiers waiting at Victoria Station for transport to the army of occupation in Germany had suddenly rebelled and marched in a mob to Whitehall. Leaders had risen spontaneously among them and had begun to dictate terms to the astounded staff of the London Command. A battalion of the Grenadier Guards and two troops of His Majesty's Household Cavalry had finally gotten them back to Victoria Station and off to Germany, but it had been a close thing. The thought of such troops now being mobilized and launched onto a prostrate nation where they would be compelled to put down insurrections, to

fire on strikers and to witness the slow starvation of women and
children gave pause to every member of the British delegation.

The attitude of the British Prime Minister, supported by the
reasoning of Smuts, was contagious. The group discussed reparations payments. Lords Sumner and Cunliffe, the British reparations
commissioners whose insistence upon immense long-term German
payments had earlier bordered on the outrageous, sat silently by
while their associates now came to the conclusion that it would be
better to demand a smaller lump sum instead.

Regarding the Rhineland occupation, the delegation suggested
that fifteen years was too long; two years would be enough. In the
matter of Germany's eastern frontiers, it was generally agreed that
Poland had been too greedy, "had behaved quite abominably and
had mismanaged her affairs."[35] The consensus was that there must
be a plebiscite in Upper Silesia; in fact, it might be well to cut back
the Polish frontiers in many areas without even bothering about
plebiscites. As for Germany's admittance to the League of Nations,
the British were now in favor of letting her in at "an earlier date
than now specified in the Treaty."[36] There was, in fact, a considerable sentiment for opening direct face-to-face negotiations with the
German delegation.

By the time the two-day meeting had adjourned, Lloyd George
was authorized—indeed, instructed—by his Cabinet to press for a
sweeping revision of the draft treaty. If the other Allies would not
agree, the British Prime Minister was to bring to bear "the full
weight of the entire British Empire, even to the point of refusing
(1) the services of the British Army to advance into Germany, (2)
the services of the British Navy to enforce the blockade of Germany."[37] Armed with this message, Lloyd George appeared that
evening before the Council of Four to face the other Allies.

The British revisionist ultimatum was a drastic one, but in order
for it to mean anything it was necessary to secure the agreement of
either the French or the Americans, and it was abundantly clear
that Clemenceau would tolerate only the most insignificant revisions.

The French now moved with dispatch to head off the British
proposals. Clemenceau himself took the lead in the Council of Four
with a bitter attack on the British position. The Tiger pointed out
that the British were making no effort to placate the Germans at the
expense of *British* interests. They offered no proposals to reduce the
number of German ships to be handed over, or to return Germany's
colonies, or to restore the German Navy, or to remove the restric-

tions on Germany's overseas trade. Instead, it was always at the expense of French interests that concessions were to be made. Clemenceau scoffed at the British fears that the treaty was too harsh. "We know the Germans better than you," he declared. "Our concessions will only encourage their resistance while depriving our own peoples of their rights. We do not have to beg pardon for our victory."[38] Clemenceau even offered to introduce Lloyd George to a group of French women aged fourteen to sixty-five who had been raped by German occupation troops.

Meanwhile the French paid great care to stiffening the backbone of the American delegation against revision. André Tardieu dispatched a note to Colonel House which began, "Very grave mistakes have been made during the past week. There is only just time to change them."[39] Tardieu went on to argue that naturally Germany objected to the peace treaty. Had anyone been so naïve as to suppose that she would *like* the treaty? Of course not. Should the treaty be changed simply because Count Brockdorff-Rantzau found it unjust? "If we change it, we admit that we think as he does. What a condemnation of the work we have done during the past sixteen weeks!"[40] The French position on revision was a simple one: "We will not accept it."[41]

The French attitude toward treaty revision came as no surprise to the British. They had never counted upon French support. It was America upon which they relied for assistance. They knew that many of the members of the United States delegation were actively sympathetic. Certain influential American "revisionists" such as Herbert Hoover and Vance McCormick had actually met to plot strategy with Smuts and John Maynard Keynes of the British delegation. Secretary of State Lansing was known to be opposed to the draft treaty. Under these circumstances, the British believed, it was almost certain that Wilson would make alliance with them.

They were wrong. To their dismay and astonishment, they found that Wilson was unwilling to endure the whole painful treaty-writing process again just to salve the belated conscience of David Lloyd George. He was nearing the end of his ordeal, and nothing would tempt him to begin it again. Moreover, the American President warned his delegation that the entire treaty was now a thicket of compromises. Virtually every article represented either a concession or a bargain which related to another article. Scarcely a single significant amendment could now be made without tearing to pieces the entire treaty. As it was, the completion of the treaty had been

practically a miracle. The Italians had left Paris and had come back
only at the last minute. The Japanese had nearly gone home. The
Chinese probably would not sign. The Belgians had barely been
coerced. And now, at this point, the British wanted to revise the
treaty! It was, in Wilson's view, madness. If a real change were
made, say, in the terms of the Rhineland occupation, all the bar-
gains made with the French would have to be renegotiated. No one
knew where such revisionism might end. It might even result in the
demise of the League of Nations, which Wilson had now convinced
himself would eventually undo the worst excesses of the treaty.

Nor was Wilson convinced that Lloyd George was really prepared
to go the limit. When Herbert Hoover appealed to him to join with
the British Prime Minister, Wilson replied, "Lloyd George will not
stand up against Clemenceau, no matter what he says."[42]

The President's point of view became known at a conference of
thirty-nine members of the American delegation on the morning of
June 3. It was a meeting which was notable for at least two other
reasons: it was the first (and last) general conference of plenipotentiaries and experts which had been held among the United States
delegation, and it took place not in the offices of Colonel House but
in the quarters of Secretary of State Lansing. Only a few weeks
before, such a meeting would unquestionably have been conducted
at House's residence. The significance of this change was not lost on
the American officials, on their European counterparts or, presumably, on House himself.

The meeting was a desultory one. The various British objections
were brought up, inspected and rejected. Then the tired President
summarized his general position to the hearers seated in a circle
about him.

"Well, I don't want to be unreasonable," he said, "but my feeling
is this: that we ought not, with the object of getting it signed, make
changes in the treaty. . . . The time to consider all these questions
was when we were writing the treaty, and it makes me a little tired
for people to come and say now that they are afraid that the Germans won't sign, and their fear is based upon things that they insisted upon at the time of the writing of the treaty; that makes me
very sick. . . . These people overrode our judgment and· wrote
things into the treaty that are now the stumbling blocks. . . . Here
is a British group made up of every kind of British opinion, from
Winston Churchill to Fisher. From the unreasonable to the reasonable, all the way around, they are all unanimous, if you please, in

their funk. Now, that makes me very tired. They ought to have been rational to begin with and then they would not have needed to funk out at the end. . . . Well, the Lord be with us."[43] Thereupon the meeting adjourned.

This lack of support by the United States ultimately overcame the resolve of the British. They obtained a few modest alterations to the draft treaty, but nothing remotely approaching the sweeping changes which Lloyd George and his Cabinet had demanded. The reparations section of the treaty was modified very slightly, and it was agreed that the plebiscite should take place in Upper Silesia. The breaking of this unpalatable news to Paderewski was left to Lloyd George, who did not mind the task in the least.

The question of the Rhineland occupation was partly answered by a letter of agreement signed jointly by Clemenceau, Lloyd George and Wilson. This inter-Allied declaration, which was not made part of the actual treaty, promised that the annual occupation costs which Germany would be required to pay would not exceed sixty million dollars. There was also a vague statement that if Germany proved to be animated by a spirit of goodwill and a sincere desire to fulfill her treaty obligations, the Allies would "be ready to come to an agreement among themselves for the earlier termination of the period of the occupation." There were no other alterations of a significant character.

On June 16 the Allies completed a booklet which constituted their reply to the German counterproposals of May 29. It is indicative of Lloyd George's mercurial temperament that he now seemed relieved of the fear that the Germans would refuse to sign. He even lent his private secretary, Philip Kerr, for the purpose of drafting the Allied reply. Kerr, known as perhaps the most rapid diplomatic draftsman in the British delegation—no small distinction among a group whose general level of proficiency in this art was quite high—swiftly produced what amounted to a complete rebuttal to the German note of May 29. From first to last, this Allied reply was a denial that the treaty was unjust in any way or violated the alleged pre-armistice agreement in any way. Extensive quotations from the wartime speeches of each of the Allied leaders were set down to establish their interest in a permanent peace of justice. Each of the German counterproposals was listed, and almost every one of them was rejected. Germany was reminded that she was held responsible for both the outbreak of the war and the "barbarous methods" and "criminal character" under which it had been fought.[44] Regarding territorial losses, the Allied note observed that Germany's own previous practices surely put her in a poor position to complain. It was noted that Germany did indeed have a different type of government now from the one which had begun and had prosecuted the war, but the German people had not brought this new government to power until after the war had obviously been lost, and there was "no guarantee that it represents a permanent change."[45]

This reply from the Allies, said the covering letter which accompanied it, constituted "their last word." Under the terms of the armistice agreement, the Allies herewith required "a declaration from the German Delegation within five days from the date of this communication that they are prepared to sign the treaty as it stands today." In default of such notification "the armistice will then terminate and the Allies will take such steps as they think needful to enforce their terms."[46]

The presentation of the Allied reply to the German delegation was made in an atmosphere of suitable formality. The Allied liaison officer, Colonel Henri, requested the presence of German representatives to receive a communication from the victors. Brockdorff-Rantzau designated representatives, who were escorted on foot by Colonel Henri out of the Hotel des Reservoirs, around the barbed-wire fence, through a crowd of silent onlookers and down a street running alongside the hotel. At this point they were ushered back into a room in the same hotel, where the secretary general of the peace conference, M. Dutasta, awaited them. After an exchange of ceremonial courtesies, Dutasta handed over the Allied reply, together with a single copy of the final treaty. The Germans, with their escort, returned as they had come.

Upon their return, Brockdorff-Rantzau convened a meeting to study the "revised" treaty. They found that there were so few changes that the Allies had not thought it worthwhile to reprint the draft treaty. The revisions had simply been written in the margin with red ink.

Brockdorff-Rantzau made a quick decision. His delegation would at once leave Versailles for Weimar. There was no further work for them here. A small staff was left at Versailles to maintain a channel of communication with the Allies. The acceptance or rejection of the Allied ultimatum was now up to the German government.

The German delegation made its hasty departure that night. The French officials, caught off balance by the abruptness of the German move, had no time to make proper preparations. There were not, at first, enough automobiles to convey the Germans to their train. When these were finally collected, the streets outside the Hotel des Reservoirs were found to be choked with members of the French Ligue des Patriots. There were not sufficient police to clear the way, and as the automobiles pushed slowly through the crowd they were hooted and jeered, rocks were thrown, and the windows of several of the cars were smashed. Some of the German delegates were cut by broken glass.

In this inauspicious manner the Germans took their departure. Before leaving, they had secured the agreement of the Allies to a two-day extension of the time limit for German acceptance. They had seven days to do whatever could be done. By 7 P.M. on Monday, June 23, a final answer must be given.

Chapter Sixteen

The Last Seven Days

Brockdorff-Rantzau permitted his delegation no rest as their train made its way east toward Weimar. Every moment of the two-day journey was taken up with the drafting of the delegation's final report to the Cabinet. No one made any effort to throw a happy light on the "revised" treaty. The delegation's report consisted of a sketch of each of the disputed treaty sections, followed by a commentary on what little had been revised. The document concluded with predictions of the calamities which each would bring to Germany. The delegates forecast that the eventual result of the treaty would be the impoverishment and enslavement of generations of Germans. The odium of guilt for beginning the war would be borne by Germans into perpetuity "in a way that is both hateful and dishonorable."[1]

The recommendation of Brockdorff-Rantzau's delegation was unanimous and clear-cut. The Allied terms were "unbearable" and "impossible of fulfillment," and the German delegation was "therefore firmly convinced that the German government must refuse the treaty."[2] The delegates had debated the possibility of signing the treaty and then telling the Allies that it could not be fulfilled, but Brockdorff-Rantzau had convinced them that this was unthinkable. As a professional diplomat, he believed that a treaty obligation was, or at least ought to be, sacred.

The delegation's report was completed and typed, and was signed just as the train pulled into a Weimar siding on the morning of June

18. Despite the fact that they were exhausted and almost stupefied by lack of sleep, Brockdorff-Rantzau, Giesberts and Landsberg stepped at once from the train and proceeded directly to the palace of the former grand dukes of Saxe-Weimar-Eisenach, where, in one of the drawing rooms, President Ebert, Chancellor Scheidemann and the rest of the Cabinet awaited their report.

Only a few weeks before, the Cabinet which Brockdorff-Rantzau now faced had been unanimous in its support of the Foreign Minister's views on the rejection of the treaty. But by now, only five days before the Allied ultimatum was due to expire, the Cabinet was deeply divided. And this was due solely to the influence of one of its members—Matthias Erzberger.

Matthias Erzberger was at this time forty-four years old. The career which had led him to his present Cabinet post had been brilliant. As a very young man he had been a village schoolteacher. A Roman Catholic, he had become a member of the Catholic Center Party and at twenty-eight had been elected to the Reichstag, where for years he was the youngest deputy. Meanwhile he had risen in his party, until now he was its leader.

It was not through personal charm that he had attained success. He was an ugly little man with stumpy legs and gross features. After meeting Erzberger for the first time, a Hungarian countess exclaimed, "Why he looks just like an ornamental beer cork!"[3] Most people actively disliked him, for the thrust of his ambition and the overwhelming energy which supported it were so raw as to be positively offensive. He was thought by many to be a sinister and malignant figure, an unprincipled opportunist of the most objectionable sort. But there was no doubt of his brilliance. Erzberger was an almost impossible man to best in a debate. His argument was always carefully reasoned and pitilessly caustic. Over the years, German politicians had found it prudent to seek his favor and avoid his enmity.

Had it not been for the fact that the Majority Socialists required the support of Erzberger's party, he would surely never have been invited to join the Cabinet. In the early days of the war, the outbreak of which he had greeted with undisguised joy, Erzberger's Pan-Germanic fervor had been exceeded by no man's. From the Reichstag speaker's table he had contributed an uncritical voice to the ambitions of Ludendorff, and without reservation he had supported the concept of offensive war. Then, in the early summer of 1917,

Erzberger had made a tour of the fighting front, and what he saw there convinced him that Germany could not defeat the Allies. On July 6 he rose in the Reichstag to announce, in a devastating speech, that the promises of Germany's military leaders could not be fulfilled. He said that he had lost confidence in the Supreme Command; he warned that Germany did not have the ability to wage an aggressive war and that she must go over to the defensive, while simultaneously negotiating for the best possible peace terms. Very few German politicians would have been capable of such an abrupt about-face, just as very few German politicians cared to find themselves at loggerheads with Hindenburg and Ludendorff. But Matthias Erzberger proved well able to take care of himself. By the end of the war, the Supreme Command was pleading for his assistance.

As Erzberger had foreseen, it was no unprofitable thing to be known as a political figure who had for some months advocated the ending of the war, and who had been openly critical of the Supreme Command. In November of 1918 he was named to head the German delegation suing for an armistice. As he passed through Spa on the way to the Forest of Compiègne, Hindenburg wrung his hand and, with tears in his eyes, thanked him for undertaking the task.*

In the turmoil which followed the armistice, Erzberger conducted his affairs with conspicuous success. While other men's careers were destroyed, Erzberger trod a careful upward path. He became the unchallenged leader of his Catholic Center Party, altered its clerical image, renamed it the Christian People's Party to conform with the spirit of the time, and captured ninety of the seats in the National Assembly elections of January, 1919. His party, which everyone persisted in calling the "Center," was second only to the Majority Socialists.

When the Scheidemann coalition government was being formed in Weimar, the Majority Socialists did not know exactly what to make of Erzberger. They distrusted his Catholicism; they were frightened of his extraordinary ambition and of his reputation as an unprincipled careerist; they frankly disliked him as a person. But, as the leader of the second largest party in Germany, he could scarcely be denied a seat in the coalition Cabinet, so he was made a

---

* Hindenburg's emotion did not stem from simple gratitude. The Supreme Command had feared that Erzberger might at the last moment decline to undertake the task. If this happened it would obviously be necessary to detail an Army officer for the job; in fact, a general had already been alerted for this duty. Thus, Hindenburg's tears resulted from his thankfulness that an Army officer would not have to head the delegation.

minister without portfolio. It was soon obvious that Erzberger was not going to content himself with that. He demanded, and got, definite responsibilities. Even the Majority Socialists admitted that Erzberger had his uses. He was privately conceded to be the most clever man in the Cabinet.

As the only member of the Cabinet who had ever had any face-to-face dealings with the victors, Erzberger was sent to Spa to supervise the German military delegation to the Allied Armistice Commission. It was generally acknowledged that he did well in this difficult job, but soon afterward he became the focus of disturbing rumors. It was believed that he was in some sort of direct communication with the Allies, quite possibly through the agency of the French "observers" in Berlin, Professors Haguenin and Hesnard. At Cabinet meetings Erzberger seemed to speak with a special authority regarding what the Allies would or would not accept and what their future intentions were. He seemed to have some kind of advance knowledge of the content of the Allied notes and of the Allies' reactions to the German protests. When Brockdorff-Rantzau and his delegation departed for Versailles, Erzberger became even more a factor to be reckoned with. In the absence of the Foreign Minister, Erzberger began to fill his role in Berlin. To the fury of Brockdorff-Rantzau, he proposed that the delegation in Versailles be denied the privilege of drafting the notes which were exchanged with the Allies. He demanded, in part successfully, that "the delegation in Versailles should deal with editing the counterproposals without making significant changes in the Cabinet's decisions."[4]

This was not the only thing which roused Brockdorff-Rantzau's enmity toward Erzberger. During the period of the exchange of notes, the German Foreign Minister began to suspect that the Allies knew what he and his delegation were going to write even before they wrote it. This could only be the result of a leak at Cabinet level. It was suspected that in his various confidential contacts with the Allies Erzberger was giving as much information as he got. Moreover, his approach to the whole question of the peace treaty was so much at variance with Brockdorff-Rantzau's that conflict between the two men was inevitable.

When the treaty was first presented to Germany, the unanimous reaction of the Cabinet was that it was unbearable and could not possibly be signed. Indeed, Erzberger himself described it as a "demoniacal piece of work."[5] He did not content himself with this denunciation, however, but managed to hold a series of private conversations with Colonel A. L. Conger, the United States military intelligence officer who had earlier been in contact with the Supreme Command. Conger and an assistant, Major Frederick Henrotin, journeyed to Berlin for the talks, which were held on May 18 and 19.

The first meeting opened with Conger disclaiming any official sanction for these talks. He stated, as he reported the incident later, that he had come to Berlin of his own volition, "having, as a General Staff Officer, authority to travel anywhere my duties took me, and . . . in consequence I was not speaking officially for any military or diplomatic authority."[6] This customary disclaimer out of the way, the men settled down for off-the-record discussions, facilitated by the fact that Conger spoke fluent German.

Conger lost no time in disabusing Erzberger of any hopes Germany might have for a moderation of the peace treaty. He declared that Woodrow Wilson was in agreement with the rest of the Allies on the matter of the terms, and that the American President fully supported the intention of the other Allies to invade Germany should she refuse the treaty. Conger denied that the United States Army had mainly gone home, and he bluntly warned that large contingents of American troops were available to take part in the invasion.

Erzberger countered by asking about France. Was it not true that the French government was helpless to demand the treaty's acceptance, because its nation would not support the reopening of the war? Conger responded that the situation was quite the contrary. The French people would surely support an invasion of Germany, and in fact the French government was not at all averse to such a prospect. It expected to get a great deal more out of Germany if the treaty was not signed than if it was.

In successive conversations, Erzberger employed the various ruses to be expected of a skillful and experienced negotiator. He implied that he had been visited by French officers and by a British emissary from Lloyd George, to whom he had dispatched a confidential message. He contrived to give the impression that he personally favored acceptance of the treaty, but that the rest of the Cabinet could not be persuaded unless the terms were modified. If the treaty was not altered, the Allies would have to invade Germany. As far as he was concerned, he said, "We will not fight you: do what you please. Come in if you wish and take over the German Government." But he went on to warn that other members of the government might not agree with this course. Perhaps the war would be resumed. He quoted Ebert as saying, "I am not so sure that we won't fight when the time comes."[7]

The American officers showed no apprehension whatever in the face of Erzberger's threats. The United States was determined to insure that Germany signed the treaty, and this determination showed plainly. The only encouragement which Conger gave Erzberger was his private opinion that "the Treaty was interpreted too literally by the Germans, that after signature, and as it became apparent that Germany was doing her utmost to live up to the terms of the Treaty, it would receive more and more a liberal interpretation favorable to Germany."[8]

These meetings made a deep impression on Erzberger. Toward the end of May he appeared before the Cabinet with a stunning announcement. He forecast—quite correctly, as it turned out—that the Allies would completely reject the German "counterproposals," and that any attempt to modify the treaty to a significant degree would be hopeless. Speaking with an air of great authority, he predicted that the Allies were prepared to invade Germany if she failed to sign, and that their strategy, inspired by the French, would then be to break Germany up into its various component states, each of which would be compelled to sign a separate treaty of peace. Erzberger announced that he was now in favor of signing the peace treaty, no matter how impossible its terms. And, to support his reasoning, he handed over to Scheidemann a lengthy memorandum which summarized the position in which Germany would find herself if she did not sign the treaty.

Erzberger's memorandum did not attempt to minimize the consequences of acceptance of the treaty. "The burdens of taxation will be extraordinarily oppressive . . . the [German] East will rise up in arms against the signing of the peace treaty. . . . It is not impossible that a military coup against the government will be attempted." On the other hand, "Bolshevism will lose its appeal . . . , employment will be possible again [and] the blockade will be lifted. The borders are opened and food and raw materials can come into the country again." Regarding the military coup, "the movement will probably fail because of the unreserved longing for peace by the great majority of the people."[9] Above all, the unity of the German Reich would be preserved. If, however, Germany refused to sign the treaty, all would be lost. The Allied blockade would be rigorously applied, and the country would be attacked on both sides—from the east by the Poles and the Czechs, and from the west by the main Allied armies, which would drive a wedge between north and south Germany. All resistance would be hopeless. Germany would be reduced to a state of famine. Bolshevik uprisings would take place in all the major cities.

> Plundering, death and murder would be the rule of the day. In the general confusion, there will no longer be a communications system. The breakup of Germany will follow. . . . The individual free cities will not be able to resist the pressure of the Allied offers to agree to peace terms with them. . . . Smaller German states too would declare themselves independent and seek to establish relations with our opponents. The map of the German Reich would then disappear, and in its place a checkered collection of little states would appear, as has always been the dream of France.[10]

The Allies, Erzberger forecast, would make no effort to administer the affairs of the prostrate Reich. They would just "dissolve Germany and leave the individual parts to look after themselves."[11]

The impact of Erzberger's document was considerable. His personal arguments at the meetings of the Cabinet were even more effective. When various ministers protested that it would surely be a crime to sign a treaty which they had no intention of fulfilling, Erzberger reduced them to silence with the observation "If someone had me handcuffed and was pointing a revolver at me, demanding that I sign a piece of paper on which I promise to fly to the moon in forty-eight hours, then any sane person, in order to save his life, would sign the paper."[12] Erzberger regarded the peace treaty much as Lenin had viewed the equally ruinous Treaty of Brest-Litovsk. The nation must have peace. And if the terms were unfulfillable, so much the better. Eventually the Allies would find this out. In the meantime the world was still turning. Many diplomatic opportunities would present themselves.

In the weeks before the return of Brockdorff-Rantzau and his delegation from Versailles, Erzberger pursued this line of reasoning mercilessly. Gradually, and ominously, all that he had predicted came to pass. The Allies did indeed reject the German counterproposals. The Allies were indeed prepared to invade Germany in the event that the government would not sign the treaty. Consequently, when, on the morning of June 18, Brockdorff-Rantzau appeared before the Cabinet in the grand-ducal palace at Weimar, he found a group of men who were no longer unanimous in their determination to defy the Allies. Some members, like Scheidemann, had adopted the public position that "the hand would wither" which signed the treaty, and they could not now reverse their view, but others were wavering, half convinced that the treaty must be signed. Even President Ebert was thought to have been deeply influenced by Erzberger's arguments, and certain other Majority Socialists in the Cabinet had now obviously been won over by the Center Party leader.

This was deeply distressing to Brockdorff-Rantzau. Not only did he believe that the treaty was so unjust that to sign it would mean the eternal ruin of Germany, but by now he had even managed to convince himself that Germany could force the Allies to revise it. It was only necessary to stall for time. Supposedly only five days remained before the treaty must be signed. By one ruse or another this period of time must be prolonged.

"There are two slogans," Brockdorff-Rantzau told the Cabinet, "which I was up against during the whole of the war: 'Hold out' and 'Time is on our side.' It is these same two slogans, strangely enough, that I now find I must adopt myself. . . . If we can hold out for two or three months, our enemies will be at loggerheads over the division of the spoils, and we shall get better terms. If we sign now, no one will trouble to ask later on whether we signed under duress or not. . . . If we refuse to sign, we shall be in purgatory for a time, for two or at most three months. If we sign, it means a lingering disease, of which the nation will perish."[13]

This was all that Brockdorff-Rantzau had to say. To a Cabinet deeply divided by the influence of Matthias Erzberger, he had offered hope: if they did not sign, perhaps they *could* get a better peace. Refusing to listen to the counterarguments of Erzberger, the Foreign Minister left the room. He walked through the palace, crossed the street in front and wandered disconsolately through a park bordering the Ilm River. As he walked, the debate in the Cabinet continued. Indeed, it was to go on until three in the morning.

Brockdorff-Rantzau had not been the only Cabinet member to leave the room. At about the same time, Gustav Noske had risen and departed for another meeting—one which was as important as that now going on in the palace, and far more ominous.

*   *   *

The attitude of the officer corps toward the signing of the peace treaty was, as the Majority Socialists were forced to concede, a crucial factor in the Cabinet's deliberations. No group had more to lose by the terms of the peace treaty than the German armed forces. Moreover, the officer corps believed that it had been betrayed by the German government, which had made only the most cursory protests against the military clauses of the treaty. According to the reports which the Army received from its representatives on the German delegation at Versailles, Brockdorff-Rantzau had given instructions to his staff that the Allies' military demands should go largely uncontested, in the hope that this could be bargained off against other objections. This precisely confirmed the fears which the officer corps had had at the time of the peace delegation's departure for Versailles. General Groener had foreseen that a Socialist government would not find the preservation of a large Army and officer corps a vital objective. In addition, the Supreme Command knew that the Foreign Minister himself was something of an antimilitarist. During his wartime service as the German ambassador to Denmark, Brockdorff-Rantzau had made quite clear his distrust of such figures as Ludendorff, as well as his conviction that the refusal of the officer corps to face reality and permit a negotiated peace was largely responsible for the position in which Germany now found herself.

Just before Brockdorff-Rantzau and his delegation left for Versailles, Groener had appeared before the full Cabinet in order to make clear the position of the Supreme Command. He urged that the maintenance of a large German Army based on universal conscription be made a cardinal objective of German diplomacy. Groener conceded that the Army had a somewhat reactionary reputation, but this, he said, was not really the point. "Only that government can govern which has military power—that is, a *Staatsgewalt*—behind it. I don't deny that there were a lot of things wrong with the old military establishment, but without power you can't rule. The Supreme Command takes the position that this is not a question of counterrevolution and reaction, but only of sound state power."[14]

Groener had then gone on to sketch out for Brockdorff-Rantzau's benefit the strategy which the Foreign Minister should adopt at Versailles: Germany should propose a general Western crusade against Russian Bolshevism, spearheaded by a strong German Army commanded by its own officer corps. If the Allies agreed to this, they would simultaneously be agreeing to the maintenance of a large German Army. It was as simple as that.

Brockdorff-Rantzau regarded Groener and his proposal with cold disdain. The spectacle of the Supreme Command again dictating foreign policy brought back unpleasant recollections. The Foreign Minister flatly rejected Groener's plan. There was no indication that the Allied governments were interested in committing themselves to a full-scale invasion of Russia, nor did Brockdorff-Rantzau himself feel that the maintenance of a large army should be a principal German aim at the peace conference. Economic recovery and industrial strength were vastly more important objectives. He could not imagine a more unattractive (or less rewarding) prospect at Versailles than arguing in favor of a large German Army.

Later Groener met privately with Brockdorff-Rantzau to renew the discussion. The interview got off to a bad start. "There is danger," Groener said, "of the government showing the white feather."[15] This remark infuriated Brockdorff-Rantzau. He had no intention of accepting either instructions or reproaches from the military. He sent at once for a stenographer to make a record of the conversation and then burst out, "What is the meaning of these charges against the government of which I am a member? If the government is in this awkward position, it is because we lost the war!"[16] The interview broke up in mutual recriminations which neither party forgot in the weeks to come.

This confrontation between the government and the Supreme Command came at a particularly unfortunate moment—a moment when a belief was beginning to sweep through the officer corps that it had been the victim of a *Dolchstoss*, a "stab in the back," by certain faithless and cowardly civilians. Had it not been for this, the argument ran, the German Army would have won the war or, at the very least, would have fought the Allies to a standstill.

Prior to the spring of 1919, the theory of the *Dolchstoss* had been taken seriously only by certain military figures of vast seniority or great conservatism. The war had ended so recently that every German could remember the famine and the intense war exhaustion that had seized Germany at the time. There were plenty of western-front veterans who could recollect without any difficulty the desperate straits to which the Imperial Army had been reduced in early November, 1918—how the Allies came smashing remorselessly forward, chewing up ground faster than the exhausted Germans could entrench, and forcing them into a retreat which narrowly escaped becoming a rout.

Nevertheless, in this period immediately preceding the departure of the German treaty delegation, it became convenient for a great many Germans, especially members of the officer corps, to adopt the comfortable view that their Army would still be fighting successfully had it not been for traitors in the rear. The exact manner in which the *Dolchstoss* legend was born is unclear. One story, perhaps apocryphal, has it that Ludendorff dined with General Sir Neill Malcolm, the head of the British military mission in Berlin, and discoursed excitedly and at some length on how his Army had been betrayed at the crucial moment by the revolutionaries. In an unfortunate attempt to coalesce Ludendorff's rambling account, Malcolm suggested, "Do you mean, General, that you were stabbed in the back?"

Ludendorff leaped at this. "Yes, yes," he cried, "that's it exactly. We were stabbed in the back!"[17]

From then on it became an article of faith among German officers that no less an authority than a British general had admitted that Germany had laid down her arms only because she had been betrayed at home. A neat web of supporting evidence was gathered to substantiate this claim. The western front had never really been broken; the German Army had merely been conducting an orderly withdrawal to more defensible positions when—due to civil riot, naval mutiny and disorder fomented among the troops of the rear— it had been compelled to accept an armistice. Even Fritz Ebert, when welcoming the troops back to Berlin in December, had hailed them as returning "unvanquished from the field." In fact, the legend went on, the Allies themselves had been close to exhaustion, and possibly it would have been Germany's enemies who collapsed had the war continued only a little longer. It was also pointed out that two out of the three officials who had gone to arrange the armistice had been civilians. The blame for Germany's defeat obviously lay on both the civil government, which had panicked at the crucial moment, and the revolutionaries, who had been directly responsible for the panic.

In short order the *Dolchstoss* legend found adherents beyond the confines of the officer corps. Gustav Stresemann announced, "Not the second of October, when Germany's decision to request an armistice was made, but the ninth of November was the death day of Germany's greatness in the world."[18] And even a great number of Germany's working class began to echo this.

Curiously, at this time only the Independent Socialists seem to have grasped the long-term implications of the *Dolchstoss* legend. The Majority Socialists made little or no effort to counteract the tale even though it should have been apparent to them that they would receive the lion's share of the blame. They chose to ignore the *Dolchstoss* charge—with the result that the officer corps was provided with a grievance which, when added to the provisions of the peace treaty, was more than enough to convince the Army that it was the victim of treachery by the civil government.

The military clauses of the peace treaty were worse than even the most pessimistic members of the officer corps had predicted. The German Navy had been a quick and easy victim. In this case, however, few Germans cared much to contest the Allied terms. The Imperial Navy had been hideously expensive to build and had produced nothing but the mutinies which triggered off the November revolution. It was now generally recognized that the supreme imperial folly had been the attempt to outbuild Great Britain in a naval race.

Under the provisions of the armistice agreement, the Allies already had in their hands the most modern elements of the German Navy. Nine German battleships, five battle cruisers, seven light cruisers and fifty destroyers had been interned at the British base at Scapa Flow. There was not the slightest chance that the British would return them. Every German submarine had been surrendered, and in late December, after a tour of German shipyards, the Allied Armistice Commission even demanded sixty-four disabled submarines, which were made seaworthy and towed away to British ports. All submarines found on the shipways in the process of construction were ordered broken up at once, and the Allies made certain that the orders were carried out.

Now, under the naval terms of the peace treaty, the German Navy was to be further reduced to no more than a few obsolescent pre-dreadnought-type battleships, six light cruisers and twelve old destroyers. For the future, the Navy was to be permitted no submarines whatever, its total personnel could not exceed fifteen thousand officers and men, and the largest vessel which could be built was only ten thousand tons. The Allies had no doubt about their ability to enforce these naval terms. The island of Helgoland was to be demilitarized, most of Germany's seaward fortifications were to be dismantled and the Kiel Canal was declared open to the traffic of all nations. In the future it would be nearly impossible for Germany to build a naval vessel of any appreciable size without Allied knowledge.

So, without much protest, Germany agreed to reduce her Navy to a shadow of its prewar glory. The Army was a different matter.

What the exact strength of the German Army was in June of 1919 is somewhat uncertain. The Army contained a number of the larger *Freikorps* units which entered and left the Provisional Reichswehr at the convenience of the Army (or sometimes merely at the convenience of the *Freikorps* commanders), so Germany's formal military strength was constantly fluctuating. But the Army could be considered at that time as controlling about 350,000 men plus between 100,000 and 200,000 troops in the better-organized but still independent *Freikorps*. The intelligence service of the French Army estimated the total German forces organized for warfare at 550,000 men.[19] This was, of course, an almost inconsequential force by the standards of contemporary warfare—especially since the German Army had handed over practically all of its heavy weapons to the victors.

But the Allies had no doubt that within the space of a decade, or at the most two decades, Germany could rebuild her Army into what it had been before, one of the largest and probably the most efficient of all the military forces in the world. New and better weapons could be manufactured in the huge arms factories. The superb German General Staff was still in existence. The cadres of experienced noncommissioned officers could always be recalled to train new levies of German youth. The backbone of the old Imperial Army, the officer corps, was still very much in existence and was prepared—indeed, anxious—to supply the leadership for a reborn Army of awesome size.

The Allies had no intention of permitting this to occur. Brockdorff-Rantzau had been quite correct in his observations to Groener that the retention of a large German Army was not a subject which could be negotiated at Versailles. The Allies had suffered far too much at the hands of the German Army, and had come too close to losing the war, to consider any appeal on behalf of German militarism. The only real questions at Versailles regarding the German military were how *small* an army Germany should be permitted and how it should be recruited—and those were matters that the Allies debated among themselves.

To prepare the treaty terms for the German Army, the Council of Ten appointed in mid-February a Committee on Naval, Military and Air Terms. This committee at first considered simply drafting a requirement that Germany completely disband her Army. But the idea was dismissed. It would be too obviously unjust—and fraught with peril to the Allies themselves. No one, not even the French in this case, was prepared to trust certain of Germany's neighbors—Poland in particular—to resist the temptation of enlarging themselves at the expense of a totally disarmed Germany. To render Germany completely defenseless would be to create a tinderbox. Then, too, the revolutionary uprisings within Germany had demonstrated that she must have an army which, functioning as a heavily armed police force, could put down a major Bolshevik insurrection.

Obviously, Germany must be permitted some sort of army, but what size was it to be? This question, it transpired, could not be separated from the question of how the German Army was to be recruited. The French, whose committee delegation was headed by Marshal Foch, came up with the astonishing proposal that the German Army should consist of 200,000 men and be recruited on the principle of short-service conscription. It was an idea which seemed to be so generous toward the Germans that the British, in particular, could scarcely believe that Foch had proposed it. *

But Foch had an explanation for his proposal which was subtle and surprising. The secret of German military success, he said, did not lie in the size of its trained reserve. This factor was secondary to the manner in which the German soldier was trained. The German Army had always been a power unto itself and had been controlled by the Prussian officer corps, which had succeeded in imbuing its Army recruits with a spirit of ferocious antidemocratic nationalism.

---

* To understand the British confusion it is necessary to recollect the period, beginning in 1806, when Napoleon crushed the army of the kingdom of Prussia. Later, in 1808, as a part of the conditions of peace, the French Emperor required that the Prussians demobilize and henceforth limit their army to 42,000 men—a third of its previous size. This the Prussians were compelled to do, but the great Scharnhorst contrived a clever innovation. The 42,000 troops were not the same men from year to year. Through a process of short-service conscription he trained class after class, dismissing them in turn to a secret reserve and calling up new classes of conscripts. Then, in 1813, when it came time to resume war against Napoleon, the Prussian Army mobilized these trained reserves and at once put into the field a force which was larger by 33,000 men than the size which Napoleon had permitted. Scharnhorst's scheme was later adopted by practically every other European army, but no nation ever made it work quite as well as did the Prussians, its inventors.

Foch claimed that this was the true basis of the German Army's success. The best way to remedy this, the Marshal announced, was to compel the German Army to be opened to all classes of citizens, who would serve only for a period of from six months to a year. The Army would thus constantly be washed through and republicanized by successive waves of recruits who would arrive with democratic convictions and would depart before the cadres had had time to instill in them the old Prussian militarism. The only alternative to this was a long-service, strictly professional army, which, the French claimed, could not help but become a citadel of the Prussian spirit. Such a force would swiftly reach such a pinnacle of efficiency that it could provide the leadership for an instant expansion of a new German Army. It would be, in the words of Foch, *"une grande armée en miniature."*

The weight of the opinion of the General in Chief of the Allied Armies was so overwhelming that the majority of the committee at once accepted the French proposal; only the British objected. With the British apprehensions duly noted, the committee forwarded its draft to the Council of Four for its approval. It happened, however, that this was at a time when Lloyd George was not in Paris, having returned briefly to London, and Clemenceau decided that the military clauses were too important to be dealt with in the absence of the British Prime Minister. To Foch's disgust, Clemenceau tabled the matter until Lloyd George's return.

Lloyd George arrived back in Paris on March 5 and instantly took exception to Foch's proposals. The theory of constant renewal and democratization of a conscript German Army was entirely too nebulous for Lloyd George. The British Prime Minister could only multiply. Two hundred thousand men times ten years would produce a trained German reserve of at least two million men. In twenty years it would be four million. Lloyd George searched for a reason why Foch would advocate such a scheme. Then he struck on it. Foch, Lloyd George suspected, wanted a sizable German conscript reserve because only with this as a threat would the French Army have an excuse for maintaining its own larger, longer-term conscription system, which would soon accumulate a better-trained French active Army and reserve of nearly five million men.[20] The mystery having been solved to his satisfaction, Lloyd George demanded, with no objection from Clemenceau, that the German Army be organized on the basis of long-service volunteers. Each soldier would be recruited for a period of twelve years, and at the end of his service he would not be permitted to pass into a reserve. Officers were to be required to serve for twenty-five years. With these instructions, the Council of Four returned the draft to the expert committee.

French officers on the committee considered the defeat of the Foch proposal a serious affront. Again the Clemenceau government had failed to support its own Army. If they had to accept the concept of a long-service professional German Army, Foch said, this force must not consist of more than 100,000 men. Over British protests that this was much too small a force to protect Germany against invasion from the most insignificant of its neighbors or even from an internal revolt, the demands of the French Army prevailed. Within a short period after the peace treaty came into effect, the German government was to reduce its Army to not more than seven infantry and three cavalry divisions—the whole amounting to not more than 96,000 soldiers and 4,000 officers. No air force was permitted.

No other section of the peace treaty was drafted with anything like the precision of the military clauses. The Committee on Naval, Military and Air Terms set down its conditions to the most finite detail. It began by writing down practically everything which was required to mobilize an army for modern war, and then, using this list as a guide, it prohibited Germany from having such items.

The most important consideration was to eliminate any possibility that a reserve force might be created, either overtly or covertly. Article 177 of the treaty specifically required that "educational establishments, the universities, societies of discharged soldiers, shooting or touring clubs and, generally speaking, associations of every description, whatever be the age of their members, must not occupy themselves with any military matters." The *Freikorps* were not overlooked. There were sweeping prohibitions insisting that no German organization of any type was to be permitted "to instruct or exercise its members in the profession or the use of arms," nor could they have any "connection with the Ministries of War or any other military authority."

The next step was to reduce Germany's stock of arms to the point where she would never have enough to operate on a major scale. As with the numbers of men to comprise the infantry and cavalry divisions, the armament for each force was spelled out to the smallest detail. A total of only 204 field guns and eighty-four howitzers was permitted—figures which allowed each division only a small artillery complement and provided the entire German Army with an artillery reserve of five guns.

A comprehensive table showing the allowed number of machine guns, trench mortars, rifles and carbines was drawn up. In each case the number was too small for modern warfare. The amount of ammunition for these weapons was similarly prescribed. Fifty-six million rounds of small-arms ammunition—a quantity which would be insufficient for any general European war—was the maximum reserve.

Germany was prohibited from owning, manufacturing or importing poison gas, armored cars, tanks, dirigibles and aircraft of any type. All German factories which had been set up to produce such material were instantly to be dismantled or converted.

The Rhineland was to be permanently demilitarized, and, so as to provide a convenient sallyport into the German heartland, all German fortifications on the east bank of the Rhine, to a depth of fifty kilometers, were to be dismantled.

The crowning triumph of German military science, the General Staff, was to be "dissolved and . . . not be reconstituted in any form." Careful steps were taken to limit the number of staff officers allowed to the German Army, in the hopes that this would prevent it from becoming a staff-and-cadre organization for eventual transformation into a much larger army.

The *Kadettenhäuser*, the cadet schools which ever since the eighteenth century had taken in generations of Prussian youth and trained them to be officers, were to be closed down. Also to be closed was the famous Kriegsakademie, where German officers had received advanced military education.

In drafting all of these terms, the Allied military experts did not anticipate that the German Army would cheerfully and honorably undertake its own reduction to one of the smallest armies in Europe. They expected that every subterfuge would be employed to evade the Allies' terms. Thus, Germany was required to provide facilities for an "Allied Commission of Control" which would have the right to go anywhere and see everything that might in any way bear on the disarmament requirements. The Allies were confident that this commission could control the production and the quantities in use of most major weapons, such as field guns. They already knew what the German stocks of these were, and the weapons would be difficult to manufacture in quantity on a clandestine basis. Other items, such as the number of rifles and the amount of rifle ammunition, would be almost impossible to control. In fact, the German Army itself hardly knew how many small arms and how much small-arms ammunition were at large in Germany.

But any evasions which the German Army might be able to make would certainly be inconsequential. The Allied terms were so sweeping that even if Germany resorted to subterfuge on a wholesale basis its Army would still be pitifully small. Germany's western frontiers would still be unfortified and her supply of heavy weapons completely inadequate for war with the Allies. Minor evasions meant nothing. Before the German Army was in a position to resume war on the victors, it would have to recruit and rearm on such an enormous scale, and for such a prolonged period, that secrecy would be absolutely impossible; and should this ever take place, either the League of Nations or the principal Allies would step in.

The German delegation at Versailles made only a halfhearted effort to contest the military provisions of the peace treaty. In part this was because the Allies announced that this German disarmament was only the forerunner of a general world reduction of armaments which would soon take place under the aegis of the League of Nations. In addition, the German delegates soon sensed that Brockdorff-Rantzau had been quite correct in his prediction that these sections of the treaty were not open to discussion. The victors had stated their military terms, and these must be accepted.

The German officer corps, quite predictably, regarded the treaty's military clauses with the most profound horror. To accept the reduction of the German Army to a size which would not do justice to the most insignificant Balkan nation was unthinkable. The officer corps would be reduced to such proportions that it could no longer serve as the exemplar of the German virtues of loyalty, honor and discipline. Besides, with places in the new Army for only four thousand officers, what would the rest of the corps do? The mere fact that the government was even considering the signing of such a treaty was positive evidence of its betrayal of the officers.

The attitude of the officer corps toward the peace treaty was no secret to the civil government and was the source of great apprehension. The Socialist leadership had long since begun to suspect that Ebert's November 9 telephone bargain with Groener, representing Hindenburg and the officer corps, had lapsed. It was surely obvious that Noske did not completely control the Supreme Command, just as it was now apparent that the Supreme Command did not truly control the various elements of the Provisional Reichswehr, the

Freikorps and such armed miscellany as the Iron Division, which was still fighting in the Baltic.

There was, therefore, a very well grounded fear that if the civilian government signed the treaty the officer corps might attempt a military coup at the head of the Provisional Reichswehr and the *Freikorps*. This was much more than just a vague suspicion. Even Matthias Erzberger had warned that when the treaty was signed the government could expect a military insurrection.

With all this in mind, the government leaders came to the conclusion that they must force the Supreme Command to tell them whether or not the Army was prepared to accept the responsibility for defending Germany against an Allied invasion. If the Army was strong enough to defend Germany's borders against invasion, the Cabinet could consider rejecting the treaty. But the Army must first tell them that it would accept responsibility for Germany's defense. Ebert had no intention of signing a peace treaty and having the officers later claim that they could have repelled an invasion. And if the Army was not willing to accept this responsibility, a way must be found to compel the obedience of the officer corps.

The government had one unusual ally in this task—General Wilhelm Groener. To be sure, Groener was no less horrified than the other members of the officer corps at the severity of the military clauses of the peace treaty. Like his brother officers, Groener believed that only the Army could engender the unique kind of spiritual discipline which stamped the German character. There was no officer in the German Army more determined to preserve the officer corps and an army large enough to support it.

But, unlike the majority of the officer corps, Groener was a realist. He knew that the existing German Army could not possibly repel any serious Allied invasion. Moreover, Groener's objective was to preserve the Army, not to destroy it. The conception of a last suicidal battle against the French, the British and the Americans, with the Army perishing in a romantic and glorious *Heldentod*, had no attraction for him. The idea of defending the honor of the officer corps at the price of its absolute destruction seemed pointless to Groener. In addition, he saw quite clearly that neither the Allies nor the German people would tolerate a military coup. Groener was a far more careful student of politics than most of his fellow officers. Germany, as a unified nation, had existed for less than fifty years. She was still a fragile thing. If Germany were to be invaded, he suspected, Bavaria, for one, would instantly conclude a separate peace. Already the Supreme Command had received indication that the Bavarian officers were more than slightly interested in such a possibility, which would restore autonomy to their Army. A recent survey of Bavarian staff officers had reported that only two could be considered reliable "in a greater German sense."[21] Whether the Prussian officer corps was willing to admit it or not, times had changed. The Kaiser was gone and would not return. The officers would have to adjust themselves to a civilian government and prepare for a future in which the Army would be reconstituted within the framework of a democratic state. For the present, the Army had no choice but to accept its subordination to the civil Cabinet. If the officer corps required a focal point for its loyalty, as it apparently did, Groener was ready to give them one. In the figure of Field Marshal von Hindenburg he had prepared a substitute monarchial figure.

In all of this there was not a particle of personal gain for Groener. He foresaw that when his task was done he would be hated and rejected by the very officer corps which he had saved against its will. (Already he was known as the central figure in what was coming to be called "the treachery of Spa"—the events of November 9, when he had been the one to tell the Kaiser that the Army would no longer honor its oath of obedience.) If Groener was successful, it would be at the price of his resignation from the Army. He had already selected a clever and realistic officer, General Hans von Seeckt, as his successor. Groener did not mind the hatred he would reap, for he believed that ultimately the Army would recognize him as its savior.

Since February the Supreme Command had been quartered in the Baltic seacoast resort town of Kolberg. From this headquarters Groener attempted to control the various forces which might be considered to make up the German Army. Groener was not, of course, the titular commander of the German Army. That was the septuagenarian Field Marshal Paul von Hindenburg, who now, in June, still preserved his attitude of almost dreamlike passivity. He signed what Groener placed before him, spoke the little speeches which were written for him and gave audience to whomever Groener suggested he receive. Groener himself said of Hindenburg that "he hardly ever took an active part in the decision which had to be made. He was informed about everything—and waited to see how things would turn out."[22]

This was not, as might be supposed, the simple torpor of old age. Nor was it just that Hindenburg had accustomed himself, both with

Ludendorff during the war and with Groener after the war, to permitting his chief of staff the widest possible latitude. The reason for his lethargy was principally that Hindenburg was still stunned by the role he had played in the flight and the subsequent abdication of the Kaiser, whom he persisted in referring to as "His Majesty, my King and my master."[23] The event had been, as Hindenburg conceived it, an indelible stain on his honor, even though the actual advice to the Kaiser had been left to Groener to give. The Field Marshal ruminated constantly about his "faithlessness" to his monarch, and he imagined that people talked about it behind his back.

The Majority Socialist government leaders were acutely aware of Hindenburg's devotion to the Kaiser, but they were helpless to do much about it. Just as they could not do without an Army, they could not do without the Field Marshal, for it was common knowledge that, as the Kaiser's military "heir," Hindenburg occupied a position of undisputed authority over the officer corps. The government knew that senior officers, when invited to serve the government in any capacity, invariably asked the Field Marshal for his permission to serve the republic. And, so far, this permission had always been given.

Hindenburg remained in his current post only because he had been entrusted with it by the Kaiser, and because he wanted to make sure that the Army made its transition to peace successfully. He referred to his office as a "martyrdom."[24] Nonetheless, he was invaluable to the Army and, in particular, to Groener. The figurehead role which he played was precisely what Groener desired. The dignity of the Field Marshal had always been imposing, and since the armistice it had grown to the point where it was positively overwhelming. Even the most prominent persons were usually afflicted with stage fright when they were ushered into the Hindenburg presence.

Cloaked with this ponderous dignity, uncontaminated with defeat (for the unlucky wartime offensives had conveniently borne Ludendorff's name, whereas the public associated Hindenburg with the glorious defense of East Prussia in 1914), the Field Marshal dwelt serenely above the sordid contentions of day-to-day political life. This was as Groener had planned it. He had determined 'that the Hindenburg legend was to be preserved at all costs. In the Field Marshal's name, Groener had rejected the pleas of the conservative German National People's Party for Hindenburg to head their ballot in the elections to the National Assembly. "The Field Marshal must not be used as an attractive source of propaganda for party purposes," Groener directed his officers. "If the Field Marshal were drawn into party politics, his historical name would acquire a reputation which might estrange him from part of the nation."[25] This was the keystone of Groener's plan. Hindenburg was to be preserved to represent the honor of the Army and the unquestionable dedication of the officer corps to future Germans. No one would be able to assail the aged Field Marshal. He would be a natural hero. His reputation was to be such that no German, of whatever political belief, would wish to attack him. And to preserve this image Groener was willing to sacrifice his own reputation and his own future.

Groener had never believed that the 350,000 men of the Provisional Reichswehr, with whatever else might be added from the *Freikorps*, could resist a serious Allied invasion of Germany. He was well aware, however, that most of the officer corps did believe this would be possible—or at least that an attempt should be made. To Groener this was sheer idiocy. It was one thing to suppress a domestic insurrection by some ill-armed Bolsheviks, or to fight Pilsudski's Polish irregulars in Posen, or to battle a scratch Baltic army of Lithuanians and Letts. It was quite another to contend with a vastly larger Allied army equipped with tanks, airplanes and every other weapon of modern warfare. Against such a force, bursting out of the fifty-mile-deep bridgeheads it occupied on the Rhine, the German Army would have no chance whatever. Even in the east—where the Allies would surely encourage the Czechs and the Poles to make a simultaneous attack on Germany—it was doubtful that the German Army could put up a successful defense.

The only possibility for a successful defense was a levee en masse. If the people were willing to sell their lives, to accept the destruction of their cities and to endure the most catastrophic sacrifices, the country might possibly be defended. Groener was sure that they were not willing.

To prove his point, he had, in the past weeks, dispatched his best staff officers to interview the commanders of the various military zones into which Germany was now divided. Each officer was instructed to obtain the answers to five questions:

   1. *Could the majority of the population be won over to taking up hostilities again?*

2. *Would the population be prepared to defend its local Fatherland?*

3. *Could a vast contingent of volunteers be counted upon?*

4. *What resistance would the population offer to the enemy occupation?*

5. *Is the populace ready and determined to remain steadfast in the face of the personal, economic and political pressure which accompanies an enemy occupation of the country?*[26]

The replies to these questions did not take long to gather. None of the staff officers could find any evidence that the German people were prepared to resume the war. Only in the east could any part of the population be found which was willing to defend Germany against attack. There was no possibility of a levee en masse to raise a huge army. The only Germans who would willingly serve were already in the Army or the *Freikorps*. As for the fourth question, it was the general opinion that the German people were still so exhausted that they would make no resistance whatever to an invasion. In fact, a left-wing insurrection could be anticipated in practically every major city. The cause was utterly hopeless.

On the sixteenth of June—the day the Allies handed over their final treaty and the German delegation left Versailles—Groener was summoned to Weimar to confer with the government. He did not have to leave until the following day, but he foresaw that he would be required to tell the government what the position of the Supreme Command was. He also anticipated the reaction of the officer corps to the acceptance of the peace treaty. So, in one of the few decisions which he had ever asked of Hindenburg, Groener laid the case before the Field Marshal, informing him of the survey and its findings.

Hindenburg, after a long pause, answered evasively. "All the same," he said, "ought we not to appeal to the officers and ask a minority of our citizens to sacrifice themselves to save our national honor?"

Groener had only this realistic reply: "The significance of such a gesture would escape the German people. There would be a general outcry against counterrevolution and militarism. The result would only be the downfall of the Reich. The Allies . . . would show themselves pitiless. The officer corps would be destroyed and the name of Germany would disappear from the map."[27] Then, quite correctly for one in his position, Groener asked Hindenburg for written instructions. What should he tell the Cabinet in the name of the Army?

It is said that the night of June 16–17 was the only time Hindenburg ever failed to sleep. He paced back and forth in his bedroom. In the early morning he handed a note to Groener. With it, Groener says, Hindenburg told him, "In point of fact I agree with you, and I don't mind saying so openly. But I cannot and will not give up those views which have guided me all my life. If the government wishes to know my viewpoint, please give them the following message."[28] The written note read:

> In case of a resumption of hostilities we are militarily in a position to reconquer, in the east, the province of Posen and to defend our frontier. In the west we cannot, in view of the numerical superiority of the Entente and its ability to surround us on both flanks, count on repelling successfully a determined attack of our enemies.
>
> A favorable outcome of our operations is therefore very doubtful, but as a soldier I would rather perish in honor than sign a humiliating peace.[29]

This was not helpful to the government: Hindenburg had left the awful decision to the civilians. Still, it was the closest thing to a definite decision which Groener was going to get—and quite possibly it was as much as he wanted. That night Groener took a train for Weimar.

In the early afternoon of June 18, only a few hours after the arrival of Brockdorff-Rantzau and his delegation, Groener debarked at the railroad station in Weimar. He was immediately driven off to a meeting with General Walther Reinhardt, who occupied the post of minister of war in the Prussian state government.° Although Reinhardt was a Württemberger, in outlook he frequently out-Prussianed the Prussians. The two men had known each other for many years and had almost always been in agreement, but now they were completely in opposition. Reinhardt felt that under no circumstances should Germany sign the peace treaty. Let the Allies invade the nation, let them split it up and make peace with the individual states. At least the unity of Prussia and the honor of the Prussian

° Reinhardt's rank had been raised from colonel to general following his appointment to this post in November, 1918.

Army would be saved. Quite possibly Posen and Danzig could be retained by Prussia, which, Reinhardt claimed, would savagely resist the advancing Allies. And, with Prussia preserved as the core, the German Reich would someday be reconstituted. Reinhardt declared that if the civilian government signed the treaty it would be the duty of the Supreme Command to lead a popular revolt against its acceptance. Hindenburg must put himself at the head of the Army, the *Freikorps* and the Prussian people and, sweeping aside the civilian government, lead a glorious insurrection in defense of the Prussian Fatherland.

Groener refused to have anything to do with such a scheme. The idea that only the Prussian state was really important was in itself repugnant to him. The whole concept of the dissolution of Germany was the antithesis of everything Groener had worked for. He foresaw quite clearly the disastrous consequences of a military mutiny against the government. It would be collective suicide on the part of the officer corps. Either the Allies or the government (or perhaps the Bolsheviks) would smash this rebellion and everyone connected with it. The Hindenburg legend, the officer corps, the General Staff and the entire Army would be destroyed.

As Reinhardt well knew, Groener lacked the authority to commit Hindenburg to any particular course of action. But, as Reinhardt knew also, the Field Marshal relied on Groener for practically every decision—so long as Hindenburg's personal honor was protected. Within these bounds Groener was the voice of Hindenburg, and now he measured his reply to Reinhardt carefully: "Speaking for myself and for the top military leadership, for whose views I am jointly responsible, I refuse all cooperation of this sort in the event that the government signs the treaty. The right to a personal decision must be reserved to the Field Marshal. Of course, if the government does not sign the treaty, and hostilities are resumed as a result, the top military leadership is obliged, as an organ of the government, to assume direction of military operations even though they know the struggle to be hopeless."[30] With this statement the meeting ended and the First Quartermaster General hurried off to join Noske, who had left the Cabinet session in order to consult with him.

The meeting between the two men was held privately, and there is no record of the conversation. All that can be surmised is that Groener told Noske of his discussion with Reinhardt. And it is fairly certain that at this time Groener gave Noske the letter which

Hindenburg had written to the government. Noske read it through and then returned to the Cabinet.

The Cabinet meeting dragged on for hour after hour. The ministers explored every conceivable avenue. What, for example, would the Allied reaction be if Germany offered to sign the treaty except for Articles 227 through 231? These included the "war guilt" clause and the others requiring the extradition of "war criminals" and the trial of the Kaiser. Erzberger, anxious to obtain the treaty's acceptance, interjected that the Allies might well agree to this. But then it was pointed out that, aside from these *"Schmachparagraphen"* (shame paragraphs), there were the matters of territory, reparations and Germany's entry into the League of Nations to be considered.

As the Cabinet debated through the afternoon and into the evening, the ministers became more and more depressed. It all seemed utterly futile. They could not possibly sign the treaty, and yet they could not refuse to sign the treaty. Brockdorff-Rantzau was called back in from his solitary pacing in the park and asked for enlightenment on a few points. He would only repeat what he had said before. Germany must not sign. The Allies would soon fall out among themselves. Germany must hold on. But the other Cabinet members, as much as they wanted to believe this counsel, could not give much credit to these comfortable words. It seemed to them that Brockdorff-Rantzau was grasping at straws. They saw no signs of Allied disunity, and they were sure that the Allies would not grant Germany any further delays.

Then Noske took the floor. He read Hindenburg's letter, with special emphasis on the final sentence which admitted that the Army could not resist an Allied invasion. In the morning Noske had been opposed to accepting the treaty. Now he declared that he still regarded the treaty as monstrous and unbearable, yet what could they do but sign it? Could the Cabinet accept responsibility for the defense of Germany against the Allied invasion? "It's all very fine for us fifteen heroes to sit here and refuse to sign. But behind us there is a nation which is down and out. What is the use of heroics on the part of fifteen leaders in that situation?"[31]

Finally, at 3 A.M. on June 19, a decision of sorts was made. The Cabinet took a series of votes on whether or not the treaty should be accepted. The opposition to signing was led by Chancellor Scheidemann. The case for acceptance was headed by Erzberger. The voting failed to produce any clear solution: the Cabinet was almost evenly divided. Scheidemann made no secret of the fact that if it was decided that Germany would sign, he and his closest associates would resign. Brockdorff-Rantzau reminded the Cabinet that when he originally entered the government he had stated that his service was contingent upon his being able to obtain a peace which would insure the German people a "decent livelihood." Because he had repeatedly declared that to accept the treaty would mean the economic ruin of Germany, Brockdorff-Rantzau also would resign if the vote was in favor of signing.

Finally Ebert declared that, lacking any consensus, the matter must be submitted to the National Assembly for debate and decision. There now remained less than five days before the Allied ultimatum would run out.

Beginning on the morning of June 19, there was a series of frantic meetings at Weimar as the individual political parties caucused to determine their attitude toward acceptance of the treaty. And while this was going on, a group of German financial and economic experts who had been part of the German delegation at Versailles presented to the government their own separate report on the treaty. Signed by some of the most famous and respected names in German finance, the report declared flatly that the Allied economic demands were utterly impossible. "Germany will collapse economically, will be incapable of providing her present population with the opportunity to earn a living, and millions of Germans will die in civil conflicts or will be forced to emigrate to foreign countries where they will live on as embittered and unwelcomed foreigners."[32] The treaty was, they said, the deliberate instrument and proof of "the desire of the Allies to ruin Germany economically."[33]

Meanwhile another event of importance was taking place at Weimar. General Reinhardt had summoned more than thirty senior military leaders to the city for a formal council of war. It was the first such council to be held since November 9 at Spa, when Groener had intimated that the Army would no longer honor its oath to the Kaiser. It was also the first council of war in the history of the Army at which the Prussian King had not presided.

A host of famous names were present: General von Maercker, the officer who had founded the first *Freikorps;* General von Lüttwitz, who had put down the Berlin uprisings; Colonel Heye, the officer who, on November 9, had read out to the Kaiser the report that the Army was defeated; the generals commanding the Provisional Reichswehr in central and eastern Germany; the military governors of Bavaria, Saxony and Württemberg; Admiral von Trotha, for the German Navy; and, of course, Groener and Noske.

Groener had had no part in calling this council of war. In fact, he viewed the meeting with anxiety, for he suspected that its only purpose was to give Reinhardt an opportunity to advance his conspiracy for an insurrection of the officer corps against the government if it signed the treaty. Groener knew his generals; most of those who were gathered for this council would be inclined to follow Reinhardt's lead, especially concerning the honor of the officer corps. The King of Prussia would be present in spirit if not in body.

As the meeting opened, Groener's worst fears were realized. His own influence over these officers had obviously waned substantially in the past few weeks. The assemblage gravitated instead toward Reinhardt, who, as the man of the hour, was proposing a course of action which was precisely attuned to their tradition of Prussian military honor. Several of the generals, particularly those with commands in the east, proclaimed themselves in favor of abandoning western Germany, withdrawing their forces behind the Elbe and sacrificing all else to a savage defense of the ancient Prussian heartland. "This old Prussia," Reinhardt urged, "must be the core of the Reich."[34] In deference to Noske's presence, none of them was so crass as to state outright that the Army would rebel against the civil government, although their intent could not have been more obvious.

Finally Noske himself spoke up. He began with the statement that he too found the treaty utterly repugnant, but, he said, it could not be more impossible than the splintering apart of the Reich which would inevitably result if the Allies invaded. Personally he doubted if Prussia itself could hold out against the Allies on the west and the Poles on the east.

It would be one thing, Noske continued, if they could all count upon a spontaneous uprising of the German people in support of the resumption of the war. If this were the case, he would not stand in the way of war. But, he assured the officers, no such prospect existed. On the contrary, the Independent Socialists and the Communists would quickly rally the workers and bring about a nightmare situation of pacifist strikes and insurrections.

Noske now invited the attention of the council of war to the political situation. The resignation of Scheidemann, Brockdorff-Rantzau and others was expected momentarily, he said. When this occurred, Germany would have no government. Perhaps President Ebert too would resign. What would be done then? Noske had an answer to his own question. It was quite possible that he himself would be asked to form a government, in which he would assume dictatorial powers. But he would do this only if he was assured of the wholehearted support of the officer corps. Archly he declared that there were some "pessimists" who actually believed that if the treaty was signed the officers would refuse to "cooperate" with the government. Noske affected to dismiss this prospect. He said that he knew the psychology of the officers best and he did not share these fears.

This little speech made a deep impression upon the generals. Noske as Germany's dictator! Certainly this was not an unpleasant prospect to them. He was the man who had suppressed the Kiel mutinies, allowed the officer corps a free hand in the recruitment of the *Freikorps* and forced the Provisional Reichswehr Law of March 6 through the National Assembly. None could fault Noske's courage. Had he not marched at the very head of the *Freikorps* column which suppressed the January Spartacist uprising in Berlin? And, more important, he had proved to be gratifyingly malleable. His loyalty to the officer corps was no longer open to question. The thought must surely have flashed into every mind that the Army could scarcely ask for a happier circumstance than to have Noske directing the affairs of the German nation. Even the most brutal peace treaty might become tolerable if this man were to rule Germany. All that was necessary was to pledge their loyalty to Noske.

Groener instantly saw the way the wind was blowing. If it had to come to a popularity contest between Reinhardt and Noske, Groener would gladly support the Minister of Defense. "What weighs most of all at this moment," he now declared, "is to maintain the unity of the Reich. . . . This is why all officers, without exception, have the duty of standing by the Minister. The Supreme Command is determined, for its part, to make common cause with him, come what may."[35]

This, it seemed, was all that it took. The best that the disgruntled Reinhardt could do was to force through a resolution that the government must reject the *Schmachparagraphen*. A few diehard generals supported him in additional demands. General von Below, commanding the Twenty-seventh Army Corps in West Prussia, and General von Lossberg, chief of staff of Armee Oberkommando Süd, announced that their officers and men would refuse to carry out any orders which involved the evacuation of German territory in favor of the Poles. They implied that Groener must expect a wholesale insurrection which the general officers would feel obliged to lead.

Groener accepted none of this. "It is an absurdity to suppose that the generals could assume the political leadership of the movement themselves," he scoffed. "From the point of view of both civil and international law, you classify yourselves as rebels. The Allies will consider you as such and treat you as such."[36] He went on to warn that in the west the Allies had an effective numerical superiority of ten to one over Germany. Even to defend the Elbe, Germany would have to raise more than a million trained troops. Probably even this would not be enough. There was coal sufficient for only ten and a half days. What would happen when this ran out? These were Groener's final words to the council of war. He departed for Kolberg, and Noske left for a meeting of his party.

The impression with which both men left this council of war was that the majority of the generals would obey Noske if the treaty was signed, providing that the *Schmachparagraphen* were deleted and in the hope that Noske would shortly assume direction of the government on a dictatorial basis. There was, to be sure, another meeting of military figures scheduled for that evening. Neither Noske nor Groener planned to attend it, for it was to deal, strictly speaking, with the internal affairs of the Prussian state and would be chaired by Wolfgang Heine, the Prussian Minister of the Interior. It was to be a confrontation between the civilian political leadership of the Prussian state government and the Prussian generals whom Reinhardt had picked for the occasion. The idea, apparently, was that the Army would explain to the civilians the sacrifice which would be required of them when the war resumed.

Groener was well content to let this conference run its course. Reinhardt's diehard generals would find out for themselves what sort of warlike spirit could be expected from the Prussian population. Groener's own survey had already revealed to him what the answer would be.

The afternoon council of war had no sooner broken up than a meeting of the Cabinet began. Appearing before it were representatives of the various states comprising the German Reich. The session did not take long. Each representative was asked to declare whether or not the people of his state were in favor of signing the treaty. The representatives of Prussia and the Hanseatic "free cities" announced their opposition. They were, however, the only ones to do so. Bavaria, Saxony and Württemberg were in favor of signing the treaty on the grounds that to refuse would mean the disintegration of Germany. The Prime Minister of Baden reported that almost ninety per cent of his war-sick population favored signing the treaty. The Hessian Prime Minister guessed that an even higher percentage of his people believed that Germany must sign.

This did little to resolve the dilemma of the Cabinet, which was now so deeply divided within itself that it was obvious that the Scheidemann government could not continue. Even as the representatives of the German states were speaking, there was a constant coming and going of Cabinet members to and from the party caucuses being held throughout Weimar. News came that the two parties of the right, the monarchist National People's Party and Stresemann's conservative German People's Party, had unanimously rejected the treaty. This had been foreseen; in any event, these parties were not represented in the coalition Cabinet. What was truly serious was that the Democratic Party, which held four Cabinet seats, also had voted unanimously to reject the treaty. Even Erzberger's own Center Party had approved it only on condition that the *Schmachparagraphen* were deleted. The Majority Socialists had voted seventy-five to thirty-five in favor of accepting the treaty.

Upon this news the Cabinet itself took a vote on the matter. Erzberger, his two Center Party associates and four Majority Socialists, among them Gustav Noske, voted for signing the treaty; Chancellor Scheidemann, the two other Majority Socialists and the four Democratic Party members voted against. The deadlock was now complete. With a tie vote nothing could be done. At one hour past midnight on that night of June 19–20 Scheidemann handed in his resignation, followed by Brockdorff-Rantzau and the four Democrats. Now, with less than four days remaining before the armistice was to expire, Germany had no government.

On that same night of June 19, the meeting of the Prussian generals and certain prominent political personalities from the east had taken place. As Groener had foreseen, the generals who took part in this meeting were supporters of Reinhardt. They told the civilians present that their troops would not accept the peace treaty, and that the officers would be obliged to join their men in this insurrection in order that the Army should not go leaderless. Thereupon they issued what amounted to an open invitation to the political leaders to arouse the Prussian people in a supporting rebellion against the central government. If the population followed the Army's lead, agreed to a levee en masse and rose up against the Poles, the Allies and the central government, the generals said, there was quite a good chance that Prussia might be left intact. At the very least, the honor of the officer corps would forever be preserved.

The civilians lost no time in enlightening these generals about the essential facts of the situation. They bore out Groener's every prediction. Whether or not the officer corps chose to realize it, they said, the Prussian people had no intention whatever of resuming the war in defense of the officers' honor. In a chorus the Prussian Minister of the Interior, the mayor of Danzig and the representatives from Upper Silesia protested that if the officers thought the people were prepared to endure any renewed suffering they were living in the past. The officials were, in fact, greatly indignant about the whole matter. What right had these generals to propose a revolution against the civil authority? The excuse that the generals must follow their soldiers was so transparent as to be laughable. Let the officers control their troops, the civilians demanded. "Since when," cried Heine, "have the officers regulated their conduct by that of their men? Do the generals obey their troops or the orders of their government?"[37] As for the civilian population, it would have nothing to do with an insurrection.

All this was received by the generals in a stony silence. Things had obviously changed in Prussia. The ritual professions of loyalty, respect and gratitude toward the officer corps were forgotten. The meeting broke up, leaving the two groups somber and embittered.

During all of June 20 and most of June 21 there was no German government. President Ebert was himself on the point of resignation. He had again been placed in a situation in which the awful decision must be made by him. All others had taken the easy road. Hindenburg, admitting that Germany could not withstand the Allies' invasion, had nonetheless given the ambiguous counsel that his soldierly honor compelled him to advise resumption of the war. The nationalist parties, including even the Democrats, from whom much had been expected, had all declined the treaty and thus absolved themselves for posterity of all responsibility. The professional diplomats, Brockdorff-Rantzau and important members of his staff, had resigned. Even the Majority Socialist Philipp Scheidemann had found it convenient to quit. This was all well and good for them—they were all out of it, free from responsibility. For Ebert, the temptation to join them and thereby escape from the misery of this predicament must have been great. To his great credit, he devoted himself to a search for a new Chancellor and a new Cabinet.

At first he considered Noske, whose candidacy was obvious and offered at least some assurance of the support of the Army and the *Freikorps*. But the prospect of Noske as chancellor brought with it other fears. The infatuation of the Minister of Defense for his officers and for the use of military force had by now become apparent to every observer. What good would it have done for Ebert to have endured these months of agony if he placed in power a man who might well abrogate the constitution, dissolve the National Assembly and become a dictator managed by the military? Having overthrown an imperial autocrat, Ebert had no intention of replacing him with a Socialist one.

And as Ebert searched for a suitable figure to form a German government, the last possibility that the Allies would modify their peace terms vanished when the High Seas Fleet sank itself at Scapa Flow.

The bulk of the German High Seas Fleet sailed to Great Britain only a week after the armistice. Five battle cruisers, nine battleships, seven cruisers and more than fifty destroyers had been prepared for the voyage in accordance with strict Allied orders: the breechblocks had been removed from the guns; all ammunition had been taken out of the shell rooms and the powder magazines and sent ashore. With only skeleton crews on board, the vessels sailed to the Firth of Forth, where the Allies inspected them to insure that they were unarmed. Then they were sailed to the immense British naval harbor of Scapa Flow in the Orkney Islands, where they were anchored for internment with their German crews still aboard.

Throughout the months of the treaty deliberations, the rusting German fleet swung idly at anchor. Although the ships were guarded by a large British squadron, few Allied officers ever set foot aboard them. The British Admiral forbade the Germans to lower boats, to send uncensored radio messages or to go ashore. The only contacts which the German fleet had with the rest of the world were the infrequent visits of transport vessels from the homeland and newspapers which the British delivered daily aboard the flagship of Vice-Admiral Ludwig von Reuter, the commander of the German fleet.

But, isolated as they were, all through the winter and into the spring of 1919 these German vessels were the scene of insurrections which duplicated remarkably the events then taking place within Germany itself. Even before they sailed for Britain the sailors had elected a "Supreme Sailors' Soviet" which claimed to be in command of the German fleet, Admiral von Reuter being merely a "technical adviser." They had demanded a special bonus for sailing, which Noske gave them, and even tried to insist that the fleet sail under the red flag—a plan which the officers frustrated with the ingenious claim that a red flag was the international symbol of piracy and that any foreign warship sighting a ship which flew it would instantly open fire.

At Scapa Flow the British refused to recognize the sailors' soviet and insisted upon dealing solely with Reuter and his officers. Understandably, the British were apprehensive about permitting any of their sailors aboard the interned German vessels; on the rare occasions when British officers found it necessary to board the German ships, they were accompanied by marines who were under orders to keep their distance from the German sailors, not to talk with them and not to accept any revolutionary pamphlets.

At its best, Scapa Flow is a bleak and depressing harbor. At its worst, during midwinter, it has daylight only four hours a day. It is so far north that an arctic wind blows constantly. It is always bitter cold. Under these circumstances it was not surprising that among the already mutinous German sailors small insurrections were constantly breaking out. They were suppressed only with great difficulty. On some ships certain sailors formed "White Guards" to contest the rebellions of the "Reds." Reuter was even driven from his flagship, *Friedrich der Grosse,* and forced to transfer his flag to the less mutinous *Emden.* He had to ask the British whether they would provide marines to restore order among the German crews if the situation grew worse.

Finally spring came, the weather moderated, and transport vessels from Germany arrived to ferry home the most rebellious of the sailors. By the middle of June the German crews had been reduced to the point where a destroyer had only a dozen officers and men left aboard. Even a battleship had a complement of only eighty. The British now considered the German fleet completely helpless; it had neither guns nor ammunition, and its crews were so small that they could not even get under way.

In reality the German fleet was not totally helpless. Like the desperately ill, it did retain one prerogative: it could commit suicide. From the British newspapers the German officers had learned that their ships were to be divided up among the victors. The Germans at Scapa Flow now consisted of a hard core of officers and kindred spirits. On June 17 Admiral von Reuter dispatched a secret letter to the officers commanding the German ships. Upon his flying a certain signal from his flagship, the officers were to perform the only act they could to cheat the Allies of their prize: they were to scuttle their ships.

It must have been apparent to Reuter that such a deed would be intensely embarrassing to his government. But, quite probably, he cared nothing for this. What had the Socialist government done for him? Nothing except condemn him and his men to a bitter winter at Scapa Flow and then hand the German Imperial Navy to its enemies. Besides, in these mid-June days Reuter was imperfectly informed of developments at home. It must have seemed quite possible, even probable, that Germany would permit the armistice to expire and compel the Allies to resume the war.

Early on the morning of June 21, the harbor at Scapa Flow presented a sight astonishing to the Germans. The entire British guard squadron except for seven trawlers and a couple of destroyers was weighing anchor and abruptly putting out to sea. From time to time in the past some of the British vessels had gone to sea for a day's training, but never before had the Germans been left practically unguarded.

Reuter had no way of knowing that the only reason the British squadron had put to sea was to get in a day of torpedo-firing practice outside the harbor's mouth. He at once assumed that the British were preparing for the resumption of the war, that their fleet was bound for the German coast and would be used to bombard the seaport cities. From his flagship the German Admiral hung out the signal "Paragraph eleven. Acknowledge." Aboard all the German vessels in the immense harbor, parties of officers raced below and opened the seacocks, smashing the mechanism with sledgehammers so that they could not be reclosed.

The first Englishman to notice that the German ships were being scuttled was a civilian artist sitting in a trawler, sketching the battleship *Friedrich der Grosse*. As he sketched he noticed that the trim of the vessel was slowly changing and that German sailors were lowering boats and throwing seabags into them. The alarm was raised, but there was little that could be done.

At 12:16 P.M. *Friedrich der Grosse* abruptly lurched over and sank. All over the huge harbor the scene was being duplicated. Even groups of German destroyers which were anchored in bays well out of sight of the flagship were sinking. The few British vessels in port were gotten under way and steered for first one and then another of the German ships as their British officers gradually realized the full extent of the sinkings. The crews aboard the German vessels lowered boats and pulled away from the sinking vessels. When British officers ordered them to go back aboard and either stop the flooding or drown, the German boat crews cast away their oars. The frantic British persisted and even fired into the boats and killed a few of the German sailors. It was pointless. By this time no one could halt the flood. The open seacocks were under many feet of water, and the sea was still bubbling in. Recognizing the hopelessness of trying to force the Germans back aboard their ships, the British concentrated upon trying to beach such German vessels as were still in moderately good trim.

At 2:30 P.M. the British squadron came steaming back into the harbor from its ill-timed torpedo practice. By then the affair was largely over. Eighteen German destroyers, one battleship and three cruisers had been beached and saved. The rest, fifty vessels in all, either had been sunk or were capsizing. The oarless German lifeboats bobbed on the bright waters of the harbor, their crews sending up thin cheers as each vessel plunged.

In Weimar on the afternoon of the same day, June 21, with less than two days left before the Allies must be given their reply, Ebert produced a government.

This new German government was not as strong politically as its predecessor. The Democratic Party refused to join the Cabinet, which now consisted only of Majority Socialists and members of the Center Party, which had wavered but had been kept in the coalition by Erzberger's merciless harassment. Theoretically, the coalition of the two parties which formed the Cabinet controlled 240 out of the 423 seats in the National Assembly. But, on the crucial issue of the treaty, it was very questionable whether the government had anything approaching a majority. A great many of the Democrats, as well as the Scheidemann sympathizers among the Majority Socialists, had warned that they would not accept the Allied terms.

Nor was Gustav Bauer, the Chancellor in the new government, an especially commanding figure. He was an experienced trade-union leader and had been minister of labor in the previous Cabinet, but he had never played a dominant role and was not particularly well known. Bauer's selection had been a disappointment to Matthias Erzberger, who could not conceal the fact that he had hoped to become chancellor. Instead he had been named minister of finance, with the additional function of deputy chancellor. The other Cabinet seats went to Majority Socialists and members of the Center Party, none of whom, significantly, was publicly on record as being categorically opposed to the signing of the treaty. Gustav Noske continued to occupy his old post as minister of defense, although he manifested his chagrin at not being named chancellor by behaving in a most independent manner toward his colleagues. He knew that, commanding as he did the support of the officer corps, he was probably the most powerful figure in the Cabinet.

The new Cabinet debated the treaty issue during the evening of June 21. The results of all the meetings with the Army and with the various political factions were summarized. The probable attitude of the Allies was considered. There now seemed no question but that the treaty must be signed. Perhaps it would mean Germany's eventual ruin—but if the government refused to sign, the Allies would surely invade and the ruin would be certain and immediate. How could the government convince the National Assembly of this, and how could a military insurrection be prevented?

Erzberger came up with a plan. He believed that the Allies might well accept a German reservation in the matter of Articles 227–231, the *Schmachparagraphen*. He was, in fact, sure about this. And it now seemed fairly certain that if these particular articles could be deleted, enough National Assembly votes could be found and the Army would not mutiny. This, then, was decided: on the following day the new Cabinet would appear before the National Assembly to demand from it both a vote of confidence and its permission to sign the treaty without accepting the "shame paragraphs."

On the afternoon of Sunday, June 22, the Bauer Cabinet confronted the National Assembly. There was now only one day before the Allied ultimatum would expire. Bauer, wasting no time, announced that he and his government favored conditional acceptance of the treaty: they were prepared to sign the treaty with the exception of Articles 227–231. To support this, the Majority Socialists and the Democrats introduced a resolution stating, "The National Assembly approves of the position of the government in the question of the signing of the peace treaty."[38]

The debate which ensued was violent. On the left the Independent Socialists objected vehemently to the attaching of any conditions to acceptance of the treaty. They held that the war guilt of Germany could not really be questioned, and they cared nothing for the fate of the Kaiser and the Army officers. They would not vote for a motion which limited the acceptance of the treaty and which might subject the German people to an invasion for the sake of the deposed monarch and the honor of the officer corps. The government's motion was thereupon amended to read, "The National Assembly is agreed as to the signing of the peace treaty"[39]—quite a different thing from the original, for it enabled the government to sign without conditions. This did not, of course, go unnoticed by the parties to the right, which rose in rage. Not only did the government propose to sign this treaty, they howled, but it was now preparing to accept even the hateful *Schmachparagraphen.* In response the courageous Bauer flung a challenge in their teeth. If they would accept the responsibility for Germany's government, he would gladly step aside. Exactly what did they propose to do? Exactly how would they defend Germany against the Allied invasion which would begin at 7 P.M. on the following day? Who would put down the insurrections of the war-sick populations of the cities when the Allied offensive started? In short, what practical alternative did the right offer in place of signing the treaty? There was, of course, no answer to such a challenge. The Assembly finally voted 237 to 138 in favor of the government's motion, but with the understanding that the government would attempt to get the treaty amended so as to exclude Articles 227–231.

The voting was actually a closer thing than the figures indicated. In favor of the motion were the bulk of the Majority Socialists, the Independents and Erzberger's Center Party. But the latter group was wavering, and there was a strong possibility that it might renege if the government could not get the five articles excluded from the treaty.

Immediately following the National Assembly session, the German Cabinet dispatched a message through Ambassador von Haniel, its representative at Versailles, offering "to sign the Treaty of Peace without, however, recognizing thereby that the German people was the author of the War, and without undertaking any responsibility for delivering persons in accordance with Articles 227 to 230 of the Treaty of Peace."[40] There was, in these last days, an open telephone connection from Weimar direct to Versailles. As a consequence the German note arrived with amazing promptness. By 7 P.M. that same day, Haniel had delivered it, together with two others, to Colonel Henri. By 7:15 it had been translated from the German and was being read out to Lloyd George, Clemenceau and Wilson, who had immediately assembled at Lloyd George's residence.

If there had ever been a possibility that the Allies might agree to waive the articles to which the Germans objected, there was none now. The news of the scuttling at Scapa Flow had been received that day, and the Allies regarded it as proof of official German perfidy. Lloyd George was particularly angry, and embarrassed as well. The scuttling having taken place in a British harbor, it was already giving rise to certain suspicions that the British, anxious to preserve the dominance of the Royal Navy, had done nothing to prevent it. Wilson drafted a brief note which flatly rejected the German offer. "The time for discussion is past," it said. The Allies demanded of the German representatives "an unequivocal decision as to their purpose to sign and accept as a whole or not to sign . . ." The note warned that less than twenty-four hours remained.

There was no doubt about the Allied determination to march. The German Rhineland was crowded with more than thirty Allied divisions, ready to pour through the occupied bridgeheads. At 7 P.M. on the twenty-third they were to move forward. French Army Intelligence reported that there were no German troop formations in frontier positions and that all railway rolling stock had been pulled back into Germany to a depth of one hundred kilometers. No one knew exactly what this meant, but it was apparent that there would at least be no immediate opposition to the Allied advance.

The plans for the Allies' invasion had not been completed without some difficulty with Marshal Foch, who had proved to be as incorrigible as ever. The week before, on June 16, the Council of Four had summoned Foch and four other Allied generals to brief it on his planning for invasion in the event Germany refused to sign. To their intense surprise, the Council members heard Foch state that his forces were insufficient for a march on the center of Germany. Due to demobilization, the Allied commander in chief claimed, he now had only thirty-nine divisions instead of the 198 which he had commanded at the time of the armistice. And he went on to say that, inasmuch as he had only enough troops to invade a portion of Germany, the Allies must make plans to sign a separate and specially lenient peace with various south-German states, such as Bavaria and

Württemberg. Only with Germany thus dismembered could he invade Prussia and occupy Berlin.

This plan was obviously another attempt to repeat the Rhineland separation scheme, but on a larger scale, and it drew down upon the Marshal a unanimous barrage of rage. In the presence of all, Clemenceau sharply warned Foch "not to intervene in political affairs."[41] The rest of the Council of Four refused to believe that the Allied forces were insufficient to invade Germany. They challenged the French Army contention that the German Reichswehr consisted of 550,000 men, and they forced Foch to concede that the German Army was actually so underarmed that it could not possibly resist thirty-nine Allied divisions. Lloyd George went even further. It was curious, he noted cynically, that Foch had only now elected to advise the Council of Four that he had not enough troops. If this was true, surely he should have come to them before this. The secretary to the Council, Sir Maurice Hankey, whipped out from his large black dispatch case the minutes of the Council's meetings of May 10 and May 11, at which Foch had been present. Lloyd George read them aloud. Foch had said nothing about military inadequacy then. He had, in fact, stated at that time that his manpower was completely sufficient to march on Berlin. It seemed very strange that the intervening few weeks had wrought such a change. If it was a case of needing some more troops, Lloyd George was sure that the British could return a few additional divisions, and certainly President Wilson would delay the scheduled return to the United States of several American divisions.

Under the sarcasm of the British Prime Minister, Foch gave way. He did not exactly mean, he said evasively, that he had too few troops—only that an invasion directed toward the occupation of Berlin might require more troops than he now had. The Council thereupon allowed him to go, and took up the matter privately. It had by now lost all patience with the meddlesome French Marshal. Clemenceau was instructed to sound out General Pétain with a view to offering him the Allied command if he would lead a march on Berlin. In the end this proved unnecessary. Foch acknowledged his military preponderance over the Germans and agreed to do whatever the Council of Four required.

Thus the morning of Monday, June 23, found the Allied army poised and ready for a thrust into Germany which would culminate in the occupation of Berlin. To the east the Czech and Polish armies were similarly prepared for invasions of their own, conforming to the orders of the Allied command. The advance into Germany was to be made in several "bounds" of about one hundred kilometers each. The first two bounds would put the Allied army on the line of the River Weser, about halfway to Berlin. It was anticipated that this would take somewhere between twelve and fourteen days. Here the army would pause and regroup. Meanwhile the Polish and Czech armies would strike for Berlin from the east and the south respectively. In order that all movements should be properly co-ordinated, the Czechs and the Poles had agreed to name Foch commander in chief of their armies. Indeed, the Czechs had gone so far as to turn over to French officers the direct command of all their units of any size. Coordination thus having been assured, the main Allied army was to sidestep to its right, form a line with the Czechs and attack Berlin from the south. In the meantime the Allied navies would resume a close blockade of the German coast. If desirable, they could even steam directly into German harbors to bombard the port cities.

Against all of this, Germany was almost completely defenseless.

The Allied refusal of the conditional German offer to sign the peace treaty was in the hands of the German government at Weimar shortly after midnight on the twenty-third. It was a terrible shock. Erzberger had assured the Cabinet that the Allies would agree to the German exceptions, and, because the Center Party leader had in the past so often been right concerning the Allies' intentions, the Cabinet had half believed, half hoped that he would be right again. Stunned by the refusal, the Cabinet hastily convened in the small hours of the morning and decided that it must again present the matter to the National Assembly, to which it had, after a fashion, pledged that it would sign only without the *Schmachparagraphen*. An emergency session of the Assembly was announced for three in the afternoon—only four hours before the armistice would expire. And then, in the midst of this frantic haste, came appalling news: Noske had defected to the generals, was refusing to sign the treaty, and was carrying with him the entire vote of Erzberger's Center Party.

On the night of June 22–23 Noske had been aboard a train bound for Berlin when he received a message to return to Weimar for the Cabinet meeting. He had come back, but he had not joined the rest of the Cabinet. Instead, in the early hours of June 23 he went to his office, where he received a visit from General von Maercker, the founder of the first of the *Freikorps* and the officer with whose troops Noske had reconquered Berlin in January. Accompanying Maercker was Major von Gilsa, Noske's personal staff officer.

Adopting the role of an old comrade, Maercker now advised Noske that if the treaty was signed without the exceptions he, together with practically every other officer, would instantly resign from the Army, and their example would be followed by every noncommissioned officer and soldier in the *Freikorps*. He pleaded with Noske not to betray the officers. Taking the hand of the Minister of Defense in his, Maercker pledged the personal loyalty of the officer corps if Noske would only let them make him dictator of Germany and reject the treaty. The Army would stand behind him to a man. It would gladly die for him. "For you, Herr Minister," said Maercker, "I would let myself be cut to pieces, and so would my infantrymen."[42]

All this was too much for Noske to withstand. The thought of being lifted to the pinnacle of power upon the shoulders of these nobly born officers was irresistible. He jumped to his feet, pounded the table and, with tears in his eyes, swore, "General, now I too have had enough of this rotten mess!"[43] Grasping Maercker's hand, he promised that he would immediately resign from the Cabinet. It would then be almost certain that the government would fall, the treaty would not be signed, and the Army would be free to appoint its own government.

Maercker lost no further time. It was apparent to him that "Noske's non-soldier's 'soldierliness' had won the upper hand," he wrote later. "I could sense his handshake only to mean his agreement that, under the right circumstances, he would become dictator."[44] At first light Maercker appeared before caucuses of the Democrats and the Center Party, telling them that Noske was now in agreement that the treaty must be rejected and that Germany would fight. The impact of this disclosure was considerable. At noon the Center Party deputies, upon whose votes the acceptance of the treaty hinged, now decided by a ballot of fifty-eight to fourteen that they would not support acceptance. In the meantime Noske appeared before the Cabinet and tendered his resignation on the grounds that to sign the treaty would mean the evaporation of the Army and chaos within Germany.

It was now up to Ebert. If Noske's resignation was accepted, the Bauer government would instantly collapse. Another could not possibly be put together in time. A last-minute appeal to the Allies for additional time had just been rejected. There was only one alternative to catastrophe. Ebert picked up a telephone and was at once connected to Groener at Supreme Headquarters in Kolberg. He spoke carefully. He now required of the Supreme Command its most precise evaluation of the situation. If the German Army had even a small chance of defending the Reich, he, Ebert, would join Noske in his refusal to sign, and Germany would again be at war. But if resistance was hopeless the Supreme Command must tell him so, with the understanding that the treaty would then be signed. Ebert would call back in a few hours to obtain the Supreme Command's reply.

In the ensuing time Hindenburg and Groener paced the latter's office and debated their reply. Hindenburg at last summed it up with the flat statement "You know as well as I that armed resistance is impossible." But, as in the past, he refused to declare himself openly. As the moment for Ebert's return call approached, Hindenburg consulted his watch and walked from the room, saying to Groener, "There is no need for me to stay. You can give the answer to the President as well as I."

Thus when the telephone again rang it was Groener who was left to tell Ebert that resistance was hopeless and that the treaty must be signed. He added that it was his personal belief that even the officer corps would recognize this. There would, in all probability, be no insurrection. When Groener had hung up, Hindenburg reentered the room, walked over to him, placed his hand on Groener's shoulder and, in an abrogation of responsibility which must surely be unique, said, "You have taken a heavy burden on yourself."[45]

That afternoon, using Groener's words as the wedge, Ebert succeeded in convincing Noske that he should remain in the Cabinet.

The Bauer government appeared before the National Assembly, the members of which by now had also heard of Groener's message. They all knew that the catastrophe was imminent: the treaty must be signed. But, like Hindenburg, they could not bring themselves to say it. They passed a devious motion resolving that the Cabinet already had the authority to sign the treaty as the result of the previous day's voting. The German government thereupon dispatched the following note to the Allies.

> *Yielding to overwhelming force, but without on that account abandoning its view in regard to the unheard-of injustice of the*

conditions of peace, the Government of the German Republic declares that it is ready to accept and sign the condition of peace imposed by the Allied and Associated Powers.[46]

German delegates would arrive at Paris to sign the treaty in five days' time.

The German acceptance arrived in Paris at a moment when the Council of Four was meeting in the study of President Wilson's residence. At 5:30 P.M., only ninety minutes before the troops were to march, Colonel Henri burst into the meeting room waving the German message. The Council at once adjourned. The last line of the minutes read, "Orders were given for guns to be fired."[47]

Across the Rhine, in Germany, a cold spring rain was falling upon a sullen and embittered nation. There was, of course, no celebration of the acceptance of the treaty. The German people could not resist, but, in unanimity, they could still hate.

A transitory peace now descended upon Germany and her conquerors.

Afterword

It is difficult to consider the events of the period between the armistice and the signing of the Treaty of Versailles as anything but a record of terrible failure. The bright hopes for a new Europe, for a new era in the relationships of men and for the secure establishment of German democracy all failed to materialize. As early as November 9, 1923, on the fifth anniversary of the German Revolution, an armed column of three thousand nationalist *Sturmtruppen* was marching through the streets of Munich. At the head of this column was the young rabble-rouser Adolf Hitler, accompanied by General Ludendorff, who by then was half insane. This attempted coup, the famous Beerhall Putsch, failed by only a narrow margin to overthrow the Bavarian state government.

Less than a decade later, Adolf Hitler became the legally appointed Chancellor of the German Republic. Shortly afterward the Treaty of Versailles was in tatters. In March, 1935, Hitler announced the restoration of conscription and the expansion of the German Army. In March, 1936, German troops reoccupied the Rhineland. In March, 1938, Germany annexed Austria.

All that Smuts had predicted in his letters to Lloyd George and Woodrow Wilson came to pass. Germany was too powerful to be suppressed for long. The World War I hatreds of the Allied populations rapidly cooled, and their governments could no longer obtain their support for the enforcement of many of the treaty's provisions. In 1919 any treaty could have been presented to Germany and she could have been compelled to sign it. But to think that its most objectionable features could be enforced against the largest, most industrious and most technically adept nation in Central Europe was to defy every law of politics, economics and common sense. As this gradually became apparent, many of the provisions of the Treaty of Versailles were modified or allowed to go unenforced. The "shame paragraphs" are a good example: the Allies made only a perfunctory demand that Holland surrender the person of Wilhelm II; when the Dutch refused, the matter was quickly dropped. It is quite possible that the Dutch refusal was based on secret assurances from the Allies that they had no real desire to press the point. Even the British, who had once been so frantic to place the Kaiser on trial in London, no longer felt the prospect so appealing.

It was much the same in the matter of the German war criminals to be handed over to the Allies under the provisions of the treaty. On February 3, 1920, the Allies submitted to Germany a list of nine hundred persons who were to be surrendered to them for trial. On the list were the names of practically all of Germany's prominent wartime leaders, including three Hohenzollern princes, four field marshals (Hindenburg was one of them) and a host of generals, among them Ludendorff. The charge under which they were to be tried ranged from the murder of prisoners to petty theft.

The fury which this demand aroused among the German people was indescribable. The Bauer Cabinet debated the question and apparently came to the quite plausible conclusion that any attempt on its part to deliver up these German "criminals" would lead to the overthrow of the government, and probably to the lynching of each Cabinet member in the streets of Berlin. The Army leaders made no secret of their intention to resume the war on their own if the Allies pressed the matter.

The government had no choice but to attempt to negotiate the matter with the Allies, who, somewhat stunned by the German popular fury, agreed to permit the German government to try the accused in its own national courts. Only six obscure Germans were actually tried and convicted, and they got very short sentences. The Allies, unwilling to resume a general war for the dubious pleasure of seeing a few hundred Germans in their docks, were forced to the official conclusion that "it was useless,"[1] and the whole matter was forgotten.

Similarly, the fears regarding Germany's economic ruin at the hands of an avaricious Reparations Commission never materialized. There were a variety of reasons for this, the most important of them being the discovery that, as the American financial experts had predicted, it was impossible to squeeze much in the way of payments in stable money out of a nation which had just endured four years of war. The only way for Germany to accumulate the gold resources or the foreign exchange necessary to make substantial reparations payments was to maintain a much higher level of exports than of imports. In a ruined Europe this was not possible, and, besides, Germany's victors did not want her to compete with them in foreign markets. The only other way Germany could have paid substantial reparations was for the Allies to have accepted manufactured articles in lieu of cash payments. But the victors did not want this either, because their acceptance of any great quantities of finished goods would have ruined their own manufacturers of similar articles. The British were among the first to realize this. To the fury of the French, Great Britain gradually lost interest in the matter of reparations, leaving only France and Belgium prepared to compel German payments. This resulted in successive moderations of the Allied demands.

In 1920 the Reparations Commission announced a decision by which Germany was required to pay a total of 269 billion gold marks over a period of thirty-five years. The Germans protested that they could not possibly meet the annual installments, and so in the following year the Allies reduced the total German liability to 132 billion marks. Even with this the Germans were soon in default, and in 1923 the French Army occupied the Ruhr to compel payments. Thereupon Germany, partly by government design and partly because of faulty economic policies, was launched into a period of wild inflation which ruined the German middle class and brought nothing appreciable to the Allies in terms of reparations payments.

In 1924 the Allies and the Germans agreed to accept the Dawes Plan, a comprehensive United States scheme which stopped inflation, reorganized the German financial system and recommenced the reparations payments by means of enormous loans (mostly American) to Germany. The reparations payments made to the victors by means of these loans were turned over to the United States to satisfy their wartime debt to America. Thus the money simply turned full circle. Germany was permitted to borrow from all sides in vast amounts; at one period, 1924–31, she borrowed eighteen billion marks, while paying out only about eleven billion. The result of this capital influx was that during the early part of this period the German economy boomed. By 1929 Germany seemed to be doing so well that another American-sponsored idea, the Young Plan, was adopted to finish off the reparations, but the worldwide depression burst the bubble. Germany could not begin to repay the debts she had so lavishly contracted in previous years, much less make reparations payments. At a conference in Lausanne in 1932 it was proposed that the whole reparations matter be settled by a token German payment of three billion marks. When Hitler came to power in 1933 even this relatively modest amount was left unpaid.

When the balance was finally added up it was found that Germany had paid approximately 36 billion marks. To offset this, she had borrowed about 33 billion from abroad. Because few of the loans were repaid, it is now generally agreed that the reparations payments had little or no adverse effect upon the German economy.

But these *de facto* modifications of the peace treaty failed to make an impression on the German people. The principal defect of the treaty was that to the vast majority of Germans it was the most vicious and wrathful document in the history of mankind. They blamed their every misfortune upon the fact that there was a Polish Corridor, a demilitarized Rhineland, a free city at Danzig. They ascribed every economic difficulty instantly to the reparations payments. They imagined themselves alone in a world of foes, surrounded by vengeful neighbors who mocked and ridiculed Germany for the military weakness which the treaty had reduced her to. They believed themselves encircled by aggressive nations. They were certain that the Germans who had been cut off from the Fatherland by plebiscites were subjected to the most awful humiliations at the hands of their barbarian and oppressive masters.

There was, of course, no shortage of people who were anxious to assure the average German that his convictions about the treaty were correct. From the moment the document was signed, there were thousands of German orators holding meetings to denounce the *Diktat* of Versailles. Attacks on the treaty were by all odds the favorite German political subject. It was the foolproof crowd-pleaser. Any speaker who denounced the victors was certain to draw an ample crowd and produce a generous response. Adolf Hitler was only one of these agitators—though in the long run the most successful. It was his first subject, and he delivered practically the same speech again and again in the early days of Nazism. This attack, first entitled "The Peace Treaty of Versailles" and then retitled "The Peace Treaties of Brest-Litovsk and Versailles," invariably fell on fertile ground, and attendance at his early speeches increased from a dozen persons to a hundred, to two hundred, and then to crowds beyond computation.

If any further proof was needed regarding the diabolical character of the treaty's reparations section, the Germans had only to consult the work of the brilliant young British economist John Maynard Keynes. At the peace conference Keynes had been the representative of the British Treasury. In early June, appalled at the treaty's terms, he resigned and fled back to Great Britain, where he at once devoted his energy and talents to the writing of a book entitled *The Economic Consequences of the Peace*. It appeared in the late fall of 1919 and established Keynes as a brilliant writer with arresting abilities as a biographer. The central thesis of his book was that Germany could not possibly pay the reparations which would be demanded of her, and that in the course of attempting to wring payments from her the Allies would so upset the economy of Central Europe that the victors along with the vanquished would go down in financial ruin. As a sort of preface to this discussion, Keynes penned an acid-etched portrait of Woodrow Wilson as a fool, a failure and a hypocrite.

The Economic Consequences of the Peace at once became a best seller in Germany. The fact that most of its dire predictions never came to pass made no difference. It was enough that an Englishman and an increasingly famous economist had denounced the treaty as a "Carthaginian peace" and had forecast the ruin which it would bring to Germany. What further proof could possibly be needed?

It is apparent that the *Freikorps* played an important role in the general disaster which ultimately befell the Weimar Republic.

The first major dilemma with which the *Freikorps* were to confront the government was their refusal to disband. Although the peace treaty specifically required Germany to disband all *Freikorps*, the government found that it lacked the power to do so. In the Baltic nations the old Iron Division continued to fight as the "Russian Army of the West." The Allies protested furiously, but the German government could do nothing about it—much as it would have liked to, since these Baltic *Freikorps* were obviously planning a march upon Berlin in the interests of a Hohenzollern restoration. These troops would neither disband nor return to Germany. And when, in November of 1919, the "Russian Army of the West" was finally surrounded by the Latvian Army, a new German *Freikorps* was openly formed in Berlin to go to its relief. Defying the orders of the government, this new force, the Rossbach Freikorps, entrained for Latvia, crossed the German frontier and cut its way through to relieve the beleaguered "Russian Army."

Much more serious were the events of March, 1920, when the government ordered the dissolution of Captain Ehrhardt's "Second Marine Brigade," one of the best-trained and -equipped of all the *Freikorps*. The result was that on the night of March 12 the three thousand troops of this elite brigade and two thousand from the Baltic formations—such as the Third Kurland Infantry Regiment—began to march on Berlin. By morning they had captured the capital, and the government had fled, first to Dresden and then to Stuttgart. The Ehrhardt Brigade, whose troops were distinguishable by the swastika painted on their helmets, met with no opposition from the Reichswehr garrison in Berlin. The Army troops were confined to barracks by order of their commander, General Hans von Seeckt, who bluntly told the civilian government that he would not defend the republic. "Troops do not fire on troops," Seeckt explained to Noske. "Do you perhaps intend, Herr Minister, that a battle be fought before the Brandenburg Gate between troops who have fought side by side against the common enemy? . . . When Reichswehr fires on Reichswehr, all comradeship between the officer corps has vanished."[2]

The arrival in Berlin of the Ehrhardt Brigade and the smaller *Freikorps* formations which joined them was not unexpected, nor was this military insurrection without a political objective. As the *Freikorps* troops marched into the Tiergarten in the small hours of March 13 they were greeted by General Ludendorff, who, he later claimed, chanced to be strolling past for a predawn constitutional. Simultaneously an obscure nationalist civil servant named Wolfgang Kapp arrived in Berlin. It was the intention of the *Freikorps* to install this nonentity as the German Chancellor. The marching orders to the Ehrhardt Brigade had been given by Kapp's unofficial military adviser, General Baron Walther von Lüttwitz, the same officer who had commanded the reconquest of Berlin following the Spartacist uprising of January, 1919. Other experienced *Freikorps* figures were much in evidence. The principal officers on Kapp's staff were Captain Waldemar Pabst, who had earlier organized the Guard Cavalry Rifle Division, and Colonel Bauer, Ludendorff's principal aide. And as the fleeing Cabinet ministers drove into Dresden they were met by General von Maercker, the organizer of the first *Freikorps,* who announced that he was putting the entire Cabinet under arrest. He was dissuaded from this project with some difficulty, but he warned the ministers that the worst was yet to come. *Freikorps* were mobilizing all over Germany to go to Kapp's assistance. In particular, Major Bischoff's Baltic formations were reported to be assembling in East Prussia for their long-awaited march on Berlin.

After five days the "Kapp Putsch" was brought to an end by a combination of the "Chancellor's" total incompetence and the astonishing effectiveness of a general strike which the Socialists called against Kapp and his "government." Kapp fled to Tempelhof, where a plane waited to take him to Sweden, and Ludendorff departed for the more congenial political climate of Munich. The sullen troops of the Ehrhardt Brigade formed columns of fours on Unter den Linden and, while a silent and obviously hostile crowd of Berliners watched from the sidewalk, prepared for their march back to Boberitz. Then, among the spectators, a boy laughed. Two *Freikorps* soldiers broke ranks, knocked the youth down with their rifle butts and kicked him where he lay in the gutter. The crowd began to hiss its hatred. In response, an officer shouted an order, and a rank of the *Freikorpskämpfer* at once raised their rifles and, at point-blank range, fired a volley into the crowd. Then they turned about, the order to march was given, and the brigade tramped off to the west, passing through the Brandenburger Tor. Before they disappeared down the Charlottenstrasse, individual troopers broke ranks, ran to the sidewalk and beat lone civilians, using their potato-masher hand grenades as clubs. It was their final gesture to the people of Berlin.[3]

The failure of the Kapp Putsch did not bring about the demise of the *Freikorps.* They were a constant threat to the government. A little song which they composed at the time explains their intentions:

> *Why should we cry when a* Putsch *goes wrong?*
> *There's another one coming before very long.*
> *So say goodbye—but remember, men,*
> *In a couple of weeks we will try it again.*[4]

It took the government many months to disband the most highly organized of the *Freikorps.* Even then they had a habit of springing up again. In 1921 General Wilhelm Reinhard recruited a brand-new

Freikorps and shortly had his men fighting a small undeclared war against the Poles in Upper Silesia. When the Ehrhardt Brigade supposedly disbanded, it actually re-formed into secret splinter corps. Among these was the infamous "Organization Consul" (Ehrhardt himself was "Consul"), which, along with other *Freikorps*-inspired murder societies, carried out the "Feme Murders" (*Fememorde*—political murders) of the early Twenties—an extensive campaign of assassinations directed at those civilians whom they called the "November criminals." By the time it ended, hundreds of persons had been murdered, including some of Germany's most famous political personalities—men such as Matthias Erzberger and Walter Rathenau. The assassins were rarely arrested, and when they were they received light sentences. Enough former *Freikorpskämpfer* occupied positions of power in the police and the judiciary to protect their old comrades. Since the commander of the Reichswehr in Bavaria, General Franz Ritter von Epp, was a former *Freikorpsführer*, it is little wonder that murders went unsolved. Early during the wave of assassinations, an informant came to the chief of the Bavarian police and whispered, "Herr Police President, political murder organizations exist in this country." "I know," whispered back the policeman, himself the Organization Consul director for Bavaria, "but not enough of them."[5]

Other *Freikorps*, not choosing to specialize in the field of political assassination, ultimately re-formed into military "clubs" calling themselves the "Association of Baltic Fighters," the "Association of Defenders of the Eastern Frontiers," etc. It was found to be almost impossible to suppress these organizations. In early 1920 the government ceased to give financial support to the *Freikorps*—or, more precisely, the government *thought* it had ceased to give them financial support; actually, the surviving *Freikorps* continued to receive money, weapons, barracks and military instruction secretly from the Reichswehr. Even though the Army command distrusted the "freebooter spirit" of the *Freikorps*, it recognized that they had their uses. They were openly referred to as the "Black Reichswehr," and for a period of years these semiclandestine formations provided a reserve troop strength almost equal to the size of the German Army itself. Both the German government and the Allied Military Control Commission made efforts to identify and disband these *Freikorps*, but the task was made exceedingly difficult by the ability of the corps to rename themselves anything they liked. The Rossbach

Freikorps, for example, transformed itself into an "agricultural labor corps" (to explain why large groups of men were living in barracks on remote East Prussian estates), then was renamed a "savings society" and finally became a "union for agricultural instruction." For recruitment in the cities, Rossbach's formation owned a night club and established a "detective bureau." With good reason Rossbach claimed, "I can form new organizations faster than the authorities can dissolve them."[6] Obtaining arms posed no particular problem, even when the Reichswehr would not provide them. It was officially estimated by the Army that no fewer than two million rifles were unaccounted for in Germany.

Throughout the harassed life span of the Weimar Republic the *Freikorps* and their legacy exercised a corrosive effect upon German national life. Actively disloyal, they constituted an endless threat to the republic and to the lives of its principal officials. Given only the faintest opportunity, the *Freikorpsführer* would at once strike his elected government in the back—all the while complaining of the government's heinous guilt in the *Dolchstoss* of November, 1918.[*]

The only reason the *Freikorps* did not pose an even more dangerous threat to the German Republic was that their intensely individualistic leaders could never agree on a single policy or subordinate themselves to another leader. Ultimately, however, this defect was remedied by Adolf Hitler, operating in the ripe political atmosphere which Munich afforded. As his star began its ascendancy, various *Freikorps* leaders took their groups en masse into the Nazi S. A. (which itself had been organized on the storm-troop pattern of the *Freikorps* and whose early leadership had drawn heavily from experienced *Freikorps* fighters). Not all the *Freikorpsführer* were anxious to do this, of course, for it meant strict subordination to another *Führer*, but the enthusiasm of their men for Adolf Hitler compelled even the most reluctant leaders to give way. And in most cases they were handsomely rewarded. The list of district leaders of the S. A. in the early days of the Nazi Party reads like a roster of old *Freikorps* officers. They marched under the swastika, which had often been their symbol long before Hitler. Then Hitler became

---

[*] Because of the *Freikorps* threat, the various major political parties also formed their own paramilitary forcs. The Communists created a "Red Veterans' League" and the Social Democrats put together their "Reichsbanner Schwarz-Rot-Gold," a uniformed but at first unarmed force which also accepted members from the Center and Democratic parties. Finally, in 1931, Reichsbanner organized select combat units called *Schufo* (defense groups), but by then it was too late to match the Nazi S. A. formations.

tired of their individualism, and in the 1934 "Blood Purge" of the S.
A. many of the most troublesome old *Freikorps* leaders were killed.
By then they had already served his purpose.

The figure of Woodrow Wilson is central to this account. When
the President appeared before the United States Senate on July 10,
1919, to report on the peace negotiations and to request ratification
of the Versailles Treaty, he was already a sick man. He was sixty-
two years old, had probably suffered a recent thrombosis, had been
bitterly disappointed at Paris and was utterly played out. The worst
flaws in his personality now seemed to magnify themselves.

It is widely thought that the peace treaty could have been ratified
by the Senate. Newspaper polls, resolutions passed by thirty-two
state legislatures, the declarations of labor unions and business and
professional organizations, and the statements of countless prominent persons all confirm the fact that a real majority of Americans
was prepared to support the treaty—which, of course, meant that
the United States would join the League of Nations. In fact, it was
generally doubted that the Senate itself was opposed to the treaty.
Of ninety-six Senators, only fourteen Republicans and four Democrats were irreconcilably against the treaty. The rest either favored
it or were prepared to accept it subject to certain minor modifications. Even though the ratification of a treaty requires a two-thirds
majority of the United States Senate, a great deal of important business has been steered through that body on far less favorable terms.

Recognizing this, Wilson's foes in the Senate knew that they could
not reject the treaty out of hand. Instead, led by Senator Lodge,
they demanded certain "reservations" to the treaty. Even then they
were forced to stall for time, in order to develop enough support to
permit their reservations to be brought to the Senate floor. Lodge's
Foreign Relations Committee strung out its hearings by devoting
two weeks to having the treaty read aloud and then spent six weeks
debating it. It summoned witnesses who opposed the treaty and
heard them at length. It badgered every witness who favored the
treaty, in the hopes of finding flaws in his testimony.

Finally, in September, 1919, the Foreign Relations Committee
submitted its report. The committee's Republican majority listed a
series of reservations, most of which were of a rather inconsequential nature and were designed to "Republicanize" a treaty which
Lodge and his followers conceived to be an overly Wilsonian docu-

ment. What was perhaps Lodge's principal reservation dealt with Article Ten of the Covenant of the League of Nations. "The United States," the reservation stipulated, "assumes no obligation to preserve the territorial integrity of any other country or to interfere in controversies between nations . . . or to employ the military or naval forces of the United States . . . unless in any particular case the Congress shall by act or joint resolution so provide."[7] Since in any case the United States could not go to war unless Congress approved, this reservation did not materially alter the treaty.

In the face of Lodge's reservations, Wilson was at his implacable worst. He had done his compromising in Paris. He would do none now. He would tolerate no opposition. In presenting the treaty to the Senate, Wilson had not referred to that body as his "colleagues," as he had often done in the past. Instead he had "informed" them of the treaty's presentation and virtually demanded its acceptance. He had made it clear that the Senate must pass the treaty exactly as it was written and without a single one of Lodge's hateful reservations, or he would go to the people; he would tell the nation what their Senators were doing to his treaty and his League of Nations.

Wilson's supporters begged him not to do this. They urged him to compromise. He would not. The French ambassador, frightened that the United States might not sign the treaty, told Wilson that France would be willing to accept the Lodge reservations and urged concession upon Wilson. "Mr. Ambassador," the American President coldly replied, "I shall consent to nothing. The Senate must take its medicine."[8] Colonel House, who had not seen Wilson since they parted in Paris, wrote to the President, advising him to accept the reservations. Wilson did not reply to the letter, and he never again received House into his presence.

On September 3, over the combined objections of his physician, his wife and his closest advisers, Wilson left Washington for a projected twenty-seven-day speaking trip in which he would take his case to the people. Even as he left, his hands were shaking and he was suffering ghastly headaches. The trip was never finished. In Pueblo, Colorado, he suffered a collapse which forced his return to Washington. One arm and a leg were partly paralyzed, and he had headaches so constant and agonizing that he could neither sleep nor eat. On October 2 another thrombosis left him paralyzed and without speech. In the following months the President of the United States lay in his White House sickroom, virtually unable to conduct the nation's business.

Ultimately the Treaty of Versailles was not ratified by the United States Senate; it failed by only seven votes to obtain the necessary two-thirds majority. The treaty of guarantee with France which had been the basis of the Rhineland settlement was also rejected by the Senate. Under the Harding Administration a separate peace treaty was made with Germany—a treaty containing no League of Nations Covenant. Thus the United States, the nation which had proposed the League and whose President had been the moving spirit in its creation, was the first to reject it.

Woodrow Wilson lived on in retirement in Washington until his death on February 3, 1924. To the end, although he was an invalid, he cherished the fantastic hope that he would again be nominated for the Presidency and that the United States would ultimately enter the League of Nations.

After his death it was apparent that even after years of illness he had not lost his remarkable capacity for hatred. Of all his many old supporters, the men who had assisted him and offered guidance in the years from Princeton to the Presidency, practically none were invited to attend the funeral services. Joseph Tumulty, his faithful political secretary during the Presidential years, had to plead for an invitation. Edward House listened to the service over a loudspeaker while he stood in the rain outside Madison Square Garden in New York.

The career and the reputation of Georges Clemenceau were also ruined by the Peace of Versailles. It was a common supposition that Clemenceau more than any other Allied figure was personally responsible for whatever violence the treaty did to the ideals of Woodrow Wilson. Clemenceau was customarily portrayed as a vicious and misanthropic old man, and this was correct. It was believed that he had influenced the French press and the Parliament to the point where they backed his exorbitant demands, and this is wrong. In Paris during 1919 it would have been difficult to find another French political figure as moderate, as open to negotiation and as congenial to compromise as Georges Clemenceau. What was not at first widely understood was the degree to which the dominant French political forces—the parliamentary right, President Poincaré, Foch and the Army—combined to press their fears and hatreds upon the leader of the French government.

By January, 1920, the Clemenceau ministry was out of power. The principal reason was that the Tiger was generally thought to have betrayed France by his "softness" at the time of the treaty negotiations—especially after the United States Senate refused to ratify the treaty of guarantee with France, with the result that the British Parliament exercised its privilege of not approving the treaty.

Clemenceau devoted the last nine years of his life to defending himself against these charges. He wrote a rambling book, *The Grandeur and Misery of Victory,* which is nothing more than a tiresome catalogue of countercharges against Foch, coupled with an attempt to prove that he had done all that he could to bring about a favorable peace treaty. It was not well received. When, in 1922, Clemenceau made a tour of the United States, he was given no official mission, message or status by the French government.

Even at his advanced age at the end of the war, Georges Clemenceau had cherished the dream of being elected president of the French Republic. As the Premier who had led France to victory, it seemed easily within his grasp. But after the events of the peace conference his election was unthinkable. He died in Paris on November 24, 1929, at the age of eighty-eight.

The only one of the principal Allied figures whose career survived the effects of the Treaty of Versailles was David Lloyd George, and he did not last long.

Lloyd George returned from Paris to a nation which, it was soon discovered, had suffered a wartime economic catastrophe far greater than had been suspected. The Prime Minister found himself required to steer Britain through massive coal and railroad strikes, as well as the crisis of Irish independence. His popularity gradually diminished, as did his hold over the coalition of Conservatives and Liberals without whose support he could not survive. By late 1921 Britain was in an economic depression, which Lloyd George met with a sharp cut in government spending, coupled with an "Anti-Waste" campaign. The only result was that the slump deepened, and there was widespread disenchantment with the Prime Minister's methods—his increasingly erratic decisions, his penchant for conducting personal diplomacy without consulting or even advising the Foreign Office, and his unconventional personal life.

In the early spring of 1922, Lloyd George came to the conclusion that the Treaty of Versailles had been an awful mistake and that it was in no small way responsible for the economic crisis in which both Great Britain and the Continental European nations now found themselves. He believed that Europe could not possibly make an effective recovery unless both the Germans and the Russians (whom practically none of the Western powers had yet recognized diplomatically) were brought to a conference. French reluctance to meet with Germany and Russia notwithstanding, Lloyd George succeeded in convoking a general meeting of European powers at Genoa, and he anticipated that a successful conference would do much to restore his diminished prestige. As was increasingly his custom, he drew practically none of his conference staff from the Foreign Office and, in fact, left his Foreign Secretary, Lord Curzon, in London. "When I reflect," Curzon wrote at the time to a friend, "that the P. M. is alone at Genoa with no F. O. to guide him . . . I can feel no certainty that we may not find ourselves committed to something pregnant with political disaster here."[9]

The Conference of Genoa ended at 1:15 A.M. on Easter Sunday, when the German delegation, which, together with the Russians, had been banished from the innermost councils of the conference, received a telephone call from the Soviet delegation, which was staying in the nearby resort town of Rapallo. The Russians suggested that these two powers, Europe's outcasts, sign an agreement by which they would reestablish diplomatic relations and Russia would agree to waive any of the reparations from Germany which the Treaty of Versailles specifically permitted her to claim at a future date.*

This Russian proposal, to which the German delegation agreed on the spot, had not come as a total surprise to the Germans. Certain rumors of a Russian desire to reach an accommodation had already been passed on to the German government, but Ebert had opposed it on the grounds that Germany must not forfeit Allied goodwill by a rapprochement with Russia, which could only appear to be an alliance against the West. Now, at Rapallo, the Germans felt that the Russian offer was too good to turn down. The threat of a Russian reparations claim had been a sword of Damocles held over the head of the German government. Diplomatic recognition of Russia seemed a small price to pay to be relieved of his threat. They signed the agreement.

The events at Rapallo came as a shattering surprise to the French and British conferees at Genoa. They were furious at what they regarded as the duplicity of these two outcast nations. To the

---

* This provision had been inserted into the treaty at the insistence of the French, who hoped that, by one means or another, it would protect the holders of imperial Russian bonds, most of whom were French.

French it was but another proof of German treachery, and in Paris there was a considerable agitation for the mobilization of the Army. For all practical purposes, the Conference of Genoa broke up while the Allied dignitaries scurried for home.

On his return to England, Lloyd George found his enemies massed in ranks. The prestige of the Prime Minister had declined precipitately as the result of Genoa. His judgment was now seriously suspect, even by the members of his own Cabinet. "Tell me which way the little man is going," Colonial Secretary Winston Churchill said of Lloyd George, "and I am off in the opposite direction."[10]

As if Genoa were not enough, there immediately followed a tragic series of events in Asia Minor. In October of 1920 King Alexander of Greece strolled out into his palace garden to watch two pet monkeys at play. One of them bit him, and soon thereafter the young King was dead. In short order, and as the result of events stemming directly from Alexander's death, Great Britain found herself deeply involved in supporting Greece's war against Turkey, which was being backed by France. Lloyd George, after maneuvering Britain into an almost inextricable position in the matter, appealed to the dominions for support. The British dominions interpreted this as the first step in another war and refused to commit themselves.

If anything else was required to complete the ruin of the Prime Minister's reputation, it was the revelation of serious irregularities in the distribution of political funds entrusted to the care of certain of his associates. In October of 1922 the Conservatives withdrew from the government, and Lloyd George was forced to resign. In the general election which followed he was left with practically no parliamentary support.

Lloyd George never managed to regain the government. Under his leadership the Liberal Party sank into decrepitude. Lloyd George himself decayed into a lecherous old man. For a time his home became virtually a seraglio. At the age of eighty-two, shortly after having been created an earl, he died.

The fate of the major German figures in the events of 1918–19 was no less sad than that of the Allied principals. Like the victors, none, save perhaps Hindenburg, lived to achieve a happy and respected old age.

Perhaps the most pitiful of all the German figures involved in the events of the revolutionary period was Gustav Noske. In the months which followed the signing of the peace treaty, it became obvious to everyone that Noske was under the spell of the officer corps. Fellow Socialists complained and laughed; they could not understand how Noske could fail to see through the facile deference which the officers paid him, and they snickered at the authoritarian airs and delusions which the Minister of Defense permitted himself.

All of this could be tolerated as long as Noske could claim to control the Army. The charade was soon over. At one o'clock on the morning of March 13, 1920, as the Ehrhardt Brigade was tramping into Berlin and the Kapp Putsch was starting, a council of war was called in Noske's office at the Ministry of Defense. The German government expected, of course, that the Reichswehr would defend it—if necessary, with a vigor similar to that with which the Spartacist uprising had been put down the year before.

Noske was beginning to outline his plans for resisting the Ehrhardt Brigade, when the voice of Colonel General Hans von Seeckt (shortly to assume the title "Chief of the Army Command") was heard. Aloof, his monocle glittering as he surveyed the group in attendance, von Seeckt made his announcement that the Army would not oppose Ehrhardt's troops. It was one thing to crush an insurrection by the left even though there were plenty of former soldiers to be found in the ranks of the proletarian uprising; it was quite another to oppose an insurrection by the right.

Astonished, Noske polled the officers in the room. They were all his old associates—the officers who had offered to make him Germany's dictator. Now he asked which of them would defend the German Republic and its Cabinet members against mutiny and insurrection. Only two of the eleven officers at the council would do so. The rest indicated that the Army should remain "neutral." It should await developments and, presumably, side with whichever faction won. With a faint smile, von Seeckt rose and left the room, to go on an extended leave.

Noske was crushed. In company with his Cabinet colleagues, the Minister of Defense was forced to flee Berlin. "This night has shown me the bankruptcy of all my policy," he despaired. "My faith in the officer corps is shattered. You have all deserted me. There is nothing left but suicide."[11]

Noske did not commit suicide. But the German Republic had no further need for a Minister of Defense who could not even persuade the generals to defend his own person against insurgents. Five days after the Kapp Putsch, Noske submitted his resignation. His party dropped him from its list of nominees to the Reichstag, and Noske would have been completely finished in public life except that an old friend appointed him president of the province of Hanover. He held this post until 1933, when the Nazis dismissed him. A man of great physical stamina, Noske was still active during his mid-seventies, when the Second World War began. The Nazis imprisoned him twice—first for a brief time at the war's outbreak, and again after the attempt on Hitler's life in 1944, when Noske's name was found among a list of officials to be appointed following the asassination. Jailed in Berlin, he managed to escape when the Russians attacked the city.

Noske died in November of 1946 just as he was about to leave for a lecture tour in the United States.

Unfortunately for the German Republic, the influence of Gustav Noske upon its future relations with the Army did not end with his resignation. The example of Noske had set a precedent for future ministers of defense in the Weimar Republic. In its fifteen-year life span the republic had fourteen chancellors but only four ministers of defense. The Army had little difficulty with two of them and virtually provided the last two. From 1919 to 1928, both Ministers were servants, whom the Army told only what it wished to tell, and from whom no interference was tolerated. Each learned that he was expected to conceal certain facts from his Cabinet colleagues, and from time to time each was forced to defend the Army against charges concerning which the Minister himself was imperfectly informed.

In this manner, the Army leadership was able to pursue policies of its own, free from intervention or control by the civil government. Traditionally the Army had conceived of itself as a state within a state, and under the Weimar Republic it continued to operate in that manner. Toward the end of 1921 the Army concluded a secret agreement with Russia by which German military-aircraft manufacturers were set up in Russia, as were also German factories for making shells and poison gas. Under the supervision of the Army's "Special Branch R[ussia]," German officers trained Russian troops and conducted maneuvers on Russian soil—all of this practically unknown to the German civil government. In late 1922, when Count von Brockdorff-Rantzau had conversations with Army representatives and indicated that he knew what was going on in Russia, they became very agitated, crying, "The President [Ebert] need not be informed."[12]

The Army leadership refrained from staging a coup from the right, but this was the only service it was prepared to render the Republic it despised. With or without the connivance of its creature, the Minister of Defense, the Army pursued its own independent policies, contracted for the illegal manufacture and importation of weapons, trained its own secret reserves (the "Black Reichswehr") and paid them with its own secret funds (the "Black Budgets"). Concerning all of this, the civil government was informed either not at all or in terms which the Army described as "in general but not in particular."[13]

The independence of the Army was, of course, attributable in great measure to the defects of Germany's civilian leadership. A fatal weakness of the Weimar Republic was the inability of its largest political party, the Social Democrats, to produce men with the near-titanic qualities which were truly required to direct the destiny of the German state in such a period. The Socialist leaders were nothing more than what they had always been—trade-unionists who had made their way up the rungs of the Social Democratic machine. They were tenacious and honest, but they were also plodding and cautious. They handled every problem as if it were a question of labor negotiation, and they were prepared always to compromise.

These Social Democratic leaders were the conditioned product of an earlier age in which German life had been dominated by a patriarchal family system, an established church and a hierarchal factory organization. They could not free themselves from those traditional values. They had developed their party organization to the point where its maintenance became an end in itself, not a means to an end. They approached national crises with a spirit of resignation and the constant complaint that conditions were not favorable for action by them.

As time went by, the inability of the Social Democratic Party to set a goal and to advance ruthlessly upon it resulted in the progressive disaffection of the young German worker. The election of January, 1919, in which the Majority Socialists received nearly forty per cent of the national vote, proved to be the party's permanent high-water mark. Even after the October, 1920, breakup of the Independent Social Democratic Party, the membership of which gradually distributed itself between the parent party and the Communists, the slow decline in Social Democratic strength continued.

Ultimately the Social Democratic Party became the home of the middle-aged worker. Its leadership paid a stiff price for its failure to cleanse the German judiciary and bureaucracy of their monarchist incumbents. The party floundered. The leaders drifted from concession to compromise. Finally, beset from the right for their "guilt" in the matter of the armistice and the Treaty of Versailles, and besieged from the left for their "bourgeois" outlook, they crumbled before the Nazis and could offer practically nothing in the way of resistance.

Friedrich Ebert did not live long after the signing of the Treaty of Versailles, and his last years were unhappy. He was the subject of constant personal persecution from the right. In 1922, while Ebert was on a formal visit to Munich, a certain Dr. Gansser shouldered his way through the crowd and spat the epithet "Traitor!" into the face of the President. Ebert felt that he had no choice but to file a legal charge of slander against Gansser, and the matter was brought to court. The nation was thereupon treated to the spectacle of the President of the German Republic being required to give testimony in a Bavarian court to establish his patriotism. The verdict was in Ebert's favor, but it had to be conceded that, in a very technical sense, he had been a "traitor" to the Hohenzollern monarchy when he called the general strike of November 9, 1918.

Now the nationalist newspapers and the right-wing speakers all combined to taunt Ebert. They sneered at his early career as a saddlemaker and café proprietor, and they renewed the charges of treason. Ebert found himself drawn into endless litigation. At one point he had slander complaints pending against nearly 150 individuals. The judges in the courts frequently showed little respect toward the person of the President of the Republic, and each legal case was viciously fought.

Under this pressure, Friedrich Ebert's health and judgment were undermined. He disregarded until too late the advice of his doctors that he be operated on for appendicitis. In February of 1925, at the age of fifty-four, Ebert died of peritonitis. It was a catastrophe for the German Republic. He was both the leader of the nation's largest political party and the man who had every right to claim the title of founder of the republic. There were no other men of his quality to replace him. Ebert was the one man in his party who might have summoned sufficient authority and prestige to prevent the rise of Adolf Hitler.

* * *

Philipp Scheidemann, the first Chancellor of the German Republic, was an altogether different case. He was an ordinary character,
given to making injudicious statements at inopportune times. His
memoirs reveal him as a rather simple fellow. He never misses an
opportunity to demonstrate his importance by recalling his private
train. He displays his courage and the dangers he faced by telling of
how he slept with a cocked pistol by his side. He chuckles at little
stories from his youth—for example, about the time when, as a poor
young worker, he dipped into a large vat of soup in company with
two friends, who suddenly stopped eating when a drip of snot rolled
off Scheidemann's nose and into the pot; with glee he tells how the
entire bowl of soup was left to him.

During his brief tenure as chancellor, Scheidemann was completely overshadowed by Ebert and showed his resentment at this in
many ways, principally through allegations that Ebert had attempted to assume a dictatorial role in the German government and
that it was only Philipp Scheidemann who had blocked this. After
his resignation, Scheidemann served for many years as a Reichstag
deputy and as mayor of Kassel, his native town. As sometimes
happens, he was more perceptive and more effective outside the
government than he had ever been within it. His experiences during
the German Revolution had led him greatly to distrust the Army
and the *Freikorps*. He had never been in favor of the Ebert-Groener
"pact," and he had never had any confidence in Noske's methods as
minister of defense. For these reasons Scheidemann decided to become the Reichstag's watchdog against militarism—an office which
badly needed filling. He was not averse to attacking his old comrades among the Majority Socialists, particularly Ebert and Noske.
Shortly after the peace treaty was signed, Scheidemann read in the
newspapers that General Wilhelm Reinhard, the famous *Freikorps*
leader who had gone into the Reichswehr with his troops, had made
a speech in which he called the Cabinet "a pack of rascals."[14]
Scheidemann immediately demanded that Reinhard be dismissed.
Noske refused to do this, giving the remarkable explanation "You
must take into account that Reinhard did not think his words to the
troops would be reported in the newspapers."[15] Scheidemann was
indignant at this reply and took care to give it wide publicity.

Scheidemann's most famous attack upon the Army took place in

1927 when, from the floor of the Reichstag, he charged that the Army had illegally purchased large quantities of artillery ammunition in Russia and was secretly importing it through the port of Stettin. The incumbent Minister of Defense, Otto Gessler, claimed that he knew nothing about it, which may well have been true. The Army denied the charge completely. The parties on the right shrieked that Scheidemann had given away a state secret. From the left the Communists screamed that it was all a lie, for they could scarcely afford to admit that Soviet Russia was secretly supplying the German Army. Nonetheless, Scheidemann persisted, and he finally obtained enough evidence to prove his charge, much to the embarrassment of practically every political party.

It is astonishing that Scheidemann managed to survive into old age, for he was one of the earliest targets of the nationalist assassins. In June of 1922, while walking through a park in his home city, he was approached by two men, one of whom threw acid at him while the other pulled out a revolver. Scheidemann, who carried a pistol of his own, flung himself to the ground and began firing at his would-be murderers, who fled. He was lucky to have escaped; few of the assassination attempts were bungled. In the following years Scheidemann was careful always to be armed and accompanied by armed friends when he appeared in public. He lived until 1939.

The assassins were more successful in the case of Matthias Erzberger. The fact that Erzberger was not a man of towering personal probity was his undoing. In late 1919, while still occupying the position of minister of finance in the Bauer government, he became involved in a series of charges and countercharges with Karl Helfferich, a prominent member of the wartime imperial government. The two men had hated each other for a long time. In 1919, from the floor of the National Assembly, Erzberger accused Helfferich of fiscal irresponsibility as minister of finance during the war. Helfferich responded with a violent personal attack on Erzberger which was published in a conservative newspaper. He charged Erzberger with having taken illegal advantage of his various official positions to become a member of certain business enterprises. Erzberger thereupon brought suit for libel against Helfferich.

The trial lasted from January until March of 1920. Technically, Erzberger won the suit and Helfferich was fined three hundred marks. In actuality, Erzberger was the loser. During the trial Helfferich was supported by the forces of the right. They were energetic and well organized, and they dredged up a tremendous amount of muck concerning Erzberger, with special emphasis on his role in signing the armistice and encouraging the acceptance of the peace treaty. The courtroom was packed with conservatives who jeered at Erzberger. The bias of the public prosecutor in favor of Helfferich was very evident. Although the original point of the lawsuit became obscured, Helfferich did succeed in proving that Erzberger had engaged in some financial dealings which, if not actually illegal, were certainly highly irregular. Even his staunchest friends had to concede that Erzberger had been very indiscreet in his use of his official contacts. His resignation as minister of finance came as a matter of course.

The nationalist parties were not content to let it go at that. They looked upon Matthias Erzberger as the epitome of all the forces which, according to them, had stabbed the monarchy and the Army in the back. Had he not headed the German armistice delegation at Compiègne? This was all it took to prove the point. On a rainy day in August, 1921, when Erzberger was on vacation at a resort in the Black Forest, two members of Organization Consul lay in wait for him beside a path in the woods. When Erzberger came along they jumped out and leveled their pistols at him. Erzberger thrust his umbrella toward the assassins, but was cut down by their bullets. Then the two murders reloaded and, standing above him, fired twelve more bullets into his head. Afterward they escaped to Hungary on passports supplied by the Munich police.

Count von Brockdorff-Rantzau went into retirement when he resigned from the Scheidemann government, but it was to be only temporary. In 1922 Germany and Russia signed the Treaty of Rapallo, and the government appealed to Brockdorff-Rantzau to become the German ambassador to the Soviet Union. He accepted the job reluctantly and with no illusions, for he regarded the Soviet government as "a gang of criminals."[16] His appointment was viciously opposed by the Army, which had not forgotten his failure to contest the military clauses at Versailles.

For all this, Brockdorff-Rantzau was brilliantly successful in his embassy to the Soviet Union. It lasted for six years, during which he displayed a remarkable ability to influence the Russian Foreign Ministry, at that time headed by the former aristocrat Grigori Chicherin. The two men, whose backgrounds and interests—fine wine, literature, and art—were absolutely harmonious, became close personal friends. Unlike the ambassadors of other nations to the Soviet Union, Brockdorff-Rantzau managed to convey to the Russians the feeling that he alone among the Western powers truly cared for their friendship. At the same time, he knew how to be tough in a way the Russians respected. When he arrived in Moscow in November of 1922, he did not feel that the official reception given him was commensurate with his position. He let it be known that he considered his welcome no better than that which would have been given "a high-class bootlegger."[17] This was just the sort of treatment the Russians understood. Three days later they made amends with a huge military review held in Brockdorff-Rantzau's honor, at which a Red Army band played a selection of aristocratic airs personally chosen by the Count.

Like humbler Germans, Brockdorff-Rantzau never forgot the peace treaty. On his deathbed, in 1928, his last words to his brother were, "Do not mourn. After all, I have really been dead ever since Versailles."[18]

In viewing the entire spectacle of the German Republic, it is impossible not to marvel at the tenacity and resilience of old habits and values in Germany—indeed, in practically all of Europe. True, the discredited monarchies all vanished, but after they had gone their people preserved the established traditions of German life. There was little real danger that Germany would become Bolshevik. It quickly became apparent that the bulk of her working class had no desire to follow a path of violent revolution.

In recent years it has become commonplace to think of the Russian Bolsheviks as possessing a cunning international apparatus of trained agents who were prepared, in the event of any upheaval in a capitalist nation, to step into the chaos and establish a Communist regime. The events of the German Revolution demonstrate the falsity of such assumptions. In 1918–19 the "worldwide Communist conspiracy" consisted of no more than a small number of Socialist extremists who had been successful in Russia only through a set of circumstances which were particularly favorable to them. They were out of touch with the rest of Europe and, as a result, grossly overestimated the degree of revolutionary ferment in the West.

The German counterparts of Lenin and Trotsky were confused and ineffective. They received no assistance from Russia and would not have accepted Russian direction if it could have been given them. When one considers Liebknecht, Luxemburg and the figures in the

Munich Commune, it is impossible not to marvel at the pathetically amateur quality of their revolutionary efforts. They were naïve, utopian and confused. The counterrevolutionary forces moved against them with the assurance of a cat stalking a cornered mouse.

Of the Communist leaders who died during the German Revolution, the most important was undoubtedly Rosa Luxemburg. She was the one who possessed the clearest view of what was going on and what needed to be done. While such figures as Liebknecht were agitating for the immediate "completion" of the German Revolution, Luxemburg continued to press for thorough Marxist education of the proletariat as a preliminary to their takeover.

With Luxemburg's death, and with the killing of most of the alternate leadership of German Communism, the party was forced to concede the necessity of a lengthy and complete reconstruction. But how should this be accomplished? In the elections of June, 1920, the Communists ran candidates and succeeded in electing only two deputies to the Reichstag. One opportunity soon presented itself when the Independent Socialists broke up. The Communists offered terms, the "Twenty-one Conditions," upon which they would admit the left wing of the Independent Socialists to their party. Some 300,000 Independents accepted the terms, and suddenly the German Communist Party became a mass party which succeeded in winning sixty-two Reichstag seats in the 1924 elections. Additional strength continued to flow into the party from the recruitment of young workers who were dissatisfied with the stodgy pace of the Social Democrats.

Counterbalancing this good fortune was a whole series of problems which stemmed from the events of 1918–19. The party found itself compelled to fight out a murderous internal battle over the corpse of Rosa Luxemburg. One section of the German Communists persisted in clinging to certain of her principles: that the Leninist conception of the dictatorship of the proletariat as manifested through a small body of theorists was incorrect; that the use of terror on the Russian Communist pattern was un-Marxist; and that Lenin and his successors had no valid claim to predominance over Communists in other nations. The Russian-influenced wing of the German Communist Party violently decried these theories. If Luxemburg had been right, then Lenin must have been wrong—a prospect too horrifying to consider.

By the early 1920s the whole question had taken on a religious fervor similar to the charges and countercharges of heresy which rent the early Christian Church. And when Stalin came to power and forced Trotsky into exile, the matter became even more tortured. Stalin, determined to exert his own direction over the Communists of every nation, demanded that German Communists agree that Rosa Luxemburg had been wrong in her assessments of the German Revolution and, for good measure, in her evaluations of practically every other Marxist question.

In due time the German Communist Party was squarely under Stalin's thumb and its Central Committee announced: "We have to speak clearly: in all these questions in which Rosa Luxemburg differed from Lenin she was wrong."[19] Stalin went even further and denounced Luxemburg as a "Trotskyite" and secured the dismissal of all "Luxemburgists" from the Communist Party.

Thus Rosa Luxemburg, once a towering revolutionary figure on a par with Lenin, sank to the position of an obscure and minor saint. The Russians insisted that the German Communists prepare themselves for violent revolution on the Russian pattern. The party bought illegal weapons, trained workers for armed revolution and made revolutionary propaganda. The result was—as Luxemburg had pointed out in the March, 1919, Berlin uprising—that the party could not escape the consequences of premature revolutionary attempts by its members. From time to time little Communist "revolutions" broke out in Germany, but each was swiftly dealt with by the Army and the police. Although the party retained the ability to produce a large vote in any election, its leadership deteriorated. Finally, when Hitler came to power, the Communist Party could offer no effective resistance, and its principal members fled to Russia or were killed in concentration camps.

The subsequent career of General Wilhelm Groener is no less instructive than the legend of Rosa Luxemburg. More than anyone else, it was Groener who prevented the officer corps from independently resuming the war in 1919 and thus destroying itself and its Army. On the day he informed Ebert that the Army could not resist and that the government must agree to the Allied peace terms, Groener proudly told his staff officers, "I have undertaken great responsibility by my action, but I will know how to bear it."[20] The consequences were not long in coming. Only three days later General von dem Borne, commanding Armee Oberkommando Sud, wrote to Noske to say that his officers "had lost confidence in General Groener on account of his attitude in the past months."[21] Soon, knowing that the officer corps now regarded him as little better than a traitor and a coward, Groener resigned from the Army.

For three years thereafter Wilhelm Groener served as minister of transport in the Socialist government, and then he quit that too. But he was still a vigorous and relatively young man. In 1922 he demanded and was given a hearing before an Army court of honor, which returned a verdict saying that at the time of the Kaiser's flight Groener had "acted in accordance with his conscience." He counted upon ultimately being rewarded, especially when Hindenburg became the President of the German Republic and when a position of great influence within the Army came to be occupied by General Kurt von Schleicher, who had been a protégé of Groener's and whom Groener regarded almost as a son.

By 1928 it appeared that Groener was finally to be repaid. He was appointed minister of defense, a post in which he functioned loyally and ably, for, unlike the still recalcitrant officer corps, Groener sincerely believed that Germany must maintain a parliamentary and democratic form of government. He was prepared to defend German democracy against the right as well as the left, and especially against the growing power of the Nazis. Groener thought them "entirely destructive. They wish to destroy the present fabric of the state, but have no constructive program with which to replace it, except a form of mad-dog dictatorship."[22]

He published a series of orders demanding that the officers cease meddling in politics and regard themselves solely as servants of a state which they were sworn to protect and defend. Aware of the formidable and increasing power of the Nazi S. A. and S. S., he was determined that these menacing organizations must be dissolved; if necessary, they must be disarmed and dispersed by the Army.

In 1931 the German government, knowing Groener's loyalty and believing that the Army would obey its former First Quartermaster General, made him minister of the interior as well as minister of defense. Groener was aware, of course, that in certain quarters he was still regarded as a "November criminal." Nevertheless, he was certain that he could control the Army. He was, as he explained it, working with "his friends, his old comrades, his colleagues."[23] He could surely expect the support of Hindenburg, he told Chancellor Brüning; after all, the Field Marshal owed much to Groener for past services.

In early April of 1932 elections were held for the Presidency of the German Republic, and Hindenburg was reelected. Shortly be-

fore the balloting, however, the Nazi S. S. and S. A. had been mobilized. More than 400,000 storm troopers had been "called to duty,"
and a cordon of these troops surrounded Berlin. The Prussian police
thereupon raided Nazi headquarters in Berlin and discovered a plan
for a Nazi *Putsch* to be carried out by the S. A.

With this proof in hand, Groener appeared before President
Hindenburg to ask for an emergency decree suppressing the S. S.
and the S. A. Previous consultation with Schleicher and other high-
ranking officers had assured Groener that the Army now recognized
the threat which the huge Nazi paramilitary forces posed and that
the officers, his friends, were prepared to back him. He anticipated
no difficulty in securing Hindenburg's agreement to the emergency
decree. Instead, Hindenburg equivocated. First he said that he
would sign the decree, then that he would not, then that he would,
but that Groener must—again—accept all the responsibility.
Deeply wounded by the Field Marshal's attitude, Groener finally
accepted these terms. Several weeks later the next blow was struck.
It was learned that General von Schleicher had held talks with
Ernst Röhm, the S. A. commander, and Count Wolf von Helldorf,
the S. A. leader in Berlin. The Army, it became apparent, would not
support the decree of dissolution and was, in fact, preparing to come
to an agreement with the Nazis. Hindenburg himself now wrote
Groener a letter in which he complained that the decree was unfair,
because it did not apply to organizations such as the Social Democrats' Reichsbanner. The Army, now anxious to do a favor for the
Nazis, gave them a copy of the letter. On May 10 Schleicher informed Groener that the Minister of Defense "no longer enjoyed the
support of the Army."

Groener resigned at once. His last letter to Schleicher could only
describe how "scorn and rage boil within me because I have been
deceived in you, my old friend, disciple, adopted son: my hope for
people and Fatherland."[24]

Wilhelm Groener died in 1939. He was not the perfect democratic
figure he is sometimes made out to be, but, more than any other
German general, he was free from the typical narrow-minded military prejudice against civil government. He was a German first, an
officer second.

Field Marshal Paul von Hindenburg resigned from the Army on
the day after the peace treaty was accepted by the government. He
departed from Supreme Headquarters on June 25, thus completely

dissociating himself from the Treaty of Versailles, which was signed three days later. It is revealing that before leaving his post Hindenburg wrote two letters of resignation. One was directed to President Ebert. The other was a private letter to the exiled Wilhelm II, begging the royal assent to Hindenburg's withdrawal from a post in which the Kaiser had placed him.

For five years thereafter the old Marshal lived in retirement in his home city of Hanover. As Germany's most respected citizen, he was constantly waited upon by delegations beseeching him to run for one office or another. He refused them all and devoted his time to the writing of his memoirs, which he and his advisers conceived as an educational work which would inspire all Germans to a renewed sense of duty and patriotism. As such, *Out of My Life* became one of the best-selling books in German history and admirably served to keep alive the Hindenburg legend—as well as the *Dolchstoss* myth, to which the author contributed with his description of the defeat of November, 1918: "Like Siegfried, slain by the treacherous spear of the grim Hagen, our exhausted front collapsed."[25]

Aside from various appearances at veterans'-association gatherings and war-memorial unveilings, Hindenburg made only one significant public appearance during his years in retirement. In the fall of 1919, the Social Democratic members of the Reichstag, suddenly realizing the extent to which the *Dolchstoss* legend was making inroads upon the German people and the implications which it had for them as, presumably, the "back stabbers" and "November criminals," created a parliamentary committee to investigate the details of wartime responsibility and the circumstances leading to the armistice. They invited Hindenburg to journey to Berlin to testify before them.

It proved to be a most ill-advised move. Hindenburg's arrival in Berlin set off a vast popular demonstration of welcome. The Army dispatched a guard of honor to greet him at the railroad station, and huge crowds of cheering Berliners jammed the streets whenever he drove out. In fact, on the day when he was to testify, a troop of cavalry had to be called out to force a passage for him through the delirious throngs. The Reichstag committee itself was not immune to the effect of Hindenburg's awesome dignity. As the Field Marshal lumbered into the committee room, every member found himself jumping to his feet. Hindenburg seated himself and, ignoring the committee's first question, proceeded to read a prepared statement in which he dwelled at length on the "stab in the back." The committee chairman attempted to recover the initiative, but Hindenburg refused to acknowledge his questions. The hearing broke up shortly afterward, its only result being that Hindenburg had succeeded in implanting the *Dolchstoss* legend more solidly than ever. Wisely the committee decided not to call him back the following day. When a Defense Ministry official inquired whether it was in order to give Hindenburg a guard of honor as he departed from the railroad station, the official answer was, "Yes, yes. Give him two, if necessary, but for God's sake get him out of Berlin!"[26]

In 1925, when Hindenburg was seventy-seven, Friedrich Ebert died. By this time most German political parties were beginning to appreciate the real importance of the Presidential office, especially since the President had the power, under Article 48 of the constitution, to suspend certain constitutional guarantees and, in emergencies, govern by decree.* The German National People's Party persuaded Hindenburg to run for the office, assuring him that he would receive the support of the parties to the right. Reluctantly, and only after confidentially seeking and receiving the approval of the Kaiser, Hindenburg allowed his name to be entered. He won the election by a narrow margin, receiving 14,600,000 votes to the Socialist candidate's 13,750,000 and the Communist candidate's 1,900,000.

Hindenburg did not enjoy the office of president. An elderly military man who had never been noted as a particularly rapid learner, he found the disorderly worlds of economics, politics and foreign affairs almost incomprehensible. But in the palmy days of the Twenties he got along nicely merely by trading on his dignity and reputation. The Thirties brought a different era. By now Hindenburg was a very old man. His mind wandered and he was apt to take the advice of the last person who called on him. He was carefully watched over by his son Oscar, who, it was well known, exerted great influence upon his father.

In 1932 Hindenburg was persuaded to stand for re-election as president of the republic. This time the Socialists supported him, because the choice was simple: Hindenburg's opponent in the elections was Adolf Hitler. On April 10, 1932, Hindenburg was re-elected by nineteen million votes to Hitler's thirteen million.

On the morning of January 30, 1933, following a prolonged period of governmental crisis, Hindenburg summoned Hitler to the Presi-

---

* During the fourteen years of its existence, Article 48 was invoked on more than 250 separate occasions, vastly more than had ever been foreseen by the framers of the Weimar Constitution.

dential Palace and asked him to accept the post of chancellor and to form a cabinet. Hitler agreed to do so.

Less than one month later, on February 28, the Reichstag Fire took place. The next day Hitler prevailed upon Hindenburg to suspend the constitutional guarantees of individual and civil liberties—a perfectly legal act under Article 48 of the constitution.

A month later, on March 23, the Reichstag deputies were summoned into session to pass the so-called Enabling Act by which they abdicated practically all of their powers to the Reich Chancellor. Outside, a mob of storm troopers shrieked, "Full powers or else!" The terrified Reichstag acquiesced, thus making Hitler the legally authorized German dictator.

On August 2, 1934, Paul von Hindenburg died, at the age of eighty-seven. Three hours later it was announced that the office of president of the republic was now merged with that of chancellor, the two being joined in the person of the Führer, Adolf Hitler.

The German Republic which had been born on November 9, 1918, was now, only sixteen years later, dead, having never attained a status of legitimacy in the minds of the German people. The disaster was complete.

Author's Notes
and Acknowledgments

I first began to write this book for the very simple reason that I had long been interested in the German Revolution of 1918–19 and I wished to know more about it. I wanted to discover for myself how the Weimar Republic became what it was and how the German Revolution set the stage for the Third Reich. At that time, six years ago, there were practically no good studies of the German Revolution to which the interested general reader might turn, and very few have been published since.

As I worked on the book it became insistently apparent that the story of the drafting of the Treaty of Versailles was inextricably bound up with any account of the German revolutionary period. The two could not possibly be separated, for most of German political and economic life was in a state of semi-suspended animation pending the presentation of the Allies' peace terms. The demands of the victors, the activities of the *Freikorps*, the personality of Woodrow Wilson and the travails of the German Social Democrats all combine into one story in this period.

Several of those who have been shown this manuscript have expressed surprise that no mention is made of the Stahlhelm (Steel Helmet) organization as a companion group to the *Freikorps*. My reason for this omission is that the Stahlhelm, which was founded in East Prussia on Christmas Day, 1918, did not grow into real prominence for many months after the events described in this book. Even then the Stahlhelm was in no sense a *Freikorps*-type organization. For several years it restricted its membership exclusively to those veterans who could prove to have had six months' wartime service at the front. The Stahlhelm never developed a terrorist section, nor did it take an armed part in the counterrevolutionary expeditions of 1919. Its membership was conservative and antirepublican (in its founder's words, the German Republic was the product of "the swinish revolution"), but it was also reasonably law-abiding and it took great pride in the organization's exclusivity. The Stahlhelm developed into a fairly strong political force (Hindenburg was its honorary commander) whose members regarded themselves as socially superior to the average *Freikorpskämpfer*. All in all, it cannot be equated with any of the *Freikorps*.

Another questioned point is the exact date of the Groener-Ebert telephone pact. Most sources say that it took place on the evening of November 9 (Volkmann, p. 68; Groener-Geyer, p. 116; Wheeler-Bennet, *Nemesis of Power*, p. 20). On the other hand, Groener's memoirs indicate (p. 124) that the conversation took place on the evening of November 10—presumably at some time after Ebert returned from the Zirkus Busch meeting. I have elected to use the November 9 date. Actually, I suppose, the exact date makes little difference. There is no dispute as to the essential facts of the conversation's occurrence and its substance.

In the preparation of this account and the encouragement to write it I owe much to my friends Professor Donald M. Murray of the University of New Hampshire and Professor Evan Hill of the University of Connecticut. Dr. Robert Cloos of Plainfield, New Jersey, gave me much valuable assistance in research.

I am also very indebted to a long list of persons and institutions upon whom I imposed shamelessly. Mrs. Agnes F. Peterson of the Central and Western Europe collection of the Hoover Institution on War, Revolution and Peace again gave me the unstinting assistance for which she has become so well-known to so many authors. Professor Ralph Haswell Lutz, this country's first and most prolific student of the German Revolution, generously loaned me material from his personal collection. Mr. Egon Weiss, the Librarian, U.S. Military Academy Library, made every facility available to me. The French Institute Library of New York permitted me to borrow books for an extraordinary period of time. The assistance of the patient staffs of the Wiener Library, London; the New York Public Library; Baker Library, Dartmouth College; and the Butler Library, Columbia University, is gratefully acknowledged.

I wish also to express my deepest appreciation to Michael V. Korda, executive editor of Simon and Schuster, for his constant encouragement and enthusiasm as well as his own very hard work on this manuscript. Finally, for me merely to express thanks to my wife, Sandra, who endured six years of my absorption with work on this book (and typed more than a half-million words in the process), would not remotely indicate the gratitude I feel toward her.

CHAPTER ONE

In addition to those works cited below, several others were of great help in the preparation of this chapter. The most frequently consulted were Link, Arthur S., *Woodrow Wilson and the Progressive Era, 1910–1917; Wilson the Diplomatist;* and *Wilson: The Road to the White House.* For certain matters on Wilson's health see Grayson, Cary T., *Woodrow Wilson: An Intimate Memoir.*

1. Nicolson, Harold, *Peacemaking: 1919,* p. 367.
2. Seymour, Charles, ed., *Intimate Papers of Colonel House,* Vol. IV, p. 487.
3. Mordacq, J.-J.-H., *Le Ministère Clemenceau: Journal d'un témoin,* Vol. III, p. 357.
4. Seymour, *op. cit.,* Vol. IV, p. 488.
5. Hoover, Herbert, *The Ordeal of Woodrow Wilson,* p. 240.
6. Nicolson, *op. cit.,* p. 371.
7. Riddell, George, Lord, *Lord Riddell's Intimate Diary of the Peace Conference and After,* p. 102.
8. Walworth, Arthur, *Woodrow Wilson: World Prophet,* Vol. II, p. 324.
9. Wilson, Edith Bolling Galt, *My Memoir,* p. 271.
10. Baker, Ray Stannard, *Woodrow Wilson: Life and Letters—Princeton, 1890–1910,* p. 150.
11. *Ibid.,* p. 258.
12. Walworth, *op. cit.,* Vol. I, p. 128.
13. Baker, *op. cit.,* p. 197.
14. *Ibid.,* p. 175.
15. George, A. L. and A. J., *Woodrow Wilson and Colonel House,* pp. 30–32.

16. Baker, *op. cit.,* p. 317.
17. Link, Arthur S., *Wilson: The Road to the White House,* p. 143.
18. McAdoo, Eleanor Wilson, *The Woodrow Wilsons,* p. 139.
19. Kennan, George F., *Russia and the West,* p. 122.
20. Smith, Arthur D. Howden, *Mr. House of Texas,* p. 26.
21. Seymour, *op. cit.,* Vol. I, p. 45.
22. *Ibid.,* p. 46.
23. Link, Arthur S., *Woodrow Wilson: A Brief Biography,* p. 65.
24. Gelfand, Lawrence E., *The Inquiry,* p. 117.
25. Seymour, Charles, "End of a Friendship," *American Heritage,* August, 1963, p. 5.
26. Owen, Frank, *Tempestuous Journey: Lloyd George, His Life and Times,* p. 22.
27. *Ibid.,* pp. 22–23.
28. *Ibid.,* p. 43.
29. Jones, Thomas, *Lloyd George,* p. 63.
30. *Ibid.,* p. 76.
31. Churchill, Winston S., *The World Crisis: Aftermath,* pp. 4–5.
32. Owen, *op. cit.,* p. 138.
33. McAdoo, William G., *Crowded Years,* p. 338.
34. *New York Times,* Jan. 8, 1918.
35. Lloyd George, David, *Memoirs of the Peace Conference,* Vol. I, p. 94.
36. Luckau, Alma, *The German Delegation at the Paris Peace Conference,* p. 140.
37. Seymour, *Intimate Papers of Colonel House,* Vol. IV, p. 75.
38. Luckau, *op. cit.,* p. 146.
39. Rudin, Harry R., *Armistice: 1918,* p. 172.
40. *Ibid.,* p. 108.

41. Seymour, *op. cit.*, Vol. IV, p. 87.
42. Lloyd George, David, *War Memoirs of David Lloyd George*, Vol. VI, p. 262.
43. Seymour, *op. cit.*, Vol. IV, pp. 162–63.
44. Bonsal, Stephen, *Unfinished Business*, p. 3.
45. Seymour, *op. cit.*, Vol. IV, p. 163.
46. Bonsal, *op. cit.*, p. 2.
47. Seymour, *op. cit.*, Vol. IV, p. 165.
48. Czernin, Ferdinand, *Versailles: 1919*, p. 31.
49. Seymour, *op. cit.*, Vol. IV, p. 189.
50. *New York Times*, Oct. 25, 1918.

CHAPTER TWO

There are, of course, countless studies of the deliberations of the Paris Peace Conference. For the most official documentation, although not necessarily the clearest exposition of the subject, see the British history Temperly, Harold W. V., *History of the Peace Conference of Paris*, and the U. S. official collection of documentage— U. S. Dept. of State, *Papers Relating to the Foreign Relations of the United States: The Paris Peace Conference, 1919*. For the French account see Mantoux, Paul, *Les Délibérations du Conseil des quatre: 24 mars–28 juin 1919*.

1. Gelfand, Lawrence, *The Inquiry*, pp. 351–52.
2. Bonsal, Stephen, *Unfinished Business*, p. 10.
3. Lansing, Robert, *The Peace Negotiations*, p. 23.
4. Hoover, Herbert, *The Ordeal of Woodrow Wilson*, p. 64.
5. Churchill, Winston S. *The World Crisis: Aftermath*, pp. 121–22.
6. Cranston, Alan, *The Killing of the Peace*, p. 39.
7. Seymour, Charles, ed., *Intimate Papers of Colonel House*, Vol. IV, p. 224.
8. Seymour, Charles, *Letters from the Paris Peace Conference*, p. 31.
9. Gelfand, *op. cit.*, pp. 23–24.
10. Shotwell, James T., *At the Paris Peace Conference*, pp. 76–78.
11. Hoover, *op. cit.*, p. 69.
12. Nicolson, Harold, *Peacemaking: 1919*, p. 225.
13. Lloyd George, David, *Memoirs of the Peace Conference*, Vol. I, pp. 110–11.
14. *Ibid.*, p. 112.
15. *Ibid.*, p. 114.
16. Keynes, John Maynard, *The Economic Consequences of the Peace*, p. 131.
17. Lloyd George, *op. cit.*, pp. 307–9.
18. Churchill, *op. cit.*, p. 38.
19. Noble, George Bernard, *Policies and Opinions at Paris, 1919*, p. 88.
20. *Ibid.*, p. 89.
21. Shotwell, *op. cit.*, p. 100.
22. Seymour, *Intimate Papers of Colonel House*, Vol. IV, p. 255.
23. Baker, Ray Stannard, *Woodrow Wilson and World Settlement*, Vol. I, p. 195.
24. Tardieu, André, *The Truth about the Treaty*, p. 91.
25. Nicolson, *op. cit.*, p. 152.
26. Lansing, Robert, *The Peace Negotiations: A Personal Narrative*, p. 201.
27. *New York Times*, Jan. 19, 1919.
28. *Ibid.*
29. Tardieu, *op. cit.*, p. 99.
30. Nicolson, *op. cit.*, pp. 225–26.
31. Bailey, Thomas A., *Woodrow Wilson and the Lost Peace*, p. 156.
32. Lloyd George, *op. cit.*, p. 140.
33. Churchill, *op. cit.*, p. 133.
34. Lloyd George, *op. cit.*, p. 141.
35. *Ibid.*, p. 152.
36. *Ibid.*, p. 175.
37. *Ibid.*, p. 177.
38. Clemenceau, Georges, *Grandeur and Misery of Victory*, p. 179.
39. Nicolson, *op. cit.*, p. 108.
40. House, Edward M., ms. diary for February 27, 1917, quoted in Kennan, George F., *Russia Leaves the War*, p. 29.
41. Trask, David, *General Tasker Howard Bliss and the "Sessions of the World," 1919*, p. 13.
42. Noble, *op. cit.*, p. 92.
43. Walworth, Arthur, *Woodrow Wilson: World Prophet*, Vol. II, p. 248.
44. Lloyd George, *op. cit.*, p. 142.
45. Baker, *op. cit.*, p. 257.
46. Thompson, Charles T., *Peace Conference: Day by Day*, p. 141.
47. Baker, *op. cit.*, p. 233.
48. Bonsal, *op. cit.*, p. 56.
49. *Ibid.*
50. Noble, *op. cit.*, pp. 117–18.
51. Walworth, *op. cit.*, Vol. I, p. 258.
52. Baker, *op. cit.*, p. 285.
53. Bonsal, *op. cit.*, p. 57.
54. Seymour, *Intimate Papers of Colonel House*, Vol. IV, p. 319.

55. Bonsal, *op. cit.*, p. 58.
56. Bailey, *op. cit.*, p. 115.
57. Watt, Richard M., *Dare Call It Treason*, p. 281.
58. King, Jere Clemens, *Generals and Politicians*, pp. 217–18.
59. King, Jere Clemens, *Foch versus Clemenceau*, p. 15.
60. Baker, *op. cit.*, p. 58.
61. Lloyd George, *op. cit.*, p. 78.
62. *Ibid.*
63. *Ibid.*
64. *Ibid.*, p. 79.
65. King, *Foch versus Clemenceau*, p. 49.
66. Baker, *op. cit.*, p. 162.
67. House, E. M., and Seymour, Charles, eds., *What Really Happened at Paris*, p. 463.

CHAPTER THREE

1. U. S. Dept. of State, *Papers Relating to the Foreign Relations of the United States: The Paris Peace Conference, 1919*, Vol. III, p. 583.
2. Thompson, John M., *Russia, Bolshevism, and the Versailles Peace*, p. 12.
3. Lloyd George, David, *Memoirs of the Peace Conference*, Vol. I, p. 222.
4. Kennan, George F., *Russia and the West*, p. 123.
5. Thompson, *op. cit.*, p. 96.
6. Chamberlain, William Henry, *The Russian Revolution*, Vol. II, p. 158.
7. Hankey, Maurice, Lord, *The Supreme Control: At the Paris Peace Conference, 1919*, p. 68.
8. U. S. Dept. of State, *op. cit.*, p. 1043.
9. *Ibid.*, Vol. IV, pp. 16–18.
10. Hankey, *op. cit.*, p. 76.
11. Seymour, Charles, ed., *Intimate Papers of Colonel House*, Vol. IV, p. 348.
12. Lloyd George, *op. cit.*, p. 247.

CHAPTER FOUR

In addition to those sources shown below, I used Temperly for background on individual points of dispute. Haskins, Charles H., and Lord, Robert H., *Some Problems of the Peace Conference*, provides a detailed study of certain questions, notably the Fiume controversy, by men who were part of the committees which worked on these matters.

1. Baker, Ray Stannard, *Woodrow Wilson and World Settlement*, Vol. I, p. 297.
2. Bonsal, Stephen, *Unfinished Business*, p. 64
3. Seymour, Charles, ed., *Intimate Papers of Colonel House*, Vol. IV, pp. 329–30.
4. Cranston, Alan, *The Killing of the Peace*, p. 67.
5. Walworth, Arthur, *Woodrow Wilson and World Settlement*, Vol. II, p. 269.
6. Cranston, *op. cit.*, p. 68.
7. Bonsal, *op. cit.*, p. 59.
8. Walworth, *op. cit.*, p. 277.
9. Hoover, Herbert, *The Ordeal of Woodrow Wilson*, p. 191.
10. *Ibid.*, pp. 193–94.
11. Seymour, *op. cit.*, p. 385.
12. Wilson, Edith B. G., *My Memoir*, pp. 245–46.
13. Baker, *op. cit.*, p. 311.
14. Lloyd George, David, *Memoirs of the Peace Conference*, Vol. I, p. 313.
15. *Ibid.*
16. Bailey, Thomas A., *Woodrow Wilson and the Lost Peace*, p. 271.
17. *Ibid.*, p. 159.
18. Nicolson, Harold, *Peacemaking: 1919*, p. 101.
19. Baker, *op. cit.*, Vol. II, p. 35.
20. Seymour, *op. cit.*, p. 396.
21. Baker, *op. cit.*, Vol. II, p. 54.
22. Seymour, *op. cit.*, p. 404.
23. House, E. M., and Seymour, Charles, eds., *What Really Happened at Paris*, p. 272.
24. Lloyd George, *op. cit.*, p. 268.
25. *Ibid.*, p. 266.
26. *Ibid.*, p. 267.
27. Seymour, *op. cit.*, p. 407.
28. Baker, *op. cit.*, Vol. II, p. 80.
29. Seymour, *op. cit.*, p. 408.
30. Nicolson, *op. cit.*, p. 160.
31. Baker, *op. cit.*, Vol. II, p. 161.
32. Hoover, Irwin, *Forty-two Years in the White House*, pp. 98–99.
33. Hoover, Herbert, *The Memoirs of Herbert Hoover*, Vol. 1, *Years of Adventure*, p. 468.
34. Lloyd George, *op. cit.*, p. 159.
35. Seymour, Charles, *Letters from the Paris Peace Conference*, p. 214.
36. Baker, *op. cit.*, Vol. II, p. 167.
37. Seymour, *Intimate Papers of Colonel House*, Vol. IV, p. 448.

CHAPTER FIVE

There are a great many studies of the German Social Democratic Party in the years before, during and after World War I. Of these, I found Schorske (referenced below) to be the most helpful. Others frequently used were Landauer, Carl, *European Socialism*, and Roth, Guenther, *The Social Democrats in Imperial Germany*. Additional useful information on Liebknecht and Luxemburg was found in the collection of Liebknecht's speeches and papers *The Future Belongs to the People* and Luxemburg's *Juniusbrochure*, published in English as *The Crisis in the German Social Democracy*. For insight into Luxemburg's personality see her *Letters to Karl and Luise Kautsky, 1896–1918*.

1. Foch, Ferdinand, *Memoirs of Marshall Foch*, p. 473.
2. Carr, Edward H., *The Bolshevik Revolution*, Vol. III, pp. 95–96.
3. Schorske, Carl, *German Social Democracy, 1905–1917: The Development of the Great Schism*, p. 4.
4. *Ibid.*, p. 5.
5. Eyck, Erich, *A History of the Weimar Republic*, Vol. I, p. 3.
6. Ludwig, Emil, *Wilhelm Hohenzollern*, p. 312.
7. Pinson, Koppel S., *Modern Germany*, pp. 216–217.
8. Frölich, Paul, *Rosa Luxemburg*, p. 68.
9. Ernst, Eugen, *The Germans and Their Modern History*, p. 13.
10. Gay, Peter, *The Dilemma of Democratic Socialism*, p. 269.
11. Manifesto of the Extraordinary International Socialist Conference "On the International Situation," Basel, November, 1912, quoted *in extenso* in Gankin, O. H., and Fisher, H. H., eds., *The Bolsheviks and the World War*, p. 84.
12. Speech of Rosa Luxemburg, "On a General Strike Against the War," in Gankin and Fisher, *op. cit.*, p. 59.
13. Scheidemann, Philipp, *Making of a New Germany*, Vol. I, p. 218.
14. Lutz, Ralph H., *Fall of the German Empire*, Vol. II, pp. 6–7.
15. *Ibid.*, p. 12.
16. Pinson, *op. cit.*, p. 327.
17. Lutz, Ralph H., ed., *The Causes of German Collapse in 1918: Sections of the Officially Authorized Report of the Commission of the German Constituent Assembly and of the German Reichstag, 1919–1928*, p. 260.
18. Pinson, *op. cit.*, pp. 325–26.
19. Lutz, *Fall of the German Empire*, Vol. II, p. 11.
20. *Ibid.*, pp. 36–37.
21. Nettl, J. P., *Rosa Luxemburg*, Vol. II, pp. 640–41.
22. Angress, Werner T., *Stillborn Revolution*, p. 7.
23. Meyer, Karl W., *Karl Liebknecht*, p. 85.
24. Nettl, *op. cit.*, p. 644.
25. Liebknecht, Karl, *The Future Belongs to the People* (a collection of speeches, letters and statements by and about Liebknecht), p. 85.
26. Nettl, *op. cit.*, p. 649.
27. Cowles, Virginia, *The Kaiser*, p. 370.
28. Hoffmann, Max, *Aufzeichnungen*, Vol. I, p. 159.
29. Ludendorff, Erich, *Ludendorff's Own Story*, Vol. II, p. 64.
30. Craig, Gordon A., *The Politics of the Prussian Army*, p. 319.
31. Benoist-Méchin, J., *History of the German Army*, Vol. I, p. 17.
32. Goodspeed, D. J., *Ludendorff*, p. 221.
33. Halperin, S. William, *Germany Tried Democracy*, p. 30.
34. *Ibid.*, p. 31.
35. Gatzke, Hans, *Germany's Drive to the West*, p. 144.
36. Rosenberg, Arthur, *The Birth of the German Republic*, p. 228.
37. *Ibid.*, p. 126.
38. Lutz, *Fall of the German Empire*, Vol. I, p. 498.
39. *Ibid.*, Vol. II, p. 233.
40. *Ibid.*, pp. 455–56.
41. *Ibid.*, pp. 459–60.
42. Max[imilian] of Baden, Prince, *The Memoirs of Prince Max of Baden*, Vol. II, pp. 11–12.
43. *Ibid.*, p. 163.
44. Eyck, *op. cit.*, p. 36.
45. Pinson, *op. cit.*, p. 321.
46. Czernin, Ferdinand, *Versailles: 1919*, p. 5.
47. Lutz, *Fall of the German Empire*, Vol. II, p. 473.
48. *Ibid.*, p. 491.
49. *Ibid.*, p. 494.
50. Halperin, *op. cit.*, p. 56.

51. Max of Baden, *op. cit.*, p. 15.
52. *Ibid.*
53. Rosenberg, *op. cit.*, p. 245.
54. Lutz, *Fall of the German Empire*, Vol. II, p. 382.
55. *Ibid.*, p. 481.
56. *Ibid.*, p. 397.
57. Niemann, Alfred, *Kaiser und Revolution*, p. 100.
58. Ludendorff, *op. cit.*, p. 412.
59. Eyck, *op. cit.*, p. 27.
60. Max of Baden, *op. cit.*, p. 181.
61. Hindenburg, Paul von, *Out of My Life*, Vol. II, p. 265.
62. Goodspeed, *op. cit.*, p. 269.
63. Max of Baden, *op. cit.*, p. 195.
64. Rudin, Harry R., *Armistice: 1918*, p. 10.
65. Ludendorff, *op. cit.*, p. 425.
66. Goodspeed, *op. cit.*, pp. 271–72.
67. Lutz, *Fall of the German Empire*, Vol. II, p. 524.

CHAPTER SIX

A very helpful account in the preparation of this chapter was Schubert, Paul, and Gibson, Langhorne, *Death of a Fleet*, which follows the German Navy from the mutinies to the Scapa Flow scuttling.

1. Rosenberg, Arthur, *The Birth of the German Republic*, p. 274.
2. Ryder, A. J., *The German Revolution of 1918–1919*, p. 101.
3. Rosenberg, *op. cit.*, p. 263.
4. In his *Memoirs* (Vol. II, p. 282), Prince Max offers an interesting comment. He was affronted by the fact that the Navy did not tell him of its plans, but he stresses the point that he *would not* necessarily have forced the Navy High Command to call off the operation. Instead, he was angry on the finer point that he, as Chancellor, *should* have been told by virtue of the prerogatives of his office. He was quite offended that the Navy did not trust him in this matter.
5. The German battle plan has been described with a host of variations. This plan outlined above is taken from Vidil, Charles, *Les Mutineries de la marine allemande*, pp. 152–54. Other accounts claim that it was the intention of the Admiral commanding to steam southeast a short distance and cover the flank of the Army as it retreated along the coast. Actually, it makes little difference what the precise plan was. It is enough that the Navy High Command intended to send the High Seas Fleet to sea under circumstances wherein they stood an excellent chance of engaging the Royal Navy in a full-scale action.
6. Fischer, Ruth, *Stalin and German Communism*, p. 80.
7. Noske, Gustav, *Von Kiel bis Kapp*, p. 11.

CHAPTER SEVEN

In addition to sources directly quoted below, I drew heavily on Ryder, A. J., *The German Revolution of 1918–1919*, Gentizon, Paul, *La Révolution allemande*, and Mishark, John W., *Friedrich Ebert and German Social Democracy*. Rosenberg, Arthur, *History of the German Republic*, was also valuable.

1. Rudin, Harry R., *Armistice: 1918*, p. 173.
2. Pershing, John J., *My Experiences in the World War*, Vol. II, p. 367.
3. Foch, Ferdinand, *The Memoirs of Marshall Foch*, p. 463.
4. Burdick, Charles B., and Lutz, Ralph H., eds., *The Political Institutions of the German Revolution, 1918–1919*, p. 27.
5. *Ibid.*, p. 35.
6. Max[imilian] of Baden, Prince, *The Memoirs of Prince Max of Baden*, Vol. II, p. 230.
7. Payne, Robert, *The Rise and Fall of Stalin*, p. 236.
8. Meyer, Karl W., *Karl Liebknecht*, p. 127.
9. Carr, Edward H., *The Bolshevik Revolution*, Vol. III, p. 566.
10. Trotsky, Leon, *The Russian Revolution*, p. 223.
11. McNeal, Robert H., *The Bolshevik Tradition*, p. 96.
12. Trotsky, Leon, *My Life*, p. 382.
13. Pinson, Koppel S., *Modern Germany*, p. 337.
14. Nettl, J. P., *Rosa Luxemburg*, Vol. II, p. 695.
15. Deutscher, Isaac, *The Prophet Armed*, p. 193.
16. Wheeler-Bennett, Sir John W.,

Brest-Litovsk: The Forgotten Peace,
p. 358.
17. Kabisch, Ernst, *Groener,* p. 53.
18. Max of Baden, *op. cit.,* p. 300.
19. *Ibid.,* p. 304.
20. Wheeler-Bennett, *Nemesis of Power,*
p. 24.
21. Noske, Gustav, *Von Kiel bis Kapp,*
p. 27.
22. Max of Baden, *op. cit.,* p. 295.
23. Burdick and Lutz, *op. cit.,* p. 38.
24. *Ibid.,* pp. 34, 37.
25. Max of Baden, *op. cit.,* p. 312.
26. *Ibid.*
27. *Ibid.,* p. 318.
28. *Ibid.*
29. *Ibid.,* p. 319.
30. Craig, Gordon A., *The Politics of
the Prussian Army,* pp. 344–45.
31. Foch, *op. cit.,* p. 471.
32. Max of Baden, *op. cit.,* p. 340.
33. Frölich, Paul, *Rosa Luxemburg: Her
Life and Works,* p. 287.
34. Max of Baden, *op. cit.,* pp. 341–42.
35. *Ibid.,* p. 342.
36. Baumont, Maurice, *The Fall of the
Kaiser,* p. 20.
37. Wheeler-Bennett, *Nemesis of Power,*
p. 10.
38. Baumont, *op. cit.,* p. 70.
39. *Ibid.,* p. 95.
40. *Ibid.,* p. 99.
41. *Ibid.,* p. 111.
42. *Ibid.*
43. *Ibid.,* p. 112.
44. *Ibid.,* p. 127.
45. *Ibid.,* p. 136.
46. *Ibid.,* p. 133.
47. Scheidemann, Philipp, *The Making
of a New Germany,* Vol. II, p. 250.
48. Baumont, *op. cit.,* p. 187.
49. Lutz, Ralph H., ed., *Fall of the
German Empire,* Vol. II, p. 535.
50. *Ibid.,* p. 537.
51. Schorske, Carl, *German Social Democracy, 1905–1917,* p. 123.
52. Max of Baden, *op. cit.,* p. 354.
53. *Ibid.,* p. 357.
54. Scheidemann, *op. cit.,* p. 264.
55. Benoist-Méchin, *History of the German Army,* Vol. I, p. 53.
56. Fischer, Ruth, *Stalin and German
Communism,* p. 60.
57. *Ibid.,* p. 63.
58. Max of Baden, *op. cit.,* p. 363.
59. Benoist-Méchin, *op. cit.,* p. 90.
60. Groener, Wilhelm, *Lebenserinnerungen,* p. 467.

CHAPTER EIGHT

On the German General Staff at this
period I used Kuhl, H. L., *Der deutsche
Generalstab;* also Caro, K., and
Oehme, W., *Schleichers Aufsteig.* For a
valuable survey of the German Revolution with emphasis on Spartacist Week I
used Coper, Rudolf, *Failure of a Revolution.*

1. Rudin, Harry R., *Armistice: 1918,*
p. 379.
2. Volkmann, E. O., *Revolution über
Deutschland,* p. 76.
3. Shartle, Samuel G., *Spa, Versailles,
Munich,* pp. 29–30.
4. Volkmann, *op. cit.,* pp. 69–70.
5. Craig, Gordon A., *The Politics of
the Prussian Army,* p. 350.
6. Wheeler-Bennett, Sir John W.,
Wooden Titan, p. 210.
7. Volkmann, *op. cit.,* p. 80.
8. Waite, Robert G. L., *Vanguard of
Nazism,* p. 31.
9. Volkmann, *op. cit.,* p. 124.
10. Groener, Wilhelm, *Lebenserinnerungen,* pp. 473–74.
11. Carsten, F. L., *The Reichswehr and
Politics: 1918–1933,* p. 14.
12. Wheeler-Bennett, *Nemesis of Power,*
p. 31.
13. *Die Rote Fahne,* Nov. 10, 1918.
14. Daniels, H. G., *The Rise of the German Republic,* pp. 60–61.
15. Scheidemann, Philipp, *The Making
of a New Germany,* Vol. II, pp.
269–71.
16. *Ibid.,* p. 268.
17. Meyer, Karl W., *Karl Liebknecht,*
p. 136.
18. Bouton, S. Miles, *And the Kaiser
Abdicates,* p. 172.
19. Fischer, Louis, *The Life of Lenin,*
p. 317.
20. Carr, Edward Hallett, *The Bolshevik Revolution,* Vol. III, p. 101.
21. Burdick, Charles, and Lutz,
Ralph H., eds., *The Political Institutions of the German Revolution,
1918–1919,* p. 92.
22. Carr, *op. cit.,* p. 101.
23. Pinson, Koppel S., *Modern Germany,* p. 375.
24. *Die Rote Fahne,* Dec. 14, 1918.
25. Ryder A. J., *The German Revolution of 1918–1919,* p. 183.
26. Meyer, *op. cit.,* p. 145.

27. Lutz, Ralph H., *The German Revolution*, p. 84.
28. Volkmann, *op. cit.*, p. 133.
29. *Die Rote Fahne*, Dec. 20, 1918.
30. Bouton, *op. cit.*, p. 213.
31. Wheeler-Bennett, *Nemesis of Power*, p. 33.
32. Burdick and Lutz, *op. cit.*, p. 109.
33. *Ibid.*, p. 110.
34. Groener, *op. cit.*, p. 475.
35. Burdick and Lutz, *op. cit.*, pp. 107–8.
36. Benoist-Méchin, J., *History of the German Army*, Vol. I, pp. 88–89.
37. Burdick and Lutz, *op. cit.*, p. 124.
38. Scheidemann, *op. cit.*, p. 289.
39. Benoist-Méchin, *op. cit.*, p. 90.
40. Volkmann, *op. cit.*, pp. 158–59.
41. Waite, *op. cit.*, p. 11.
42. Carr, *op. cit.*, p. 97.
43. *Ibid.*, p. 103.
44. Craig, *op. cit.*, p. 360.
45. Nettl, J. P., *Rosa Luxemburg*, Vol. II, p. 471.
46. *Ibid.*, p. 731.
47. *Ibid.*, p. 757.
48. Meyer, *op. cit.*, p. 151.
49. Noske, Gustav, *Von Kiel bis Kapp*, p. 68.

CHAPTER NINE

Several valuable works on the *Freikorps*, although not directly quoted from in this chapter, are Salomon, Ernst von, *Das Buch vom deutschen Freikorpskämpfer* and *Die Geächteten*. In addition, see Schmidt-Pauli, Edgar von, *Geschichte der Freikorps 1918–1924*.

1. *Times*, London, Dec. 10, 1919.
2. *Ibid.*, Dec. 13, 1919.
3. *Morning Post*, Jan. 20 and 22, 1919.
4. Pinson, Koppel S., *Modern Germany*, p. 384.
5. Waldman, Eric, *The Spartacist Uprising*, p. 28.
6. Benoist-Méchin, J., *History of the German Army*, Vol. I, p. 112.
7. Maercker, Ludwig R. von, *Vom Kaiserheer zur Reichswehr*, p. 64.
8. Heiden, Konrad, *Der Führer*, p. 20.
9. Waite, Robert G. L., *Vanguard of Nazism*, pp. 25–26.
10. *Ibid.*, p. 23.
11. *Ibid.*, p. 28.
12. *Ibid.*, p. 29.

13. Maercker, *op. cit.*, p. 46.
14. *Ibid.*, p. 53.
15. *Ibid.*
16. *Ibid.*, p. 55.
17. Waldman, *op. cit.*, p. 161.
18. Ryder, A. J., *The German Revolution of 1918–1919*, p. 201.
19. Waldman, *op. cit.*, p. 177.
20. Carr, Edward H., *The Bolshevik Revolution*, Vol. III, p. 108.
21. Burdick, Charles, and Lutz, Ralph H., eds., *The Political Institutions of the German Revolution, 1918–1919*, p. 181.
22. *Ibid.*, p. 178.
23. This account is largely drawn from Roden, Hans, ed., *Deutsche Soldaten*, pp. 39–44 (account by Major von Stephani, who commanded the troops storming the *Vorwärts* building).
24. Benoist-Méchin, J., *History of the German Army*, Vol. I, pp. 108–9.
25. Noske, Gustav, *Von Kiel bis Kapp*, pp. 69–70.
26. Ames, Knowlton L., Jr., *Berlin after the Occupation*, p. 36.
27. Nettl, J. P., *Rosa Luxemburg*, Vol. II, p. 767.
28. Fischer, Ruth, *Stalin and German Communism*, p. 74.
29. Waldman, *op. cit.*, p. 192.
30. *Die Rote Fahne*, Jan. 7, 1919.
31. Waldman, *op. cit.*, pp. 190–91.
32. Angress, Werner T., *Stillborn Revolution*, p. 35.
33. Lutz, Ralph H., *The German Revolution*, p. 97.
34. Meyer, Karl W., *Karl Liebknecht*, p. 167.
35. Lutz, *op. cit.*, p. 97.
36. Frölich, Paul, *Rosa Luxemburg: Her Life and Works*, p. 326.
37. Nettl, *op. cit.*, p. 779.
38. Burdick and Lutz, *op. cit.*, p. 192.
39. Lutz, *op. cit.*, p. 98.
40. Goodspeed, D. J., *Ludendorff*, p. 280.

CHAPTER TEN

For the German constitution I used Brunet, René, *The New German Constitution*. I found Mitchell's *Revolution in Bavaria, 1918–1919* to take precedence over all other sources on the Munich uprisings, just as Waite's *Vanguard of*

Nazism is the principal account of *Frei-korps* activity. Ryder was again valuable in this chapter.

1. Kaufmann, Walter H., *Monarchism in the Weimar Republic*, p. 54.
2. Lutz, Ralph H., *The German Revolution*, p. 117.
3. Noske, Gustav, *Von Kiel bis Kapp*, p. 78.
4. Wheeler-Bennett, Sir John W., *Nemesis of Power*, p. 44.
5. Craig, Gordon A., *The Politics of the Prussian Army*, p. 347.
6. Gentizon, Paul, *La Révolution allemande*, p. 22.
7. Heiden, Konrad, *Der Führer*, Vol. I, p. 20.
8. Nettl, J. P., *Rosa Luxemburg*, p. 21.
9. Gentizon, *op. cit.*, p. 57.
10. *Ibid.*, p. 63.
11. Mitchell, Allan, *Revolution in Bavaria, 1918–1919*, p. 120.
12. Gentizon, *op. cit.*, pp. 99–100.
13. *Ibid.*, p. 14.
14. Mitchell, *op. cit.*, p. 139.
15. Gentizon, *op. cit.*, p. 77.
16. *Ibid.*, p. 76.
17. *Ibid.*, p. 80.
18. Mitchell, *op. cit.*, pp. 171–72.
19. Heiden, *op. cit.*, pp. 19–21.
20. Got, Ambroise, "L'Assassinat de Kurt Eisner," *La Revue de France*, Vol. I (1922).
21. Benoist-Méchin, *The History of the German Army*, Vol. I, pp. 149–50.
22. Burdick, Charles, and Lutz, Ralph H., eds., *The Political Institutions of the German Revolution, 1918–1919*, p. 198.
23. Noske, *op. cit.*, p. 82.
24. Hulse, James W., *The Forming of the Communist International*, pp. 25–26.
25. *Die Rote Fahne*, Mar. 3, 1919.
26. Lutz, *op. cit.*, p. 127.
27. Waite, Robert G. L., *Vanguard of Nazism*, p. 73.
28. Benoist-Méchin, *op. cit.*, p. 200.
29. Waite, *op. cit.*, p. 75.
30. Benoist-Méchin, *op. cit.*, p. 203.
31. *Ibid.*, p. 202.
32. Waldman, Eric, *The Spartacist Revolution*, p. 194.
33. Burdick and Lutz, *op. cit.*, p. 266.
34. Czernin, Ferdinand, *Versailles: 1919*, p. 226.
35. Eyck, Erich, *A History of the Weimar Republic*, Vol. I, p. 66.
36. *Ibid.*, p. 69.
37. Benoist-Méchin, *op. cit.*, p. 164.

CHAPTER ELEVEN

Déak's *Hungary at the Paris Peace Conference* was the most helpful for that section of this chapter. An additional source was Low, Alfred D., *The Soviet Hungarian Republic and the Paris Peace Conference*.

1. Károlyi, Mihály, *Memoirs of Michael Karolyi*, pp. 31–32.
2. Jaksch, Wenzel, *Europe's Road to Potsdam*, p. 192.
3. Károlyi, *op. cit.*, p. 153.
4. Hulse, James W., *The Forming of the Communist International*, p. 45.
5. Seymour, Charles, ed., *The Intimate Papers of Colonel House*, Vol. IV, p. 405.
6. Seymour, Charles, *Letters from the Paris Peace Conference*, p. 185.
7. Trask, David F., *General Tasker Howard Bliss and the "Sessions of the World,"* 1919, p. 41.
8. Baker, Ray Stannard, *Woodrow Wilson and World Settlement*, Vol. III, pp. 238–44.
9. Bonsal, Stephen, *Unfinished Business*, p. 124.
10. Nicolson, Harold, *Peacemaking: 1919*, p. 298.
11. *Ibid.*, p. 299.
12. *Ibid.*, p. 304.
13. Volkmann, Erich, *Revolution über Deutschland*, p. 222.
14. Mitchell, Allan, *Revolution in Bavaria, 1918–1919*, p. 311.
15. Noske, Gustav, *Von Kiel bis Kapp*, p. 136.
16. Mitchell, *op. cit.*, p. 319.
17. Got, Ambroise, *La Terreur en Bavière*, p. 168.
18. Mitchell, *op. cit.*, p. 326.
19. Lutz, Ralph H., *The German Revolution*, p. 141.
20. Got, *op. cit.*, p. 177.
21. Hitler, Adolf, *Mein Kampf*, p. 208.
22. Mitchell, *op. cit.*, p. 322.
23. *Ibid.*
24. Got, *op. cit.*, p. 178.
25. Mitchell, *op. cit.*, p. 326.
26. *Ibid.*, p. 327.

27. Toller, Ernst, *I Was a German*, pp. 196–97.
28. Got, *op. cit.*, p. 181.
29. Mitchell, *op. cit.*, p. 329.
30. *Ibid.*, p. 130.
31. Waite, Robert G. L., *Vanguard of Nazism*, p. 89.
32. Got, *op. cit.*, p. 276.
33. Waite, *op. cit.*, p. 92.
34. The question of how many persons were killed in the Munich suppression is, as usual in this sort of thing, open to question. Benoist-Méchin says 700, Got says about 600, Waite says 1,200, Mitchell says 600; but these figures were all *before* the "cleansing" of Munich began. A final figure of about 1,200 is therefore reasonable and probably conservative.
35. Benoist-Méchin, *History of the German Army*, Vol. I, p. 282.

CHAPTER TWELVE

For the section on Poland and Pilsudski I drew most heavily on Humphrey, Grace, *Pilsudski: Builder of Poland;* Pilsudska, Alexandra, *Pilsudski: A Biography by his Wife;* Temperly for the Paris Peace Conference activity; Donald, Sir Robert, *The Polish Corridor and the Consequences;* Korbel, Josef, *Poland Between East and West;* and Leslie, R. F., *The Polish Question: Poland's Place in Modern History*.

In the section on the Baltic states, Benoist-Méchin's *Histoire de l'armée allemande,* Vol. II, was particularly valuable.

1. Burdick, Charles, and Lutz, Ralph H., *The Political Institutions of the German Revolution*, p. 199.
2. Komarnicki, Titus, *Rebirth of the Polish Republic*, p. 94.
3. Haskins, C. H., and Lord, R. H., *Some Problems of the Peace Conference*, p. 154.
4. Gelfand, Lawrence E., *The Inquiry*, pp. 146–47.
5. Hooker, Nancy, ed., *The Moffat Papers: Selections from the Diplomatic Journals of Jay Pierrepont Moffat, 1919–1943*, p. 13.
6. Czernin, Ferdinand, *Versailles: 1919*, p. 202.
7. Lloyd George, David, *Memoirs of the Peace Conference*, p. 189.
8. Wandycz, Piotr, *France and Her Eastern Allies: 1919–1925*, p. 32.
9. Lloyd George, David, *The Truth about the Peace Treaties*, Vol. I, p. 693.
10. Nelson, Harold I., *Land and Power*, pp. 98–99.
11. Bonsal, Stephen, *Suitors and Suppliants*, p. 124.
12. Seymour, Charles, ed., *The Intimate Papers of Colonel House*, Vol. IV, p. 462.
13. Trask, David F. *General Tasker Howard Bliss and the "Sessions of the World," 1919*, p. 24.
14. Baker, Ray Stannard, *Woodrow Wilson and World Settlement*, Vol. II, p. 60.
15. Lloyd George, *Memoirs of the Peace Conference*, Vol. II, p. 644.
16. Nelson, *op. cit.*, p. 286.
17. Birdsall, Paul, *Versailles Twenty Years After*, p. 187.
18. Wandycz, *op. cit.*, p. 42.
19. Lloyd George, *Memoirs of the Peace Conference*, Vol. II, p. 646.
20. *Ibid.*, p. 647.
21. *Ibid.*, p. 648.
22. Laqueur, Walter, *Russia and Germany*, p. 31.
23. Waite, Robert G. L., *Vanguard of Nazism*, p. 101.
24. Many sources imply that there was an actual agreement to give Latvian land to German soldiers. This was not the case, although the rumor was successful in attracting recruits for *Freikorps* duty in the Baltic. See Du Parquet, Lieut. Col., *L'Abenture allemande en Lettonie*, pp. 55–58, in which the treaty is quoted *in extenso*.
25. Noske, Gustav, *Von Kiel bis Kapp*, pp. 177–78.
26. Salomon, Ernst von, *Die Geächteten*, p. 70.
27. Waite, *op. cit.*, p. 110.
28. Goltz, Rüdiger von der, *Meine Sendung in Finnland und im Baltikum*, p. 128.
29. *Ibid.*, p. 128.
30. Du Parquet, *op. cit.*, p. 43.
31. Waite, *op. cit.*, p. 131.
32. Du Parquet, *op. cit.*, p. 44.
33. Waite, *op. cit.*, p. 115.
34. *Ibid.*, p. 117.
35. Miller, David Hunter, *My Diary at the Peace Conference*, Vol. XVI, pp. 363–64.

CHAPTER THIRTEEN

1. Nowak, Karl, *Versailles*, p. 259.
2. Luckau, Alma, *The German Delegation at the Paris Peace Conference*, p. 55.
3. Burdick, Charles, and Lutz, Ralph H., eds., *The Political Institutions of the German Revolution, 1918–1919*, pp. 100–101.
4. Luckau, *op. cit.*, p. 186.
5. *Ibid.*, pp. 182–88.
6. *Ibid.*, p. 209.
7. *Ibid.*
8. *Ibid.*, p. 210.
9. *Ibid.*

CHAPTER FOURTEEN

1. Luckau, Alma, *The German Delegation at the Paris Peace Conference*, p. 116.
2. Schiff, Viktor, *The Germans at Versailles*, pp. 31–32.
3. Tardieu, André, *The Truth about the Treaty*, pp. 192–93.
4. Hoover, Herbert, *The Ordeal of Woodrow Wilson*, p. 234.
5. *Ibid.*, p. 240.
6. *Ibid.*, pp. 241–42.
7. *Ibid.*
8. Hankey, Maurice, Lord, *The Supreme Control*, p. 153.
9. Nowak, Karl, *Versailles*, p. 217.
10. *Times*, London, May 8, 1919.
11. Nowak, *op. cit.*, p. 220.
12. *Times*, London, May 8, 1919.
13. Riddell, George, Lord, *Lord Riddell's Intimate Diary of the Peace Conference and After*, pp. 73–74.
14. *Ibid.*, p. 74.
15. *Ibid.*, p. 76.
16. Luckau, *op. cit.*, p. 124.

CHAPTER FIFTEEN

For the section on the Saar I used Russell, Frank M., *The Saar: Battleground and Pawn*; Temperly, Vol. II; Haskins and Lord; and House and Seymour, eds., *What Really Happened at Paris*. For reparations the best study is Burnett, Philip M., *Reparations at Paris Peace Conference*.

1. Scheidemann, Philipp, *The Making of a New Germany*, Vol. II pp. 310–12.

2. Lutz, Ralph H., *The German Revolution*, p. 149.
3. *Ibid.*
4. Luckau, Alma, *The German Delegation at the Paris Peace Conference*, p. 98.
5. Lutz, *op. cit.*, p. 148.
6. Burdick, Charles, and Lutz, Ralph H., eds., *The Political Institutions of the German Revolution: 1918–1919*, p. 286.
7. U. S. Dept. of State, *Papers Relating to the Foreign Relations of the United States: The Paris Peace Conference, 1919*, Vol. VI, p. 459.
8. Luckau, *op. cit.*, p. 308.
9. *Ibid.*, p. 332.
10. *Ibid.*, p. 335.
11. Tardieu, André, *The Truth about the Treaty*, pp. 253–54.
12. *Ibid.*, p. 253.
13. *Ibid.*, p. 265.
14. *Ibid.*
15. House, E. M., and Seymour, Charles, eds., *What Really Happened at Paris*, p. 464.
16. *Ibid.*
17. Luckau, *op. cit.*, p. 246.
18. *Ibid.*, pp. 267–68.
19. King, Jere Clemens, *Foch versus Clemenceau*, p. 62.
20. Birdsall, Paul, *Versailles Twenty Years After*, p. 217.
21. King, *op. cit.*, p. 62.
22. Allen, Henry T., *The Rhineland Occupation*, p. 195.
23. King, *op. cit.*, p. 100.
24. Luckau, *op. cit.*, p. 409.
25. Thompson, Charles T., *Peace Conference Day by Day*, p. 388.
26. Tillman, Seth, *Anglo-American Relations at the Paris Peace Conference*, p. 239.
27. Luckau, *op. cit.*, p. 242.
28. *Ibid.*, p. 242.
29. Baker, Ray Stannard, *Woodrow Wilson and World Settlement*, Vol. III, p. 459.
30. *Ibid.*, p. 461.
31. *Ibid.*, p. 463.
32. *Ibid.*, pp. 464–65.
33. *Ibid.*, pp. 466–68.
34. *Ibid.*, Vol. II, p. 109.
35. Lloyd George, David, *Memoirs of the Peace Conference*, Vol. I, p. 467.
36. *Ibid.*, p. 480.
37. *Ibid.*, pp. 480–81.
38. Tardieu, *op. cit.*, p. 120.
39. Seymour, Charles, ed., *The Intimate*

Papers of Colonel House, Vol. IV, pp. 476–77.

40. Tardieu, *op. cit.*, p. 121.
41. *Ibid.*, p. 122.
42. Hoover, Herbert, *The Ordeal of Woodrow Wilson*, p. 248.
43. Baker, *op. cit.*, Vol. III, pp. 503–4.
44. Luckau, *op. cit.*, pp. 418–19.
45. *Ibid.*, p. 468.
46. *Ibid.*, p. 419.

CHAPTER SIXTEEN

For a survey of the drafting of the disarmament terms I found Temperly, Vol. II, pp. 129–36 to be the most complete. On the scuttling of the German fleet see Schubert and Gibson. The Allied plans for an invasion of Germany are covered in U. S. Dept. of State, *The Paris Peace Conference, 1919*, Vol. VI, pp. 543–56. Additionally on Erzberger I consulted Epstein, Klaus, *Matthias Erzberger and the Dilemma of German Democracy.*

1. Luckau, Alma, *The German Delegation at the Paris Peace Conference*, p. 483.
2. *Ibid.*, p. 488.
3. Goodspeed, D. J., *Ludendorff*, p. 209.
4. Erzberger, Matthias, *Erlebnisse im Weltkrieg*, p. 370.
5. Lutz, Ralph H., *The German Revolution*, p. 150.
6. U.S. Dept. of State, *Papers Relating to the Foreign Relations of the United States: The Paris Peace Conference, 1919*, Vol. XII, p. 124.
7. *Ibid.*, pp. 126–27.
8. *Ibid.*
9. Erzberger, *op. cit.*, p. 371.
10. *Ibid.*, pp. 372–73.
11. *Ibid.*, p. 373.
12. *Ibid.*, p. 374.
13. Nowak, Karl, *Versailles*, pp. 264–65.
14. Craig, Gordon A., *The Politics of the Prussian Army*, pp. 366–67.
15. Nowak, *op. cit.*, p. 197.
16. *Ibid.*
17. Wheeler-Bennett, Sir John W., *Wooden Titan: Hindenburg*, p. 238.
18. Turner, Henry A., Jr., *Stresemann and the Politics of the Weimar Government*, p. 13.
19. U. S. Dept. of State, *op. cit.*, Vol. VI, p. 548.
20. Lloyd George, David, *Memoirs of the Peace Conference*, pp. 391–94.

21. Carsten, F. L., *The Reichswehr and Politics: 1918–1933*, p. 38.
22. Dorpalen, Andreas, *Hindenburg and the Weimar Republic*, p. 5.
23. *Ibid.*, p. 30.
24. *Ibid.*, p. 31.
25. Groener, Wilhelm, *Lebenserinnerungen*, p. 477.
26. *Ibid.*, p. 496.
27. Wheeler-Bennett, Sir John W., *Nemesis of Power*, p. 52.
28. Dorpalen, *op. cit.*, p. 39.
29. *Ibid.*
30. Volkmann, Erich, *Revolution über Deutschland*, p. 282.
31. Nowak, *op. cit.*, p. 267.
32. Luckau, *op. cit.*, p. 492.
33. *Ibid.*, p. 489.
34. Dorpalen, *op. cit.*, p. 40.
35. Benoist-Méchin, *History of the German Army*, Vol. I, p. 331.
36. *Ibid.*, p. 332.
37. *Ibid.*, p. 333.
38. Noske, Gustav, *Von Kiel bis Kapp*, p. 152.
39. *Ibid.*
40. Hankey, Maurice, Lord, *The Supreme Control*, p. 177.
41. U. S. Dept. of State, *op. cit.*, Vol. VI, p. 504.
42. Noske, *op. cit.*, p. 154.
43. Maercker, Ludwig R. von, *Vom Kaiserheer zur Reichswehr*, p. 289.
44. *Ibid.*
45. Wheeler-Bennett, *Wooden Titan*, p. 220.
46. Hankey, *op. cit.*, p. 181.
47. *Ibid.*

AFTERWORD

1. U. S. Dept. of State, *The Treaty of Versailles and After*, p. 379.
2. Craig, Gordon A., *The Politics of the Prussian Army*, p. 377.
3. Morgan, John, *Assize of Arms*, p. 92.
4. Waite, Robert G. L., *Vanguard of Nazism*, p. 166.
5. *Ibid.*, p. 213.
6. Benoist-Méchin, J., *Histoire de l'armée allemande*, Vol. II, p. 155.
7. Lodge, Henry Cabot, *The Senate and the League of Nations*, pp. 201–2.
8. Link, Arthur S., *Wilson the Diplomatist*, p. 131.
9. Kennan, George F., *Russia and the West*, p. 215.

Beaverbrook, Lord, *The Decline and Fall of Lloyd George*, p. 139.

Wheeler-Bennett, Sir John W., *Nemesis of Power*, pp. 76–77.

Carsten, F. L., *The Reichswehr and Politics: 1918–1933*, p. 141.

Ibid.

Scheidemann, Philipp, *The Making of a New Germany*, Vol. II, p. 325.

Ibid.

Hilger, Gustav, and Meyer, Alfred C., *The Incompatible Allies*, p. 90.

17. *Ibid.*, p. 97.
18. *Ibid.*, p. 90.
19. Nettl, J. P., *Rosa Luxemburg*, Vol. II, p. 819.
20. Craig, *op. cit.*, p. 373.
21. Carsten, *op. cit.*, p. 45.
22. Craig, *op. cit.*, pp. 433–34.
23. *Ibid.*, p. 430.
24. Craig, *op. cit.*, p. 453.
25. Hindenburg, Paul von, *Out of My Life*, p. 440.
26. Wheeler-Bennett, *op. cit.*, p. 68.

Bibliography

Allen, Henry T., *The Rhineland Occupation*. Indianapolis, 1927.

Ames, Knowlton L., Jr., *Berlin after the Occupation*. Chicago, 1919.

Angress, Werner T., *Stillborn Revolution: The Communist Bid for Power in Germany, 1919–23*. Princeton, 1963.

Bailey, Thomas A., *Woodrow Wilson and the Lost Peace*. New York, 1944.

Baker, Ray Stannard, *Woodrow Wilson and World Settlement*, 3 vols. Gloucester, Mass., 1930.

————, *What Wilson Did at Paris*. New York, 1919.

————, *Woodrow Wilson: Life and Letters*, 8 vols. New York, 1927–39.

Baumont, Maurice, *The Fall of the Kaiser*, translated by E. I. James. New York, 1931.

Beaverbrook, Lord, *The Decline and Fall of Lloyd George*. New York, 1963.

Benoist-Méchin, J., *History of the German Army*, Vol. I of two, translated by Eileen R. Taylor. Zurich, 1939.

————, *Histoire de l'armée allemande*, Vol. II. Paris, 1938.

Birdsall, Paul, *Versailles Twenty Years After*. New York, 1941.

Bonsal, Stephen, *Suitors and Suppliants: The Little Nations at Versailles*. New York, 1946.

————, *Unfinished Business*. Garden City, N.Y., 1944.

Bouton, S. Miles, *And the Kaiser Abdicates*. New Haven, 1920.

Brunet, René, *The New German Constitution*. New York, 1922.

Burdick, Charles, and Lutz, Ralph H. eds., *The Political Institutions of the German Revolution: 1918–1919*. New York, 1966.

Burnett, Philip M., *Reparations at the Paris Peace Conference*, 2 vols. New York, 1940.

Caro, K., and Oehme, W., *Schleichers Aufsteig*. Berlin, 1933.

Carr, Edward Hallett, *The Bolshevik Revolution*, 3 vols. New York, 1951–53.

Carsten, F. L., *The Reichswehr and Politics: 1918–1933*. Oxford, 1966.

Chamberlin, William Henry, *The Russian Revolution*, 2 vols. New York, 1935.

Churchill, Winston S., *The World Crisis: The Aftermath*. New York, 1929.

Clemenceau, Georges, *Grandeur and Misery of Victory*. New York, 1930.

Coper, Rudolf, *Failure of a Revolution*. Cambridge, England, 1955.

Cowles, Virginia, *The Kaiser*. New York, 1964.

Craig, Gordon A., *The Politics of the Prussian Army*. Oxford, 1956.

Cranston, Alan, *The Killing of the Peace*. New York, 1945.

Czernin, Ferdinand, *Versailles: 1919*. New York, 1964.

Daniels, H. G., *The Rise of the German Republic*. New York, 1928.

Déak, Ferencz, *Hungary at the Paris Peace Conference*. New York, 1942.

Deutscher, Isaac, *The Prophet Armed*. New York, 1965.

Donald, Sir Robert, *The Polish Corridor and the Consequences*. London, 1929.

Dorpalen, Andreas, *Hindenburg and the Weimar Republic*. Princeton, N.J., 1964.

Du Parquet, Lieutenant Colonel, *L'Aventure allemande en Lettonie*. Paris, 1926.

Epstein, Klaus, *Matthias Erzberger and the Dilemma of German Democracy*. Princeton, N.J., 1959.

Ernst, Eugen, *The Germans and Their Modern History*, translated by Charles M. Prugh. London, 1966.

Erzberger, Matthias, *Erlebnisse im Weltkrieg*. Berlin, 1920.

Eyck, Erich, *A History of the Weimar Republic*, 2 vols., translated by Harlan P. Hanson. Cambridge, Mass., 1962.

Fischer, Louis, *The Life of Lenin*. New York, 1964.

Fischer, Ruth, *Stalin and German Communism*. Cambridge, Mass., 1948.

Foch, Ferdinand, *Memoirs of Marshal Foch*, translated by Colonel T. Bentley Mott. Garden City, N.Y., 1931.

Frölich, Paul, *Rosa Luxemburg: Her Life and Works*, translated by Edward Fitzgerald. London, 1940.

Gankin, Olga, and Fisher, H. H., editors, *The Bolsheviks and the World War*. Stanford, Calif., 1960.

Gatzke, Hans, *Germany's Drive to the West*. Baltimore, 1950.

Gay, Peter, *The Dilemma of Democratic Socialism*. New York, 1952.

Gelfand, Lawrence E., *The Inquiry*. New Haven, 1963.

Gentizon, Paul, *La Révolution allemande*. Paris, 1919.

George, A. L. and J. L., *Woodrow Wilson and Colonel House: A Personality Study*. New York, 1956.

Goltz, Rüdiger von der, *Meine Sendung in Finnland und im Baltikum*. Leipzig, 1920.

Goodspeed, D. J., *Ludendorff*. Boston, 1966.

Got, Ambroise, *La Terreur en Bavière*. Paris, 1922.

———, "L'Assassinat de Kurt Eisner," *La Revue de France*, Vol. I. Paris, 1922.

Grayson, Cary T., *Woodrow Wilson: An Intimate Memoir*. New York, 1960.

Groener, Wilhelm, *Lebenserinnerungen*, edited by Friedrich Hiller von Gätringen. Göttingen, 1957.

Groener-Geyer, Dorothea, *General Groener—Soldat und Staatsmann*. Frankfurt-am-Main, 1955.

Halperin, S. William, *Germany Tried Democracy: A Political History of the Reich from 1918 to 1933*. New York, 1946.

Hankey, Maurice, Lord, *The Supreme Control: At the Paris Peace Conference*. London, 1963.

Haskins, C. H., and Lord, R. H., *Some Problems of the Peace Conference*. Cambridge, Mass., 1922.

Heiden, Konrad, *Der Führer*, translated by Ralph Manheim. Boston, 1944.

Hilger, Gustav, and Meyer, Alfred C., *The Incompatible Allies*. New York, 1953.

Hindenburg, Paul von, *Out of My Life*, 2 vols. New York, 1919.

Hitler, Adolf, *Mein Kampf*, translated by Ralph Manheim. Boston, 1943.

Hoffmann, Max, *Die Aufzeichnungen des Generalmajor Max Hoffmann*, edited by Karl Nowak. Berlin, 1930.

Hooker, Nancy, editor: *The Moffat Papers: Selections from the Diplomatic Journals of Jay Pierrepont Moffat, 1919–1943*. Cambridge, Mass., 1956.

Hoover, Herbert, *The Memoirs of Herbert Hoover*, Vol. I, *Years of Adventure*. New York, 1951.

———, *The Ordeal of Woodrow Wilson*. New York, 1958.

Hoover, Irwin, *Forty-two Years in the White House*. Boston, 1934.

House, Edward M., and Seymour, Charles, editors, *What Really Happened at Paris*. New York, 1921.

Hulse, James W., *The Forming of the Communist International*. Stanford, Calif., 1964.

Humphrey, Grace, *Pilsudski: Builder of Poland*. New York, 1936.

Jaksch, Wenzel, *Europe's Road to Potsdam*, translated by Kurt Glaser. London, 1963.

Jones, Thomas, *Lloyd George*. Cambridge, Mass., 1951.

Kabisch, Ernst, *Groener*. Leipzig, 1932.

Károlyi, Mihály, *Memoirs of Michael Karolyi*. New York, 1957.

Kaufmann, Walter H., *Monarchism in the Weimar Republic*. New York, 1953.

Kennan, George F., *Russia and the West under Lenin and Stalin*. Boston, 1961.

————, *Russia Leaves the War*. New York, 1967.

Keynes, John Maynard, *The Economic Consequences of the Peace*. New York, 1920.

King, Jere Clemens, *Generals and Politicians*. Berkeley, Calif., 1951.

————, *Foch versus Clemenceau*. Cambridge, Mass., 1960.

Komarnicki, Titus, *Rebirth of the Polish Republic*. London, 1957.

Korbel, Josef, *Poland Between East and West*. Princeton, 1963.

Kuhl, H. L., *Der deutsche Generalstab in Vorbereitung und Durchfürung des Weltkrieges*. Berlin, 1920.

Landauer, Carl, *European Socialism*, 2 vols. Berkeley, Calif., 1959.

Lansing, Robert, *The Peace Negotiations: A Personal Narrative*. Cambridge, Mass., 1921.

Laqueur, Walter, *Russia and Germany*. Boston, 1965.

Leslie, R. F., *The Polish Question: Poland's Place in Modern History*. London, 1964.

Liebknecht, Karl, *The Future Belongs to the People*. New York, 1918.

Link, Arthur S., *Wilson: The Road to the White House*. Princeton, 1947.

————, *Wilson the Diplomatist*. Baltimore, 1957.

————, *Woodrow Wilson: A Brief Biography*. Cleveland, 1963.

————, *Woodrow Wilson and the Progressive Era*. New York, 1954.

Lloyd George, David, *Memoirs of the Peace Conference*, 2 vols. New Haven, 1939.

————, *The Truth about the Peace Treaty*, 2 vols. London, 1938.

————, *War Memoirs of David Lloyd George*, 6 vols. Boston, 1937.

Lodge, Henry Cabot, *The Senate and the League of Nations*. New York, 1925.

Low, Alfred D., *The Soviet Hungarian Republic and the Paris Peace Conference*, Transactions of the American Philosophical Society, New Series, Vol. 53, Part 10, Philadelphia, 1963.

Luckau, Alma, *The German Delegation at the Paris Peace Conference*. New York, 1941.

Ludendorff, Erich, *Ludendorff's Own Story*, 2 vols. New York, 1919.

Ludwig, Emil, *Wilhelm Hohenzollern*, translated by Ethel Mayne. New York, 1927.

Lutz, Ralph H., *The German Revolution: 1918–1919*. Stanford, Calif., 1922.

————, *Fall of the German Empire, 1914–1918*, 2 vols. Palo Alto, Calif., 1932.

————, *The Causes of German Collapse in 1918: Sections of the Officially Authorized Report of the Commission of the German Constituent Assembly and of the German Reichstag, 1919–1928*. Stanford, Calif., 1934.

Luxemburg, Rosa, *et al.*, *The Crisis in the German Social Democracy*. Brooklyn, N.Y., 1918. *Letters to Karl and Luise Kautsky, 1896–1918,* edited by Luise Kautsky, translated by Louis P. Lochner. New York, 1925.

McAdoo, Eleanor Wilson, *The Woodrow Wilsons.* New York, 1937.

McAdoo, William Gibbs, *Crowded Years.* Boston, 1931.

McNeal, Robert H., *The Bolshevik Tradition.* Englewood Cliffs, N.J., 1963.

Maercker, Ludwig R. von, *Vom Kaiserheer zur Reichswehr.* Leipzig, 1921.

Mantoux, Paul, *Les Délibérations du Conseil des quatre: 24 mars – 28 juin 1919.* Paris, 1955.

Max[imilian] of Baden, Prince, *The Memoirs of Prince Max of Baden,* 2 vols. New York, 1928.

Meyer, Karl W., *Karl Liebknecht: Man Without a Country.* Washington, D.C., 1957.

Miller, David Hunter, *My Diary at the Peace Conference of Paris,* 21 vols. New York, privately printed, 1925.

Mishark, John W., *Friedrich Ebert and German Social Democracy.* Ann Arbor, Mich.: University Microfilms, 1954.

Mitchell, Allan, *Revolution in Bavaria, 1918–1919: The Eisner Regime and the Soviet Republic.* Princeton, 1965.

Mordacq, Jean-Jules-Henri, *Le Ministère Clemenceau: Journal d'un témoin,* 4 vols. Paris, 1931.

Morgan, John H., *Assize of Arms.* New York, 1946.

Nelson, Harold I., *Land and Power: British and Allied Policy on Germany's Frontiers.* Toronto, 1963.

Nettl, J. P., *Rosa Luxemburg,* 2 vols. London, 1966.

Nicolson, Harold, *Peacemaking: 1919.* New York, 1933.

Niemann, Alfred, *Kaiser und Revolution.* Berlin, 1922.

Noble, George Bernard, *Policies and Opinions at Paris, 1919.* New York, 1935.

Noske, Gustav, *Von Kiel bis Kapp.* Berlin, 1920.

Nowak, Karl Friedrich, *Versailles.* New York, 1929.

Owen, Frank, *Tempestuous Journey: Lloyd George, His Life and Times.* New York, 1955.

Payne, Robert, *The Rise and Fall of Stalin.* New York, 1965.

Pershing, John J., *My Experiences in the World War,* 2 vols. New York, 1931.

Pilsudska, Alexandra, *Pilsudski: A Biography by his Wife.* New York, 1941.

Pinson, Koppel S., *Modern Germany.* New York, 1954.

Riddell, George, Lord, *Lord Riddell's Intimate Diary of the Peace Conference and After.* New York, 1934.

Roden, Hans, editor, *Deutsche Soldaten.* Leipzig, 1935.

Rosenberg, Arthur, *The Birth of the German Republic,* translated by I. F. D. Morrow. London, 1931.

———, *History of the German Republic,* translated by I. F. D. Morrow and L. M. Sieveking. London, 1936.

Roth, Guenther, *The Social Democrats in Imperial Germany.* Totowa, N.J., 1963.

Rudin, Harry R., *Armistice: 1918.* New Haven, 1944.

Russell, Frank M., *The Saar: Battleground and Pawn.* Stanford, Calif., 1951.

Ryder, A. J., *The German Revolution of 1918–1919.* Cambridge, 1967.

Salomon, Ernst von, *Das Buch vom deutschen Freikorpskämpfer.* Berlin, 1938.

———, *Die Geächteten.* Berlin, 1930.

Scheidemann, Philipp, *The Making of a New Germany,* 2 vols. New York, 1929.

Schiff, Viktor, *The Germans at Versailles,* translated by Geoffrey Dunlap. London, 1930.

Schmidt-Pauli, Edgar von, *Geschichte der Freikorps 1919–1924*. Stuttgart, 1936.

Schorske, Carl, *German Social Democracy, 1905–1917: The Development of the Great Schism*. Cambridge, Mass., 1955.

Schubert, Paul, and Gibson, Langhorne, *Death of a Fleet*. New York, 1932.

Seymour, Charles, "End of a Friendship," *American Heritage*, August, 1963.

———, *Letters from the Paris Peace Conference*, edited by Harold B. Whiteman, Jr. New Haven, 1965.

———, editor, *Intimate Papers of Colonel House*, 4 vols. New York, 1926–28.

Shartle, Samuel G., *Spa, Versailles, Munich*. Philadelphia, 1941.

Shotwell, James T., *At the Paris Peace Conference*. New York, 1937.

Smith, Arthur D. Howden, *Mr. House of Texas*. London, 1940.

Tardieu, André, *The Truth about the Treaty*. Indianapolis, 1921.

Temperly, Harold W. V., *History of the Peace Conference of Paris*, 6 vols. London, 1920–24.

Thompson, Charles T., *Peace Conference Day by Day*. New York, 1920.

Thompson, John M., *Russia, Bolshevism and the Versailles Peace*. Princeton, 1966.

Tillman, Seth, *Anglo-American Relations at the Paris Peace Conference*. Princeton, 1961.

Toller, Ernst, *I Was a German*. New York, 1934.

Trask, David F., *General Tasker Howard Bliss and the "Sessions of the World,"* *1919*. Transactions of the American Philosophical Society, New Series, Vol. 56, Part 8, Philadelphia, 1966.

Turner, Henry Ashby, Jr., *Stresemann and the Politics of the Weimar Government*. Princeton, N.J., 1963.

Trotsky, Leon, *My Life*. New York, 1930.

———, *The Russian Revolution*. Garden City, N.Y., 1959.

United States Department of State, Papers Relating to the Foreign Relations of the United States: The Paris Peace Conference, 1919, 13 vols. Washington, 1942–47.

———, *The Treaty of Versailles and After*. Department of State Publication 2724, Conference Series 92. Washington, 1947.

Vidil, Charles, *Les Mutineries de la marine allemande*. Paris, 1931.

Volkmann, Erich Otto, *Revolution über Deutschland*. Oldenburg, 1930.

Waite, Robert G. L., *Vanguard of Nazism: The Free Corps Movement in Postwar Germany, 1918–1923*. Cambridge, Mass., 1952.

Waldman, Eric, *The Spartacist Uprising*. Milwaukee, 1958.

Walworth, Arthur, *Woodrow Wilson: World Prophet*. New York, 1958.

Wandycz, Piotr, *France and Her Eastern Allies: 1919–1925*. Minneapolis, 1962.

Wheeler-Bennett, Sir John W., *Brest-Litovsk: The Forgotten Peace*. New York, 1939.

———, *Nemesis of Power: The German Army in Politics, 1918–1945*. New York, 1953.

———, *Wooden Titan: Hindenburg*. New York, 1936.

Wilson, Edith Bolling Galt, *My Memoir*. Indianapolis, 1939.

NEWSPAPERS

The Morning Post, London. *The New York Times*. *Die Rote Fahne*. *The Times*, London.

Index

Groener, Gen. Wilhelm (*cont.*)
Ebert and, 525
economic powers of, 140
Hindenburg and
conflict on Nazis, 527
equivocation by Hindenburg, 477, 496
fostering of Hindenburg legend, 473, 474–75
latitude of Groener, 474
prospect of resistance, 475–76
query of officers and, 475
supports signing of treaty, 496
later years of, 525–27
Ludendorff and, 176–77
Majority Socialists and
direct wire to Ebert, 199–200
friendliness, 176–77
Kaiser's abdication demanded, 177, 183–84, 189–92
meeting on Kaiser's abdication, 177
ultimatum to Max of Baden, 183–84
Noske and, 280
opposes Hamburg Points, 229–30
on plans to forestall Communists, 238
soldiers' councils and, 207–8
Versailles Treaty and
meeting with Brockdorff-Rantzau, 463
meeting with Noske, 478–79
problem of military coup, 472–73
prospect of resistance, 475–77
realism of Groener, 472
Reinhardt military conspiracy, 477–78, 480–83
Grosser Kurfürst (German battleship), mutiny on, 162–63
Gruppe Internationale
antiwar policies of, 123, 125–26, 127–28
development of, *see* Spartacists
formation of, 125
"Guiding Principles" of, 125–26
Independent Socialists and, 128
Lenin on, 128
Guard Cavalry Rifle Division (*Freikorps* detachment)
formation of, 253
in second Communist uprising, 307
"Guiding Principles" (Gruppe Internationale), 125–26, 127–28
Guldein School (Munich), 283

Haase, Hugo
on armistice demands, 145
on Berlin Executive Council, 217
at Berlin workers' and soldiers' council, 216
on Council of People's Commissioners, 215
held by Peoples' Naval Division, 231
as Independent Socialist, 122
Leninist views of, 221
supports war, 118
on Versailles Treaty, 415
Hague Peace Conferences (1899, 1907), 63
Haguenin, Prof., 244, 457
Hall of Mirrors in Versailles
German emperor crowned in, 10
signing of peace treaty at, 9
Halle, Germany, 300
Freikorps repression in, 299, 300–302, 303
rioting in, 226
Haller, Gen. Józef, 352
Haller's Army, 96
contingents in France, 365
expansionist activities of, 366–67
military campaigns of, 352
size of, 352
Halstein, Germany, revolution in, 186
Hamburg, Germany
Communist-Independent uprising in, 258, 298
Communist influence, 242
rioting, 226
naval harbor at, 158
November Revolution in, 167
Hamburg *Freikorps*
formation of, 379
informality of, 379–80
Hamburg Points
opposition of officer corps to, 229–30
passage of, 229
Hammerstein, von (*Freikorps* leader), 246
Haniel von Haimhausen, Edgar, 491, 492
Hankey, Sir Maurice, 55, 493
Hanover, Germany, troops join strikers in, 193
Hanseatic "free cities"
Baltic trade of, 370
Versailles Treaty and, 483
Hapsburgs (royal family), 317

ABOUT THE AUTHOR

Richard M. Watt is the author of *Dare Call It Treason*, a widely acclaimed history of the French Army mutinies in 1917. Born in 1930, he was educated at Dartmouth College and lives in Glen Ridge, New Jersey.